Capitalisms and Democracies

This book focuses on the economic and social inequalities that have grown within Western capitalist democracies, examining with care the differences between countries rooted in their culture and institutions.

It highlights the reaction of advanced democracies to the new challenges brought about by globalization and technological innovation, pointing to the role of endogenous institutions that affect social inequalities as well as the relationship between redistribution and economic growth. The book presents extensive comparative research on institutional factors such as industrial relations, welfare systems, training, and innovation policies.

Paying attention to diverse types of democracies and to the main features of left-wing parties, this contribution also emphasizes the generally overlooked role of politics, and of different types of democracies, in shaping social inequalities and diverse development paths. It will appeal to students and scholars interested in economic and labour sociology, welfare studies, comparative political economy, comparative welfare, varieties of capitalism, and comparative politics.

Carlo Trigilia is Emeritus Professor of Economic Sociology at the University of Florence and member of the Italian "Accademia Nazionale dei Lincei". He served as Minister for Regional Development in the national Government in 2013–2014. He worked in various universities and was De Bosis professor at Harvard. His research interests and publications include local development (*Social Capital and Local Economic Development*, 2001; *Local Production Systems in Europe*, co-author, 2001; *Changing Governance of Local Economies*, co-author, 2004); economic sociology and political economy (*Economic Sociology: State, Market, and Society in Modern Capitalism*, 2002; *Italy: Rise, Decline and Restructuring of a Regionalised Capitalism*, co-author 2009; *Politics against market: The hard way of Italian capitalism*, co-author 2012; *Is there a future for democratic capitalism*, 2022).

Routledge Advances in Sociology

This series presents cutting-edge developments and debates within the field of sociology. It provides a broad range of case studies and the latest theoretical perspectives, while covering a variety of topics, theories and issues from around the world. It is not confined to any particular school of thought.

Debates Around Abortion in the Global North
Europe, North America, Russia and Asia
Fabienne Portier-Le Cocq

Class Boundaries in Europe
The Bourdieusian Approach in Perspective
Johs Hjellbrekke, Cédric Hugrée, Étienne Penissat, Alexis Spire

Covid-19 Responses of Local Communities around the World
Exploring Trust in the Context of Risk and Fear
Khun Eng Kuah, Gilles Guiheux, Francis K.G. Lim

Space, Mobility, and Crisis in Mega-Event Organisation
Tokyo Olympics 2020's Atmospheric Irradiations
Rodanthi Tzanelli

Capitalisms and Democracies

Can Growth and Equality be Reconciled?

Edited by Carlo Trigilia

Routledge
Taylor & Francis Group
LONDON AND NEW YORK

First published 2023
by Routledge
4 Park Square, Milton Park, Abingdon, Oxon OX14 4RN

and by Routledge
605 Third Avenue, New York, NY 10158

Routledge is an imprint of the Taylor & Francis Group, an informa business

British Library Cataloguing-in-Publication Data
A catalogue record for this book is available from the British Library

Library of Congress Cataloging-in-Publication Data
Names: Trigilia, C. (Carlo), editor.
Title: Capitalisms and democracies: can growth and equality be reconciled? / edited by Carlo Trigilia.
Description: Milton Park, Abingdon, Oxon; New York, NY: Routledge, 2023. |
Series: Routledge advances in sociology | Includes bibliographical references and index.
Identifiers: LCCN 2022025966 (print) | LCCN 2022025967 (ebook) |
ISBN 9781032285122 (hardback) | ISBN 9781032285153 (paperback) |
ISBN 9781003297130 (ebook)
Subjects: LCSH: Income distribution–Western Hemisphere. |
Equality–Western Hemisphere. | Western countries–Economic conditions. |
Capitalism–Western Hemisphere.
Classification: LCC HC94.Z9 I533 2023 (print) | LCC HC94.Z9 (ebook) |
DDC 339.209181/2–dc23/eng/20220613
LC record available at https://lccn.loc.gov/2022025966
LC ebook record available at https://lccn.loc.gov/2022025967

Published in Italian by Il Mulino *Capitalismi e democrazie. Si possono conciliare crescita e uguaglianza* 2020

ISBN: 978-1-032-28512-2 (hbk)
ISBN: 978-1-032-28515-3 (pbk)
ISBN: 978-1-003-29713-0 (ebk)

DOI: 10.4324/9781003297130

Typeset in Times New Roman
by Newgen Publishing UK

Contents

List of figures vii
List of tables xiii
List of contributors xv
Acknowledgements xviii

Introduction 1
CARLO TRIGILIA

PART I
Growth and inequalities in advanced democracies 39

1 Four models of growth and inequality 41
ALBERTO GHERARDINI

2 Production structure, employment, and corporate governance 55
MARCO BETTI AND CECILIA MANZO

3 Industrial relations 74
DARIO RASPANTI

4 Labour market policies 92
ROBERTO RIZZA

5 Welfare systems 110
GIOVANNI AMERIGO GIULIANI

6 Education and innovation policies 131
ALBERTO GHERARDINI

7 Political institutions, governments, and parties 145
VITTORIO MARTONE AND DANIELA R. PICCIO

PART II
Comparative historical analysis 171

8 Industrial relations: representation, inclusion, and competitiveness 173
LUIGI BURRONI AND MARCELLO PEDACI

9 Labour market policies: de-regulation, inclusion, and dualisation 208
ROBERTO RIZZA, NICOLA DE LUIGI, AND BARBARA GIULLARI

10 Welfare, social policies, and redistribution models 235
EMMANUELE PAVOLINI AND ANTONINO SORRENTI

11 The influence of innovation and education policy on inclusive growth 277
ALBERTO GHERARDINI, CECILIA MANZO, AND DARIO RASPANTI

PART III
Institutional structure, politics, and policies 307

12 Processes of political convergence and divergence in advanced democracies 309
ALFIO MASTROPAOLO, FRANCA RONCAROLO, AND ROCCO SCIARRONE

13 Social stratification and electoral behaviour 336
ALBERTO GHERARDINI AND GIOVANNI AMERIGO GIULIANI

14 Politics and policies of left-wing parties 369
ALFIO MASTROPAOLO, VITTORIO MARTONE, DANIELA R. PICCIO, ROCCO SCIARRONE, AND LUCA STORTI

Index 407

Figures

0.1 Types of democracy, models of capitalism, and paths of development 2
0.2 Redistribution features, education and innovation policies, and development paths 6
0.3 Challenges, adjustments, and development paths 11
1.1 Dispersion of disposable income after taxes and transfers (Gini index, 2018 and 1980s) 42
1.2 Share of income held by the 40% of the population with the lowest incomes (2018 and 2004) 43
1.3 Relative poverty rate (2018 and 2000s) 44
1.4 GDP per capita and income inequalities in advanced democracies (2018) 45
1.5 GDP per capita (2018) and percentage change in GDP per capita (2001–2018) 46
1.6 Dualisation index for inclusive growth countries (2019 and 1999) 47
1.7 Four models of growth and inequality 48
1.8 Public consumption and investment expenditure as a percentage of total expenditure (2013) 49
1.9 Taxes and social contributions per country and per growth model (average 2010–2017) 50
1.10 Change in taxes and social contributions between 2008 and 2017 by country and model as a percentage of GDP 51
1.11 Public deficit by country and by model (average value 2009–2018) 51
1.12 Public debt by country and model (average value 2009–2018) 52
2.1 Employment in the industrial sector as a percentage of total employment (2009–2018 average) 56
2.2 Incidence of employment in services on total employment (average 2009–2018) 57
2.3 Number of manufacturing firms with fewer than 20 employees (2016) 58

2.4 Percentage of workers employed in small enterprises (one to nine employees) over total employment (2016) 58
2.5a High-tech exports as a percentage of manufacturing exports (average 2009–2017) 59
2.5b Incidence of medium and high-tech exports on manufacturing exports (2017) 59
2.6 Employment rate, age range 15–64, percentage values (average values for 2009–2018) 60
2.7 Number of employees with fixed-term contracts, percentage values (2017) 61
2.8 Incidence of NEETs on the youth population, percentage values (2017) 62
2.9 Undeclared economy as a percentage of GDP (year 2015) 62
2.10 Labour productivity (GDP per hours worked, in 2010 PPP dollars, 2018) 63
2.11 Percentage of workers employed in publicly owned or controlled enterprises over total number of employees 67
2.12 Credit to the private sector from bank deposits as a percentage of GDP (2016) 68
2.13 Equity market capitalisation as a percentage of GDP (2017) 69
2.14 Financial structure. Ratio of bank credit to financial credit (2017) 70
3.1 Centralisation of collective bargaining, average values 78
3.2 Presence and characteristics of open clauses, average values 79
3.3 Collective bargaining coordination, average values 80
3.4 Adjusted coverage of collective bargaining, average values 81
3.5 Mandatory extension of collective agreements (2019) 82
3.6 Ordinary involvement of social partners in government decisions, average values 83
3.7 Trade union density, average values 84
3.8 Trade union density per country, average values 85
3.9 Share of labour income as a percentage of GDP, average values 86
3.10 Income dispersion, average value 2016–2010 87
3.11 Collective bargaining coverage (standardised, average values 2000–2009) and income dispersion (standardised, average values 2010–2016) 87
4.1 Expenditure on active labour market policies by growth model, as a percentage of GDP (2017) 95
4.2 Expenditure on active labour market policies by country, as a percentage of GDP (2017) 96
4.3 Expenditure on training policies by growth model, as a percentage of GDP (2017) 96
4.4 Expenditure on training policies by country, as a percentage of GDP (2017) 97

4.5 Expenditure on employment services by growth model, as a percentage of GDP (2017) 98
4.6 Expenditure on employment services by country, as a percentage of GDP (2017) 98
4.7 Participation in non-formal job-related training by growth pattern, as a percentage of the population aged 25–64 (2016) 99
4.8 Participation in non-formal job-related training by country, as a percentage of the population aged 25–64 (2016) 100
4.9 Participation in formal education by growth pattern, as a percentage of the population aged 25–64 (2016) 100
4.10 Participation in formal training by country, as a percentage of the population aged 25–64 (2016) 101
4.11 Expenditure on passive policies by growth model, as a percentage of GDP (2017) 101
4.12 Expenditure on passive policies by country, as a percentage of GDP (2017) 102
4.13 Net replacement rate of unemployment benefit at the second and 24th month, % average salary, individual without children (2017) 103
4.14 Share of workers involved in short-time work schemes during the crisis by growth pattern 103
4.15 EPL fixed-term workers by growth pattern (2013) 104
4.16 EPL fixed-term workers by country (2013) 105
4.17 EPL permanent workers by growth pattern (2013) 105
4.18 EPL permanent workers by country (2013) 106
5.1 Total public expenditure as % of GDP (2017) 112
5.2 Public expenditure for social policies by growth model as % of GDP (2015) and public expenditure *per capita* for social policies by growth model at constant prices, PPP, 2010 dollars (2015) 113
5.3 Expenditure on social benefits by type of function as % of total social expenditure (2015) 113
5.4 Pension expenditure as a percentage of GDP (2015) 115
5.5 Net replacement rate of mandatory pensions (public and private) as a percentage of average income (2017) 116
5.6 Poverty rate before and after taxes and transfers (2016) 118
5.7 Minimum income adequacy, % of median income (2017) 119
5.8 Expenditure on family policies as a percentage of GDP, monetary transfers, and services (2015) 120
5.9 Public expenditure on early childhood care, crèches and nursery schools (2015), and crèche enrolment rate for children 0–2 (2016) 121
5.10 Duration of maternity and paternity leave, number of weeks (2016) 121

5.11 Replacement rate, maternity and paternity leave, as a percentage of gross average salary (2014) 122
5.12 Government/mandatory health expenditure, as a percentage of GDP (2017) 123
5.13 Distribution of health expenditure among sources of financing as a percentage of the total (2012) 124
5.14 Gini index before and after transfers and percentage variation (2016) 127
6.1 Public expenditure on education by growth model, as a percentage of GDP (2015) 133
6.2 Public expenditure on tertiary education by growth model as a percentage of GDP per capita (2015) 134
6.3 Public expenditure on primary education by growth model as a percentage of GDP per capita (2015) 135
6.4 Population with university degrees as a percentage of the total number in 25–64 years age group (2018) 136
6.5 Public expenditure on R&D by growth model, as a percentage of GDP (2016) 137
6.6 Governmental organisations' expenditure on R&D by growth pattern, as a percentage of GDP (2016) 138
6.7 R&D expenditure of the university system by growth model, as a percentage of GDP (2016) 139
6.8 Publicly financed private R&D expenditure and private R&D expenditure by growth pattern as a percentage of GDP (2016) 140
6.9 Publicly funded private R&D expenditure and private R&D expenditure by countries and growth patterns, as a percentage of GDP (2016) 141
6.10 Direct funding of corporate R&D, as a percentage of GDP (2015) 142
6.11 Indirect support to business R&D through tax incentives, as a percentage of GDP (2015) 143
7.1 Index of concentration of political power, comparison between countries and growth models (1981–2010) 147
7.2 Electoral disproportionality, comparison between countries and growth models (1980–2015) 148
7.3 Number of political parties, comparison between countries and growth models (1980–2015) 149
7.4 Indices of concentration of political power and of concertation (1990–2015) 151
7.5 Left-, centre- and right-wing parties in government, by growth pattern (1960–1979; 1980–2015) 153
7.6a Left in government, comparison of models 156
7.6b Left in government, country comparison 157
7.7 Left in government and social expenditure per capita 158

7.8 Left in government and Gini index 159
7.9 Relative weight of the main party of the "reformist" left and electoral strength of the left (average 1960–1979) and average 1980–2015, comparison of growth patterns (index and % values) 161
8.1 Trend of union density, 1980–1999 176
8.2 Collective bargaining coverage, average values per period 176
8.3 Characteristics of industrial relations systems, GDP per capita and Gini index 186
8.4 Trend of union density, years 2000–2019 187
8.5 Trend in collective bargaining coverage, years 2000–2019 188
8.6 Inclusion of trade unions in policymaking 190
8.7 Industrial relations, competitiveness, and inequality in countries with inclusive egalitarian growth 194
8.8 Industrial relations, competitiveness, and inequality in countries with dualistic inclusive growth – the case of Germany 195
8.9 Industrial relations, competitiveness, and inequality in high-growth inclusive dualistic countries – the case of France 196
8.10 Industrial relations, competitiveness, and inequality in non-inclusive medium growth countries – the case of the UK 197
8.11 Industrial relations, competitiveness, and inequality in non-inclusive low growth countries – the case of Italy 198
9.1 Participation in life-long learning (percentage of employed 25–64 years old) 221
9.2 Long-term unemployment (share of total unemployed) 223
10.1a Public expenditure on social protection per capita in PPP (2015/18) 236
10.1b Generosity index of public pensions (2015/18) 237
10.1c Public expenditure on social protection as a percentage of GDP (2015/18) 237
10.2a Public expenditure on social protection per capita in PPP (1980) 240
10.2b Percentage change in social protection expenditure per capita (1980/1990) 240
10.2c Generosity index of public pensions 241
10.2d Public expenditure on social protection as a percentage of GDP 241
10.3a Public expenditure on social protection per capita in PPP (1990) 244
10.3b Percentage change in public expenditure on social protection per capita 244
10.3c Generosity index of public pensions 245

10.3d Public expenditure on social protection as a percentage of GDP 245
10.4a Public expenditure on social protection per capita in PPP (year 2000) 250
10.4b Percentage change in public expenditure on social protection per capita 250
10.4c Generosity index of public pensions 251
10.4d Public expenditure on social protection as a percentage of GDP 251
10.5a Public expenditure on social protection per capita in PPP 2010 (2015/18) 255
10.5b Percentage change in social protection expenditure per capita (2015/18) 256
10.5c Public expenditure on social protection as a percentage of GDP 256
13.1 Share of workers in manufacturing sectors in the active population, percentage values (1970–2010) 342
13.2 Share of workers in the service sectors in the active population, percentage values (1970–2010) 342
13.3 Incidence of service workers on the active population by type of service, percentage values (2010) 343
14.1 A typology of relations between left-wing parties and trade unions 384

Tables

1.1 Growth models and macroeconomic variables 52
3.1 Key dimensions of the bargaining structure, average values 2010–2019 88
5.1 Voluntary supplementary pensions, percentage of workers involved (2017) 117
8.1 Coordination and prevailing level of collective bargaining, years 1980–1999 (average values for periods) 177
8.2 Coordination and predominant level of collective bargaining (average values per period) 188
9.1 Expenditure on active and passive labour market policies as a percentage of GDP 218
9.2 Inequality indices calculated on gross monthly wages 219
9.3 Expenditure on active labour market policies (% of GDP) 221
9.4 Expenditure on public employment services in terms of percentage of total expenditure on active labour market policies as a percentage of GDP 224
9.5 Expenditure on passive labour policies (% of GDP) 228
9.6 Expenditure on active labour policies (% of GDP) 228
9.7 In-work poverty by sector of productive activity 229
10.1 Policy sectors and types of institutional change: a comparative view 261
10.2 Trend of public expenditure on social protection (1980–2018) 265
10.3 Income, pensions, and poverty 267
10.4 Net costs for parents sending their children to early childhood education services (% of net household income) (2015) 268
10.5 Regulation of leave (2018) 269
10.6 Inequalities in terms of access to health services (2018) 270
11.1 Tertiary education policies in different growth models 296
11.2 Innovation policies in the various growth models 298
13.1 The 16-item post-Fordist occupational class schema proposed by Daniel Oesch 340

13.2 Oesch's collapsed eight-class schema 341
13.3 Social stratification in some advanced democracies, percentage values (second half of the 2010s) 344
13.4 Voting for left-wing parties of the post-Fordist social classes (early 2000s and late 2010s) 349
13.5 The most voted parties by the production workers, late 2010s 351
13.6 The four most voted parties by the traditional bourgeoisie (late 2010s) 355
13.7 Changes in constituencies of left-wing parties in the four growth models (% of each class over the whole constituency), early 2000s, late 2010s 357
13.8 Weight of each social class within the constituency of the left-wing parties in the eight countries, late 2010s (values) 360
13.9 Composition of the coalition formed by the first three classes supporting the left-wing parties and overall weight on their electorate 360
14.1 Years of main programmatic shifts and policy positions 373
14.2 Social composition of the parliamentary groups of left-wing parties, comparison between "working class" and "middle class" (percentages) 374
14.3 Average votes obtained by left-wing parties, comparison by decade (percentages, 1960–2015) 377
14.4 Main features of political and institutional frameworks (1980–2015) 378

Contributors

Marco Betti is a researcher fellow at *Federsanità*. He has previously worked at the University of Siena and the University of Florence. His research interests concern comparative financial systems and their relationship with corporate governance. He has also carried out research on local development and industrial relations, and more recently on health policies and regional health systems.

Luigi Burroni is Professor of Economic Sociology at the University of Florence. His research focuses on comparative political economy and industrial relations. He is the co-editor of *Economy and Society in Europe*. He recently edited the volume *Mediterranean Capitalism Revisited* with Emmanuele Pavolini and Marino Regini.

Nicola De Luigi is Professor of Sociology at the Department of Political and Social Science, University of Bologna. His research focuses on social policies, labor market policies, and social practices. Among his publications (co-authored with Ilaria Pitti, 2021) are: *Young Italians and the Crisis: Emerging Trends in Activism and Self-organisation*.

Alberto Gherardini is Associate Professor at the University of Turin, where he teaches "Society, Policies and Innovation in Advanced Economics" and "Industrial Relations". His main research interests include innovation policy, university-business relations, regional development, and industrial relations. He is the author of *Torn in Ivory: Italian Universities and Economic Innovation* (2015).

Giovanni Amerigo Giuliani is a research fellow at the Department of Political and Social Sciences, University of Bologna. His research focuses on comparative welfare state analysis, party politics, and social stratification. His most recent publication was "The family policy positions of conservative parties: A farewell to the male-breadwinner family model?" (*European Journal of Political Research*, 2021).

Barbara Giullari is Assistant Professor of Economic Sociology at the Sociology and Business Law Department, University of Bologna where she teaches "Local Social Planning" and "Labour and Care Regime". Her main research interests concern transformations of work and employment trajectories, social work, welfare systems, and local social planning.

Cecilia Manzo is Assistant Professor of Economic Sociology at the University Cattolica del Sacro Cuore, in Milan. Her research focuses mostly on innovation, platform economy, and local development. In 2021, with Routledge, she published *The Economy of Collaboration: The New Digital Platforms of Production and Consumption* (with F. Ramella).

Vittorio Martone is Associate Professor of Environmental Sociology at the University of Turin. His main research interests include environmental policies, local development and sustainability, political ecology, and green criminology.

Alfio Mastropaolo is Professor Emeritus of Political Science at the University of Turin. He taught at this university and at the University of Palermo. His most recent book is: *Is Democracy a Lost Cause? Paradoxes of an Imperfect Invention* (2012).

Emmanuele Pavolini is Professor in Economic Sociology and Social Policy at the University of Macerata (Italy). As an economic sociologist he has focused his research interests in two fields: welfare state studies from a comparative perspective; labour market research and economic development, with a particular attention on the changing roles of professionals, firm networks, strategies for competitiveness, and the role of migrants in the labour market.

Marcello Pedaci is Associate Professor of Economic and Labour Sociology at the University of Teramo. His research interests include the field of comparative industrial relations and sociology of work, with a focus on union strategies, working conditions, and precarious work.

Daniela R. Piccio is Assistant Professor at the Department of Cultures, Politics and Society of the University of Turin. Her main research interests include political representation, party organisations, and party and political finance regulation from a national and comparative perspective.

Dario Raspanti is a research fellow at the University of Florence, Italy. His research focuses on policy implementation from a street-level perspective, sociology of work, and labour market policy. His most recent publication is "Trapped into reverse asymmetry: Public employment services dealing with employers" (co-authored with T. Saruis, *Journal of Social Policy*, 2022).

Roberto Rizza is Professor of Economic Sociology and Labour Market Policies at the University of Bologna. His research focuses on work careers, labour market policies, and social inclusion. His most recent publication is "Organization matters: Policy entrepreneurship among Street-Level Bureaucrats in public employment services. Insights from an Italian case-study" (co-authored with S. Lucciarini, *International Review of Sociology*, 2021).

Rocco Sciarrone is Professor of Economic Sociology and Co-director of the Center "Luigi Bobbio" for Public and Applied Social Research at the Department of Culture, Politics and Society of the University of Turin, Italy. Among his latest publications is *Italian Mafias Today: Territory, Business and Politics* (co-authored with F. Allum, I. Clough Marinaro, 2019).

Antonino Sorrenti is a post-doc research fellow. His main research interests include comparative social policy, EU governance of social policy, childcare and family policy.

Luca Storti is Associate Professor of Economic Sociology at the University of Turin and research fellow of the Ralph Bunche Institute for International Studies in the Graduate Center at The City University of New York. His main research interests and publications include international organised crime groups at boundaries between legal and illegal markets, and the relationships between institutions and the economy.

Franca Roncarolo is Professor of Political Science at the University of Turin where she teaches courses in Public and Political Communication. Her research interests focus on election campaigns, the role of media in the contemporary democracies, populism, and the relationship between political leadership, public opinion, and journalism.

Acknowledgements

The research on which this volume is based was funded by the Italian Minister of University and Research (PRIN: Research Projects of Relevant National Interest 2015). Carlo Trigilia was the principal investigator. He also served as coordinator for the Research Unit of the Universiy of Florence, which included Marco Betti, Luigi Burroni, Alberto Gherardini, Giovanni Amerigo Giuliani, Laura Leonardi, Cecilia Manzo, Marcello Pedaci, Angela Perulli, and Dario Raspanti. Roberto Rizza was associated investigator for the Research Unit of the University of Bologna, which included Nicola De Luigi and Barbara Giullari. Emmanuele Pavolini was associated investigator for the Research Unit of the University of Macerata with the collaboration of Antonio Sorrenti. Alfio Mastropaolo was associated investigator for the Research Unit of the University of Turin, which included Vittorio Martone, Daniela Piccio, Franca Roncarolo, Rocco Sciarrone, and Luca Storti.

I wish to thank all the members of the research team for their commitment and their contribution to the research project, and for their comments and critical remarks that helped me in writing the introduction to this book. Arnaldo Bagnasco, Marino Regini, and Michele Salvati made helpful comments on earlier versions of the book. I am particularly grateful to Alberto Gherardini, Cecilia Manzo, and Dario Raspanti for their generous collaboration at various stages of this work. Special thanks to Giovanni Amerigo Giuliani for his patience and his competent collaboration in the preparation of this volume.

Finally, I am particularly grateful to Giulia Gray for her committed and careful translation of the text, which is not an easy task.

Introduction

Carlo Trigilia

0.1 The research questions

During the post-war era, the advanced democracies experienced a long period of growth. Until the late 1970s, economic development was accompanied by a reduction in social inequalities. Things changed considerably in subsequent years due to economic globalisation. In recent decades, internationalisation has been bolstered by liberalisation of trade, improvements in material and immaterial communications, delocalisation of production, and foreign investments. These trends have undoubtedly contributed to reducing income inequality between advanced and developing countries by increasing production and export in the less developed regions and improving people's living standards. However, during this same period, there has been a constant increase in inequality within the advanced countries that has worsened the conditions for low-income social groups.

Have growth and equality thus become incompatible in the advanced democracies? And is this tendency gradually affecting all the developed countries? Or will the differences in the levels of inequality and in the rates at which it increases persist? Certainly, one could argue that these differences are simply the heritage of an institutional structure established in the past, and are therefore bound to disappear; however, we might also think that some of these structures are more stable and resilient than others.

It is difficult to provide a precise answer to these questions. The first step necessarily involves a comparative analysis. The main objective of our study is thus to highlight the differences between the advanced democracies in their degree of inclusive growth, and to identify the main causes of these diversities. We first selected some ideal types, each representing a different *path of development*, based on a set of economic and social data. This general assessment, focused on the last 20 years, reveals significant differences in the income inequality found in the advanced democracies, and in their relationship with economic growth. We then identified those countries that fit more closely to these ideal-types and reconstructed the main policies and institutional factors that have impacted these paths (*outcomes*), the paths of

DOI: 10.4324/9781003297130-1

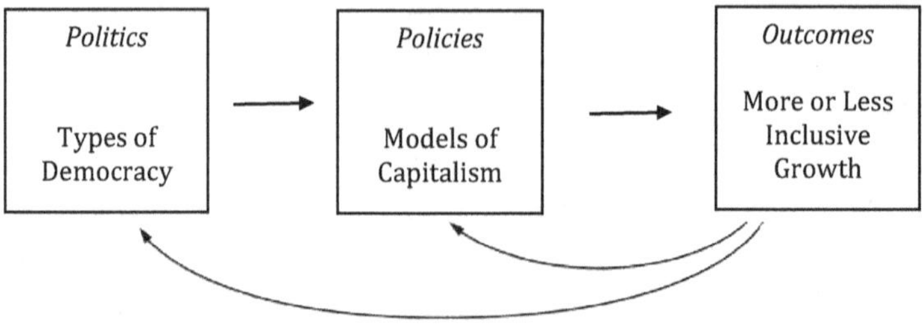

Figure 0.1 Types of democracy, models of capitalism, and paths of development.

development. We focused on those factors with the greatest influence on the redistribution of wealth, and hence on inequality, and assessed their effects on economic growth (especially welfare systems and social and labour policies, industrial relations, education, and innovation policies). This led us to identify different *models of capitalism*, understood as the economic and social regulations of a market economy. However, unlike the "varieties of capitalism" approach, we did not stop at this point. We also sought to investigate the relationship between models of capitalism and *types of democracy*, to shed light on how politics influences, through policies, the institutional regulations of the economy. As a consequence, different models of capitalism may favour or hinder paths of inclusive development (Figure 0.1). Of course, this perspective also required taking into account the feedback effects, in terms of political consensus and electoral support, created by different paths. These in turn affect politics and political choices (as shown by the two arrows in Figure 0.1).

0.2 The analytical perspective

In the last decade a wide literature has investigated the causes of the growing inequalities in advanced democracies. Many factors come into play: changes in the organisation of production and the demand for more specialised skills, which tend to penalise less qualified workers; globalisation and the delocalisation of production, which have further weakened the bargaining power of the workforce, by shifting production towards countries with lower labour costs and less stringent regulations for business; and the effects of the increasing financialisation of the economy. However, while these processes have had a similar impact on the economies of the advanced democracies, their consequences in terms of inequality seem to vary. It is therefore plausible that endogenous institutional factors play a significant role. Scholars have focused their attention on various factors: labour market reforms designed to bring about wider flexibility; weakened industrial relations; the reduction of progressive taxation and the overall tax burden, along with a trend to downscale governments' commitment to social policies, in terms of both financial transfers and the provision of social services.

This volume therefore aims to provide a better understanding of the role played by endogenous institutional factors in the rise in income inequality that has affected the advanced democracies. As mentioned above, however, our main question concerns the combination of inequality and economic growth. Analysing the role of institutional factors in this perspective led us to deal with various strands of literature which in recent years have addressed this issue from different viewpoints. Therefore, it is worth underlining briefly to what extent our perspective overlaps with, but also differs from, these strands.

First, we focused on studies of inequality, which have mushroomed in recent years due to the increasing visibility of this phenomenon.[1] These contributions are valuable because they provide a detailed picture of current trends and show how different social classes are affected, while also offering hypotheses on the causes of increasing inequality. In this respect they draw attention to institutional frameworks and their impact on economic and social regulations. Our analysis relies on this approach with reference to the role of institutions. However, we put more emphasis on the comparative analysis of national cases to better highlight similarities and differences among countries. In addition, this strand of literature deals with the relationship between inequality and economic growth but does not specifically analyse this issue, whereas this is precisely the focus of our study.

Another research field of interest for us is what could be defined as comparative welfare systems analysis.[2] These studies have also contributed significantly to our understanding of the impact that welfare systems have on the forms and degrees of redistribution, and thus on inequality. In this case, comparative analysis is widely used to assess how different models of welfare influence inequality. However, there is a main difference with our perspective. These contributions addressed the relationship between economic growth and redistribution, but this is not their main research focus.

Lastly, the comparative political economy is particularly important for our work. This strand ranges from studies of neo-corporatism and concertation to comparative research on the varieties of capitalism.[3] Unlike the other approaches, the focus is here on growth rather than on inequality. Initially, the studies that pioneered this literature analysed the influence of institutional settings such as neo-corporatism on employment and inflation; later, the attention shifted to the relationship between firms and institutions as a key factor to explain innovative capacity and competitiveness. In this perspective, two main ideal types of capitalism were identified: the "liberal market economies" or "Anglo-Saxon capitalism", and the "coordinated market economies" or "Rhine capitalism" rooted in Continental Europe. Within this framework, the "varieties of capitalism" approach deals with the relationship between growth and redistribution, and provides interesting insights, but the main focus remains on the institutional bases of growth rather than on inequality, although some contributions clearly tend to combine the two dimensions.[4]

Our research, therefore, draws considerably on the approaches mentioned above. However, it also differs from them in focusing on a comparative study of the relationship between growth and inequality. In this respect, it is important to stress that we do not intend to offer a comprehensive analysis of economic growth, but we rather try to evaluate to what extent it is influenced by the institutional settings (e.g., welfare systems, industrial relations, education, etc.) in which redistributive measures, designed to reduce inequality, take shape. In this way, we aim at assessing whether politically generated redistribution must always be seen as hindering economic growth (as some economic theorists maintain), or whether – and under what conditions – it can be a successful means not only of reducing inequality but also of sustaining growth itself.

This is also important for shedding light on another, even more neglected issue: the relationship between different types of democracy – for example "majoritarian", "consensus", or "negotiation" democracy – and models of capitalism, or more generally speaking the relationship between politics and policies.[5] Our central concern here is the role of institutional frameworks, governments, parties, and interest groups in building up support for different kinds of redistribution that influence growth and inequality. In dealing with this problem, we have moved away from the path usually followed in the literature. This is certainly a more complex and difficult task. However, it is particularly important to assess whether growth and inequality are bound to become increasingly incompatible in all advanced democracies,[6] or whether a more inclusive growth can take place, and under what conditions.

0.3 The research design

In carrying out our research within the aforementioned framework, the first problem was the definition of development paths based on a particular combination of growth and inequality over the last two decades (see Chapter 1). In order to deal with this issue, we did not consider the multiple forms of inequality, focusing instead on income. This kind of inequality has increased throughout the advanced world, albeit to different degrees in diverse countries. To evaluate these differences, we turned to several indicators found in the literature: the Gini coefficient, the relative poverty rate, the share of income going to the 10% of the population earning the most, and the share going to the 40% earning the least. Nearly all of the indicators considered show a trend towards an increase in income inequality. The figures for the various countries in question, however, are significantly different, as was generally the case in previous decades as well. To mention just a few significant examples, levels of inequality are higher in the USA and United Kingdom than elsewhere, followed by the Southern European countries (Spain and Italy). At the opposite end of the spectrum we find Nordic countries such as Sweden and Denmark, which boast the lowest rate of inequality according to all of the indicators. France and Germany, in contrast, are ranked in an intermediate position, between the Nordic countries on the one hand and the Anglo-Saxon and Southern European countries on the other.

How do these differences in the degree of inequality align with economic growth? One simple way of evaluating this relationship is to compare per-capita income with the rate of income inequality (Gini coefficient). Considering 18 advanced democracies, three ideal types emerge*: high* (above average) *income/high inequality*; *high income/low inequality*; *low income/high inequality*.[7] We should bear in mind that the two types with above average per-capita income are also generally characterised by an above-average increase in per-capita income over the last two decades. The opposite is true for lower-income countries, which are also the least dynamic ones.

At this point, we were able to define our ideal types and determine which cases come closest to them: *non-inclusive growth* (NIG), marked by high income, high growth and high inequality, generally typical of Anglo-Saxon countries; *non-inclusive low growth* (NILG), close to the Southern European countries' performance, with low income, low growth and high inequality; and, lastly, inclusive growth, which is found in the Nordic and Continental European countries.

This basic framework needs some qualifying. First, the amount of income and its rate of growth refer to the last two decades. During different periods of time, the rates of growth differed from those considered by our ideal types. To mention but one example, over the last two decades Italy and Spain ranked among those countries closest to the non-inclusive low growth type, whereas in previous periods both countries displayed higher rates of growth. Second, it seemed appropriate, based on the literature and the data presented in Chapter 1, to distinguish between *egalitarian inclusive growth* (EIG), which comes closer to the situation seen in Nordic countries, and which displays a weaker effect in terms of inequality, and *dualistic inclusive growth* (DIG), which is closer to the type of growth found in Continental European countries, where there is a larger gap in the job market between poorly protected (outsiders) and well protected groups (insiders), in terms of labour and social policies, and therefore of income inequality.[8]

Lastly, it should be taken into account that our study was completed not long after the income levels and the rate of growth on the one hand, and inequality on the other. At present, we have estimates of trends in income; these point to a drastic short-term deterioration in income, presumably followed by a period of substantial recovery in coming years. It is difficult to estimate the pandemic's long-term effects on income inequality, although an immediate turn for the worse is foreseeable due to the on-going economic crisis. It remains to be seen whether the measures taken by the various countries (some of them also supported by the European Union) can curb and offset these effects, without altering their position within the different path of development (more or less inclusive), or whether, on the contrary, some will succeed in acting more effectively. Our analysis is based on an assessment of long-term structural tendencies, which are unlikely to be affected by short-term fluctuations. Nevertheless, due to the serious feature of this crisis, we cannot rule out the possibility that individual countries may change their position in terms of development paths. In any case, our analysis of the institutional factors may provide some tools to analyse any possible "shifts".

This brings us to the question of the "independent variables", i.e., the institutional factors that influence the different paths (our "dependent variables"). We have mainly focused on three dimensions which may have a significant impact on the redistribution of wealth: industrial relations, welfare policies, and education and innovation policies. The first two dimensions have a direct influence on a country's capacity for redistribution, that is, on its capacity to reduce income inequality and the effects this has on growth, and therefore on the different development paths. Education and innovation policies are important since they can improve firms' ability to innovate, and thus can help to sustain the costs of redistribution without compromising growth (Figure 0.2).

The initial chapters (in particular, Chapters 1 and 2) analyse a few basic macro-economic indicators (public spending, social spending, taxation, deficit, and public debt) together with other micro-economic indicators (productive structure and employment, presence of high-tech sectors, productivity, corporate governance, and financial systems, etc.). This data helps us to improve our picture of the various paths by highlighting the economic fundamentals that best characterise single countries. The income level and its rate of growth undoubtedly influence redistribution and thus the possibility of reducing inequality. However, these economic factors are not sufficient

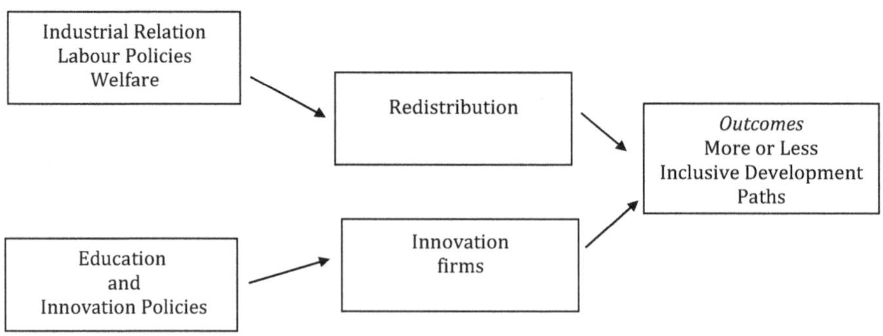

Figure 0.2 Redistribution features, education and innovation policies, and development paths.

to explain redistribution and inequality. Actually, there are countries with similar income levels, such as, for instance, the UK and the USA, on the one hand, and the Central and Northern European countries, on the other, which display different levels of inequality. Thus, the degree of economic dynamism is not sufficient to explain the feature of inequality.

For this reason, in the remaining chapters of the first section, we tried to assess the influence of the following variables: industrial relations (Chapter 3), labour policies (Chapter 4), welfare and social policies (Chapter 5), and education and innovation policies (Chapter 6).

A distinct profile thus emerged for the countries closest to each path. As we shall see, inclusive development seems to be associated with extended and institutionalised industrial relations, including widespread concertation practices; active and well-conceived labour policies; comprehensive and universal welfare models; effective education and innovation policies.

Obviously, the institutional configuration of single countries does not always completely fit the analytical framework. Each country may be more or less close to the features that characterise the different development paths. For these reasons the single paths are considered as ideal types to which individual countries, to a greater or lesser degree, draw near. This is also true for the role of politics analysed in Chapter 7 of the first section. In this case, we hypothesise that the forms of regulation – or models of capitalism – most favourable to inclusive development are those influenced by a political-institutional framework close to the "negotiation democracy" type. To verify this hypothesis, we analysed the relationship between the various development paths and factors such as the type of democracy (majoritarian or negotiation), the composition of governments, the main features of left-wing parties (electoral support, unity or fragmentation, relations with unions), and the competition between parties in different polities.

The first part of the volume is based on the analysis of a number of advanced democracies (18 countries). We found significant links between the different paths of development taken by such countries and the institutional factors concerning industrial relations, policies, and politics. These, however, are to be considered as simple associations helpful for formulating hypotheses subject to further exploration. Thus, the aim of the second part of our study was to reconstruct more in depth the complex causes underlying different development paths. The results are presented in the second and third sections of this volume. We focused on four pairs of countries, selected to represent the various types of developmental paths: the United States and the United Kingdom in the case of NIG, Sweden and Denmark in the case of EIG, Germany and France as regards DIG, and Italy and Spain with regard to NILG. The second part of this volume provides a comparative analysis of how these countries dealt with the challenges that arose in the 1980s and discusses the factors already considered in the first section in greater detail: industrial relations (Chapter 8); labour policies (Chapter 9); welfare policies (Chapter 10); education and innovation policies (Chapter 11). Lastly, the third part focuses on changes in social stratification and electoral behaviour (Chapter 13), the transformation of the political-institutional framework (Chapter 12), and more specifically the programs and policies proposed by left-wing parties who have traditionally played a central role in fostering redistribution (Chapter 14).

The countries examined are clearly different. This is also true for those selected as representative of each of the four development paths (especially France and Germany). This is the reason why some scholars maintain that comparisons are appropriate only in terms of a mere "contrast of contexts",[9] i.e., by analysing their historically specific features and diversities and contrasting them (Salvati, 2020). However, there is another way of conceiving comparisons between countries: the "causal macro-analysis". This approach has traditionally been used in the social sciences: it is based on the formulation of hypotheses through the comparison itself. This is the approach we applied. Basically, it requires the selection of specific features distinguishing one or more cases from the others considered. Then, such outcomes are related to factors which, in turn, are either present or absent in each case. In this way, it is possible to formulate causal hypotheses by replicating the procedures used for experiments in the natural sciences. Obviously, we are aware that in macro-social analysis single units are never entirely similar, except in terms of the factor identified as a specific cause. Therefore, there is always the risk that other differences, difficult to keep under control, will interfere with a given outcome. Furthermore, the limited number of cases available for this kind of research makes such generalisations even riskier. The results of this kind of comparison must therefore be taken with caution. At the same time, however, this approach may be particularly useful in testing general theories, such as for example, in our case, the theory that foresees an increasing convergence of advanced democracies towards a uniform model of deregulated capitalism.

0.4 Politics, policies, and development paths

In the subsequent part of this introduction, I shall present an overview of our main research findings. The aim is to provide an analytic framework based on a comparison of the various cases, and to point to the main causal factors that influenced the responses to the challenges and the paths of (more or less inclusive) growth. First, I shall focus on changes in the different models of capitalism – in the main features of economic and social regulation – and then I shall try to assess how such changes have influenced the relationship between growth and inequality, that is, the development paths. Lastly, some key aspects of politics will be discussed – with reference to the type of democracy, the composition of governments, the role of parties (especially the left-wing parties) – to shed light on their impact on the regulatory choices.

0.4.1 The challenges

First of all, we have to consider the challenges that the advanced democracies have had to face from the 1980s onwards. The roots of these challenges lie in the decline of an institutional framework that had characterised the 30-year period of intense economic growth (Les Trente Glorieuses) after the end of World War Two. The "Keynesian social state" at the macro level with new public policies, together with "Fordism" at the micro level with mass production organised through large firms, had brought about a significant reduction in inequality, during a phase of high economic growth. Public policies aiming at full employment were extensively pursued (after being introduced in some countries to face the 1930s disruptive crisis). Industrial relations and the extension of collective bargaining mechanisms led wages and salaries to rise, but they also reduced dispersion in income among workers, and therefore inequality. With the further extension of welfare policies, wages were supplemented by benefits offered directly or indirectly by the State through social services. This contributed considerably to reducing inequality, and also raised the demand for consumer goods in the Fordist economy, which needed a stable and large market for mass production. But how was this result achieved? What were the social bases that favoured this institutional framework?

Representative organisations (parties, unions) provided a democratic channel for the demands of a large class of wage earners with highly uniform working and living conditions. This class grew, driven by Fordist industrialisation based on large factories and industrial cities. What took shape was referred to by Peter Gourevitch (1986) as the great "historical compromise". The labour movements accepted a capitalist economy in exchange for the promise of full employment, collective bargaining, and welfare. Obviously, there were differences in the institutional configuration of the post-war compromise. However, all advanced democracies went in the same direction, and the effects were similar. These consequences included the silent, yet rapid and vigorous rise of the middle class, favoured by the "mid-century social contracts" (Bagnasco, 2016).

The 1970s crisis and the ensuing "stagflation" put an end to the Trente Glorieuses and destabilised the balance between growth and inequalities. Two major processes defined the new challenges: first, the decline of Fordism and the advent of new ways of organising production, which were to lead to a decrease in numbers, and the geographical dispersion of the industrial working class; second, the later process of economic globalisation and the massive shift of production to the emerging countries. These changes affected social stratification with the dramatic decline of a large working class, characterised by high social and political cohesion, which was the trigger to the compromise between democracy and capitalism of the post-War period. New forms of employment appeared in the variegated world of services.

A significant number of such services were characterised by their low added value and the notable discontinuity of employment. This new world is one of highly fragmented employment and individual living conditions. Those who were part of it – often young people, women, immigrants – had much more difficulty sharing their experiences with others. Thus, the new inequalities, unlike previous ones, did not favour social and political mobilisation and collective action. It was now more difficult to build social coalitions and to find electoral support for reforming the welfare state and dealing with the new social risks. Overall, in the advanced democracies there was a weakening of the less privileged groups' capacity to have their voices heard. What did increase, on the contrary, was the influence of the strongest economic interests on political decision-making processes and the shaping of public opinion (see, among others, Hacker & Pierson, 2010; Crouch, 2011)

Thus, new challenges emerged within this profound social change. On the one hand, they were brought about by the decline of Fordism, reorganisation of production, technological innovation, and globalisation, which reduced the size and political strength of the traditional working class. It was necessary to find new opportunities for employment in other activities, especially in the service sector. On the other hand, advanced democracies had to face the increasing costs of welfare policies covering old risks and, at the same time, had to deal with new social risks that required a comprehensive reform. The various development paths were shaped by the response to these challenges arising in different contexts.

0.4.2 The search for causal factors

A variety of responses emerged in advanced democracies leading to different development paths. They were not the result of real strategies but decisions based on contingencies influenced by the severity of the problems and constrained by the previous institutional framework (path-dependence). They were rather adjustments, that is, adaptations to variable circumstances. We identified four types of response to the challenges of the 1980s. All of them involve regulatory measures that leave more room for the market, albeit in different forms[10] (Figure 0.3). The first is the overall de-regulation that was to mark the path of non-inclusive growth most typical of the Anglo-Saxon countries. It involves an overall retrenchment of the redistribution mechanisms introduced during the period of post-war development (industrial relations, welfare provisions), leaving more leeway for market forces. The response of the Nordic countries went in the opposite direction, towards an overall re-regulation. In this case, redistribution was maintained, although significant changes were made in the institutional framework, making such regulation more sustainable for the state and firms, as well as more capable of reducing inequality and favouring an inclusive egalitarian growth. In other countries, a compromise took shape that maintained the basic redistribution

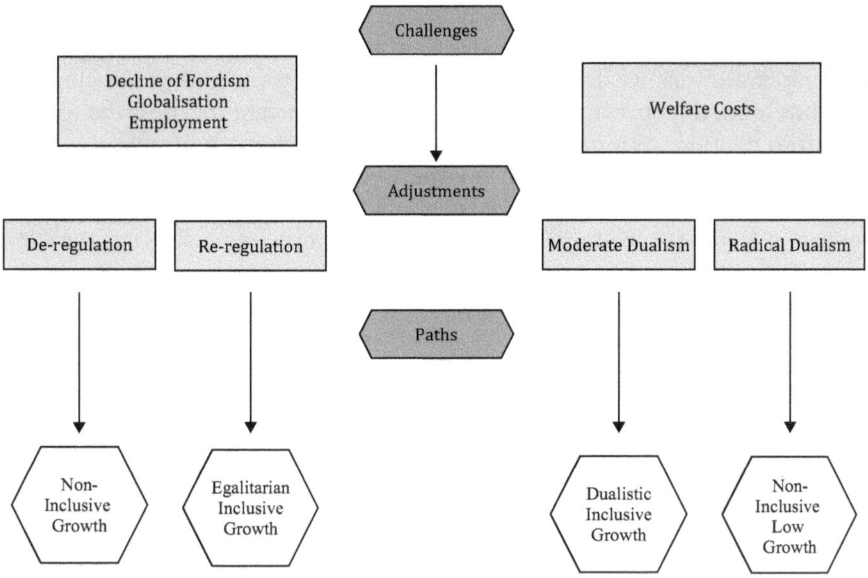

Figure 0.3 Challenges, adjustments, and development paths.

mechanisms introduced in the Fordist era, but limited their benefits to those involved in certain sectors (workers of medium-large industrial companies and public employees), while new service workers with lower skills (young people, women and the unemployed) remained less protected or without any protection at all. Thus, a dualist adjustment took shape in these cases. A moderate dualism is more typical of countries in Continental Europe, where reduced levels of inequality are accompanied by high economic growth. A more radical dualism, marked by non-inclusive low growth, can be seen in Mediterranean countries.

I shall now try to summarise the explanation for these different paths offered by our research. I shall first point to the influence of regulation – that is, of different models of capitalism – on redistribution and its relationship with growth. Second, the role of politics and types of democracy in shaping development paths will be discussed.

0.4.2.1 Regulations, adjustments, and paths

Industrial relations, labour policies and welfare provisions certainly had a significant impact on redistribution, as well as education, human capital endowments, and innovation policies. However, the overall influence of these factors on inclusive growth should not be assessed through simple quantitative indicators. For instance, the role of industrial relations should not be evaluated only through the figures of unionisation and collective bargaining. It is necessary to consider to what extent they improve wages and working conditions without being too onerous for firms and public finance, and thus hindering growth. In this respect, it is important to assess the role of industrial relations as a means of increasing productivity at firm level.

The same considerations hold for the welfare system and for social and labour policies. Measuring welfare spending only as a GDP percentage or in per capita terms may be misleading. On the one hand, we must assess the capacity of the welfare system to reduce inequality and poverty, and to counter old and new risks. On the other hand, the burden on public and corporate finances has to be considered. This means ascertaining whether public policies favour a good supply of human capital and actually encourage firms to innovate, thus raising their chances of sustaining higher standards of redistribution and regulation.

Clearly, the set of institutional factors most closely related to inclusive development is based on a complex blend that is difficult to find in the concrete reality. This configuration can also be used as a sort of benchmark against which other development paths can be assessed. In these cases, we may expect fewer positive outcomes in terms of inclusion and growth.

0.4.2.2 The political-institutional framework

I shall now discuss the influence of some key political factors on the regulatory decisions. A useful starting point is the well-known distinction made by the political scientist Arend Lijphart (1999; 2012) between "majoritarian democracy" and "consensus democracy" (Chapter 7 contains a more detailed discussion of Lijphart's distinction and the debate it triggered). The main difference between these two types of democracy is based on the idea of a greater or lesser concentration of political power. Lijphart aims to demonstrate through various indicators that the non-majoritarian democracies, where political power is less concentrated, perform relatively better in terms of economic growth and social cohesion.

Majoritarian democracy is the prevalent form of democracy in the Anglo-Saxon world. It is characterised by a greater concentration of political power due to a number of factors: the majoritarian electoral system; the usual presence of two main parties favoured by electoral rules; one-party governments; the greater power of governments vs parliaments;[11] and a pluralistic system of interest representation that hinders "concertation" (that is, the participation of interest groups together with governments in the policy-making and implementation of the main economic and social choices). On the other hand, in the consensus democracy, more commonly found in Continental and Northern Europe, political space is shared to a larger extent by a higher number of actors. This institutional configuration includes: a proportional electoral system; a larger number of parties and the prevalence of coalition governments; a more balanced division of powers between governments and parliaments; and a corporatist system of interest representation that favours concertation between governments and interest groups.

Lijphart's classification has been criticised in many respects (some critiques seem well grounded, see Armingeon (2002). However, it seems useful for us, as a starting point, because it provides a promising link between types of democracy and development paths. We thus attempted to relate the different types of democracy to our paths (Chapter 7). The results confirmed that countries with a majoritarian democracy are largely the same as those characterised by non-inclusive growth (the only significant exception being France) and can be mainly identified with the Anglo-Saxon nations. At the same time, however, the performance of the countries classified by Lijphart as closer to the consensus democracy model (or in any case, not clearly classifiable as majoritarian) is more variable.[12] In the Nordic and Continental Europe, a more inclusive form of economic growth was found, while Mediterranean countries were affected by non-inclusive low growth. In trying to explain these differences among those countries classified by Lijphart as consensus democracies, one variable seems to play a key role: the presence of institutionalised concertation. In Nordic and Continental Europe, concertation was – and remains – extended and well-established, whereas in Mediterranean countries it was less stable and institutionalised. Therefore, Central and North European countries can be better defined as "negotiation democracies" (Armingeon, 2002).

Another problem with the Lijphart's classification concerns causal explanation. Why is majoritarian democracy accompanied by non-inclusive growth while negotiation democracy combines growth and reduced inequality? What link is there between the features of politics and non-inclusive low growth? In trying to find an answer to these questions, we need to reconstruct the behaviour and interaction of the main actors involved. Comparing the four pairs of countries (see the second and third part of this volume) is of particular interest to analyse the causal factors that have influenced different development paths.

From this point of view, it seemed appropriate to focus on the most important left-wing parties (in terms of electoral results and presence in governments) in each country. This particular attention is justified by the importance traditionally given in their programs to redistribution and reduction of inequality by parties on the left. The role of such parties in favouring redistribution is clearly confirmed by the data presented in the first part (Chapter 7). The left as a whole (including reformist and moderate forces together with the more radical parties) has governed for a greater amount of time from 1960 until the most recent period precisely in those countries displaying more inclusive growth, while the opposite is true for nations with non-inclusive growth. Mediterranean countries are situated in an intermediate position.

Major left-wing parties boasting electoral strength and governmental presence are thus important, since they sustain redistribution to a greater extent than the other parties (Iversen & Soskice, 2006). Nevertheless, these factors are not sufficient to explain the different forms of redistribution and their effects on inequality and growth.[13] It is necessary to assess how diverse strategies and outcomes take shape even with similar levels of electoral support and influence on governments for the left. In this perspective, aspects should be considered such as ideological tradition, party constituencies, relations with the unions, and above all the competition from other political forces on the left (i.e., the degree of unity or fragmentation of the left as a whole).

Other factors more exogenous to left-wing parties are also important. The institutional structure of "negotiation democracy" generally offers more opportunities for the emergence and consolidation of concertation practices, which in turn can bring about more favourable conditions for fulfilling demands for redistribution. Furthermore, this form of democracy is characterised by a proportional electoral system that fosters redistribution, contrary to what happens in a majoritarian system. With proportional electoral rules, parties on the left are less inclined and induced to compete for the moderate vote at the centre to win elections and go to power. Therefore, they do not need to curb considerably the demand for redistribution to attract the vote of the middle classes. As a matter of fact, these social groups are generally less favourable for bearing the costs, in terms of taxation, of extended welfare provisions and significant redistribution.

Another important factor discussed in the literature on welfare systems (see Esping-Andersen, 1993), is the influence of previous welfare architecture, created during the Fordist era, on the response to the new challenges (rising costs, new risks). In this respect, attention is drawn to a path-dependence dimension that seems to play an important role. In addition to the already mentioned aspects, one should also take into account the strength, influence, and orientation of the main conservative parties as well as the characteristics of social stratification and the potential for attracting support of new groups.

This complex set of internal and external factors conditioned the strategies deployed by left-wing parties to deal with the new challenges thrown up during the 1980s. In this situation, left-wing parties had to face a dilemma. If they wanted to go to power, they would need to modify their political supply by leaving more room for market forces in the models of capitalism. This change was necessary to gain support among the new middle classes and moderate voters, and to offset the erosion of their traditional electoral bases due to the decline of the working class (Kirchheimer, 1966). However, if they were to move more decisively and rapidly in this direction, they would risk compromising their representation of the traditional working-class electorate together with that of the new low-skilled workers, on the rise in the service sector.

As shown in the third part of this volume (Chapters 12 and 14), in facing these challenges left-wing parties generally converged towards political programs that were more open to the market and oriented towards reducing the cost of welfare by limiting social protection for wage workers. This tendency was accompanied by changes in their internal organisation and leadership. The power of central structures increased. New leaders were more and more often recruited from the middle/upper classes. Relations between unions and parties weakened. These general trends, however, were more or less marked in different national settings and had diverse impacts on actual policies pursued by left-wing parties and on their effects on development paths. In fact, party strategies were influenced by the opportunities and constraints inherited from the previous institutional framework (the complex mix of endogenous and exogenous factors mentioned before), and they thus worked out different solutions to the electoral dilemma.

0.4.3 De-regulation and "compliant left-wing parties"

The two countries we chose in order to analyse the adjustment based on de-regulation – the USA and the United Kingdom – when examined more closely are obviously quite different, as are in fact, the countries making up the other pairs. Their differences also concern the political dimension. This becomes even clearer if we look at their main left-wing parties. They significantly differ in terms of their respective ideological traditions and history: the UK's Labour Party is linked to the history of European socialism, while the US Democratic Party is closer to liberal-democratic traditions. A socialist outlook never took root in the USA, a vast country that grew thanks to successive waves of immigration, with its unique frontier spirit and strong ethnic and linguistic cleavages within the nation's working class. Industrial relations have traditionally been heavily institutionalised in the United Kingdom (at the firm level), but emerge as more voluntarist and uneven in the United States. What, then, brings the two countries together and sets them apart from those nations that followed other development paths?

First, in the late 1970s both the UK and the USA were experiencing a serious "stagflation", with the manufacturing sector rapidly shrinking, and serious problems concerning unemployment and high inflation. During the 1960s and 1970s both countries had been governed by a series of left-wing governments, who were increasingly considered responsible for these negative outcomes. Unlike other European countries, neither the USA nor the UK could implement an effective concertation as a means of controlling inflation and sustaining the economy and employment. The main reason was the same in both cases, namely the lack of a neo-corporatist infrastructure representing the interests of firms and unions. Despite the strengthening of industrial relations during post-war years, the unions were still bound to decentralised, rather uncoordinated forms of organisation. The organisation of unions was based on professional categories, rather than a more general representation of workers. Peak structures were usually very weak. Left-wing parties thus lacked credible strategies when faced with the new challenges of stagflation, and were accused of supporting tax and spending policies, responsible for the serious economic crisis.

This was the backdrop to the emergence of neoliberalism during the 1980s, both at the political and cultural level (especially in economic thought). In short, the conservatives took the lead and triggered a process of de-regulation that left greater room for the operation of market forces. From the 1980s onwards, a significant retrenchment of the welfare systems and industrial relations took place in comparison to the Fordist era (Chapters 8 and 10). Even though redistribution had been less marked in the post-war decades, especially in the USA, due to the residual nature of welfare provisions aimed at those in conditions of particular need, and to the more decentralised and uncoordinated nature of industrial relations. It is generally agreed that this downscaling process took place through the introduction of radical, rather than gradual, measures,[14] but what is the relationship between these trends and economic growth?

Social policies did not hinder growth for the simple reason that they were reduced, thus becoming less onerous to public finances, while tax rates fell, in particular those paid by wealthier taxpayers. Industrial relations were weakened while an overall de-regulation of the job market (Chapter 9) made labour in traditional sectors more flexible and less costly (as a result of the reduced costs of lay-offs). De-regulation also favoured the strong growth in employment in low-productivity services (primarily in the consumer service sector, and in that of personal services), thus offsetting the rapid and significant decline in manufacturing jobs that characterises this model (Chapter 13). Indeed, productivity was low in many service sectors, and there was limited space for growth. This meant that employment in these activities could only be increased through low wages and considerable flexibility. Deregulating the service sector job market, in which unions and collective bargaining were rare or entirely absent, thus offered an alternative to the adoption of more expensive social and labour policies, and allowed tax rates to be cut, at the price, however, of growing inequality. Nevertheless, one should not forget that in this development path skilled employment also rose in high value-added services to firms and in financial activities (the latter also benefited from the radical de-regulation introduced in the 1980s). The increased profits coming from the financial sector, and the substantial bonuses paid to senior management in large firms, heightened the gap between skilled services and personal and consumer services, together with what remained of the traditional manufacturing sector. The dramatic weakening of unions, and the fragility of employment, compared to other models, did not counter wage dispersion and the lower income of wage workers and the middle-classes, damaged by technological and organisational innovation. The result has been a higher increase in income inequality.

Lastly, attention is to be given to the significant amount of public spending on education and research and development (Chapter 11). This is a specific feature of countries close to the NIG model, which is often overlooked. Public investments in these activities contributed to increasing human capital and sustaining research, through financing universities and research institutions. Thus, the creation of human capital and the application of new knowledge in the field of production are fostered in many ways. They generated, in turn, a significant number of innovative, high-technology companies (especially in the USA). The mechanisms of corporate governance and business financing, based on the key role of listed public companies and the stock market, also sustained the drive towards a more radical kind of innovation (Hall & Soskice, 2001). Labour market regulations moved in the same direction and favoured rapid adjustments to the new opportunities of innovation.

Income growth and low unemployment (albeit subject to rapid and profound cyclical fluctuations, depending on market trends) were thus driven by de-regulation and the central role of the market, as well as by considerable investment policies. However, they were accompanied by increasing social inequality. Serious crises affected the more fragile and traditional sectors, just as the old Fordist scenario was transformed by new ways of organising production and services, and globalisation fully displayed its effects.

How did left-wing parties react to this situation? After the long domain of conservative governments in the 1980s, they redesigned political programs (especially under Clinton's presidency in the USA and Blair's leadership in the UK), in the attempt to overcome their cultural and political isolation and increase electoral support. Their political supply did not substantially depart from the market-oriented stance of previous conservative-led governments but simply tried to mitigate its harsher social effects through measures designed to protect the weaker categories; more attention was also given to education (Chapter 10).[15] Why did left-wing parties essentially support the path of non-inclusive growth? Why did they appear to be so compliant?

In addition to the already-mentioned lack of concertation practices, another political-institutional factor has to be considered: the majoritarian electoral system. As we know, the majority of votes is required to win an election in this system. This results in electoral campaigns focused on attracting support from voters at the centre of the political spectrum, where the pivotal votes of the more moderate middle-class lie. A two-party system is also more likely to appear in the context of majoritarian democracies and both parties try to bag the middle-class vote to go to power. But the middle-class electorate is increasingly unwilling to foot the bill for a form of welfare that gives it little or no benefits (especially in the USA).

Summing up, left-wing parties had to face a peculiar set of constraints and opportunities. Agreements and concertation were not an option in the two Anglo-Saxon countries for the reasons mentioned above, neither was an extensive welfare system (due to the increased spending and taxation this system would imply and the opposition of middle-class voters). As a consequence, left-wing parties were less likely here than elsewhere to challenge the main features of the neo-liberal turn towards de-regulation and market dominance.

Of course, the risks underlined by the electoral dilemma remain. Convergence towards the centre can alienate the traditional working-class electorate and makes it difficult to attract the new service workers. From this point of view, however, another aspect, often overlooked, must be taken into account. The majoritarian system is not only projected towards the centre, but it also protects – to a certain extent – left-wing parties from competition. The reason is that minor parties face very strong difficulties to get represented in parliaments. Therefore, electoral rules offer no credible alternatives to voters and disaffection can be expressed mainly through abstention or by sustaining critical positions within the two traditional major parties. That is clearly demonstrated by the split over Brexit within the Conservative Party, or the changing fortunes of Corbyn within the Labour Party, or the rise of Trump in the American Republican Party. This does not happen in other contexts, such as in Europe, where proportional electoral systems do allow the foundation of new parties (as we will see in the third section of the volume).

0.4.4 Re-regulation and "resilient parties"

In the Scandinavian countries, strong left-wing parties have a long and deeply rooted "social-democratic" tradition. They have pursued full employment and redistribution since the 1930s. In both Sweden and Denmark, they quickly rose to power and in the phase of post-war development their presence in governments was larger than that of other left-wing parties. During this period, concertation and a universal welfare system were established. Centralised, multi-sector concertation between government, unions, and business organisations was fostered by a highly concentrated and centralised representation of interests (a "neo-corporatist system of representation"). The welfare system can be defined as "institutional-redistributive". This is a universal model: extensive services are provided as citizenship rights, social spending is quite high and is concentrated on services rather than transfers, financing is based on fiscal revenues.

The strength (in terms of electoral success and presence in government) of the social-democratic parties is a specific feature of the Scandinavian countries' political-institutional framework, which distinguishes them and involves three main factors. First, the greater degree of unity shown by the left, which reinforced its social-democratic orientation and led it to accept the market economy quite early on, in exchange for full employment, workers' rights, and a universal welfare system. Second, owing to the original features of agriculture in these countries, with the rise of mass politics in the late nineteenth and early twentieth century, the prevalence of small–medium independent farmers led to the formation of agrarian parties. These latter allied with left-wing parties (the "red–green" alliance) pushing for redistribution and for more extensive welfare provisions financed through taxation, rather than social contributions (after World War II the agrarian parties became centrist parties). Lastly, the main conservative parties were liberal and non-religious, meaning that there was no conflict between state and Church when the nation-state was established, while support was provided to the state by protestant churches. This feature limited the conservatives' ability to compete with socialist parties for votes among the lower classes which in turn curbed the division and radicalisation of the left. Consequently, alliances between conservative and centrist parties – more in favour of redistribution – were unlikely, while the left-wing parties were particularly strong (Manow, 2009; Iversen & Soskice, 2015).

Summing up, we could say that the Scandinavian scenario is based on a "negotiation democracy" with extensive and institutionalised concertation practises sustained by strong left-wing parties. This institutional framework had a significant influence on the strategy devised by social-democratic parties to deal with the new challenges arising in the 1980s with the decline of Fordism, new employment problems, and the increased costs of welfare. Scandinavian parties too had to reformulate their programs. In this case as well, the influence of neo-liberalism brought about a greater openness to the market regulation of economic activities, together with an increased commitment to reducing the costs of welfare and high fiscal pressure. There were also changes in party organisation and political leadership, but relations with unions remained relatively closer than in other European countries and concertation practices continued to influence the policymaking (Chapter 14). The role of the proportional system must also be considered. Actually, this limited the need for left-wing parties to seek votes among the moderate middle classes, as is the case in a majoritarian system, and favoured the formation of coalition governments. Furthermore, the proportional electoral rules reduced the personalisation of leadership and the weakening of parties.

This peculiar institutional context influenced the adjustments to the new challenges in the Scandinavian countries. Growth of low value-added services and low wages, as in the Anglo-Saxon world, was hindered, while the welfare system centred on public services offered an alternative. This was based on the growth of more skilled employment, with a strong female component, in social and personal services.[16] The problem of the overall costs of social policies, with consequences for fiscal pressure, was dealt with measures designed to "recalibrate" welfare,[17] by reducing funds for passive policies (mainly pensions and unemployment benefits) and shifting resources towards protection of new social risks and unstable employment (Chapters 9 and 10). Active labour market policies (ALMPs) thus attracted an increasing amount of social expenditures. What were the consequences of these adjustments on growth?

The EIG model entails a high fiscal pressure for financing an extended welfare system. However, public deficit and public debt remained under control. The debt-to-GDP ratio is, on average, one of the lowest among the advanced democracies. Pension spending as a percentage of the total social expenditure is lower than the average, while supplementary pensions gained ground quite early, helping to lighten the burden on public finances. Despite these macroeconomic performances, there is no doubt that this development path also entails high costs for firms, due to fiscal pressure together with market regulation and collective bargaining. However, several kinds of compensation for firms are also at work. True, firms must bear higher costs, but these are partly offset by "collective competition goods" (Crouch et al., 2001) produced by the public sector, often in collaboration with interest groups (unions, business associations). They include – in addition to general infrastructure – education and training policies to enhance human capital, and measures to support innovation through investment in research and development (Chapter 11). In this way, firms are encouraged to compete along the high road of innovation, rather than in production that is more vulnerable to cost competition (the low road). Signs of this particular interest in supporting innovative activities can also be seen in the presence of an active sector for financing innovation (venture capital), sustained by public measures, and in the wider role played by the stock market in financing firms (Chapter 2), compared to traditional "Rhine capitalism" (of which the Nordic version can be considered a variant).

Industrial relations point in a similar direction. During the era of Fordism, they were already marked by active policies favouring job mobility. This trend continued and was developed during the post-Fordist period towards flexicurity, involving those who lose their jobs and those with unstable careers and temporary jobs, especially in the service sector (mainly young people and women). These people are included in training and re-training programmes, in which considerable investment has been made (following the "social investment" approach). The beneficiaries of such programmes are afforded income support and other benefits such as childcare and conciliation policies sustaining women's employment, and supplementary pension plans.

Overall, the EIG model has responded to the new challenges through re-regulation, that is, by adapting the forms of regulation originally established in Nordic capitalism. A new integration between the market and a recalibrated welfare state has been accomplished. Economic growth has been favoured through an efficient and effective redistribution. Efficiency is linked to sustainability for public finances and for businesses. Redistribution does not have a negative impact on the economy, but on the contrary it favours growth by means of policies centred on education, research, and innovation, and through industrial relations that foster productivity and competitiveness. At the same time, effectiveness is higher in comparison to other development paths due to the greater impact of redistribution on reducing inequality (even though inequality has risen in Scandinavia as well, and especially in Sweden [Chapter 1]).

To conclude, while changing their programs and organisational structure, and loosening their original ties with unions in order to meet the new challenges, social-democratic parties have contributed to a more inclusive and egalitarian path of growth that can be defined as re-regulation. As regards electoral trends, these parties have maintained their considerable support among the traditional working classes in both Sweden and Denmark (the highest in all European countries examined). They have also been more successful than other parties in attracting votes among the less skilled new service workers (many of whom are women), as well as among the new middle class, especially in the socio-cultural sector (teachers, social workers, physicians, public employees in general) (Chapter 13). We noted that this service sector has grown more here than elsewhere, because of the peculiar adjustment discussed above. These trends indicate that Scandinavian parties have proved to be more resilient. That is, they have succeeded in effectively combining the support they enjoy among less privileged social groups and a significant component of the new middle class (socio-cultural workers), with policies that have maintained the emphasis on redistribution and countering inequality. Nevertheless, not even the social-democratic parties have managed to avoid the loss of voters experienced by all left-wing parties in Europe. As shown in the third section, this trend has been accompanied by a shift to the new radical right populist parties, for whom almost one fifth of the working class now votes in both Sweden and Denmark. I shall return to this issue later.

0.4.5 Dualism and "left-wing parties at risk"

Let us now consider the two types of readjustment that respond to challenges through compromise and an increased dualism, which may be more moderate (France and Germany) or radical (Spain and Italy). In both cases more room is left for the market, albeit mainly in less protected activities, especially in the service sector, where a tendency to de-regulate temporary work and fixed-term contracts has grown. More extended regulations and protection persist in manufacturing (especially in larger firms) and in the public sector. As illustrated in the second and third sections of this volume, the countries involved in dualist adjustments present many differences. The main left-wing parties have also distinct stories and traditions. However, they all share two main features: they have been challenged by Christian-Democratic parties competing for the votes of the working class, and they generally share a tormented history of divisions and conflicts that have weakened the political left as a whole.

The left-wing parties' influence on the welfare system and industrial relations, as well as on concertation practices, has therefore been more limited than in the Nordic countries. Consequently, redistribution was weaker during the post-war growth. Except for Germany, negotiation democracy has not been institutionalised (in the late 1950s, France moved towards a majoritarian model democracy, while Spain and Italy remained in a hybrid position). Welfare state building was more influenced by Christian-Democratic parties and was based on a "Bismarckian" model, financed through social contributions[18] (with the important exception of the National Health Services in Italy and Spain). The outcome was a framework of social protection less capable of reducing inequality. This institutional infrastructure had also a strong influence on the responses to the challenges of the 1980s.

In actual fact, the Bismarckian system makes boosting employment in low-productivity services more difficult, because of the higher labour costs related to social contributions. However, the path followed in the Anglo-Saxon countries, based on the overall de-regulation of the job market, was not feasible in the eyes of left-wing parties, due to their relations with unions and their commitment in favour of industrial relations. Nor was the Scandinavian adjustment based on extending public services, because the Bismarckian model is traditionally more oriented towards transfers than to public services. This is due to the importance given by Christian-Democratic parties to the role of the family and women as caregivers, and to the Church's provision of services (education, social assistance, etc.). Consequently, serious problems and political tensions arose with the growth of unemployment during the 1980s. Left-wing parties were particularly affected by this issue, whether governing in a position of greater electoral strength, as in Spain and France, or leading coalition governments as in Italy (albeit with a weaker electoral support), or aspiring to a return to power, as in Germany. Despite all the differences, left-wing parties were influenced by the constraints mentioned above and pushed towards a similar response. Thus, they gave an important contribution to dualistic adjustments.

It is true that initially some of them insisted on various combinations of traditional policies (for instance, early retirement, lowering of retirement age and reduced working hours, under the Mauroy government in France; high levels of public expenditure and debt under the Socialist-led governments in Italy during the 1980s). However, in the end a common stance was adopted towards the de-regulation of labour market and of fixed-term contracts. Apparently, there was a shared conviction that there were no feasible alternatives in terms of an overall de-regulation, such as in the Anglo-Saxion countries, or of an overall re-regulation, such as in the Nordic countries. After all, the new political ideas and proposal put forward by the Third Way or the New Centre in the 1990s, provided support for this choice.[19]

At this point, Continental and Southern European parties were faced with two challenges. Their response strongly influenced their countries' adjustments. The first relates to the ability to reorganise the traditional welfare system, and to reduce its costs and impact on public finances. This is not an easy task for left-wing parties, taking into account that the welfare reorganisation will inevitably create tensions in the relationship with a considerable component of their electorate (especially the traditional working class). The second challenge concerns the ability to shield the new outsiders, excluded from traditional social protection (especially young people, women, and the unemployed) from the new social risks.

Under the influence of the inherited political-institutional framework, two different models emerged from the 1980s onwards. The Continental model took the path of a moderate dualism, more efficient in protecting against old and new risks. Here dualism can be defined as moderate insofar as those facing new risks were given some forms of limited (but on the rise) public protection (Chapter 10). This adjustment is more efficient because it maintains some basic regulations and social provisions of the Fordist past, but at the same time manages to reduce costs and avoid any additional burden on public finances with a negative impact on growth. This attempt, however, did not protect left-wing parties against the political cost of their traditional electorate's reaction. Such voters did not feel adequately represented, and they reacted to the (limited) attempt at reducing previous levels of protection by shifting towards new radical left-wing parties or – more frequently – to the new radical right parties.

A different path was followed by the Southern European model, involving a more radical, less efficient, and effective dualism. This adjustment was based on a larger presence of outsiders in employment and a lower degree of protection against the new risks they faced, which reduced its effectiveness in countering inequality. At the same time, serious difficulties were found in reorganising traditional forms of protection and reducing the corresponding costs. The result was less efficiency with a heavier burden on public finances and on growth. In this case, once again, the political cost paid by left-wing parties was particularly high.

To explain the different reaction between the Continental and Southern countries from a comparative point of view, we might mention three key factors that all involve significant legacies of the past: the features of the welfare state built during the previous Fordist phase; the nature of industrial relations; and the solidity of the productive system and of economic development.

As for the welfare state during the Fordist era, in the Continental European countries the path taken was characterised by the greater responsibility of the main parties competing for power. Thus, the use of the welfare state to raise electoral support was more limited, fragmentation of social policies was reduced, as well as the burden on public finances (Chapters 5 and 10). In the two Mediterranean countries, on the other hand, the influence of particularisms and clientelism on social policies was stronger, while the burden on public finances was greater (Ferrera, 1996; 2005; Manow, 2009; 2015). The generosity of the pension system remained considerable, despite various reforms, and supplementary pensions did not gain much ground, unlike in the Continental European countries. These features contributed to reducing the effectiveness of redistribution, that is, the ability to curb inequality despite non-negligible levels of public expenditure, as well as the efficiency due to the higher burden on public finance (Chapters 5 and 10). Important shortcomings included increased fiscal pressure and reduced availability of resources for new policies aimed at protecting outsiders, as well as for innovation policies, thus making redistribution more sustainable (Chapter 11).

With regard to industrial relations, the overall trend was towards a weakening (Chapter 8). However, in the moderate dualism model a high degree of protection remained for workers in large companies and for the employees in the public sector (in France unionisation has always been quite low and contractual protection provided through state intervention). Constraints to firms coming from the old regulations – especially in certain countries such as Germany – could be at least partially offset by an efficient system of professional training, publicly supported and jointly managed between business associations and unions. This system was able to enhance the human capital available for firms and fosters innovation and competitiveness. A non-negligible role was also played by decentralised agreements, at the firm level, between unions and companies. Under such agreements, job security was provided to workers in exchange for greater flexibility in the use and organisation of labour, so as to increase productivity and competitiveness.[20] Consequently, the higher labour costs for business coming from institutionalised industrial relations and extended protections for workers could – at least partly – be offset by the involvement of unions in activities that contributed to raising productivity.

This was not generally the case in those countries where a more radical dualism has grown. Industrial relations, in fact, continue to play an important role here, above all in medium-sized and large companies and in the public sector. The degree of contractual protection has remained relatively high, as well as collective bargaining at sectoral level (even though decentralised bargaining has increased and is now conducted more often at company level). Centralised concertation remains sporadic, unstable, and non-institutionalised in both Italy and Spain. Conversely, the level of conflict (measured through number and duration of strikes) continues to be rather high in comparative terms. Employment protection for permanent employees, while weakened, is still considerable, as with the continental model. Much less widespread, in contrast, is the workers' involvement in the management of firms, as well as the role of industrial relations in activities sustaining human capital formation and productivity growth at firm level.

Lastly, an important factor affecting the sustainability of redistribution is to be found in the strength of the productive system (Chapter 2). Economic dynamism has certainly been more marked in Continental Europe, where it has traditionally been supported by robust education, training, and innovation policies, as in the Nordic countries (Chapter 11). In Mediterranean countries, in contrast, the productive system is not as solid (although there are significant differences between Italy and Spain, and within Italy at a regional level). In the latter two countries, after a previous period of dynamism of small manufacturing firms and industrial districts (especially in Italy), the productive structure has been hit by increasing competition in traditional sectors brought about by globalisation. However, innovation and the shift to the high road, less vulnerable to cost competition, have often been hindered by the strong presence of small, family-managed firms, as well as by the shortcomings of public policies and financing channels available for innovation (Chapter 11). As a result, the need for innovation has been only partially fulfilled. Public policies, in particular, were affected by the lack of resources, in turn due to the inefficiency of the welfare system and the costs generated by a higher level of public debt. In addition, as a consequence of the international economic crisis, and the budget restraints imposed by the EU austerity approach, the macroeconomic situation has worsened to a greater extent, reinforcing the vicious circle of non-inclusive low growth.

Considering the three dimensions we have discussed above, we can assume that the more radical dualism found in the Mediterranean countries, in comparison with the Continental ones, has proved less effective in countering inequality, and less efficient and sustainable from the point of view of its costs and consequences on growth. However, despite these differences between the two variants of dualism, electoral and political losses for the left-wing parties have been considerable and similar in both kinds of dualism. They have paid the highest electoral price, and seem to be most at risk, regardless of their actual responsibilities in shaping dualistic adjustments. Data on the changes in their electoral support show relatively similar trends (Chapter 13). These parties have not succeeded in attracting the votes of outsiders, i.e., the new, low-skilled service workers, due to their involvement in the dualist response and their hostility towards immigration. At the same time, they have also lost considerable ground among working-class voters, i.e., the insiders who formed their traditional electoral base and reacted against the weakening of traditional protections and the increase in immigration. The decline in electoral support has been neither sufficiently offset nor slowed down by middle-class or upper-class voters, despite their growth in the constituency of left-wing parties. This is clearly a key issue that also concerns the future of policies designed to reduce inequality.

0.5 Capitalisms and democracies: concluding remarks

0.5.1 Redistribution and growth

I shall now discuss a few theoretical and political implications of our findings. Our research began with the observation that in recent decades, inequality – especially income inequality – has increased within developed countries, while it has decreased between the more advanced economies and the less advanced ones. Nevertheless, there are significant, often overlooked, differences in the rates of growth and the levels of inequality of the advanced democracies themselves. Two important, interrelated questions ensue from this observation. Which factors underlie these differences? Is a process of convergence going on that is making equality and growth increasingly incompatible?

As regards the first question, many observers see the process of globalisation, the reorganisation of productive systems driven by technological innovation and the financialisation of the market economy as the main underlying causes of increasing inequality within the advanced democracies. In this respect, however, we have drawn attention to a set of endogenous institutional factors that have influenced the advanced democracies' responses to the considerable challenges of recent years, They can help explain the different forms that such responses to external changes have taken. A set of significant factors emerged: welfare systems and social policies, industrial relations and labour policies, public intervention in the crucial fields of education and innovation. These forms of economic and social regulation shaped models of capitalism in which the role of redistribution changed, depending on the resources available and the organisational models that were implemented. In some cases, redistribution continued to play a significant role. While undoubtedly undergoing considerable change, it was still combined favourably with economic growth. Through the new forms of integration with the market, it sustained inclusive growth. In other cases, in contrast, redistribution was considerably downscaled and contributed to increasing inequality.

In analysing the institutional factors that influence inequality, we thus focused on the relationship between growth and redistribution from a comparative perspective. A first theoretical implication of our research can be formulated in the following terms. Our reconstruction of non-inclusive growth confirms that *there are no solid grounds for the "trickle-down" theory, according to which a de-regulated economy that reduces the amount and the scope of redistribution and leaves more room for the market (reducing public spending, in particular welfare provisions, lowering fiscal pressure and down-sizing industrial relations) is able to reduce inequality.* In short, the argument based on the idea that "a rising tide lifts all boats" does not hold, nor does the expectation that lowering taxes and leaving firms more freedom to hire and fire helps to counter inequality.[21] Our research confirms that economies less burdened by taxation and regulation may bring about income and employment growth but at the price of increased inequality.

There is a second theoretical implication. Unlike what is maintained by some economic theorists, redistribution designed to counter inequality is not necessarily a factor hindering the efficiency of the market and economic growth. *Under certain conditions, redistribution can, on the contrary, stimulate the dynamic efficiency of markets innovation and growth.*

It is therefore important to focus on those conditions allowing for a positive combination of redistribution and growth. In this respect, an analysis of economic and social regulations and of their different effects on growth and inequality is necessary. Such an approach is usually found in *comparative political economy*, which includes studies of the relationship between models of capitalism and inclusive development. However, it is important to go beyond this approach of comparative statics, in order to better understand how a political-institutional framework influences regulatory decisions and their reproduction over time. We thus formulated a few hypotheses as to how specific types of democracy can influence different models of capitalism. We focused on the relationship between negotiation democracy and the type of redistribution that supports growth by favouring inclusive development. This perspective calls for a closer link between political economy investigations and studies of politics, taking also into account changes in social stratification and their influence on regulation.[22] We therefore decided to pursue a more complex and difficult objective, in the belief that focusing on different relationships between capitalisms and democracies can be fruitful not only in shedding light on the different forms taken by inequality in advanced countries but also in dealing with future trends. The use of the plural seems more appropriate since our findings point to the operation of different models of capitalism fostered by different types of democracy.

These differences are important. Not all countries have followed the same path in their attempts to meet the challenges emerging during the 1980s. The case of Northern Europe shows that redistribution can be effective in lowering income dispersion, ensuring that a higher proportion of national income goes to employees, significantly reducing the poverty rate, and hedging the new social risks without overlooking the old ones. This case is even more significant since it was accompanied by one of the highest rates of growth in terms of per capita income, in addition to a high rate of employment. What was behind this performance? Clearly, a solid and innovative production system was important. This was able to reduce the exposure to cost competition that increased in developed countries because of globalisation. However, a dynamic productive structure was in turn favoured by three main institutional factors: industrial relations and labour market policies; the welfare system; and training and innovation policies.

0.5.2 The conditions of inclusive development

One distinct feature brings together these different institutional factors in cases of inclusive growth. Not only do they all contribute to a redistribution more capable of countering inequality, but they also offer resources that "offset" the ensuing higher costs for firms, both in terms of more stringent labour regulation and higher fiscal pressure.[23] As regards the welfare system, the underlying idea is that social policies can work as a "social investment" (see, for example, Morel, Palier, & Palme (2012) and Hemerijck (2013)). In other words, they can be not only a cost, but also a positive externality that increases firms' competitiveness through education, training, and higher endowments of human capital. This same idea could be applied to industrial relations. The higher costs and restrictions for firms that they entail for countering inequality can be offset by the industrial relations' contribution to the productivity growth made by trade associations. Lastly, education and innovation policies may be seen in a similar perspective. They constitute "collective competition goods" for firms: important externalities that sustain innovation. In addition, one should also consider that these supply-side effects, related to external economies, may be accompanied by other effects on the demand-side. In actual fact, reduced inequality and higher incomes for less privileged social groups tend to have a positive impact on the demand for goods and therefore stimulate, in turn, investment and growth.

Another significant theoretical and political implication of our research emerges here. Redistribution oriented towards social investment and the provision of collective competition goods, instead of being simply a constraint or a cost, can become a resource by combining the capability to counter inequality with active support for growth. This target can be achieved through a form of liberalisation that offers more room to the market, while at the same time protecting society from new risks and negative externalities linked to market regulations.

Of course, not all forms of redistribution have these positive effects. There are cases in which redistribution is not efficient (it is onerous for public finances and for firms), without being effective in countering inequality. In the last decades, the Mediterranean countries came close to this situation and attracted the European Union's attention, as well as that of important international organisations (the International Monetary Fund, the World Bank, the OECD). Since the 1990s, and in particular after the 2008 global economic crisis, these institutions have frequently made recommendations encouraging national governments to carry out "structural reforms". These should aim at improving competitiveness by cutting public expenditure and reducing and reorganising welfare spending, by lowering taxation, and above all by de-regulating the labour market to render it more flexible. This would lead to employment growth while countering dualism. These recommendations were more motivated by concern for efficiency (unemployment, job creation) rather than for growing inequality. They often entailed criticism of the so-called "European social model", due to its considerable rigidity compared to the American model (Regini, 2018). This pressure had a significant impact on the redistribution mechanisms, as will be shown in the following chapters. However, in the last years a rethinking of the austerity approach has emerged, especially by some important international organisations, as a result of the destabilising economic and political consequences of increased inequality.[24] Recently, the UE also has taken a step back from the austerity approach to face the dramatic consequences of the pandemic. It is too early to assess whether this turn is temporary or will consolidate over time. In this latter perspective, a different approach focusing on the relationship between redistribution and economic growth could attract more attention and interest, both theoretically and politically.

0.5.3 Political-institutional framework and inclusive growth

As already mentioned above, our research also aimed at a better understanding of the role of politics in fostering inclusive growth. Comparative analysis drew our attention to a peculiar institutional framework, that is the importance of a type of democracy that favours compromise between the interests of labour and those of business, through a stronger representation of labour and a less unbalanced relationship between capital and labour. This political-institutional framework is what we term "negotiation democracy". Two series of factors seem to be particularly important in explaining how this type of democracy can encourage a form of redistribution that supports growth. The first includes the proportional electoral system and some other features of left-wing parties that influence their choices on redistribution and growth. The second concerns the presence of concertation practices and their effects on the parties' strategy.

Unlike majoritarian democracy, the proportional model does not encourage a two-party system and a convergence towards the centre to win elections and go to power. It is possible to govern by way of coalitions, and this is a rather common feature of European polities. Significant consequences result for the main left-wing parties, which are usually the promoters of redistribution, at times together with other actors, such as the Christian Democrats. A proportional system encourages the left-wing parties to curb their shift towards the centre, in an attempt to meet the new challenges, thus limiting the erosion of their traditional support among the working-class voters.[25] These parties are also less likely to loosen their ties with unions in the attempt to attract moderate voters.

The capacity of the main left-wing parties to remain closer to their traditional roots, while at the same time generating support among new service workers and the middle classes, seems an important condition for redistribution and inclusive growth. To explain these peculiar features, in addition to the electoral system, a number of other concurrent factors must be considered. These include: a consolidated social-democratic tradition of compromise; electoral strength and a substantial governmental presence; reduced internal conflict and divisions within the left; wide electoral support of the traditional working class, less challenged by the centre-right or by the radical left; persisting close relations with unions. The left-wing parties' political choices can be also influenced by social stratification (Beramendi et al., 2015) (Chapter 13). For example, the stronger presence of people working in the socio-cultural sector can create more favourable conditions for building a coalition that brings together both traditional and new voters. On the contrary, social stratification characterised by a greater number of self-employed and independent middle class – traditionally more hostile to redistribution – makes it more difficult to construct a new coalition to sustain inclusive growth.

Thus, a complex set of interdependent factors influences the parties' choices that in turn play an important role in the shaping of a more inclusive development path, such as in the case of Nordic countries. In other contexts, the outcomes have been different, pushing the left-wing parties towards moderate or radical dualist paths. This is what happened especially to weaker parties, in contexts affected by a long history of cleavages within the left. Such parties tried to increase their votes by moving more clearly towards the centre[26] and adopting policies oriented towards labour market de-regulation, welfare retrenchment rather than recalibration, and downsizing of industrial relations. But in this way, they have not been able to attract the new less skilled service workers (outsiders), while facing, at the same time, a loss of traditional working-class voters, for whom the old forms of labour protection could not be completely maintained (insiders). In addition, the middle classes' support remained limited, if not declining (Chapter 13).

A second series of factors fostering inclusive growth concerns the presence of well-established concertation practices in negotiation democracies. As we have seen, this factor is not present in majoritarian democracies, or is unstable and poorly institutionalised as in South European contexts. Concertation was generally established and/or reinforced during the Fordist era, under the pressure of the stronger bargaining power acquired by the working class. Concertation among unions, business associations and government strengthen workers' representation, especially when interest organisations are large, encompassing, and highly centralised. They can therefore represent not only narrow groups, but the more general interests of wage workers.[27] In this situation, in fact, the unions are more driven to internalise the benefits of decisions aimed at a more general representation of collective interests (Olson, 1982).

Our research (Chapters 3 and 8) shows that these features of interest representation have weakened in the last decades. Nevertheless, to the extent to which negotiation democracies can keep alive forms of centralised concertation with a considerable capacity of representing collective interests, the main left-wing parties can rely on a key resource to sustain inclusive growth. This leads us, in conclusion, to another question that our study may raise. Should we expect a progressive convergence towards a model of de-regulated capitalism? Or will the institutional differences persist, with diverse combinations of capitalisms and democracies?

0.5.4 Convergence or diversity?

Answering this question is clearly difficult. Our research shows different institutional trends. In some settings, especially in industrial relations, there are signs of a weakening of traditional regulations. However, the influence of path-dependence can also be seen, and the diversity between various contexts persists. In other areas, the differences remain or become even more pronounced, for example, in the field of welfare and labour policies, where expectations for extended protection seem to be generalised and shared by various social groups, cutting transversally across social stratification and political parties. In this respect, we might underline the rise of welfare chauvinism: that is, the tendency to demand more limited protection for immigrants (Chapter 10). Trends in inequality are also difficult to interpret. On the one hand, income inequality is rising in all advanced democracies. On the other hand, the differences in both its entity and rate of growth remain relatively stable. In short, the trends we have analysed suggest that caution is needed in making predictions for the future.

There is, however, one clear change that ought to be acknowledged. It concerns all the European development paths, also including the more inclusive ones. We have emphasised the greater capability of some Central and North European countries to combine growth and redistribution, economic development, and the reduction of inequality. However, we must not underestimate the tensions and changes affecting these experiences as well, which may compromise their previous outcomes. One important dimension concerns the weakening of left-wing parties who have played an important role in the promotion of welfare and industrial relations. This trend has also affected other political actors, such as the Christian Democrats, who have supported redistributive measures to varying degrees.

In recent years, a large number of voters have changed their choices. Many of them come from the less privileged classes, including the traditional working class, the new service workers and the self-employed. They have shown an increasing detachment from traditional political parties, especially left-wing parties. This trend can be found not only in countries with less inclusive growth, such as the UK and USA, or Spain and Italy in Southern Europe, but also in Central and Northern European countries closer to the model of inclusive growth. Immigration is a key issue to understand these changes. It has been cleverly used by new political entrepreneurs as a catalyst for increasing disaffection and thus opening the way for new parties and movements who are highly critical of the traditional political establishment and sustain new demands for social protection. These forces are usually classified as part of a new radical right, although in some countries – notably in Southern Europe – they also have left-wing origins and connotations. In any case, the literature underlines the rising influence of the cultural dimension (with the crucial theme of immigration). Cultural cleavages tend to become more influential, vis-à-vis the traditional economic conflict over redistribution, in shaping political preferences and divisions (see, for example, Inglehart (2018). This makes it more difficult for left-wing parties to maintain their electoral support even in contexts, such as in the Nordic countries – where their strategy was more successful in sustaining inclusive growth.

However, while there is no guarantee that more inclusive growth will continue to be promoted, this does not mean that it is necessarily bound to disappear. An important implication of our study, in fact, is that the problems hindering the reproduction and extension of inclusive development paths are more political than economic. These problems are influenced to a lesser extent by factors such as technological innovation or globalisation, which are often thought to ineluctably drive all countries towards de-regulated capitalism. Actually, their impact is mediated and influenced by the political-institutional framework at national and supranational level, that is, by its capability to find and mobilise support for regulations (models of capitalism) that sustain inclusive growth.

Notes

1 To mention but a few of the more influential contributions: Stiglitz (2012; 2015); Piketty (2013, 2020); Deaton (2013); Atkinson (2015); Milanovic (2016; 2019). A discussion of this approach is found in Franzini and Pianta (2016).
2 See, for instance, Flora and Heidenheimer (1981); Esping-Andersen (1990; 1999); Ferrera (1993; 1996; 2005); Pierson (2001). Of particular interest for our analysis are Armingeon and Bonoli (2006), Bonoli Natali (2012), and Manow, Palier, and Schwander (2018).
3 On neo-corporatism and concertation, see Berger (1981); Schmitter and Lehmbruch (1979); Lehmbruch and Schmitter (1982). For models of capitalism, see: Albert (1991); Hollingsworth and Boyer (1997); Crouch and Streeck (1997); Dore (2000); Regini (2000). For the varieties of capitalism, see Hall and Soskice (2001); Hancké, Rhodes, and Thatcher (2007); Hall (2007, 2009).
4 See Sapir (2005), Regini (2009; 2018); Burroni (2016); Hassel and Palier (2021).
5 Attention has occasionally been given to the correspondence between democracies and models of capitalism, in particular between "majoritarian democracies" and "liberal market economies" on the one hand, and "consensus democracies" and "coordinated market economies" on the other (Amable, 2003; Ido, 2012; Schmitter & Todor, 2014). Nevertheless, with a few exceptions (Iversen & Soskice, 2006; 2015; Thelen, 2014), this topic has not been explored in depth. The importance of establishing a close relationship between comparative political economy and politics, to develop a more dynamic perspective, has been recently underlined (see Hall, 2022a; 2022b; Trigilia, 2016; 2022). A useful starting point can be found in the work of the political scientist Arend Lijphart (1999; 2012). His typology distinguishes between majoritarian and consensus democracies.
6 See, for example, the highly debated contribution by Streeck (2013).

7 A fourth type, based on a combination of low income and low inequality, is found, though not to a significant degree, within the advanced democracies. Eastern European countries, which shifted to a market economy model when their communist regimes fell, seem closer to these conditions.

8 In recent literature, especially that concerning welfare systems, four types have been identified that are similar to those used in our research. See, for example, Beramendi et al. (2015), Manow, Palier, and Schwander (2018). These typologies are based on the influential contribution originally made by Esping-Andersen (1990), which distinguished between three "worlds of welfare". Later, other typologies have generally also considered a fourth type represented by Southern European countries.

9 Skocpol and Somers (1980) proposed a distinction between three types of comparative analysis: a "contrast of contexts", "causal macro-analysis", and a "parallel demonstration of theories". See also Paci (2013).

10 Esping-Andersen (1990; 1993) provided a significant contribution to the analysis of new challenges and different paths. Works by Thelen (2014) and Beramendi et al. (2015) followed a similar perspective.

11 Lijphart does not explicitly refer to it, but the more significant role of personal leadership in parties and governments could also be considered as a more characteristic feature of majoritarian institutional frameworks.

12 Moreover, even in Lijphart's analysis, the positions of countries such as Italy, Spain, and Greece seemed not to meet expectations (Lijphart, 2012, 268–269).

13 These differences are neglected by the Power Resource Theory. See, for example, Korpi (1983).

14 See, for example, the reconstruction of this process by Thelen (2014). For the welfare retrenchment, see Pierson (1994).

15 A significant exception to this trend was the health sector reform that President Obama later succeeded in introducing in the USA.

16 On the distinctive features of this adjustment, see Esping-Andersen, Assimakopulou, and van Kersbergen (1993).

17 On welfare recalibration, see Ferrera, Hemerijck, and Rhodes (2000); Pierson (2001).

18 According to Manow and Palier (2009), the Christian Democrats' influence was also very important in France during the period in which the welfare system was established, in the 1950s, when the Republican Popular Movement was particularly active.

19 Mudge (2018) noted the change that generally came about in the economic orientations of socialist parties from the 1980s on. This was due to the greater role of economists who, unlike their colleagues from the previous generation, were educated not in parties but in academic environments critical of Keynesianism and more open to neo-liberalism.

20 Palier and Thelen (2010) insist on this aspect in reference to the situation in Germany and France.

21 See the excellent overview of the evidence against the trickle-down theory in Stiglitz (2016).

22 Bagnasco (2016) called attention to this aspect, pointing to the need to combine the "institutional matrix" and the "social bases" of regulation, generally neglected by comparative political economy.

23 Crouch (2013) underlined these features of redistribution, also pointing to their importance for renewing the left-wing parties' political proposal.
24 An interesting example of this current rethinking can be found in the Manifesto for Renewing Liberalism, published by *The Economist* on 13 September 2018 (Trigilia, 2019).
25 Iversen and Soskice (2006) noted that in a context of competition between parties based on a proportional electoral system, parties come closer to the model of a "representation party" with a more integrated constituency, made up of less contrasting interests, while in the majoritarian system "parties of leaders" prevail, with a more important role of personal leadership in bringing together the contrasting interests represented by the same party. We might add that in the latter case, parties as organisations are weakened to a greater degree, to the advantage of personal leadership (Aarts et al,. 2011; Trigilia, 2018), while a more influential role in political communication is played by the media (see Chapter 12).
26 An interesting discussion of this aspect can be found in Watson (2015). Manow (2009, 2015) has repeatedly focused on the influence of divisions within the left on welfare policies, in Mediterranean countries.
27 Rueda (2007) underlined an overall tendency, shared by social-democratic parties and trade unions, to defend the interests of insiders at the expense of outsiders. Our comparative data show that the trends indicated by Rueda are not found in all contexts.

References

Aarts, K., Blais, A., & Schmitt, H. (2011) (Eds). *Political leaders and democratic elections*. Oxford: Oxford University Press.

Albert, M. (1991). *Capitalisme contre capitalism*. Paris: Seuil.

Amable, B. (2003). *The diversity of modern capitalism*. Oxford: Oxford University Press.

Armingeon, K. (2002). The effects of negotiation democracy: A comparative analysis. *European Journal of Political Research*, 41(1), 81–105. DOI: 10.1111/1475-6765.00004

Armingeon, K. & Bonoli, G. (2006) (Eds). *The politics of post-industrial welfare states: Adapting post-war social policies to new social risks*. London and New York: Routledge.

Atkinson, A.B. (2015). *Inequality: What can be done?*, Cambridge, MA: Harvard University Press

Bagnasco, A. (2016). *La questione del ceto medio. Un racconto del cambiamento sociale*. Bologna: Il Mulino.

Beramendi, P,. Häusermann S., Kitschelt H., & Kriesi H. (2015) (Eds). *The politics of advanced capitalism*. London and New York: Cambridge University Press.

Berger, S. (1981) (Ed.). *Organizing interests in Western Europe: Pluralism, corporatism, and the transformation of politics*. Cambridge: Cambridge University Press.

Bonoli, G. & Natali, D. (2012) (Eds). *The politics of the new welfare state*. Oxford: Oxford University Press.

Burroni, L. (2016). *Capitalismi a confronto. Istituzioni e regolazione dell'economia nei paesi europei*. Bologna: Il Mulino.

Crouch, C. (2011). *The strange non-death of neoliberalism*. Cambridge: Polity Press.

Crouch, C. (2013). *Making capitalism fit for society*. Bristol: Polity.
Crouch, C. & Streeck, W. (Ed.) (1997). *Political economy of modern capitalism: Mapping convergence and diversity*. London: Sage.
Crouch, C., Le Galès, P., Trigilia, C., & Voelzkow, H. (2001). *Local production systems in Europe: Rise or demise?* Oxford: Oxford University Press.
Deaton, A. (2013). *The great escape: Health, wealth, and the origins of inequality*. Princeton, NJ: Princeton University Press.
Dore, R. (2000). *Stock market capitalism, welfare capitalism*. Oxford: Oxford University Press.
Esping-Andersen, G. (1990). *The three worlds of welfare capitalism*. Princeton, NJ: Princeton University Press.
Esping-Andersen, G. (1993) (Eds). *Changing classes: Stratification and mobility in post-industrial societies*. London: Sage.
Esping-Andersen, G. (1999). *Social foundations of postindustrial economies*. Oxford: Oxford University Press.
Esping-Andersen, G., Assimakoupulou, Z., & Van Kersbergen, K. (1993). Trends in contemporary class structuration: A six-nation comparison. In G. Esping-Andersen (Eds), *Changing classes: Stratification and mobility in post-industrial societies* (pp. 32–57). London: Sage.
Ferrera, M. (1993). *Modelli di solidarietà. Politica e riforme sociali nelle democrazie*. Bologna: Il Mulino.
Ferrera, M. (1996). Il modello sud-europeo di welfare state. *Rivista Italiana di Scienza Politica*, 26(1), 67–101. doi:10.1017/S0048840200024047
Ferrera, M. (2005) (Eds). *Welfare state reform in Southern Europe: Fighting poverty and social exclusion in Italy, Spain, Portugal and Greece*. London and New York: Routledge.
Ferrera, M., Hemerijck, A., & Rhodes, M. (2000). *The future of social Europe: Recasting work and welfare in the new economy*. Report for the Portuguese Presidency of the European Union, Oeiras, Celta.
Flora, P. & Heidenheimer, A.J. (1981) (Eds). *The development of welfare states in Europe and America*. London: Transaction.
Franzini, M. & Pianta, M. (2016). *Disuguaglianze. Quante sono, come cambiarle*. Roma/Bari: Laterza.
Gourevitch, P. (1986). *Politics in hard times: Comparative responses to international economic crises*, Ithaca, NY: Cornell University Press.
Hacker, J.S. & Pierson, P. (2010). *Winner-take-all politics: How Washington made the rich richer – and turned its back on the middle class*. New York: Simon and Schuster.
Hancké, B., Rhodes, M., & Thatcher, M. (2007) (Eds). *Beyond varieties of capitalism: Conflict, contradictions, and complementarities in the European economy*. Oxford: Oxford University Press.
Hall, P.A. & Soskice, D. (ed.) (2001). *Varieties of capitalism: The institutional foundations of comparative advantage*. Oxford: Oxford University Press.
Hall, P.A. (2007). *The evolution of varieties of capitalism in Europe*. In B. Hancké, M. Rhodes & M. Thatcher (Eds), *Beyond varieties of capitalism: Conflict, contradictions, and complementarities in the European economy* (pp. 39–88). Oxford: Oxford University Press.
Hall, P.A (2022a). The shifting relationship between postwar capitalism and democracy. *Government & Opposition*, 57(1), 1–30.

Hall. P.A. (2022b). Why and how do growth strategies change? *Stato e Mercato*, 1, 3–52.

Hall, P.A. & Gingrich D.W. (2009). Varieties of capitalism and institutional complementarities in the political economy. *British Journal of Political Science*, 39(3), 449–482. doi:10.1017/S0007123409000672

Hemerijck, H. (2013). *Changing welfare states*. Oxford: Oxford University Press.

Hollingsworth, J.R. & Boyer, R. (1997) (Eds). *Contemporary capitalism: The embeddedness of institutions*. Cambridge: Cambridge University Press.

Ido, M. (2012) (Ed.). *Varieties of capitalism, types of democracy and globalization*. London/New York: Routledge.

Inglehart, R. (2018). *Cultural evolution: People's motivations are changing, and reshaping the world*. Cambridge: Cambridge University Press.

Iversen, T. & Soskice, D. (2006). Electoral institutions and the politics of coalitions: Why some democracies redistribute more than others. *The American Political Science Review*, 100(2), 164–181. DOI: 10.1017/S0003055406062083

Iversen, T. & Soskice, D. (2015). Democratic limits to redistribution: Inclusionary versus exclusionary coalitions in the knowledge economy. *World Politics*, 67(2), 1–41.

Kirchheimer, O. (1966). The transformation of western European party systems. In J. LaPalombara & W. Myron (Eds), *Political parties and political development* (pp. 177–200). Princeton, NJ: Princeton University Press.

Korpi, W. (1983). *The democratic class struggle*. London and New York: Routledge & Kegan Paul.

Lehmbruch, G. & Schmitter, P (1982) (Eds). *Patterns of corporatist policy-making*. London: Sage.

Lijphart, A. (1999). *Patterns of democracy: Government forms and performance in thirty-six countries*. New Haven, CT: Yale University Press.

Lijphart, A. (2012). *Patterns of democracy: Government forms and performance in thirty-six countries*, 2nd ed. New Haven, CT: Yale University Press

Manow, P. (2009). Electoral rules, class coalitions, and welfare state regimes, or how to explain Esping-Andersen with Stein Rokkan. *Socio-Economic Review*, 7(1), 101–121. doi:10.1093/ser/mwn022

Manow, P. (2015). Workers, farmers and Catholicism: A history of political class coalitions and the South-European welfare state regime. *Journal of European Social Policy*, 25(1), 32–49. https://doi.org/10.1177/0958928714556969

Manow, P. & Palier, B. (2009). *A conservative welfare state regime without Christian democracy? The French Etat-Providence, 1860–1960*. In K. van Kersbergen and P. Manow (Eds), *Religion, class coalitions, and welfare states* (pp. 146–175). Cambridge: Cambridge University Press.

Manow, P, Palier, B. & Schwander, H. (2018) (Eds). *Welfare democracies and party politics: Explaining electoral dynamics in times of changing welfare capitalism*. Oxford: Oxford University Press.

Milanovic, B. (2016). *Global inequality: A new approach for the age of globalization*. Cambridge, MA: Harvard University Press;

Milanovic, B. (2019). *Capitalism, alone: The future of the system that rules the world*. Cambridge, MA: The Belknap Press of Harvard University Press.

Morel, N., Palier, B., & Joakim, P. (2012). *Towards a social investment welfare state?* Bristol: Bristol University Press.

Mudge, S.K. (2018). *Leftism reinvented: Western Parties from socialism to neo-liberalism*. Cambridge, MA: Harvard University Press.

Olson, M. (1982). *The rise and decline of nations: Economic growth, stagnation and social rigidities*. New Haven, CT: Yale University Press.

Palier, B. & Thelen, K. (2010). Institutionalizing dualism: Complementarities and change in France and Germany. *Politics & Society*, 38(1), 119–148. DOI: 10.1177/0032329209357888

Paci, M. (2013). *Lezioni di sociologia storica*. Bologna: Il Mulino.

Pierson, P. (1994). *Dismantling the welfare state? Reagan, Thatcher and the politics of retrenchment*. Cambridge: Cambridge University Press.

Pierson, P. (2001) (Eds). *The new politics of the welfare state*. Oxford: Oxford University Press.

Piketty, T. (2013). *Le capital au XXI siècle*. Paris: Seuil.

Piketty T. (2020). *Capital e idéologie*. Paris: Seuil

Regini, M. (2000). *Modelli di capitalismo. Le risposte europee alla sfida della globalizzazione*. Roma and Bari: Laterza.

Regini, M. (2009). *Ascesa e declino del modello sociale europeo*. in L. Sciolla (Ed.), *Processi e trasformazioni sociali. La società europea dagli anni Sessanta ad oggi* (pp. 65–88). Roma and Bari: Laterza.

Regini, M. (2018). *Il mutamento del modello sociale europeo*. In M. Lazar, M. Salvati & L. Sciolla (Eds), *Europa*, vol. III, *Cultura e società* (pp. 165–173). Roma: Istituto della Enciclopedia Italiana.

Rueda, D. (2007). *Social democracy inside out: Partisanship and labor market policy in industrialized democracies*. Oxford: Oxford University Press.

Salvati. M. (2020). *Commento alla relazione di Carlo Trigilia "Politiche, classi e diseguaglianze: le basi istituzionali della regolazione*. Accademia Nazionale dei Lincei, conference on "Diseguaglianze classi sociali. La ricerca in Italia e nelle democrazie avanzate", Roma, 12 December 2018.

Sapir, A. (2005). *Globalisation and the reform of European social models*, paper presented at the "Ecofin Informal Meeting", Manchester, 9 September.

Schmitter, C.P. & Todor, A. (2014). Varieties of capitalism and types of democracy. *Stato e mercato*, 100, 87–116.

Schmitter, P. & Lehmbruch, G. (1979) (Eds). *Trends toward corporatist intermediation*. London: Sage.

Skocpol, T. & Somers, M. (1980). The uses of comparative history in macrosocial inquiry. *Comparative Studies in Society and History*, 22(2), 174–197. doi:10.1017/S0010417500009282

Stiglitz, J.E. (2012). *The price of inequality: How today's divided society endangers our future*. London: Norton.

Stiglitz, J.E. (2015). *The great divide: Unequal societies and what we can do about them*. London: Penguin.

Stiglitz, J.E. (2016). Inequality and economic growth. In M. Jacobs & M. Mazzucato (Eds), *Rethinking capitalism: Economics and policy for sustainable and inclusive Growth* (pp. 134–155). Chichester, Wiley,

Streek, W. (2013). *Gekaufte Zeit. Die vertagte Krise des demokratischen Kapitalismus*. Berlin: Suhrkamp

Thelen, K. (2014). *Varieties of liberalization and the new politics of social solidarity*. Cambridge: Cambridge University Press.

Trigilia, C. (2016). Tipi di democrazia e modelli di capitalismo. Un'agenda di ricerca. *Stato e Mercato*, 107, 183–213.

Trigilia, C. (2018). *La personalizzazione della leadership politica.* In D. D'Andrea & C. Trigilia (Eds), *Max Weber oggi. Ripensando politica e capitalismo*, (pp. 19–38). Bologna: Il Mulino.

Trigilia, C. (2019). Il Manifesto dell' "Economist". Un cambiamento di rotta tardivo? *Iride*, 32(1), 13–24.

Trigilia, C. (2022). Is democratic capitalism bound to disappear? *Stato e Mercato*, 1, 53–64.

Watson, S.E. (2015). *The left divided: The development and transformation of advanced welfare states*. Oxford: Oxford University Press.

Part I

Growth and inequalities in advanced democracies

Chapter 1

Four models of growth and inequality

Alberto Gherardini

1.1 Introduction

The issue of income inequality has increasingly become an object of interest as globalisation has progressed. Two different trends have distinguished themselves in the literature. The first concerns the curtailing of differences between advanced and underdeveloped economies. One of the main interpreters of this perspective is Angus Deaton (2013), the Nobel laureate in economics. According to Deaton, global economic growth has had positive effects on the incomes and well-being of less advanced economies, producing an improvement in the living conditions of that part of the global population that has succeeded in the great escape from poverty (Deaton, 2015). While highlighting the progressive convergence between countries, he does not conceal, however, that the narrowing of the gap is, to a large extent, attributable to the marked improvement in the economic conditions of Asian countries, while the permanence of disparities is still strongly conditioned by the lagging development of the African continent.

The second trend highlighted by studies on inequality concerns the growth of differences within countries. Among the many authors who have dedicated time to this area of study, we can refer to the work of Branko Milanovic (2016; 2019). He argues that the third wave of globalisation, the one that gained momentum with the 1980s and which the economist Dani Rodrik (2011) has termed "hyper-globalisation", has produced completely different effects compared to the previous ones. If, as Deaton points out, the distance between countries has been reduced, hyper-globalisation has increased inequality within countries. This is the result of the tendency towards social polarisation that has been evident in the major advanced economies at least since the second half of the 1990s. Where income and wealth are concentrated at the top of the social pyramid, the share of income available to the middle classes shrinks and the conditions of the less well-off deteriorate.

We aim to analyse the institutional causes of this phenomenon, with two specifications. First, we will focus on the welfare model and industrial relations, namely on the redistributive interventions that characterise the different

DOI: 10.4324/9781003297130-3

countries. Second, unlike other approaches that focus only on inequality and welfare, or exclusively on institutional factors affecting growth (e.g. studies on the "varieties of capitalism"), we propose to focus on the relationships between growth and redistributive policies. We will thus propose a typology that is based on more or less dynamic and more or less inclusive models of growth.

1.2 Inequality and economic growth: a typology

To move in this direction, it may prove valuable to ponder the observation that income inequality in advanced countries, albeit a general trend, neither increases with the same intensity nor reaches the same levels. This suggests that besides the common exposure to the effects of globalisation (offshoring, growth of international trade, and cost competition, etc.), a major role is played by differences in endogenous institutional factors, such as welfare and industrial relations.

We took the significant differences in income inequality levels in advanced countries as a starting point. Examining the 18 major advanced economies[1] between the mid-1980s and 2018, the Gini index[2] of disposable income after taxes and transfers shows that inequality increased from around 0.27 to 0.30.[3]

Over the past 30 years, the social structure has forked wider and wider, both in countries that were already characterised by strong inequality – such as the United States and the United Kingdom – and in the countries that in the early 1980s had more egalitarian societies – such as Sweden and Germany (Figure 1.1). However, also noteworthy is the fact that significant

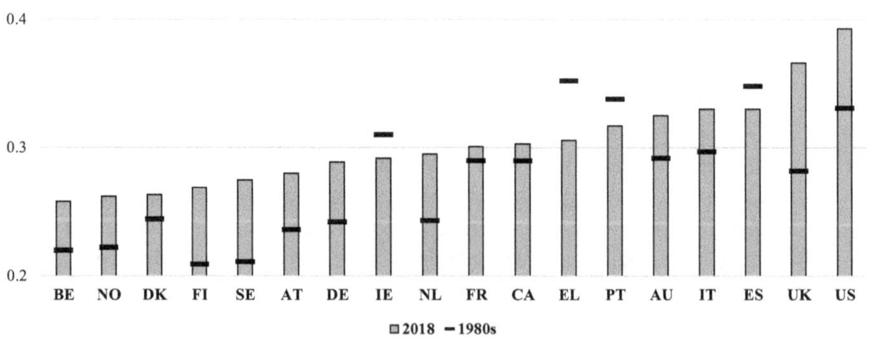

Figure 1.1 Dispersion of disposable income after taxes and transfers (Gini index, 2018 and 1980s).

Note: The value for the 1980s may vary from 1983 to 1987. The source is the Gini project, with the exception of Finland, Greece, and Norway (OECD data), and Portugal, where the source is the World Bank.

Source: OECD.

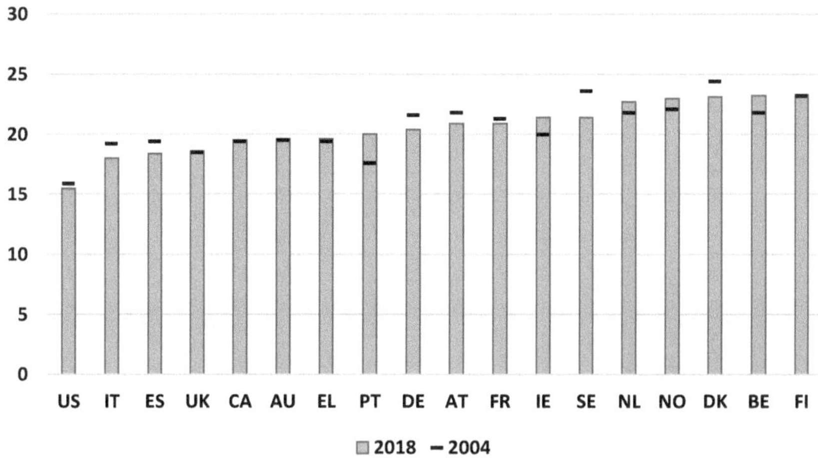

Figure 1.2 Share of income held by the 40% of the population with the lowest incomes (2018 and 2004).

Note: Income is the disposable income of households after taxes and transfers. The indicator measures the amount of income available to the two lowest quartiles of each country's income distribution.

Source: World Bank.

differences in overall levels of inequality within the more advanced countries have persisted, suggesting that this is not just a legacy of the past but that the phenomenon is influenced by institutional and regulatory setups well worth investigating.

Looking at other indicators of inequality – the share of income available to the poorest 40% of the population and the relative poverty rate (Figures 1.2 and 1.3) – these trends are confirmed. Albeit for a diminished time span, both point to a widening gap between the richest and poorest segments of the population and, at the same time, to persistent differences between countries.

From a diachronic perspective, inequality has not grown in a linear fashion. As early as 2005, the Gini index for economically advanced countries reached its current level (0.30). This might suggest that the economic and financial crisis of 2008 has only had a cyclical influence on inequalities and that, consequently, their ultimate must be sought in factors of a structural nature. What we do know is that between the mid-1980s and the mid-2000s, almost all the countries we have considered (14 out of 18) increased their internal inequalities: the Gini index rose by 11.8%, representing an average annual increase of 0.6%.

According to the OECD (2011), the disposable income of households increased over that period, but it was the richest 10% of the population whose

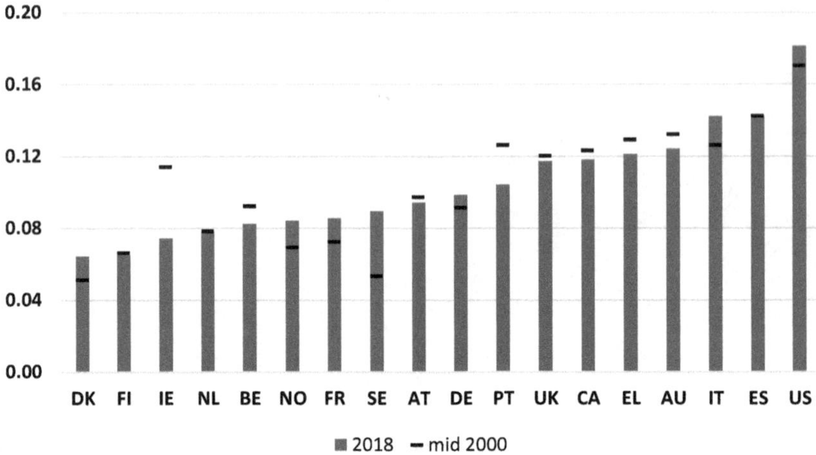

Figure 1.3 Relative poverty rate (2018 and 2000s).

Note: Relative poverty is calculated as the incidence of the population with an income at or below half the median income. Income is the disposable income of households after taxes and transfers. The relative value for the mid-2000s refers mostly to the year 2005, in some cases earlier (Netherlands, Denmark, Canada, Greece) and in others later (Finland and Italy).

Source: OECD.

share of income rose faster than that of the poorest 10%, so much so that in 2007 the average income of the richest decile was about nine times that of the poorest decile. Conversely, the most recent data show that over the last decade, the trend towards income concentration has slowed down (the Gini has increased by only 0.7%), although it has not reversed.

Nevertheless, the benefits of slowing growth in inequality have affected the lower strata of the population less. Suffice it to say that in the decade under review, the relative poverty index increased by 7.4%, the available income of the poorest 40% of the population fell by 1.3%, and the ratio between the income of the richest 20% of the population and the poorest 20% increased by 2.8%. In other words, if the society of the period of the Glorious Thirties could be broadly represented by a pyramid, since the 1980s it has increasingly taken the form of an hourglass.

Only in recent years has this trend diminished, the middle class has started to grow again, but this is rather due to a shift (or perhaps a sliding) in the upper classes than to a rise in the lower classes.

The data presented above show distinctly that levels of social inequality vary significantly from country to country, allowing us to clearly distinguish between different groups: at one end of the spectrum the Mediterranean and Anglo-Saxon countries, which show more marked inequalities, and

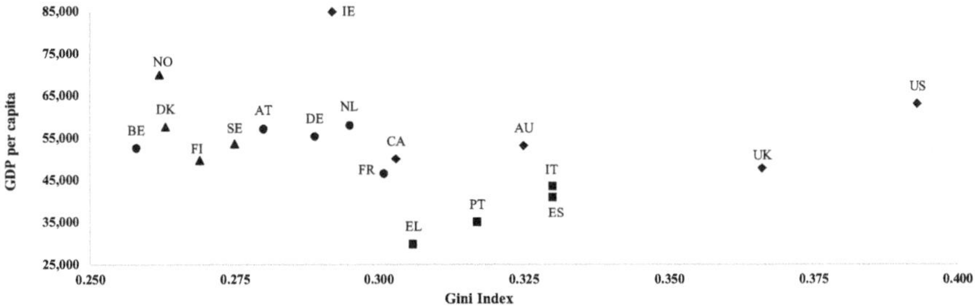

Figure 1.4 GDP per capita and income inequalities in advanced democracies (2018). Legend: Countries belonging to the high income/high inequality growth model are marked with the rhombus-shaped indicator. Countries with high income/low inequality countries are marked with the triangle indicator. Low income/high inequality countries are marked with the square indicator.

Note: GDP per capita is expressed in dollars, calculated at current prices and expressed in purchasing power parity (PPP). Income inequality is measured by the Gini coefficient on household disposable income after taxes and transfers.

Source: OECD.

at the other end the northern European countries, in which the social structure continues to be less polarised. The continental European states stand halfway between these two types. But how do the different levels of inequality combine with the degree of development of the economy and its growth rates?

Correlating the levels of inequality measured by the Gini index to the income of the population (Figure 1.4), we may hypothesise a first answer. Considering 18 cases of advanced economies, three ideal types emerge: high income/high inequality; high income/low inequality; low income/high inequality.

We should bear in mind that the two types with higher-than-average per capita income are also those that, generally speaking, have shown higher-than-average income growth over time in the last two decades. The opposite is true for the lowest income countries, which are also the least dynamic (Figure 1.5).

Three clearly distinguishable types of growth emerge from this perspective. On the one hand, there is a first group of countries that we define as "inclusive growth"; on the other hand, there is a second group characterised by "non-inclusive growth". To these two groups should be added the model that gather the Southern European countries that, being characterised by low competitiveness and high inequality, can be defined as countries with "low, non-inclusive growth".[4]

In order to analyse the relationship between growth and inequality, however, it would be opportune to introduce a further dividing dimension within the inclusive growth countries. In the literature, it is well established that

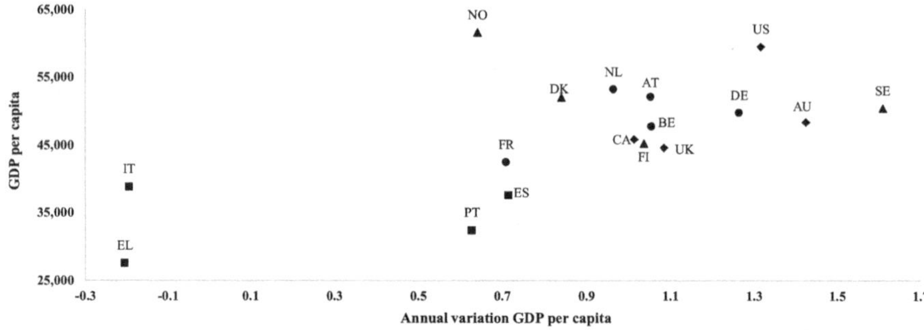

Figure 1.5 GDP per capita (2018) and percentage change in GDP per capita (2001–2018).

Legend: See Figure 1.4.

Note: GDP per capita is in dollars, calculated at current prices and expressed in purchasing power parity (PPP).
The average annual change in GDP is calculated at constant 2010 prices.

Source: OECD.

reforms since the 1990s have diversified the structure of the labour market in continental European countries compared to the Nordic countries and, consequently, the distribution of their incomes (Emmenegger, 2012; Palier & Thelen, 2010; Rueda, 2014; Thelen, 2014). As will be seen in more detail in Chapter 4, continental European countries have witnessed a deregulation of the labour market in the service sector, which, however, has not reduced protection for industrial workers.

In the Scandinavian countries, on the other hand, the lower level of commitment to the safeguarding of traditional work (which nevertheless remains high in comparative terms) has been accompanied by greater protection for flexible workers, ensured by more generous interventions in terms of vocational training, job placement, and social benefits. Based on this different level of labour market "dualisation", it is therefore possible to distinguish between countries with a more unequal distribution of incomes and others where such differences are less pronounced (Figure 1.6).

The typology used throughout the pages to come is described as follows. The first model is that of the countries with non-inclusive growth (NIG), that is, those characterised by high income, high economic growth, and high inequality. The second is that of the inclusive growth (IG) countries because they are characterised by high income, high growth, and lower inequality. In view of the above-mentioned regarding the differences in terms of dualisation, the model can be divided into two variants: egalitarian inclusive growth (EIG), typical of the experience of Northern European countries, and dualistic inclusive growth (DIG) closer to that of continental European countries.

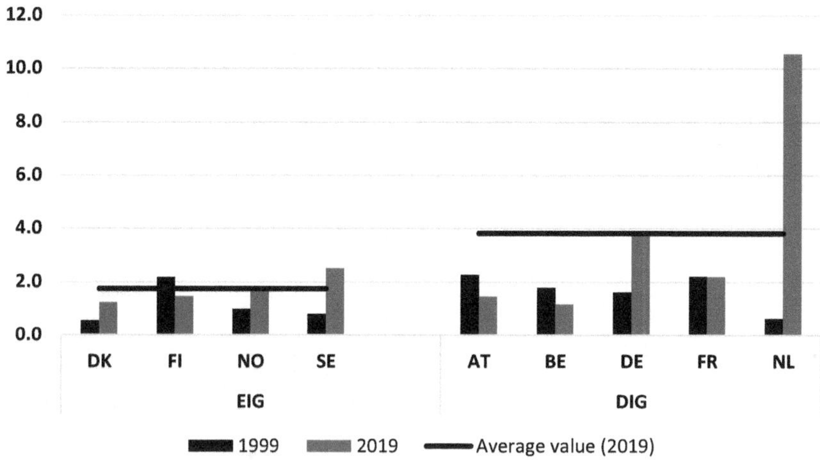

Figure 1.6 Dualisation index for inclusive growth countries (2019 and 1999).

Note: the dualisation index corresponds to the ratio between the EPL (Employment Protection Legislation) for workers with permanent employment contracts and the largesse of the social policy of the job market, calculated as ratio between expenditure for active policies and unemployment rate (Rueda, 2014).

Finally, the non-inclusive low growth countries (NILG) are those in Southern Europe that respond to the configuration of low income, low growth, and high levels of inequality (Figure 1.7).

1.3 Macro-economic differences between growth types

These four types of growth outlined above will be examined more in depth in the chapters to come. Here we introduce some preliminary differences, related to macro-economic variables of particular importance: public expenditure, revenues from taxation, and debt.

In order to identify public spending behaviour, we use two indicators to reveal the quantity of resources governments have devoted to a selected set of items concerning "investment" and "consumption" expenditure. The "consumption" component includes spending on pensions, health, unemployment, and social housing; that is, it refers to traditional social policies implemented to cover what can be termed traditional social risks.

Expenditure on "investment", on the other hand, covers interventions that are also referred to as social investment and includes: expenditure on kindergarten and childcare, education (including tertiary education), active labour policies (training and upgrading/retraining, support for vulnerable groups), as well as research and development policies.[5] The combination of the two

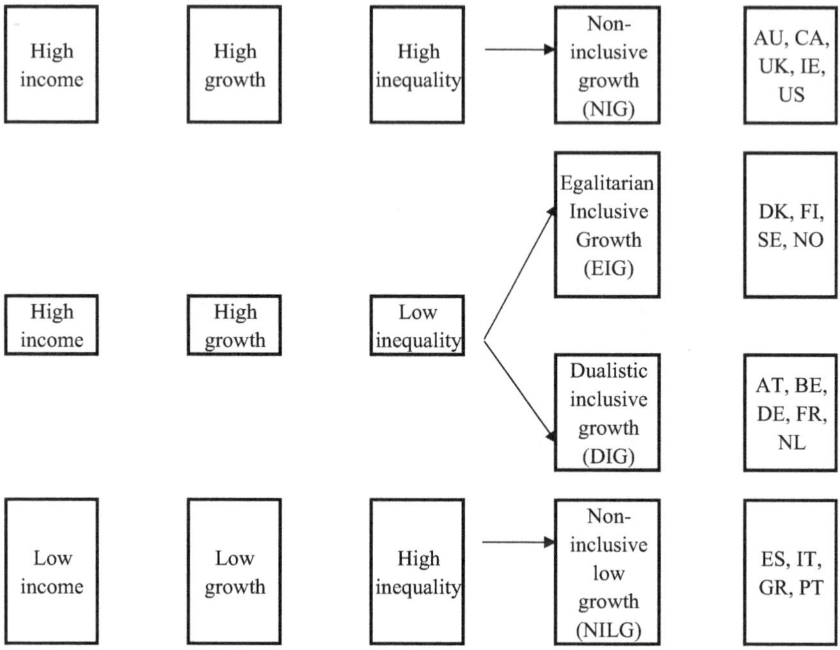

Figure 1.7 Four models of growth and inequality.

indicators defines different styles of intervention that characterise types of growth, highlighting the significance of our typology. NIG countries have relatively low levels of public spending (23.7% of GDP) but show a high incidence of investment in support of social and economic development (0.40). In contrast, EIG countries are characterised by high public spending (34.0% of GDP) combined with a high incidence of investment in consumption (0.50).

The DIG and NILG countries generate yet another configuration. As in the EIG model, they show a high level of public spending (32.7% and 31.5% of GDP, respectively), which, however, tips the balance on the side of consumption compared to investment. Specifically, the incidence of the latter on the former is limited to 0.33 in the DIG and 0.23 in the NILG (Figure 1.8).

The four types also show significant divergences in relation to taxation (Figure 1.9). The group of NIG countries shows significantly lower tax revenues compared to the other types (28.8% of GDP), in line with the levels of public spending outlined above. Conversely, inclusive growth countries offset higher public spending with higher tax revenues. The difference between egalitarian and dualistic variants is marked by the difference in the source of revenues. The dualistic model, with a Bismarckian/occupational welfare

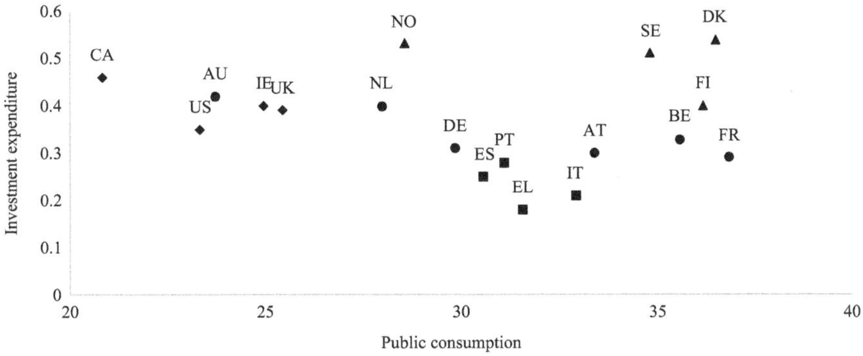

Figure 1.8 Public consumption and investment expenditure as a percentage of total expenditure (2013).

Legend: countries belonging to the NIG model are marked with the rhombus-shaped indicator. Countries in the EIG model are marked with the triangle-shaped indicator. DIG countries are marked with the circle-shaped indicator. Finally, NILG countries are marked with the square indicator.

Note: The consumption and investment considered here cover only a limited number of items. In particular, consumption concerns expenditure on different types of pensions, health, disability, unemployment, and housing, as well as allowances, family allowances, and maternity and family leave. Investment covers public expenditure on active labour market policies, family, children and childcare, education (including tertiary education), research, and development. Public expenditure indicates total consumption and investment expenditure as defined above.

Source: consumption and households: OECD (SOCX); education: World Bank elaboration on UNESCO data; research and development: OECD, MSTI (Main Science and Technology Indicators).

matrix, weighs more in terms of social contributions, which reach 14.6% of GDP, against an overall taxation of 41.7%. In EIG countries, where taxation corresponds to 42.8% of the GDP, social security contributions have a lower average weight (8.0%), ranging from 0.04% of the Danish GDP to 12.1% of the Finnish GDP. The taxation of NILG countries has a matrix more similar to that of DIG countries. In this case, the average incidence of social contributions is 11.2% while tax revenues from taxes and social contributions stand at 37.3%. Within this group, however, the case of Italy is remarkable, with revenue from taxation that is comparable to that recorded in inclusive growth countries.

With a few exceptions, the ten-year trend in income from taxes and contributions is increasing (Figure 1.10). However, a high level of intra-group variance emerges conspicuously. Rather than structural constraints, this indicator therefore seems to be more subject to variances that depend on national political economy choices (as in the case of Ireland and Norway) and exogenous pressures (as in the case of Greece). Last but not least, this

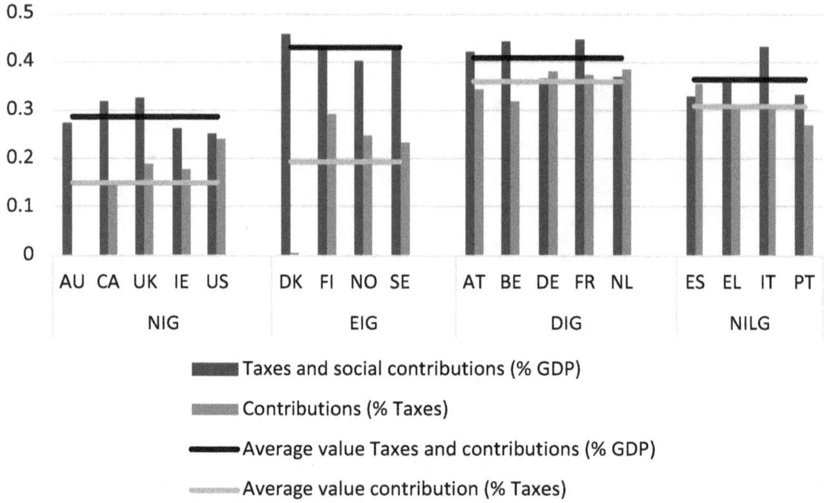

Figure 1.9 Taxes and social contributions per country and per growth model (average 2010–2017).

Note: For Australia, the time range does not include 2017.

Source: Elaboration on ICTD/UNU-WIDER, Government Revenue Dataset, 2018.

indicator is also affected by the effects of the economic recovery of previous years, which increases the tax base of different countries and, consequently, revenues at the same tax rates.

The macro-economic picture that derives from the analysis of consumption and revenues is completed by indicators concerning public budget deficit (Figures 1.11 and 1.12). The average value of the budget deficit over the ten-year period 2009–2018 indicates that the EIG countries have a greater capacity for controlling public accounts, equal only to some of the DIG countries. On the contrary, the NILG countries have recorded decidedly higher deficits, although in the decade considered Italy has settled at levels similar to those of continental European countries, thanks also to a primary surplus that is among the lowest in advanced economies. Countries with non-inclusive growth, some of which (the United States and Ireland) have deficit levels similar to those of the NILG, are characterised by greater irregularity, while in other cases resource management has been more severe. Using the indicator for the stock of public debt, the differences between types are more pronounced. At one end of the spectrum, NILG countries have, on average, accumulated public debt corresponding to about 134% of GDP. At the other end, EIG countries have an extremely low level of debt, corresponding to 54.8% of GDP. The other two growth types are in an intermediate position,

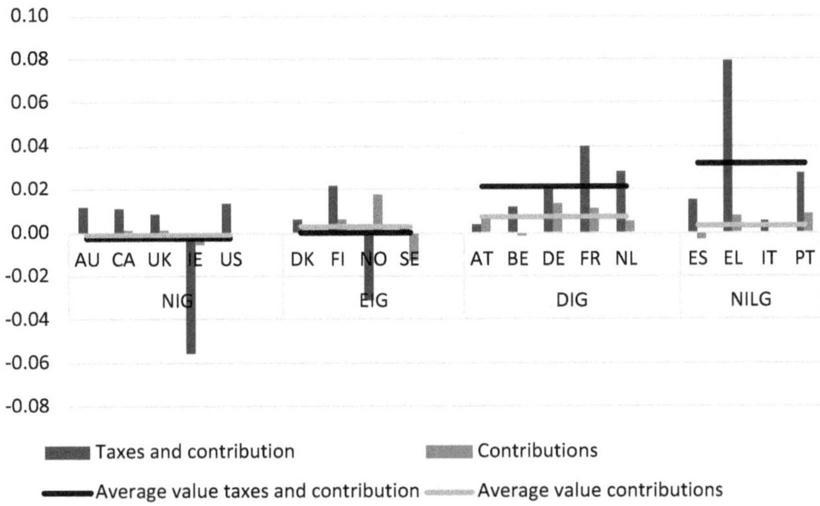

Figure 1.10 Change in taxes and social contributions between 2008 and 2017 by country and model as a percentage of GDP.

Note: for Australia, the time range does not include 2017.

Source: elaboration on ICTD/UNU-WIDER, Government Revenue Dataset, 2018.

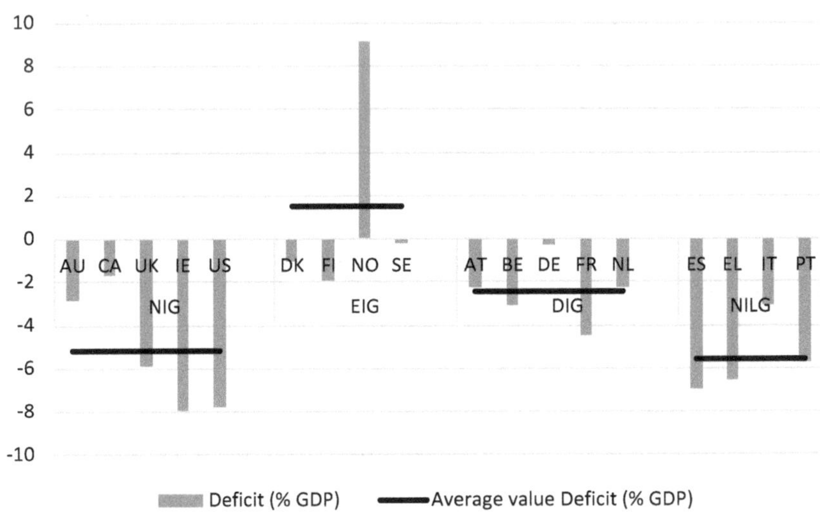

Figure 1.11 Public deficit by country and by model (average value 2009–2018).

Source: OECD data, general government deficit.

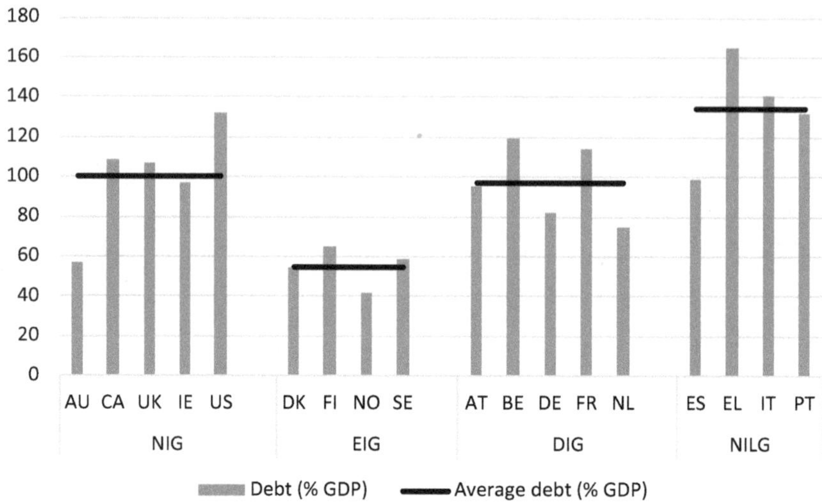

Figure 1.12 Public debt by country and model (average value 2009–2018).

Source: OECD data, general government debt.

Table 1.1 Growth models and macroeconomic variables

	Expenditure	*Revenues from taxation*	*Indebtedness*
NIG	Low but investment-oriented	Low and fiscal	Medium-high with differences
EIG	High and investment-oriented	High and fiscal	Low
DIG	High and consumption-oriented	High and contributory	High with differences
NILG	High and consumption-oriented	High and contributory	High

although, in both cases, some countries can be clearly identified as departing significantly from the average value. Specifically, Germany and the Netherlands are characterised by much lower debt than the other DIG countries, while the US debt is significantly above the average for its group.

Overall, four differentiated profiles emerge from a cross-reading of macro-economic indicators (Table 1.1). The NIG model is characterised by a combination of low expenditure (but investment-oriented), low taxation, and medium-high debt. The EIG countries have a completely different profile: high investment-oriented public spending, but with a significant share also for consumption, which is matched by high taxation. In this case, deficits and public debt remain under control. The inclusive capacity of DIG countries is supported by expenditure with a higher consumption-oriented component. Revenues from taxation are higher in this case and there is a higher incidence of social contributions. Public debt is higher, especially in the French-speaking area. Finally, the overall picture of the NILGs shows a system based on a more limited redistributive capacity and even more prone towards consumption than in the countries neighbouring the DIG. As we shall see later, this tendency is accompanied by less effectiveness in reducing inequalities and by greater imbalances between services/benefits and revenues, which must be offset by public finance, with consequences for deficits and debt.

Notes

1 The reference is to countries considered in this research: Australia (AU), Austria (AT), Belgium (BE), Canada (CA), Germany (DE), Denmark (DK), Spain (ES), Finland (FI), France (FR), the United Kingdom (UK), Ireland (IE), Italy (IT), the Netherlands (NL), Norway (NO), Portugal (PT), Sweden (SE), and the United States (US).

2 The Gini index ranges on a scale from 0 to 1, where the lowest extreme represents the greatest dispersion of income and the highest, the greatest concentration.

3 Only four countries (Ireland, Portugal, Greece, and Spain) have curtailed internal differences, most probably due to sluggish economic development. See, among others, Andreosso-O'Callaghan, Lenihan, and McDonough (2014) and Ó Riain (2014) for an interpretation of the exceptional case in Ireland, which in our analyses often emerges as an outlier.

4 "Low growth" refers here to a recent phase and does not exclude that in earlier periods growth may have been more considerable.

5 This is a similar elaboration, with some modifications, to the one presented by Beramendi et al. (2015, 9–10). The "expenditure" indicator used here also includes public expenditure on health, social housing and "passive" household support (family allowances). The "investment" indicator adjoins expenditure on primary and secondary education while, conversely, excluding the private expenditure on research and development.

References

Andreosso-O'Callaghan, B., Lenihan, H., & McDonough, T. (2014). The evolving model of capitalism in Ireland: An insight into enterprise development and policy. *Economic and Industrial Democracy*, 37(2), 319–344. doi:10.1177/0143831X14547116

Beramendi, P., Häusermann, S., Kitschelt, H., & Kriesi, H. (2015) (Eds). *The politics of advanced capitalism*. Cambridge: Cambridge University Press.

Deaton, A. (2015). *La grande fuga. Salute, ricchezza e origini della disuguaglianza*. Bologna: il Mulino.

Deaton, A. (2013). Assessing the impact of the memoranda on Greek labour market and labour relations. ILO Working Paper, n. 53. Geneva: International Labour Office.

Emmenegger, P. (2012). Job security regulations in Western democracies: A fuzzy-set analysis. *European Journal of Political Research*, 50(3), 336–364. doi.org/10.1111/j.1475-6765.2010.01933.x

Milanovic, B. (2016). *Global inequality: A new approach for the age of globalization*. Cambridge: Harvard University Press.

Milanovic, B. (2019). *Capitalism, alone. The future of the system that rules the world*. Cambridge: Harvard University Press.

OECD (2011). *Divided we stand: Why inequality keeps rising*. Paris: OECD Publishing.

Ó Riain, S. (2014). *The rise and fall of Ireland's Celtic tiger: liberalism, boom and bust*. Cambridge: Cambridge University Press.

Palier, B. & Thelen, K. (2010). Institutionalizing dualism. *Politics & Society* 38(1), 119–148. doi.org/10.1177/0032329209357888

Rodrik, D. (2011). *The globalization paradox: democracy and the future of the world economy*. New York, WW Norton.

Rueda, D. (2014). Dualization, crisis and the welfare state. *Socio-Economic Review*. 12(2), 381–407. doi.org/10.1093/ser/mwu015

Thelen, K. (2014). *Varieties of liberalization and the new politics of social solidarity*. Cambridge, Cambridge University Press.

Chapter 2

Production structure, employment, and corporate governance

Marco Betti and Cecilia Manzo

2.1 Introduction

The data regarding the discrete development paths presented in the previous chapter illustrate that the correlation between the highest level of GDP per capita and, on the one hand, its greater increase over time, and, on the other, the extent of income inequality, cannot be reduced to a simplistic univocal equation. In other words, high income conditions are not necessarily associated with lower inequality. Nevertheless, situations of stagnation or low growth are more uniformly associated with high inequality. Clearly, a competitive production structure, based on innovation, productivity growth, and the ability to export quality products with high technological content, may provide greater scope for effective redistributive measures to combat inequality. It is therefore important to distinguish our own paths from this point of view and identify the key aspects in which they differ.

This, however, is not enough. Good income levels and stronger development would seem to be conditions that are favourable, yet not sufficient, for more inclusive growth. We hypothesise that they should therefore be integrated with other institutional factors, in particular redistributive interventions linked to industrial relations and the welfare model, which in turn bring up the significance of the political-institutional structure, and which will be analysed later.

To proceed in this direction, it would therefore be advisable to first pose a few questions. What is the degree of solidity of the productive apparatus and what is it based on? How do the quantity and quality of employment vary in the different development paths? How do corporate governance and financing mechanisms differ? We will address these questions in a very schematic way, with the sole aim of outlining the main features of the productive engine that differentiates our ideal-typical paths of more or less dynamic and inclusive growth.

DOI: 10.4324/9781003297130-4

2.2 Production structure

Examining the production structure in the years between 2009 and 2018, a general shift of the economy towards services can be observed, along with diminishing employment in the industry sector. These trends, however, take a variety of forms. The data on employment in industry (Figure 2.1) illustrates that the significance of the industrial sector has dropped in recent years where non-inclusive growth (NIG) and egalitarian inclusive growth (EIG) are concerned, while higher peaks have been recorded in the other two types of growth, with the greatest values reached by Germany (27.9) and Italy (27.2) respectively.

In relation to the incidence of services on employment (Figure 2.2), this can be noted as generally lower in countries with greater growth difficulties non-inclusive low growth economies (NILG), including Italy, while it reaches the highest levels in those cases where greater dynamism is manifest, both with low (EIG) and high (NIG) inequality.

Later, we will see how the numerical composition of those employed in services varies in some countries that reflect the different development pathways. Here, we can anticipate how different profiles emerge. Notwithstanding the greater significance of personal services (which include public services) in all the cases considered, NIG countries are characterised by the higher incidence of both more specialised services with high wages (business services) and less specialised and lower added value services (consumer services), as well as by the considerable significance of personal services. Only the Scandinavian countries with an EIG trend are characterised by even higher peaks of personal services, linked to the high incidence – as we shall see – of public

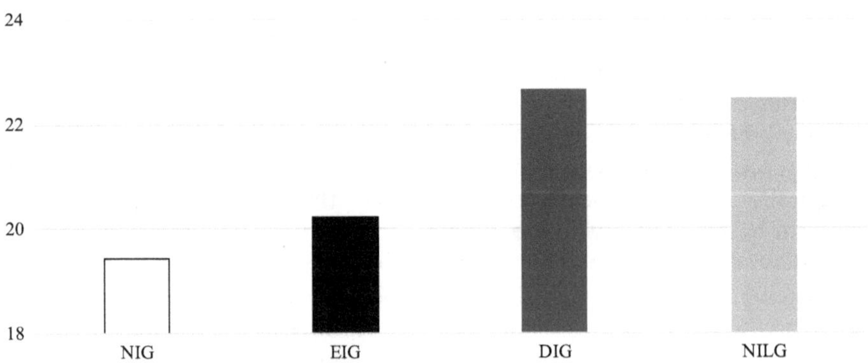

Figure 2.1 Employment in the industrial sector as a percentage of total employment (2009–2018 average).

Source: World Bank.

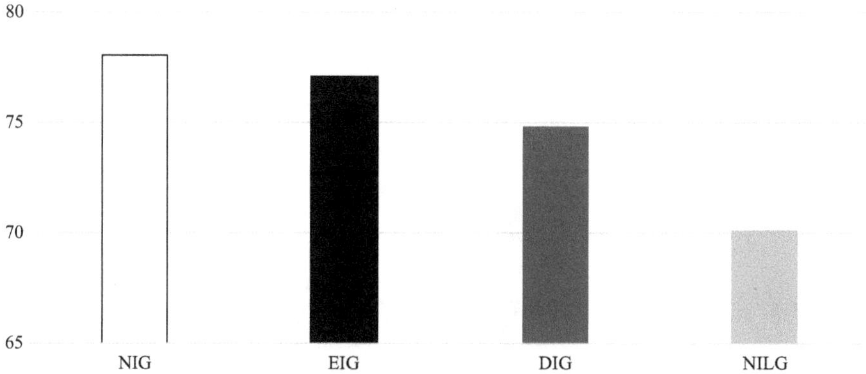

Figure 2.2 Incidence of employment in services on total employment (average 2009–2018).

Source: World Bank.

employment. But in this case lower values for consumer services emerge, as is the case for the dualistic inclusive growth (DIG). Finally, in NILG countries, there is a lower incidence of business and personal services and a substantial presence of consumer services with low added value.

The dynamism measured by the level and growth of per capita income over the last two decades would thus seem associated with a lower industrial connotation in terms of employment and with the presence of, and increase in, more specialised services. However, let us return to the industrial structure for a moment to highlight some differential features in the different contexts.

Considering first the size of industrial enterprises, NILG countries turn out to have the highest proportion of manufacturing enterprises with fewer than 20 employees (Figure 2.3), with peaks reached by Greece (96.8%) and Italy (92.5%). A glance at the number of employees by company size reveals even more clearly the significance of the small companies in the various contexts. In this respect, the dividing line is essentially between the NILG and all other models. In countries with the former trend, the number of workers in firms with fewer than ten employees is roughly twice as high as in the other cases (Figure 2.4).

The significance of small enterprises can be considered an indicator of greater weakness and more limited innovative capacity in the production structure – not that all small enterprises necessarily have these characteristics, especially when they are integrated into local systems or districts at a regional level. In order to explore this dimension further, and to check whether, and to what extent, it differs from our models, let us consider the incidence of the export of high technology goods, and of medium and high technology goods, on total exports.

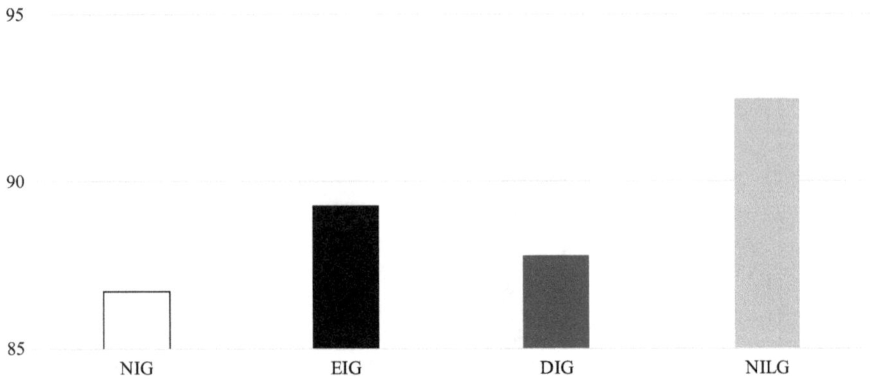

Figure 2.3 Number of manufacturing firms with fewer than 20 employees (2016).

Note: The figure for the United States and Canada refers to 2015.

Source: OECD.

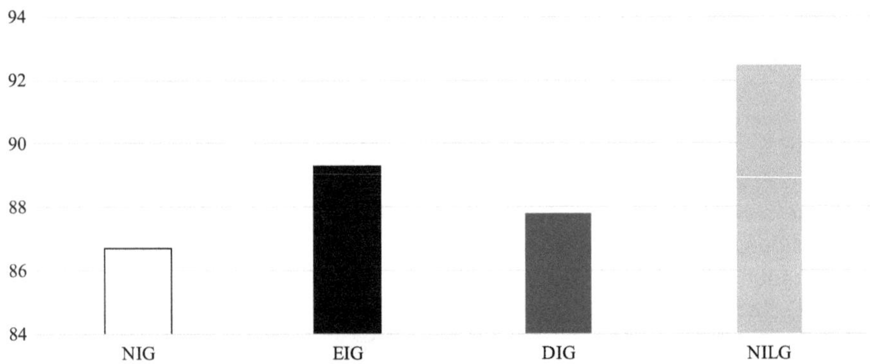

Figure 2.4 Percentage of workers employed in small enterprises (one to nine employees) over total employment (2016).

Source: OECD (SDBS).

For the first indicator (relating only to products classified as high-tech), the United States and the United Kingdom are the countries that stand out the most, while, with the exception of France, which reaches the highest peak, the values of EIG and DIG countries are lower – not, however, Germany, the export country par excellence.

It should be noted that the data from Ireland is influenced by the strong presence there of foreign multinationals for tax purposes. NILG countries reveal a considerably more modest performance (Figure 2.5a).

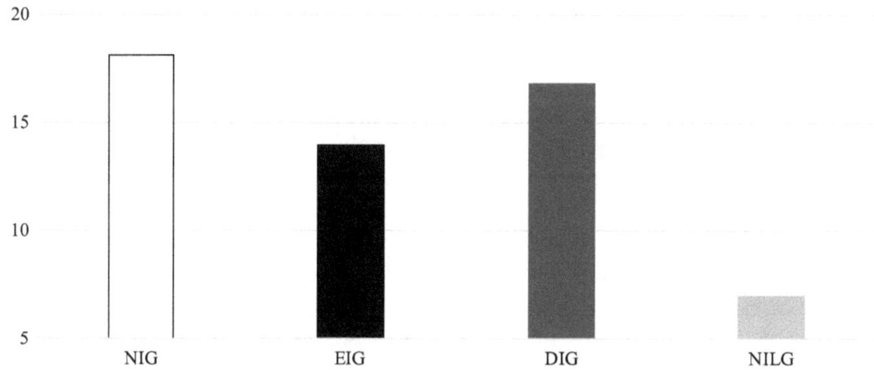

Figure 2.5a High-tech exports as a percentage of manufacturing exports (average 2009–2017).

Source: United Nations Industrial Development Organization (UNIDO), Competitive Industrial Performance (CIP).

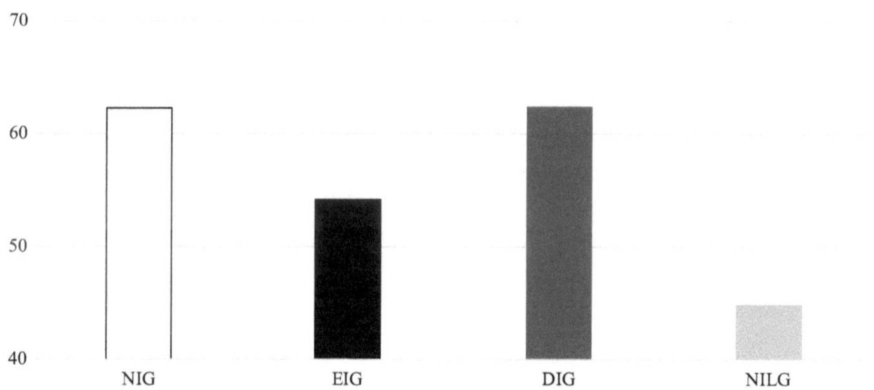

Figure 2.5b Incidence of medium and high-tech exports on manufacturing exports (2017).

Source: See Figure 2.5a.

Looking at the export figure that includes medium as well as high-tech, the balance between NIG countries (especially the USA and the UK) and inclusive growth countries is redressed, thanks mainly to the performance of Germany and France. The position of Italy and France also improves (Figure 2.5b).

Overall, this data points to an initial, very clear divide between countries with low growth or stagnation and those with higher growth capacity. The former show elements of greater weakness in the production structure linked to the lower development of specialised services and the greater persistence of industry, characterised by the much more widespread presence of small businesses and a modest specialisation in high, but also in part medium, technology production.

The second divide concerns countries with higher non-inclusive growth, on the one hand, and dynamic and more inclusive countries, on the other. The former have seen more significant industrial downsizing in favour of services, with the great, though not exclusive, presence of (low-skilled) consumer services. Industrial firms, however, reveal greater capacity to move into high-tech production, in the field of what has also been called "radical innovation" (Hall & Soskice, 2001).

Conversely, the countries of the two more inclusive growth models seem to share a lower presence of consumer services and an industrial base that in some cases, such as Germany, remains more substantial in terms of employment. In general, this latter performs well in the production and export of medium-technology goods (such as, for example, German cars) linked to the world of "incremental innovation".

2.3 Employment and productivity

Over the last two decades, the employment rate has varied significantly between the different groups of countries analysed (Figure 2.6). The EIG and DIG countries (in particular, Germany and the Netherlands) show a high level of participation in the labour market, with higher values than the NIG countries (74–75%). The gap with the NILG is even greater, with significantly lower rates.

Figure 2.6 Employment rate, age range 15–64, percentage values (average values for 2009–2018).

Source: OECD, Labour Market Statistics.

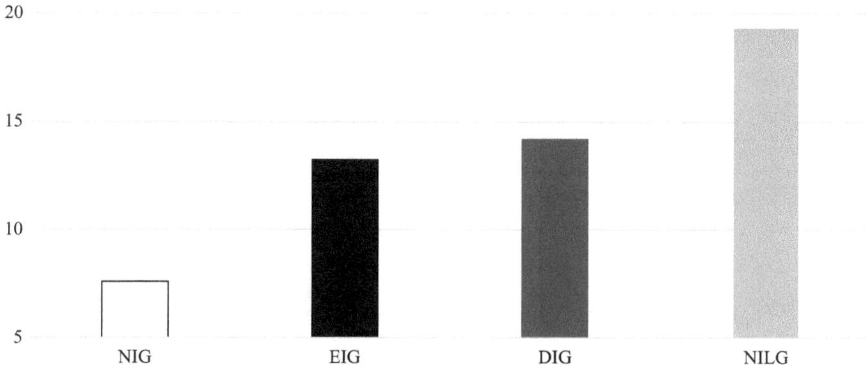

Figure 2.7 Number of employees with fixed-term contracts, percentage values (2017).

Source: OECD, Labour Market Statistics.

The Scandinavian EIG countries are also characterised by a higher presence of women in the labour market (a trend that has been observed since the 1960s), the diffusion of voluntary part-time work, and flexibility combined with low precariousness. The economic crises of the early 1990s (in particular, in Finland and Sweden) and 2008 thus found countries with robust labour markets featuring a distinctive capacity for generating employment (Sapir, 2005).

The number of people employed with permanent contracts varies widely across our models (Figure 2.7). This figure is influenced not only by the organisational culture of work in the various countries examined but also by the fact that different programmes are implemented to encourage the spread of fixed-term contractual formulas and thus introduce greater labour market flexibility, especially on entry (Rizza & Scarano, 2019). The Netherlands (21.5%) has the longest tradition of fixed-term work while the NIG countries resort less to temporary employment (7.6%); this can be correlated – as will be seen in more detail in Chapters 4 and 9 – with the broader regulation entrusted to the market that does not require the expedient of searching for atypical work in order to obtain more flexibility. On the other hand, the strong protection of permanent employment over the years has led, especially in NILG countries, to greater recourse to fixed-term work in order to favour labour market entry flexibility.

The incidence of young people not in education and employment (NEETs), with reference to the youth population (Figure 2.8), is greater in the countries that, as we have seen, are characterised by a lower overall employment rate, and in NIG countries where, notwithstanding a high employment rate, there is a high level of youth unemployment, especially in the United States and Canada.

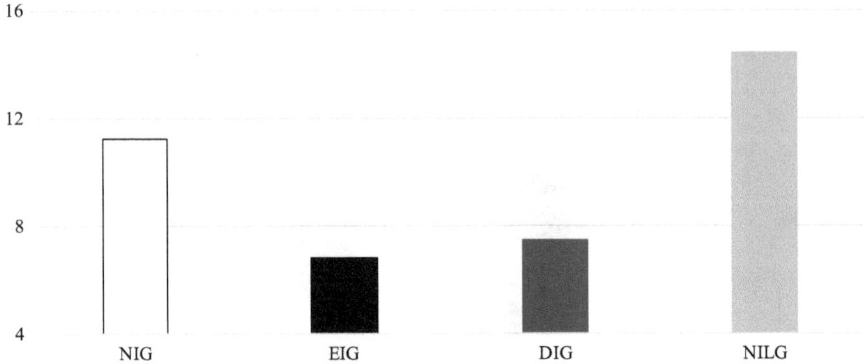

Figure 2.8 Incidence of NEETs on the youth population, percentage values (2017).

Source: OECD, Employment and Labour Market Statistics.

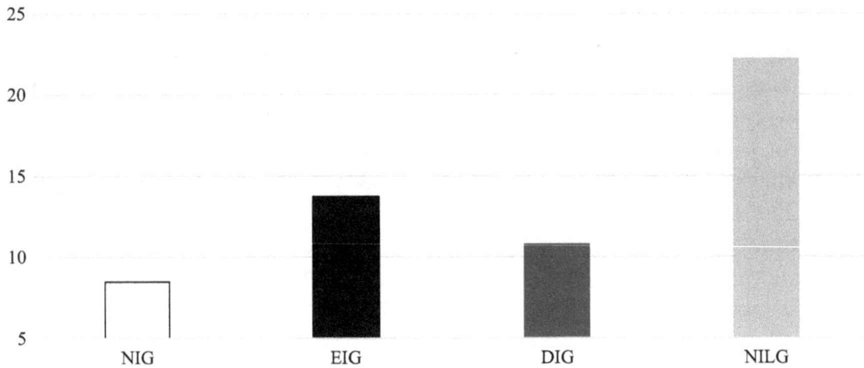

Figure 2.9 Undeclared economy as a percentage of GDP (year 2015).

Source: Medina and Schneider [2018].

Another striking indicator concerns "unofficial" economic activity, i.e. the hidden or shadow economy (Figure 2.9). As might be expected, the incidence of the shadow economy on GDP is highest in the NILG countries (22.3%), with particularly high values in Greece (26.5%) and Italy (23%). With rates lower by more than half, the European countries come closest to inclusive growth while those with non-inclusive growth trends are lower still.

With regard to labour productivity in 2018 (Figure 2.10) significant differences emerge between the various cases considered. First, there is a strong gap between the Mediterranean NILG countries and the others. But substantial differences also appear within the different types of development. Italy and Spain have markedly higher values than Greece and Portugal. The

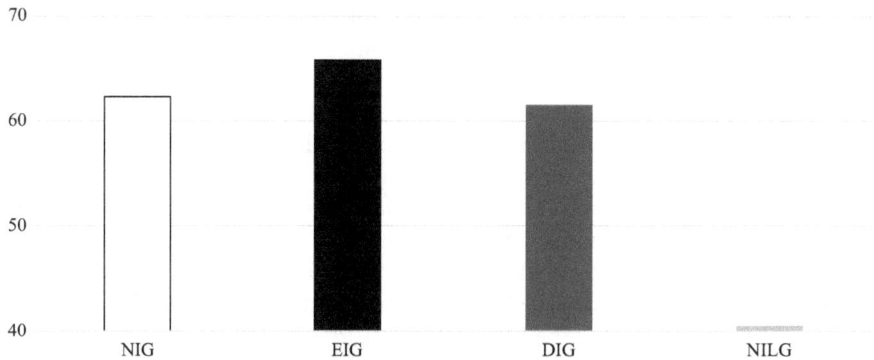

Figure 2.10 Labour productivity (GDP per hours worked, in 2010 PPP dollars, 2018).

Note: data regarding the United States and Canada refers to 2017.

Source: OECD, Labour productivity growth in the total economy.

United States is well above the UK and better than the EIG (with the exception of Norway) and DIG countries. The latter also perform well overall in comparison with the Nordic countries with an EIG trend.

Overall, the data on employment and productivity confirm and reinforce the picture that has already emerged from the consideration of some indicators relating to the structure of production. The employment level is higher in the inclusive growth areas (EIG and DIG, especially Germany and the Netherlands), while lower values are recorded for the NILG. Atypical employment is more widespread in the context of the NILG, but also in some inclusive growth countries (the Netherlands and France, less so in Germany). In this respect, it is conceivable that a dualisation of the labour market (insiders/outsiders) has emerged more significantly due to the expedient of atypical work as a resort to make employment more flexible and more remunerative in sectors with highly variable patterns of demand, especially in the field of low-productivity services.

The positive performance of employment in the inclusive growth countries is confirmed by the low number of young people not in education or employment (NEETs), which in contrast reaches high values in the Mediterranean European countries (NILG). Similar trends can be observed in youth unemployment and more generally in the shadow economy, as well as in productivity levels and trends over time.

2.4 Corporate governance and financing mechanisms

The fact that production specialisation, innovation paths, and competitiveness may be affected by the governance of firms and the way they are financed is not a new consideration. In the literature on the variety of capitalisms, this dimension has been identified as one of the most important factors for identifying models such as "Anglo-Saxon capitalism" and "Rhineland capitalism" (Albert, 1991) or distinguishing between "coordinated market economies" and "non-coordinated economies" (Hall & Soskice, 2001).

Comparative studies have pinpointed some variables helpful in defining the main models, such as the shareholding structure of firms and the role and functioning of capital markets (Allen & Gale, 2000; Bosetti, 2010; Zattoni, 2015). Corporate governance interacts with the type of financial system, centred on markets or intermediaries; with the relationships created between firms and workers, collaborative and long-term or distant and flexible (Trento, 2012); and with the role of the State (Burroni, 2016).

The prevailing legal regime is one of the first elements to take into account. In common law countries, where the law is unwritten and case law is the source of law, corporate governance guidelines tend to be significantly influenced by the indications expressed by stock exchange supervisory bodies. This regime predominates in Anglo-Saxon countries, where extensive recourse to the financial market is common, along with a prevalence of large, widely owned public companies and a marked separation between ownership and management. In contrast, in civil law countries, greater centrality is reserved for the legislator, who defines the orientation rules and constraints for formalising governance structures and processes. Public regulation, however, is part of a "closed" context, where ownership of risk capital is essentially transferred through agreements between the parties, while the financial market plays a less important role.

Therefore, a second factor to consider is the roles played by the markets and the banks. In the Anglo-Saxon markets, resources flow quickly, following stock market price movements, and thus stable majorities interested in the long-term management of the company are infrequent ("impatient capital"). In such a situation, managers assume a powerful leadership position. However, shareholder pressure to seek short-term results that satisfy investors may discourage innovative processes with long-term yields. Indeed, management can only maintain its position if the shareholders' results are deemed satisfactory.

In contrast, banks have historically played a more important role in continental Europe and Scandinavian countries. Banks have participated in formulating business strategies, acting both as partners – in the capacity of permanent shareholders, holding a considerable part of the risk capital and therefore authorised to appoint directors – and as creditors. In this case, a more "patient" capital makes possible the pursuit of longer-term innovation processes but may encounter more difficulties in monitoring the effectiveness of management action (Rajan & Zingales, 2001).

Finally, a third element concerns the openness of the institutional bodies (composed by employees and employers). The most significant example of this, which will be looked at in more detail in the following chapters, is provided by Germany, where employee representatives are present on the supervisory board of the largest companies.

Based on these elements, we can identify two criteria of classification: on the one hand, the type of monitoring to which managers are subjected and, on the other, how powers of administration and control are distributed.

In the first case, we will distinguish between an outsider system ("external" monitoring) carried out by the market and an insider system ("internal" monitoring) carried out by the main stakeholders. The outsider system – also called the market-oriented system – is implemented in the presence of many large listed companies, with widespread ownership, in which the market regulates the potential conflict of interest between shareholders and management. The capital market thus plays a relevant role for savings transformation, institutional investors, and venture capital funds (Allen & Gale, 2000; Deeg, 2010; Zattoni, 2015; Burroni, 2016; Amable, 2003). It should also be noted that, in this case, the legal system accords high protection to investors (Trento, 2012, 45; Doing Business, 2018).

Nonetheless, it has recently been highlighted in the literature how the emphasis placed on the creation of shareholder value as a guiding criterion for all business decisions may not only, as mentioned earlier, hinder innovation processes because of impatient capital: it has also been one of the determining factors behind the increase in inequality over the last 30 years. On the one hand, it has contributed to transferring wealth from the remuneration of labour to the remuneration of capital; on the other, it has shifted much of the income to the top managerial and professional positions, where remuneration is correlated with shareholder value. In fact, inequalities in disposable income are affected by the primary distribution of "market income", both because redistribution cannot intervene beyond a certain degree and because, if the primary distribution is highly unbalanced in favour of the holders of capital, the latter will have more strength to influence tax policy and prevent effective redistribution (Sacconi et al., 2019).

On the other hand, Insider systems are characterised by underdeveloped financial markets, concentrated and stable ownership and strong links between companies and banking institutions. Since only one shareholder, or a few, constitute the "hardcore" of ownership, often only a marginal part of the capital is traded on the market – which would not allow management to be replaced by external takeovers. In the countries where the insider system has been established, historical and economic events have, nevertheless, contributed to the evolution of partially divergent forms (Bosetti, 2010; Zattoni, 2015): the "Rhineland" type systems (relationship-based or network-oriented), characterised by a high degree of participation in control by the banks and, in part, by the employees; and the "Latin" type, in which the majority shareholder controls the management, exercising considerable influence through the board of directors.

The Latin system (as adopted in Italy, Spain, Portugal, Greece, Belgium, and France) has some essential elements in common with the Rhineland system: the limited role of the stock market in financing companies and controlling management; ownership of capital concentrated within a family or group and protected through voting agreements and cross-ownership of shares. However, in this case, bank and worker representatives, both seen as external stakeholders in government and control functions, exert a different role. The relationship with banks does not take on strategic significance: the banks are not involved in the ownership of the companies but merely provide financing by way of credit and sometimes offer assistance in "special" operations but are unlikely to have an enduring influence on the decision-making processes (only, indirectly, by limiting credit). At the same time, the employees seem to tend more towards the Anglo-Saxon context than that of the Rhineland. Neither system, indeed, institutionalises the role of employees within the company, although the Latin system offers greater protection thanks to the role of the trade unions (Bosetti 2010, 30–38).

2.5 Corporate governance and development paths

In the light of the above considerations, we will now endeavour to define how the more or less dynamic and inclusive development paths fit in with the different types of corporate governance and financing.

To this end, we focus on the presence of the smallest firms (one to nine employees) and those – fully or partially – owned publicly. The former can be seen as a proxy for the role of family-owned firms, while the latter constitutes a relevant mode, especially in some contexts, of state intervention in the economy.

As illustrated in Figure 2.2, small enterprises (one to nine employees) are mainly present in the group of NILG economies with about 50% of employees working in this bracket, while the lowest values are recorded in NIG and EIG countries and following these in DIG countries. In short, it can be assumed that the presence of small family-owned businesses, with low differentiation between ownership and management, and with traditional credit financing channels, significantly conditions the governance of businesses in the NILG countries and influences their path, often holding back both innovative processes and competitiveness. Of course, this is not necessarily the case, as the literature on industrial areas has pointed out in past years. Nevertheless, the intensification of competition from emerging countries in the more traditional areas of production, and the constraints imposed by family control on the process of management renewal, are all factors that influence the competitive trajectory of small enterprises.

Public enterprises (Figure 2.11) have played an essential role in some countries, such as Italy and France, in the early post-war decades. Public enterprises

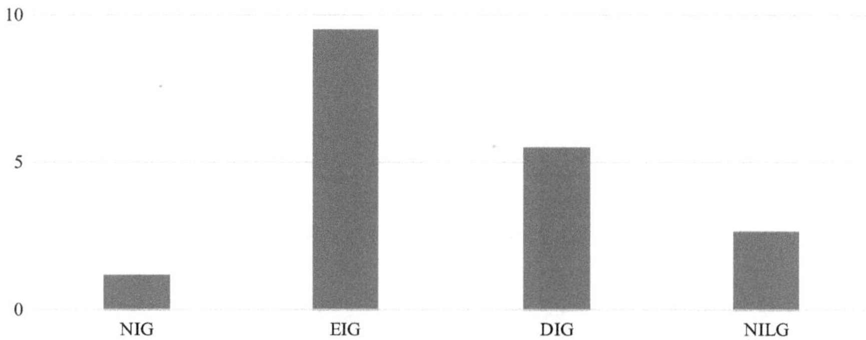

Figure 2.11 Percentage of workers employed in publicly owned or controlled enterprises over total number of employees.

Source: OECD.

or SOEs (state-owned enterprises) are legal entities owned or controlled by the national government on whose behalf they operate. Usually concentrated in sectors such as transport, utilities, or finance, they have recently become increasingly active at the national level (OECD, 2017). Although their role has been somewhat downsized over time, it still appears relevant, at least in terms of employees, particularly in countries reflecting DIG and EIG trends.

Among DIG countries, France stands out, while Austria and Germany have values closer to those of Italy. There is also a specific variance in EIG countries, with Sweden, Finland, and, above all, Norway showing a central role for public enterprises. Low values, with the sole exception of Ireland, are observed in NIG countries.

The previous discussion on corporate governance and financing presented the distinction between outsider and insider systems as the "Rhineland" and "Latin" variants. Our models confirm this typology, especially concerning specific indicators determining how firms are financed, making it possible to point out the different countries that are more "bank-centric" or market-oriented.[1]

The first dimension examined is financial depth, which enables us to approximate the size of financial markets and institutions.

As far as the financial institutions are concerned, the variable that has come most under the spotlight is private credit, defined as a credit to the private sector from bank deposits as a percentage of the GDP.[2]

Concerning financial markets, the variable used is stock market capitalisation to GDP (%). From these measures, it is possible to calculate the ratio of private credit to market capitalisation (financial structure ratio), which defines the degree to which a financial system can be considered more or less bank-centric.[3]

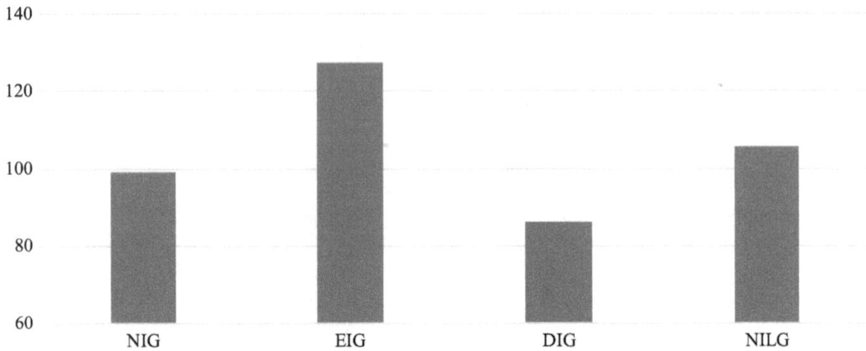

Figure 2.12 Credit to the private sector from bank deposits as a percentage of GDP (2016).

Source: (G)DFDD.

Credit to the private sector from bank deposits (Figure 2.12) is high in the EIG group but lower in the DIG countries. The other two groups show similar intermediate values.

In more detail, the NILG countries show similar levels, as do the DIG countries, with Belgium – with the lowest value – and France at the extremes. There is a steep variance in the EIG countries, where the average, although high, is led by Denmark. Finally, regarding NIG countries, two subgroups can be distinguished: Ireland and the United States, with low values, and Canada, the United Kingdom, and Australia, with similarly high values.

These values identify the relationship between savers' deposits and credit with the private sector and may be seen as a proxy for corporate financing and household saving and investment patterns. The link between saving and financing is strongest in the EIGs and some countries of the NILG groups. In other contexts, however, this may indicate, on the one hand, different ways of raising funds from businesses – especially large ones – and, on the other, diversified investment strategies on the part of banking institutions. In Germany, for example, financing channels for SMEs would appear to continue to follow a bank-based model while this no longer seems to be the case for larger companies (Deeg, 2010).

Shifting the focus to market capitalisation (Figure 2.13), a substantial gap can be observed opening between the NIG and NILG group of countries. The other two groups, demonstrating intermediate values, show similar results, while minor variance emerges in the distribution of values in individual countries. On the one hand, NILG countries show similar levels. Only the case of Spain shows a higher percentage, closer to that of the DIG

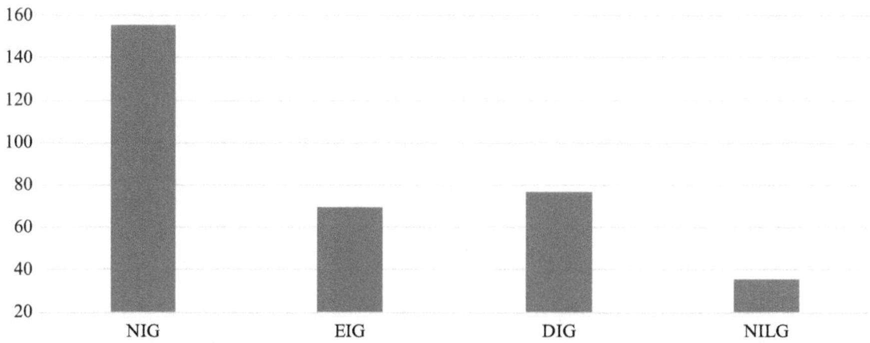

Figure 2.13 Equity market capitalisation as a percentage of GDP (2017).

Source: (G) DFDD.

countries in comparison with Greece, Italy, and Portugal. The variance within the two intermediate groups is small, ranging between the values of Austria and the Netherlands. At the same time, in Germany, although the reforms of the 1990s have accentuated the relevance of "markets", savings banks and cooperative banks continue to maintain a particular relevance (Schnyder & Jackson, 2013), while the French case seems similar to the British one (Deeg, 2010). Finally, as might be expected, stock market capitalisation is much stronger in the Anglo-Saxon countries, with Ireland showing low values, in line with those of the NILG countries.

The next step is to calculate the financial structure ratio, which makes it possible to distinguish between a more bank-centric model, like that of the NILG countries, and a more market-oriented model, like that of the NIG group (Figure 2.14). Individual countries align with the reference set: the lowest values are recorded for the United States and Australia, the highest for Italy, Portugal and especially Greece. However, in the other groups, the highest values are observed in Austria and Denmark.

2.6 Concluding remarks

In conclusion, by integrating the characteristics identified by the indicators on financing mechanisms with those on ownership and management of firms, we can characterise our models as follows.

In NILG economies, we observe a strong presence of small enterprises as a proxy for family-based governance. The primary funding sources are self-financing and commercial credit, while medium and large enterprises, based on shareholder control, are fewer in number and closer to the insider model,

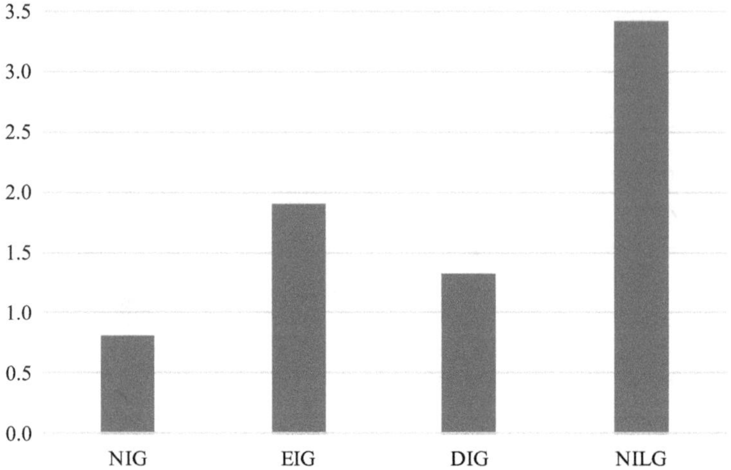

Figure 2.14 Financial structure. Ratio of bank credit to financial credit (2017).

Source: (G) DFDD.

with a stable ownership structure that tends to be "closed" to the outside world. Therefore, the relationship with banks tends to be medium-long term, but without a shared vision of business ownership, and as such there is more involvement in pursuing a strategic perspective of growth. The role of finance for innovation is particularly lacking in some countries, including Italy.

In essence, we are close to what the literature has called a "Latin" variant of the insider system. Its limitations are that its encouragement for innovation and efficient business management is weak. On the one hand, there is no "impatient capital" to keep management under pressure as in market-oriented models and, on the other, the longer-term oriented mechanisms characterising the classical Rhineland model, with forms of bank co-ownership and "patient capital", are lacking. As a result, growth in size, diversification of savings and investments and economic innovation are inhibited.

The context of the DIG countries represents the core of what has been called the classic "Rhineland" insider system. Larger firms have a significant weight, relationships with banks are structured in the medium to long term, often with forms of participation in the ownership of firms, and a greater centrality of financial intermediation emerges. As the literature has shown, this creates an ideal ecosystem for incremental innovations, which in turn are supported by forms of "institutional complementarity" (Hall & Gingrich, 2009) in the arenas of industrial relations, labour, and education policies, as we shall see further on.

However, some differences between the main countries can be observed in this context. In France, there is a more significant presence of financial markets and publicly owned or controlled firms (Deeg, 2010; OECD, 2017). In contrast, in Germany, notwithstanding the implementation of market-oriented strategies by larger firms and more internationalised banks (see, for example, the case of Deutsche Bank), there is a greater centrality of the banking system and a lower level of capitalisation of stock markets in relation to the GDP (Schnyder & Jackson, 2013; Jackson & Sorge, 2012).

On the other hand, the EIG economies represent what we might call a "Nordic variant" of the insider model. In this case, state-owned enterprises prevail (especially in Norway), but the banking system's importance is confirmed more generally. Nevertheless, from this point of view, a more "open" relationship emerges vis-à-vis both financial markets and finance tools for innovation, such as private equity and venture capital (Burroni, 2016). For example, in 2018, in terms of the weight of venture capital in relation to the GDP (OECD data), after the United States, we find Finland, Denmark, and Sweden.

Thus, in Northern European capitalism, banks have played a similar role to that played in some continental countries, such as Germany, by actively acting as investors in specific sectors and influencing the structure of firms through direct participation and other forms of influence that have facilitated mergers and acquisitions and strengthened dimensional growth. This blend of more traditional and market-oriented credit instruments, together with the growth of innovative forms of financing, i.e. venture capital, has afforded a helpful combination for supporting economic activities in general and innovation activities in particular. Thanks to a peculiar synthesis of a liberal approach and coordinated institutions (Boyer, 2004), Northern European economies have grown in the ICT sector.

Elements of the stakeholder model have also been traced in the Nordic model, balanced by an ownership structure with a concentrated shareholder base that is sensitive to the role of the trade unions (realised through pension funds) (Thomsen, 2016).

Lastly, in NIG economies, larger and more diffusely owned firms (public companies) come to light, while under the impetus of governance devoted to the creation of shareholder value, the roles of the stock exchange and the stock market acquire greater importance, and there are fewer employees in "public" companies. These countries can thus be traced back to the model of the outsider system, where incremental innovation, requiring stability, is frustrated by "impatient capital" in favour of radical innovation, which is more likely to generate significant returns in the short term. As we have already mentioned, these features condition the trend of inequality and present a high institutional complementarity with some policy areas – such as labour policies and industrial relations – which we will explore in detail in the following pages.

Notes

1 To classify financial systems, we will use some of the measures developed by Čihák et al. (2012) and discussed by the World Bank (2013). The original methodology identifies four dimensions, distinguishing between financial institutions and markets: financial depth, accessibility, efficiency in service provision, and stability. The choice of variables falls, on the one hand, on indicators with greater coverage across countries and, on the other, on variables analytically linked to the literature on poverty reduction and economic growth (World Bank, 2013; 2015).

2 An alternative measure is total banking assets to GDP, which, compared to private credit, includes credit to governments and banking assets other than loans. Although this measure allows a better approximation of the size of the banking system, it is less widely used in the literature. Moreover, the two variables are closely correlated (r=0.98), so private credit can provide a reasonable approximation of total assets (World Bank, 2013, 25). Data on private credit, as well as on GDP, in the GFDD (Global Financial Development Database) comes from International Financial Statistics (IFS), published by the International Monetary Fund (IMF).

3 In this regard, although the economic literature provides some evidence concerning the link between the stage of economic development and the financial system, with bank-centric models more present in the first stage, the sociological literature proposes a different reflection. See Dore (2000; 2009) and Mutti (2008).

References

Albert, M. (1991). *Capitalismo contro capitalismo*. Bologna: il Mulino.

Allen, F. & Gale, D. (2000).*Comparing financial systems*. Cambridge MA: MIT Press.

Amable, B. (2003). *The diversity of modern capitalism*. Oxford: Oxford University Press.

Bosetti, L. (2010). *Corporate governance e mercati globali*. Milano: Franco Angeli.

Boyer R. (2004). New growth regimes, but still institutional diversity. *Socio-Economic Review*, 2(1), 1–32. doi.org/10.1093/soceco/2.1.1

Burroni, L. (2016). *Capitalismi a confronto: istituzioni e regolazione dell'economia nei paesi europei*. Bologna: il Mulino.

Cihak, M., Demirguc-Kunt A., Feyen E., & Levine R. (2012). *Benchmarking financial systems around the world*. Policy Research working paper, WPS 6175, Washington, DC: World Bank.

Deeg, R. (2010). Institutional change in financial systems. In Morgan, G., Campbell, J. L., Crouch, C., Pedersen, O. K., & Whitley, R. (Eds), *The Oxford handbook of comparative institutional analysis*. Oxforf: Oxford University Press, 309–333.

Doing Business (2018). *Doing business 2018. Reforming to create jobs, international bank for reconstruction and development*. Washington, DC: The World Bank.

Dore, R. (2000). *Stock market capitalism, welfare capitalism*. Oxford: Oxford University Press.

Dore, R. (2009). *Finanza pigliatutto*. Bologna: il Mulino.

Hall, P.A. & Gingrich D. (2009). Varieties of capitalism and institutional complementarities in the political economy. *British Journal of Political Science*, 39(3), 449–482. doi:10.1017/S0007123409000672

Hall, P.A. & Soskice, D. (2001). *Varieties of capitalism: The institutional foundations of comparative advantage*. Oxford: Oxford University Press.

Jackson, G. & Sorge, A. (2012). The trajectory of institutional change in Germany, 1979–2009. *Journal of European Public Policy*, 19(8), 1146–1167. doi.org/10.1080/13501763.2012.709009

Mutti, A. (2008). *Finanza sregolata? Le dimensioni sociali dei mercati finanziari*. Bologna: il Mulino.

OCSE (2017). *The size and sectoral distribution of state-owned enterprises*. Paris: OECD Publishing.

Rajan, R. & Zingales., L. (2001). Financial systems, industrial structure, and growth. *Oxford Review of Economic Policy*, 17(4), 467–482. doi-org.eres.qnl.qa/10.1093/oxrep/17.4.467

Rizza, R. & Scarano, G. (2019). *Nuovi modelli di politica del lavoro*. Milano: Egea.

Sacconi L., Denozza F. & Stabilini A. (2019). Democratizzare l'economia, promuovere l'autonomia dei lavoratori e l'uguale cittafinanza nel governo di impresa: una proposta. *Studi Organizzativi*,1, 149–178. 10.3280/SO2019-001006

Sapir, A. (2005). *Globalisation and the reform of European social models*. Background document for the presentation at ECOFIN Informal Meeting in Manchester, 9 September 2005. Brussels: Bruegel.

Schnyder, G. &Jackson, G. (2013). Germany and Sweden in the crisis: Re-coordination or resilient liberalism? In Schmidt, V. & Thatcher, M. (Eds), *Resilient liberalism in Europe's political economy*. Cambridge: Cambridge University Press, 313–345.

Thomsen S. (2016). The Nordic corporate governance model. *Management and Organization Review*, 12, 189–204. doi.org/10.1017/mor.2015.55

Trento, S. (2012). *Il capitalismo italiano*, Il Mulino, Bologna.

World Bank (2013). *Global financial development report: Rethinking the role of the state in finance*. Washington, DC: World Bank.

World Bank (2015). *Global financial development report 2015–2016: Long-term finance*. Washington, DC: World Bank.

Zattoni, A. (2015). *Assetti proprietari e corporate governante*, Egea, Milano.

Chapter 3

Industrial relations

Dario Raspanti

3.1 Introduction

Industrial relations constitute a crucial regulatory arena in contemporary capitalist economies. They are the locus of the collaborative and conflictual relationships over employment-related issues, such as remuneration, working time, training, and working conditions. Unions, employers' associations, or single employers are also the subjects of collective bargaining. Industrial relations have a conspicuous impact on economic growth since they contribute to establishing labour costs. At the same time, they help in curtailing social inequalities through union action on wages and supplementary welfare provisions.

This chapter will compare industrial relations systems of growth and inequality models by looking at their "bargaining structure" (Cella & Treu, 2009), the set of relatively stable relations between trade unions and employers' organisations, and the different levels constituting the representative organisations themselves. The state participates in the bargaining structure as an employer in the public sector and defines the fundamental juridical framework of industrial relations.

The bargaining structure has four basic dimensions that could be analytically employed to illustrate the characteristics of the industrial relations system of a country. First, bargaining structures' centralisation depends on the number of bargaining levels involved in determining labour regulations. Second, bargaining coverage indicates the number of employees covered by collective agreements. The third dimension is the social partners' involvement in government decisions on policies that are more or less directly related to industrial relations, e.g. economic, pension, and social policies. Fourth, the union density rate illustrates the number of unions members in the workforce.

The degree of centralisation is crucial since industrial relations are forged at different levels that interact according to hierarchical relationships. The most comprehensive level is the inter-sectoral or national level, also referred to as central. The main actors operating at this level are national confederations, whose inter-confederal agreements are valid in different sectors throughout

DOI: 10.4324/9781003297130-5

the country. The intermediate level is the sectoral level, also valid nationwide, where multi-employer collective agreements are concluded between trade unions and sectoral employers' organisations. This level may also include agreements at lower administrative levels (regional, provincial, or local). Lastly, single-employer agreements resulting from company bargaining are considered the most "decentralised" level. The purpose of company agreements is to regulate those aspects of the employment relationship specific to a given company, whose effects are limited to that company's employees. Scholars agree on a common trend in mature economies towards decentralising industrial relations (Traxler, Blaschke, & Kittel, 2001). Single-employer agreements become pivotal in determining employment conditions to the detriment of sectoral and central level bargaining. Accordingly, two more measures must be considered in evaluating a bargaining structure centralisation. The first is the degree of coordination between the different levels of negotiation. Coordination refers to the ability of higher-level agreements to influence the content of lower-level contracts and thus ensure uniform working conditions both within the same sector (vertical coordination) and between different sectors (horizontal coordination).

The second measure concerns the presence and content of derogation clauses. Under certain circumstances, social partners could override higher-level collective agreements. While derogation allows the social partners to adjust bargaining to local working conditions, it could also lead to less favourable firm-level settlements weakening the capacity of collective bargaining to tackle social inequalities. Derogation agreements from central and sectoral regulation have increased in importance (Baccaro & Howell, 2017). The literature identifies two patterns of decentralisation (Traxler, 1995). Organised decentralisation refers to a situation in which economy-wide agreements are absent. Still, some coordination mechanisms extend the agreements reached in one sector to the other sectors. Disorganised decentralisation is the proliferation of single-employer and local arrangements without sectoral coordination. Organised decentralisation is assumed to sustain employment standards, while disorganisation relates to a deterioration of collective bargaining and unilateral employer wage-setting (Grimshaw et al., 2017).

Coverage represents the second fundamental dimension of the bargaining structure. The number of workers whose conditions of employment are covered by collective bargaining measures the capacity of union action to affect working conditions both collectively and individually. Coverage is thus a measure of collective bargaining's impact on the economy and social inequalities. Since collective agreements apply to employers who are members of signing organisations, coverage will depend on how encompassing bargaining is: the greater the centralisation, the higher the degree of coverage. However, bargaining coverage may also rely on automatic mechanisms of agreement extension or institutionalised practices that extend coverage beyond sectoral boundaries.

The third dimension is social partners' involvement in ordinary government policy-making on topics related to labour regulation, such as pensions, employment, health, and training policies. Defined as "social" to underline the role taken on by trade unions and employers' associations beyond their involvement in regulating labour relations, this involvement presupposes the social partners' legitimacy in representing the interests of workers and society in general. For its relevance during the industrial readjustment processes in the 1970s and 1980s, Lange and Regini (1989) included social concertation among the forms of regulation of the economy, alongside the State, the market, and the community. However, social partners' involvement is intermittent in most European countries, activated only in the face of specific political conjunctures when the need to obtain consensus on politically sensitive issues comes into play or in the event of institutional crises (Guardiancich & Molina, 2017). Agreements reached by concertation are then converted into legislation by the government or parliament. Although concertation refers mainly to trilateral relations at the national level, this does not rule out that such practices may also be observed at regional and local levels (Trigilia, 1999). Another matter is the advisory and informative role of employers and trade union organisations with regard to economic or social measures. This role is absent in some countries while decreed by law[1] in others. Among the topics discussed by concertation are the rules governing collective bargaining. These rules identify the actors entitled to participate in bargaining and determine the manner and timing of the negotiations, the right to strike, and the rules governing dispute resolution bodies.

The fourth dimension, workforce unionisation, does not concern the bargaining structure but rather one of its most significant components, the trade union. It measures a union's capacity to represent workers and thus the union's power against employers, though not necessarily a union's ability to mobilise. The significance attributed by a union's members to membership varies from one case to another, especially in terms of their involvement in the union's activities (Gumbrell-McCormick & Hyman, 2013). By way of example, the ability of trade unions in France to mobilise workers derives from their members' high degree of activism. However, membership is a minimal share of the workforce (Sullivan, 2009). Similarly, trade union participation in Spain is promoted by a system that recognises the most representative trade unions, as established by law, and the only ones allowed to participate in collective bargaining. Only those trade unions that elect their own representatives in participation and company representation bodies are defined as representative. Consequently, members actively participate in union life (Martínez Lucio, 2017). In contrast, Scandinavian trade union members are generally described as "passive" since the decision to join a trade union can be linked, among other reasons, to the possibility of accessing unemployment benefits, according to the "Ghent system" (Vandaele, 2019).[2]

The bargaining structure of growth and inequality models will be compared to the four dimensions sketched above in the following sections. The quantitative analysis builds upon the work of Jelle Visser and his colleagues at the University of Amsterdam. The Data Base on Institutional Characteristics of Trade Unions, Wage Setting, State Intervention and Social Pacts (ICTWSS), now in its sixth version (Visser, 2019), gathers extensive data on collective bargaining from 1960 onwards. This chapter considers data from 1990 to the last year for which data are available, namely, 2017, if not otherwise indicated.

However, a comparative analysis of bargaining structures is incomplete without discussing the effects on overall wage developments. Trade union action has two essential functions. One is to protect workers' living conditions with regard to the dynamics of the economy. The other function regulates the employment relationship within the market itself (Crouch, 1993). Accordingly, two additional variables will be discussed in the present chapter. These are the percentage of labour income on GDP and wage dispersion.

The chapter is structured as follows. The second section is devoted to bargaining centralisation. The third section deals with collective bargaining coverage. Section four shows data about the routine involvement of social partners in policy-making. The fifth section looks at trade union density. The sixth section discusses the effects of the labour market on industrial relations systems regarding the redistribution of labour income. Lastly, the conclusions will jointly analyse the dimensions discussed in the previous paragraphs and link them to model outcomes.

3.2 Bargaining centralisation

Figure 3.1 shows the level of bargaining centralisation in the four models during different periods, 1990–1999 and 2010–2019. The egalitarian inclusive growth (EIG), dualistic inclusive growth (DIG), and non-inclusive low growth (NILG) models register a similar level of centralisation. Bargaining mainly takes place at the sectoral level in Germany, Austria, the Netherlands, France, Italy, Spain, EIG countries, Sweden, and Denmark. Belgium represents an exception among coordinated economies since bargaining occurs mainly at the central and level. Unlike the other models, bargaining in the NIG model and Greece is company-based.

Regarding diachronic differences, it should be noted that the NIG (-1.0) and NILG (-0.5) models show the most marked decrease in the indicator's values between the two periods. Among NIG countries, the downswing observed here can be attributed to the decentralisation of bargaining in Australia and Ireland. In contrast with the other countries in the model, sectoral bargaining was predominant in these two countries. However, while company bargaining was already prevalent in Australia in the 1990s, the central level was abandoned only during Ireland's economic crisis. Here, this marked decentralisation of bargaining can be explained by the social partners' legitimacy crisis due to the

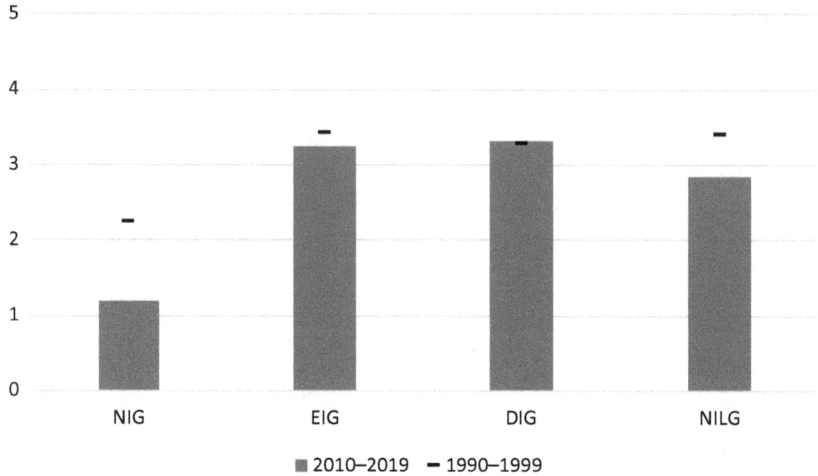

Figure 3.1 Centralisation of collective bargaining, average values.

Note: The figure shows the values assumed by the level indicator, which is coded as follows: 5 if bargaining takes place at a central or inter-sectoral level; 4 if bargaining takes place alternately between central and sectoral levels; 3 if bargaining is sectoral; 2 if bargaining takes place between sectoral and company levels; 1 if bargaining takes place exclusively at a company or local level.

Source: ICTWSS data (OECD & AIAS, 2021).

collapse of the development model that the unions had endorsed with their employer counterparts as a consequence of Irish economy collapse between 2008 and 2012 (Regan, 2017). In contrast, the United States, the United Kingdom, and Canada show no changes by virtue of their long tradition of decentralised bargaining. Regarding NILG countries, the decline of the indicator value is driven by Greece, where centralised collective bargaining was dismantled during the economic crisis (Koukiadaki & Kokkinou, 2016). On the other hand, the predominant level in Italy, Spain, and Portugal has been sectoral.

The formal coordination ensured by sectoral bargaining is not devitalised by the interposition of derogation per se but by the type of the clauses introduced. Deviations from the norm may be allowed in exceptional cases, such as a company crisis or a reorganised production process. They may concern different aspects of the employment relationship: from wage levels to working hours. In some cases, coordination results from the voluntary adoption by representative organisations of similar solutions in different companies and sectors. However, there is no coordination of any kind in others, and the decentralisation process proceeds in a disorganised manner. For all these reasons, the indicator illustrating the extent of exceptions and the coordination indicator between bargaining levels were also examined to furnish a clear picture of the relationship between centralisation and decentralisation in collective bargaining.

The decentralisation process of industrial relations described in the literature does not derive from the radical redefinition of bargaining institutions but is offset through their diverse implementation (Pedersini, 2014; Baccaro & Howell, 2017). To identify its effects, we should look at the introduction of exceptions to sectoral and inter-sectoral collective agreements. Bargaining continues to occur formally at the sectoral level but affects working conditions at the decentralised level. In the second half of the first decade of the 21st century there was an increasing convergence towards implementing exceptions in all countries (see Figure 3.2). Open clauses have become generalised in EIG countries, especially Denmark (since 2004) and Sweden (since 2008). Collective agreements in these two countries establish the regulatory framework necessary for company bargaining or its replacement if the latter should fail (Visser, 2013). In NILG countries, where derogations in the 1990s were reserved solely for cases of company crises, derogations have also been introduced but are limited to working hours. Notwithstanding their status of coordinated economies, DIG countries also show the presence of open clauses. In NIG countries, exception clauses are non-existent as sectoral bargaining is extremely limited, if not absent.

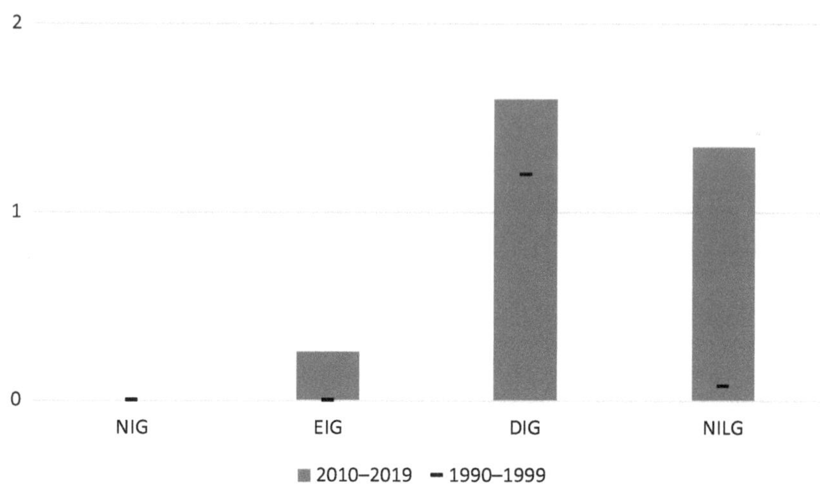

Figure 3.2 Presence and characteristics of open clauses, average values.

Note: The figure shows the values of the OCG indicator. The indicator assumes the value of 2 if sectoral agreements contain opening clauses, allowing the renegotiation of contractual wages at enterprise level; 1 if sectoral agreements contain opening clauses, allowing the renegotiation of contractual non-wage issues at firm-level; 0 if open clauses are absent, as there is no sectoral or inter-sectoral bargaining.

Source: ICTWSS data (OECD & AIAS, 2021).

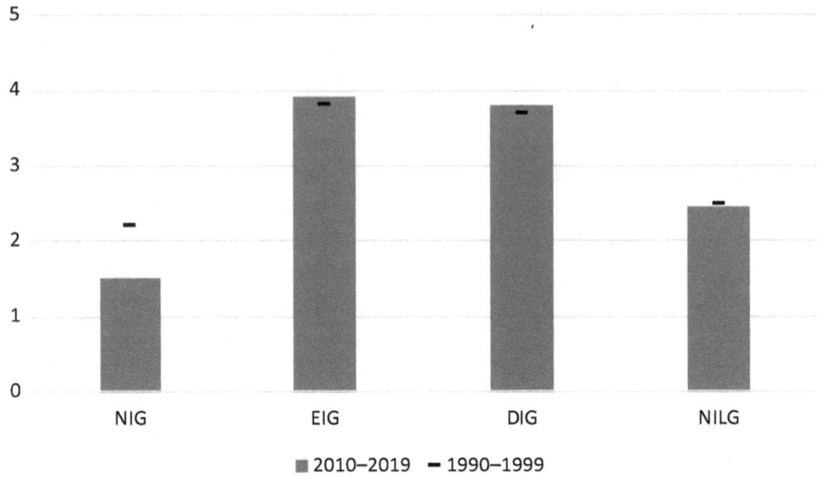

Figure 3.3 Collective bargaining coordination, average values.

Note: The figure shows the values assumed by the coordinate indicator and looks at the coordination between bargaining levels regarding wage levels. It is coded as follows: 5 if binding norms regarding maximum or minimum wage rates or wage increases exist; 4 if non-binding norms and/or guidelines exist; 3 if procedural negotiation guidelines (recommendations on, for instance, wage demand formula relating to productivity or inflation) exist; 2 if some coordination of wage setting, based on pattern setting by major companies, sectors, government wage policies in the public sector, judicial awards, or minimum wage policies exist; 1 if fragmented wage bargaining, confined largely to individual firms or plants, as well as no coordination, exist.

Source: ICTWSS data (OECD & AIAS, 2021).

The discussion about coordination concludes the analysis of bargaining centralisation. Figure 3.3 shows the degree of coordination between the different bargaining levels. Coordination was stable in all the growth models in contrast to the degree of effective centralisation. Except for the NIG model, it also declined, with Australia and Ireland converging towards the other countries in the model. NILG countries show an intermediate level between the "fragmented bargaining" of NIG and the much more coordinate bargaining of EIG and DIG models. In the latter, coordination is ensured either by the presence of rules laid down by the government or through the action of representative organisations, particularly employers' organisations.

High coordination levels may be achieved by encompassing employers' organisations with the capacity to influence the decisions of registered companies to adhere to collective agreements. By way of example, despite a decline in centralisation and the extensive use of open clauses, EIG countries continue to be characterised by a high degree of coordination. In Sweden, decentralised bargaining is matched by cohesive interest organisations that ensure a certain degree of inter-sectoral homogeneity in working conditions and retribution levels (Baccaro & Howell, 2017). Besides, coordination may be achieved by law, e.g. establishing minimum and maximum wage regulations. This is the case in DIG countries, except France, representing a case of uncoordinated bargaining (Pedersini, 2014). Germany (Bordogna & Pedersini, 2019) and Denmark (Thelen, 2014) are characterised by pattern bargaining whereby an agreement signed by a relevant company (or groups of companies) in terms of size or symbolic value is used as a reference for bargaining in other companies and sectors.

3.3 Collective bargaining coverage

Looking at Figure 3.4, a high collective bargaining coverage rate emerges in the different growth models, above 75%, except for the NIG model, where only a third of the workforce is covered by collective agreements (29.9%). DIG countries have the highest values of bargaining coverage (85.3%), while EIG and NILG models show values in line with the DIG model, 82.8% and 76.9%, respectively. The figure permits assessing the changes over the last 25 years between the average values of the last period considered (2010–2019) and those of the period 1990–1999. It is possible to note substantial stability of the coverage rate in all models, except for the NILG model, where the average value decreases by ten percentage points. It is the consequence of the substantially reduced coverage in Greece (from 100% in 1990 to 14.2% in

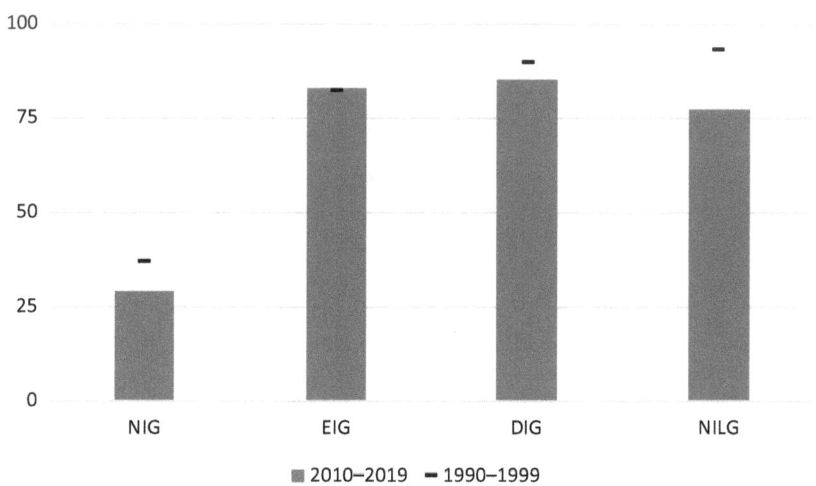

Figure 3.4 Adjusted coverage of collective bargaining, average values.

Source: ICTWSS data (OECD & AIAS, 2021).

2017), with the decrease concentrated in the years of the economic crisis, from 2011 on.[3] On the other hand, the coverage rate in Italy remains unchanged in the considered period due to the resilience of the trade union movement, employers' organisations unwillingness to question sectoral bargaining, and the weakness of national governments, which have not challenged (with some exceptions) the traditional autonomy of the social partners (Regalia & Regini, 2018). Particularly noteworthy is the sharp decline in coverage in Germany (-31%, 1990–2018), where, despite the sectoral level continuing to represent the main level of bargaining in Germany, the slow process of the progressive weakening of German industrial relations, especially in the manufacturing sector, produced a system "full of holes, and only about 30 per cent of German manufacturing establishments are now covered by a collective agreement of any type" (Baccaro & Howell, 2017, 115).

As pointed out in this chapter's introductory section, different degrees of institutionalisation of industrial relations can be observed among European countries. Institutionalisation affects bargaining coverage where there are mechanisms for the automatic extension of contracts to various sectors. Figure 3.5 shows the spread of the collective bargaining extension clause in those countries making up the growth models. Belgium and France (DIG model countries), Finland (EIG), and Spain (NILG) are the only ones to have automatic extension systems for labour contracts. Austria and Italy have no automatic contract extension institutions, but there are practical alternatives that ensure high levels of coverage. In Austria, these alternatives stem from the obligation for enterprises to join employers' organisations. In Italy,

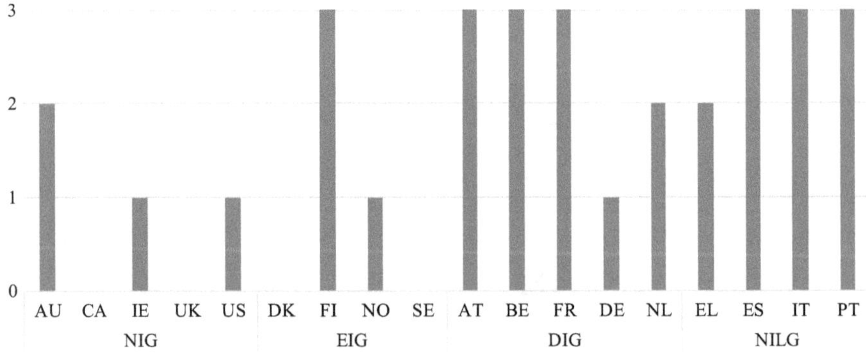

Figure 3.5 Mandatory extension of collective agreements (2019).

Note: The "Ext" variable is coded as follows: 3 if the extension is automatic; 2 if the extension is used in most sectors but with limitations, and ministers can decide not to extend (clauses in) collective agreements; 1 if extension it is used exceptionally because of the absence of sectoral contracts; 0 if there are neither legal provisions for mandatory extension, nor is there a functional equivalent.

Source: ICTWSS data (OECD & AIAS, 2021).

bargaining coverage is extended by applying the collective agreement to non-signatory companies in court proceedings, originating from the constitutional obligation to pay workers a "remuneration that is proportionate" to work carried out.[4] No form of automatic extension emerges in any of the NIG-model countries, apart from Ireland, and Greece. In Denmark and Sweden, one of the highest collective bargaining coverage rates in Europe (82% and 88%, respectively, in 2018) is accomplished via the coordination mechanisms described above.

3.4 Routine involvement of social partners

Notwithstanding the decentralisation of bargaining, social partners' consultation continues to be common in EIG countries, where concertation is stable and steady over time (see Figure 3.6). At the other extreme are the NIG countries, where involvement is absent. However, Ireland hosts tripartite national social dialogue between 2000 and 2008. The objective was to create the best conditions to lure foreign firms and investments, i.e. the disposition of a high-skilled workforce at low costs and favourable tax treatments to foreign capital inflows (Burroni, 2016). The DIG model shows a high value of routine involvement. However, DIG countries could be separated into two groups. On the one hand, Austria, Belgium, and the Netherlands are much more similar to Denmark and Sweden, while, on the other hand, involvement with

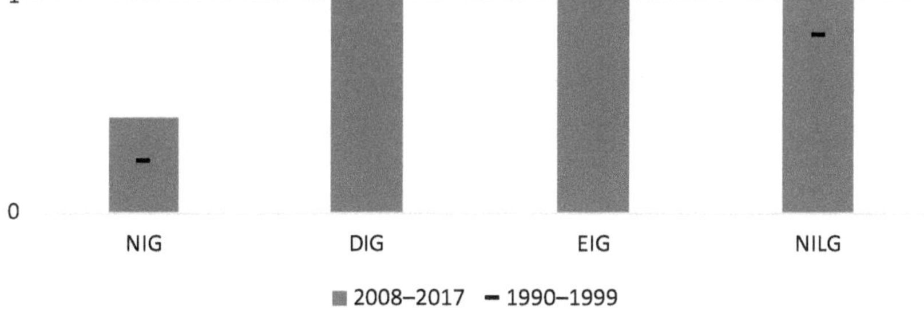

Figure 3.6 Ordinary involvement of social partners in government decisions, average values.

Note: The figure shows the values of the RI indicator: 2 if consultation is stable and frequent; 1 if it is episodic; 0 if it is completely absent.

Source: Based on the ICTWSS data (Visser, 2016).

social partners in Germany and France is lower. Social partners in Germany are only involved at certain times, as in NILG countries. At the same time, engagement in France is virtually absent due to the particular model of industrial relations, based on the solid regulatory role of the State and those confrontational trade unions traditionally excluded from the political decision-making (Burroni, 2016). The higher level of concertation in NILG countries depends on a strong involvement of trade unions in Portugal from 2013 onwards and the resilience of concertation in Spain. During the years 2000 to 2009, there was a period of intense social dialogue in Spain, which was then interrupted due to disagreements between trade unions and business organisations on labour market reforms and social cooperation during the economic crisis (Godino & Molina, 2011).

3.5 Trade union density

Trade union density is the number of employees who are members of a trade union per total number of employees. The term expresses a trade union's associative and representative capacity in the workplace. Over the last 30 years, the unionisation rate has declined in all four growth models (Figure 3.7). In particular, the most significant cutback is observed in the NIG (-12.4%) and EIG countries (-11.1%). Notwithstanding huge decreases in Sweden (-17.2%) and Finland (-11.7%), EIG countries show a significantly higher unionisation rate than the others (62.5%). On the other hand, the NILG model shows the smallest reduction in density (-4.8%) due to the significant resilience of

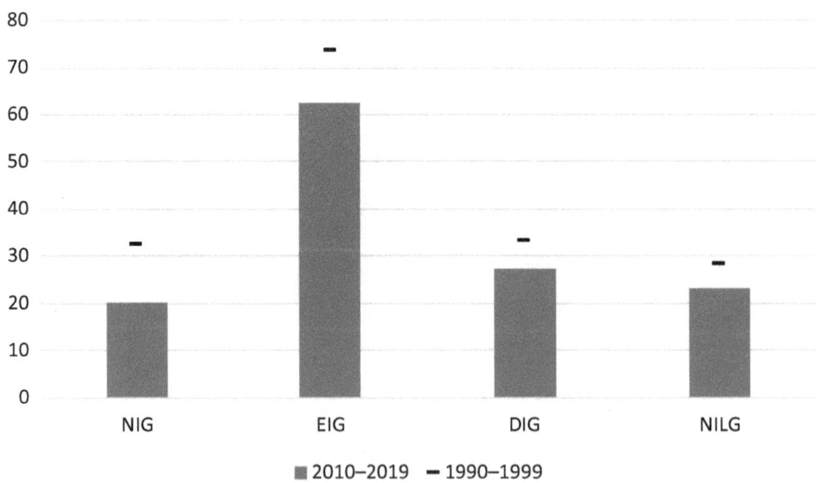

Figure 3.7 Trade union density, average values.

Source: Based on the ICTWSS data (OECD & AIAS, 2021).

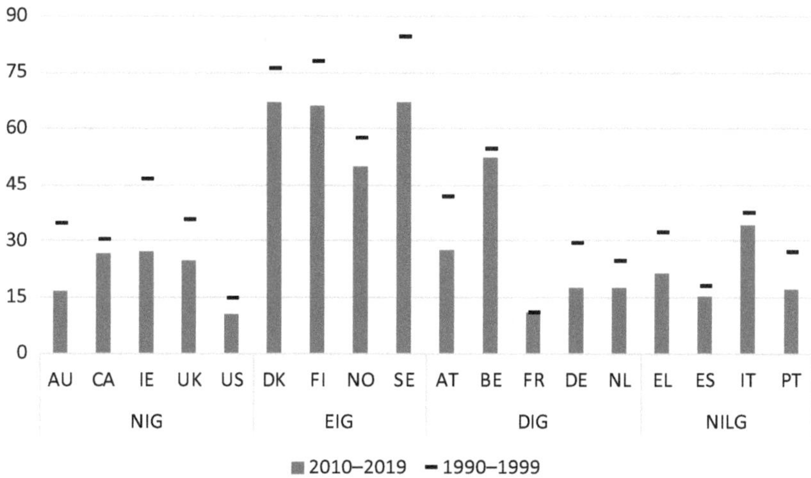

Figure 3.8 Trade union density per country, average values.

Source: ICTWSS data (OECD & AIAS, 2021).

unionisation in Italy (-2.7%) and Spain (-1.1%). The decrease marked by the DIG model (-5.6%) stems from the considerable reduction of union membership in Austria (-27.6% between 1990 and 2018) and Germany (-14.6% over the same period).

Examining the countries individually (Figure 3.8), significant decrements are shown in the NIG countries of Australia (-17.8%) and Ireland (-19.2%). Regarding DIG countries, since the 1990s, German trade union membership has declined by a third.[5] Trade unions in France have gained around 12% more members, while they rose in Belgium by 18%. The former, however, remains a country with very low unionisation (10.9% as an average value between 2010 and 2019); the latter has the highest union density (52.1%) among DIG countries. The NILG countries of Greece and Portugal saw a reduction of around ten percentage points in the unionisation rate. Compared to the 1990s, trade union membership in Italy increased steadily until 2012, only to decline gradually. However, Italian unions had 1.4 million more members in 2017 compared to 1990.[6] Spanish trade unions manifested the same tendency, with membership burgeoning until 2009.

3.6 Collective bargaining effects on income levels

The capacity of social partners to support worker income through industrial relations has been marred by changes involving the bargaining structure (Gumbrell-McCormick & Hyman, 2013). The share of labour income

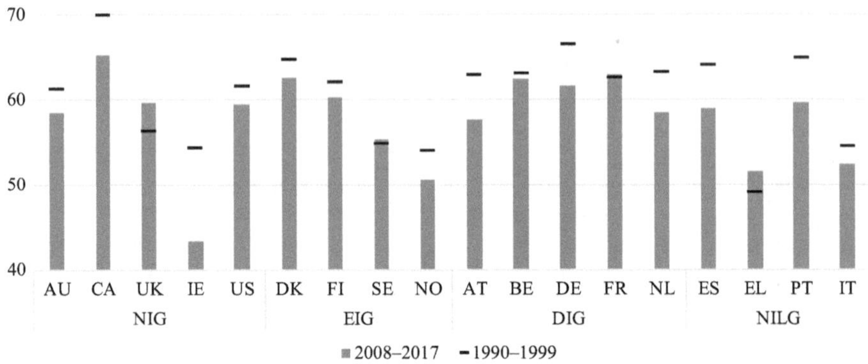

Figure 3.9 Share of labour income as a percentage of GDP, average values.

Note: The share of labour income is calculated as the nominal total of compensation in cash or services paid by businesses to their employees as a percentage of nominal GDP.

Source: Feenstra, Inklaar, & Timmer (2015).

as a percentage of gross domestic product has steadily decreased over the last 20 years (Figure 3.9) in all the countries in the sample. The exceptions are the United Kingdom (+3.3%) and Greece (2.5%). The single country with the most marked downturn is Ireland (-11.0%). In addition, this decline characterises the countries with inclusive growth, such as the DIG countries of Austria (-5.2%), Germany (-5.0%), and the Netherlands (-4.7%).

The second indicator to assess the ability of industrial relations to affect a worker's living conditions is income dispersion measured by the Gini coefficient (see Figure 3.10).[7] The NIG and NILG models are where the dispersion coefficient is most significant, i.e. the most income is concentrated in the upper deciles of the income distribution. On the other hand, wage dispersion in inclusive growth models is lower, and incomes are more evenly distributed.

Industrial relations affect income distribution in the population. As established in the literature, collective bargaining has dispensing effects on income dynamics and positive effects on wage increase restraint (Crouch & Traxler, 1995). According to Rueda and Pontusson (2000), there is a negative relationship between inequality and the unionisation rate, regardless of institutional differences between countries and the various exposures to international competition (Mahler, 2004). High levels of trade union density are associated with more even income distributions, hence with lower social inequalities, both in centralised and decentralised systems. Insomuch as income dispersion constitutes the main product of bargaining, it has been associated with bargaining coverage rate rather than with trade union density. Figure 3.11 shows the negative relationship between collective coverage and income dispersion in the sample countries for the periods 2000–2009 and 2010–2016.[8]

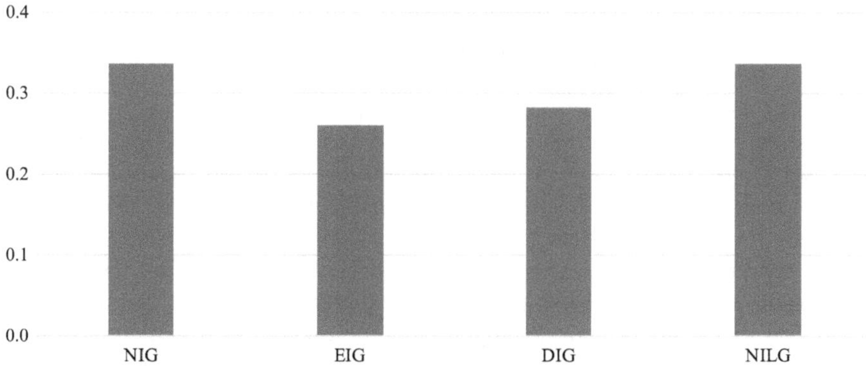

Figure 3.10 Income dispersion, average value 2016–2010.

Note: The Gini coefficient is used as a concentration index to measure inequality in income distribution. The coefficient ranges between 0 (perfect income equality) and 1 (perfect inequality).

Source: Elaboration on OECD data (OECD, 2015).

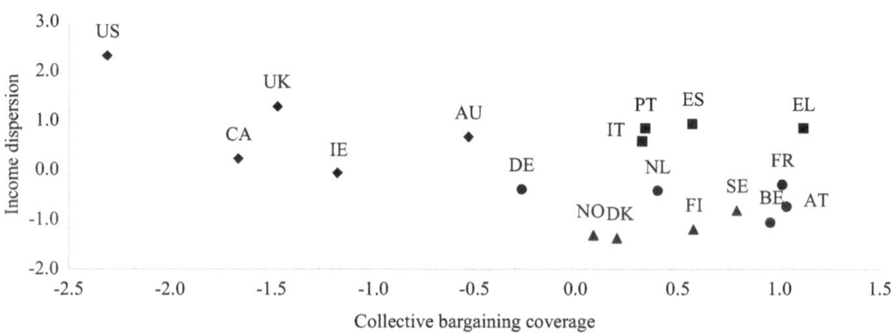

Figure 3.11 Collective bargaining coverage (standardised, average values 2000–2009) and income dispersion (standardised, average values 2010–2016).

Source: ICTWSS data (OECD & AIAS, 2021) and OECD (2015).

It is assumed that the ability of industrial relations to protect incomes in a given period depends on the coverage offered by labour contracts in the previous period since bargaining coverage acts with a certain lag on the general level of incomes. Indeed, income dispersion is higher in countries with the lowest bargaining coverage values, such as in the NIG model countries. Conversely, the EIG and DIG countries have a higher coverage rate than the sample average and lower-income dispersion. However, considerable variability within the models can be observed when looking at the individual countries. Germany, for example, shows a dispersion comparable to that of

France but with a much lower coverage rate. This is a sign that income dispersion and, more generally, inequality do not depend exclusively on industrial relations. The solid institutional coordination characterising some countries can offset an apparently weaker but substantially fragmented industrial relations system with some sectors more covered than others.

These intra-model differences will be discussed in more detail in Chapter 8. The NILG countries, on the other hand, are characterised by combinations of high coverage and high dispersion compared to the sample average. The effect of the bargaining structure in these countries is not the same as in the others, whether the NIG, EIG, or DIG model. The literature on the various capitalisms offers a possible explanation for this result. The institutional configuration of these countries, described in the literature as a mixed market economy (Molina & Rhodes, 2007), defines them as weak in terms of institutional complementarities between the different institutional arenas of the production system, the welfare system, and industrial relations. Thus, there is a mix of solid industrial relations and poorly coordinated economic systems, the effect of which on economic efficiency and inequality is not uniform. Moreover, the countries themselves are characterised by many self-employed workers who are not covered by collective bargaining (Pedaci, Raspanti, & Burroni, 2017).

3.7 Concluding remarks

This chapter has presented a comparative analysis of the industrial relations systems of the growth and inequality models looking at the element composing their bargaining structure. Table 3.1 summarises the combinations of centralisation and coverage of bargaining, routine involvement of social partners, and workforce unionisation for each model of growth and inequality. Collective bargaining in NIG countries occurs mainly at the enterprise level, resulting in low labour-force coverage and low involvement of social partners in national policy-making. Conversely, countries with inclusive growth show high levels of coverage and participation by social partners. The DIG and

Table 3.1 Key dimensions of the bargaining structure, average values 2010–2019

Growth and inequality model	*Centralisation (presence of open clauses)*	*Bargaining coverage (%)*	*Routine involvement (2008–2017)*	*Trade union density (%)*
NIG	1.20 (0.0)	29.2	0.4	20.0
DIG	3.32 (1.6)	85.3	1.4	27.5
EIG	3.25 (0.26)	82.9	1.8	62.5
NILG	2.85 (1.35)	77.0	1.1	23.4

Source: ICTWSS data (OECD & AIAS, 2021) and OECD data.

EIG models differ in the extent of the open clauses in collective agreements – limited in DIG countries, generalised in the EIG model – and in the weight of trade unions in the workforce – lower in the former than in the latter. NILG model countries reveal less bargaining centralisation than the inclusive growth models. Still, collective agreements are less easily derogated at the local level, given the limited presence of open derogation clauses. The workforce's lower unionisation corresponds to social partners being less involved than the DIG model, which has the same union density.

In conclusion, this chapter has provided a general overview of the bargaining structures of these growth models. The differences and similarities identified here stem from several factors, such as the distinctive features of bargaining in each growth model, each actor's interests and logic of action, and the different challenges industrial relations face in each model (disintermediation and deregulation, first of all). These features will be explored in more detail in Chapter 8.

Notes

1 One example is the Socio-economic Council (SER) of the Netherlands, which has an advisory role (de facto binding for the government) on social protection and macro-economic policies, as well as the annual determination of the minimum wage. The SER is made up of delegates from the most representative trade unions, employers' associations, and economic experts appointed by the government, including the President of the Bank of the Netherlands.

2 The "Ghent system" refers to the management of unemployment insurance funds by trade unions. It is associated with high unionisation rates since, in most cases, trade union membership is required to access benefits. The countries where this system is active are Belgium, Denmark, Finland, and Sweden.

3 This result is explained by the abolition of the automatic extension mechanism in sectoral labour contracts and the rapid decentralisation to the company level of bargaining; hence the increase in the number of workers covered by national contracts setting minimum wage levels (Dedoussopoulos et al., 2013).

4 The notion of 'proportionate remuneration' is contained in Article 36 of the Italian Constitution. Among other things, it states that "[t]he worker has the right to remuneration commensurate with the quantity and quality of his work and in any case sufficient to ensure a free and dignified existence for himself and his family".

5 Between 1990 and 1999, 11.5 million workers on average were members of German trade unions. Between 2008 and 2017, however, membership declined to 7.9 million. Despite this, the main German trade union, IG-Metall, increased its membership (Schmalz & Thiel, 2017).

6 For a more detailed discussion, see Vandaele (2019).

7 The OECD defines 'income' as an individual's disposable income in a given year derived from employment, self-employment, capital, and public cash transfers; fewer taxes and contributions paid by the individual (OECD, 2015).

8 Of the two variables, the standardised variable of the mean value in the indicated time intervals was calculated. The distribution of a standardised variable has a mean equal to zero and a variance equal to one.

References

Baccaro, L. & Howell, C. (2017). *Trajectories of neoliberal transformation: European industrial relations since the 1970s*. Cambridge: Cambridge University Press.

Bordogna, L. & Pedersini, R. (2019). *Relazioni industriali. L'esperienza italiana nel contesto internazionale*. Bologna: Il Mulino.

Burroni, L. (2016). *Capitalismi a confronto. Istituzioni e regolazione dell'economia nei paesi europei*. Bologna: Il Mulino.

Cella, G. P. & Treu, T. (2009). *Relazioni industriali e contrattazione collettiva*. Bologna: Il Mulino.

Crouch, C. (1993). *Industrial relations and european state traditions*. Oxford: Clarendon.

Crouch, C. & Traxler, F. (1995) (Eds). *Organized industrial relations in Europe: What future?*. Aldershot: Ashgate

Dedoussopoulos, A., Aranitou, V., Koutentakis, F. & Maropoulou, M. (2013). *Assessing the impact of the memoranda on Greek labour market and labour relations*. ILO Working Paper, n. 53. Geneva: International Labour Office.

Feenstra, R. C., Inklaar, R., & Timmer, M. P. (2015). The next generation of the Penn world table. *American Economic Review*, 105(10), 3150–3182. DOI:10.1257/aer.20130954

Godino, A. & Molina, O. (2011). *Failed remedies and implications of the economic crisis in Spain*. Brussels: OSE Research Paper n. 6.

Grimshaw, D., Johnson, M., Marino, S., & Rubery, J. (2017). Towards more disorganised decentralisation? Collective bargaining in the public sector under pay restraint. *Industrial Relations Journal*, 48(1), 22–41. DOI:10.1111/irj.12166

Guardiancich, I. & Molina, O. (2017) (Eds). *Talking through the crisis: Social dialogue and industrial relations trends in selected EU countries*. Geneva: ILO.

Gumbrell-McCormick, R. & Hyman, R. (2013). *Trade unions in Western Europe: hard times, hard choices*. Oxford: Oxford University Press.

Koukiadaki, A. & Kokkinou, C. (2016), Deconstructing the Greek system of industrial relations. *European Journal of Industrial Relations*, 22(3), 205–219. DOI:10.1177/0143831X16643206

Lange, P. & Regini, M. (1989) (Eds). *State, market and social regulation: New perspectives on Italy*. Cambridge: Cambridge University Press.

Mahler, V. A. (2004). Economic globalization, domestic politics, and income inequality in the developed countries: A cross-national study. *Comparative Political Studies*, 37(9), 1025–1053. DOI:10.1177/0010414004268849

Martínez Lucio, M. (2017). Organising without knowing it? The curious case of para-organising style campaigns in Southern Europe and the case of trade union elections in Spain. *Transfer*, 23(1), 89–94. DOI:10.1177/1024258916684324

Molina, O. & Rhodes, M. (2007). The political economy of adjustment in mixed market economies: A study of Spain and Italy. In B. Hancké, M. Rhodes & M. Thatcher (Eds), *Beyond varieties of capitalism: Conflict, contradictions, and complementaries in the European economy* (pp. 223–252). Oxford: Oxford University Press.

OECD (2015). *In it together: Why less inequality benefits all*. Paris: OECD.

OECD and AIAS (2021). *Institutional characteristics of trade unions, wage setting state intervention and social pacts*. Paris: OECD.

Pedaci, M., Raspanti, D., & Burroni, L. (2017). *Autonomous, atypical, hybrid forms of employment: Aspects of social protection in Italy*. Hans-Böckler-Stiftung WSI, National Report, no. 10.

Pedersini, R. (2014). European industrial relations between old and new trends. *Stato e Mercato,* 102, 341–368. DOI:10.1425/78527

Regalia, I. & Regini, M. (2018). Trade unions and employment relations in Italy during the economic crisis. *South European Society and Politics,* 23(1), 63–79. DOI:10.1080/13608746.2018.1430608

Regan, A. (2017). Post-crisis social dialogue and economic governance in Ireland. In I. Guardiancich & O. Molina (Eds), *Talking through the crisis: Social dialogue and industrial relations trends in selected EU countries*, pp. 151–170. Geneva: ILO.

Rueda, D. & J. Pontusson (2000). Wage inequalities and varieties of capitalism. *World Politics*, 52(3), 350–383. DOI:10.1017/S0043887100016579

Schmalz, S. & Thiel, M. (2017). IG Metall's comeback: Trade union renewal in times of crisis. *Journal of Industrial Relations*, 59 (4), 465–486. DOI:10.1177/0022185617714818

Sullivan, R. (2009). Density matters: The union density bias and its implications for labor movement revitalization. *Mobilization*, 14(2), 239–260. DOI:10.17813/maiq.14.2.l67816x747x47q32

Thelen, K. (2014). *Varieties of liberalization and the new politics of social solidarity*. Cambridge: Cambridge University Press.

Traxler, F. (1995). Farewell to labour market associations? Organized versus disorganized decentralization as a map for industrial relations. In C. Crouch & F. Traxler (Eds), *Organized industrial relations in Europe: What future?*. (pp. 3–19). Aldershot: Ashgate.

Traxler, F., Blaschke, S., & Kittel, B. (2001). *National labour relations in internationalized markets*. Oxford: Oxford University Press.

Trigilia, C. (1999). Capitale sociale e sviluppo locale. *Stato e mercato*, 57, 419–440. DOI:10.1425/435

Vandaele, K. (2019). *Bleak prospects: Mapping trade union membership in Europe since 2000*. Brussels: ETUI.

Visser, J. (2013). *Data base on institutional characteristics of trade unions, wage setting, state intervention and social pacts, 1960–2011 (ICTWSS). Version 4.0: Codebook*. Amsterdam: Institute for Advanced Labour Studies (AIAS).

Visser, J. (2016). What happened to collective bargaining during the great recession?. *IZA Journal of Labor Policy*, 5(1), 1–35. DOI:10.1186/s40173-016-0061-1

Visser J. (2019). *ICTWSS database. Version 6.1*. Amsterdam: Amsterdam Institute for Advanced Labour Studies (AIAS).

Chapter 4

Labour market policies

Roberto Rizza

4.1 Introduction

Labour market policies come into play in the context of the broader social regulatory function exerted by labour market institutions. Their rules and norms take the shape of concrete practices, guiding and constraining action, legitimising it, thereby reducing uncertainty (Gualmini & Rizza, 2013). Labour market policies counteract market failures (Solow, 1994), and their concrete interventions modify the distribution of income and labour.

The scope of labour market policies could be confined to those interventions aimed at reducing unemployment and providing social protection for the unemployed, as well as promoting and maintaining a high and stable level of employment. However, some interventions may be differently motivated from those oriented towards curtailing or boosting employment. For example, an excessive shrinking of consumption in periods of economic recession may be averted by the implementing of unemployment benefits, which at the same time have a role in backing businesses and checking unemployment expansion. Similarly, working time reduction schemes involving wage compensation can safeguard jobs while ensuring a certain stability of household income.

The nature of the resources employed and the actors involved represent a further criterion to consider when defining labour policies. In particular from the 1990s onwards, non-public actors have also gained ground in the dispensing of labour policies. Hence, referring to labour market policies as state-implemented interventions no longer suffices, although it must be pointed out that the resources draw on the public budget.

More specifically, labour market policies can be divided into three macro-categories, depending on the purposes and instruments used (Reyneri, 2011; Gualmini & Rizza, 2013; Samek-Lodovici, 2014; Vesan, 2014):

1. the regulation of work relations, i.e. the set of interventions that regulate the interaction between labour supply and demand;

DOI: 10.4324/9781003297130-6

2. passive policies, i.e. the interventions that aim to ensure a form of income support in the event that the beneficiaries are unemployed or at risk of unemployment;
3. active policies, namely, the set of measures designed to remove non-legislative obstacles that may preclude entering and remaining in the labour market.

Labour market policies can also be distinguished from more general employment policies – such as interventions aimed at lowering labour costs through the general cutback of taxes and/or social security contributions – because they incorporate a precise guiding criterion: that of selectivity, addressing specific groups of individuals (*target groups*).

In this regard, the target groups are:

1. the unemployed, i.e. people who are out of work but actively looking for a job and willing to accept a job opportunity should one arise;
2. people at risk of unemployment, i.e. those who have not yet lost their job but who are at risk of losing it involuntarily because of the critical economic situation or a period of sectoral and/or company crisis;
3. discouraged workers, i.e. those who are not currently in the labour force but who would be willing to join it under certain conditions. These are people who have looked for a job in the past and would be willing to work but do not expect to be able to access a job; or people who are overburdened with care duties – often women – who, having changed their circumstances and been relieved of their domestic obligations, would be ready to enter the labour market.

Historically labour policy trends and comparative data have revealed a wide divergence among countries, not only in terms of the greater or lesser employment protection provided by legislation, and in terms of public expenditure reserved for labour market policies, but also regarding the subjects to whom employment protection and promotion policies are addressed. While devoting little attention to labour market policies as an autonomous question, the vast body of comparative literature on the welfare state has shed light on the variety of policy development paths. In a first phase, up to the 1970s, the introduction and development of labour market programmes were explained through economic and demographic independent variables: the GDP growth rate, the structure of the population in terms of age, the level of industrialisation and urbanisation (Wilenski, 1975). Subsequently, "power resource theory" focused on the plurality of political actors and interest organisations to the fore, concluding that large and entrenched trade unions, strong left-wing parties and pro-labour government coalitions were key explanatory variables for understanding the variety and extent of interventions in different countries (Korpi, 1978). From the 1980s onwards, the role of the state, its administration and the efficiency of its bureaucracy came under the spotlight (Flora & Alber, 1981).

Investigating the relationship between change and stability in the long term represents the most appropriate perspective for understanding similarities and differences between labour policy regimes, where by "regimes" we mean "relatively coherent and stable schemes of social regulation, differentiated according to certain models and variants that in part resume old differences and in part develop new profiles" (Mingione, 1997, 111–112). In this respect, the institutionalisation of a certain labour policy regime and its stability can be accounted for by the consideration that margins of manoeuvre in the field of labour market policies will be conditioned by the "institutional paths" defined in the past (Weishaupt, 2011). The stability of particular institutions generates "winners" who will have an interest in preserving the status quo. Pierson (2004) has called this situation "institutional inertia", the positive feedbacks of which, in terms of policy outcomes and political mobilisation, lead to a certain equilibrium that will be resistant to change. Hence a "lock-in" phenomenon of labour market institutions is engendered that governments will tend not to change in order to not risk generating negative effects for the consensus they need.

By observing the level of "complementarity" and the extent to which institutions tend to reinforce each other through mutual interaction, Hall and Soskice (2001) offer a perspective that identifies a particular mechanism to account for their continuity. According to this perspective, two varieties of capitalism can be identified: the so-called "liberal market economies" and the so-called "co-ordinated market economies", each responding to a different logic, the ultimate basis of which lies in the greater or lesser ability of firms to co-ordinate with each other and with workers. Labour market policies will consequently be embedded in the variant of national capitalism and constitute an integral part of the same set of complementary institutions that partake in distinguishing the specific variant.

More recently, Thelen (2014) proposed three trajectories of liberalisation in the field of labour policies. These depend on the coalitions between interest groups that have strengthened over time, resulting in different distributional outcomes that hinge on the capacity of actors to coordinate and the degree of inclusion, i.e. the extent to which welfare interventions are encompassing.

4.2 Labour market policies in different growth models

Labour market policies feature different institutional orientations and routes that trace the various development paths ensuing from the combination of economic growth and inequality patterns, presented here in Chapter 1. The cross-country comparison shows that each labour policy regime tends to be associated with a specific institutional configuration linked to a consistent underpinning logic. Hence, limited economic support and weak legislative

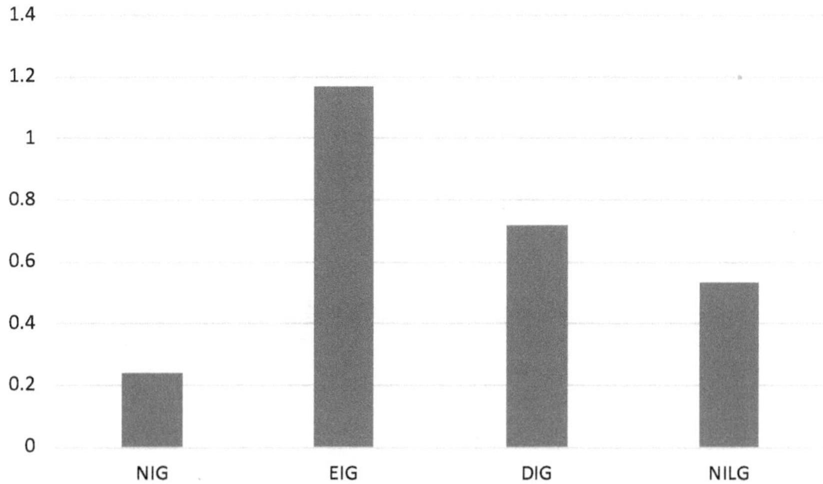

Figure 4.1 Expenditure on active labour market policies by growth model, as a percentage of GDP (2017).

Note: Missing countries: Greece. United Kingdom: 2011 data. Italy: 2015 data.

Source: Elaboration on OECD data.

protections, combined with underdeveloped active labour market policies in some cases endorse the supremacy of the market as a mechanism for regulating labour relations (*non-inclusive growth*). Substantial interventions in active policies and training, addressing a wide range of employed and unemployed, as well as the pursuit of greater equality, are manifest in other national cases (*egalitarian inclusive growth*). In other countries, there are protection insurance schemes and integrated education and training policies, with rights linked to employment status and tendencies towards dualisation between insiders and outsiders (*dualistic inclusive growth*), while a historical lack of training policies and employment services and the displacement of protection schemes condition other national cases (*low non-inclusive growth*).

Figure 4.1 shows how the egalitarian inclusive growth model exhibits higher spending on active labour market policies. This is a long-term trend corroborated by the 2017 data.

Through the analysis of some of the characteristic and important areas such as training and employment services, expenditure on active policies can be further investigated (Figures 4.2 and 4.3). These interventions have different objectives. Training is related to investments in human capital and skills development, while employment services are aimed at job seekers. In the latter case, the focus is on activating recipients of income support to push them to return to work quickly (Busemeyer & Garritzmann, 2019; Garritzmann et al., 2018).

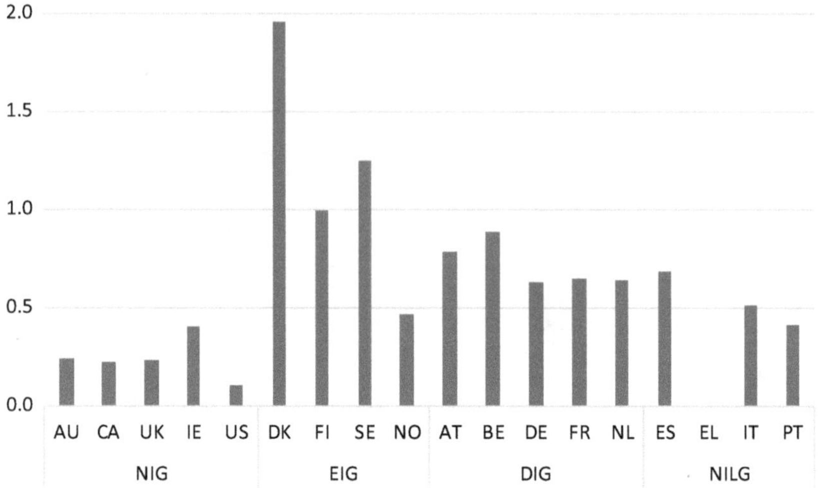

Figure 4.2 Expenditure on active labour market policies by country, as a percentage of GDP (2017).

Note: Missing countries: Greece, United Kingdom: 2011 data. Italy: 2015 data.

Source: OECD (2020), Labour market programmes: expenditure and participants, OECD Employment and Labour Market Statistics (database).

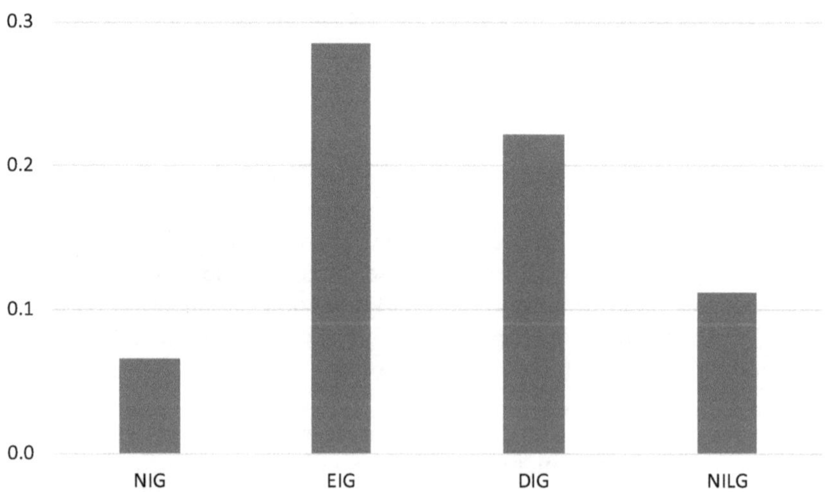

Figure 4.3 Expenditure on training policies by growth model, as a percentage of GDP (2017).

Note: United Kingdom: data from 2011. Italy: data from 2015.

Source: Data OECD.

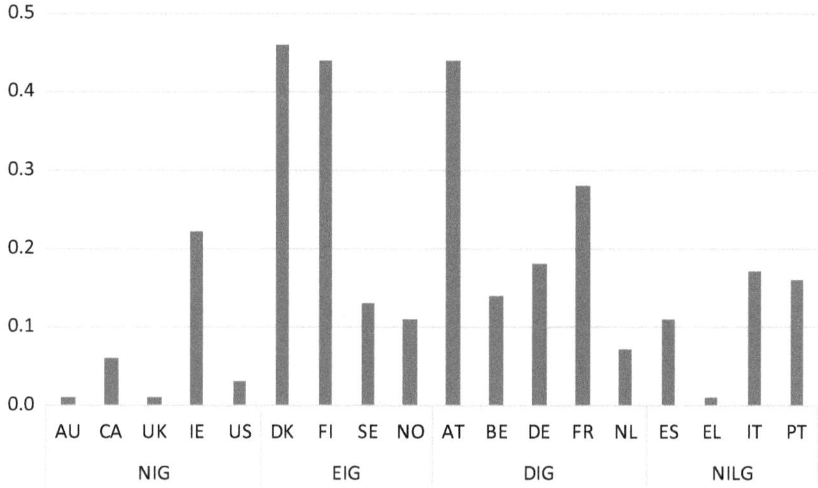

Figure 4.4 Expenditure on training policies by country, as a percentage of GDP (2017).

Note: United Kingdom: 2011 data. Italy: 2015 data.

Source: OECD (2020), Labour market programmes: expenditure and participants, OECD Employment and Labour Market Statistics (database).

Of note is the fact that the egalitarian inclusive growth model invests more in training (especially in Denmark) (see Figures 4.4 and 4.5), while dualistic inclusive growth countries focus on employment services (especially Germany) (see Figure 4.6). The non-inclusive growth (NIG) model shows similar levels of expenditure for both policy areas, at a very low level. In countries with low and non-inclusive growth, little is invested in training policies and employment services compared to the two inclusive growth regimes (egalitarian and dualistic), though slightly more in training compared to the NIG countries.

The OECD defines formal training as an activity that a person undertakes within an adult learning institution or centre, or by following an education or training programme within a company. A closer inspection of the data available on *formal* and *non-formal* training reveals that the distinguishing feature of formal training is the issuing of a certificate upon completion of the course. The activity is institutionalised and structured, has learning objectives, and is delivered by a trainer or educator (Werquin, 2007).

Alongside formal learning there is non-formal learning, which can be described as a process of *learning by doing*, i.e. learning through *"hands-on"* experience. Also this activity is structured and follows predefined learning objectives, but unlike formal learning it does not lead to certification and may take place in companies but may also be pursued externally.

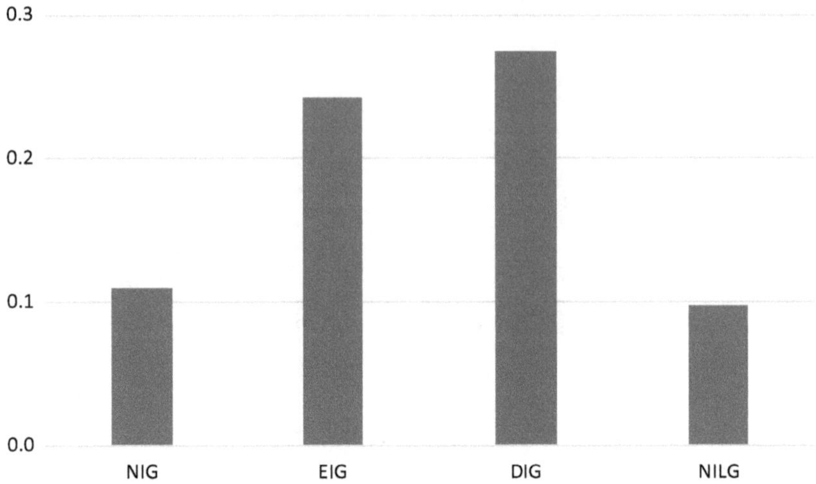

Figure 4.5 Expenditure on employment services by growth model, as a percentage of GDP (2017).

Note: Missing countries: Greece. United Kingdom: 2011 data. Italy: 2015 data.

Source: Elaboration on OECD data.

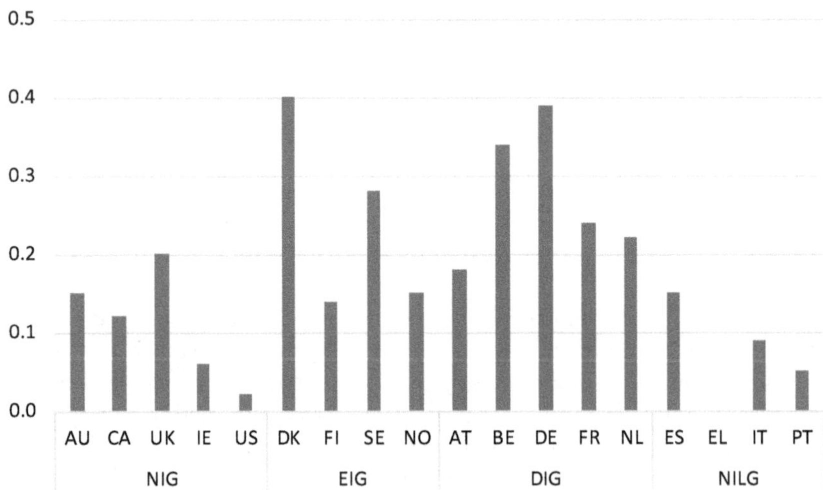

Figure 4.6 Expenditure on employment services by country, as a percentage of GDP (2017).

Note: Missing countries: Greece. United Kingdom: 2011 data. Italy: 2015 data.

Source: Elaboration on OECD data (2020). *Labour market programmes: expenditure and participants, OECD Employment and Labour Market Statistics* (database).

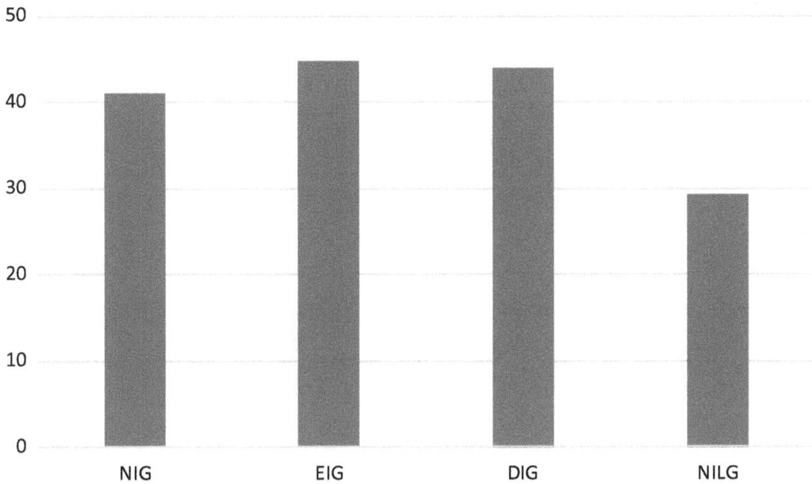

Figure 4.7 Participation in non-formal job-related training by growth pattern, as a percentage of the population aged 25–64 (2016).

Note: United States, Ireland, and Canada: 2012 data.

Source: Elaboration on OECD data.

Generally speaking, formal training schemes are less implemented to provide training for individuals in the 25–64 age group. This is hardly surprising, if we consider that formal training, especially that which takes place within educational institutions, is more important for the lower age groups. However, from a comparative perspective, there are some interesting reflections to express on growth models (Figures 4.7, 4.8, 4.9, and 4.10).

In the first place, the model based on EIG is confirmed as that which invests most in training, both formal and, in particular, non-formal. Worthy of note is that in the case of formal training, the gap between the EIG and the NIG countries narrows, confirming the important role of educational institutions in skills training in Anglo-Saxon countries (Estevez-Abe, Iversen & Soskice, 2001).

In the case of the DIG model, however, formal training is revealed as having significantly less weight. This also seems to corroborate the claim in the literature on types of capitalism that within coordinated market economies the training of workers' skills takes place mainly in-house.

The comparison of NIG and NILG trends leads us to a further consideration. Notwithstanding the fewer resources in the former type devoted to training in terms of expenditure on GDP compared to the latter, participation in training activities is higher, confirming the critical issues distinguishing the non-inclusive low growth model (Figures 4.11 and 4.12).

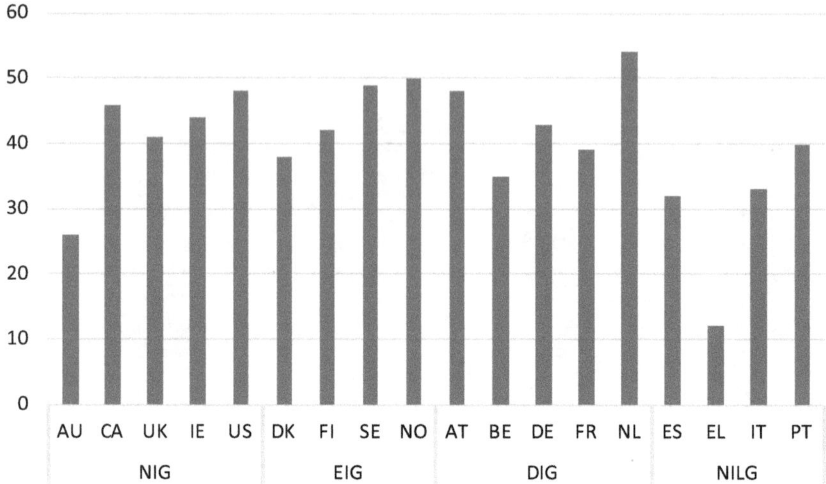

Figure 4.8 Participation in non-formal job-related training by country, as a percentage of the population aged 25–64 (2016).

Note: United States, Ireland, and Canada: 2012 data.

Source: Survey of Adult Skills (PIAAC).

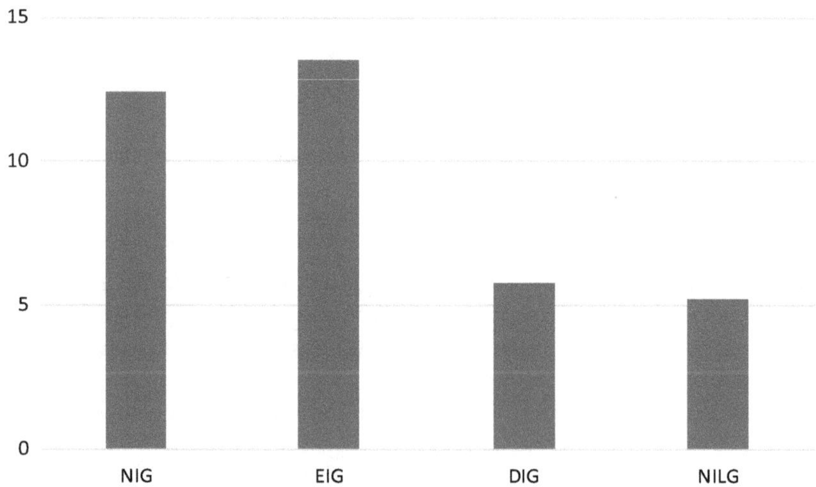

Figure 4.9 Participation in formal education by growth pattern, as a percentage of the population aged 25–64 (2016).

Note: Canada and the United States: 2012 data.

Source: Elaboration on OECD data.

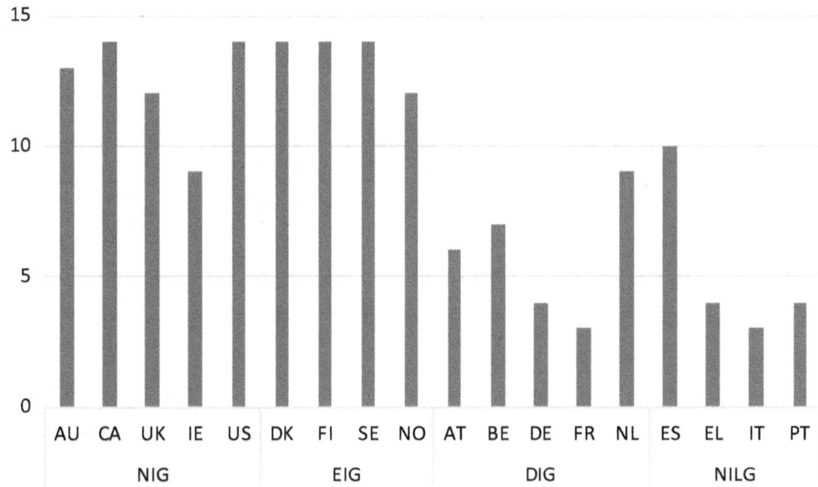

Figure 4.10 Participation in formal training by country, as a percentage of the population aged 25–64 (2016).

Note: Canada and the United States: 2012 data.

Source: Survey of Adult Skills (PIAAC).

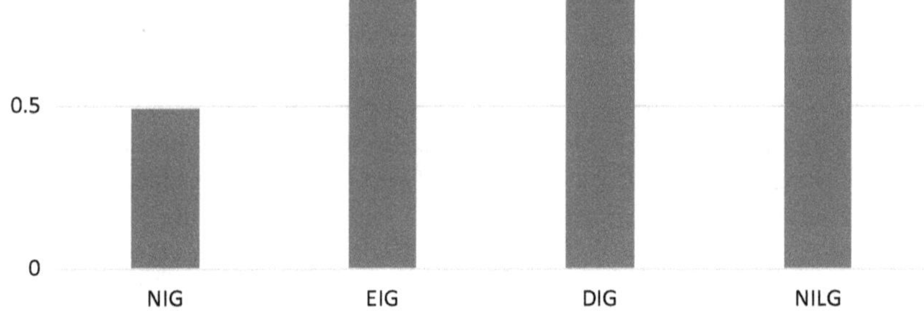

Figure 4.11 Expenditure on passive policies by growth model, as a percentage of GDP (2017).

Note: United Kingdom: 2011 data.

Source: Elaboration on OECD data.

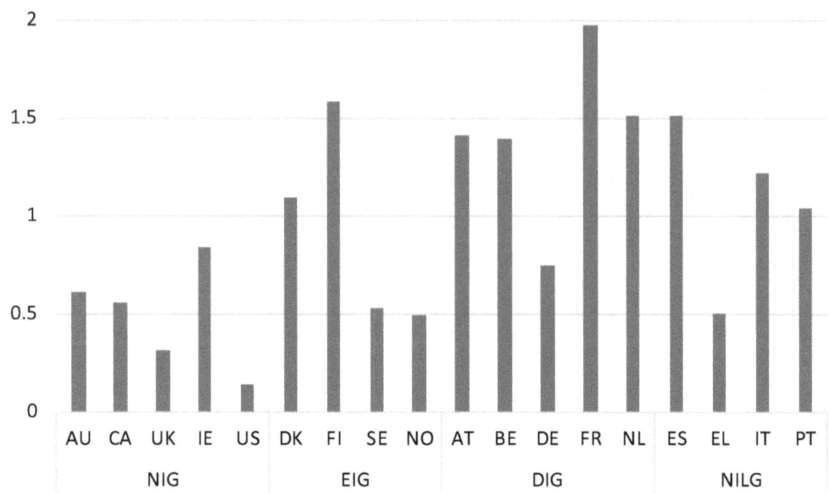

Figure 4.12 Expenditure on passive policies by country, as a percentage of GDP (2017).

Note: United Kingdom: 2011 data.

Source: Elaboration on OECD data.

As far as the *passive policies* are concerned, dualistic and non-inclusive low-growth countries devote relatively more resources to this policy instrument, even in the face of averagely high levels of unemployment, especially in the non-inclusive low-growth model.

With regard to the question of entitlement to benefit, Figure 4.13 shows the net replacement rate at the second month of unemployment and at the 24th month.

The NIG countries are the least generous, with a replacement rate of 42.6% during the second month of unemployment and 28% after 24 months. The value for the USA, which falls to 6% in the 24th month, is worthy of note. In contrast, the DIG countries provide the highest replacement rates during both time-points considered, while similar but slightly lower values are those of the EIG countries. The values of the NILG countries invite reflection: the replacement rates (56.2% at month 2 and 41.2% at month 24) are lower than those of the egalitarian inclusive growth and dualistic inclusive growth countries but higher than the non-inclusive growth countries. It should be noted that, compared to the Scandinavian and Continental countries, the difference between the replacement rates at the second month are modest, while the gap widens when we compare the replacement rates at the 24th month (the gap with the DIG countries is about 12 points, while with the EIG countries about 15 points). In other words, despite the fact that the phenomenon is particularly widespread, the risk of long-term unemployment is less well protected in these countries.

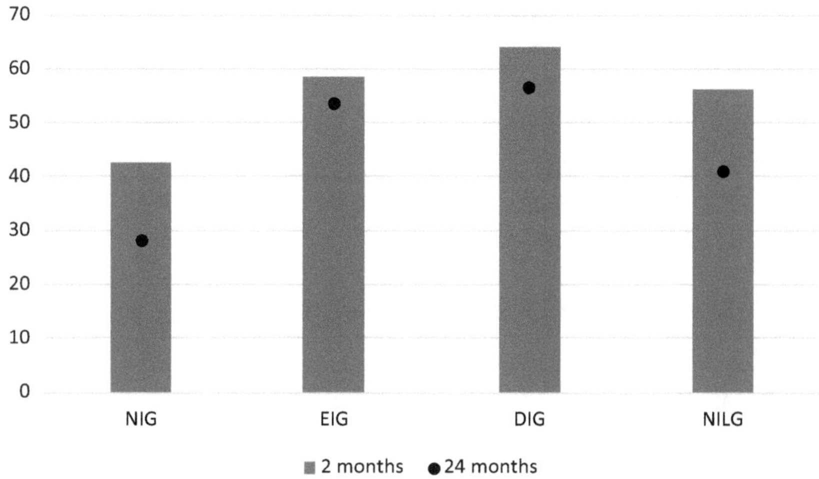

Figure 4.13 Net replacement rate of unemployment benefit at the second and 24th month, % average salary, individual without children (2017).

Source: Elaboration on OECD-SOC data.

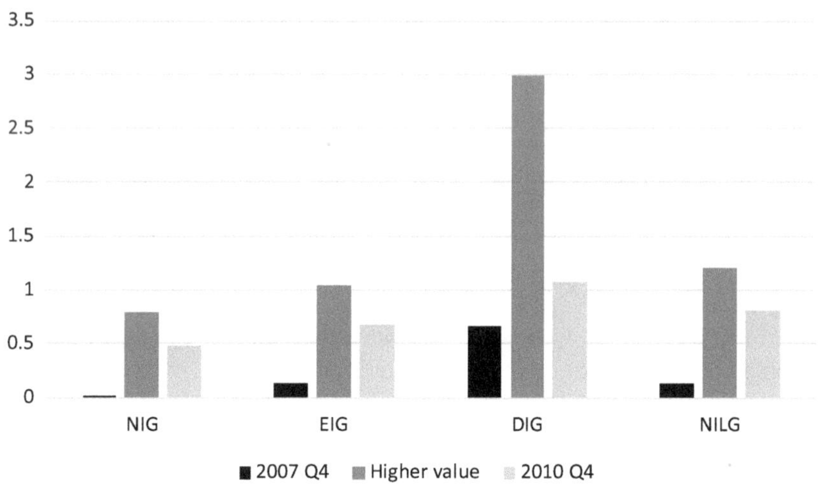

Figure 4.14 Share of workers involved in short-time work schemes during the crisis by growth pattern.

Note: Missing countries: UK, USA, Greece, Sweden. Denmark: No data for 2010.

Source: Hijzen and Martin (2013).

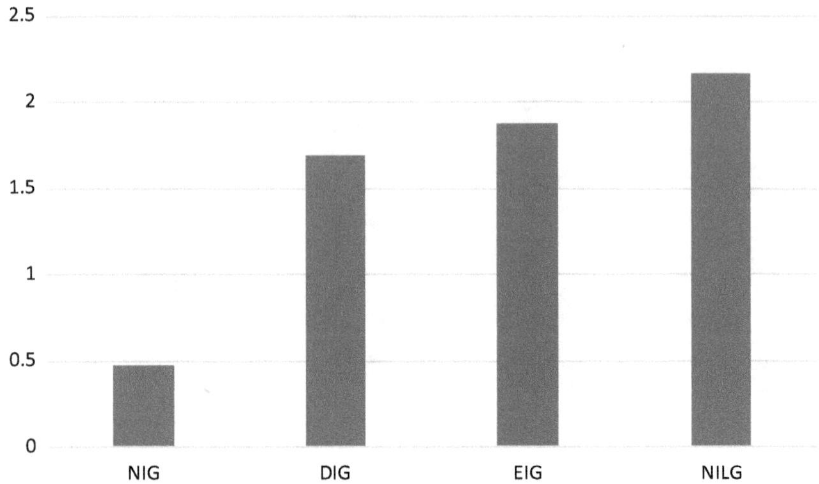

Figure 4.15 EPL fixed-term workers by growth pattern (2013).

Source: Elaboration on OECD data.

Figure 4.14 shows the percentage of workers who participated in short-time work programmes, i.e. those interventions that support wages and simultaneously safeguard jobs for those who have suffered reductions in their working hours as a result of an economic crisis. These interventions are particularly widespread in the industrial sector (Thelen, 2014). The data refer to the last quarter of 2007, immediately preceding the crisis, to the last quarter of 2010, following the "responses" given by the various countries to the employment crisis and, finally, to the period when the highest values were recorded, i.e. around the third quarter of 2009 (Hijzen & Martin, 2013; Hijzen & Venn, 2010). It is clear from this figure that dualistic inclusive growth countries are the ones to make most use of short-time work schemes, followed by NILG countries. In particular, the countries that have made the most use of these schemes are Belgium, Germany, and Italy, the only ones where the percentage of workers involved exceeds 2% of employees.

The following figures (4.16, 4.17, and 4.18) present data on Employment Protection Legislation (EPL), which measures, first, the constraints contained in the legislation in relation to recruitment and dismissal procedures in the case of permanent employment, and second, the rules relating to the temporal extension of employment relationships and the definition of hours (EPL fixed-term employment).

The EPL index is higher for workers with permanent contracts (Figure 4.15), regardless of the growth pattern, with one important exception, however, France (Figure 4.16). Regarding the EPL aimed at permanent workers, it can

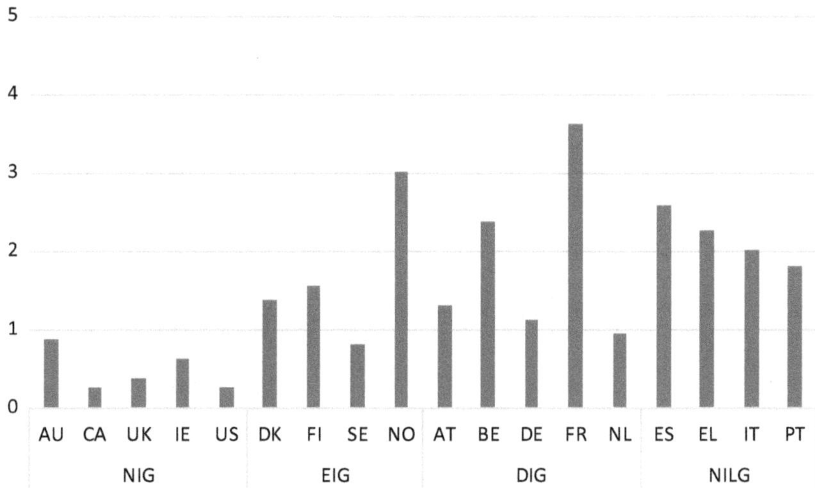

Figure 4.16 EPL fixed-term workers by country (2013).

Source: OECD.

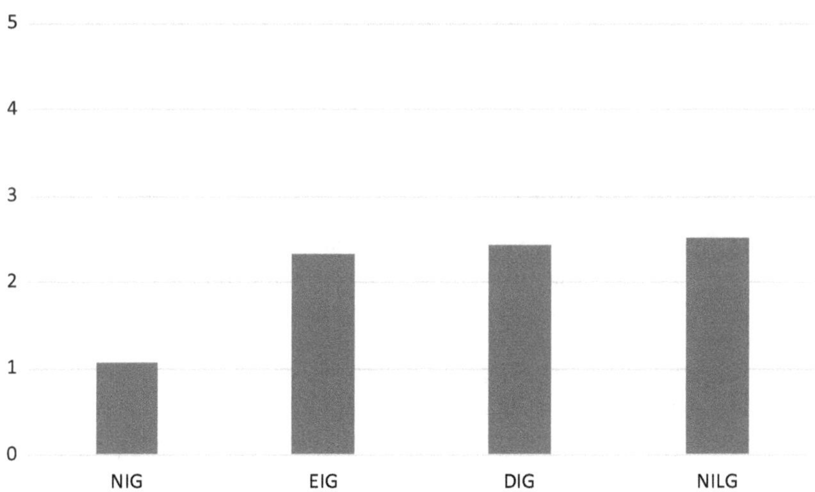

Figure 4.17 EPL permanent workers by growth pattern (2013).

Source: Elaboration on OECD data.

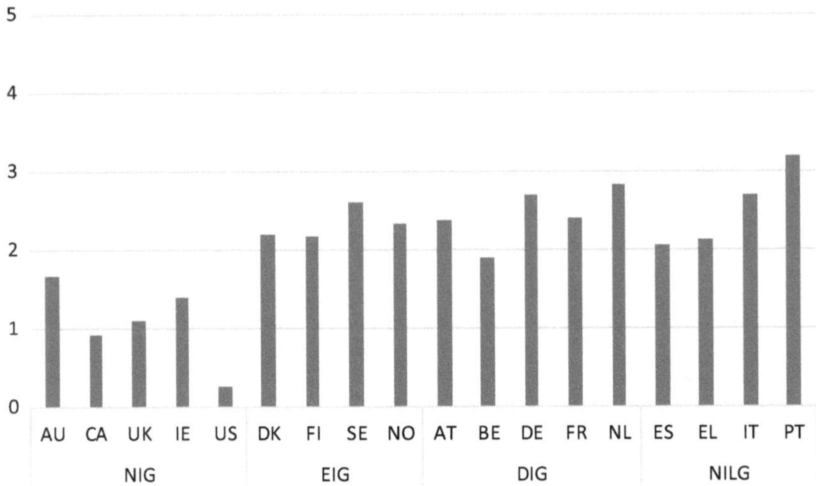

Figure 4.18 EPL permanent workers by country (2013).

Source: OECD.

be seen that the main difference is between the low level of the NIG type and the other three. Nonetheless, it should be noted that as no post-2013 data are available, the effect of major labour market reforms implemented in some countries that have reduced the EPL index more recently (Italy and Spain, for example) does not emerge.

4.3 Concluding remarks

Summarising, in conclusion, the characteristics of labour policy interventions, it is useful to underline the distinction regarding the incidence of public consumption or investment expenditure on the gross domestic product (Beramendi et al., 2015; see also Chapter 1). Also in this policy arena there is a different weight of measures oriented towards investment (active labour and human capital development policies and employment services) or measures oriented towards consumption (unemployment benefits and short-time work schemes), depending on the growth patterns.

In cases of non-inclusive growth, all areas of labour market policies are underdeveloped. Low legislative employment protection, low income protection interventions in favour of the unemployed, combined with almost non-existent short-time work schemes to support workers during cyclical crises, and little intervention in active policies. The only policy areas showing significant interventions are employment services, especially in the UK, and formal training, chiefly in the US. This confirms the importance in those countries of educational institutions in skills training, on the one hand, and of employment services that encourage the unemployed to return to work as soon as possible, even in low-wage areas, on the other.

A broad array of interventions to develop active labour market policies is what most distinguishes the inclusive and egalitarian growth model. In particular, the role of formal and non-formal training is pinpointed, demonstrating the importance of the acquisition of general and specific skills required by an innovation-oriented production system in the context of a labour market featuring high mobility. Furthermore, the intensive training programmes in the EIG model target both the employed and the unemployed, while low spending on employment services shows that the activation of income support recipients is of secondary importance compared to increasing qualification levels. As far as passive policies are concerned, the EIG model illustrates scarce use of short-time work schemes addressing only workers already employed and a preference for universalistic supports such as unemployment benefits, which, integrated with active policies and training that focus on all, workers and non, help develop a strong institutional complementarity with a coordinated and innovation-oriented business system (as shown by the data presented in this volume with reference to innovation policies). Finally, the considerable turnover in the labour market (especially in Denmark) is favoured by the lower value of the EPL index for permanent employment in comparison with the dual inclusive growth model and the non-inclusive low growth model.

Compared to the other models, the dualistic inclusive growth model has the highest expenditure per GDP on passive labour market policies and the most largesse in the net replacement rate of unemployment benefits. The protection of employed workers threatened by cyclical downturns with working time reductions is also strong, as shown by ample compensation schemes linked to short-time work, combined with high legislative protection of insiders with full-time, permanent jobs. In the field of active policies, there are only two significant areas of intervention: non-formal training, which mostly targets adult employees in industrial enterprises – the *insiders* – and employment services. The latter have been strengthened, especially in Germany, with the aim of accompanying workers supported by welfare schemes to reintegrate into the labour market in low-skilled services, as shown, among other things, by the high number of low-wage workers in that sector (Thelen, 2014).

Finally, the low-growth, non-inclusive model differs from the others in its meagre use of active labour market policies, with lower spending than in the EIG and dual models and slightly higher spending than in the NIG model. Expenditure on training is also scant and much lower than in the EIG and DIG models. Moreover, employment services are underdeveloped, meaning that spending as a proportion of GDP is the lowest of all the growth models. As a result, the support offered by labour market policies for re-entering the labour market is very low, excluding a very large share of the active population ensnared in long-term unemployment. Participation in formal and non-formal job-related training among the population aged 25–64 is also weak, the lowest of all the growth models. Labour market policies in the low-growth, non-inclusive model thus focus on protecting those who are already in employment, as confirmed by the higher EPL index for permanent employment and the high expenditure on short-time work schemes in favour of the employed during economic downturns.

References

Beramendi, P., Häusermann, S., Kitschelt, H., & Kriesi, H. (2015) (Eds). *The politics of advanced capitalism*. Cambridge: Cambridge University Press.

Busemeyer, M. R. & Garritzmann, J. L. (2019). Compensation or social investment? Revisiting the link between globalisation and popular demand for the welfare state. *Journal of Social Policy*, 48(3), 427–448. doi:10.1017/S0047279418000569

Estevez-Abe, M., Iversen, T., & Soskice, D. (2001). Social protection and the formation of skills: A reinterpretation of the welfare state, in Hall, P. A. & Soskice, D. (Eds), *Varieties of capitalism: The institutional foundations of comparative advantage*. Oxford, New York: Oxford University Press, 145–183.

Flora, P. & Alber, J. (1981). Modernization: Democratization and the development of welfare states in Europe and America, in Flora, P. & Heidenheimer, A. J. (Eds), *The Development of Welfare States in Europe and America*. New Brunswick: Transaction, pp. 37–80.

Garritzmann, J. L., Busemeyer, M. R. & Neimanns, E. (2018). Public demand for social investment: New supporting coalitions for welfare state reform in Western Europe? *Journal of European Public Policy*, 25(6), 844–861. doi.org/10.1080/13501763.2017.1401107

Gualmini, E. & Rizza, R. (2013). *Le politiche del lavoro*. Bologna: Il Mulino.

Hall, P. A. & Soskice, D. (2001). *Varieties of capitalism: The institutional foundations of comparative advantage*. Oxford: Oxford University Press.

Hijzen, A. & Martin, S. (2013). The role of short-time work schemes during the global financial crisis1 and early recovery: A cross-country analysis. *IZA Journal of Labor Policy*, 2 (5), 1–31.

Hijzen, A. & Venn, D. (2010). *The role of short-time work schemes during the 2008–09 recession, OCED social, employment and migration working papers no. 2010/15.* Paris: OECD Publishing.

Korpi, W. (1978). *The working class in welfare capitalism: Work, unions and politics in Sweden*, London: Routledge & Kegan Paul.

Mingione, E. (1997). *Sociologia della vita economica*. Roma: Carocci.

Pierson, P. (Eds) (2004). *Politics in time: History, institutions and social analysis*. Princeton: Princeton University Press.

Reyneri, E. (2011). *Sociologia del mercato del lavoro. Le forme dell'occupazione*. Bologna: Il Mulino.

Samek-Lodovici, M. (2014). *Le politiche del lavoro*, in R. Semenza (Eds) *Il mondo del lavoro. Le prospettive della sociologia*. Torino: UTET, 261–294.

Solow, R. (1994). *Il mercato del lavoro come istituzione sociale*. Bologna: il Mulino.

Thelen, K. (2014). *Varieties of liberalization and the new politics of social solidarity*. Cambridge: Cambridge University Press.

Vesan, P. (2014). *La politica del lavoro*, in M. Ferrera (Eds), *Le Politiche sociali*, III ed., Bologna: il Mulino, 183–201.

Weishaupt, J. T. (2011). *From the manpower revolution to the activation paradigm: Explaining institutional continuity and change in an integrating Europe*. Amsterdam: Amsterdam University Press.

Werquin, P. (2007). Moving mountains: Will qualifications systems promote lifelong learning? *European Journal of Education,* 42 (4), 459–484. doi.org/10.1111/j.1465-3435.2007.00327.x

Wilenski, H. L. (1975). *The welfare state and equality: Structural and ideological roots of public expenditure*. Berkeley: University of California Press.

Chapter 5

Welfare systems

Giovanni Amerigo Giuliani

5.1 Introduction

As already underlined in the Introduction and Chapter 1, the welfare state represents a key topic in our research.

The organisational characteristics of social policies and their relevance in terms of expenditure significantly influence the redistributive capacities of a given country and, consequently, affects the level of social inequalities. Yet, social policies also condition the development path, depending on their greater or lesser financial sustainability, besides their effects on the labour market.

The three welfare regimes – liberal, conservative-corporative, and social-democratic – have a long and well-established tradition in the comparative welfare state literature. They were initially introduced by Richard Titmuss (1974) and subsequently developed by Gøsta Esping-Andersen (1990), using the concepts of de-commodification and de-stratification.[1] The effectiveness of modifying the distribution of life opportunities produced by the market and the family sphere varies considerably among these three regimes (Ferrera, 2019). This effectiveness is greatest in the social-democratic regime, average in the conservative-corporatist cluster, and at a minimum in the liberal one.[2]

Following the criticism by feminist scholars on the lack of a gender perspective in conceptualising the welfare state, a further differentiating aspect between welfare regimes was introduced, namely, de-familialism (see Lewis, 1992; Leitner, 2003; Esping-Andersen, 2009).[3] Since the 1960s, the social-democratic regime has pursued de-familialising policies that promote a family model based on both women and men at work and on men's greater involvement in caregiving tasks. The other two regimes, notably the conservative-corporative one (except France), have historically been exemplified by a high degree of familialism. The resulting "male breadwinner family model" is thus based on a solid differentiation of men's and women's roles, with the latter being relegated to caring tasks (Lewis, 1992).

The Mediterranean model has come into play as a fourth regime, following a more extensive in-depth analysis of southern European countries.

DOI: 10.4324/9781003297130-7

Notwithstanding a Bismarckian imprint and hence traits similar to the conservative-corporatist regime, the Mediterranean regime differs from the latter for at least three reasons.[4] First, historically speaking, the protection system is more dualised than in those countries belongining to the conservative-corporative regime. The level of decommodification is particularly disproportionate, with excessive protection of the *insiders* – i.e. the labour market'core workers – while the more peripheral worker group – the *outsider*s – has weaker coverage. Second, the Catholic Church's strong influence accentuates the family's role as a "social buffer". Lastly, with state structures open to manipulation by organised interests, especially political parties, the Mediterranean-regime welfare states typically feature high levels of *particularism* and a low degree of *stateness*.

The concept of four welfare regimes has been consolidated with time in comparative welfare analysis and, more generally, the *comparative political economy* (Beramendi et al., 2015; Manow et al., 2018).

An analysis of how our development paths differ regarding welfare policies has disclosed a distinct overlapping of the relatively dynamic and inclusive development types and the welfare regimes. The non-inclusive growth (NIG) countries present the typical features of a liberal regime. The egalitarian inclusive growth (EIG) countries are similar to social-democratic regimes with universalistic, new social risk-oriented welfare states. In contrast, the continental DIG countries shows the features of the corporatist-conservative regime. Lastly, the non-inclusive low growth (NILG) countries manifest characteristics typical of the Mediterranean welfare regime.

The following pages focus on the correlation between welfare models and types of development, examining more closely cross-type differences in terms of expenditure and organisational characteristics and discussing the most recent change trends.

5.2 An overview

This chapter provides an overview of the welfare systems in the four growth models. Despite the methodological limitations,[5] general indicators (mainly *public* and *social expenditure*) provide a preliminary outline of the "macro" differences between the four *ideal growth* models.

Figure 5.1 shows the total public expenditure in 2017. The NIG countries display the lowest average value, with Ireland recording the minimum at ten percentage points (*pp*) below the average. In the other three growth models, the data are more homogeneous. The EIG countries have the highest expenditures, followed by the DIG first and the NILG countries next. Historically, the state's role in the economies of the Anglo-Saxon countries is more contained. Therefore, the low value of public spending is not surprising as the neo-liberal paradigm has strongly influenced economic and financial choices, including the state budget, since the 1980s. Similarly, the expenditure

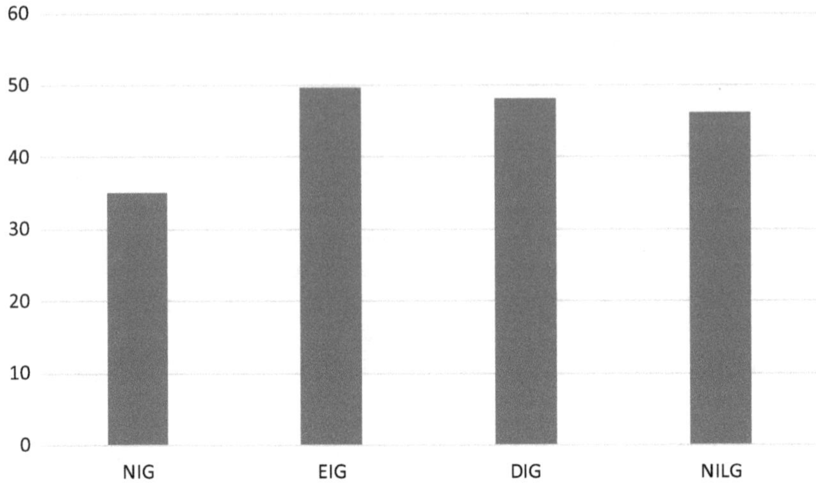

Figure 5.1 Total public expenditure as % of GDP (2017).

Source: Elaboration of IMF Data.

amount for the Scandinavian countries, where the state has always played a significant role,[6] is consistent with their social-democratic tradition.

Figure 5.2 shows total social expenditure and social expenditure per capita data in 2015. Regarding the percentage of GDP, the NIG countries indicate the lowest value of social-policy spending, while the EIG countries record the highest, followed closely by the DIG and NILG countries. Among the continental countries, social expenditure is significantly higher than the group average in France (32%) and considerably lower than in the Netherlands (17.7%).

Comparing these results with the social expenditure per capita data reveals an interesting picture. Indeed, measuring the resources invested for each individual citizen enables us to highlight the differences between the various growth models concerning total social spending more effectively. The highest per capita social expenditure is recorded in the EIG countries, followed by the DIG countries. In contrast, spending in the NIG and NILG models is lower. The Mediterranean countries show a lower value than the Anglo-Saxon countries, albeit with higher social spending of GDP. It can be inferred that in the NILG countries, notwithstanding the relatively high level of overall public expenditure on social policies, the impact of welfare policies on single individuals is moderate.

To conclude this general overview of the "macro" characteristics of welfare states in the four growth models, Figure 5.3 shows the composition of social expenditure in 2015 by type of function.

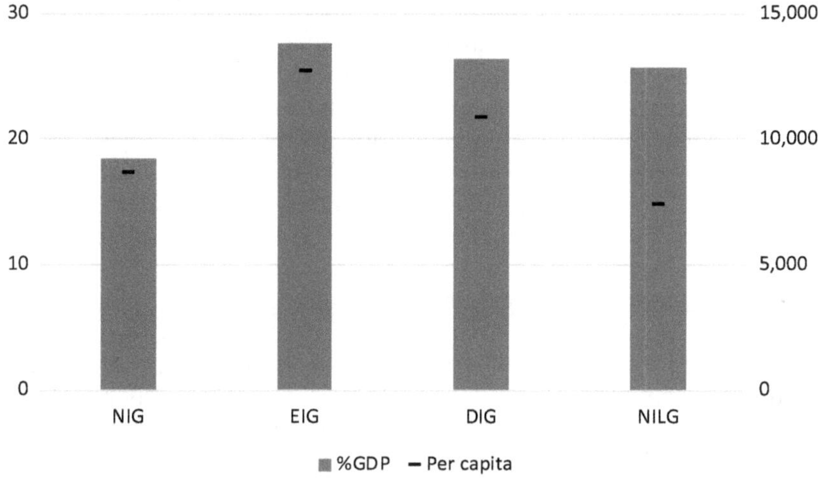

Figure 5.2 Public expenditure for social policies by growth model as % of GDP (2015) and public expenditure *per capita* for social policies by growth model at constant prices, PPP, 2010 dollars (2015).

Source: Elaboration of OECD-SOC data.

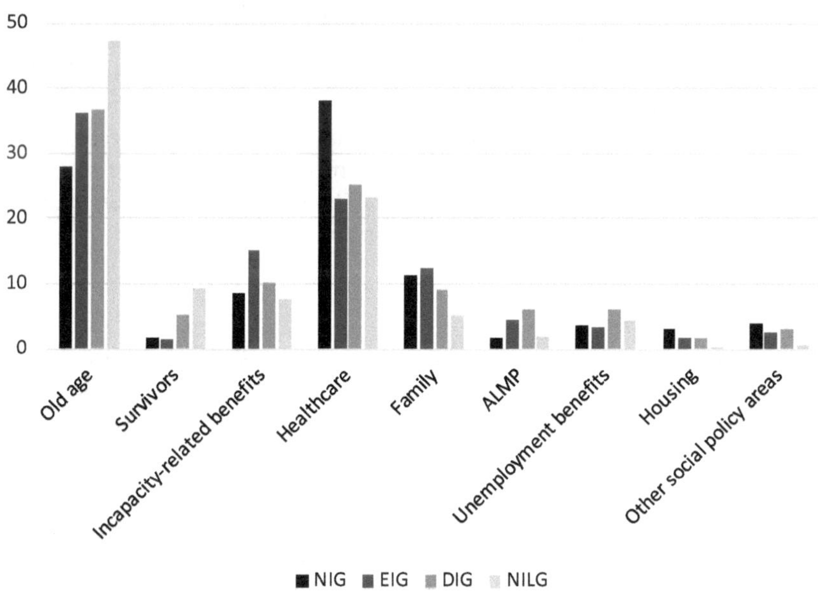

Figure 5.3 Expenditure on social benefits by type of function as % of total social expenditure (2015).

Source: Elaboration of OECD-SOC data.

The largest share of social spending is pension expenditure, except for the NIG countries where more is spent on health. However, the proportion of spending devoted to *old-age* risk varies considerably across models. For the EIG and DIG countries, the value is around 36% of total expenditure, while in the NILG countries, it accounts for almost half of all social spending. This latter value is not surprising, given that historically the Mediterranean countries – Italy first of all – have over-protected the old age risk while disregarding the *new social risks.*[7] As pointed out in the literature, these latter ones are mainly covered by the *family* function,[8] *Labour Market Policies* (ALMPs), and *housing*.

In this respect, the EIG countries have the highest expenditure on family policies and ALMPs. The DIG group's expenditure for these two functions is also high, though less than the Scandinavian countries (except for ALMP expenditures in the Netherlands, which is 4.3%). Continental countries indeed allocate a relatively high percentage of the social expenditure on the "unemployment" risk, thus preferring monetary transfers (mainly unemployment benefits) to activation. The NIG countries, on the other hand, devote a large share of social spending to the family function and housing policies, while ALMPs account for only 1.5%. Finally, as already mentioned, public spending on family policy, ALMPs, and housing for the NILG countries is particularly low – though both Spain and Portugal display higher values than Italy and Greece.

In short, in the Scandinavian countries, the *new social risks* have become a new priority. Moreover, since the end of the 1970s, they have begun to absorb a significant share of social expenditure. In contrast, social spending in the Mediterranean countries continues to be directed almost exclusively to the *old social risks*, in particular the old-age risk, thus leaving few resources available to cover the *new social risks.*[9] In an intermediate position, we find the continental and Anglo-Saxon countries, which have begun to reorient public spending, albeit with different spending priorities.

5.3 Pensions

Pension policies constitute one of the most critical areas for all advanced economies. As already noted, old-age risk accounts for a large share of social spending in Western countries. However, differences persist between the four growth models.

Figure 5.4 shows pension expenditure as a percentage of GDP in 2015. The lowest values are shown by the NIG countries, followed by the EIG group. Pension expenditure in the DIG countries is higher, with the Netherlands below average (5.1%) and France above average (13.9%). As already noted, the share of expenditure for pensions in the NILG countries is particularly high. Comparatively, both continental and Mediterranean countries have the highest values, which can be explained by considering that their pension

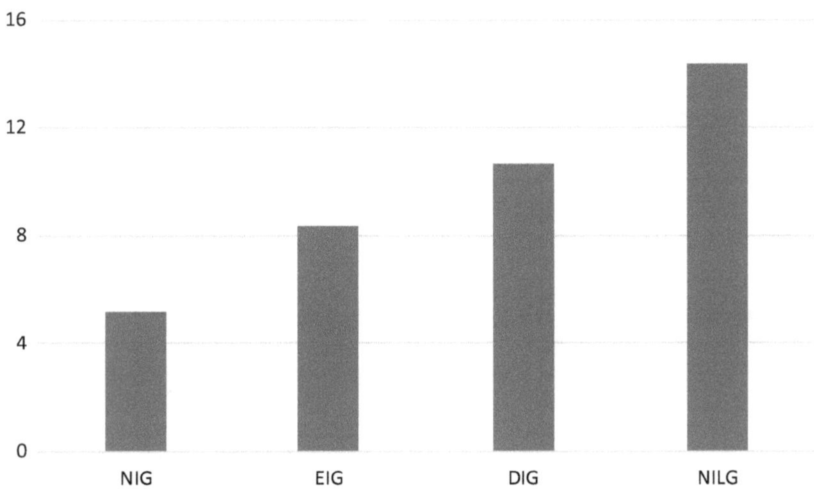

Figure 5.4 Pension expenditure as a percentage of GDP (2015).

Source: Elaboration of OECD-SOC data.

systems are historically built around the social insurance model. Indeed, the public pillar (and therefore the state) in these countries guarantees that a pensioner's income is (often) maintained through benefits linked to past earnings and financed through the social contributions of workers and employers.[10] Given the public pillar's central role, pension expenditure in the DIG and NILG groups has remained historically high, while supplementary pensions (occupational and private) have been established relatively recently.[11] From the 1990s onwards, extensive reforms of pension systems in the continental and Mediterranean countries have been carried out to cope with demographic changes, particularly the aging population and changes in the labour market. However, the DIG countries have managed to offset pension expenditure more efficiently than the NILG[12] countries.

Switching the focus to more qualitative data, Figure 5.5 shows the net replacement rate of mandatory public and private pensions.[13]

Once again, differences between growth patterns are evident.

Replacement rates in the NIG countries are the lowest, especially in the United Kingdom (29%).

The EIG countries follow, but with a gap of about 20 points, and the DIG group is at a marked distance from them. Within this model, the Netherlands demonstrates itself to be particularly generous (100%), whereas Germany guarantees a more limited replacement rate (50%). German governments, since the 1990s, have implemented a series of institutional cuts to the public pillar – in parallel with the development of the complementary pillars.[14]

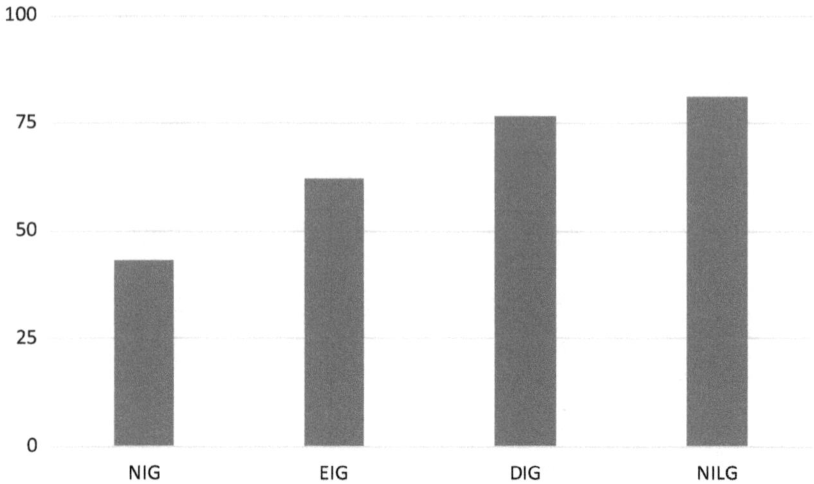

Figure 5.5 Net replacement rate of mandatory pensions (public and private) as a percentage of average income (2017).

Source: Elaboration of OECD data.

Finally, the NILG countries still offer the highest replacement rates (80%) – with Italy and Portugal recording values above 90%. For many years, the generosity of the pension system in these countries has been accompanied by large budget deficits, countervailed directly by public finance.[15].

Lastly, Table 5.1 shows the percentage of citizens covered by non-compulsory supplementary pensions (occupational and/or private).[16]

In the NIG countries, this percentage turns out to be particularly high, approximately over 40%, excluding Australia, for which the value is not available. The data suggest that, in these countries, the *voluntary* complementary pillar is essential for maintaining income in old age, given the low replacement rate provided by the compulsory pillar (both public and private).

In contrast, in the EIG countries, values for the voluntary supplementary provision are much lower (around 25%). This relatively small percentage may be explained by the fact that the supplementary pillars in these countries are compulsory.

The picture for DIG countries is more heterogeneous. Voluntary supplementary pension provision plays a powerful role in Germany and Belgium – following reforms initiated in the 1990s – while it is more limited in Austria, France, and the Netherlands. In general, however, it appears that all the continental countries have relinquished (or are relinquishing) the classic single-pillar system that distinguished them during the expansionary phase of the welfare state.

Table 5.1 Voluntary supplementary pensions, percentage of workers involved (2017)

	Voluntary –occupational	*Voluntary –personal*	*Voluntary total*
NIG			
Australia	X	ND	ND
Canada	26.3	25.2	ND
UK	38.3	12.6	46.7
Ireland	ND	ND	43
United States	40.8	19.3	ND
EIG			
Denmark	X	18	18
Finland	6.6	19	25.6
Sweden	X	24.2	24.2
Norway	ND	26.7	ND
DIG			
Austria	13.9	18	ND
Belgium	59.6	ND	ND
Germany	57	33.8	70.4
France	24.5	5.7	ND
The Netherlands	X	28.3	28.3
NILG			
Spain	3.3	15.7	18.6
Greece	1.3	ND	ND
Italy	9.2	11.5	20
Portugal	3.7	4.5	ND

Source: Elaboration of OECD data.

Finally, in the NILG countries, voluntary supplementary pension provision has very low coverage rates, especially in Greece and Portugal. In these countries, resources for boosting the implementation of these supporting structures have dwindled. Furthermore, pension systems are still based almost exclusively on the first public pillar, despite its ever-diminishing capacity to provide an adequate replacement rate in the future, especially for those with interrupted working careers.

5.4 Poverty

In parallel with the change in the economic structure of advanced economies and the consequent emergence of new social risks, citizens have increased their demand for policies to reduce poverty. However, the ability of Western countries to effectively implement such policies varies considerably (Figure 5.6).

Mediterranean countries show the highest poverty rates among the four growth models before and after transfers. However, the welfare state in these countries proves to be more effective in lowering the poverty rate than in the NIG countries.[17] Irish welfare is the most effective (-73.9%, after transfers)

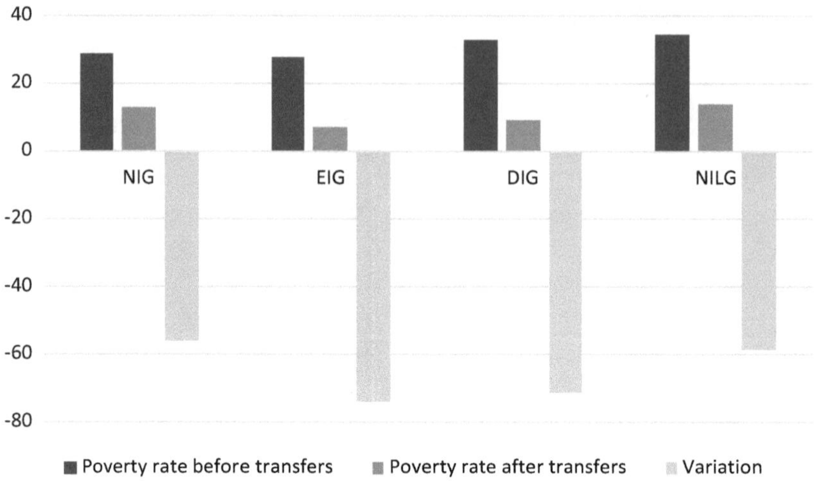

Figure 5.6 Poverty rate before and after taxes and transfers (2016).

Source: Elaboration of OECD-SOC data.

compared to the US (-33.1%). The situation in the EIG and DIG groups is different. The Scandinavian countries are the most successful in reducing poverty (-73.9%). Among them, Finland has the highest poverty rate (35%) but has the most success in reducing it (-83%). Welfare policies in the continental countries also effectively lower the poverty level (-71%), from 32% to 9.3% after transfers.

Finally, regarding new social risks and social investment, Hemerijck (2017) has stressed the importance of guaranteeing a minimum income in a historical period characterised by interrupted careers and periods of long-term unemployment. The adequacy of this measure, i.e. its replacement rate, varies across growth models (Figure 5.7).

In the NILG countries, the minimum income turns out to be the least generous, and the measure was introduced nationally much later compared to the other growth models. Higher but still moderate replacement rates have been provided by the NIG countries. Data are nevertheless somewhat disparate within the group. The US offers a meagre minimum income replacement rate of 6% of median income, while replacement rates in the UK and Ireland are above the group average (55% and 65%, respectively). Minimum income is more generous in the EIG and DIG countries than in the others. The Scandinavian countries provide the highest replacement rates, with Denmark having the highest (63%) and Norway the lowest (35%). The replacement rate in the EIG countries, on the other hand, stands at 45.6%, with the Netherlands showing an above-average value (60%).

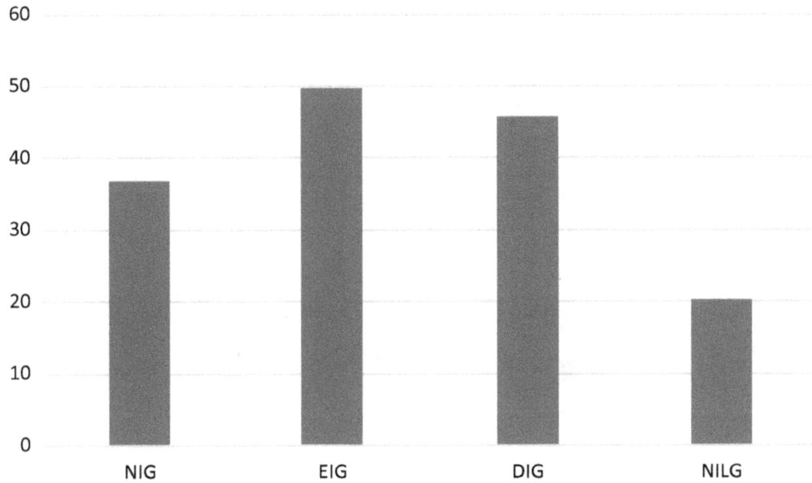

Figure 5.7 Minimum income adequacy, % of median income (2017).

Source: Elaboration of OECD-SOC data.

5.5 Family

In recent decades, in parallel with the social change in Western countries, the family policy[18] has played an increasingly essential role in the transition from the *male breadwinner family model*, with women relegated to the caregiver role, to the *dual-earner family model*, which promotes women's full-time participation in the labour market. However, the transition to this new model is still in the making in many countries, and the "family revolution" is far from accomplished (Esping-Andersen, 2009). The marked differences in the family policies of the four growth models demonstrate this unfinished revolution.

Figure 5.8 shows the social expenditure on the family function as a percentage of GDP. Total spending has been disaggregated into expenditure on services and monetary transfers.

The EIG countries are the most generous in total expenditure (3.4%), while the NILG countries are the least generous (1.4%). The NIG and DIG countries show intermediate values (2.1% and 2.4%, respectively).

If we analyse the disaggregated expenditure data,[19] only the EIG countries spend more on services (2%) than on monetary transfers (1.4%). Moreover, the percentage of expenditure devoted to services is the highest among the four growth models. The other models show inverse values, with a higher weight for monetary transfers than services. In the NIG countries, the imbalance of expenditure favouring monetary transfers is particularly evident (1.4%, twice as much as that for services, which stands at 0.7% of GDP). Family policy

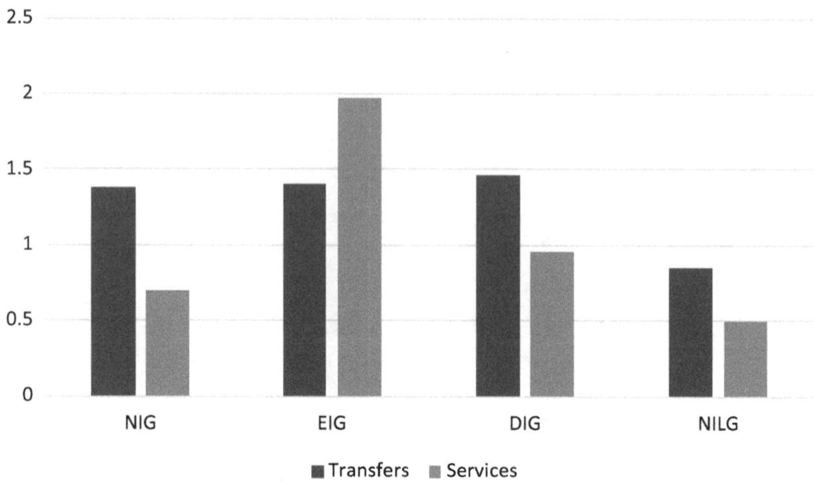

Figure 5.8 Expenditure on family policies as a percentage of GDP, monetary transfers, and services (2015).

Source: Elaboration of OECD-SOC data.

expenditures are the more balanced in the CID group (1.5% of GDP devoted to monetary transfers and 1% to services). Nevertheless, in these countries, expenditure on services is precisely half that of the Scandinavian countries. Only France spends almost equally on services and monetary transfers (1.5% and 1.4%, respectively). Finally, the NILG countries show very low values for spending on monetary transfers (0.9%) and services (0.5%).

Differences emerge in public spending on early childhood education care (ECDC) among all four growth models[20] (Figure 5.9).

The EIG countries devote the highest proportion of expenditure, significantly distancing themselves from the other three models. The NIG countries spend the least as childcare care has historically been left in the hands of the private sector. Next are the NILG countries. Compared to these two groups, the DIG countries spend a slightly higher amount but still much less than the Scandinavian countries.

Figure 5.9 also highlights the impact of social spending on the enrolment rate of children aged 0–2 in early childhood services. The data show that the enrolment rates are also low in the face of low expenditure. Indeed, the EIG countries show the highest enrolment rate (48.5%), followed by the DIG countries (46%). The NILG (29.5%) and NIG (28.8%) countries have low rates.

Finally, Figures 5.10 and 5.11 show, respectively, data on maternity and parental leave and paternity leave (including the quota of parental leave reserved for fathers).

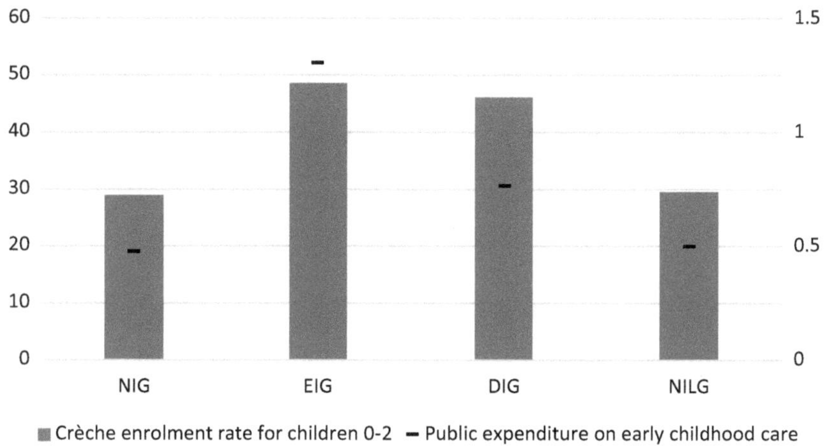

Figure 5.9 Public expenditure on early childhood care, crèches and nursery schools (2015), and crèche enrolment rate for children 0–2 (2016).

Source: Elaboration of OECD-SOC data.

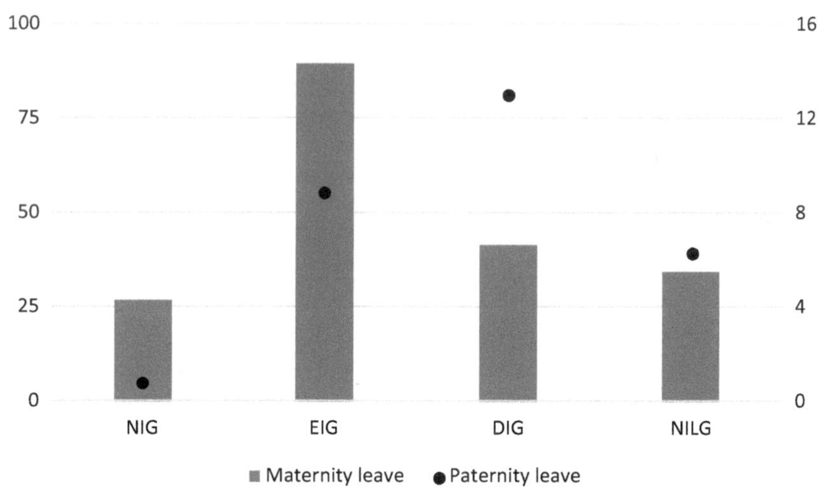

Figure 5.10 Duration of maternity and paternity leave, number of weeks (2016).

Note: OECD-SOC data are aggregated. Weeks of paid maternity leave are added to weeks of (paid) parental leave. Weeks of paid paternity are added to weeks of parental leave for fathers (if any). As regards the replacement rate, the data refer to the maternity leave (thus excluding parental leave) and paternity leave, i.e. the weeks of parental leave reserved for fathers, if any, are included).

Source: OECD-SOC data.

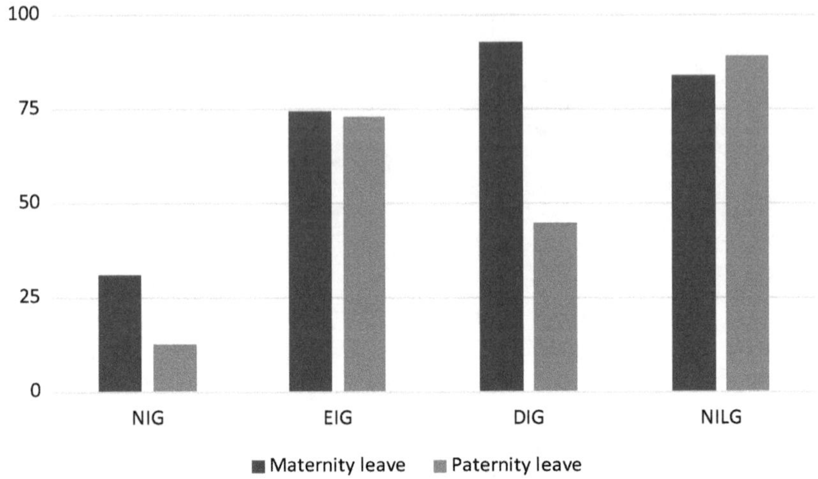

Figure 5.11 Replacement rate, maternity and paternity leave, as a percentage of gross average salary (2014).

Note: see note, Figure. 5.10.

Source: Elaboration of OECD-SOC data.

The NIG countries are the least generous, offering only 27 weeks of paid maternity and parental leave and less than one week of paternity leave. The replacement rates for maternity leave[21] are the lowest of the four growth models. The same applies to paternity leave, which is only paid in Australia (with a 40% substitution rate) and the UK, while Canada, Ireland, and the United States offer no monetary compensation. There is no mandatory paid maternity or paternity leave at the federal level in the United States. The EIG countries offer the longest paid maternity and parental leave – almost 90 weeks – with a high replacement rate (74%). However, in terms of generosity, there is a considerable difference within this area, with the replacement rates of Denmark (53%) and Norway (91%) at the two extremes. In terms of paternity leave, these countries provide, on average, almost nine weeks of leave, with the highest replacement rate among the four growth models (72.5%). The redistribution of caregiving tasks within the family is thus promoted by these policies, encouraging fathers to take paternity leave. The DIG countries provide for a much shorter duration of maternity leave compared to the EIG (41.3 weeks), but with an exceptionally high replacement rate (92.6%), except Belgium (63%). On average, paternity leave is the longest (13.2 weeks), but its replacement rate is low (around 44% of the gross salary). Finally, in the NILG, maternity and parental leaves are a combined 43 weeks, slightly longer than the average for the EIG countries, and a high replacement rate (83%). On the other hand, paternity leave is very short (6 weeks). The value is influenced by Portugal, which provides 22 weeks of paid leave. The other countries in this group are less generous by far, with values well below the average (Spain offers 2.1 weeks of paid paternity leave, Greece and Italy only 0.4). The replacament rate is the highest among the four growth models (89%), but this value must be analysed in relation with the short leave duration. As the literature points out, such short paternity leaves, even if paid, have no effect on the redistribution of caregiving tasks within the household.

5.6 Healthcare

Healthcare is one of the main items of expenditure in advanced Western economies. In terms of social spending on GDP (Figure 5.12), the NILG countries show the lowest expenditure (6%), while the three other growth models record similar values, around or above 8%. As for the NIG countries, the average value is affected by the very high health expenditure in the United States (14%).

Universal, or near-universal, coverage has been achieved in all the countries of the four models, with the exception of the United States, where only 35.9% of the population is automatically covered by the free public healthcare system (means-tested), whereas 54.9% is covered by private insurance. A total of 9% of the population remains uninsured (OECD, 2019).[22]

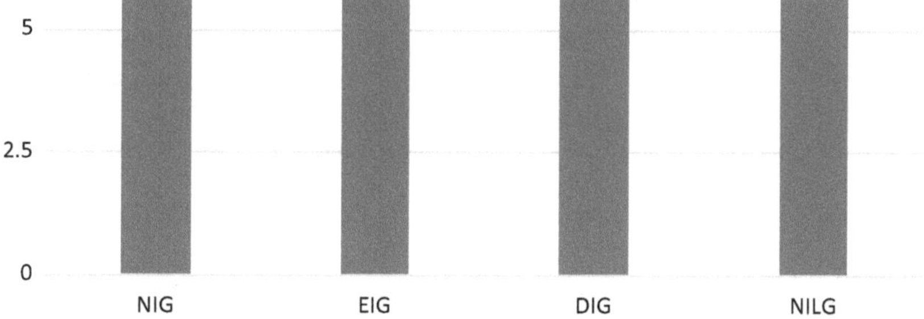

Figure 5.12 Government/mandatory health expenditure, as a percentage of GDP (2017).

Source: Processing of OECD data.

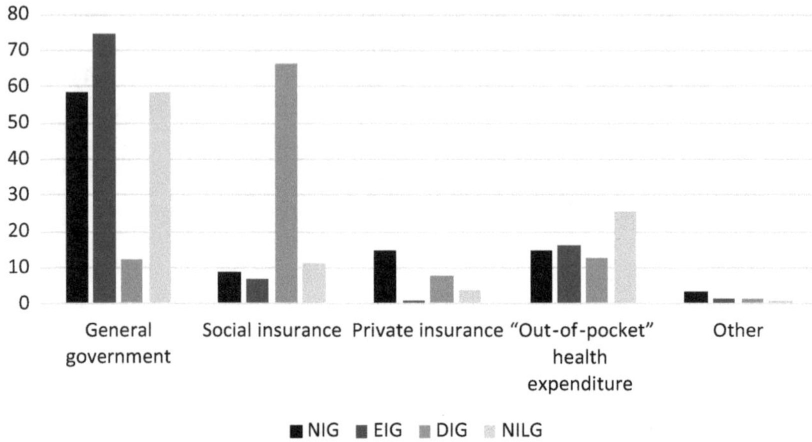

Figure 5.13 Distribution of health expenditure among sources of financing as a percentage of the total (2012).

Source: Processing of OECD data.

Finally, Figure 5.13 shows the distribution of current health expenditure among the sources of financing, including private insurance and the "out-of-pocket" spending.

The general government is the first source of financing for health expenditure in NIG, EIG, and NILG countries, although the percentages vary considerably. The government's role in financing health expenditure is particularly robust in the Scandinavian countries (around 75%), while the values are about 58% in the NIG and NILG countries. Concerning the Anglo-Saxon countries, the percentage of expenditure financed directly by the central government in the United States is very low (6%). On the opposite side, the government's role is well above the group's average (84%) in the United Kingdom. Public expenditure among the NILG countries is below average in Greece (29%), while the levels in Italy reflect those reported in the Scandinavian countries (77%). In the continental countries, where the health system has historically developed around the principle of social insurance, the role of the central government as a funder of health expenditure is minimal (12.2%). However, it has been growing since the 1990s.In contrast, social insurance funds in these countries make up the primary source of financing. These funds play a marginal role in the other three growth models, except in the United States (44%) and Greece (39.3%).

Regarding the role of private insurance, the percentage of expenditure financed by the latter is modest in the EIG and NILG countries. At the same time, it is higher in the DIG countries (7.6%) and relatively high in the NIG countries, by a comparative standard. Within this group, the US shows the highest value (around 35%) and the UK the lowest (2.1%). Among the DIG countries, in Belgium and Austria private sector is a key sources of financing (16.7% and 20.4%, respectively).

Finally, it is interesting to highlight the "out-of-pocket" health expenditure, i.e. that paid directly by the families. The lowest value is recorded in DIG (12.6%) and NIG (14.72%) countries, where the private sector manages to compensate sufficiently for the public sector's shortcomings. The expenditure in EIG countries is relatively higher (16.2%). Among these countries, Finland is above average (around 19%). Finally, the NILG countries have the highest level of "out-of-pocket" health expenditure (25%), with Portugal and Greece well above average (28.8% and 31.7%, respectively).

5.7 Concluding remarks

In this chapter, the main features of the welfare systems in the four growth models have been analysed quantitatively, with the analysis revealing substantial differences between the groups in all the policy areas investigated.

The EIG countries have the highest public and social expenditure values at the macro level, while we find the NIG countries on the opposite end. High values are also found among the DIG and NILG countries. The latter, however, display a comparatively lower per capita social expenditure, with the actual impact of welfare policies on citizens in these countries more limited. Moreover, while the Scandinavian countries have long devoted a significant share of their spending to the protection against new social risks and needs, the priorities of the Mediterranean countries continue to be the old social risks typical of the Fordist economy (especially old age and pensions).

Regarding pension policy, the NILG countries show the highest share of social spending on old-age risk and guarantee very generous replacement rates in the first public pillar, followed by the DIG countries. The values displayed by the EIG countries, where there are mandatory supplementary pillars, and in the NIG are more limited in terms of both expenditure and generosity. In the latter, a voluntary supplementary pension provision is particularly widespread, unlike in the NILG countries. The reforms of the 1990s in the continental countries are gradually encouraging the spread of voluntary supplementary pensions.

Concerning anti-poverty policies, the welfare systems most effective in lowering poverty rates are those of the EIG countries, followed by the DIG countries. In contrast, the NIG and NILG countries show high poverty rates before and after transfers. A similar picture can be seen when analysing minimum income adequacy. Again, the most generous are the Scandinavian countries, followed by the continental ones, with a very low replacement rate in the Anglo-Saxon and Mediterranean countries. Long-term unemployment in the Southern countries has not been a government priority for many years, and adequate policy responses are still lacking.

Shifting the focus to family policy, Scandinavian countries are the only ones that spend more on services than on monetary transfers, in contrast to the other three growth models. Expenditure on family policies is particularly low in the NILG countries. With regard to maternity leave, the most generous in terms of duration are those provided by the EIG countries. In contrast, the highest replacement rate is for leave in the DIG countries, followed by the NILG countries. The Anglo-Saxon countries have short, not very generous leaves. Finally, the Scandinavian countries' transition from the male breadwinner model to the dual-earner family one has (almost) been completed. Although shorter than in the DIG, they offer relatively long paternity leaves (although shorter than in the EIG) and high replacement rates. In contrast, paternity leave in the NIG and NILG countries is extremely short and, in the case of Anglo-Saxon countries, with little or no paid compensation.

Finally, healthcare policy coverage in almost all the three models is universal or nearly universal, except for the United States. However, the sources of funding for health expenditure are different. The state continues to be the primary funder in the EIG, NIG, and NILG countries, i.e. those with a tradition of universalism in health (again, except for the USA). In contrast, social insurance and, therefore, workers'contributions in the DIG countries are the main funding sources following the Bismarckian tradition. Private insurance plays a significant role only in the DIG and NIG countries, but the data for the latter are biased by the US. Lastly, as far as out-of-pocket expenditure is concerned, this is relatively high in the NILG countries, despite *de jure* universal coverage.

In conclusion, a careful analysis of the welfare policies of these 18 countries has corroborated the existence of four well-defined and discrete welfare state profiles, which imply equally distinct redistributive capacities.[23] Figure 5.14 shows the variation of the Gini index before and after transfers.

The NILG countries show the highest inequality value before and after transfers. It is worth noting that the values are slightly higher than those of the NIG countries, commonly acknowledged as the most unequal. This would seem to result from the economic crisis, whose consequences have had a more significant impact than in the other growth models. However, the capacity to reduce inequalities after transfers in these countries is slightly higher than in NIG countries. The situations in the EIG and DIG countries are different. The Scandinavian countries show lower Gini index values before and after transfers. Inequality reduction capacity is also high. Compared to the Scandinavian countries, the continental countries have a higher Gini index before transfers, but welfare policies drastically reduce the figure. Generally speaking, it may be argued that, considering all four growth models, the

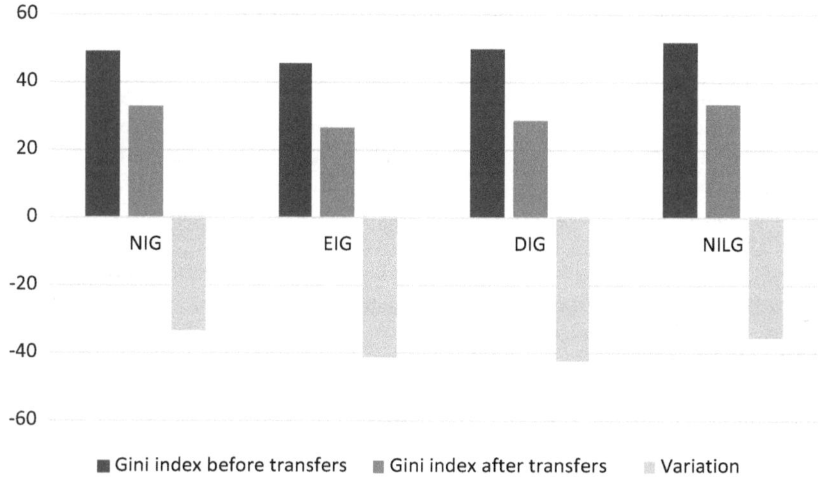

Figure 5.14 Gini index before and after transfers and percentage variation (2016).

Source: processing of OECD data.

continental countries have managed to reduce inequality more effectively. However, inequality remains higher than in the Scandinavian countries even after transfers.

Notes

1 The concept of de-commodification refers to the degree to which individuals can freely and, without potential loss of job, income, or general, welfare, opt out of work when they consider it necessary. The concept of de-stratification connotes the degree to which the structure of social benefits provided by the state absorbs, employment status, or social class differentials, to the point of nullifying, employment status, or social class differentials.
2 Clearly, there has been an evolution over time in the characteristics of these schemes.
3 The concept of de-familialism refers to the extent to which a country's welfare state reduces women's dependence on the family, maximising their access to and management of economic resources regardless of family or marital reciprocity. For more detailed discussions, see Lewis (1992) and Leitner (2003).
4 For a more in-depth analysis of the Mediterranean regime, see Ferrera (1996; 2005).
5 Using social expenditure as the only variable to measure a welfare system's generosity has often been criticized in the literature (see Esping-Andersen, 1990). Moreover, studies based exclusively on public expenditure data very often fail to correctly assess the impact of reforms involving institutional cuts (see Pierson, 2001 and Green-Pedersen, 2002).

6 For an overview of the liberal and social-democratic welfare regimes, particularly the reforms introduced between the 1980s and 1990s, see Pierson (2001).
7 For more on social risks, see Armingeon and Bonoli (2006) and Bonoli and Natali (2012).
8 The family function includes direct and indirect financial support measures for families (monetary transfers and tax relief), work-life balance measures (e.g. parental leave), and measures that support children's cognitive development (childcare). The literature on new social risks only considers the last two measures as policy instruments aimed at covering the new social risks (see Häusermann, 2012; 2018).
9 Among the Mediterranean countries, in the last few decades, Spain and Portugal have started an institutional recalibration of their welfare states, allocating more resources to childcare and ALMPs. However, the expenditure remains low by a comparative standard.
10 The Netherlands represents an exception. Its pension system has historically been a multi-pillar system.
11 For a more detailed discussion of the pension system classification and their historical evolution, see Natali (2008).
12 Pension system reforms in countries similar to the Bismarckian model have been discussed extensively by Bonoli and Shinkawa (2005), Häusermann (2010), and Palier (2010).
13 The replacement rate is defined as the percentage ratio between the first pension annuity and the last annual income immediately prior to retirement.
14 Concerning the evolution of the pension system in Germany, see Hinrichs (2010).
15 For an in-depth look at pension reforms in the NILG countries, see Jessoula and Alti (2010) for the Italian case, Maylonas and de la Maisonneuve (1999) for the Greek case, Ferreira (2003) for the Portuguese case, and Guillen (2010) for the Spanish case.
16 It is methodologically problematic to present average values for the four growth models, as data are either not available in some countries or the complementary pillars are not provided *de jure*. Therefore, we only provide individual values for each country and comment on them in aggregate.
17 The *welfare effectiveness* in reducing poverty is measured as percentage variation and not as simple difference in percentage points.
18 The definition of family policy is much debated in the literature (see Eydal and Rostgaard, 2018, for a discussion). In this chapter, we consider three different policy instruments as family policies: (a) financial support measures to families (e.g. family allowances and child benefits), (b) parental leave, and (c) childcare.
19 The choice of spending more on cash transfers rather than services (or vice versa) has substantial implications for family policy. Monetary transfers tend to reinforce dependency among family members. On the other hand, services play a key role in the de-familialising process. See Leitner (2003) and Knijn and Saraceno (2010) for a more detailed discussion.
20 Feminist literature and research on social investment have highlighted that access to early childhood services has a positive influence on female employment rates (consequently incentivizing the de-familialisation of care) and children's cognitive development (Hemerijck, 2013; 2017).

21 The replacement rate indicates the ratio between the amount of maternity leave benefit and the amount of the worker's last gross salary or wage (taking into account the average salary).
22 In this respect, it should be noted that Barack Obama's 2010 health reform had the effect of increasing the rate of health insurance coverage.
23 The Gini index was chosen as the instrument to measure the capacity to reduce inequalities and thus indirectly redistribute wealth.

References

Armingeon, K., Bonoli, G. (2006) (Eds). *The politics of post-industrial welfare states: Adapting post-war social policies to new social risks.* London/New York: Routledge.

Beramendi, P,. Häusermann S., Kitschelt H., & Kriesi H. (Eds) (2015) *The politics of advanced capitalism.* New York: Cambridge University Press.

Bonoli, G. & Shinkawa, T. (2005) (Eds). *Ageing and pension reform around the world: Evidence from eleven countries.* Cheltenham: Edward Elgar.

Bonoli, G. & Natali, D. (2012) (Eds). *The politics of the new welfare state.* Oxford: Oxford University Press.

Esping-Andersen, G. (1990). *The three worlds of welfare capitalism.* Princeton: Princeton University Press.

Esping-Andersen, G. (2009). *The incomplete revolution: Adapting to women's new roles.* Cambridge: Polity Press.

Eydal, G. B. & Rostgaard, T. (Eds.). *Handbook of family policy.* London: Edward Elgar.

Ferrera, M. (1996). Il modello sud-europeo di welfare state. *Rivista Italiana di Scienza Politica*, 26(1), 67–101. doi:10.1017/S0048840200024047

Ferrera, M. (2005) (Ed.). *Welfare state reform in Southern Europe: Fighting poverty and social exclusion in Italy, Spain, Portugal and Greece.* London/New York: Routledge.

Ferrera, M. (2019). *Le politiche sociali.* Bologna: Il Mulino

Ferreira, F. (2003). *The past in the present Portuguese social security reform.* Article presented at the 1st annual ESPAnet Conference "Changing European Societies – The Role for Social Policy", 13–15 November. Danish National Institute of Social Research (SFI), Copenhagen, Denmark.

Green-Pedersen, C. (2002). *The politics of justification: Party competition and welfare-state retrenchment in Denmark and the Netherlands from 1982 to 1998.* Amsterdam: Amsterdam University Press.

Guillen, A. (2010). Defrosting the Spanish welfare state: The weight of conservative components. In B. Palier (Ed.), *A long goodbye to Bismarck? The politics of welfare reforms in Continental Europe* (pp. 183–206). Amsterdam: Amsterdam University Press,

Hemerijck, H. (2013). *Changing welfare states.* Oxford: Oxford University Press.

Hemerijck, H. (2017) (Eds). *The uses of social investment.* Oxford: Oxford University Press.

Hinrichs, K. (2010). A social insurance state withers away. Welfare state reforms in Germany – Or: Attempts to turn around in a cul-de-sac. In B. Palier (Eds), *A long goodbye to Bismarck? The politics of welfare reforms in Continental Europe* (pp. 45–72). Amsterdam: Amsterdam University Press

Häusermann, S. (2010). *The politics of welfare state reform in Continental Europe: Modernization in hard times*. Cambridge: Cambridge University Press.

Häusermann, S. (2012). The politics of old and new social policies. In G. Bonoli & D. Natali (Eds), *The new welfare state in Europe* (pp. 111–132). Oxford: Oxford University Press.

Häusermann, S. (2018). The multidimensional politics of social investment in conservative welfare regimes: Family policy reform between social transfers and social investment. *Journal of European Public Policy*, 25(6). 862–877. doi.org/10.1080/13501763.2017.1401106

Jessoula, M. & Alti, T. (2010). Italy: An uncompleted departure from Bismarck. In B. Palier (Eds) *A long goodbye to Bismarck? The politics of welfare reforms in Continental Europe* (pp.157–181).Amsterdam: Amsterdam University Press.

Knijn, T. & Saraceno, C. (2010). Changes in the regulation of responsibilities towards childcare needs in Italy and the Netherlands: Different timing, increasingly different approaches. *Journal of European Social Policy*, 20(5), 444–455. doi.org/10.1177/0958928710380481

Leitner, S. (2003). Varieties of familialism: The caring function of the family in comparative perspective. *European Societies*, 5(4), 353–375. doi.org/10.1080/1461669032000127642

Lewis, J. (1992). Gender and the development of welfare regimes. *Journal of European Social Policy*, 2(3), 59–173.

Manow, P., Palier, B. & Schwander, H. (2018). *Welfare democracies and party politics: Explaining electoral dynamics in times of changing welfare capitalism*. Oxford: Oxford University Press.

Maylonas, P. & de la Maisonneuve, C. (1999). *The problems and prospects faced by pay-as-you-go pension systems: A case study of Greece*. OECD Economics Department Working Papers, no. 215.

Natali, D. (2008). *Pensions in Europe, European pensions: The evolution of pension policy at national and supranational level*. Brussels: PIE-Peter Lang.

OECD (2019). *Health at a glance 2019: OECD indicators*. Paris: OECD Publishing.

Palier, B. (2010) (Eds). *A long goodbye to Bismarck? The politics of welfare reforms in Continental Europe*. Amsterdam: Amsterdam University Press.

Pierson, P. (2001) (Eds). *The new politics of the welfare state*. Oxford: Oxford University Press.

Titmuss, R. (1974). *Social policy: An introduction*. London: George Allen & Unwin.

Chapter 6

Education and innovation policies

Alberto Gherardini

6.1 Introduction

Two apparently different but extremely related policy arenas are discussed in this chapter: education and innovation. Over the years, their relations have become increasingly intertwined, forging a strong liaison in contemporary capitalism. Defined by Schumpeter as the ability of an entrepreneur to introduce economically relevant changes, innovation maintained for a long time certain independence from high educational attainment. In the past, the innovator may undoubtedly have had the characteristics of the great intellectual applying his knowledge to the technological improvement of certain products or machines, or even of the researcher working for the large companies that dominated the technological scene, yet his profile did not necessarily have to include a high level of education (Ramella, 2016). In other words, innovation was not based on formal education through which the innovators could learn a basic technology to apply to new products. The biographies of many entrepreneurs disclose an innovativeness that evolved more from know-how acquired "hands-on" in the workplace than in university classrooms.

However, as the international competitiveness of markets and the sophistication of demand have increased, the innovator has increasingly found the need to combine their abilities with codified skills. Nowadays, more specialist knowledge is required – whether it is technical or humanistic. State intervention has hence interlinked education and innovation increasingly. On the one hand, as emphasised by the Lisbon Strategy, raising education levels has become one of the main levers for bolstering economic development and strengthening the knowledge society.

On the other hand, a broad awareness that globalisation would hit the most ordinary productions in advanced countries, due to growing competition from emergent economies with low labour costs, has brought about more attention to innovation policies.

Since the second half of the 1990s, therefore, education and innovation policies have become progressively strategic pivots around which to

DOI: 10.4324/9781003297130-8

generate economic policy in advanced countries. They have emerged as typical instruments of the supply-side approach, which considers public spending as public investment that buttresses private investment.

However fundamentally entwined, substantial differences nonetheless appear in these two policy areas, one of which concerns those who implement and those who receive the policies. The promotion of education is a typical area of public intervention, albeit with significant differences between countries, with a significant presence of the private sector in some cases (e.g. the United States). Encouraged by democratic values, advanced countries invested in education even before this evolved into a full-blown driving force of economic development, setting up complex and differentiated education systems that span from early childhood to university specialisation. This is therefore a predominantly public sphere of action which, however, since the end of the 1980s has been undergoing a progressive, albeit slow, process of greater privatisation. In contrast, innovation has traditionally been considered an activity to be managed by private entrepreneurs. The state was left with a residual role of solving market failures, as a guarantor of adequate funding for basic or pre-competitive research activities.

Here, however, compared to that observed in the field of education, an antipodal process has taken shape. Innovation policies have grown in size and scope since research results showed that public intervention is a necessary condition for private competitiveness (Block, 2008; Nelson, 1993; Mazzucato, 2013). They have expanded far beyond the mere incentivisation of business R&D towards public infrastructures supporting private innovativeness and, at the same time, the weaving of public–private networks.

A second difference concerns the effect of these two types of policies on inequalities. Education policies have a direct effect on curtailing inequalities, especially when construed as those interventions that aim to remove the socio-economic obstacles that prevent young people from achieving the desired higher levels of education. As the level of education increases, so does employability, together with income and the possibility of upward social mobility.

Nevertheless, the relationship between public investment in education and inequality curtailment rather than evolving in a linear fashion is mediated by multiple intervening factors, the key elements of which are the quality of the educational regime and the institutional characteristics of the national education system. The reference here is to the distinguishing traits within the different national education systems, arising from the possible early channeling of students into vocational paths, or relating to dualised university systems, between elite and popular paths. Dual and/or early-channeling education regimes are more likely to reproduce the ascribed socio-economic status of students and, consequently, even with generous public or private funding, the impact on reducing inequalities diminishes. Conversely, educational regimes that are more responsive to the needs of students with greater difficulties, combined with open and democratic education systems, can produce meritocratic effects. In the latter case, growth in public funding may have a stronger impact on upward social mobility.

The abatement of inequality is only indirectly affected by innovation policies, however. In this case, there are two mechanisms at work. First, the intensification of innovative activities corresponds to a significant increase in employment, both in those sectors where innovation is implemented and for the economy as a whole (Moretti, 2012). Second, innovation policies trigger trajectories of economic development that are more shielded from international competition, consequently enhancing the health of firms and, with it, their ability to bear higher taxation, generally directed at financing the welfare state. As such, these policies can offset the costs of reducing inequality (Trigilia, 2016).

While acknowledging their joint contribution in influencing development and inequality, these two policies will be handled separately in the following pages to better understand how the 18 advanced economies considered in our research differ under this aspect.

6.2 Education

The diversity among the four growth models emerges also in consideration of the level of public expenditure on education (Figure 6.1). The highest proportion of GDP spent on education (7.5%) is among the countries with inclusive

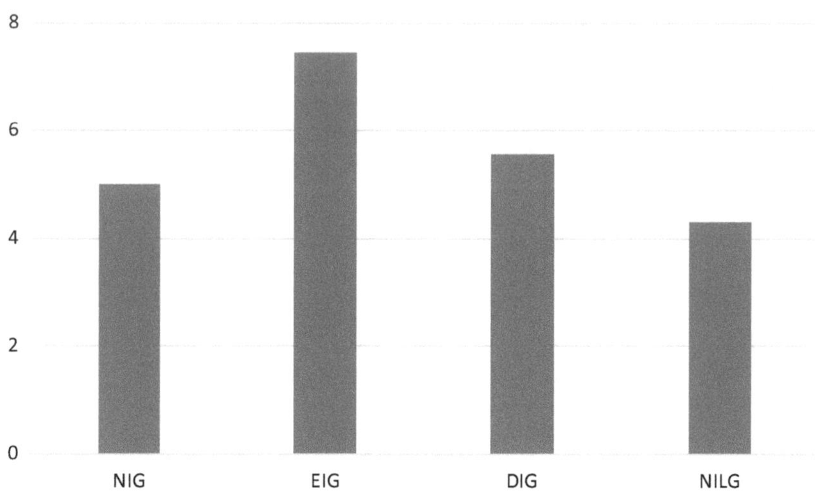

Figure 6.1 Public expenditure on education by growth model, as a percentage of GDP (2015).

Source: Elaboration on World Bank data, World Development Indicators.

and egalitarian growth. In this case, the EIG countries have quite homogeneous features, with expenditure ranging from 7.6% in Denmark to 7.1% in Finland.

In the other cases, spending on education is lower in the shift from growth to low growth models. Specifically, countries with dualistic inclusive growth are characterised by an average expenditure of 5.6 GDP points, two points below the EIG type. Within this grouping, the internal variance is pronounced: Belgium spends about 6.5% of GDP while Germany barely reaches 4.8%.

In the non-inclusive growth countries, the average value of expenditure (5.0%) is still significantly lower than with dualistic inclusive growth (DIG). Here, the average value is strongly influenced by the outlay in Ireland (3.8%), the lowest of the whole sample considered. In the other cases, the level of expenditure is entirely in line with that of the DIG countries (5.5%).

Overall, however, the group of countries that spend less on education belong to the non-inclusive low growth model. Only Portugal (4.9%) is above the average value of this group – at 4.3% – while the other three Mediterranean economies have extremely low levels of spending at around 4%.

Considering the expenditure devoted only to the tertiary level of education, the order of the growth patterns presented above does not change (Figure 6.2). Once again, the EIG countries are the ones to invest the most (39.5% of per capita GDP), followed by the DIG (33.7%) and non-inclusive growth (NIG)

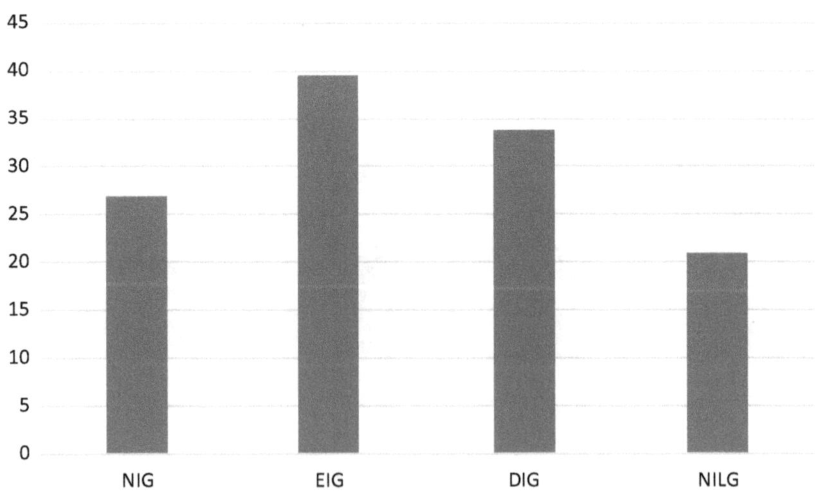

Figure 6.2 Public expenditure on tertiary education by growth model as a percentage of GDP per capita (2015).

Source: Elaboration on World Bank data, World Development Indicators.

(26.8%). The last group by total expenditure is the non-inclusive low growth (NILG) (21.0%).

The expenditure in higher education is more susceptible to strong country-level fluctuations in comparison with the overall spending. Excluding the DIG countries, higher education expenditure shows a high intra-group variation. This is especially true for those that belong to the NILG and NIG models, except for the UK and Canada. However, even in the EIG model, there are countries with an expenditure above the average value of the group: Denmark and Sweden have the highest value among the 18 countries considered (43.1%). On the other hand, within the NILG model, the average value of expenditure on tertiary education would be around 25% were it not for Greece, which considerably lowers the average of the group due to an outlay that is decidedly below the countries considered here (9.2%).

Going back to the differences between models, less variance comes to light in spending on primary education (Figure 6.3). In particular, the clear recovery of the NILG countries (20.3%) is worth noting, just below the EIG model (22.5%), outstripping even the DIG (19.5%) and NIG (18.6%) countries.

Here again, it is interesting to highlight certain national specificities. The most significant of these is the United Kingdom, whose expenditure (25.1%) is more similar to that of the inclusive growth countries than to the NIG model. Internal differences also characterise the DIG countries – here Germany, France, and the Netherlands spend around 17% of their GDP per capita, while Austria and Belgium spend relatively more (around 22.5%). The

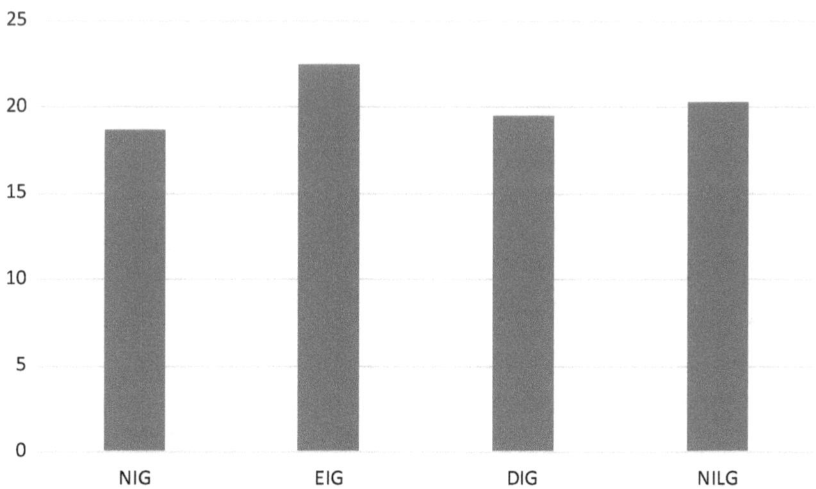

Figure 6.3 Public expenditure on primary education by growth model as a percentage of GDP per capita (2015).

Source: Elaboration on World Bank data, World Development Indicators.

NILG countries show more internal homogeneity, with only Spain (17.3%) presenting levels significantly below the group average.

Overall, the countries that invest the most in the education system, from primary schools to universities, are those with an inclusive egalitarian growth trend. Of particular interest to our research is the fact that much of the diversity between the models relates to spending on university education. This attests that primary education is one of the most typical and cross-cutting functions of governments in advanced economies while confirming that only a few countries, those that are most concerned with spending as an investment, focus on higher levels of education.

Moreover, in contrast with what emerges in most of the policies considered in our research, spending on tertiary education is also high in the NIG countries that invest almost as much as happens in the DIG model.

Concerning the share of the population aged 25-64 with a university degree, it is hardly surprising that the graduation rate is low in the NILG countries (27%), and equally unremarkable that in the inclusive growth models the rate is higher (see Figure 6.4). Worthier of note is the fact that NIG countries have the highest graduation rate (47%), followed by EIG countries (41%) and DIG countries (34%). In the light of these data, the level of public spending on education conditions the qualification of human capital, but at the same time, there are cases, such as those in the NIG countries, where the same conclusion is reached only if the sum of public funding and private contribution is considered.

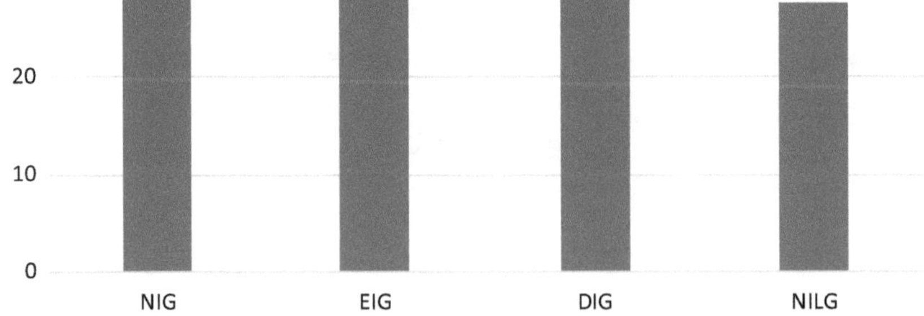

Figure 6.4 Population with university degrees as a percentage of the total number in 25–64 years age group (2018).

Source: Elaboration on OECD data (2019).

If the source of funding (public or private) has no bearing on the extent to which economic development is affected by the qualification of human capital, the same cannot be said for the relationship between education and the curtailing of inequality. It is precisely in this area that we find the main cleavage between the two models of inclusive and non-inclusive growth. On the one hand, we have the countries of the EIG model, and to a lesser extent of the DIG model. Here the state ensures everyone access to the highest levels of education, thanks to low, if any, university fees. On the other hand, in the countries of the NIG model, where enrolment in university courses is extremely expensive, scholarships are granted only to the most deserving, and access to university education for the majority depends on family heritage or borrowing capacity.

6.3 Innovation

Data on public spending on innovation policies in advanced economies confirm the trends highlighted for education policies. Higher levels are associated with the EIG countries (0.99%), while the NILG countries register the lowest spending (0.56%). The other two groupings are positioned on an intermediate level (Figure 6.5). In general, the variation of expenditure on innovation policies within the growth models is low, except for the NIG countries. The average value associated with this group hides different spending behaviours.

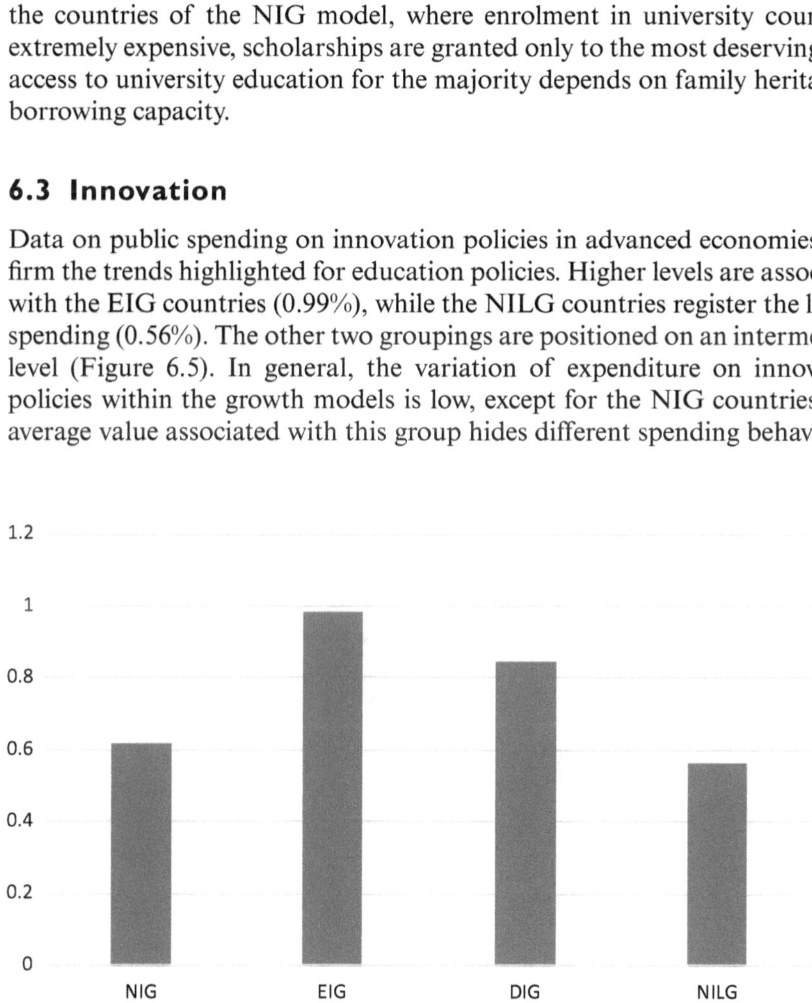

Figure 6.5 Public expenditure on R&D by growth model, as a percentage of GDP (2016).

Note: "R&D expenditure" refers to expenditure by governments (GOVERD) and universities (HERD).

Source: Elaboration on OECD data.

On the one hand, Australia and Canada show levels of investment similar to that of the DIG countries (0.80%); on the other, the United Kingdom and Ireland present quite low expenditure – 0.52% and 0.32% respectively. Between these two extremes is the United States, with an expenditure of just over 0.6% of GDP.

The taxonomy of public expenditure on research and development provided by the "Frascati Manual" – which guides the statistical definitions for the OECD countries – distinguishes between the spending exercised directly by the government (and its administrative units) and that exercised by the university system. In general, compared to those of the government the interventions of the university system are always financially more substantial: in advanced economies, the ratio between the two is almost three to one. Although government spending on R&D is highest in the DIG countries (0.27%) (Figure 6.6), specific national patterns are noticeable. First, the German case shows the highest figure among advanced economies (0.4%). It outlines a peculiar mode of intervention, which adds to the funding of the university system that of some research institutes, such as the Fraunhofer (dealing with applied research), the Max-Planck (which instead carry out basic research, often with an interdisciplinary approach) and the Leibniz institutes.

Also within the NIG model differences emerge. In the US, in the face of low levels of public spending on university R&D, the government invests a considerable part of its GDP (0.28%) in supporting a system of federal

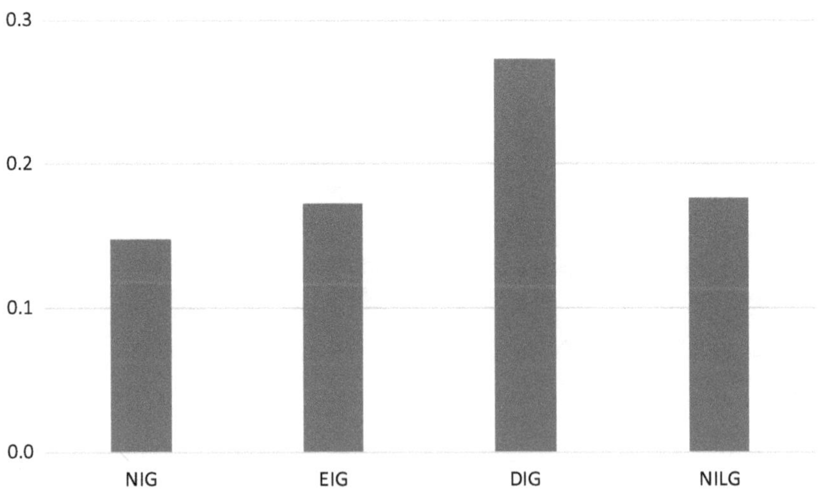

Figure 6.6 Governmental organisations' expenditure on R&D by growth pattern, as a percentage of GDP (2016).

Source: Elaboration on OECD data, Main Science and Technology Indicators.

agencies that carry out, among other things, mission-oriented research and development (e.g. DARPA, National Science Foundation, NASA, National Institutes of Health, Department of Energy, etc.). Finally, there are some countries that, regardless of the growth model, are characterised by a somewhat negligible intra-governmental research expenditure. This is the case with Ireland (0.05%), Denmark and Portugal (0.07%), Sweden and the United Kingdom (0.11%).

An appraisal of the amount spent on R&D by the (public) university system confirms that advanced economies fit the four types of growth thoroughly (Figure 6.7). The countries with inclusive, egalitarian growth, implementing an innovation system that is notoriously university-centric, disclose the highest expenditure. Within this group, spending levels are comparatively elevated; among these prevails Denmark, the country whose universities spend the most on R&D (1% of GDP). This is followed by the DIG countries (0.57%), the NIG countries (0.47%), and finally the NILG (0.39%). In this last growth pattern, the average value is propelled by Portuguese expenditure (0.57%), while Spain, Greece, and Italy are just above 0.3%.

In the NIG model, the two countries that invest the most (Australia and Canada are almost at the level of the DIG countries) offset those with much lower expenditure, ranging from 0.4% in the United Kingdom to around 0.3% in Ireland and the United States. However, in the latter cases, it is not a matter of weak university systems, as with the NILG model, but rather of strong, yet predominantly privately funded, university systems.

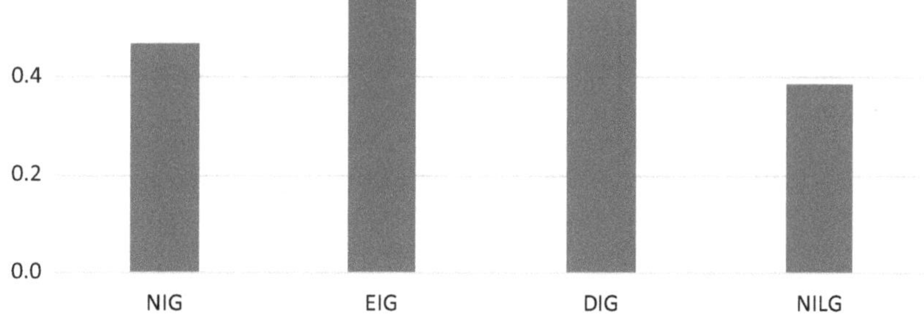

Figure 6.7 R&D expenditure of the university system by growth model, as a percentage of GDP (2016).

Source: Elaboration on OECD data, Main Science and Technology Indicators.

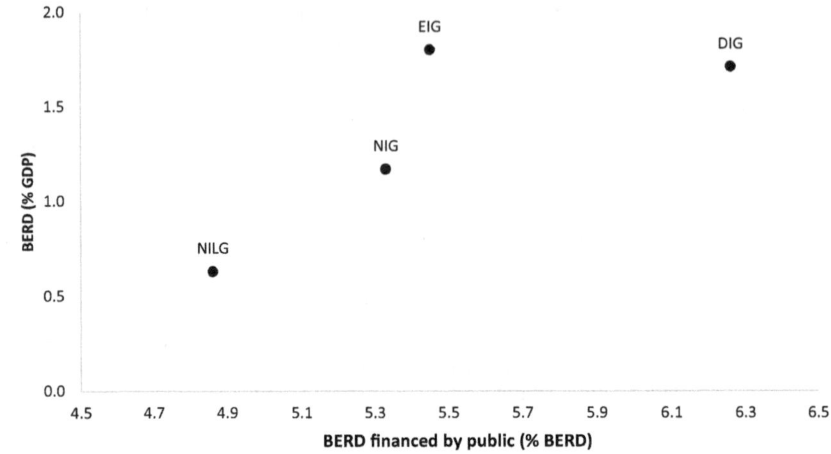

Figure 6.8 Publicly financed private R&D expenditure and private R&D expenditure by growth pattern as a percentage of GDP (2016).

Note: Private R&D expenditure financed by the public is calculated as a percentage of private expenditure (BERD).

Source: Elaboration on OECD data, Main Science and Technology Indicators.

The degree of innovativeness of the different growth models may nevertheless be still further appreciated upon an exploration of two other indicators. The first concerns research and development expenditure by private actors, the second the percentage of these activities financed by governments (Figure 6.8). Crossing these two indicators, four configurations can be clearly distinguished. The EIG model shows a prominent level of private expenditure where the public contribution is below the average of the 18 countries considered. The DIG model always shows high private R&D but is highly supported by public funding. The NIG and NILG models, on the other hand, share a low level of public funding for private R&D but reveal a different degree of business commitment, high in the NIG model and extremely low in the NILG model.

However, it is necessary to bear in mind that the variance within the four growth models can, in some cases, lead to misleading conclusions (Figure 6.9). Within the NIG countries, only Canada, Ireland, and Australia can be properly considered as being in the bottom left quadrant, while the US and the UK are notable exceptions. In the American case, private R&D expenditure is unusually high (2.0% of GDP), and, at the same time, there is a high incidence of public funding (6.4%). In the British case, on the other hand, investment in R&D by private individuals is modest (1.1%) while it is upheld more firmly by the state (7.8%).

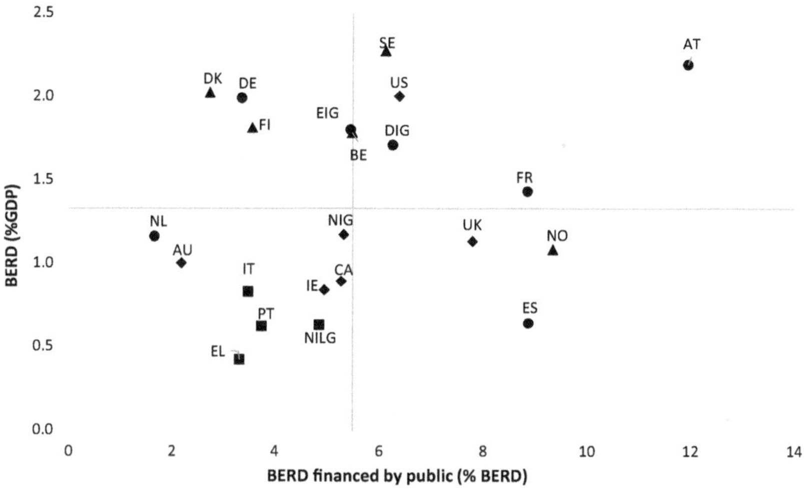

Figure 6.9 Publicly funded private R&D expenditure and private R&D expenditure by countries and growth patterns, as a percentage of GDP (2016).

Note: Private publicly funded R&D expenditure is calculated as a percentage of private expenditure (BERD).

Legend: see Figure 6.8.

Source: Elaboration on OECD data, Main Science and Technology Indicators.

In Finland and Denmark private activity in the field of R&D is high (1.8% and 2.0% respectively), mainly financed by companies themselves. In the case of Sweden, for the same level of private activity (2.3%), the incidence of public support increases considerably (6.1%). Finally, the Norwegian model includes state aid more than Sweden (9.3%) but with a business system that is less inclined to spending on R&D (1.1%).

In the DIG model, Austria and France show high private R&D activities and, at the same time, high public support for businesses. In particular, Austrian firms undertake activities worth 2.2% of GDP but, here more than in any other country, public funding is extremely high (11.9%). Compared to Austria, French companies conduct less private research and development (1.4%) and receive relatively less public funding (8.8%). Germany and Belgium are characterised by high private strength (2% in the former, 1.8% in the latter) with significant but below-average public support (3.4% in Germany and 5.5% in Belgium). Finally, in the Netherlands, private initiative in R&D is low (1.2%) and, at the same time, there is a negative record of public support (1.7%).

In contrast, the countries of the NILG model manifest more homogeneous values (low expenditure–low aid). Only Spain differs, placing the country in

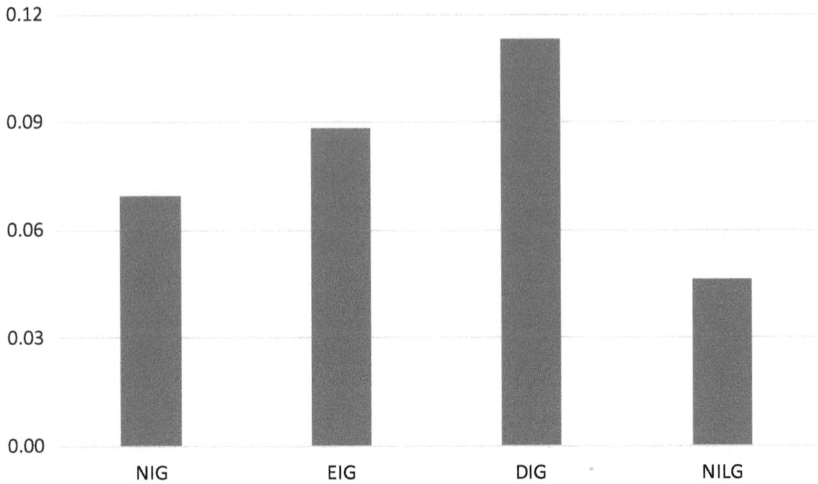

Figure 6.10 Direct funding of corporate R&D, as a percentage of GDP (2015).

Source: Elaboration on OECD data, Main Science and Technology Indicators.

the bottom right quadrant. Here public funding for private R&D is considerably higher than the average for the group (8.9%).

Upon closer inspection of how governments support private companies, another distinction emerges. In innovation policies discrimination between direct and indirect interventions is commonplace. Direct interventions allocate funds to firms that have passed a selection process, while indirect types of intervention denote automatic measures, i.e. measures granted whenever firms adopt certain behaviours identified as needing incentives, such as carrying out research and development.

Direct funding prevails in inclusive growth models, while indirect funding tends to be more widespread in both the DIG and NIG groups (Figures 6.10 and 6.11). More specifically, the countries making the most use of direct interventions are Austria (0.26%) and, to a lesser extent, Sweden (0.14%). In contrast, indirect interventions such as tax incentives for R&D activities are particularly common in two DIG countries – Belgium and France (0.28%) – as well as in Ireland (0.29%).

These initiatives are both implemented to a lesser extent in the NILG countries. The only exception is Portugal, where tax incentives for enterprises are above the group average (0.10%).

In conclusion, innovation policies would seem to respond more to national policy styles than to similar growth patterns. However, some relevant elements are worthy of comment. First, for all the indicators considered, the NILG countries always record lower levels of investment than the other countries.

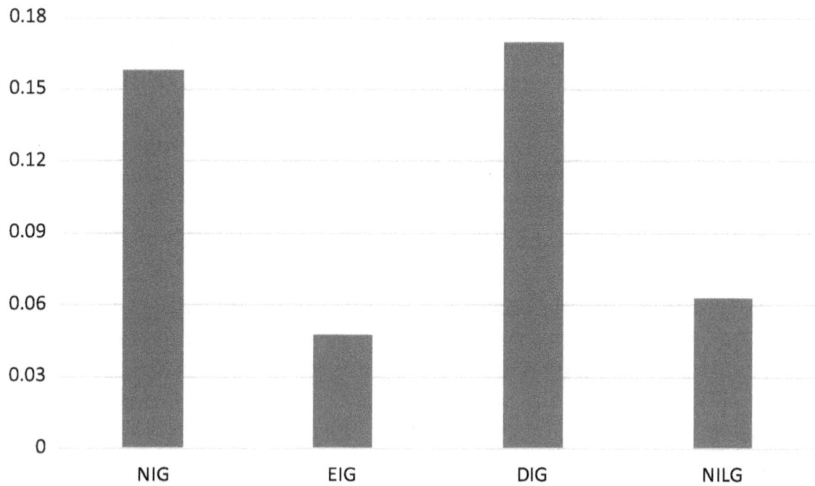

Figure 6.11 Indirect support to business R&D through tax incentives, as a percentage of GDP (2015).

Source: Elaboration on OECD data, Main Science and Technology Indicators.

Second, innovation is supported the most by the public sector, in particular universities, in the EIG model. Third, the DIG countries are characterised by a high degree of public intervention which, however, is more varied: there is leverage from the university system and government bodies, as well as public funding for private initiatives. Fourth, in the NIG model, innovation policies receive fewer resources than in the other models of inclusive growth, but more than in the NILG countries. In this case, more space is left to the market, although, as the US case shows, well below what one would expect.

6.4 Concluding remarks

This chapter commenced with a description of the pertinence of spending on education and innovation. For both policy areas our research illustrates how public funding is higher in inclusive growth countries, especially in the cases of the EIG, but also the DIG models. In these contexts, the university – understood as an organisation engaged in the training of human capital and generating research – constitutes a fundamental pivot on which development policy hinges, but also provides an indispensable contribution to the curtailing of inequality. Indeed, it has emerged how in these growth models the state intervenes to remove socio-economic obstacles and allow access to the highest levels of education. At the same time, particular emphasis has been given to the research infrastructures as representing a significant resource for businesses, which is a factor of systemic competitiveness that may well be worth a higher level of taxation.

In the NIG model, public investment in education and innovation is limited and the competitiveness of the economic system is ensured by private investment. In this case, therefore, the public sector could be said to play a more subsidiary role than the market. As a result, conditions to support the competitiveness of the economic system being equal, the effects on the abatement of inequalities are more limited.

In the case of the NILG model, low competitiveness can be attributed to low investment in education and innovation, also generating, however, a lower capacity to scale down inequalities. However, it is worth pointing out that in this case social mobility is thwarted more by low levels of university enrolment than by a segregating education system. Finally, in the NILG countries limited spending on innovation policies hinders growth and, ultimately, does not legitimise the high taxation endured by firms, forcing them inevitably to demand cutbacks, which thus, in turn, generate less likelihood to spend on welfare.

References

Block, F. (2008). Swimming against the current: The rise of a hidden developmental state in the United States. *Politics & Society*, 36(2), 169–206. DOI: 10.1177/0032329208318731

Nelson, R.R. (1993) (Eds). *National innovation systems: A comparative analysis*. Oxford: Oxford University Press.

Mazzucato, M. (2013). *The entrepreneurial state: Debunking the public vs private myth in risk and innovation*. London: Anthem.

Moretti, E. (2012). *The new geography of jobs*. Boston and New York: Houghton Mifflin Harcourt.

Ramella F. (2016), Sociology of Economic Innovation, London and New York: Routledge.

Trigilia, C. (2016). *Tipi di democrazia e modelli di capitalismo: un'agenda di ricerca. Stato e Mercato*. 107, 183–213.

Chapter 7

Political institutions, governments, and parties

Vittorio Martone and Daniela R. Piccio

7.1 Introduction

The focus of this chapter is on the political institutions that can be linked to the various development processes or paths. More specifically, through a comparative analysis, our aim is to shed light on the role of the political-institutional frameworks of governments and parties in helping define the conditions for economic growth and curbing inequalities. The variety of processes undertaken by the various capitalisms – including their capacity to integrate growth, income and inequalities – has given rise to an extensive body of literature. Nonetheless, these studies lack in-depth investigation as to the influence of politics, that is, the impact on regulatory choices made by factors pertaining to government systems, political parties and the mechanisms of constructing and forming consensus.[1]

The importance of the party composition of governments, and of the political-institutional set-ups within which they operate, has long been stressed (Schmidt, 1996). Particularly noteworthy was Lijphart's contribution (1999; 2012) on different types of democracy, which illustrated the utility of institutional frameworks in better appreciating how the socio-economic performance of individual countries is forged by politics.

From this perspective, we will present the results of a comparative analysis targeting some characteristics of the political institutions associable with the various models of growth having more or less dynamic and inclusive traits. More specifically, relying on different databases, we analyse some variables that portray the political-institutional structures typifying the models of growth in the 18 advanced-economy countries researched over the last 50 years (1960–2015). Reference is made to the electoral systems, the number of political parties in parliament, the strength of governments with different political compositions, and the electoral strength and extent of fragmentation of the parties, in particular those of the left wing.

The chapter is divided into five sections. The second section considers a series of political-institutional factors, examining how they are related to the different growth models. In the third we take a look at how governments are

DOI: 10.4324/9781003297130-9

structured. The fourth focuses on the role of left-wing political groups as the key medium through which to advocate redistribution. The last section draws some conclusions, recapping the traits of the political-institutional frameworks relating to the various paths of development.

7.2 Types of democracy and models of growth

Several scholars have highlighted the significance of the fact that politics and policies are markedly influenced by variables relating to the institutional framework, that is, the set of rules defining the balance of power in a democratic government.

In the following analysis we shall refer mainly to the seminal contribution of Arend Lijphart to this debate. In his Patterns of Democracy (Lijphart, 1999; 2012), the Dutch political scientist not only sought to extend the traditional classifications of democracies, but he also – through an empirical analysis of institutional variables – examined the nature of the balance of power in different countries. Lijphart identified two main types of democracy, "majoritarian" and "consensus", according to the extent to which a concentration of political power is supported by the institutional regulations and the extent to which instead a more widespread political power shared by a plurality is guaranteed. The majoritarian model, characterised by a more exclusive and competitive nature, prevails in Anglo-Saxon countries, while the consensus model, tending more towards inclusion and open to compromise, is predominant in Central and Northern Europe.

Lijphart endorses the utility of these different institutional frameworks also for appreciating the socio-economic results achieved by the single countries, concluding that the consensus model has the edge over the majoritarian in terms of social and economic performance.[2] His work is particularly relevant for our research as we aim to identify the associations between politics and the policies influencing the various paths of a more or less inclusive development.

Can the political-institutional characteristics and the four models of growth and inequality presented in Chapter 1 thus be said to be correlated? We formulate an answer to this question with an appraisal of the positioning of the 18 countries under study on Lijphart's "executives-parties" dimension. The latter serves to summarily measure the concentration of political power within each country by taking into account five main variables: cabinet type (single-party versus multi-party cabinets); executive dominance in the executive-legislative relations; electoral system (dis)proportionality; system of interest representation (pluralist versus corporatist).[3] Figure 7.1 shows how a higher degree of concentration of power associates with countries belonging to the non-inclusive model of growth. Indeed, in a range between -2 and +2 (maximum and minimum concentration of power, respectively), the average score for this group of countries is -0.7, as opposed to the +1.2 average of the inclusive growth model in the egalitarian variant, +0.2 of the inclusive growth

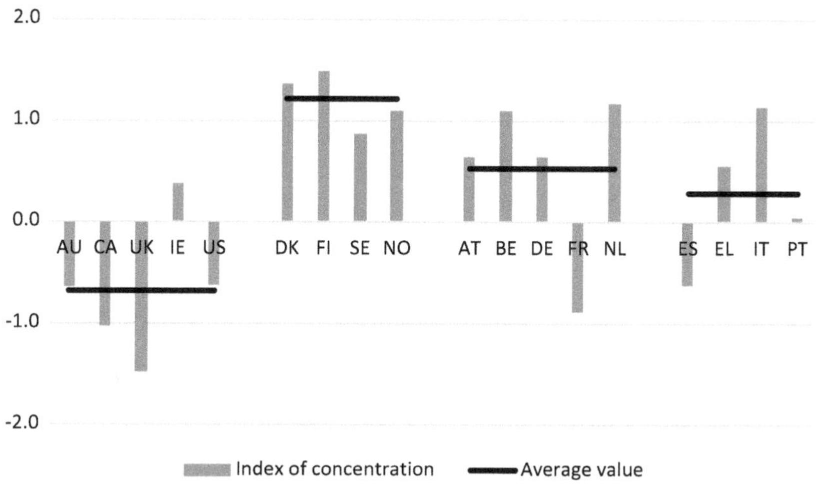

Figure 7.1 Index of concentration of political power, comparison between countries and growth models (1981–2010).

Note: Data refer to the "executives-parties" dimension. Values range from -2 (maximum concentration of power) to +2 (maximum distribution of power).

Source: Authors' elaboration from Lijphart (2012, 304–306).

model in the dualistic variant, and +0.3 of the non-inclusive low growth model. Particularly striking is the contrast between the non-inclusive and the inclusive growth models in the egalitarian variant.

On the whole, as with Lijphart, a correlation between concentration of political power and socio-economic performance comes to light. Where the decisional power is concentrated in the hands of a few, non-inclusive growth prevails. In contrast, better results in terms of inclusive development can be found in consensus democracies where decisional power is more widespread and more inclined to admit negotiation and compromise. Nevertheless, here a problem arises: consensus democracies prevail in the Mediterranean countries, with the exception of Spain, yet their economic and social performance (non-inclusive low growth) differs significantly from that of the Scandinavian countries and continental Europe, in which inclusive growth is predominant. As such, we need to seek other variables that may explain these differences. More generally speaking, there remains the issue (none too satisfactorily resolved by Lijphart) of explaining the correlation between types of democracy and socio-economic performance (for further details on this matter, see the Introduction).

We therefore examined in greater detail two variables that distinguish majoritarian form consensus democracies. The first one is the electoral system

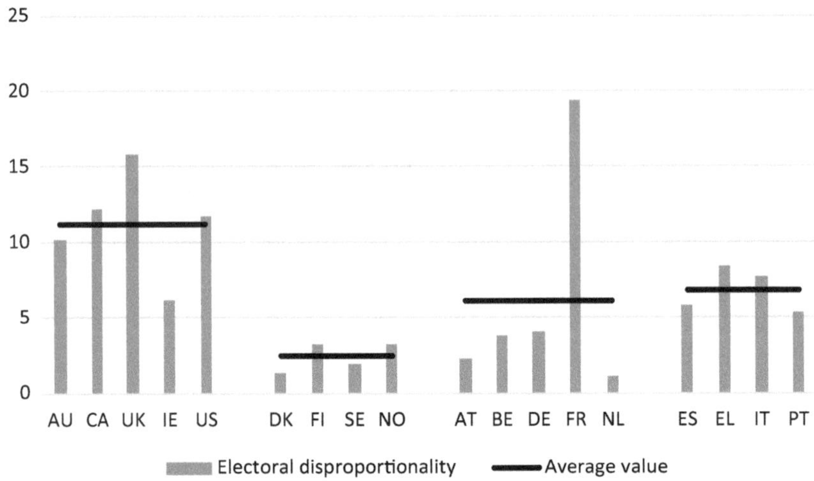

Figure 7.2 Electoral disproportionality, comparison between countries and growth models (1980–2015).

Source: Authors' elaboration from Gallagher (2017), *Election indices dataset.*

(included in Lijphart's aggregated index), one of the institutional variables with the greatest impact on the functioning of the party systems and on the very quality of public policies.[4] Figure 7.2 shows the degree of disproportionality of the electoral systems in the 18 countries under consideration and the average values of the four models of growth. With an average disproportionality of 11.2, the countries included in the non-inclusive growth model present significantly higher values than those in other models (2.4 for countries with egalitarian inclusive growth; 6.1 in countries with dualistic inclusive growth; and 6.8 in countries with non-inclusive low growth). This finding is hardly surprising considering that all the countries included in the non-inclusive growth model – except for Ireland[5] – have majority systems. The second group of countries reporting relatively high disproportionality values are those included in the non-inclusive low growth model. This may be seen as a consequence of the effects of the reinforced proportionality system in Greece (that envisaged a majority bonus to the party obtaining a relative majority), the strong majoritarian tendencies of the Spanish electoral system and also of the shifts towards a majority system that took place in Italy from the 1990s onwards.[6]

Hence, we may confirm the correlation between majority electoral systems – with an elevated level of disproportionality – and less inclusive economic yield. In contrast, proportional electoral systems, notably those with lower levels of disproportionality, are associated with inclusive types of economic performance (Trigilia, 2016). We could speculate that countries with a proportional electoral system encourage redistribution, while majoritarian institutional rules hinder it, pressing for bipartisanship and urging the parties who aim to govern to champion the preferences of a middle-class central electorate that is less inclined to bear costs in terms of taxing to achieve greater redistribution (Iversen & Soskice, 2006). Nevertheless, the electoral system variable does not seem to afford an answer to the problem, already earmarked, of the differences between the countries that Lijphart held to be close to a consensual democracy. A lower disproportionality is what largely characterises these countries (France being a conspicuous exception), although their paths of development diverge: in central-northern Europe the trend is towards inclusive growth, while in the south there is less dynamism and greater social inequalities prevail.

Nor is the second institutional variable – the number of political parties present in parliament – of much use alone in disentangling this problem. This variable is closely related to the characteristics of the electoral system. As known, electoral systems have a significant impact on political representation in both technical and psychological terms. It is no coincidence that the data in Figure 7.3 almost perfectly mirror those of the previous figure.

Two-party systems – where the political offer is less pronounced – generally correspond to majority systems with high electoral disproportionality, whereas multi-party systems, featuring wider-ranging and pluralist political offers, correspond to proportional electoral systems.

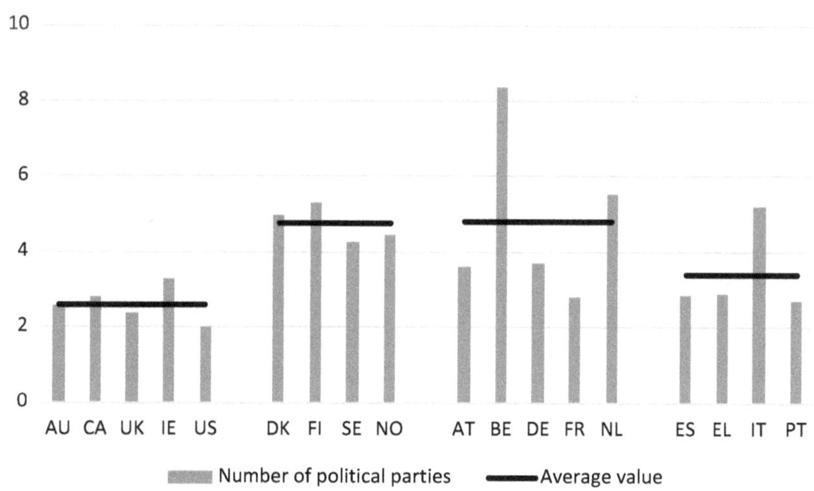

Figure 7.3 Number of political parties, comparison between countries and growth models (1980–2015).

Source: Authors' elaboration from Gallagher (2017), *Election indices dataset*.

With regard to the four models of growth, the data show a markedly lower political offer in countries with non-inclusive growth (with an average of parties in the government amounting to 2.6), almost half compared to the number of political parties in parliament in the two groups of countries with inclusive growth (presenting averages of around 4.7 and 4.8).[7] Low numbers of political parties in countries with non-inclusive low growth, presenting an average of 3.4 parties in parliament, can thus be correlated with the majoritarian leanings of their electoral systems and may afford an explanation for the lower redistribution and greater inequalities. Nonetheless, neither does the number of parties manifestly distinguish countries with inclusive growth from less dynamic countries with non-inclusive low growth.

Analysing the involvement of social groups in government decisions on economic and social policies could allow us to take a crucial step forward. As seen in Chapter 3, in countries with inclusive growth, concertation takes place regularly and continuously, while it is virtually non-existent in non-inclusive growth economies (with the exception of Ireland). This phenomenon is considerably less present and institutionalised in Mediterranean countries with non-inclusive low growth.

Coming back to Lijphart's index of concentration of political power, Figure 7.4 illustrates a strong connection between the extent of the concentration/dispersion of power within the state (the cardinal dividing line in majoritarian and consensus democracies) and the extent to which the social partners participate in policymaking.

Countries with majoritarian democracies feature extremely low levels of concertation, whereas countries with inclusive growth, in both the egalitarian and the dualistic variants, present significantly greater levels of concertation (except for France, which stands out from the other countries with inclusive growth for the elevated disproportionality of its electoral system and the considerable dominance of government over parliament).[8] In the countries that Lijphart would describe as approaching a consensus democracy, this figure differentiates more clearly, however, between those with high levels of concertation, characterised by inclusive development, and those with non-institutionalised concertation, featuring non-inclusive low development (see Chapters 3 and 8). Hence, we might conjecture that in majoritarian democracies redistribution and the countering of inequalities are hampered by the lack of concertation as well as the by electoral system. In contrast, in countries with no majoritarian democracy we should discern between those with high institutionalised concertation – correlated to inclusive development – and those with low concertation (countries in southern Europe with non-inclusive low development). This distinction underpinning the concertation/neo-corporatism aspect would provide a sounder explanation for the differing policies and economic-social yields in non-majoritarian contexts in non majoritarian contexts, as indeed suggested by some critiques on Lijphart's two types of democracy (Armingeon, 2002; Vassallo, 2016).

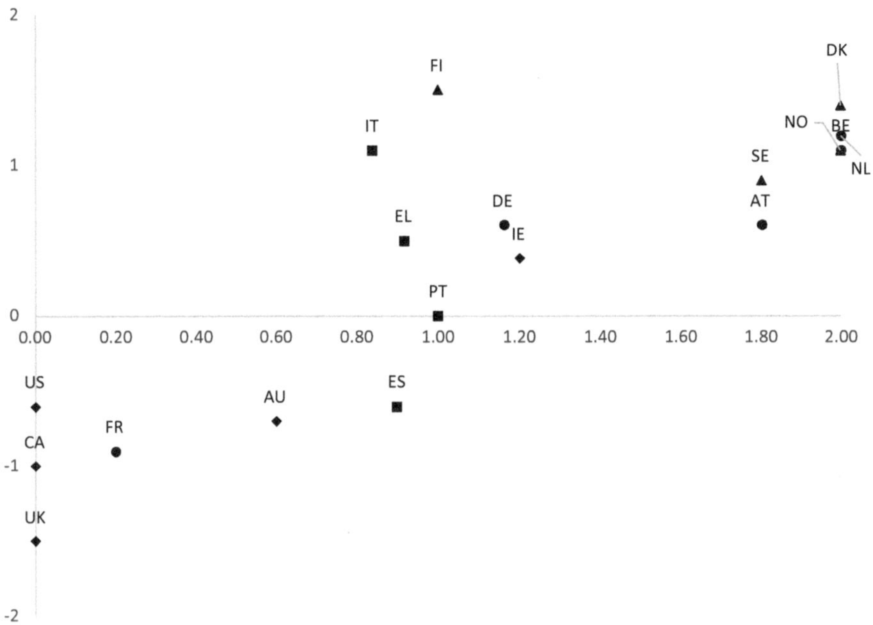

Figure 7.4 Indices of concentration of political power and of concertation (1990–2015).

Legend: Countries belonging to the non- inclusive growth model are marked with the rhombusshaped indicator. Countries with egalitarian inclusive growth are marked with the triangleshaped indicator. Dualistic inclusive growth countries are marked with the circle- shaped indicator. Finally, non-inclusive low growth countries are marked with the square indicator.

Note: Visser's index measures the regularity of social partners' participation in government decisions on social and economic policies on a scale of 0–2, where "0" indicates no participation and "2" indicates regular and frequent participation.

Sources: For the index of concentration of political power, source and data processing as for Figure 7.2. For the concertation, ICTWSS data (Visser, 2019).

After pinpointing an important institutional variable that throws light not only on the differences between the diverse types of democracy but also on the various performances within non-majoritarian democracies, the next step is to examine in detail which factors are associated with concertation. The significance of the system of interest representation is well known, particularly the role of organisations representing employment and businesses in ensuring strength and a more centralised bargaining power (Chapters 3 and 8). Here the emphasis will be on the impact that institutional factors, such as the governmental framework and the parties' distinguishing features, may exert.[9]

7.3 Government composition

From the second half of the 1970s onwards, the role of the leading actors on the political stage – political parties, trade unions, and governments – has come under the spotlight in the three main lines of research characterising welfare state studies. A first strand of inquiry, commonly referred to as the partisan politics theory, has perused the differences between the social and economic policies advanced by left-wing parties and those advanced by right-wing parties on the political spectrum, pinpointing their differences. A second strand, known as the power resource theory, considers the overall resource potential of working-class actors, trade unions and social democratic political parties, which by mobilising and entering the parliamentary arenas countervail the power of capital with redistributive social and economic policies. A third strand of studies, investigating the partisan difference theory, has appraised the political composition of governments and the impact that different governmental compositions have had on the formulation of social policies.[10] Deferring the discussion of political parties to the next section, we will now focus our attention on this impact.

A more redistributive and inclusive political offer has been attributed in the literature to governments composed of left-wing or Christian-democratic parties, both of which are considered decisive forces for the development of the welfare state.[11] Conversely, an offer of the opposite orientation has been accredited to governments composed of conservative and liberal right-wing parties (Castles, 1982). Figure 7.5 presents the composition of governments in the four ideal-types of growth and inequality comparing the period 1960–1979 with the period 1980–2015.[12]

The great post-war development and the upswing in welfare comprise the first period considered (1960–1979). Bearing in mind that our four types of development paths refer to the situation seen in the last two decades, contemplating the institutional factors that emerged at a much earlier stage may help to analyse contemporary development patterns through an exploration of the institutional conditioning that may have unfolded in the long run and thus influenced more recent paths as well.

As such, investigating the period 1960–1979, in the non-inclusive growth (NIG) model a prevalence emerges of conservative (right-wing) parties in government (62% of the overall total of government days), more than twice as much as central parties (30%) and four times as much as left-wing parties (15%).[13] An almost identical picture appears in the egalitarian inclusive growth (EIG) model. Here, left-wing political parties were in government more than 60% of the time overall, three times higher than the presence of right-wing political parties in government (18%). In contrast, in the composition of governments in continental European countries with dualistic inclusive growth (DIG), the role of governments with a greater presence of centre parties is conspicuous, in this context

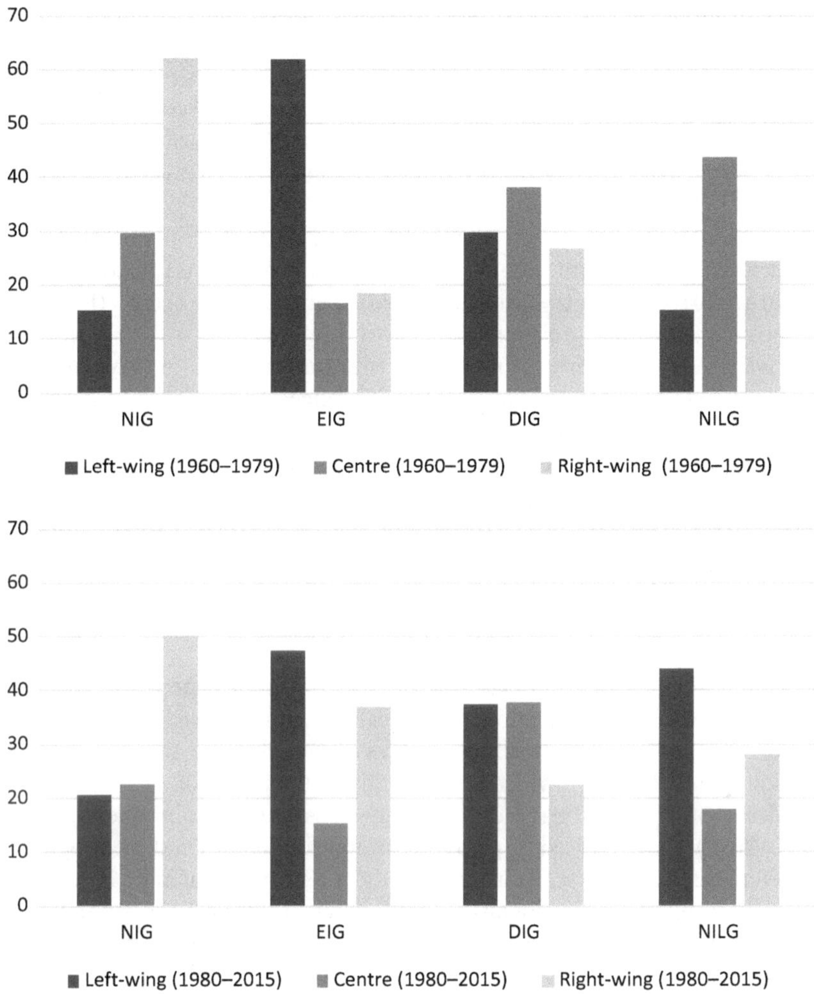

Figure 7.5 Left-, centre- and right-wing parties in government, by growth pattern (1960–1979; 1980–2015).

Legend: NIG = Non-inclusive growth; EIG = Egalitarian inclusive growth; DIG = Dualistic inclusive growth; NILG = Non-inclusive low growth.

Note: The figure is calculated as the percentage of ministerial posts allocated to right, centre and left parties weighted by the number of days in office in each year.

Source: Authors' elaboration from Armingeon et al. (2018).

potentially attributable to the bearing of the Christian-democratic parties, as well exemplified by the case of Germany.

This phenomenon appears even more pronounced in the non-inclusive low-growth (NILG) countries of Southern Europe, with parties of the centre more present in government and a weaker participation of those of the left.[14] Differences in the presence of varying types of parties in government thus appear to be clearly associated, in this first phase, with diverse development paths.

The correspondence between the political orientation of governments and patterns of growth and inequality seems less pronounced in the period from 1980 to 2015. While the association between the presence of the right wing in government and non-inclusive growth remains high – the right wing was in government on average for 50% of the total number of days in government, against 20% for the left – the differences in the composition of governments with ministerial presence of left, centre and right-wing parties in the remaining three ideal-types are less significant. Nevertheless, the increased and high presence of left-wing parties in government in the non-inclusive low-growth countries (corresponding to 44% of the total time) is worth noting, outstripping that of the continental countries and closer to the Nordic countries, where a decrease is evident.

These data offer some points for reflection:

1. in democratic majority contexts, the majority electoral system and the tendency towards bipartisanship are associated with a clear prevalence of conservative parties in government. This concerns both the first period considered (1960–1979), which corresponds to the phase of the great post-war development and the rise of welfare systems, and the subsequent period (1980–2015), characterised by greater economic difficulties and the problems of welfare reorganisation. It can reasonably be assumed that in both periods, redistribution, and hence inclusive development through concertation and welfare, is not favoured by the prevalence of conservative parties;
2. the path pursued of more egalitarian inclusive growth in the Nordic countries in recent decades seems to be associated with a strong presence of the left in government, which chiefly manifested, however, in the phase preceding the Glorious Thirties. We have seen how the presence of the left in government is associated with high concertation; we will see in the following section how it is also associated with high social spending and lower inequalities;
3. differences emerge between the Nordic countries where development is more inclusive, and the continental countries, which are characterised by greater dualism. In this case it can be assumed that the continental growth model was also influenced by the initial phase of development and welfare construction, featuring a situation of prevalence in government of the centrist forces from the Christian-democratic area and a greater balance

and compromise between social-democratic and Christian-democratic parties. As we know (see Chapters 5 and 10), this was accompanied by the construction of a welfare model less inclusive than the Nordic one, based on employment (the Bismarckian model). However, as we shall see, despite the increased participation of left-wing parties in government, in the period 1980–2015, social expenditure remained lower in Germany and the Netherlands (higher in Austria and France) and inequalities measured by the Gini index higher (especially for Germany, France, and the Netherlands);

4. as regards the Mediterranean countries, characterised in the most recent phase by low non-inclusive growth, it can first be noted that the weaker presence of the left in government in the first period (1960–1979) was compatible with reduced concertation, low redistribution, and greater inequalities. However, the situation changed radically in the following phase, when the presence of the left in government was much higher and approaches the Scandinavian peaks (which were instead decreasing). However, the results in terms of inequality reduction do not change much: in the following section we will empirically investigate the association between social spending and inclusive growth paths in the countries of Central and Northern Europe, where, in the most recent phase, the welfare model had even stronger dualising effects than in the continental model (Chapters 5 and 10).

There is therefore no doubt that the presence of left-wing political parties in government is linked to more inclusive development paths. However, it is also necessary to better understand why the influence of this variable does not seem to be linear. In other words, the effects of redistribution on the more inclusive nature of economic growth do not necessarily increase with the greater participation of left-wing political parties in government (according to the expectations of power resource theory), as shown by the case of Mediterranean countries in the most recent period, and to a more limited extent that of continental countries. And at the same time, the impact in a less inclusive sense does not increase with the diminishing presence of the left in government, as the case of the Nordic countries shows.

7.4 The left in government: policies and inclusion

To proceed in this direction, we shall now focus on the left-wing political parties,[15] long considered in the literature as vehicles of redistributive demands. As mentioned in the previous section, in a partisan theory approach the formulation of expansive and welfare-oriented policies is associated with the presence in government of parties of the left or – with different specificities – of the centre. Starting from this hypothesis, the available data were investigated to examine the relationship between the degree of participation in government of left-wing parties and the consistency of redistributive policies, measured as per capita expenditure on social policies. The outcomes of these configurations will be considered with respect to the concentration of inequality, as measured by the Gini index. Before doing so, we first summarise the incidence of left-wing party participation in government, recapping in detail the figure observed in the previous section and focusing only on left-wing political forces, compared across the four development paths and individual countries (Figures 7.6a and 7.6b).

Taking into account the entire period considered (1960–2015), in the countries with egalitarian inclusive growth the incidence of left-wing parties in government was significantly higher than in the other models, with a higher concentration in the period 1960–1979 (61.9%). Excluding Finland, the average for the Scandinavian countries exceeds 70 percentage points in the first period (71.4%) and remains above 50 percentage points even in the second period (50.3%). At the other end of the scale, the average figure for the whole period in the non-inclusive growth countries is clearly lower, at 15.1% for 1960–1979 and 20.6% for the following period. Internal differentiations linked to electoral systems can be observed here, with the UK showing higher values in the period 1960–1979 (54.2%), and Australia in the period 1980–2015 (52.2%). For the other two models, the figure remains below 40 percentage points, with a slightly higher overall incidence in non-inclusive low-growth countries. In both models, the post-1980 period shows an increase in the number of governing left-wing parties, which is much more evident in

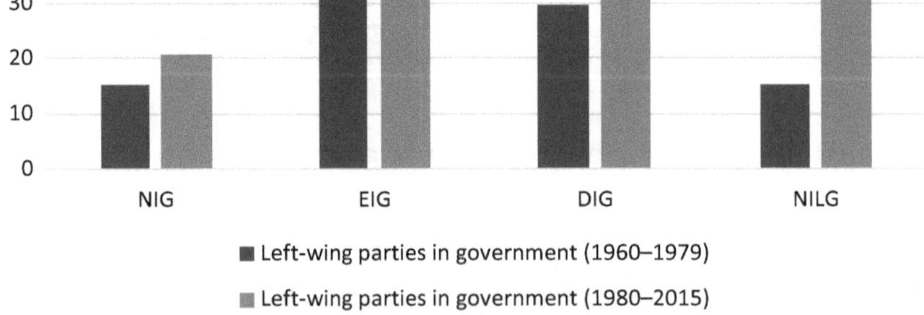

Figure 7.6a Left in government, comparison of models.

Legend: NIG = Non-inclusive growth; EIG = Egalitarian inclusive growth; DIG = Dualistic inclusive growth; NILG = Non-inclusive low growth.

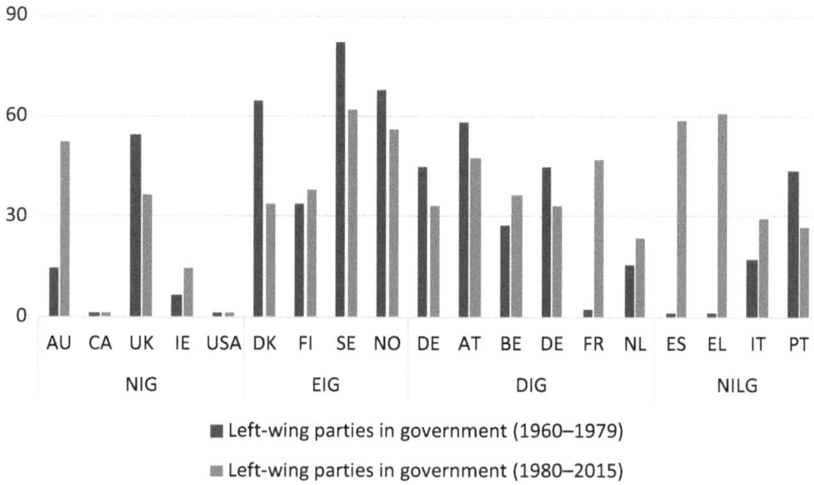

Figure 7.6b Left in government, country comparison.

Source: Authors' elaboration from Armigeon et al. (2018).

the Mediterranean countries. Among these, as mentioned above, the historical events in Greece, Portugal, and Spain weigh heavily on the first period, while the figure for Italy is affected by the experience of the Socialist Party and the subsequent transformation of the Communist Party towards parties that would come to have a greater impact through government positions. Therefore, precisely for the countries of the Mediterranean area, the weight of the left in terms of configuring the original features of the development and welfare models, was considerably weaker. Looking at the relationship between left wing parties in government and the promotion of redistributive policies, as measured by the indicator of social expenditure per capita for the period 1980–2015 (Figure 7.7), an overall positive correlation is clear. The countries in which a high incidence of the left wing in government was associated with higher per capita social spending – belonging to the inclusive growth models of both variants – appear in the upper right quadrant. Sweden and Norway have the strongest association, followed by Denmark where, as mentioned earlier, the left-wing participation in government was much lower after 1980 than in the previous period (Figure 7.6b).

Further down, the countries with dualistic inclusive growth are clustered, including Finland which, as seen above, is among the Nordic countries with the lowest presence of the left in government over the period. In Austria and France, the left governed for almost half the period, 47.4% and 47.1% respectively, while spending remained above $11,000 per capita. Belgium, Germany, and the Netherlands show lower values both for the incidence of the left in

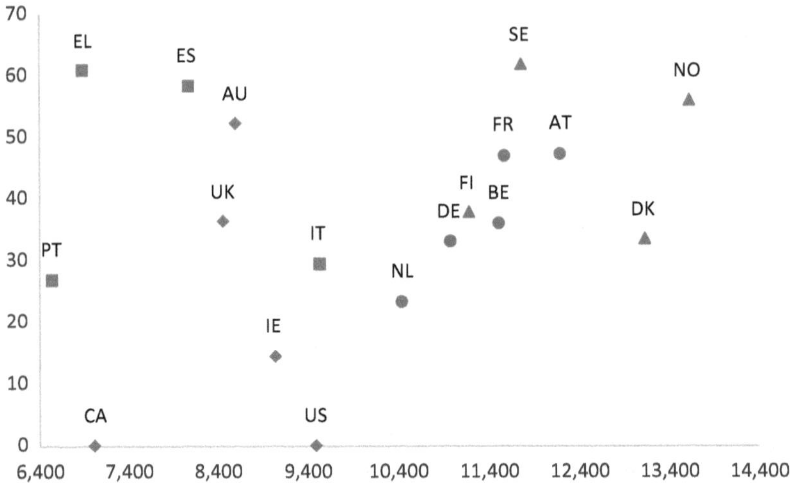

Figure 7.7 Left in government and social expenditure per capita.

Legend: countries belonging to the non-inclusive growth model are marked with a rhombus. Countries with egalitarian inclusive growth are marked with a triangle. Dualistic inclusive growth countries are marked with a circle. Finally, non-inclusive low growth countries are marked with a square.

Source: Authors' elaboration from Armingeon et al. (2018) and OECD data.

government and for social spending. Conversely, much lower levels of social spending per capita are recorded among the non-inclusive low-growth countries, which spend even less than the non-inclusive growth countries, with the partial exception of Italy. In these cases, therefore, the presence of the left in government has effects that differ from those found in the Nordic and continental countries.

The prevalence of left-wing governments is thus linked to more inclusive policies only for the Nordic and Continental models. This is reflected in the level of inequality, measured here by the Gini index of household disposable income after taxes and transfers (Figure 7.8).[16] Inclusive growth countries are grouped in the left-hand quadrant, characterised by low inequality and a high incidence of left-wing parties in government positions. Overall, the non-inclusive growth countries are on the opposite side, with low incidence of left-wing parties in government and high inequality, with the exception of Ireland. The non-inclusive low-growth countries, on the other hand, show higher levels of inequality with the same overall presence of the left in government.

The prevalence over the period 1980–2015 of left-wing parties in government in non-inclusive low-growth models thus seems to contradict the hypothesis that a greater left-wing presence would be associated with greater

Figure 7.8 Left in government and Gini index.

Legend: Countries belonging to the non-inclusive growth model are marked with the rhombus-shaped indicator. Countries with egalitarian inclusive growth are marked with the triangle-shaped indicator. Dualistic inclusive growth countries are marked with the circle-shaped indicator. Finally, non-inclusive low growth countries are marked with the square indicator.

Sources: Authors' elaboration from Armingeon et al. (2018) and OECD data.

redistributive measures and higher levels of equality. On the other hand, the downsizing of the influence of the left in the Nordic countries does not seem to have had a proportional influence on expenditure levels and welfare characteristics. Obviously, in order to analyse the different outcomes of similar amounts of presence of left-wing political forces, other variables need to be taken into account. These may concern the state of the economy in terms of available resources that may or may not favour redistributive interventions (see Chapter 2). Here we shall refer in particular to the parties' margins of action.

It can first be assumed that the historical legacies of different development paths influenced more recent changes (Mahoney & Thelen, 2015). As we have seen in the previous section, the strength of the left in government is exercised with different results depending on whether it appeared in the phase of the great post-war development and welfare construction, as for the Nordic and continental countries, or rather in the subsequent phase, more difficult overall due to economic growth and the problems of reorganising welfare with respect to its growing costs. If we situate the transition between the 1970s and the 1980s as the beginning of the transition to post-Fordism, in the model of inclusive egalitarian growth the left-wing parties have a stronger prominence in configuring the original traits of the development paths and the related social protection approaches matured, precisely, above all in the years of the so-called "Glorious Thirty Years".

We can therefore glimpse a variable that we could consider "path-dependency" in welfare systems, which conditions the possibilities of manoeuvre of left and centre-left parties with the same presence in government, and that influences the development paths seen in recent decades, the focus of our research. The original institutional framework can be conditioned in different forms. Among these, particular attention will be given in the following part of our historical-comparative study to the interests that are constituted in relation to certain choices in the original construction of welfare, and therefore to the costs that may involve decisions involving more or less radical change in relation to the resulting social stratification.

A final key to interpretation concerns the areas of competition between parties and coalition spaces within the left, associated with the level of fragmentation of consensus. We have therefore tried to measure the degree of division of the left by calculating the weight of the main parties of the "reformist" left (excluding communists and post-communists) in relation to the overall consensus obtained by left-wing parties (electoral strength), in each country and for all electoral rounds from 1960 to 2015, in order to maintain uniformity in the analysis carried out so far.[17] The data point to a general downward trend in the electoral strength of the left as a whole. This trend would be even more pronounced if we had used more recent, post-2015 data. But here we are interested in trying to measure the degree of division as a long-term structural phenomenon.

As can be seen from Figure 7.9, the non-inclusive growth countries show lower values of consensus fragmentation in both periods considered, a result that can be related to the effects of the majoritarian electoral system. For the countries with inclusive egalitarian growth, in the period 1960–1979, while the average support obtained by left-wing parties was 47.1%, there was relatively low internal fragmentation, with the main reformist party obtaining almost 80% of the votes. This does not change in the subsequent period, even though there was a significant reduction in the overall support of the left (from 47.1% to 41.3%). In the countries with dualistic inclusive growth, fragmentation appears even lower and decreases between the two periods (between 1980 and 2015 the main party obtained on average almost 90% of the votes), but one must also consider the overall lower electoral strength of the left and the decrease in the two periods considered.

In contrast, the non-inclusive low-growth countries have the highest fragmentation of all the other models. The main reformist party reached on average about 60% of the votes on the left (40.3%) in the constitutive phase of welfare (1960–1979). In the subsequent period, the average figure rose to around 70%, in the context of a 5 percentage point growth in the left-wing vote.

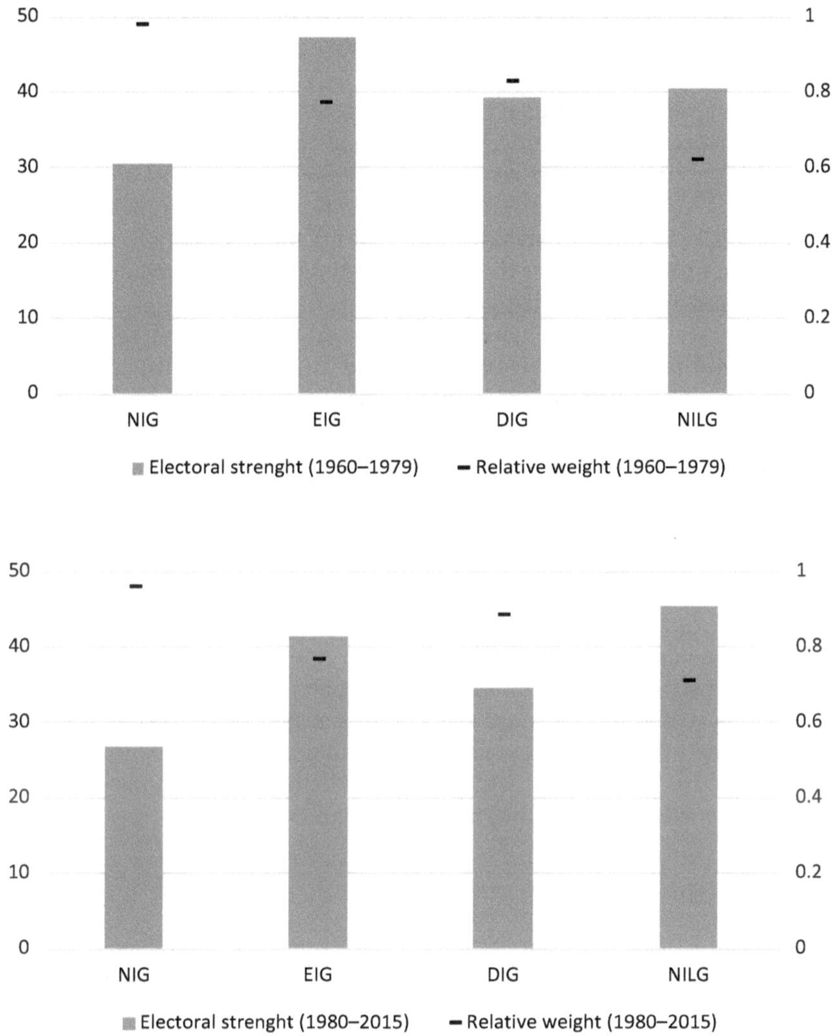

Figure 7.9 Relative weight of the main party of the "reformist" left and electoral strength of the left (average 1960–1979) and average 1980–2015, comparison of growth patterns (index and % values).

Legend: NIG = Non-inclusive growth; EIG = Egalitarian inclusive growth; DIG = Dualistic inclusive growth; NILG = Non-inclusive low growth.

Source: Authors' elaboration from Armingeon et al. (2018).

The division of left-wing forces in the various phases is therefore an element to be considered carefully when assessing the impact of the left-wing's strength on the welfare model. Particular attention should be given to this factor, especially in relation to the constitutive phase of welfare systems which, as we have seen, also exerted an influence that in terms of path-dependency should not be disregarded. A more united and stronger left certainly contributed, together with the presence of minor parties – first agrarian and then liberal – to building the "red-green" coalition that laid the foundations for the extended and universalistic welfare, financed by general taxation, which characterises the Nordic countries. It was on this basis that the most egalitarian response to the challenges of post-Fordism evolved.

In the continental context, a social-democratic left less fragmented than that of the southern European countries had to contend with Christian-democratic forces competing for political space, particularly with regard to the poorer classes. The result was a compromise that, through the diffusion of a (Bismarckian) occupational welfare, contributed to an inclusive but less egalitarian development than the Nordic one. Finally, the strong divisions of the left in the Mediterranean countries are a crucial element in understanding the welfare of these countries and the effects on the development path. As some studies have pointed out (Manow, 2009; 2015; Watson, 2015), the divisions and the presence of a strong communist party, as well as the experience of non-democratic regimes for many of the countries until the late 1970s, delayed the construction of welfare and weakened the capacity of the left to influence its structure in a more egalitarian sense, precisely because of its internal conflicts. The result was a welfare system highly fragmented in the protection it offered, more exposed to a strong dualism between insiders and outsiders, and costly for public finances (see Chapters 5 and 10).

7.5 Concluding remarks

This chapter illustrates the results of a comparative analysis that focuses on the political dimension of inclusive development, i.e. considering some associations between the characteristics of political systems and types of socio-economic development in 18 advanced economies. We have discussed the results by distinguishing four ideal-types of growth and measuring, for each of them, the degree to which they can be linked to a number of political-institutional factors.

Our starting point was Lijphart's hypothesis of a link between majority and consensual democracies on the one hand and economic and social performance on the other. Cross-checking our data with the four development models, we verified that while for majority democracies there is an link with the model of non-inclusive development established in recent decades, the relationship between consensual democracy and inclusive development seems to be more problematic. In fact, the cases which, according to

Lijphart's scheme, are to be ascribed to the latter type of democracy present results in terms of performance which only in some cases came close to inclusive development.

We therefore went in search of variables that could discriminate between countries belonging to majority democracies, finding them first of all in the presence of institutionalised concertation practices, considered as an important channel of redistribution. We then asked ourselves what other factors could be linked to concertation between governments and large interest representation organisations. We know that from the point of view of interest representation, concentration and the centralisation of representation are very important. However, we have drawn attention in this chapter to the role of left-wing parties, not only in activating consultation, but also in supporting social spending. The presence of left-wing parties in government is therefore crucial to characterise the more inclusive development that combats inequalities most strongly. However, we also noted that the influence of this variable does not manifest itself in a linear way. First of all, it is conditioned by the historical phase: for example, it appears stronger in the period of the Glorious Thirty Years, characterised by great development and the upward phase of welfare, than in the more recent period.

This suggests that the influence of the left must in any case be measured in the most recent phase with elements of path-dependency linked to concerted practices and to previously constructed welfare models. Second, the impact of the left in government appears to be strongly conditioned by the degree of fragmentation and division between the political forces that make up the area of the left as a whole. These aspects can be better explored in the more in-depth comparative analysis of some cases presented in the next section.

We will now conclude with a summary of the results that emerged for the different development models.

Particularly clear results emerged with respect to the consistency of the model of non-inclusive growth countries, which are characterised by the following properties:

- They are majoritarian systems (all except Ireland), as opposed to proportional electoral systems seen in eight of the nine inclusive growth countries.
- They have high levels of electoral disproportionality, with an average spread between the distribution of votes and the distribution of seats coming to 11.2.
- They are characterised by the highest concentration of political power according to the Lijphart indcx (-0.7).
- They tend to be two-party systems, in which political competition is concentrated around two main parties, with the others playing a subordinate role.

- They have a lower actual number of political parties in parliament (with an average overall figure of 2.6) than those with inclusive growth (4.8).
- They have the lowest percentage of government positions held by left-wing parties (18.6%).
- They do not experiment with forms of consultation with interest representation organisations. Their system of representation is more pluralist than neo-corporatist in character.
- They have lower levels of per capita social expenditure and higher levels of inequality.

Egalitarian inclusive growth countries present an almost mirror-image configuration of political arrangements, and:

- They are all proportional electoral systems, characterised by a high effective number of parties (4.7), which without Belgium would be the highest.
- They have the lowest average spread between the distribution of votes and the distribution of seats, with an average electoral disproportionality of 2.4.
- They have the lowest degree of concentration of power (+1.2) in relation to the proportional electoral system, multipartyism and relations between parliament and government.
- In particular, these are the contexts with the most significant concertation practices with the social partners, supported by the greater weight of the left in government and a more neo-corporative system of representation.
- They show the highest percentage of incidence of government positions held by left-wing parties (61.9 in the 1960–1979 period and 47.2 in the 1980–2015 period), which is reflected in a greater propensity towards redistributive policies, with an extended universalistic welfare.
- The left-wing political area is less fragmented and divided: the average consensus obtained by left-wing parties appears more concentrated, with the main reformist party obtaining almost 80% of the votes.
- They have higher levels of per capita social spending and lower levels of inequality.

The profile of Dualistic inclusive growth countries differs from the former inclusive variant in some features. Let us see them in detail:

- They are predominantly characterised by proportional electoral systems, with a higher actual number of political parties (4.8) than in non-inclusive growth countries (except for France, which has a majority electoral system).

- They have a higher degree of concentration of power than countries with inclusive egalitarian growth, but still less than those with non-inclusive growth.
- They also have a higher degree of concentration of power than countries with inclusive, egalitarian growth, but still less than countries with non-inclusive growth; here, too, consultation is a widespread and consolidated practice, supported by a neo-corporatist system of representation.
- The average incidence of the left in government was 29.7 in 1960–1979 and 37.4 in 1980–2015, with a high concentration of electoral consensus towards the main reformist party.
- The participation of a cohesive left in government is associated with high levels of social spending per capita, second only to those of countries with inclusive growth in the egalitarian variant.

The profile of non-inclusive low-growth countries is not markedly different from what we have just seen, although some variables of political arrangements and policy seem to characterise their institutional configuration and growth and development performance. In further detail:

- The low growth non-inclusive countries are all proportional but have a lower actual number of parties (3.4); only Italy has average values above 5 points (5.2) while Greece, Portugal and Spain are not far from the average number recorded in the non-inclusive growth countries.
- The values concerning electoral disproportionality (6.8), although distant, are second only to the non-inclusive growth countries, as a consequence of the majoritarian effects of Greece's reinforced proportional system and the strong majoritarian propensities of the Spanish electoral system, and of the changes occurred in Italy since the 1990s.
- Lower degrees of disproportionality also correspond to comparatively lower levels of consultation, although in absolute terms higher than in non-inclusive growth countries.
- They have high levels of consensus for the left (over 40 points, second only to countries with inclusive egalitarian growth).
- The experiences of left-wing governments have been prevalent since the 1980s (43.9% in 1980–2015, compared to 15.3 in 1960–1979, thus +28.6 points) and the consensus expressed for the left is comparatively much more fragmented.
- This pattern is associated with much lower levels of per capita social spending, even below the non-inclusive growth countries, with the partial exception of Italy.

Notes

1 The institutional frameworks and the regulatory structures marking the development paths have been considered in several valuable contributions (among others, Streeck, 2012; Thelen, 2014; Burroni, 2016), which have also identified the correlation between "coordinated economies" and "consensus democracies" as well as between "liberal market economies" and "majoritarian democracies" (for example, Amable, 2003; Ido, 2012; Schmitter & Todor, 2014). Nevertheless, empirically based analyses that problematise "political sustainability" are still lacking, i.e. those factors that affect the forming of political and electoral consensus (Trigilia, 2016).

2 Lijphart's work has often come under criticism for his selection of cases, the indicators, their operationalisation, and therefore also for the complex theoretical outcomes of his research (see Giuliani [2016] for an in-depth discussion). Note the contribution by Armingeon (2002), who applies the concept of negotiation democracy (to which also Lijphart refers [2012]), as opposed to that of consensus democracy and Lijphart's response (2002).

The correlation between Lijphart's models of democracy and macroeconomic yield was examined in depth by Vassallo (2016, chap. V) who refuted the validity of the association between consensualism and economic performance, advocating rather that this outcome would depend on the choice to include an indicator regarding the way of representing economic interests among the essential features that characterise consensualism. As such, it would be rather the degree of corporativism that is more specifically related to improved economic yield (on this point see also Anderson [2001]).

3 The variables making up the index are considered as continuums along which different countries may be placed. Alongside the "executives-parties" dimension, Lijphart uses another that targets the form of the more or less centralised state, (the "federal-unitary" dimension). The analysis shown in this chapter regards the first dimension.

4 See Iversen and Soskice (2001; 2006) as well as Lijphart.

5 The Irish electoral system is at times classified as a majority system (Iversen & Soskice, 2006, 172–173), at others as a proportional one (Norris, 1997).

6 For Italy, data refers to three different electoral systems: proportional up to 1993; a combination of majority and proportional from 1993 to 2005; proportional with a majority bonus from 2005.

7 Belgium has one of the most splintered party systems in Europe as a consequence of the lack of integration and coordination between French and Flemish political parties at a federal level. It is thus a double party system split into two linguistic segments (for further details see De Winter, Dumont, & Swyngedouw, 2006). With the exclusion of Belgium, the average number of political parties in the dualistic inclusive model would amount to 3.9.

8 Just as pronounced is the correlation between extent of concertation and electoral disproportionality. Here the data are omitted, since the results are very similar to those presented in Figure 7.4.

9 The importance of the pro-labour governments has been recorded in the literature on neo-corporatism and concertation (Lehmbruch & Schmitter, 1982), though it has been less investigated in research.

10 For a review of the main approaches in the welfare state literature contemplating the role of policy actors, see Van Kersbergen and Becker (2002); Kittel and Obinger (2003); Hausermann et al. (2013).
11 On left-wing governments, e.g. Cameron (1978); on centrist governments, see Wilensky (1981) and van Kersbergen (1995).
12 As a way of measuring the composition of governments, we use, as do numerous authors, including Gallie (2013), the Comparative Politics Data Set ("gov_right1"; "gov_cent1" and "gov_left1"), calculated as the percentage of ministerial positions assigned to the parties of the right, centre, and left, and weighted by the number of days in office in each year. For details on the allocation criteria of political parties with respect to the categories of "right", "left" and "centre", see Armingeon et al. (2018).
13 The American Democratic Party, typically labelled as a centre party (Armingeon et al., 2018), contributes to the incidence of this group of parties.
14 The figure for non-inclusive low-growth countries is affected by the historical events in Greece, Portugal, and Spain. As is well known, Greece was ruled by the Greek junta (also known as the Regime of the Colonels) between 1965 and 1974; Portugal and Spain only transitioned to democratic regimes in the mid-1970s (Figure 7.6b).
15 We refer to the set of parties labelled as social democratic, left-socialist, communist, and post-communist by Armingeon et al. (2018).
16 The Gini index varies on a scale from 0 to 1, where the lowest extreme represents the highest distribution of income and the highest the highest concentration. See Chapter 1 for a detailed analysis of income inequality across the four development paths.
17 The 'F' figure is obtained by dividing, for each election year in each country, the percentage of votes obtained by the main 'reformist' left-wing party by the total sum of votes obtained by left-wing parties (labelled 'social democratic', 'left socialist', 'post-communist', 'communist' by the Comparative Political Data Set 1960–2015). Green parties are not included, as they have altered the structure of left-wing electoral competition in many national contexts. It should also be taken into account that: (1) given the particular structure of the competition for the federal elections in Belgium where two socialist parties compete in two different regions (Flanders and Wallonia), the weight of the main reformist party is the result of the sum of their votes, divided by the total consensus obtained by the left-wing parties; (2) for Greece the reference period is 1974–2015, for Spain it is 1977–2015; (3) for Italy the evolution of the acronyms has been taken into account, as follows: the Socialist Party was the main reformist party in the elections of 1983, 1987, 1992: the Left Democrats were so in 1994, 1996 and 2001; Uniti per l'Ulivo in the elections of 2006; the Democratic Party in those of 2008 and 2013.

References

Amable, B. (2003). *The diversity of modern capitalism*. Oxford: Oxford University Press.

Anderson, L. (2001). The implications of institutional design for macroeconomic performance. *Comparative Political Studies*, 34(4), 429–452. doi.org/10.1177/0010414001034004004

Armingeon, K. (2002). The effects of negotiation democracy: A comparative analysis, *European Journal of Political Research*, 41(1): 8–105. doi.org/10.1111/1475-6765.00004
Armingeon, K., Wenger, V., Wiedemeier, F., Isler, C., Knöpfel, L., & Weisstanner, D. (2018). *Supplement to the comparative political data set – government composition 1960–2016*. Bern: Institute of Political Science, University of Berne.
Burroni, L. (2016). *Capitalismi a confronto: istituzioni e regolazione dell'economia nei paesi europei*. Bologna: Il Mulino.
Cameron, D. (1978). The expansion of the public economy: A comparative analysis. *American Political Science Review*, 78, 1243–1261. doi.org/10.2307/1954537
Castles, F. (Ed.) (1982). *The impact of parties: Politics and policies in democratic capitalist states*. London: SAGE.
De Winter, L., Dumont, P., & Swyngedouw, M. (2006). Party system(s) and electoral behaviour in Belgium: From stability to balkanisation. *West European Politics*, 29(5), 933–956. doi.org/10.1080/01402380600968836
Gallie, D. (Eds) (2013). *Economic crisis, quality of work and social integration: The European experience*. Oxford: Oxford University Press.
Giuliani, M. (2016). Patterns of democracy reconsidered: The ambiguous relationship between corporatism and consensualism. *European Journal of Political Research*, 55, 22–42. doi.org/10.1111/1475-6765.12117
Häusermann S., Picot, G., & Geering, D. (2013). Rethinking party politics and the welfare state: Recent advances in the literature. *British Journal of Political Science*, 43(1), 221–240. doi:10.1017/S0007123412000336
Ido, M. (Eds.) (2012). *Varieties of capitalism, types of democracy and globalization*. Abingdon/New York: Routledge.
Iversen, T. & Soskice, D. (2001). An asset theory of social policy preferences. *American Political Science Review*, 95(4), 875–893. doi:10.1017/S0003055400400079
Iversen, T. & Soskice, D. (2006). Electoral institutions and the politics of coalitions: Why some democracies redistribute more than others. *American Political Science Review*, 100(2), 164–181.
Kittel, B. & Obinger, H. (2003). Political parties, institutions, and the dynamics of social expenditure in times of austerity. *Journal of European Public Policy*, 10(1), 20–45. doi.org/10.1080/1350176032000046912
Lehmbruch, G. & Schmitter, C.P. (1982). *Patterns of Corporatist Policy Making*. London: SAGE
Lijphart, A. (1990). The political consequences of electoral laws, 1945–1985. *American Political Science Review*, 84, 481–496. doi:10.2307/1963530
Lijphart, A. (1999). *Patterns of democracy: Government forms and performance in thirty-six countries*. Yale: Yale University Press.
Lijphart, A. (2002). Negotiation democracy versus consensus democracy: Parallel conclusions and recommendations. *European Journal of Political Research*, 41, 107–113. doi.org/10.1111/1475-6765.00005
Lijphart, A. (2012). *Patterns of democracy: Government forms and performance in thirty-six countries* II ed.. Yale: Yale University Press.
Mahoney, J. & Thelen, K. (Eds) (2015). *Advances in comparative-historical analysis*. Cambridge: Cambridge University Press.

Manow, P. (2009). Electoral rules, class coalitions, and welfare state regimes, or how to explain Esping-Andersen with Stein Rokkan. *Socio-Economic Review*, 7(1), 101–121. doi.org/10.1093/ser/mwn022
Norris, P. (1997). *Passages to power: Legislative recruitment in advanced democracies*. Cambridge: Cambridge University Press.
Schmidt, M.G. (1996). A review of the possibilities and limits of partisan influence on public policy. *European Journal of Political Research*, 2, 155–183.
Schmitter, C.P. & Todor, A. (2014). Varieties of capitalism and types of democracy. *Stato e Mercato*, 1, 87–116.
Streeck, W. (2012). How to study contemporary capitalism? *European Journal of Sociology*, 53, 1–28.
Thelen, K. (2014). *Varieties of liberalization and the new politics of social solidarity*. Cambridge: Cambridge University Press.
Trigilia, C. (2016). Tipi di democrazia e modelli di capitalismo: un'agenda di ricerca. *Stato e Mercato*, 2, 183–213.
Van Kersbergen, K. (1995). *Social capitalism: A study of Christian democracy and the welfare state*. London: Routledge
Van Kersbergen, K. & Becker, U. (2002). Comparative politics and the welfare state. In H. Keman (Ed.), *Comparative democratic politics: A guide to contemporary theory* (pp. 185–212). London: SAGE.
Vassallo, S. (2016). *Sistemi politici comparati*. Bologna: Il Mulino.
Visser, J. (2019). *ICTWSS Database. Version 6.1, Amsterdam, Amsterdam Institute for Advanced Labour Studies (AIAS)*. Amsterdam: University of Amsterdam, November 2019.
Watson, S.E. (2015). *The left divided: The development and transformation of advanced welfare states*. Oxford: Oxford University Press.
Wilensky, H. (1981). Leftism, Catholicism, and democratic corporatism: The role of political parties in recent welfare state development, In P. Flora & A. Heidenheimer, A. (Eds), *The development of the welfare states in Europe and American* (pp. 345–382). New Brunswick: Transaction.

Part II

Comparative historical analysis

Chapter 8

Industrial relations

Representation, inclusion, and competitiveness

Luigi Burroni and Marcello Pedaci

8.1 Introduction

In the first part of the book, we analysed the main features of industrial relations in a large number of cases (and more precisely in 18 countries), focusing mainly on some fundamental dimensions of the collective bargaining structure and their relationship with labour income and its distribution (see Chapter 3). In this chapter we will examine them in further detail, concentrating on a small number of cases, with the aim of pinpointing the role of industrial relations in the development paths taken by advanced democracies in the last 20 years. As explained in the preceding pages, two significant countries have been chosen for each development path: the United Kingdom and the United States for non-inclusive growth (NIG), Sweden and Denmark for inclusive egalitarian growth (EIG); Germany and France for inclusive dualistic growth (DIG); Italy and Spain for low non-inclusive growth (NILG). This selection makes no claim to statistical representativeness: the cases were chosen for their relevance and proximity to different development paths.

A high degree of diversity characterises the industrial relations systems in the countries surveyed. There are countries with high unionisation and countries with low unionisation, countries with institutionalised concertation and countries with neo-voluntary and unstable concertation, countries with highly centralised and coordinated collective bargaining, and countries where decentralised and disorganised bargaining predominates. Whether and how these differences affect the "dependent variables" studied here, namely economic competitiveness and income inequality, are interesting questions to investigate. As such, to proceed in this direction, it may be useful to refer first of all to some fundamental dimensions of industrial relations systems.

First, economic competitiveness has to do with the relationship between industrial relations, politics, and polity, taking into due consideration the action of the state, which directly or indirectly influences the outcome and functioning of industrial relations. An example might be the regulation of representation and collective bargaining, or the rules that institutionalise social concertation practices, understood not only as trilateral negotiations

DOI: 10.4324/9781003297130-11

for social pacts, but also as the presence of trilateral institutions. For instance, in France there is a high coverage of collective bargaining thanks to the extension mechanisms set down by the public actor, despite weak collective bargaining and trade unions and employers' associations with low membership. Even in countries with a model forged on the pattern of neo-voluntarism and low institutionalisation of concertation, at times extensive use has been made of tripartite negotiation with the social partners for substantial, instrumental reforms, as in Spain and Italy during the 1990s.

We shall moreover investigate further how the action of the "*enabling state*", as defined by Wolfgang Streeck, helps to explain the configuration of industrial relations in the case of Germany. In some Scandinavian European countries instead, the widespread practising of institutionalised concertation is directly bolstered by the institutional configuration that allows the formation of minority governments. In essence, therefore, both polity and politics influence the structure of industrial relations. Yet in part also the opposite is true. Due to the structure of associative regulation the policy space has been persistently occupied by the public actor in the case of France, while the presence of strong and encompassing associations has favoured the consolidation of consensual democracies such as those of the Nordic countries.

Second, the very logic of action that characterises the actors in industrial relations should be taken into account, i.e. the organisations representing the interests of workers and businesses (Burroni & Scalise, 2017). It is worth remembering that not all the actions of trade unions and employers' associations succeed in reducing inequality or increasing competitiveness. Their impact is in fact influenced by the logic of action that is pursued. If, for example, trade unions have a high degree of influence over policy but follow an occupation-based representation model that aims to safeguard the interests of particular groups, then their actions may contribute to increasing inequality and dualism in terms of working conditions. A different matter is the case of unions following an *encompassing* representation model, where the objective is to protect the interests of all workers. It is also important to understand whether the logic followed is mainly defensive, with a view to maintaining acquired positions, or rather more proactive, and whether a cooperative or conflictual logic prevails.

In addition to the actions of the actors, it is also necessary to look at the practices they implement. The functioning and structure of collective bargaining are of particular value, which can contribute both to curtailing inequalities and to bolstering economic competitiveness. Likewise, social concertation practices, i.e. the sharing of policy space between social partners and governments, which leads to the development of reforms that have a direct bearing on competitiveness and inequality, such as reforms of the labour market, the welfare system, training, and so on.

These three dimensions, the relationship of industrial relations with polity and politics, the logics of action and the characteristics of the practices implemented will be considered in the next paragraphs in the following order. First we will focus on the historical features that since the 1980s have characterised the four models analysed in our research (Section 8.2). Examining the historical roots of the models is useful to better outline the main trends and challenges that the four models face during the 2000s (Section 8.3). In Section 8.4, we shall study the effects of the above mentioned three dimensions on the relationship between competitiveness and inequality that characterises the four models analysed. Finally, we will open up to the most recent challenges that face the industrial relations actors, also formulating some hypotheses about the impact of these challenges on the relationship between competitiveness and inequality.

8.2 The historical roots of the four models

In terms of industrial relations models, the four ideal types have profoundly different historical characteristics, especially with regard to the dimensions that we have seen to be relevant to inequality and economic competitiveness. Therefore it may be helpful to recall the main characteristics of the models, namely, the inclusive non-dualistic growth model of northern Europe, the inclusive dualistic growth model of continental Europe, the non-inclusive growth model of Anglo-Saxon origin, and the non-inclusive low growth model of the Mediterranean countries.

The indicators most often used to describe the main dimensions of collective bargaining and unionisation (Visser, 2019) expertly outline the characteristics and dynamics of industrial relations in the countries/models considered in the 1980s and 1990s. Throughout this period, Northern European countries record much higher rates of unionisation than the others and are fairly stable (Figure 8.1); membership declines instead in Central European and Mediterranean countries, with the exception of Spain. The decline is particularly marked in the United Kingdom and Italy, countries that until the mid-1980s were characterised by a medium–high level of membership, around 50%. There is also a significant reduction in Germany and France, which are, however, characterised by a lower level of unionisation; in the case of France, membership of workers' organisations halved, falling to 10%.

The differences in terms of collective bargaining coverage are less marked in the 1980s and 1990s, with an increase in many cases (Figure 8.2). As mentioned above, with reference to this dimension, account should be taken of the presence of extension mechanisms, often promoted by legislation, which have kept contractual coverage high even in cases, such as France, characterised by low unionisation. The important difference is with the Anglo-Saxon countries. In the United States, over the period under consideration, contractual coverage remained low and on a declining trend; in the early 1980s about 23% of workers were covered by collective agreements; by the end of the 1990s this percentage had fallen to 15%. In the United Kingdom, where collective

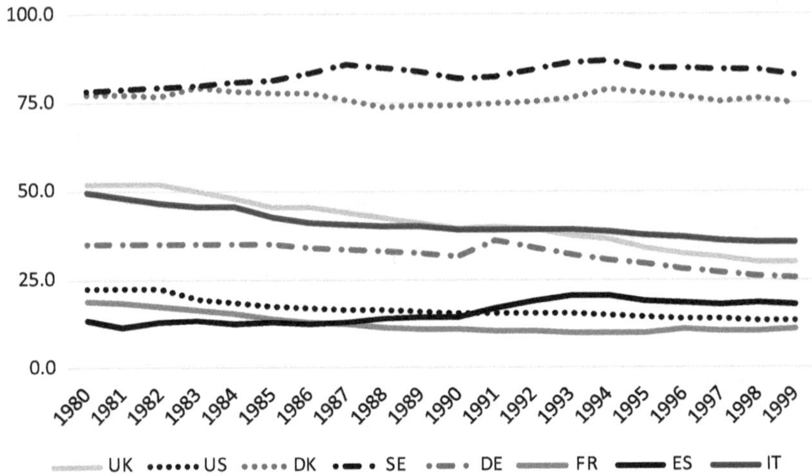

Figure 8.1 Trend of union density, 1980–1999.

Source: Elaboration on ICTWSS data (OECD & AIAS, 2021).

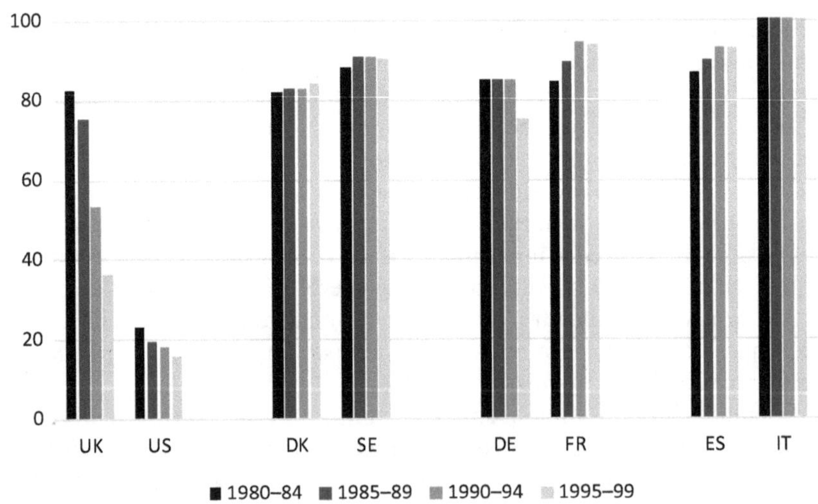

Figure 8.2 Collective bargaining coverage, average values per period.

Source: Elaboration on ICTWSS data (OECD & AIAS, 2021).

Table 8.1 Coordination and prevailing level of collective bargaining, years 1980–1999 (average values for periods)

Country	*Bargaining coordination*				*Prevailing level of bargaining*			
	1980–84	*1985–89*	*1990–94*	*1995–99*	*1980–84*	*1985–89*	*1990–94*	*1995–99*
Denmark	4.2	3.6	4.0	4.2	4.2	3.6	3.0	3.2
Sweden	4.2	3.6	3.8	3.4	4.2	4.2	3.4	3.0
Germany	4.0	4.0	4.0	4.0	3.0	3.0	3.0	3.0
France	2.0	2.0	2.0	2.0	3.0	3.0	3.0	3.0
Spain	3.8	2.4	2.0	2.0	4.6	3.4	3.0	3.0
Italy	2.8	1.4	3.4	3.0	3.4	3.0	3.0	3.0
United Kingdom	2.0	2.0	2.0	1.0	3.0	2.4	1.8	1.0
United States	1.8	1.0	1.0	1.0	1.0	1.0	1.0	1.0

Source: Elaboration on ICTWSS data (OECD & AIAS, 2021).

agreements covered more than 80% of the employed in the early 1980s, the Conservative governments' anti-labour and anti-union interventions caused contractual coverage to fall to just over a third of workers, far below the levels in other European countries.

Finally, let us consider an indicator on the extent/type of coordination of collective bargaining, and one on the main level at which it takes place (Table 8.1). The Anglo-Saxon countries constitute the cases with the lowest values on both indicators. The United States, as we shall discuss in more detail below, has been characterised since the early 1980s by the prevalence of a single-employer, very low coordination, highly decentralised model of bargaining, in which collective agreements, when present, are signed at company level. The values recorded for the UK, on the other hand, describe a gradual shift in the UK over the two decades from a multi-employer, multi-sectoral bargaining model to the US model. Looking at the values of the other countries, there is a clear trend of a gradual convergence towards models in which the main level of collective bargaining is the sectoral one; also the northern European countries, characterised at the beginning by the important role of inter-sectoral agreements, are moving in this direction. Important differences remain in the degree of coordination, which remains high, although slightly decreasing, in the Scandinavian countries, especially in Sweden, and in Germany; it is instead intermediate in Italy, but has been so only since the early 1990s, while it is low in France and Spain; in the latter case the values collected are markedly diminished in the degree of coordination, i.e. the presence of centralised forms of negotiation, especially on wages.

8.2.1 The Northern European model of inclusive egalitarian growth

The Northern European countries, characterised by social cohesion and economic competitiveness, share a long tradition of neo-corporatism, with a strong workers' movement and consolidated participatory institutions at central and decentralised levels. These are constantly involved, formally or informally, in the regulatory processes related to the labour market, income policies, welfare, and the provision of services. Moreover, as shown by the indicators discussed above, relations between social actors have long been predominantly centralised, with a high degree of coordination, although more recently they have experienced a significant growth in decentralised bargaining at sector and enterprise levels (Dølvik, 2009; Crouch, 1996).

As mentioned above, one of the distinctive features of this model is the high level of unionisation and the low fragmentation of organisations representing interests. At the beginning of the 1990s the level of unionisation was around 80% (over 85% in Sweden) and also the membership of employers' associations was very high. One of the factors contributing most to the high level of unionisation was the so-called Ghent system, named after the Belgian town where it was first implemented. The Ghent system was – and still is – based on the involvement of trade unions in the management of unemployment funds: membership of trade unions was necessary in order to obtain certain forms of welfare provision, such as unemployment benefits. This system favoured the consolidation of a model of industrial relations based on a few large organisations.

With regard to the logic of action of the representative organisations, well aware of the difficulties faced by firms exposed to international competition, the trade unions have adopted a proactive approach since the early 1990s, accepting both strong labour flexibility and practices of the organisation of work to enhance productivity. Equally important, however, was the role of the employers' associations, which at least in part sacrificed the goal of labour market de-regulation over the benefits of promoting marked wage moderation through centralised and coordinated bargaining (Martin & Swank, 2012; Dølvik, 2009). At the same time, participatory industrial relations at the corporate level have favoured negotiated flexibility and the emergence of innovative and shared models of human resource management. Precisely because of these "beneficial constraints" (for firms) (Streeck, 1997), demands for de-regulation by employers' associations have been less pronounced than in other countries.

Polity played an important role in this model, encouraging the consolidation of cooperation between government and social partners. The institutional set-up and "politics", were significantly influenced indirectly, allowing trilateral negotiation practices to emerge. The so-called "consensual democracy", a system that developed in both countries and that favoured collaboration between civil society organisations, the economy and the state, had a key role in this. This system was also strengthened by the specific type of parliamentarianism that characterises these countries, defined as "negative"; in this system, governments need no investing (the vote of confidence) by parliament, – the absence of a majority against them is sufficient. If there is no vote against on the part of an absolute majority, confidence is deemed to have been granted. Thus minority governments can be formed – a typical feature of Nordic democracies, which leads to continuous confrontation between the various parties and with possible allies, present and future: important decisions are difficult to make without consulting the other political parties and social actors (Manow, 2009).

Moreover, as pointed out, this trait of the Nordic democracies drives the "operativeness" of governments (Pasquino, 2009). In principle, each party is willing to create a coalition with others, which makes it important to discuss specific measures and the emergence of widespread cooperative behaviour, without any deep-seated fractures (Bergholm & Bieler, 2013).[1]

Besides polity, also historical tradition played an important role; first, the Lutheran tradition, which played a "very close role to that of civil service within the state (…) with the consequence that in Lutheran faith countries the state has never had any significant inhibitions about sharing political space with interest organisations" (Crouch, 1996, 340–341). The organisational structure and logic of action of the associations, few in number, very inclusive and with a tradition of general interest representation, also favoured concerted agreements. However, also the specific geography of the countries studied here is a key aspect: territorially extensive, with a total area equal to that of Italy, Germany, and France, but with a very low and territorially concentrated population density. A smaller population size may mean a greater homogeneity of interests, making representation easier (Katzenstein, 1985).

Lastly, the fact that collective bargaining with a high level of centralisation and coordination has historically characterised Sweden and Denmark should be underlined. As Dølvik (2009) points out, already with the onset of industrialisation, trade unions promoted the creation of a centralised bargaining system that was capable of standardising wage and working conditions at an intersectoral and inter-firm level. This set-up hinged on solidarity-based income policies along the lines of the so-called Rehn-Meidner model, named after the two Swedish trade union economists – Gösta Rehn and Rudolf Meidner – who during the 1950s theorised a model based on central wage setting, based on the principle of "same pay for the same work", careful to ensure that real wages did not grow more than productivity. Wage increases did not reflect the specific conditions of a sector or a company, thus motivating companies to increase their productivity. In spite of the strong centralisation, the system did not exclude forms of decentralisation of industrial relations; but this decentralisation was both organised, with high unionisation and high coverage of collective bargaining, and centralised, with company bargaining developing on issues delegated and regulated directly by the national sectoral level.

8.2.2 The dualistic inclusive growth model of continental Europe

The case of countries with dualistic inclusive growth is different, but important distinctions have to be made. These countries have very different industrial relations structures. In Germany, industrial relations have always given rise to beneficial ties, which since the mid-1980s have supported a model centred on the so-called diversified quality production (Streeck, 1992). At the national level, relations between trade unions and employers' associations have produced collective goods for competitiveness and have contributed to the design and implementation of labour and welfare policies; at the enterprise level, they have fostered ways of organising work that have led to high productivity. More generally, in Germany (as in other countries of the continental model, such as Austria, Belgium, and the Netherlands) industrial relations have always been characterised by a high degree of institutionalisation, a high degree of articulation between the sectoral and company levels, highly regulated consultation, strong links between trade unions and political parties, participatory and co-decision-making institutions at the sectoral and company levels. These date back to the 1950s and have promoted long-term commitment on the part of workers to the company (Gumbrell-McCormick & Hyman, 2013; Keller & Kirsch, 2011; Hassel, 2011; Hall, 2007) – in short, a strongly organised system of interest representation, which, however, in more recent years, as we shall see, has seen important changes.

Nevertheless, unionisation in Germany has always been low to medium, and in any case much lower than in the Nordic countries (see Figure 8.1, discussed above). Moreover, it is concentrated in certain categories of members: predominantly men, in permanent jobs, in the industrial and public sectors. One strength of the representative organisations, which facilitated participation in public policy decision-making processes, was their low fragmentation: the confederal organisation DGB (*Deutscher Gewerkschaftsbund*) represents about 6.1 of the 7.4 million members, and within it the two main organisations, *IG-Metall* (metal sector) and *Ver.Di* (services) have over 2 million members each. Also the employers are highly compact, with four main organisations, among which an important role is played by the confederations *DBA (Bundesvereinigung der Deutschen Arbeitgeberverbände)* and *BDI (Bundesverband der Deutschen Industrie)*.

As mentioned, strong participation of the representative organisations in policy-making mechanisms is another feature of this model. This was advantaged by the presence of a system of labour relations regulation based on one side on a combination of the "activist state" – which promoted the activation and inclusion of the social partners – and on the other, interest representation organisations with a quasi-public connotation (Streeck, 1995, 2015; Baccaro & Howell, 2011). With the exception of France the inclusion of trade unions has always been very high in the continental model, despite lower unionisation rates compared to other countries. Crouch (1996) traced the origins of the participation of representative organisations in policy-making back to the period of the Prussian-German state and the fact that the Catholic component was then a minority. This explained why the state never bothered to defend and maintain control of the political space, thus leaving a legacy similar to that of Scandinavia, very different from the case of France, for example. In fact, under Bismarck's government, during the first impetus of industrialisation the German state had opened up to – and cooperated with – organised employer interests.

France differs not only from the perspective of involvement in policy-making processes but also enormously from the point of view of membership (Goetschy & Jobert, 2011). And it is precisely because of its specificity that traditionally it has never been included among continental models of industrial relations (Gumbrell- McCormick & Hyman, 2013; Pedersini, 2014). As far back as the 1980s its unions featured very low membership and predominantly conflictual logics of action, disinclined to the practice of concertation at the national level and with little cooperation from the companies, which rather focused their action on mobilisation. In this panorama, where interest representation was also highly fragmented, the state played a significant role (more than in many other European countries), as a consequence of a tradition of less propensity to share political space, intervening on relevant measures such as the minimum wage (*Salaire Minimum Interprofessional de Croissance – SMIC*), and on issues that in other countries are mostly managed by the social partners (an example is the introduction of the 35-hour working week by legislation). The weakness of the divided and somewhat ineffectual trade unions, was thus matched by the strength of the state.

Moreover, there has also been a significant decline in the importance of mobilisation and workplace elections, the forms of representation that have traditionally constituted an element of legitimacy for French trade unions (Gumbrell-McCormick & Hyman, 2013; Goetschy & Jobert, 2011). Workplace elections have always been less participatory and with an increasing share of elected members from outside the union. In contrast with the trade unions, there is greater unity on the employer side, although here too there is weak participation with regard to the regulatory aspect. This is also because top-down industrialisation, typical of France in the 1980s, went hand in hand with the emergence of larger companies adhering to the US model of human resources management, with authoritative style and rigid division of labour, in order to favour flexible mass production. This model found its strength not so much in associative coordination mechanisms, but in the role of the state on one side and of large individual enterprises on the other. The pressure of companies on employers' associations to create conditions that would bolster productivity and wage moderation was much lower in France than in Germany (Goetschy & Jobert, 2011).

8.2.3 The non-inclusive growth model of the Anglo-Saxon countries

Low and declining unionisation, bargaining chiefly at company and individual level, together with the absence of social concertation are the key features that characterise industrial relations in the Anglo-Saxon model. Hyman (2008) identifies five historical features of the British model of industrial relations. The first has to do with the Anglo-Saxon system of law based on common law, which emphasises the freedom to enter into contracts without state intervention or other forms of regulation, and with which it is consequently difficult to include collective actors. In this context, Hyman notes, state intervention has a "corrective" role that aims to facilitate the functioning of the market, rather than regulatory. The second characteristic is high voluntarism, in the sense that labour relations have few externally imposed constraints (e.g. laws). The third feature concerns collective organisations, which do not have a public status, but are considered private entities in the same way as sports clubs or residents' associations. The fourth feature is that collective bargaining has, since the 1980s, been centred on the company level, with the consequence that industrial relations tend to have a "micro-regulatory" dimension. Finally, the fifth characteristic features a clear distinction between the regulation of wages and working conditions and the regulation of issues related to social protection and citizenship rights, resulting in a clear difference between the regulatory dynamics of industrial relations and those of social and economic policies (Hyman, 2008).

It is also a model that has long been undergoing a disorganised process of further decentralisation of collective bargaining, in a context of declining coverage of national/industry contracts and reduced unionisation. It is no coincidence that Crouch defined the UK model, back in the early 1990s, as a model of " collective bargaining in disintegration" in which "the government rejects almost all triangular cooperation strategies, reduces contacts with unions to a minimum and abandons all income policies" and in which there is a strong shift of the centre of gravity of regulation towards the firm level (Crouch, 1993, 293). The level of inclusion in policy-making processes is traditionally lower here than in other models of capitalism.

The rise to power of Margaret Thatcher and the beginning of the long season of conservative governments engendered an important transition phase for industrial relations in the United Kingdom. As known, the governments of those years waged a battle of multiple interventions in the arena of interest representation that severely debilitated trade unions and employers' associations. One example is the series of Trade Unions Acts (1980, 1982, and 1984), which tightened the regulation of conflict, changed the rules on representation and favoured decentralised bargaining (Marchington et al., 2011; Wren, 2001; Howell, 2007). In those years, some mechanisms for extending collective bargaining were also cancelled. Once again this confirms that the process of shifting towards a more neo-liberal model was directly guided and promoted by the state through targeted policies (Howell, 2007); for the years of conservative governments one can speak of a neo-liberal interventionist state, i.e. the intervention of the state to limit associative regulation in order to increase the role of the market (Marchington, Waddington, & Timming, 2011). The effect is, as mentioned above, and as well illustrated by Hall and Soskice, the collapse of sectoral collective bargaining, a decentralisation of a disorganised kind (Traxler, 1995), and a decline in membership (Hall & Soskice, 2001; Wren, 2001).[2]

Even weaker is the industrial relations system in the United States; the country is often considered a model of "pure and simple de-regulation" of labour relations (Thelen, 2014). Albeit with some variation between states in the federation (it is highest in the northern states), unionisation, as we have seen, is low; higher rates are recorded in the public sector, around 40%, which now gathers more than half of the union membership. Moreover, representation is very fragmented. The *AFL-CIO* (*American Federation of Labor and Congress of Industrial Organisations*), the main organisation, is a federation of more than 50 national/sectoral unions, with extensive power and autonomy in collective bargaining. In 2005, following internal conflicts over the direction of the organisation, some unions, including some of the largest and most active, walked out and formed a new federation, the *CTW* (*Change to Win*); however, in the following years many rejoined the *AFL-CIO* (Masters et al., 2006; Katz & Colvin, 2016). In addition, there are also a number of independent unions, accruing to more than 30 by the late 1990s, which accounted for almost a quarter of the membership. The United States is often mentioned as a case of business unionism, with workers' organisations focused pragmatically on the benefits of their members (Kassalow, 1974).

On the other side, employers' associations have always had little bearing (Adams, 1980). Until the 1970s, the most significant experiences were in some manufacturing sectors, such as metalworking and mining, partly because of the presence of strong trade unions; but even these associations languished gradually, often to the point of disappearing. Attempts at coordination, forging alliances and organisations with the aim of avoiding unionisation have been more consequential (Katz & Wheeler, 2004).

Collective bargaining ensues on a company level, in particular within the plant/workplace, but its coverage is modest (see Figure 8.2). The process of decentralisation intensified in the 1970s with the upsurge of international competition (particularly from Japanese firms) (Katz, 1993; Kochan et al., 1994). Firms saw labour regulations as the problem of their competitiveness and began the "assault" on collective bargaining and trade union rights (Godard, 2009). The process of decentralisation was further strengthened in the following decades, with plant/workplace bargaining gradually supplanting company-level bargaining. Even where this latter exist, as in the automobile sector, plant-level agreements are left with ample scope for variation and *in pejus* deviations (Katz & Colvin, 2016).

Also in the case of the United States, the arrival of governments with a strongly neo-liberal orientation marked an important transition phase, starting with those of Ronald Reagan, who promoted and supported a series of initiatives aimed at reducing the role of trade unions and collective bargaining, constituting an institutional context that offered many opportunities for employers to resist workers' organisations (Western, 1997; Kaufman, 1993). Subsequent attempts, especially in the 1990s, to reverse the trend, to increase union rights and the role of collective bargaining were unsuccessful (see, for instance, the report of the so-called Dunlop Commission), with scarce results. From the 1980s onwards the lack of polity support for industrial relations has been accompanied by an increasing differentiation of regulations at the sub-national level, of individual federal states; an example can be seen in the so-called "right-to-work" laws, which regulate, more often limiting, union prerogatives in the workplace (Katz & Colvin, 2016).

8.2.4 The Mediterranean model of non-inclusive low growth

The role of the state in labour regulation in the Mediterranean countries has been highlighted in many studies, as well as its different functions as mediator of conflicts between the parties, employer in the public sector and regulator through the promulgation of regulations that influence, directly or indirectly, the functioning of industrial relations. However, it should be noted that some of these studies include France among the southern European countries, which, as we have seen, is indeed characterised by a strong prominence of the public actor in a wide range of issues and activities that elsewhere are the domain of the social partners. If we exclude France to focus only on Spain and Italy, we can see that the role of the state is much less marked and, above all, less stable, oscillating between periods of greater and lesser "protagonism".[3] In Italy and Spain, the state has shared more of the political space with the representative organisations compared to France, despite there being no institutionalisation of this involvement, as instead occurred in northern European countries or in continental countries such as Austria and Germany.

As far as unionisation is concerned, the weight of representative organisations compared to other European models is intermediate, with Italy having medium–high unionisation and Spain lower. Worthy of note, however, is the fact that consensus towards industrial relations actors remains high even where unionisation is lower.[4] In both countries there is nonetheless high unionisation in the public sector and a high share of inactive (retired) workers. The high capacity of trade unions to mobilise members is another common aspect. Moreover, while in both Italy and Spain workers' organisations have effectively participated in social concertation practices, it should be underlined that there are components less favourable to involvement in policy-making processes and more hostile to concertation practices, and that at certain stages, these two countries have been characterised by intense social conflict.

The structure of interest representation reveals some differences. In Italy, for instance, it is manifestly fragmented. The employer side encompasses different cleavages, ranging from the sector of activity (agriculture, craft, industry, services) to the size of the company (craft, small, medium–large), to the type of ownership (private capital, cooperatives, etc.); within each cleavage there is further fragmentation, e.g. the representation of the interests of crafts companies is carried out by several associations including *Confartigianato* (Italian representative organisation of Artisanal Handicrafts) and *CNA* (Italian Confederation of Craft Trades and Small- and Medium-Sized Enterprises). Even the trade unions are markedly splintered, with associations that follow a logic of general representation, such as *CGIL* (Italian General Confederation of Labour), *CISL* (Italian Confederation of Workers' Trade Unions), *UIL* (Italian Labour Union), UGL (General Labour Union), and others that represent specific groups of workers.

Other interesting trends emerge examining the characteristics of the relationship mechanisms between the actors. The sectoral level is the most important one in all countries with regard to collective bargaining, although the role of bargaining at the decentralised-firm level has grown in recent years. Bargaining coverage is high (Lampousaki, 2014; Sanz, 2014; Pedersini, 2014). Alongside the high bargaining coverage, however, there has been an increase in the possibility of opting out of collective agreements: in Spain, for example, as early as the mid-1990s Law 11/1994 provided for the possibility of derogating from the national collective agreement.

8.3 Industrial relations in the 2000s

As can be seen from Figure 8.3, some of the historical features of the industrial relations systems in the countries under consideration continue to play an important role in the 2000s. The countries with the highest unionisation are still Sweden and Denmark. In Germany, on the other hand, trade union density is medium–low, although trade unions retain a significant influence in the policy-making process, as we shall see. The United States and France are the two countries with the lowest membership. Collective bargaining coverage is very low in the Anglo-Saxon countries, intermediate in Germany and high in the other countries. Interestingly, France has low unionisation but high coverage, confirming a model of political economy in which the state intervenes with "supplanting" mechanisms, such as the extension of collective baragaining coverage. In this case, therefore, an interesting aspect of the relationship between polity and industrial relations emerges: some typical

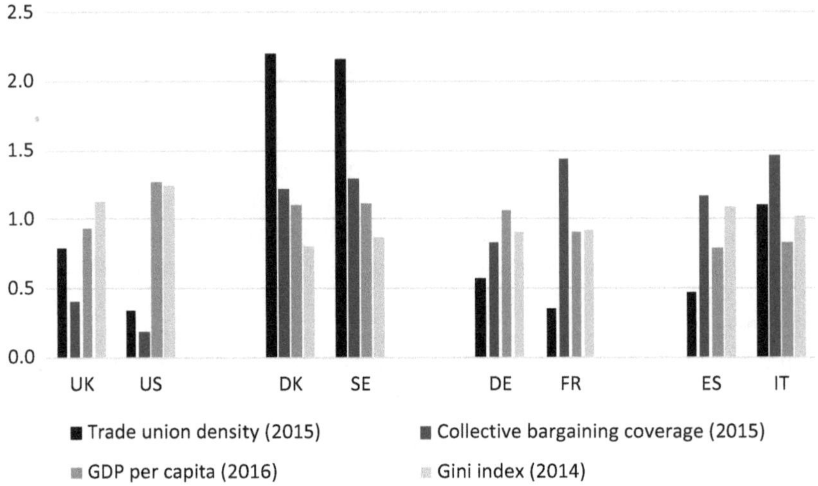

Figure 8.3 Characteristics of industrial relations systems, GDP per capita and Gini index.

Note: Values standardised on the averages of the countries considered.

Source: Elaboration on ICTWSS (OECD & AIAS, 2021) and OECD data.

features of the industrial relations system, such as coverage, can play a positive role in reducing inequality but more for the action of the state than for that of the social partners. More contained in Scandinavia, income inequality remains higher in Anglo-Saxon countries and the Mediterranean, while the level of GDP per capita is higher in Denmark, Sweden, Germany – what is traditionally called coordinated capitalism – but also in the United States.

Unionisation has followed a relatively similar trend in the various countries in the 2000s. A clear decline is evident in some of the cases analysed – especially in coordinated capitalism, but also in the United Kingdom – albeit with different intensities. Yet unionisation has also receded in non-dualistic inclusive growth capitalism, partly because the importance of the Ghent system has declined, following the introduction of new benefit mechanisms that do not require union membership and the progressive growth of non-monetary forms of benefits (Kjellberg, 2006; Van Rie et al., 2011). In Sweden, the unionisation rate shifted from 87% in the early 1990s to 65% in the most recent years and, for the first time, membership among non-manual workers exceeded that of manual workers in 2013 (Arvidsson, 2014). In contrast, the decline in membership was more moderate in Denmark. In Germany, the unionisation rate has never risen above 40%, but there has been a significant downturn for some years now, becoming more acute immediately after reunification: in the period 1992–2000 unionisation halved in the eastern Länder, while in the western Länder it fell to 25%, about 10 percentage points below the average values that had characterised the country until the end of the

1980s (Visser, 2007). In Italy and Spain, unionisation has remained fairly stable. Noteworthy is the negative impact of the recent economic crisis on the consensus and legitimacy of organisations representing workers' interests, especially in Spain, where in the first phase the trade unions were harshly attacked by the *indignados* movement, which held them responsible for having shared many of the reforms that contributed to the flexibilisation of the Spanish labour market.

Analyses of unionisation levels illustrate that there is no association between unionisation and economic dynamism. As already noted, it is possible to identify countries with low membership and high dynamism, such as the United States or Germany, and countries with high membership and high dynamism, such as the Scandinavian countries (Burroni, 2016; Crouch, 2015). Thus, unionisation *per se* does not necessarily play a role in curbing or promoting economic competitiveness; it is rather, as we shall see, the overall structure of the industrial relations system that influences the sign of the relationship between competitiveness and unionisation (Figure 8.4).

With regard to the predominant level of bargaining, also in the 2000s a significant difference persists between the Anglo-Saxon countries and the other countries: in the UK and the US the company level remains, while in the other countries considered it is the sectoral level that holds the fort (see Figure 8.5). In some cases such as Germany, however, there has been a strong increase in the use of open derogation clauses from national contracts. Also in Spain, some recent interventions (in 2010 and 2012) have expanded the room for

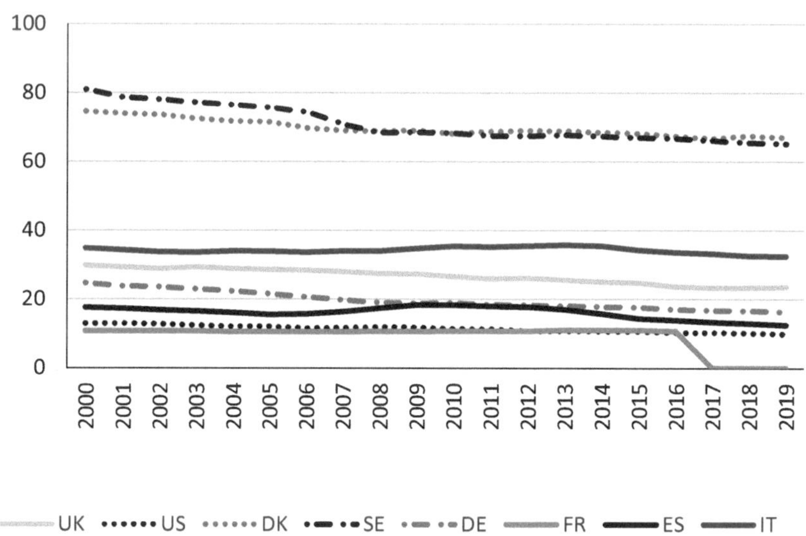

Figure 8.4 Trend of union density, years 2000–2019.

Source: Elaboration on ICTWSS data (OECD & AIAS, 2021).

Table 8.2 Coordination and predominant level of collective bargaining (average values per period)

Country	*Coordination of bargaining*				*Pre-dominant level of bargaining*			
	2000–04	*2005–09*	*2010–14*	*2015–19*	*2000–04*	*2005–09*	*2010–14*	*2015–19*
Denmark	4.0	4.0	4.0	4.0	3.0	3.0	3.0	3.0
Sweden	4.0	4.0	4.0	4.0	3.0	3.0	3.0	3.0
Germany	4.0	4.0	4.0	4.0	3.0	3.0	3.0	3.0
France	2.0	2.0	2.0	2.0	3.0	3.0	3.0	3.0
Spain	2.6	2.8	3.0	3.0	3.6	3.8	3.0	3.0
Italy	3.0	3.0	3.0	3.0	3.0	3.0	3.0	3.0
United Kingdom	2.0	2.0	2.0	2.0	1.0	1.0	1.0	1.0
United States	1.0	1.0	1.0	1.0	1.0	1.0	1.0	1.0

Source: Elaboration on ICTWSS data (OECD & AIAS, 2021).

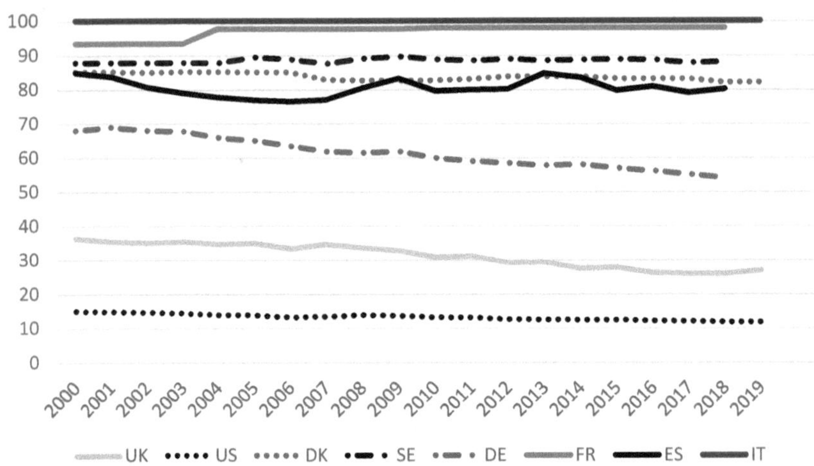

Figure 8.5 Trend in collective bargaining coverage, years 2000–2019.

Source: Elaboration on ICTWSS data (OECD & AIAS, 2021).

manoeuvre for companies that want to break away from the national/sectoral collective agreement: in 2012, 60% of contracts, covering 76% of employees, included exit clauses (Sanz, 2014). Similar clauses have also been introduced in Italy, for example with proximity bargaining, introduced by legislative decree 138/2011, which allows for agreements for certain issues such as responsibilities or working hours, notwithstanding the law and collective bargaining at territorial and individual company level.

On the other hand, also countries with traditionally higher levels of centralisation such as Denmark and Sweden are affected by the trend towards decentralisation of collective bargaining. In the first case, the national interest representation organisations *DA* (*Dansk Arbejdsgiverforening*) and *LO* (*Landsorganisationen i Danmark*) signed two different agreements, the basic agreement (*Hovedaftalen*) and the cooperation agreement (*Samarbejdsaftalen*). These comprise a cross-sectoral regulatory framework (on issues such as procedural rules, organisational rights, how to cooperate at company level, etc.), within which collective bargaining operates, in the sector on wages and work conditions. In turn, these sectoral agreements form the framework within which agreements at company level operate. In the private sector, wages are therefore mainly determined at the company level. This supports the thesis of the importance of the decentralised/firm level of regulation there, but within a framework of organised decentralisation. It is in this context that collective bargaining begins to explore new issues, such as initial and continuous training (Ibsen & Mailand, 2009, 106), supplementary pensions and other welfare measures: thus producing benefits in terms of money and services that, at least in part, compensate for the reduction of some benefits of the public actor (Trampusch, 2007a; 2007b).

In Sweden similar trends can be observed. After representing the example *par excellence* of centralisation, since the 1990s here too a process of decentralisation has been taking hold. For many years, the centralised, cross-sectoral basic agreement (*Saltsjöbaden*, after the place where it was signed in 1938) between the Swedish Confederation of Trade Unions (*LO – Landsorganisationen i Sverige*) and the Swedish Confederation of Employers (*SAF – Svenska Arbetsgivareföreningen*, now *Svenskt Näringsliv*) governed Swedish income policies, favouring wage moderation and solidarity-type redistribution (Bowman, 2014). After the mid-1990s, however, the trend was reversed, with the signing of an agreement on wage setting between trade unions and employers' associations in the manufacturing sectors in 1997. This agreement, which was later reproduced in other sectors, marked the transition to more internal coordination within sectors. However, it is worth underlining that inter-sectoral coordination has also persisted and still supports wage moderation. The high level of centralisation, which still remains a feature of the Swedish model, albeit in a different way (Bowman, 2014), has worked well for a long series of contract renewals (2001, 2004, 2007, and 2010); another agreement was reached in 2011 that fine-tuned some changes aimed precisely at strengthening inter-sectoral coordination. Thus, in Sweden, there has been a process of progressive decentralisation towards the sectoral and company level (Arvidsson, 2014), but this path has taken place within a framework that can be described as one of highly coordinated decentralisation (Anxo & Niklasson, 2008).

Marked decentralisation can also be found in the case of France, where the 2004 reform tweaked the balance between sectoral and company bargaining in favour of the latter. In the French model, traditionally the principle of favouring the worker (*principe de faveur*) applied, implying that a collective

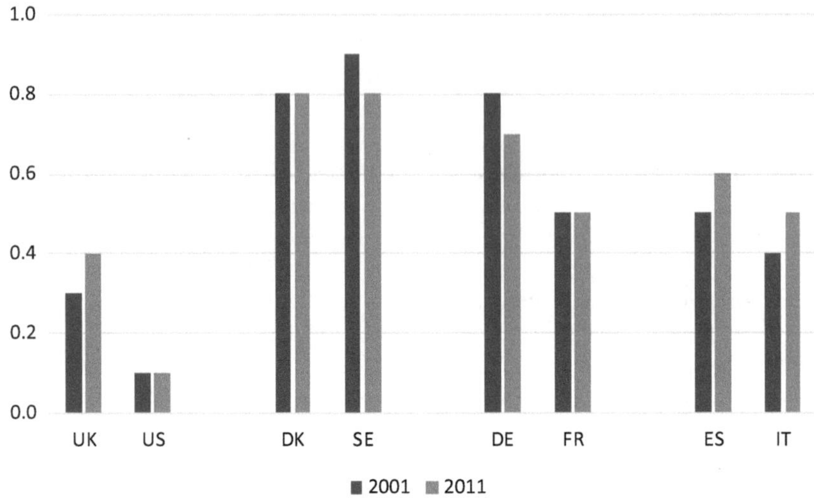

Figure 8.6 Inclusion of trade unions in policymaking.

Source: Crouch (2015).

agreement could not introduce worse rules for workers than those established at a higher level. In essence, company-level bargaining could not decree watered-down rules compared to those laid down in the sectoral contract. Under the 2004 reform (Fillon Act), this principle remains valid for only four issues (minimum wage, grading, supplementary pensions, inter-company or inter-sectoral training funds), while for the rest, company agreements can derogate from the sectoral contract, unless explicitly prevented by the latter. This reform, which had the support of the employers' association (*Mouvement des entreprises de France – Medef*) and some trade unions, significantly changed the relationship between contractual levels, affording substantial autonomy to the company level.

With regard to concertation, the Nordic countries continue to feature a high degree of cooperation among actors and the inclusion of trade unions in policymaking (Figure 8.6). Concertation practices significantly institutionalised in both formal and informal ways are adopted extensively in this model. In the case of Denmark, concertation is pursued with variable geometries and ad-hoc modalities on specific issues, though few formal institutions exist for this practice. In the 2000s there have been many experiences of concertation, from the 2002 labour market reform to the development of the Strategy for Denmark in the Global Economy (*Strategi for Danmark i den globale økonom*), together with the establishment of some tripartite institutions (Jørgensen, 2014). In Sweden, on the other hand, there is a clear-cut separation between government and social partners, with the latter retaining strong autonomy on many issues that are the subject of bargaining, although there is no lack of mechanisms to foster the inclusion of social partners in policy-making processes (Johansson & Talme, 2014). Hence, bargaining practices in the Nordic countries are still well established, tending to manifest more static rather than dynamic traits, despite some recent changes (Mailand, 2009).

Recourse to consultation since the beginning of the 2000s has been either less systematic or decidedly in decline in the other countries under consideration, that is, in the Mediterranean. Scant organisation and inconstancy characterise the use of concertation in Italy (Carrieri, 2008; Regini, 2003). Initially, under the appropriate institutional conditions that facilitated the search for consensual solutions with the social partners on a number of important issues, such as income policies, labour market regulation or the pension system, the low extent of institutionalisation of concertation favoured recourse to this policy-making practice. This was the case for a long period during the 1990s. But then, paradoxically, the pact that at the end of the 1990s aimed to promote an institutionalisation of concertation practices (the Christmas pact of 1998), marked the beginning of its decline (Carrieri, 2008; Cella & Treu, 2009). These trends at national level were nonetheless accompanied by many experiences of concertation at territorial level, where industrial relations actors actively participated in the identification of local development plans (Regalia, 2006; 2015; Cella & Treu, 2009). These (local) negotiations developed in a context of low vertical coordination and institutionalisation. As such, at the local level the typical characteristics of national concertation, i.e. a high degree of voluntarism and instability reappeared, only partly mitigated by the fact that some regions autonomously provided themselves with their own regulation of concertation practices.

Similar indications on the ebb and flow of concertation practices can be seen looking at the case of Spain, where relations with PSOE-led governments from the early 1980s to the mid-1990s were often conflictual (Botti & Field, 2014; Godino & Molina, 2011). In the mid-1990s, however, trilateral concertation picked up momentum. This revival continued into the 2000s, as shown for example by the signing of the Declaration for Social Dialogue in 2004, an agreement that aimed to increase economic competitiveness, productivity, employment, and social cohesion, or the Declaration for the Promotion of the Economy, Employment, Competitiveness, and Social Progress, and the subsequent establishment of the *Comisión de Segumento y Evaluación del Diálogo Social*, made up of the main social partners. However, in the most recent period in Spain, along with experiences of tripartite concertation, such as the pension and welfare reform of 2011, there have been important measures in the field of welfare and the labour market that have not been concerted. These have often been the subject of bitter confrontation with the trade unions, as in the case of hiring freezes and the 5% pay cut for civil servants or the labour market reforms of 2011 and 2012.

Tripartite negotiation practices still do not prevail in the United Kingdom and the United States; likewise, concertation is struggling to establish itself in France, where efforts have been made to strengthen social partner involvement practices. Law 130/2007 on the modernisation of social dialogue, for example, established that it is not possible to modify the labour code without first consulting the social partners; in other words, a limit has been placed on the unilateral regulation of labour relations. However, it should be noted that the outcome of this intervention on subsequent reforms (such as those related to the labour market and vocational training) was uncertain and not fully effective. At the same time, an important reform changed the rules on representation, with the intention of reducing their fragmentation. For many years, all unions could participate in bargaining regardless of the number of members. As early as 2004, legislation stipulated that, in order to be valid, an agreement had to be supported by a majority of the most representative trade unions. Later, the Law for the Reorganisation of Social Democracy and the Reform of Working Time (*Loi pour la rénovation de la démocratie sociale et la réforme du temps de travail*) stipulated that in order to be representative and participate in bargaining, a trade union must have at least 10% of the votes at company level and at least 8% of the members in the sector. Law 288/2014 also intervened on the representation of employers: in order to be considered representative, an association must have companies with at least 8% of the sector's employees as members.

8.4 The relationship between industrial relations, inequality and competitiveness

What is the relationship between industrial relations on the one hand and cohesion and competitiveness on the other? What are the effects of the transformations we have seen in the logic of action of the social partners? How and why can collective bargaining increase competitiveness and bring about a retrenchment of social inequality? And what can the role of social concertation practices be? These questions allow us to explore the contribution of industrial relations to the two dependent variables dealt with in this volume, competitiveness and cohesion, while at the same time shedding light on the role played by the state and its policies.

For the purpose of safeguarding the interests of all workers, in the countries with a non-dualistic inclusive growth trend an encompassing logic of action prevails in trade unions. Here more than in the other countries surveyed, trade unions maintain a high membership, despite a recent decline, and low fragmentation. Also the employer side is characterised by elevated levels of membership and low fragmentation. In this context, while accepting some decentralisation the social partners have continued to rely on centralised collective bargaining, thus contributing to the retrenchment of income disparities. Moreover, at both sectoral and company level, bargaining has taken a proactive approach, touching on relevant issues such as organisational innovation, life-long learning and support for labour productivity. And it has pushed for high wages, thwarting the so-called *dumping* processes, and hence handicapping competition based on a "low cost-low quality" hybrid. Thus, in these countries, the institutionalisation of industrial relations has turned out to be a kind of beneficial constraint, contributing to a shift towards the high road of competitiveness. Also the presence of institutionalised consultation has lent strength to this model, generating an exchange between firms' demands for flexibility, workers' security, and the competitiveness of the economic system. Policies to make the labour market more flexible have been concerted, and likewise the development of an adequate network of guarantees for workers exposed to flexibility, active policies to promote the matching of labour supply and demand, and massive investment in education policies and life-long learning. In this way, industrial relations have favoured the emerging of a welfare system defined as a "productive factor", i.e. a system that maintains high labour protection, but which at the same time develops individualised services that underpin a dynamic remodelling of firms and workers to the changing needs of the markets. It is precisely the increased security for firms and their workers that has endorsed the "release" of innovation resources (Mjøset, 2011; Miettinen, 2013; Kristensen & Lilja, 2011).

Lastly, as mentioned, in this case concertation has advocated extensive investment in training policies, reinforcing the availability of advanced and specific skills, widely relied on by high-tech firms (Figure 8.7).

In essence, therefore, consultation and the involvement of interest representation organisations, which are decidedly sensitive to the issue of competitiveness, have helped to develop effective development policies that have given rise to important collective assets, which, together with the services offered by an efficient administrative machine, have supported innovation activities. Participatory models of industrial relations at the enterprise level have increased the involvement and productivity of a highly professional workforce, which is also the result of massive public investment in education and training. All these elements have contributed to promoting the adoption of strategies aimed at an "high road" to competitiveness and economic development (Figure 8.7).

In contrast, two different paths emerge in the continental model. The first is closer to coordinated capitalism, as with Germany (Figure 8.8), where there are trade unions with medium–low membership but low fragmentation, medium–strong employer associations and an activist state. Sectoral bargaining continues to be very important, although opt-out clauses have increased in recent years. At the same time, the leverage of trade unions and employers' organisations on politics continues to be significant. Here, industrial relations have managed to sustain medium-high productivity. Participatory models implemented at the enterprise level, together with greater decentralisation of regulation and policies for promoting innovation, have led to an enhancement

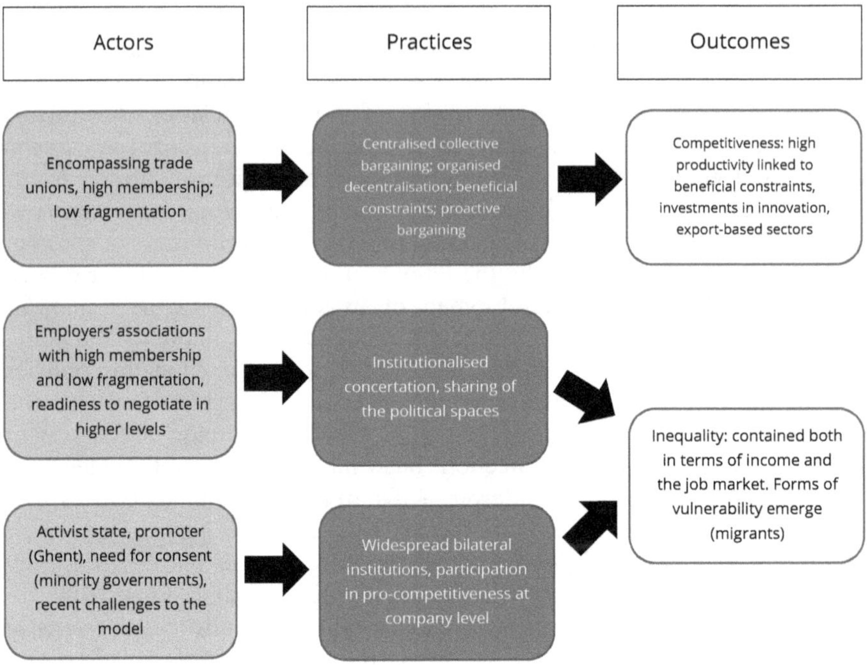

Figure 8.7 Industrial relations, competitiveness, and inequality in countries with inclusive egalitarian growth.

in labour productivity. By means of consultation and coordination of industrial relations actors, the support of a training system that offers targeted skills in line with the needs of the production system has also been essential. Nevertheless, while collaboration at the sector and company level has, on the one hand, afforded stabilisation and security for some segments of the labour force, in particular for professional figures strategic and necessary (or considered as such) to sustain productivity, on the other, it has resulted in the acceptance of an increasing recourse to outsourcing practices, especially of low-skilled services, to providers with lower costs, and to non-standard employment relationships, in particular for the weaker segments of the labour market (on this subject see Chapter 9). A different situation emerges in France (Figure 8.9), where trade unions continue to be characterised by a very low membership, associated with a more pronounced propensity towards social mobilisation rather than cooperation. Representation is also characterised by medium to high fragmentation, which further reduces the bearing of the social partners. Collective bargaining remains weak, although it maintains a high degree of coverage thanks to procedures for its extension by legislation. In this context, the state plays a substitutive role for the social partners

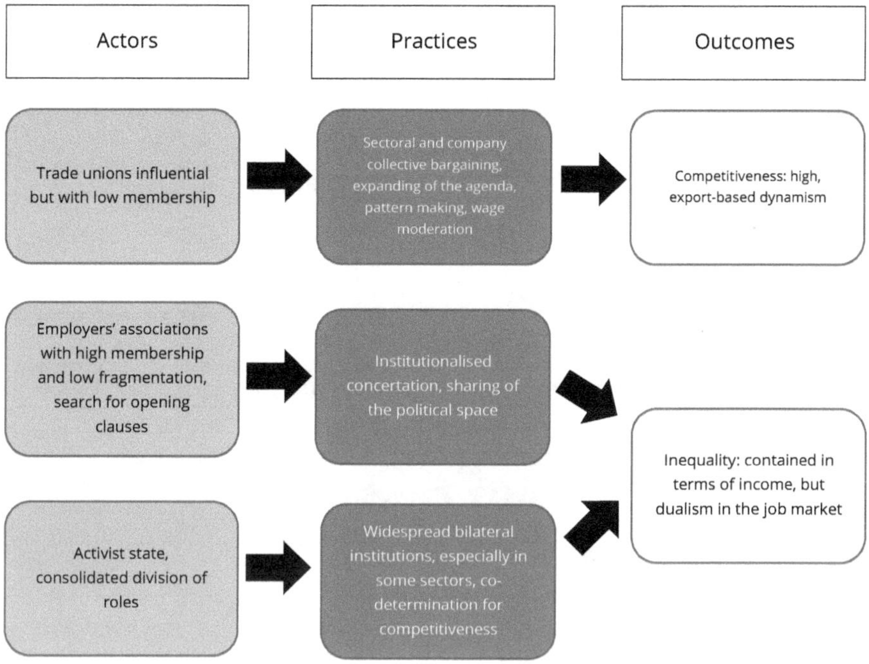

Figure 8.8 **Industrial relations, competitiveness, and inequality in countries with dualistic inclusive growth – the case of Germany.**

and, as we have pointed out, even the interventions aimed at promoting institutionalised forms of concertation seem to have not changed the main features of the case in this country.

Conversely, in the Anglo-Saxon model (Figure 8.10) trade unions have a medium-sized membership, even low in the United States and on the wane. Also the employers' associations have low membership, with a high degree of fragmentation. Collective bargaining is conducted mainly at company, workplace or individual level and the state does not intervene to buttress the industrial relations arena. In such a pluralist model, interest organisations have developed in a kind of "free market organisation", with no participation in the political space, meaning that recourse to concertation is practically non-existent. In the United Kingdom, the production system has been characterised by low productivity, while in the United States productivity has been high almost exclusively in the new technology sectors, often dominated by large companies. As far as inequality is concerned, the low weight of industrial relations is associated with weak welfare policies, as well as a higher presence of low status, poor, vulnerable work, and high disparities in income and socio-economic well-being. The contraction of union membership, the

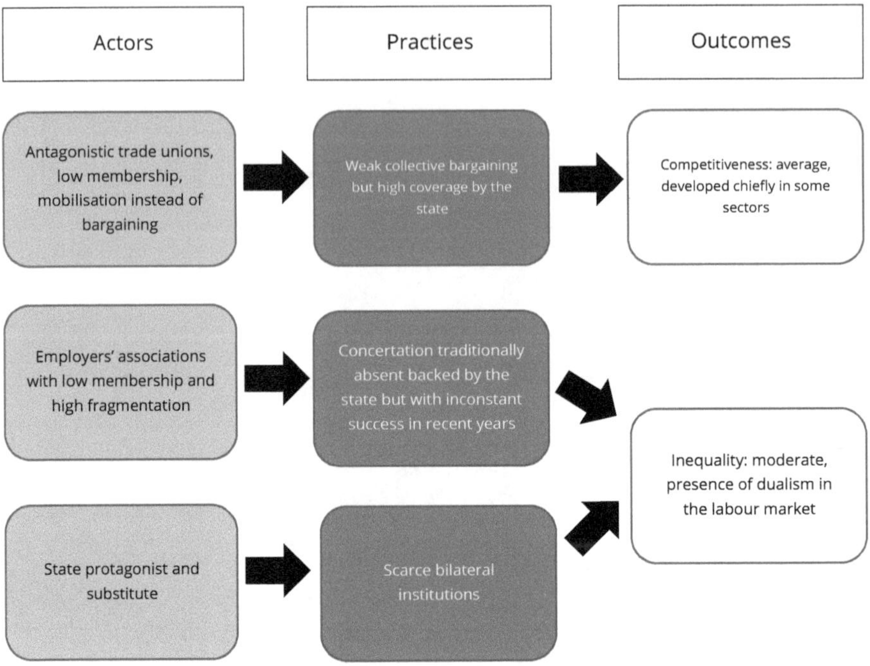

Figure 8.9 Industrial relations, competitiveness, and inequality in high-growth inclusive dualistic countries – the case of France.

extensive power of entrepreneurs to hire and fire, the low presence of workers' representatives in the workplace, also due to the lack of obligations to do so, the lower cohesion and coordination among trade unions, all have led to a long season of wage moderation, but without significant growth in labour productivity (Hall, 2007), save in the high-tech sectors (see Chapter 2).

Lastly, the Mediterranean model (Figure 8.11). While in the 1990s concertation afforded the possibility of a broad set of reforms leading towards labour flexibility and wage moderation, in the 2000s there was an about-face in all the Mediterranean countries, with concertation playing an increasingly marginal role (especially in Italy and Spain). The national structure of political economy did not favour an upward shift in the competitive strategies of enterprises, with few autonomous resources to make the necessary investments, mainly because of the small average company size, and hence these had to rely on collective goods and external economies produced by other actors. In this context, there was very little room for manoeuvre for industrial relations actors. As far as labour regulation is concerned, politics has tried more to promote competitiveness with labour market reforms, which, however, have not focused on training and active policies but on a marked flexibilisation,

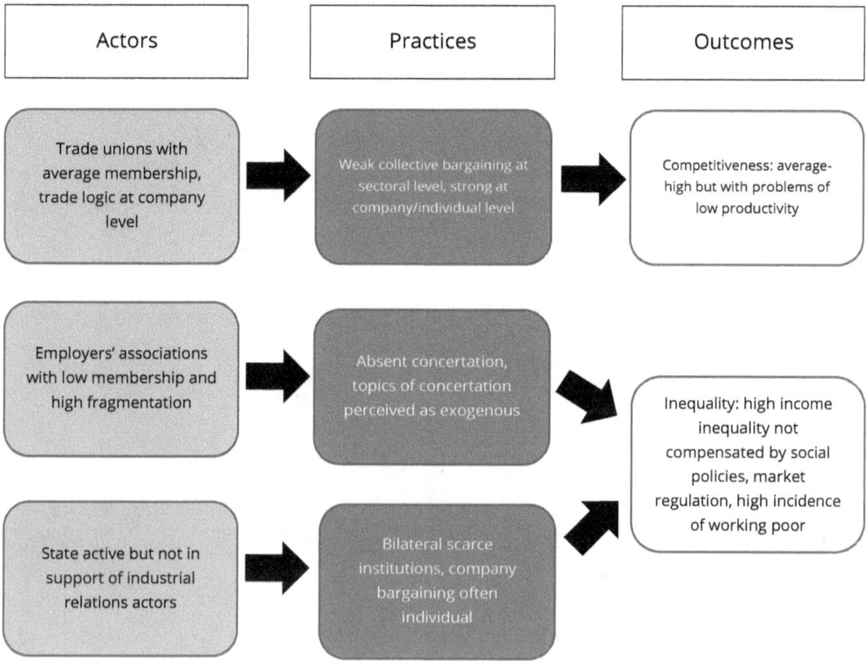

Figure 8.10 **Industrial relations, competitiveness, and inequality in non-inclusive medium growth countries – the case of the UK.**

without favouring the increase of productivity and the shift upwards. From this viewpoint, the industrial relations system, in turn, did not assist productivity growth, also because of the low recourse to decentralised bargaining, carried out often with either downward or defensive aims, even in the years preceding the crisis, instead of proactively, i.e. in support of reorganisations with the aim of increasing innovation and product quality. Moreover, the high wage moderation indulged the illusion of cost competitiveness, up to a certain point. With regard to inequality, the 2007/08 crisis reinforced the climate of "permanent austerity" (Pierson, 1998), especially in Mediterranean capitalist countries, with higher public debt, more dependent on external financial support and with more stringent public finance control requirements. This hindered the development of reforms of welfare systems that would increase their efficiency and their capacity to protect the various social groups from old and new risks, also complicating the adoption of interventions under the banner of social investment, much encouraged by the European Commission. The pressures of the so-called Troika (including the Commission itself) for an economic and financial adjustment pushed in the opposite direction, as shown, for example, by the agreements signed together with the governments

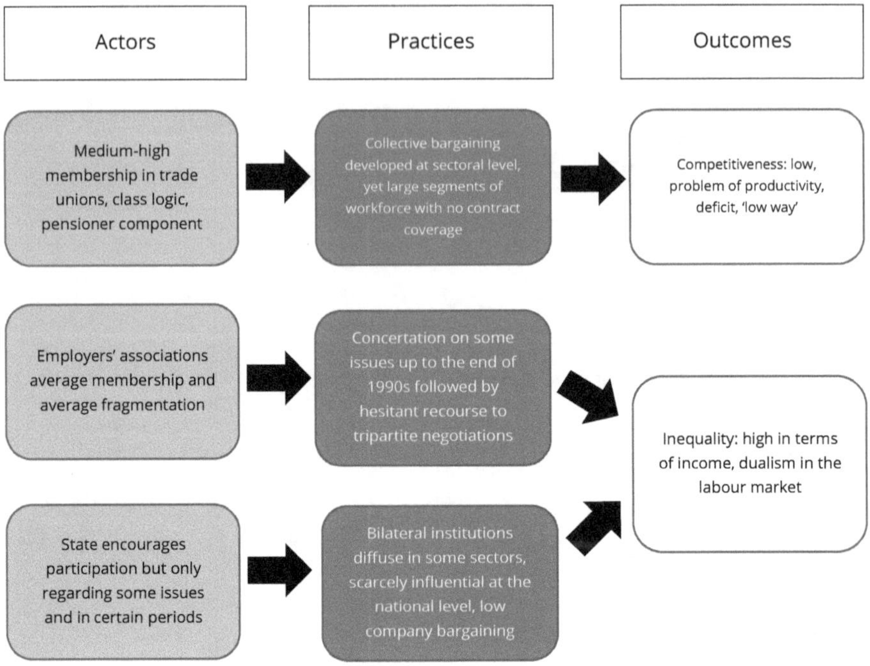

Figure 8.11 Industrial relations, competitiveness, and inequality in non-inclusive low growth countries – the case of Italy.

of Greece and Portugal. The resulting combination of measures concerning the labour market and the welfare state significantly increased flexibility, yet without redressing the balance with new forms of security (as strongly demanded by trade unions), as such creating significant criticalities for the maintenance of social cohesion.

8.5 New challenges

In more recent years the institutions of industrial relations have come under more intense pressure. Recent studies have emphasised the pressures arising from the financialisation of firms and increased competition (internationally), and especially from what has been termed "marketisation", i.e. the extension of price/cost-based competition (Greer & Doellgast, 2017: Larsen, Mailand, & Schulten, 2019). These fuel de-verticalisation processes of firms and fragmentation of "value chains". Outsourcing practices intensify, including online outsourcing via digital platforms (Drahokoupil, 2015; Haidar & Keune, 2021), which often create complex inter-organisational networks for the production of goods/services, with workers and trade unions trapped in the relationships/conflicts between "formal" employers (the legal owners of labour relations) and "substantive" employers (those who use the labour provision or its outcomes) (Marchington et al., 2005; Havard et al., 2009; Dorigatti, 2015). It also extends the use of non-standard employment relationships and self-employment in its various configurations, including partial and false self-employment (Eichhorst & Marx, 2015; Eurofound, 2020). In other words, attempts by firms to exit from the regulations prevailing in the sector/country and first and foremost from collective bargaining become more frequent (Arrowsmith & Pulignano, 2013; Greer & Doellgast, 2017), in search of looser regulations, more advantageous for the employer. Various studies have thus looked at the expansion of labour force segments not covered by representation and/or collective bargaining. But in addition to decreasing contractual coverage, its segmentation is also increasing, with the multiplication of the number of competing contracts (even at national level), providing different levels of protection, often introducing new possibilities for dumping in terms and conditions of work (Leonardi & Pedersini, 2018; Godino & Molina, 2019).

In addition to this trend there is the persistent pressure to decentralise collective bargaining in favour of the company level, with the possibility to deviate from conditions and terms set at the national/sectoral level (European Commission, 2015; Leonardi & Pedersini, 2018). But in this case it has been mainly national governments who push for it (Bordogna & Pedersini, 2019). As has been observed, a "new" element of the post-crisis years is the unilateral intervention of governments in industrial relations, no longer with the aim, as happened in the past, of supporting the autonomy of social partners and collective bargaining, but with the aim of replacing, limiting, excluding industrial relations processes (Pedersini, 2014). Many interventions in this direction have been carried out under pressure from supranational institutions, such as the European Commission, the European Central Bank, and the International Monetary Fund, which are strongly convinced of the need to reduce the role of industrial relations, especially in wage setting processes. Governments have promoted "corrective" measures chiefly in countries under the strongest pressure for economic adjustment, such as Greece, Portugal, Spain, and Ireland, but also Italy and France: more frequently, mechanisms for extending collective bargaining and wage indexation have been devitalised. Furthermore there has been a push for a decentralisation of bargaining, extending opting-out clauses, derogation clauses, expanding the possibilities for decentralised company-level contracts to envisage less favourable terms and conditions than those established by national/sectoral agreements (Marginson & Welz, 2014; Marginson, 2015; Guardiancich & Molina, 2017; Leonardi & Pedersini, 2018). State interventionism on industrial relations issues has been particularly intense in the public sector, where it has promoted a shift towards greater unilateralism (Bach & Pedersini, 2013; Keune, Ramos Martín, & Mailand, 2020).

Nonetheless, the growing pressures on industrial relations institutions should also be to the "cultural change" represented by the spread of neo-liberal ideas (Streeck, 2008) and by the prevailing of a discourse based on a deep faith in market efficiency, capital mobility, and in individuals' responsibility for their employment and economic situation (Keune & Serrano, 2014). In such a discourse, social actors, especially trade unions, and industrial relations are portrayed as obstacles to economic and employment growth. These ideas have conditioned choices and behaviours of a large part of political and socio-economic actors (Streeck, 2008; Crouch, 2011). Starting from business schools, they have prevailed in the academic debate, among governments and in international organisations, including the European Union (see, for example, European Commission, 2012)[5].

The increasing spread, in most European countries, of pro-populist orientations and the emergence of populist or neo-populist parties and movements have triggered further tensions for industrial relations actors and institutions (Gidron & Hall, 2017; Norris & Inglehart, 2018). The neo-populist discourse is based on a simplified view of society, which divides it into two homogeneous and antagonistic groups: on the one hand the "population", composed of the vast majority of people, and on the other hand the "corrupt elites". A central element of this discourse is dis-intermediation in the political-institutional and socio-economic spheres. As has been observed, neo-populist parties and movements affirm the irrelevance, if not even the harmfulness, of intermediate representative bodies, including trade unions and business associations, advocating instead the direct relationship between "the people" and the leader and his party/government (Cella, 2018; Pavolini, 2018). In such a perspective, social actors, social dialogue, and collective bargaining occupy an entirely marginal space. And, in many cases, a rhetoric against industrial relations and, in particular, against trade unions, has been disseminated – and has gained wide acceptance.

8.6 Concluding remarks

The institutions of industrial relations, starting with collective collective bargaining, are under intense pressure. "New" sources of pressure have been added to the "old" examined in the previous pages, linked to the consequences of the "great recession" and above all to the choices and initiatives of political and socio-economic actors to deal with them (Pedersini, 2014). These thrusts of pressure, taken together, threaten the structures of industrial relations, from the level of coordination and coverage of collective bargaining, to unionisation and workers' representative capacity. They also challenge the ability of industrial relations institutions and actors to influence the dependent variables considered in this volume, to promote economic dynamism and equality.

However, despite the pressures to which they are subjected and some signs of weakening, industrial relations systems have resisted in the majority of European countries, showing sound resilience, maintaining their key characteristics, with an important effect of path dependency, of continuity with the institutional models developed in previous decades. In fact, the typologies based on differences in the density of interest representation organisations, in the structure and degree of coverage of collective bargaining, in the involvement of social actors in public decisions, etc., still seem to hold out. (Pedersini, 2014; Marginson & Welz, 2014; Guadiancich & Molina, 2017; Leonardi & Pedersini, 2018). But what is more important to underline is that – in a framework characterised by the common trajectory towards a (re)enlargement of asymmetries between workers and employers (Arrowsmith & Pulignano, 2013; Baccaro & Howell, 2017) – more structured industrial relations systems, with strong and encompassing trade unions, more inclusive collective bargaining, have been able to better cope with the pushes towards labour segmentation, and to contain the deterioration of working conditions, the increase in precarious situations, gaps in social protection and unequal treatment. These trends have been analysed by many empirical studies (Antón, Fernández-Macías, & Muñoz de Bustillo, 2012; Prosser, 2016; Grimshaw et al., 2016; Fernández-Macías & Arranz-Muñoz, 2017). These industrial relations systems, we can say, have managed to more effectively contain the trend of increasing inequality while allowing for a certain economic dynamism at the same time – a topic that appears to be of great relevance with the intensification of economic crises, technological transformations, in particular those summarised by the term "digitalisation", new trends towards the fragmentation of production systems and the expansion of the so-called "*gig economy*".

Notes

1 This institutional set-up may favour a negotiated and incremental reformism that ensures, on the one hand, the curbing of radical institutional change, and on the other reforms that are unlikely to create the conditions for a very marked transformation of the constitutive features of some important institutional arenas such as labour, welfare, or industrial relations.
2 Some scholars also point to internal causes of trade union decline in the UK, including: low ability to recruit qualified union staff, low ability to effectively offer benefits to members, low commitment of union leaders to effective organisational reform, and low ability to adapt to the changing needs of workers in terms of representation (Marchington et al., 2011).
3 For example, during the 1990s there was a massive recourse to concertation in both Italy and Spain, with the state often delegating to the social partners some important decisions in the field of the labour market and welfare (Alacevich, 2004). Similarly, at the local level one can find important experiences of sharing political space, especially in more dynamic regions such as Catalonia or the regions of the Third Italy (Regalia, 2006; 2015).

4 See for example, with regard to Spain, the analyses on the elections of works councils in workplaces (Botti & Field, 2013; Godino & Romo, 2011).
5 By now there is broad consensus among scholars on the relevant influence that the introduction in 2011 of the so-called European Semester system, for example, had in promoting, through analyses and recommendations to member countries, a weakening of industrial relations institutions, in particular collective bargaining (Marginson, 2015; Marginson & Welz, 2014; Bongelli, 2018; Bordogna & Pedersini, 2019).

References

Adams, R.J. (1980). *Industrial Relations Systems in Europe and North America.* Hamilton, Ontario: McMaster University

Alacevich, F. (2004). *Promuovere il dialogo sociale. le conseguenze dell'Europa sulla regolazione del lavoro*. Firenze: Firenze University Press.

Antón JI, Fernández Macias, E., & and Muñoz de Bustillo, R. (2012). Identifying bad-quality jobs across Europe. In C. Warhust, F. Carré, P. Findlay, & C. Tilly (Eds) *Are bad jobs inevitable? Trends, determinants and responses to job quality in the twenty-first century* (pp. 25–44), London: Palgrave Macmillan.

Anxo, D. & Niklasson, H. (2008). *The Swedish model: Revival after the turbulent 1990s?*. Geneva: ILO.

Arrowsmith, J. & Pulignano, V. (2013). *The transformation of employment relations in Europe: Institutions and outcomes in the age of globalization.* New York-London: Routledge

Arvidsson, M. (2014). *Changes to the Swedish model: Trade unions under pressure.* Berlin: Friedrich-Ebert-Stiftung.

Baccaro, L. & Howell, C. (2017). *Trajectories of neoliberal transformation: European industrial relations since the 1970s*. Cambridge: Cambridge University Press.

Baccaro, L. & Howell, C. (2011). A common neoliberal trajectory: The transformation of industrial relations in advanced capitalism. *Politics & Society*, 39(4), 521–563. doi:10.1177/0032329211420082

Bach, S. & Pedersini, R. (2013). The consequences of the crisis for public sector industrial relations. In European Commission (Eds), *Industrial relations in Europe 2012* (pp. 129–161). Luxembourg: Publications Office of the European Union.

Bergholm, T. & Bieler, A. (2013). Globalization and the erosion of the Nordic model: A Swedish-Finnish comparison. *European Journal of Industrial Relations*, 19(1), 55–70. doi:10.1177/0959680112474747

Bongelli, K. (2018). The impact of the European Semester on collective bargaining and wages in recent years. In S. Leonardi & R. Pedersini, *Multi-employer Bargaining under pressure: Decentralisation trends in five European countries* (pp. 263–289). Brussels: ETUI.

Bordogna, L. & R. Pedersini (2019). *Relazioni industriali: L'esperienza italiana nel contesto internazionale*. Bologna: Il Mulino.

Botti, A. & Field, B.N. (2014) (Eds). *La Spagna di Rajoy*. Bologna: Il Mulino.

Bowman, J.R. (2014). *Capitalisms compared: Welfare, work, and business*. London: Sage.

Burroni, L. (2016). *Capitalismi a confronto, Istituzioni & regolazione dell'economia nei paesi europei*. Bologna: Il Mulino.

Burroni, L. & Scalise, G. (2017). Quando gli attori contano: Agency, eredità storiche e istituzioni nei modelli di capitalismo. Stato e Mercato, 109, 133–172.

Carrieri, M. (2008). *L'altalena della concertazione Patti & accordi italiani in prospettiva europea*. Rome: Donzelli.

Cella, G.P. (2018). Il popolo fra invenzione & finzione. *Stato & mercato*, 112, 3–36. doi:10.1425/89848

Cella, G.P. & Treu, T. (2009). *Relazioni industriali & contrattazione collettiva*. Bologna: Il Mulino.

Crouch, C. (1993). *Industrial relations and european state traditions*. Oxford: Clarendon.

Crouch, C. (1996). *Relazioni industriali nella storia politica europea*. Rome: Ediesse.

Crouch, C. (2011). *The strange non-death of neoliberalism*. Cambridge: Polity Press.

Crouch, C. (2015). *Governing social risks in post-crisis Europe*. Cheltenham: Edward Elgar.

Dølvik, J.E. (2009). Percorsi nordici di trasformazione del mercato del lavoro. *Stato & Mercato*, 86, 217–234.

Dorigatti, L. (2015). Strategie di rappresentanza del lavoro nelle catene del valore: al di là della distinzione fra datore di lavoro "formale" & "ostanziale". *Stato & mercato*, 104, pp. 281–307.

Drahokoupil, J. (2015). *The outsourcing challenge: Organizing workers across fragmented production networks*. Brussels: ETUI.

Eichhorst, W. & Marx, P. (2015) (Eds). *Non-standard employment in post-industrial labour markets*. Cheltenham: Edward Elgar.

Eurofound (2020). *Labour market change: Trends and policy approaches towards flexibilisation, challenges and prospects in the EU series*. Luxembourg: Publications Office of the European Union.

European Commission (2012). *Labour market developments in Europe, 2012*. Brussels, Report of the Directorate-General for Economic and Financial Affairs, European Economy, n. 5/2012.

European Commission (2015). *Industrial relations in Europe 2014*. Luxembourg: Publications Office of the European Union.

Fernández-Macías, E. & Arranz-Muñoz, J. M. (2017). *Occupational change and wage inequality: European job monitor 2017*. Luxemburg: Eurofound.

Gidron, N. & Hall, P.A. (2017). The politics of social status: Economic and cultural roots of the populist right. *The British Journal of Sociology*, 68(S1), S57–S84. doi:10.1111/1468-4446.12319

Godard, J. (2009). The exceptional decline of the American labor movement. *Industrial and Labor Relations Review*, 63(1), 82–108. doi:10.1177/001979390906300105

Godino, A. & Molina, O. (2011). *Failed remedies and implications of the economic crisis in Spain*. OSE Research Paper n. 6.

Godino, A. & Molina, O. (2019). *The impact of outsourcing on collective bargaining coverage: A comparative analysis in six countries*. Research Report – RECOVER project. (https://ddd.uab.cat/record/202675).

Goetschy, J. & Jobert, A. (2011). Employment relations in France. In G.J. Bamber, R.D. Lansbury, & N. Wailes (Eds), *International and comparative employment relations: Globalization and change (Fifth Edition)* (pp. 176–210). London: Sage.

Greer, I. & Doellgast, V. (2017). Marketization, inequality, and institutional change: Toward a new framework for comparative employment relations. *Journal of Industrial Relations* 59(2), 192–208. doi:10.1177/0022185616673685.

Grimshaw, D., Johnson, M., Rubery, J., & Keizer, A. (2016). *Reducing precarious work: Protective gaps and the role of social dialogue in Europe*. Manchester: European Work and Employment Research Centre, University of Manchester.

Guardiancich, I. & Molina, O. (Eds) (2017). *Talking through the crisis: Social dialogue and industrial relations trends in selected EU countries.* Geneva: ILO

Gumbrell-McCormick, R. & Hyman, R. (2013). *Trade unions in Western Europe: Hard times, hard choices*. Oxford: Oxford University Press.

Haidar, J. & Keune, M. (Eds) (2021). *Work and labour relations in global platform capitalism*. Cheltenham: Edward Elgar

Hall, P.A. (2007). The evolution of varieties of capitalism in Europe. In B. Hancké, M. Rhodes & M. Thatcher (Eds), *Beyond Varieties of Capitalism: Conflict, Contradictions, and Complementarities in the European Economy*. Oxford: Oxford University Press.

Hall, P.A. & Soskice, D. (2001) (Eds). *Varieties of capitalism: The institutional foundations of comparative advantage*. Oxford, Oxford University Press.

Hassel, A. (2011). *The paradox of liberalization – understanding dualism and the recovery of the german political economy*. LSE 'Europe in Question' Discussion Paper n. 42.

Havard, C., Rorive, B., & Sobczak, A. (2009). Client, employer and employee: Mapping a complex triangulation. *European Journal of Industrial Relations*, 15(3), 257–276. doi:10.1177/0959680109339406

Howell, C. (2007). The British variety of capitalism: Institutional change, industrial relations and British politics. *British Politics*, 2 (2), 239–263. doi:10.1057

Hyman, R. (2008). *Britain and the European social model: Capitalism against capitalism?* IES Working Paper n. WP19.

Ibsen, C.L. & Mailand, M. (2009). *Flexicurity and collective bargaining – balancing acts across sectors and countries*. FAOS Forskningsnotat 102.

Johansson, E. & Talme, L. (2014). *Sweden: Industrial relations profile*. Dublin: European Foundation for the Improvement of Living and Working Conditions.

Jørgensen, C. (2014). *Denmark: Industrial relations profile*. Dublin: European Foundation for the Improvement of Living and Working Conditions.

Kassalow, E.M. (1974). The development of western labor movements: Some comparative considerations. In L.G. Reynolds, S.A. Masters, & C. Moser (Eds), *Readings in labor economics and labor relations* (pp. 61–88). Engelwood Cliffs, NJ: Prentice-Hall

Katz, H. & Wheeler, H. (2004). Employment relations in the United States of America. In G. Bamber, R. Lansbury & N. Wailes, *International and comparative employment relations: Globalisation and the developed market economies* (pp. 67–90). London: Sage

Katz, H.C. (1993). The decentralization of collective bargaining: A literature review and comparative analysis. *Industrial and Labor Relations Review*, 47(1), 3–22

Katz H.C. & Colvin A.J.S. (2016). *Employment relations in the United States*. In G. Bamber, R. Lansbury, N. Wailes & C.F. Wright (Eds), *International and comparative employment relations: National regulation, global changes* (pp. 62–87). London: Sage.

Katzenstein, P. (1985). *Small states in world markets: Industrial policy in Europe*. Cornell: Cornell University Press.

Kaufman, B.E. (1993). *The origins and evolutions in the field of Industrial Relations in the United States*. Ithaca: Cornell University Press

Keller, B.K. & Kirsch, A. (2011). Employment relations in Germany. In G. Bamber, R. Lansbury & N. Wailes, *International and comparative employment*

relations: Globalisation and the developed market economies (Fifth Edition) (pp. 176–253). London: Sage.
Keune, M. & Serrano, A. (2014) (Eds). *Deconstructing flexicurity and developing alternative approaches: Towards new concepts and approaches for employment and social policy*. London: Routledge.
Keune, M., Ramos Martìn, N., & Mailand, M. (2020). *Working under pressure: Employment, job quality and labour relations in the public sector in Europe since the crisis*. Brussels: ETUI
Kjellberg, A. (2006). The Swedish unemployment insurance: Will the Ghent system survive? *Transfer*, 12(1), 87–98. doi:10.1177/102425890601200109
Kochan, T.A., Katz, H.C. & McKersie, R.B. (1994). *The transformation of American industrial relations*. Ithaca, NY: Cornell University Press
Kristensen, P.H. & Lilja, K. (2011) (Eds). *Nordic capitalism and globalization: New forms of economic organization and welfare institutions*. Oxford: Oxford University Press.
Lampousaki, S. (2014). *Greece: Industrial relations profile*, www.eurofound.europa.eu/it/default/observatories/eurwork
Larsen, T.P., Mailand, M., & Schulten, T. (2019). Good intentions meet harsh realities: Social dialogue and precarious work in industrial cleaning. *Economic and Industrial Democracy*. https://doi.org/10.1177/0143831X19880265
Leonardi, S. & Pedersini, R. (2018). *Multi-employer bargaining under pressure: Decentralisation trends in five European countries*. Brussels: ETUI.
Mailand, M. (2009). *Corporatism in Denmark and Norway – Yet another century of Scandinavian corporatism?*, WSI Mitteilungen: Monatszeitschrift des Wirtschafts- und Sozialwissenschaftlichen Instituts in der Hans-Böckler-Stiftung, n. 1/2009.
Manow, P. (2009). Electoral rules, class coalitions and welfare state regimes, or how to explain Esping-Andersen with Stein Rokkan. *Socio-Economic Review*, 7(1), 123–144. doi:10.1093/ser/mwn022
Marchington, M., Grimshaw, D., Rubery, J., & Willmott, H. (2005). *Fragmenting work: Blurring organizational boundaries and disordering hierarchies*. Oxford: Oxford University Press.
Marchington, M., Waddington, J., & Timming, A (2011). Employment relations in Britain. In G. Bamber, R. Lansbury, & N. Wailes, *International and comparative employment relations: Globalisation and the developed market economies (Fifth Edition)* (pp. 176–253). London: Sage.
Marginson, P. & Weltz, C (2014). *Changes to wage-setting mechanisms in the context of the crisis and the EU's new economic governance regime*. Dublin: Eurofound
Marginson, Paul (2015). Coordinated bargaining in Europe: From incremental corrosion to frontal assault? *European Journal of Industrial Relations* 21(2): 97–114. doi:10.1177/0959680114530241
Martin, C.J. & Swank, D. (2012). *The political construction of business interests: Coordination, growth, and equality*. Cambridge: Cambridge University Press.
Masters, M.F., Gibney, R., & Zagenczyk, T. (2006). The AFL- CIO v. CTW: The competing visions, strategies and structures. *Journal of Labor Research*, 27(4). 473–504.
Miettinen, R. (2013). *Innovation, human capabilities and democracy: Towards an enabling welfare state*, Oxford, Oxford University Press.
Mjøset, L. (2011). Nordic political economy after financial deregulation: Banking crises, economic experts, and the role of neoliberalism. In L. Mjøset (Ed.). *The Nordic model of capitalism* (pp. 365–420). Bingley, Emerald.

Norris, P. & Inglehart, R. (2018). *Cultural backlash and the rise of populism: Trump, Brexit, and the rise of authoritarianism populism.* New York: Cambridge University Press.

OECD and AIAS (2021). *Institutional characteristics of trade unions, wage setting, state intervention and social pacts.* Paris: OECD Publishing.

Pasquino, G. (2009). *Nuovo corso di scienza politica.* Bologna: Il Mulino.

Pavolini, E. (2018). Il populismo fra offerta politica & radici socio-economiche. *Stato & Mercato*, 1, 127–140. doi:10.1425/89853

Pedersini, R. (2014). European industrial relations between old and new trends. *Stato & Mercato*, 3, 341–368.

Pierson, P. (1998). Irresistible forces, immovable objects: Post-industrial welfare states. *Journal of European Public Policy*, 4, 539–560.

Prosser, T. (2016). Dualization or liberalization? Investigating precarious work in eight European countries. *Work, Employment and Society*, 30(6), 949–965. doi:10.1177/0950017015609036

Regalia, I. (2006). *Regulating new forms of employment: Local experiments and social innovation in Europe*. London: Routledge

Regalia, I. (2015). Oltre la contrattazione di secondo livello: Note sulla concertazione a livello locale. *Rivista Giuridica del Lavoro & della Previdenza Sociale*, 46(1), 97–111.

Regini, M. (2003). *Modelli di capitalismo: Le risposte europee alla sfida della globalizzazione*. Rome–Bari: Laterza.

Sanz, P. (2014). *Spain: Industrial relations profile*, www.eurofound.europa.eu/it/default/observatories/eurwork

Streeck, W. (1992). *Social institutions and economic performance*. London: Sage.

Streeck, W. (1995). *German capitalism: Does it exist? Can it survive?*. MPIFG Working Paper, n. 5.

Streek, W. (1997). Beneficial constraints: On the economic limits of rational voluntarism. In R.J. Hollingsworth & R. Boyer (Eds), *Contemporary capitalism: The embeddedness of institutions* (pp. 197–219). Cambridge: Cambridge University Press.

Streeck, W. (2008). *Industrial relations today: Reining in flexibility*. MPIfG Working Paper.

Streeck, W. (2015). The German political economy today. In B. Unger (Ed.), *The German model – Seen by its neighbours* (pp. 81–86). Berlin: SE Publishing.

Thelen, K. (2014). *Varieties of liberalization and the new politics of social solidarity*. New York: Cambridge University Press.

Trampusch, C. (2007a). Industrial relations as a source of solidarity in times of welfare state retrenchment. *Journal of Social Policy,* 36(2), 197–215. doi:10.1017/S0047279406000560

Trampusch, C. (2007b). Industrial relations as a source of social policy: A typology of the institutional conditions for industrial agreements on social benefits. *Social Policy & Administration*, 41(3), 251–270. doi:10.1111/j.1467-9515.2007.00551.x

Traxler, F. (1995). Farewell to labour market associations? Organised versus disorganised decentralisation as a map for industrial relations. In C. Crouch & F. Traxler (Ed.), *Organised industrial relations in Europe: What future?* (pp. 3–19). Aldershot: Avebury.

Van Rie, T., Marx, I., & Horemans, J. (2011). Ghent revisited: Unemployment insurance and union membership in Belgium and the Nordic countries. *European Journal of Industrial Relations*, 17(2), 125–139. doi:10.1177/0959680111400895

Visser, J. (2007). Trade union decline and what next: Is Germany a special case? *Industrielle Beziehungen: Zeitschrift für Arbeit*, 14(2), 97–117. doi:10.1688/1862-0035_indb_2007_02_visser.

Visser, J. (2019). *ICTWSS Database, version 6.1*. Amsterdam: Amsterdam Institute for Advanced Labour.

Western, B. (1997) *Between class and market: Postwar unionisation in the capitalist democracies.* Princeton: Princeton University Press

Wren, A. (2001). The challenge of de-industrialisation: Divergent ideological responses to welfare state reform. In B. Ebbinghaus & P. Manow (Eds), *Comparing welfare capitalism social policy and political economy in Europe, Japan and the USA* (pp. 239–269). London and New York: Routledge.

Chapter 9

Labour market policies

De-regulation, inclusion, and dualisation

Roberto Rizza, Nicola De Luigi, and Barbara Giullari

9.1 Introduction

The labour policy frameworks of Western countries had to deal with unprecedented and complex challenges generated by the crisis of the Fordist model, urging governments to introduce significant reforms in the regulation of national labour markets. Driven by technological automation, the extensive changes in the organisation of production, together with the de-industrialisation processes at work in developed Western countries, led to a considerable decline in employment in the manufacturing sector, where the weight of the trade unions had facilitated access to social citizenship rights also for the least qualified sectors of the workforce.

The growth dynamic generated by tertiarisation, propagating at specific times and in specific ways from country to country, partly managed to offset the decline in industrial employment. However, the new jobs in the service sector, both in low value-added jobs (consumer services) and in more skilled activities (business services, education, research, and personal services such as health and training), were not sufficient to reabsorb a manufacturing workforce with individual characteristics and professional qualifications different to those required by the tertiary sector. Thus, unemployment re-emerged as a structural problem in many advanced Western economies. The effects of the process of tertiarisation exacerbated the employment issue, triggering in many countries an increase in the number of people working in low value-added services, in addition to skilled and well-paid jobs. Given the nature of these occupations, characterised by low productivity growth, labour policies in many instances focused on reducing labour costs and introducing greater flexibility in the hours and length of contracts.

In terms of underlying logic and institutional arrangements, three labour policy models can be outlined according to a typological approach with which the different countries confronted the crisis of the 1980s:

1. The countries of continental Europe, represented in our analysis by Germany and France and corresponding to the dual inclusive growth

DOI: 10.4324/9781003297130-12

model, adopted measures similar to the countries of southern Europe, such as Italy and Spain, belonging to the non-inclusive low growth model. These chiefly intervened on passive policy instruments for income protection and dismissal procedures, as well as implementing labour supply reduction measures through early retirement and focusing on hourly flexibility.

2. The Scandinavian countries, exemplified by Denmark and Sweden and characterised by an inclusive egalitarian growth model, stood out not only for the income support measures (managed in close cooperation between government and trade unions), but also for the ample space given to active policies, in particular through training programmes to extend the possibilities of occupational reintegration of categories affected by the economic crisis;
3. the United States and the United Kingdom, belonging to the non-inclusive growth model, endorsed labour policies with a low level of regulation (in particular regarding protection from dismissal) and limited compensation, subject to means testing. The implementation of active policies was also low.

In the following pages, we analyse in more detail the most relevant developments in the labour policies of the countries under review, to better understand the similarities and differences. Finally, we will illustrate how the three labour policy regimes studied have risen to four since the 2000s, as the model shared by the continental and southern European countries forked with Italy and Spain developing their own configuration.

9.2 Changes in the 1980s and 1990s

9.2.1 The continental and Mediterranean European model

In the early 1980s the conditions that had evolved induced the continental European states to choose to broaden the range of contractual forms available. It became a common trend to introduce "atypical" employment relationships to curtail the rigidity of industrial labour market regulation. As the variability of demand escalated quantitatively and qualitatively, with the consequent tendency towards expansion of the ensuing "flexible specialisation" (Piore & Sabel, 1984) that superseded Fordism, companies were in need of tools to manage this upswing with more efficiency. The introduction of new employment relationships – such as part-time, fixed-term, and home-based forms of work – was also spurred by the expansion of the service sector, in particular of low-skilled services requiring a more flexible and low-cost workforce.

9.2.1.1 France

The country's government was taken over in 1981 by the Socialist Party under Mitterand. The most commonly implemented forms of contract in this period as "social shock absorber" for unemployment were solidarity contracts that envisaged a reduction in working hours agreed between companies, trade unions, and local authorities, with the dual aim of avoiding redundancies and promoting new employment opportunities. Solidarity contracts were also adopted for the early retirement of workers aged 55 and over, where companies undertook to maintain the same level of manpower. In the same vein, in 1983 (Auroux Law), the legal retirement age was reduced from 65 years to 60. Nonetheless a certain austerity on public accounts characterised the socialist government, which opted to increase social contribution rates to cope with the deficit of the social security system (Palier, 2010).

Also, passive policies were affected by attempts at reform. In 1982 the institution of unemployment benefits was modified: the period during which job losers received benefits was reduced and these were more closely bound to the previous contribution period. Two years later, an important dividing line between insurance and welfare benefits was introduced: access to insurance benefits was even further tied to claimants' contribution payments and financed only through social contributions; a support allowance (Allocation de solidarité spécifique – ASS) was instead reserved for unemployed people who had exhausted the possibility to access insurance benefits.

The prolonged economic crisis and the lack of an adequate social protection system generated conditions of vulnerability and exclusion, leading to the emerging of a new class of poor that prompted further changes as it irrupted forcefully during the 1988 presidential campaign.

The introduction of a national social assistance scheme formed the most significant response at this stage. Under the second Mitterrand presidency the Revenu Minimum d'Insertion (RMI) was launched, a measure providing access to a minimum income following a means test. A mutual commitment pact was also contemplated, with the objective of professionally and socially reintegrating applicants.

In the mid-1990s the unemployment rate reached 12.5%. In the wake of the economic crisis of the early 1990s, concern for public finances led to a reorganisation of both insurance and welfare benefits. The Allocation Unique Dégressive offered a new single insurance-type scheme but with cuts in coverage and duration. Unemployed people without insurance cover were progressively diverted to other social protection schemes. The unemployment insurance system remained comparatively generous for those with a long and stable contributory history, while those who had accumulated low levels of contributions due to low wages and fragmented careers were forced to rely on the social assistance. Thus, a real dualisation of access to benefits took shape.

In this period, some active labour policy measures were also introduced, such as access to training opportunities for those without a job, but they remained substantially marginal compared to an overall system in which rather traditional features, centred on passive policies, continued to prevail.

9.2.1.2 Germany

Similarities can be drawn between the dynamics unfolding in France in the 1980s and those in the case of Germany. From 1983, with the end of the social democrat-liberal coalition and the beginning of the long collaboration between Christian democrats and liberals under the leadership of Helmut Kohl, Federal Germany adopted the strategy of early retirement for workers aged 58 and over, with the intention of pursuing a generational turnover and supporting employment. At the same time, the possibility of using atypical forms of work was extended. The maximum duration of temporary contracts was extended from 6 to 18 months, and two different forms of part-time work were introduced: "on-demand" work, aimed at rescheduling working hours according to flexible tasks and objectives, and "shared" work, in which the tasks of a single job were divided between two or more workers. Some constraints slackened in labour relations regulation, increasing the share of redundancies needed to make the formulation of a social plan mandatory and exempting new firms from doing so.

In the early 1990s the high level of spending on passive policies represented a determining trait in Germany, where the main challenge was the reunification of the country following the annexation of the former German Democratic Republic. Unemployment in the eastern territories was twice as high as in the west. This consequently led to a surge in spending on passive policies leaving a reduced budget for active policies, mostly concentrated in public job creation schemes that were specifically aimed at unemployed people from the East. It was also necessary to step up the employment services and in 1994 the employment system was reformed by allowing private intermediary agencies.

9.2.1.3 Italy

Large-scale recourse to early retirement was also implemented in Italy during the 1980s, with distortions in social security contributions and a burden on public finances that would come to a head in the following years. An agreement between the government and the social partners then extended atypical contracts, such as training and work experience contracts – a temporary employment relationship of a maximum of two years remunerated with a variable wage. Solidarity contracts were also fairly successful. Two variants can be distinguished: in cases where solidarity was externally oriented, the reduction in working time targeted new recruitment while in the case of internally oriented solidarity it was aimed at curbing redundancies.

This measure was financed through state contributions and tax rebates for companies.

Afflicted by a deep economic and political crisis, the country had to weather a very particular phase in the 1990s. The collapse of the old party system created the political space for launching a broad wave of de-regulation, in which concertation became a necessary strategy for consensus in technically led government coalitions. The agreements signed by the governments of Amato (1992) and Ciampi (1993) introduced more flexibility in income policy, primarily by reducing the wage indexation mechanism.

These agreements also laid the groundwork for reforming other labour market institutions, which were considered responsible for creating too much rigidity. The first step in the employment reform was the abolition of the so-called "numerical call", i.e. the obligation for companies to recruit in a predetermined order from the employment lists, based on seniority.

In 1996, for the first time a centre-left coalition came to power, which made its mark by approving a series of measures that delineated a de-regulatory approach. The so-called "Treu Package" of 1997 introduced the institution of temporary work, opening up to temporary agencies and thus marking the definitive abolition of the public employment monopoly. This reform also removed some constraints on fixed-term employment relationships, in particular by relaxing the criteria concerning the repetition of the same contracts over time.

9.2.1.4 Spain

The 1982 elections in Spain saw the victory of the Socialist Party. In an attempt to respond to the consequences of the economic crisis brought about by the oil shocks, the government led by Felipe Gonzales brought into play a weighty agenda of reforms that targeted de-regulation of the labour market. Unemployment reached 20% in the early 1980s and the new government was called upon to satisfy a growing expectation of new jobs. A massive injection of flexibility was implemented under negotiation with the social partners, together with some initially modest forms of active policy. Restrictions on temporary work were lifted, with dramatic consequences in terms of labour market dualisation (temporary workers in the early 1990s accounted for 30% of the employed workforce). In addition, there were job creation schemes, training programmes for the long-term unemployed, incentives for self-employment and insertion programmes for young unemployed people.

The intention to increase employment levels also featured significantly in the nineties. In 1993–1994, the main focus was on tax and social security reductions for particular groups, such as young people, the long-term unemployed, or the elderly. At the same time, subsidised employment measures linked to particular forms of contract, such as insertion contracts and part-time work, were promoted. Mid-decade, in 1995, the public employment monopoly was abolished.

9.2.2 *The North European model*

9.2.2.1 *Sweden*

In response to the economic crisis of the 1970s the Scandinavian countries provoked an initial discontinuity in the development trajectory of their labour policies, albeit a modest one. In particular Sweden, under pressure from the trade unions, first fortified employment protection and then pursued support for employment levels, extensively implementing the active policy system set up after World War II. This was also possible thanks to the presence of a large area of public employment, with a particular role played by part-time employment (accounting for about a quarter of the working population). As such, strong passive and active labour market policy regimes were maintained in Sweden until the 1990s, the beginning of a phase that marked a sharp downtrend in the peculiar features of the country, which until then had boasted the lowest unemployment rates in Europe. In the context of a fiscal crisis that forced the governments to cut public spending, the number of unemployed people rose significantly, from 1.6% in 1989 to 10.1% in 1997. The cuts chiefly entailed reducing the coverage and generosity of unemployment benefits, containing public employment schemes and reconfiguring active policies more efficiently.

The time window established for accrual of contributory requirements was reduced and compensation, from 1993 onwards, was cut to 80% of the previous wage instead of 90%. As for the active policies, in this period Sweden opened up to influences from the workfare approach, moving away from a tradition that was more focused on increasing employability. In this sense, the mechanisms determining the conditions of the benefits were toughened, requiring likewise greater control by the employment services. Nevertheless, these changes were achieved while maintaining a tradition of industrial relations that allowed these decisions to be negotiated with the social partners, thus ensuring that wages were contained.

9.2.2.2 *Denmark*

The case of Denmark confirms the special role of active policies in the Nordic model, becoming a benchmark for Europe in the late 1990s. During this period the country attracted international interest and succeeded in developing strategies that slashed unemployment figures from 9.6% in 1993 to 4.3% in 2001, while at the same time setting a record employment rate of 76.2%. Between 1994 and 1999, with a minority government the Social Democrats introduced significant "recalibrating" measures in the area of labour policies. On the one hand, the duration of unemployment benefits was markedly reduced (from a maximum period of four years in 1994 to one year in 1999). On the other hand, assistance was accompanied by some activation measures. As a result of these interventions, recipients were obliged to accept any job offer that fitted the criteria, including mobility. Failure to find a job after one year of unemployment (six months for under 30s), led to the so-called activation phase, during which the unemployed worker had the right/duty to take part in more exacting education or training programmes. The regionalisation of active policies comprised a further element of reform. Regional tripartite labour councils were set up to design policy solutions that were more responsive to the needs of local labour markets.

More generally, the so-called "flexicurity model" was implemented in this period (Wilthagen & Tros, 2004), in which the generosity and duration of subsidies, together with active policy interventions designed to increase professional profiles in the light of job reintegration, led income security to replace job security. In addition, the wide variety of vocational training programmes was managed with a strong focus on inclusion of the unemployed and young people. In fact, the Danish school-to-work transition system can be considered very similar to the German model in terms of the high level of participation of the state and enterprises. In Denmark however, in contrast with what happened in Germany, the role of the state was decisive in averting the risk of dualisation between skilled and well-paid workers and low-skilled and marginal workers. In this regard, two peculiarities of the Danish context were determining. One was the close relationship between high school and technical-professional education. The second involved the consolidated tradition of continuous training, based on a virtuous competition between the trade unions of skilled and unskilled workers, both of which were concerned with providing adequate opportunities for their members to update and develop their professional profiles and thus making the system inclusive and opening up also to outsiders.

9.2.3 The model of the Anglo-Saxon countries

9.2.3.1 The United States

The paradigm shift that in the field of labour policies singularised the ingress to the eighties can be understood through the emblematic experiences of the United Kingdom and the United States. In the case of the latter, promoting a clean break with the past, the Reagan administration had the explicit intention of countering the rigidities of the labour market and removing obstacles to the accumulation of capital necessary for fuelling employment-oriented economic growth. With regard to labour policy, these economic policy strategies comprised a series of reforms that were designed to reduce passive policies, both in terms of coverage and generosity and duration, besides promoting activation measures strongly based on work incentives, especially negative ones. On the first front, the minimum wage introduced by the social legislation of the 1930s was cut by ten percentage points (from 50% to 40% of average earnings). Generally speaking, in the area of passive policies, a logic of intervention was attempted that aimed to re-organise benefits as far as possible on an insurance basis. Unemployment benefits were cut and included in the minimum income calculation of the beneficiaries. Similarly, the entitlement criteria for extended benefits, i.e. welfare-type benefits for those without access to insurance schemes or who had exhausted the possibilities of having recourse to them, were tightened. The welfare-type scheme established in 1962 against the risk of unemployment due to cyclical fluctuations in the private sector (Trade Adjustment Assistance) was permanently abrogated. The same fate befell the first activation strategies pursued under the Carter administration (Public Service Employment), intended chiefly for the most disadvantaged.

Alongside the drastic downsizing of passive policies, the Reagan administration introduced a workfare approach, adopting active policies based on benefit conditionality mechanisms and extensive use of incentives for active job searching. In particular, a federal assistance and work programme (Family Support Act) was established, amending the Social Security Act by linking the granting of benefits to the acceptance of a suitable job or participation in training programmes. While succeeding in lowering unemployment, these reforms also contributed to increasing poverty, low-wage employment and inequality. During the 1990s, the United States recorded an increase in the employment rate (from 70% in the late 1980s to 74% in the mid-1990s), but in the public debate the nature of the new jobs was called into question, to the point of coining a neologism, the "McJobs" (with reference to the well-known McDonald's fast-food chain), to indicate the large number of low-skilled jobs in the service sector, low-paying and less stable than the higher-skilled service sector jobs and the higher-productivity industrial sector jobs (Kalleberg, 2011).

Some timid signs of a turnaround materialised in both passive and active policies with the return to power of the Democrats under Clinton's leadership. The budget's purse strings were loosened for unemployment benefits, new measures were introduced to encourage business start-ups, and the vocational training system was reorganised (School to Work Opportunities Act, Apprenticeship for Young People, Cooperative Training), to facilitate the transition from school to work for young people.

9.2.3.2 The United Kingdom

Measures very similar to those of the Reagan presidency were taken by the governments led by Margaret Thatcher, in pursuit of a markedly neoliberal economic policy strategy. This triggered a spill-over effect in the labour market reforms designed to diminish passive policies and strengthen active policies in terms of workfare. With regard to unemployment benefits, the automatic indexation mechanism was abolished in 1982. The British system continued to provide two types of benefits, insurance and welfare, but with much stricter eligibility requirements, both in terms of willingness to work and active search, and in terms of demonstrating the involuntary nature of unemployment and implementing new rules for means testing. An active policy scheme for young people (Youth Training Scheme) was approved in 1983, aimed at getting early school-leavers into work and training activities.

Thatcher's strategy in reforming labour policies was ambivalent: on the one hand, resources were increased, but on the other, the trade union component was ousted from management. The measures implemented in this period were inspired by a workfare approach: refusal to participate in training programmes led to loss of benefit, while non-attendance in the case of training courses gave rise to a curtailment of the same. By way of accomplishing the reorganisation of the labour policy model, the possibility for firms to use atypical forms of contract was extended. Two significant reforms characterised this front: the Job Splitting Scheme, offering incentives to employers who transformed one full-time job into two part-time jobs; and the Part Time Job Release Scheme, granting incentives to increase part-time work. Broadly speaking, the overall picture of the reforms developed in the UK during the 1980s delineated an approach oriented towards employment rather than to employability. The neo-liberal recipes launched in the 1980s would by and large continue throughout the following decade. The trajectory outlined featured the containment of unemployment benefits and activation strategies based chiefly on work incentives, in a framework where unemployment remained at low levels. The most significant innovation of this period was the introduction by the Conservative government of the Jobseeker's Allowance, a single unemployment benefit that replaced all previous schemes and entailed a means test for recipients after six months.

9.3 The 2000s

The manifold labour policy regimes continue throughout the 2000s to follow different paths in the wake of their historical heritage and previous institutional setups. The three models illustrated – continental Europe, the Nordic countries, and the United Kingdom and the United States (Anglo-Saxon) – change and persist in differing from each other in a perpetual game of continuity and transformation. In the case of the continental European model, the peculiar path of the two Mediterranean countries – Italy and Spain – should be noted, which justifies the identification of a fourth labour policy regime, the traits of which will be highlighted later.

9.3.1 Sectoral dualisation in continental Europe

As illustrated above, for Germany and France the response to the economic crisis of the 1970s and 1980s entailed the safeguarding of the manufacturing sector, the strategic nucleus of the two countries' economic competitiveness and the priority area around which their social model was built (Palier & Thelen, 2010). This strategy generated a side-effect in the form of a secondary labour market, with non-standard employment relationships on a large scale, particularly in services. At the same time, labour policies were developed that involved an increasing dualisation of forms of protection: an insurance pillar on the one hand (for those paying contributions), and welfare schemes on the other (for the long-term unemployed and "atypical" workers).

9.3.1.1 Germany

In Germany, employment protection legislation for permanent employment maintained its safeguarding capacity. In addition, temporary supports were widely implemented in response to cyclical crises (short-time work) for workers employed on permanent contracts in core industrial sectors (Thelen, 2014).

Furthermore, in the 2000s a bifurcation developed and became more pronounced: while the majority of blue-collar workers in industry were employed in full-time, permanent jobs (74%), among low-skilled service workers only 37% could rely on standard contracts, the remainder being engaged in atypical occupations (Eichhorst & Marx, 2012). Also the distribution of part-time work in different sectors differed in Germany and France, with a much higher level of part-time work in services. In the 2000s in Germany, the "Hartz reforms"[1] revised unemployment benefits with the reshaping of the two pillars: the insurance pillar, calibrated on the amount of the last wage received before dismissal, called "Arbeitslosengeld I" (unemployment benefit I), and the programme "Arbeitslosengeld II" (unemployment benefit II), calibrated on the means test with very reduced amounts.

Between 2004 and 2005, the proportion of unemployed people receiving insurance benefits linked to previous earnings dropped from 58% to 25%. This was a major change in German passive labour policies, shifting from the principle of safeguarding of status and income maintenance to a basic income for the long-term unemployed. The expansion of the welfare pillar led to a dualisation of the social protection system, dividing the conditions of those assisted according to whether they were supported by insurance or assistance schemes. The restriction of short-time work (Kurzarbeit) to industrial workers made the sectoral dualisation of labour policies even more tangible. The expansion of low-wage work was one of the outcomes of this impetus towards dualisation (Grabka & Schröder, 2019).

Using ECHP and EU-SILC data for European countries, and the Luxembourg Income Study (LIS) for the US, an in-depth analysis of the

Table 9.1 Expenditure on active and passive labour market policies as a percentage of GDP

	2004	*2005*	*2006*	*2007*	*2008*	*2009*	*2010*	*2011*
Passive policies								
Continental	1.9	1.7	1.5	1.2	1.1	1.4	1.3	1.1
Nordic	1.9	1.7	1.4	1.1	0.8	1.2	1.2	1.1
Anglo-Saxon	0.2	0.2	0.2	0.2	0.5	0.7	0.5	0.4
Mediterranean	1.0	1.1	1.1	1.0	1.3	2.1	2.2	2.0
Active policies								
Continental	1.0	0.9	0.9	0.9	0.8	0.9	1.0	0.8
Nordic	1.3	1.3	1.3	1.1	1.0	1.2	1.5	1.5
Anglo-Saxon	0.2	0.2	0.2	0.2	0.2	0.2	0.2	0.1
Mediterranean	0.6	0.6	0.6	0.6	0.6	0.6	0.6	0.6

Source: Elaboration on OECD data.

Note: Passive labour policies included insurance and income support to the unemployed and those at risk of losing their jobs. Active policies included expenditure on training, incentives for companies to hire specific categories of unemployed, direct job creation with publicly supported programmes, incentives for start-ups.

dynamics of inequality in gross monthly earnings of workers aged 18–64 who had worked for at least 7 months in the reference year illustrates that wage dispersion increased more in Germany than in all the other countries considered (Table 9.1).

Generally speaking, wage inequality as measured by the Gini index is higher in the Anglo-Saxon countries than in the others, but looking at the dynamics, the greatest increase occurred in Germany, where the ratio of the 50th to the 10th percentile (p50/p10) is the highest among the eight countries analysed, while the increases were smaller in the Anglo-Saxon countries.

In the 2000s, the German service union (Ver.Di) – in competition with low-skilled service workers – tried to react to this situation and pressed the government to reduce or abolish occupations exempt from contributions and benefits, and lower the threshold for paying contributions. Given that it was convenient for workers to earn less than €800 as higher earnings would push them into a fully contributory scheme, thus reducing their net earnings, the service union's demand was based on the fear that Mini- and Midi-Jobs[2] would lower wages even further.

This position was not fully supported by the most representative unions in the industrial sector, first and foremost because their members were not competing with Mini and Midi-Jobbers. On the contrary, in many cases male industrial workers had a partner employed in Mini and Midi-Jobs, profiting from the additional tax-free income brought into the family. Rather, the fear of industry unions was that an increase in Mini-Jobs, chosen by companies to

Table 9.2 Inequality indices calculated on gross monthly wages

Country	*Year*				*Year*		
Germany	1997	2007	2015	*France*	1997	2007	2015
Gini	0.315	0.355	0.356		0.298	0.289	0.285
P90/P50	1.833	1.900	1.970		1.943	1.907	1.841
P50/P10	3.399	4.962	4.067		2.078	2.064	2.005
Denmark	1997	2007	2015	*Sweden*	1995	2007	2015
Gini	0.24	0.232	0.233		0.256	0.296	0.274
P90/P50	1.556	1.569	1.617		1.617	1.680	1.696
P50/P10	2.213	1.816	1.694		2.164	3.058	2.330
Italy	1997	2007	2015	*Spain*	1997	2007	2015
Gini	0.212	0.252	0.247		0.335	0.291	0.363
P90/P50	1.522	1.644	1.656		2.232	1.983	2.132
P50/P10	1.643	1.832	1.935		2.344	1.978	3.089
United Kingdom	1997	2007	2015	*United States*	1997	2007	2016
Gini	0.359	0.359	0.379		0.368	0.373	0.389
P90/P50	2.142	2.188	2.289		2.341	2.343	2.410
P50/P10	3.488	2.797	2.813		2.800	2.748	2.767

Source: Elaboration on ECHP, EU-SILC and LIS data.

avoid paying social security contributions, could undermine the financial stability of insurance funds, given that the number of Mini and Midi-Jobs, even as a form of second job, grew during the 2000s to about 7.5 million.

From a political standpoint, the trade unions initially supported the then ruling coalition of Social Democrats and Greens in Germany, especially with regard to the first acts of the Hartz reforms. However, the second wave of reforms (2002–2005), based on a strong retrenchment of passive insurance-type labour policies (Table 9.2), endorsed a rift between the red–green coalition and the industry unions, parallel to the emergence of a new party, the Linke, to the left of the SPD (Schwander & Manow, 2017).

The Agenda 2000 programme was pursued at a significant political cost for the German Social Democrats, with a shift of votes from the SPD to the Linke. As reconstructed by Carlin et al. (2015), they were forced into a corner as a consequence of a severe financial crisis suffered by municipal governments and Länder, which were forced to increase expenditures in the face of decreasing revenues. Indeed, since 2000, local governments have had to bear rising welfare costs due to rising unemployment. In addition, they have had to cope with declining revenues due to cuts in corporate taxes – the main source of their resources – as a result of a tax reform that took effect in 2000. The only possible choice was therefore the reorganisation of unemployment benefits along with the activation of the unemployed prescribed by the supply-side approach that the Hartz Commission had developed.

9.3.1.2 France

The trend towards dualisation escalated in France, too, as a result of the metamorphosis fuelled by the labour policy reforms in the 2000s (Palier & Thelen, 2010; Clegg, 2011), contributing to a significant increase in flexibility within firms as well as in the labour market. Changes in the taxation system lowered the payroll taxes paid by employers, while the Contribution Sociale Généralisée (CSG), initially envisaged as a policy to support families, was later extended to various forms of income support (minimum pensions, disability assistance). Also these adjustments had an impact on dualism, inaugurating a shift from traditional insurance policies towards interventions supported by general taxation. Moreover, the CSG, levied on the basis of a fixed percentage of income and initially conceived as a progressive tax, became regressive when the right-wing government capped individual taxes at 60% of income in 2005. In 2007, the right-wing government went even further with the TEPA package (Travail, emploi, pouvoir d'achat), abolishing all forms of taxation of overtime, which sparked the perverse effect of incentivising overtime in favour of insiders rather than providing for new recruitment.

The approach encompassing "sectoral dualising liberalisation" that characterised Germany and France was thus incorporated in various interventions. These processes came into play through an "institutional drift" – to use the interpretative categories suggested by Thelen (2014) – based on the fact that the practices and institutional arrangements developed for the industrial sector were not extended to be implemented externally in other sectors. A further aspect to consider with reference to the trends in Germany and France is the shift of labour policy costs from the compulsory public insurance system to the general taxation system.

9.3.2 The Nordic regime of learnfare flexibilisation

The Nordic models followed a different path from the French and German models. A wide range of public services that increased paid work for women in services formed the backbone of the response to the reduction in industrial employment. A large class of public service workers (above all female workers) was thus formed, which constituted a second pillar of the trade union movement, representing a significant counterbalance to the strength of manufacturing interests. This approach, which aimed to attain high levels of employment, was accomplished through the development of active labour policies (as shown in Table 9.3), and in particular training.

While in Denmark the focus on human capital enhancement (learnfare) is no new phenomenon, historically accompanied by reduced employment protection legislation, giving rise to what is known as the learnfare flexibilisation of the Nordic regime, these trends have also been followed more recently in Sweden.

Table 9.3 Expenditure on active labour market policies (% of GDP)

	2005	*2010*	*2015*
Nordic	1.3	1.5	1.7
Continental	0.9	0.9	0.7
Anglo-Saxon	0.2	0.2	0.2
Mediterranean	0.6	0.6	0.6

Source: Elaboration on OECD data

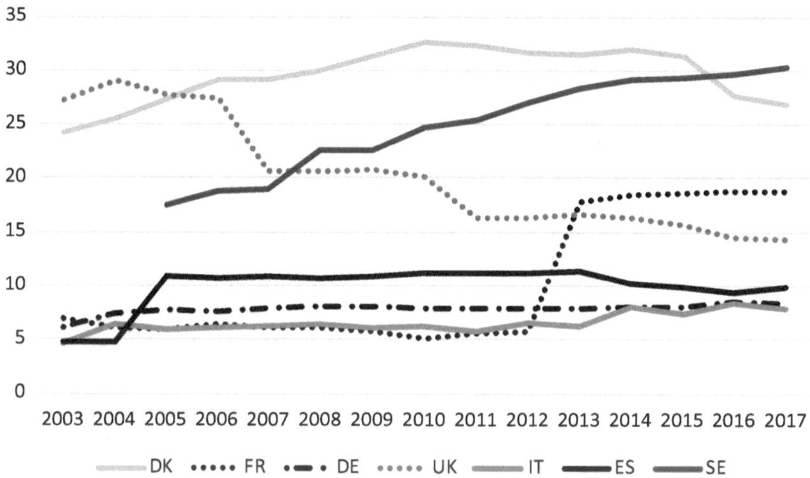

Figure 9.1 Participation in life-long learning (percentage of employed 25–64 years old).
Source: OECD.

An important feature of the Nordic retraining model is the centrality of training for both the employed and the unemployed, as shown in Figure 9.1.

In Denmark, a series of social reforms was implemented in 2009 by the new governing centre-right coalition, combining limitation of unemployment benefits, tax cuts, welfare chauvinism (through targeted and selective cuts in social programmes aimed at immigrants), and anti-unionism (exclusion of social partners from the implementation of labour policies and rejection of the "Ghent system" in the administration of unemployment insurance). In particular, the duration of unemployment benefit support was reduced, while the requirements regarding retraining obligations for the unemployed were reinforced.

More stringent conditions for recipients of social assistance measures under 30 years of age were introduced, alongside means-tested controls for unmarried couples, adopting more rigorous criteria than those reserved for traditional families. Benefits for workers in flexible jobs were cut and reductions in social services funding initiated. Incentives to set up independent funds were implemented to weaken the "Ghent system" and disband the trade union monopoly in the management of unemployment funds. As well as causing a decline in funds membership, these measures also resulted in a reduction in union membership, to the extent that Denmark's largest blue-collar union lost a quarter of its members between 1995 and 2010 in the face of the expansion of other organisations providing only legal support (Dølvik & Martin, 2015). With regard to the chauvinist approach to welfare, a series of cuts in social assistance programmes for immigrants, also approved by the nationalist Danish People's Party, were implemented while criteria were introduced to make benefits conditional on accepting low-wage jobs.

This was a fundamental turning point for Denmark. Indeed, although spending on active labour policies was still comparatively high, these reforms diverted the country from the flexicurity system established in the 1990s and nudged it towards a work-first regime, where benefits were depreciated in terms of duration and largesse, where sanctions were at least as important as incentives (Jørgensen & Schulze, 2012), and tendencies to exclude trade unions from the implementation of labour policies were manifest. In Sweden, the return of the centre-right coalition to government in 2006 led to a cutback in labour taxes and the introduction of new restrictive measures with regard to passive labour policies. Unemployment benefits were slashed still further and the screws tightened on the requirements for accepting even low-paid jobs. As unemployment increased, expenditure on passive policies as a share of GDP decreased. A similar pattern in this respect emerged also in Denmark from 2008 onwards, while for both countries, spending on active policies was vigorous and on the rise.

As far as labour market outcomes are concerned, it is clear that the traditionally high level of employment for both men and women in Sweden and Denmark was not affected by the 2008 crisis (see Figure 9.2). Since 2010, employment has started to grow again, especially in Sweden, returning to pre-crisis levels, while it has contracted in Denmark, although still remaining at high levels. The level of unemployment also increased after the crisis but decreased from 2013 onwards. What is most important to consider, however, because it is closely related to the effectiveness of the high level of spending on active labour market policies in Sweden and Denmark, is the abatement of long-term unemployment.

Another significant outcome can be observed with reference to wage inequality, which is rather low (see Table 9.1). Thus, despite some tendencies to introduce more conditionality in the Nordic system and to weaken the role of trade unions as actors in labour policies, the emerging regime continued to combine economic efficiency and equality. In this respect, it is possible to say that the change in labour policies followed a path of conversion of

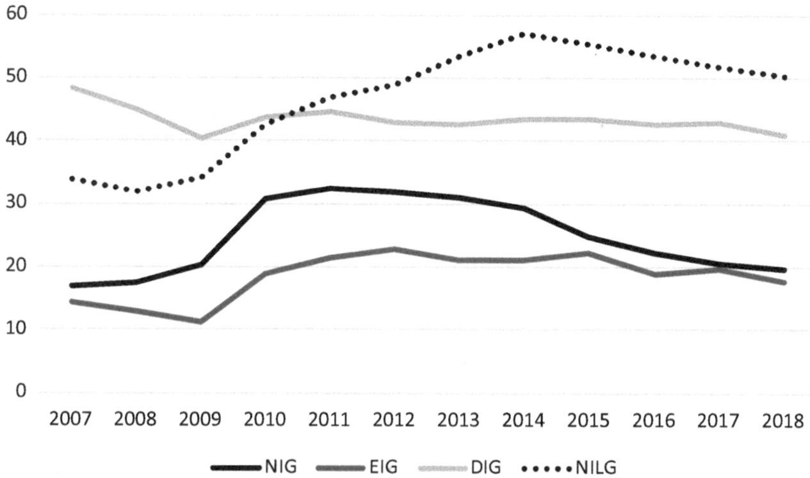

Figure 9.2 Long-term unemployment (share of total unemployed).

Source: OECD.

institutions to the new conditions that has not distorted the original structure (Thelen, 2014).

9.3.3 The regime in the Anglo-Saxon countries: de-regulation

9.3.3.1 The United Kingdom

In the United Kingdom, back in government in 1997, the Labour Party announced its intention to bring 250,000 unemployed young people into the labour market. To this end, action was taken on three fronts: increased investment in human capital and training, reorganisation of employment policies, especially those geared towards job placement, by enhancing job centres, and an increase in the legal minimum wage.

With reference to training, the so-called "Train to Gain" programme launched in 2006 provided subsidies to companies that offered training opportunities to people with low qualification levels. This approach was part of the Labour Party's view at the time that focusing on upgrading workers' skills was the only possible strategy for competing in a globalised economy (Mayhew & Wickham-Jones, 2015). However, the British context lacked an institutional structure that targeted the strengthening and enhancing of technical and vocational training, along the lines of the German model. The government therefore aimed to invest in generalist education, i.e. in schools and universities, by significantly increasing investment in these areas: spending on education increased by a quarter between 2000 and 2009 and that on tertiary education by 30% (OECD, 2012).

Throughout the first decade of the 2000s, the Labour leadership implemented policies that emphasised the duties and responsibilities of income support recipients, increasingly conditional on finding and accepting jobs. The goal of getting recipients of welfare into work (workfare) was reinforced by tax incentives to companies hiring unemployed people (in-work benefits). However, the results were not particularly satisfactory: employment in low-skilled and highly unstable occupations increased.

According to Toynbee and Walker (2010) 40% of those who found a low-skilled job then found themselves out of work and again supported by benefits. In 2010 the share of low-wage workers in the UK was 20.6%, the highest among advanced economies after the US.

New Labour, under the leadership of Tony Blair, placed great emphasis on training. As Blair emblematically stated in a speech in Manchester in 2007 (Mayhew & Wickham-Jones, 2015, 156): "Workers should be protected not through greater bargaining power in the workplace, nor through union intervention, but rather through the position gained in the labour market as a result of their education and training". However, the results were modest. The aspect to evolve the most in active policies was that regarding assistance programmes conditional on finding and accepting employment positions (Table 9.4), which as shown were concentrated among low-skilled and highly unstable jobs.

Worthy of note is the fact that the picture has not significantly changed since the introduction of the minimum wage in 1998. Set initially at a low level, it had little impact except on the first decile of the wage distribution. Subsequently, it was raised but remained below the international definition of a "low wage", i.e. less than 2/3 of the median hourly wage.

Ultimately, the transition between Conservative and Labour governments did not structurally change labour policies. The main difference can be seen

Table 9.4 Expenditure on public employment services in terms of percentage of total expenditure on active labour market policies as a percentage of GDP

	1997	*2004*	*2011*
United Kingdom	62.4	87.4	87.0
Nordic	10.1	20.6	20.0
Continental	16.0	21.9	36.7
Mediterranean	n.a	14.5	20.7

Source: OECD.

Note: Expenditure on public employment services includes placement and services for employers, employees and the unemployed, including services provided by private providers with public funding.

in the shift from the workfare system of the Conservative governments of the 1980s and early 1990s, in which income support was heavily dependent on the willingness to accept any job opportunity, to a system directed more towards "welfare-to-work", focused on strengthening the human capital of jobseekers. The return of the Conservatives to government in coalition with the Liberal Democrats (in 2010) led to the Welfare Reform and Work Act of 2016, which stepped up the penalties for those who did not accept, or cooperate with, the proposed work integration measures, and obliged benefit recipients to increase their working hours, even accepting a second job.

Looking at the outcomes, labour policy reforms favoured a stabilisation of wage inequality in the early 2000s. In fact, as the Gini index of wages presented in Table 9.1 shows, inequality remained stable between 1997 and 2007, with a decrease at the lower end of the distribution, probably due to the introduction of the legal minimum wage. Subsequently, however, wage inequality resumed an uptake, with an increase in the Gini index calculated on gross wages between 2007 and 2015, confirming the UK as the country with the highest level of wage inequality in Western Europe.

9.3.3.2 The United States

In the second half of the 1990s labour policies encompassed a workfare approach in the United States. In 1996, Clinton launched the Personal Responsibility and Work Opportunities Reconciliation Act (PRWORA), based on the reinforcement of employment assistance services and training, though destined to not last long. PRWORA also introduced the Temporary Assistance for Needy Families programme, which removed legal entitlements to assistance for poor families, reduced the period of coverage, and linked compensation to willingness to accept work. This resulted in growing competition for low-skilled occupations, a reduction in lower wages and an expansion of short-term work.

The tangible effects of these labour policies were seen in the accretion of the percentage of in-work poverty[3] from 10.57% to 12.36% between 1997 and 2007 in industry and from 10.75% to 11.45% in services.

The Obama presidency (2009–2017) marked a reversal of the trend of previous administrations, with a focus on industrial and health policies. The discontinuity in labour policies is less evident, although the data show a downtrend in the wage inequality ratio p50/p10 in both the service and industrial sectors (Table 9.1), while unemployment benefits increased and USD 3.5 billion were invested in vocational training. After the 2010 midterm elections, in which the Democrats were defeated and lost control of the House of Representatives, a compromise was reached between the Obama Administration and the Republicans on the Tax Relief, Unemployment Insurance Reauthorization and Job Creation Act, a package of stimulus measures worth 858 billion dollars. In exchange for a two-year extension of all tax cuts (including those for income earners above $200,000 a year that Obama initially intended to repeal), the Republicans accepted a 13-month extension of long-term unemployment benefits. In 2013, Obama urged Congress to increase the federal minimum wage, which stood at $7.25 an hour, much lower than in 1968 (when it reached its highest value net of inflation). The Republican-dominated Congress did not act, and the president issued an executive order to raise the minimum wage for employees on federal contracts to $10.10 an hour.

9.3.4 The Southern European regime: the two-fold dualisation

In the 2000s labour policies in the southern European countries had distinct elements in common. Both attempted to reduce the common problem of youth unemployment by expanding contractual flexibility through the liberalisation of temporary incoming employment relationships. The process initiated in the 1990s was to continue in the same direction in the 2000s.

9.3.4.1 Italy

Italy's labour market regulation policies presented two main elements of dualisation, in reference to the particular protection guaranteed by regulations to different groups of workers. The first element dated back to the early 1970s and referred to the employment protection legislation defined by the 1970 Workers' Statute, guaranteeing much more protection for workers employed in enterprises with more than 15 employees compared to those working in firms with less than 15. Added to this was the main instrument for protecting the income of workers affected by employment crises, the Cassa Integrazione Guadagni Ordinaria e Straordinaria, (Ordinary and Extraordinary Wages Guarantee Fund), relating to workers with open-ended contracts employed in medium to large enterprises.

The second, common also in Spain, originated in the 1990s when a model of de-regulation in the phase of entry into employment was pursued (Esping-Andersen & Regini, 2000), which increased the number of workers with temporary contracts, especially young people.

Upon closer analysis of the labour policies of the 2000s, the measures implemented by the centre-right coalition led by Silvio Berlusconi can be seen to mark a break with consultation and social dialogue, which incidentally had never been institutionalised in Italy. The measures introduced further changes to the regulation of the labour market, chiefly affecting flexible contracts. The so-called "Biagi law" (Legislative Decree No. 276 of 2003, issued pursuant to Law No. 30), supported by the CISL (Italian Confederation of Trade Unions) and UIL (Italian Labour Union), but not by the CGIL (Italian General Confederation of Labour), envisaged the bolstering of the redundancy fund as its main intervention. Enterprises were allowed to extend and cumulate

CIGO (Ordinary Wages Guarantee Fund) and CIGS (Extraordinary Wages Guarantee Fund) beyond the limits set by the legislation up to that moment, and social security "for exceptional cases" from the national legislation was provided, including micro enterprises which had been excluded up to then, also providing coverage for workers with temporary contracts. Implementation of the redundancy fund was justified by the general consensus it received. That the trade unions were in favour of the instrument was understandable: it gave protection to industrial workers, historically the most unionised, while the trade unions (together with the employers' associations) had to be consulted on its use. Also businesses were in favour of the lay-off fund since the cost for them was lower compared to other instruments. From the government's point of view, the use of the redundancy fund reduced the impact of unemployment compared to what would have happened if it had opted for other interventions.

In 2012, the "technical government" headed by Mario Monti passed Law No. 92, the so-called "Fornero Law". In the early months of 2012, negotiations between the government and the social partners began. Agreement was found on the re-regulation of temporary work and "bogus self-employment", but the government was forced to backtrack on the intention to abolish the "cassa integrazione" (redundancy fund) due to the opposition of the social partners, particularly Confindustria (Confederation of Italian Industry). In relation to employment protection legislation, the Prime Minister proposed to amend Article 18 of the "Workers' Statute" with the provision that even with the judge ruling in favour of the worker in the case of discriminatory dismissal, monetary compensation should be the only option, abolishing the possibility of reinstatement at work. Following opposition from the CGIL and threats to strike, a compromise was found to resolve the situation (Sacchi et al., 2011). With reference to unemployment benefits, the old legislation established in 1919 was modified, alongside the introduction of the ASpI (Social Insurance for Employment). This replaced the ordinary unemployment benefit, as of 2013, borrowing its access criteria and extending it to apprentices from 2015 onwards.

In 2015, the centre-left government led by Matteo Renzi re-examined the issue of employment and launched a measure known as the Jobs Act. This intervention proceeded along the lines of de-regulation of the legislative protection of employment, establishing that only the newly hired would be covered by the "contract with increasing protections": a new form of open-ended employment relationship that provided for minimum and maximum thresholds of compensation in case of dismissal, differentiating the compensation system for companies with fewer than 15 employees. The Confindustria (Confederation of Italian Industry) was somewhat hostile to the idea of applying it only to new employees, as in its view this would risk further toughening up and partitioning labour legislation. The real clash came, however, with the trade unions, especially with the CGIL and UIL, over the amendment to Article 18 of the "Workers' Statute" that in the event

Table 9.5 Expenditure on passive labour policies (% of GDP)

	2005	*2010*	*2015*
Italy	0.67	1.32	1.29
Spain	1.43	3.05	1.98

Source: Elaboration on OECD data.

Table 9.6 Expenditure on active labour policies (% of GDP)

	2005	*2010*	*2015*
Italy	0.54	0.42	0.51
Spain	0.76	0.90	0.59

Source: Elaboration on OECD data.

of "illegitimate" dismissal – whether economic or disciplinary – established the impossibility of reinstating the employee in the workplace, granting only a monetary compensation equal to a number of months' pay in proportion to seniority. Strikes were threatened and signatures collected for a referendum to repeal the law, but the change requested by the government passed.

In summary, the contents of the labour policies conducted in Italy during the 2000s chiefly concerned interventions on passive policies (Table 9.5), aiming to reduce the protection of workers employed in the most guaranteed sectors and to maintain a wide recourse to fixed-term forms of work. Little changed on the active policies front, marginal also in terms of expenditure (Table 9.6).

The shortcomings of the active labour market policies in the Mediterranean European countries emerge not so much in relation to wage inequality, which is lower than in almost all the countries examined here (as shown in Table 9.1), but in relation to in-work poverty.

In the case of Italy, the high rate is explained, on the one hand, by the low participation of women in the labour market, depriving households of a second income (Barbieri et al., 2018) and, on the other hand, by the phenomenon of the selective combination (Schwartz, 2013) of subjects with low levels of education employed precariously and at low wages.

9.3.4.2 Spain

Spain entered the 2000s after the right-wing Popular Party government had implemented cutbacks in unemployment benefits and legalised private non-profit employment agencies. In the wake of these measures, the reforms regarding the public employment services were in 2003 were strongly oriented towards decentralisation and the autonomy of the independent communities. In 2006, the socialist government, in agreement with the social partners proposed a legislation to lower the share of temporary work and to provide incentives to prolong working life beyond the legal retirement age. In 2007, legislation on gender equality was introduced to promote measures in favour of women in the sphere of work and social protection.

In 2012, under the leadership of Rajoy, the People's Party government enacted the so-called "Copernican revolution", launching a de-regulation programme without seeking agreement with the social partners. The reform concerned the reduction of dismissal costs and the introduction of a new type of collective agreement for companies during periods of crisis with fewer guarantees and social contributions aimed at reducing labour costs and making firing easier. Furthermore, compensation for discriminatory discharge was reduced and exemption clauses to national bargaining introduced, along with the simplification of collective lay-off and the amplifying of the grounds for just causes for individual lay-off.

In terms of the effects of labour policies on wage inequality, the outcomes reveal that there was a much greater expansion of inequality in Spain compared to Italy, chiefly ascribable to the changes in the ratio p50/p10, signalling an expansion in the lower tail of the distribution concentrated in services. The situation of individuals in a state of in-work poverty instead represents a similar picture (see Table 9.7).

In the 2000s, Italy and Spain show a parallel trend based on passive labour policy interventions with low investment in active policies. Similar measures were also taken to lower the level of employment protection for permanent workers. However, the two countries differ with respect to the specific passive

Table 9.7 In-work poverty by sector of productive activity

	Years				*Years*		
Germany	1997	2007	2015	*France*	1997	2007	2015
Industry	6.40%	6.40%	7.01%		8.89%	6.00%	5.93%
Services	6.55%	6.96%	8.23%		6.71%	5.94%	6.22%
Denmark	1997	2007	2015	*Sweden*	1995	2007	2015
Industry	2.78%	4.81%	1.10%		n.a.	5.43%	6.83%
Services	4.36%	3.39%	3.58%		n.a.	7.03%	6.90%
Italy	1997	2007	2015	*Spain*	1997	2007	2015
Industry	12.99%	10.04%	9.77%		15.17%	10.69%	7.35%
Services	10.69%	8.88%	8.92%		11.85%	9.65%	9.36%
United Kingdom	1997	2007	2015	*United States*	1997	2007	2016
Industry	6.85%	6.26%	5.82%		10.57%	12.36%	11.68%
Services	9.73%	8.18%	6.87%		10.75%	11.45%	11.66%

Source: Elaboration on ECHP, EU-SILC and LIS data.

policy instruments launched in response to the 2008–2009 crisis. Italy, in keeping with the past trend, reveals extensive use of short-time work schemes ("cassa integrazione guadagni" or wage support measures) thanks to an "interclass" alliance between firms and trade unions (Perez & Rhodes, 2015), both of which were in favour of adopting such a measure. In Spain, where the insurance pillar of unemployment support was much more developed and in the absence of a cross-class coalition supporting the status quo, short-time work did not have a strong role and the right-wing Spanish government proceeded more decisively with a de-regulatory reform of the labour market.

9.4 Concluding remarks

With the decline of Fordism, the reduction in manufacturing employment in large companies was partly offset by the accretion of services. These last had a higher-skilled but quantitatively more limited component, and a low-skilled but potentially larger component that was decisive in maintaining a high employment rate. In order to seize the potential for employment growth in the area of lower-skilled services, it was necessary to lower the standards of labour protection that existed in the Fordist phase because given the low productivity of these services, growth through employment of new workers would be possible only if labour costs remained low, and in view of the temporal discontinuity of demand, only if flexibility was high.

Implementation of active and passive policies in different countries influenced this redeployment of labour, as the analysis so far shows, and this is where our cases differ.

The Anglo-Saxon non-inclusive growth model reduced the overall standard of labour protection through a process of de-regulation that embraced the old and downsized manufacturing sectors as well as the low-skilled service area on the rise. A key feature of this process was a radical restructuring (Thelen, 2014), fostered by an overall weakness of trade union and political representation in the world of work. The process of dualisation in the labour market was contained, but this outcome was the result of the enfeeblement of the traditionally more protected sector. Passive policies were scaled down, yet without proceeding to increment active policies. With the centre-left political forces in government, this approach softened in favour of greater emphasis on human capital formation, but on the whole the variances remained nonetheless limited.

In the Scandinavian model of inclusive and egalitarian growth a process of "recalibration" modestly reduced guarantees for those employed in the most protected sectors (large manufacturing industry, public employment) while increasing protection in terms of social policies and interventions in training and retraining (learnfare) for those employed in the low-productivity services sector, and for the unemployed expelled from struggling manufacturing sectors, for whom mobility was encouraged. Hence a new balance was fashioned between passive policies, on which expenditure was reduced, albeit not to the point of dismantling them, and active policies, on which the countries in question spent more than others, giving rise to an "institutional conversion" [ibid.]. Other instruments were also implemented to contain the risks of dualisation. Scandinavian welfare has traditionally favoured service provision over cash transfers. The peculiar expansion of personal services limited the growth of low-skilled consumer services and the results show there was also lower growth in inequality. It should be noted that the rise of centre-right governments in Sweden and Denmark during the 2000s does not alter the overall picture, despite restrictions in passive policies (unemployment benefits), chauvinist measures against immigrants, and attempts to weaken the role of the trade unions.

In the continental European model of inclusive dual growth, the possibility of seizing the new opportunities for employment growth in services required labour regulation and protection standards to be slackened. The difficulty of moving in this direction led to an increase in the unemployment rate in the 1980s and 1990s, because the weight of subsidies on labour costs was not profitable for the growth of low-productivity services and public services. Furthermore, the preference of these systems for transfers over services limited the Scandinavian approach related to the growth of employment in public services. Hence a process of adaptation developed that was based on compromise. Trade unions and companies defended the traditional protection standards inherited from the Fordist phase in export-oriented manufacturing (and public employment). In the area of low-skilled services, on the other hand, a process of de-regulation (or non-regulation) or "drift", to cite Thelen (2014), lowered the standards of labour protection in order to make such services profitable. In this context the unions were feeble, while the stronger organisations in traditional manufacturing sectors actually endorsed the compromise, concerned with not weakening their traditional base through rising unemployment and economic hardship. Over time, however, interventions and programmes were taking shape that sought to mitigate the lack of protection of the social groups involved in the area of highly discontinuous services. These measures were paid for by general taxation. The continental variant together with the non-inclusive low-growth Mediterranean variant were both characterised by the path of sectoral dualisation. The latter differed from the former chiefly in three key features. In the first place, the dualisation was more extensive, involving also the many smaller manufacturing firms as well as the black economy and undeclared work. Since the weight of large and medium-sized enterprises was lower in the Mediterranean model, the area of outsiders was larger.

Second, despite various attempts to reduce the impact, the safeguarding of the most protected sectors was particularly costly in terms of passive policies supported by public finances. Third, active policies concerning the social groups involved in the new forms of employment were less incisive than those of the continental variant, partly because of the greater overall difficulties of public finances in the Mediterranean countries. Analysis of the labour policy regimes would seem to show that the logic of models prevailed over the weight of programmatic distinction between parties oriented more towards the left- and right-wing. Undoubtedly changes in government, in one direction or another, introduced shifts in the balance between active and passive policies and in the characteristics of these policies, but they did not alter the overall path and trajectory of the various models. An interpretation might thus be that a key role was played by the interest groups active in the various countries with their capacity to coalesce. From this perspective, the more radical de-regulatory turning point in the United Kingdom and the United States could be correlated to the greater weakness and lower compactness of labour representatives and the lack of coordination between companies, which leads them to thwart any form of concertation. In the face of the serious crisis in which both countries involved found themselves in the 1970s, the absence of labour market institutions complementing a skilled, high value-added manufacturing sector (e.g. vocational training policies involving companies and trade unions, stringent employment protection rules to ensure the career continuity of skilled industrial workers), laid the foundations for a coalition between declining manufacturing companies and emerging service companies, both of which, albeit for different reasons, were pushing for strong de-regulation.

In continental European countries, the loss of importance of the interclass coalition that dominated manufacturing in the Fordist era, determining the incapacity of maintaining a leadership role in today's service economy, might have had a direct bearing on sectoral dualisation. The Mediterranean model reveals an even more pronounced tendency in this direction, by dint of the ineffectual weight of the large manufacturing companies and extensive trade union and employer fragmentation. The Nordic model mitigated the drive towards dualisation, enabling service workers, including women and low-skilled workers, to be as well organised as industrial workers. Here, in addition to the interest organisations, the state also had an important role, acting as a mediator and supporting coalitions in favour of greater public sector involvement in social investment policies (Morel, Palier, & Palme, 2012) that took the form of active and training policies, as well as support services for dual-career families with children.

Notes

1 The Commission informally took the name of President Peter Hartz, former Director of Human Resources at the automobile company Volkswagen.

2 These refer to low-wage jobs targeting both the unemployed and people who already have a marginal but regular job. Wages, which must not exceed €400 in the case of Mini-Jobs and €800 for Midi-Jobs, do not include social security contributions for workers.

3 An individual is considered to be in-work poor if he/she declares to have been employed for at least seven months in the reference year and if he/she lives in a household with an equivalised disposable income below 60% of the national median income.

References

Barbieri, P. Ciabuschi, F., Fratocchi, L., &Vignoli, M. (2018). What do we know about manufacturing reshoring? *Journal of Global Operations and Strategic Sourcing*, 11(1), 79–122. doi:10.1108/JGOSS-02-2017-0004

Carlin, W., Hassel, A., Martin, A., & Soskice, D. (2015). The transformation of the German social model. In J. Dølvik & A. Martin (Eds), *European Social models from crisis to crisis* (pp. 49–104). Oxford: Oxford University Press.

Clegg, D. (2011). France: integration versus dualization. In J. Clasen & D. Clegg (Eds) *Regulating the risk of unemployment: National adaptations to post-industrial labour markets in Europe* (pp. 34–54). Oxford: Oxford University Press.

Dølvik, J. & Martin, A. (2015). *European social models from crisis to crisis.* Oxford: Oxford University Press.

Eichhorst, W. & Marx, P. (2012). *Non-standard employment across occupations in Germany: The role of replaceability and labour market flexibility*, Bonn, IZA Discussion Paper 7662.

Esping-Andersen, G. & Regini, M. (2000) (Eds). *Why deregulate labour markets?* Oxford: Oxford University Press.

Grabka M. & Schröder, C. (2019). *The low-wage sector in germany is larger than previously assumed.* DIW Weekly Report, DIW Berlin, German Institute for Economic Research, 9(14), 117–124.

Jørgensen, H. & Schulze, M. (2012). A double farewell to a former model? Danish unions and activation policy. *Local Economy*, 27(5–6), 637–644. doi:10.1177/0269094212451552

Kalleberg, A. L. (2011). *Good jobs, bad jobs: The rise of polarized and precarious employment systems in the United States, 1970s–2000s*. New York: Russell SAGE Foundation.

Mayhew, K. & Wickham-Jones, M. (2015). The United Kingdom's social model: From Labour's New Deal to the economic crisis and the coalition. In J. Dølvik & A. Martin (Eds), *European social models from crisis to crisis* (pp. 144–176). Oxford: Oxford University Press.

Morel, N., Palier, B., & Joakim, P. (2012). *Towards a social investment welfare state?* Bristol: Bristol University Press.

OECD (2012). *Education at a glance 2012: Highlights*. Paris: OECD Publishing.

Palier, B. (2010) (Eds). *A long goodbye to Bismarck? The politics of welfare reform in Continental Europe*. Amsterdam: Amsterdam University Press.

Palier, B. & Thelen, K. (2010). Institutionalizing dualism. *Politics & Society*, 38(1), 119–148. doi:10.1177/0032329209357888

Perez, S.A. & Rhodes, M. (2015). The evolution and crisis of the social models in Italy and Spain. In J. Dølvik & A. Martin, A. (Eds), *European social models from crisis to crisis* (pp. 177–218). Oxford: Oxford University Press.

Piore, M.J. & Sabel, C.F. (1984). *The second industrial divide: Possibilities for prosperity*. New York: Basic Books.

Sacchi, S., Pancaldi, F., & Arisi, C. (2011). The economic crisis as a trigger of convergence? Short-time work in Italy, Germany and Austria. *Social Policy and Administration*, 45(4), 465–487. doi:10.1111/j.1467-9515.2011.00785.x

Schwartz, C.R. (2013). Trends and variation in assortative mating: Causes and consequences. *Annual Review of Sociology*, 39, 451–470. doi:10.1146/annurev-soc-071312-145544

Schwander, H. & Manow, P. (2017). Modernize and die? German social democracy and the electoral consequences of the agenda 2010. *Socio-Economic Review*, 15(1), 117–134. doi:10.1093/ser/mww011

Thelen, K. (2014). *Varieties of liberalization and the new politics of social solidarity*. Cambridge: Cambridge University Press.

Toynbee, P. & Walker, D. (2010). *The verdict: Did Labour change Britain?* London, Granta.

Wilthagen, T. & Tros, F. (2004). The concept of "flexicurity": A new approach to regulating employment and labour markets. *Transfers*, 10(2), 166–186. doi:10.1177/102425890401000204

Chapter 10

Welfare, social policies, and redistribution models

Emmanuele Pavolini and Antonino Sorrenti

10.1 Introduction

In the wake of a series of challenges that placed the traditional post-World War II Fordist welfare systems under strain, from the 1980s onwards Western countries sought to intervene in their social protection systems. Alongside the challenge relating to the economic sustainability of these systems (resulting from an increase in needs accompanied by a simultaneous reduction in the capacity for economic growth compared to the Glorious Thirties), three other challenges emerged: the challenge of social cohesion, linked to ensuring coverage for traditional socio-economic needs (an adequate income in the case of old age, inability to work, or unemployment); the challenge of care, linked to "old" care needs (regarding illness) and "new" ones (regarding non-self-sufficiency); the challenge of socio-cultural investment, strengthening human capital endowments (education) and the possibility to participate in the labour market (reconciliation).

These challenges gave rise to reform trajectories that not only differed substantially from country to country but also within the four development paths we have identified. The debate on the weighty transformations of the welfare systems is ongoing, and the hypothesis of a generalised trend in Europe towards the liberalisation and privatisation of these systems has yet to find unequivocal confirmation in the research. In particular, in these decades there was not so much a simple process of generalised welfare retreat, definable in terms of "liberalisation" or "privatisation", as rather a twofold process: firstly, the reallocation of resources to address some challenges before others (this process is usually referred to as "recalibration"); second, the "dualisation" of social and labour market rights, with an increasing differentiation between more protected workers and citizens, defined as "insiders", and less protected workers and citizens, defined as "outsiders" (Emmenegger et al., 2012).

The chapter is dedicated to reconstructing the dynamics and trends that occurred in the four models under review in the volume, and to shedding light on the consequences they generated in terms of social inequalities. To this end, the focus is on three social policies, chosen because each responds to

DOI: 10.4324/9781003297130-13

one of the above challenges: pension policies, health policies, and policies to support families with children.

10.2 Changes in policies

10.2.1 The overall picture

To understand the welfare model of the various countries under analysis, the data on expenditure in the three areas of social protection constitute a useful starting point: namely, pensions, health, and interventions in support of families with children (Figure 10.1). The data refer to 2015 (2018 in the case of gross expenditure as a percentage of GDP). In the case of pensions, since the reported expenditure item is more the result of past choices than of more recent policy effects, an index of the generosity of the public pension system, calculated by Scruggs, Jahn, & Kuitto (2017),[1] has also been added. "Net" public expenditure corresponds to how much the state spends annually on goods and services offered as social protection after subtracting the effect of taxation on social transfers: countries tax income from social transfers in different ways. In addition, another indicator considered is related to the per capita expenditure in terms of purchasing power parity: with this indicator we measure how much each resident of a country actually receives for his/her protection. Analysis of the data shown in Figures 10.1a, 10.1b. and 10.1c allows some preliminary considerations.

First, moving from the "gross" incidence of social protection on GDP to the "net" incidence, the eight countries considered appear much more similar

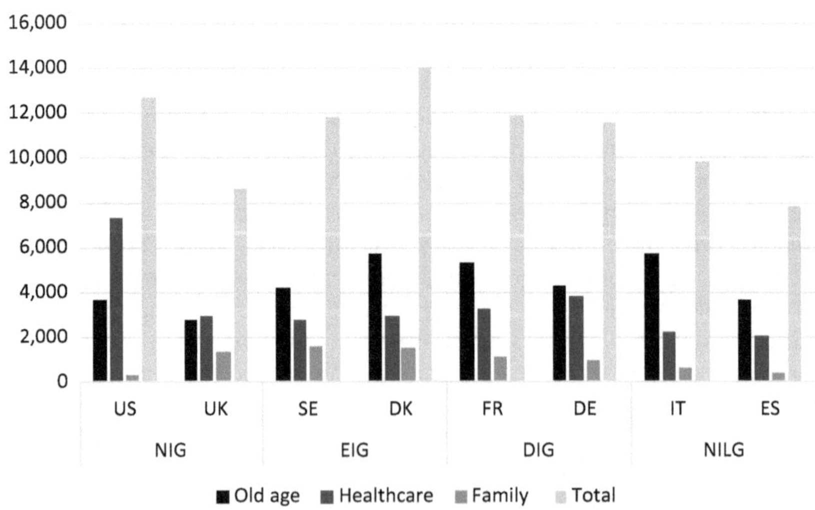

Figure 10.1a Public expenditure on social protection per capita in PPP (2015/18).

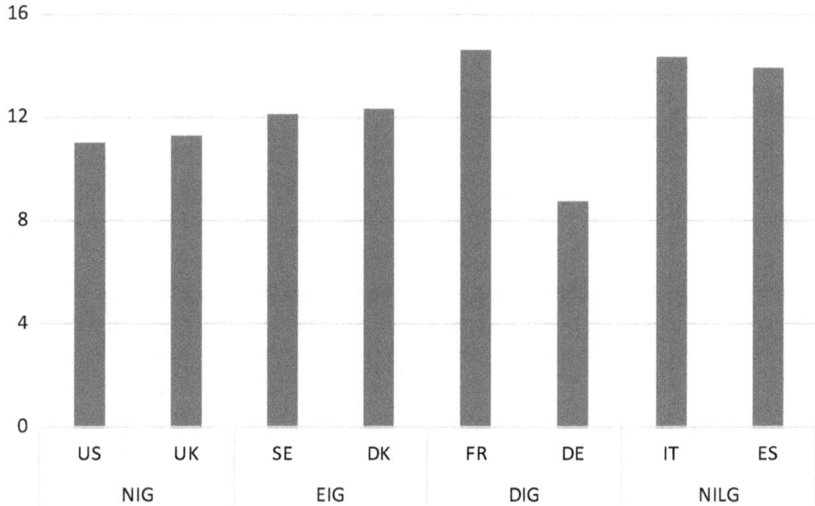

Figure 10.1b Generosity index of public pensions (2015/18).

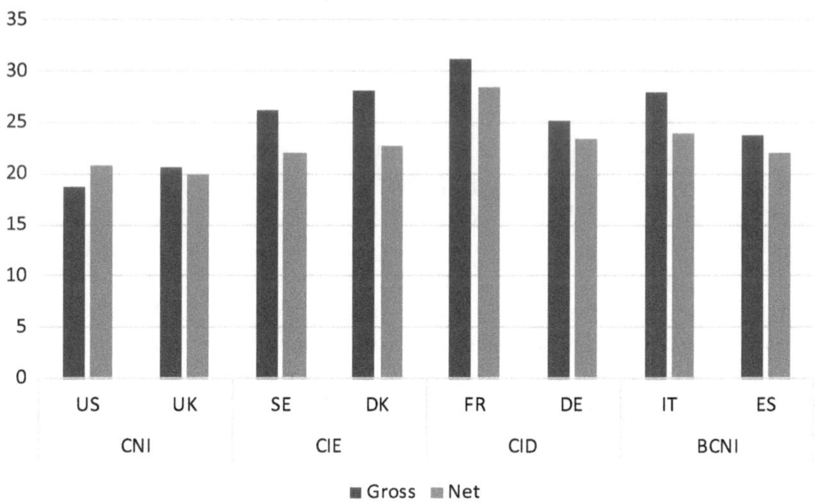

Figure 10.1c Public expenditure on social protection as a percentage of GDP (2015/18).

Source: Elaboration on OECD data and Scruggs et al. (2017).

to each other. The only real outlier is not the United States with its relatively low expenditure, but rather France (due to a relatively much higher expenditure than all the others). If we turn to public spending per capita on a par with purchasing power, Denmark is the country that invests the most per resident, followed by the United States and then, at similar levels, France, Germany, and Sweden. In order, Italy, the UK, and Spain are the countries that spend the least.

Second, the image generally offered of the United States, i.e. of a state with a "residual" welfare state, is not reflected in the one that emerges. There are basically two reasons for this. Compared to much of Europe the US reveals much higher levels of GDP per capita and GDP growth, meaning that a lower incidence on GDP corresponds in absolute terms to a substantial level of public intervention (which can be better appreciated by looking at per capita spending). Moreover, the "Obamacare" effect in the first part of this decade must be held in consideration: a comparison between the 2010 and 2015 data shows that expenditure in terms of GDP, but above all per capita expenditure, increased sharply. This change can basically be ascribed to what happened in the health sector (per capita expenditure almost doubled in five years) following the ACA (American Medical Association) reform, which will be discussed later in this section.

Third, not only countries, but also models tend to resemble each other more, or differ, depending on the welfare areas considered. In the area of pensions, the Southern European model, and to some extent the continental model (France), are the ones that apparently spend the most in terms of GDP and also in terms of the generosity index of the public pension system. However, it should be remembered that in most of the remaining countries the generosity index is not much lower, or at least it considers only public pensions and not the other pillars of social protection. In the field of healthcare, apart from the strong acceleration of the US in recent years, the main difference is between countries with systems based on compulsory health insurance in continental Europe (France and Germany) and national health systems (Nordic, UK and Southern Europe). Finally, in the field of family policies, the United States emerge as having a very limited level of development of these interventions, while on the contrary the Nordic countries invest considerably in this area. The continental countries, but also the United Kingdom, invest in resources, while Southern Europe appears to lag behind, though still remaining at a higher level than the United States.

Aside from the levels of spending on social protection, looking at what has happened in many countries over a period of 40 years represents a complex undertaking. Here we propose to outline the general lines of reform in the main fields of welfare policy, following a chronological order, decade by decade, and considering the development paths identified in the first part of our research. We will examine the development of public expenditure on social protection in the three policy areas identified above, and the reforms and the main regulatory changes ensuing in the four models over a period of 40 years. To assess the extent of the reforms carried out, we use the well-established scheme proposed in the 1990s by Peter Hall (1993), which distinguishes between first-, second- and third-order changes. According to this scheme, first-order changes are those that concern the simple regulation of the instruments of government and intervention in the field of social protection, second-order changes concern the introduction or abolition of instruments, while third-order changes concern a paradigm shift in the functioning of welfare systems.

The last 40 years of evolution of the various national welfare systems have followed trajectories in part similar which can be framed within four phases, each of them lasting approximately ten years. In many areas of welfare policy the 1980s denote a period of substantial continuity and stability in terms of the institutional framework of policies in a socio-economic context that was undergoing radical changes. The welfare system offered, or tried to adapt, "old" answers to the new problems posed by the transition to a post-industrial society and economy while maintaining sufficient resilience in terms of institutional design to resist attempts at radical change, such as those attempted by conservative governments in Anglo-Saxon countries. During this period, essentially first- and second-order reforms were introduced.

Some of these trends of the 1980s will be considered in the context of the discussion regarding the following decade – the 1990s – which rather represents a period of far-reaching innovation and transformation in welfare systems, with the institution of radical reforms of the second (and often third) order in many policy fields. The 2000s emerge as a period in which innovations are introduced, often designed to consolidate and implement reforms of the previous decade, again of the first and second order. Owing to the diverse effects that the economic crisis and austerity had on the countries under review, study of the last decade reveals an amalgam of radical innovations in some policy areas (second and third order) while there are more incremental interventions in other spheres, as well as increasing diversification across countries and models in the type of response administered.

10.2.2 The 1980s: a frozen landscape

The analysis of the policies described in these pages is accompanied by the data contained in Figures 10.2a, 10.2b, 10.2c and 10.2d. Overall expenditure during the 1980s is seen to continue to increase consistently in all models and practically in all policy areas considered, with few exceptions.

10.2.2.1 The non-inclusive growth model of the Anglo-Saxon countries

Despite an overall increase of 26–30%, social protection expenditure in this model was comparatively low. An attempt was made to significantly reduce the

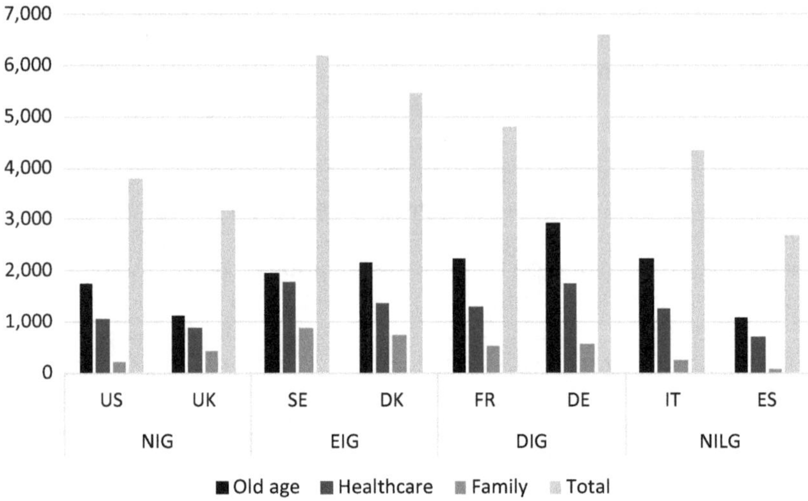

Figure 10.2a Public expenditure on social protection per capita in PPP (1980).

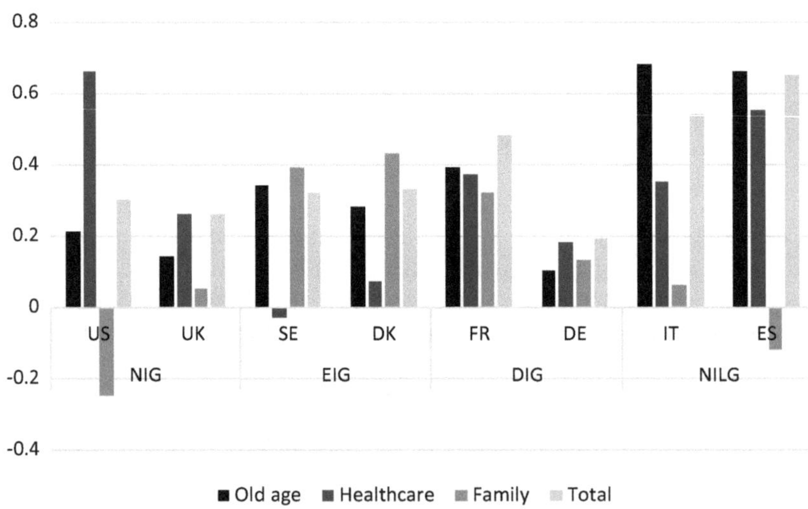

Figure 10.2b Percentage change in social protection expenditure per capita (1980/1990).

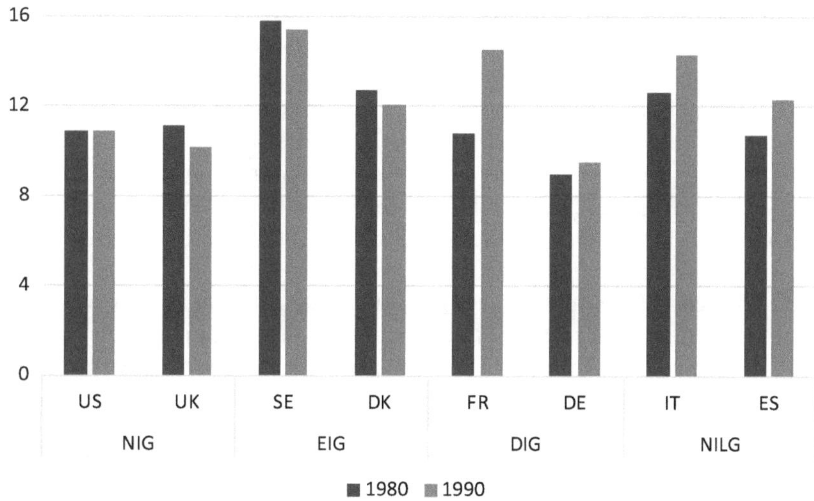

Figure 10.2c Generosity index of public pensions.

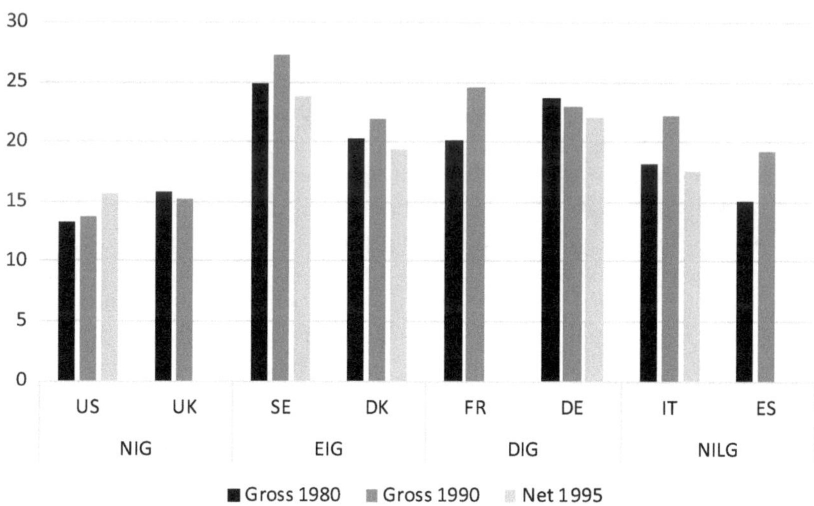

Figure 10.2d Public expenditure on social protection as a percentage of GDP.

Source: Elaboration of OECD online databank and Scruggs et al. (2017).

burden of the social security system on public expenditure with the pension reforms in the 1980s. Nevertheless, the publicly declared reform ambitions of Reagan and Thatcher were much more difficult to implement and the outcomes, in terms of retrenchment, of the changes introduced in both countries to the public pillar turned out in fact to be much more limited than they were designed to be, especially in the US (Pierson, 1994). In healthcare, too, the 1980s were characterised more by theoretical elaboration than by actual regulatory transformation. In the UK, after an initial attempt to promote alternative methods of financing the NHS, the focus shifted to promoting the efficiency of expenditure and quality of provision.

In the United States debate was inadequate; the main intervention programmes in the health sector (Medicare and Medicaid), historically much more privatised than in Europe, were not affected by any transformations worthy of note. The family policy framework in the Anglo-Saxon model was aimed in the 1980s at supporting market-based defamilisation (Woods, 2012). Besides limited spending on public services and the moderate use of monetary transfers and tax relief, this model featured little protection through maternity and parental leave (Béland et al., 2015). The almost residual nature of public interventions in this policy area is clearly visible when looking at the low level of spending and its trend (even strongly negative in the US).

10.2.2.2 The model of inclusive egalitarian growth in the Nordic countries

In the 1980s those that spent the most on social protection and where spending continued to grow at a very fast rate were the Nordic countries (+32–33%). In Sweden and Denmark, limited changes took place in the area of pensions in this period. In the area of healthcare, the problem emerged of completing a truly universalistic coverage, as well as the issue of decentralisation of competencies in healthcare. In terms of family policies, high levels of development of services for early childhood had already determined a key feature of this model, in combination with generous maternity leave, and hence the care-based policies defined in the previous decade essentially continued to be implemented: per capita expenditure increased by around 40% during the 1980s. Both countries were pioneers in introducing more generous parental leave that also incentivised fathers to take care of their children, fostering a real gender balance in the sharing of family tasks.

10.2.2.3 The dualistic inclusive growth model of continental European countries

Expenditure on social protection increased considerably in the continental model, particularly in France (+49%). In comparison with the approach that had been pursued in previous decades in the field of pensions, the 1980s represented a period of relative continuity, if not further expansion. In healthcare, continental countries with compulsory health insurance began to face the problem of cost retrenchment (Busse & Riesberg, 2004). However, insufficient for blocking the growth rate of public expenditure, the measures introduced succeeding only in reducing it. With regard to family policy, the 1980s saw an increasing divergence between the approaches followed in France and Germany. In particular, France by the mid-1980s had a highly developed early childhood services system, almost rivalling Nordic levels (Morgan, 2003). In addition, the socialist government in France introduced paid parental leave for families with three children in 1985 and a measure to support informal care services in 1986 by adopting a contribution – *Allocation de Garde d'Enfant a Domicile* (AGED) – for families who employed qualified and registered domestic helpers. Instead, in Germany family policies focused on generous parental leave and a pension credit for one year's care, introduced by the CDU in 1986 and 1987 respectively.

10.2.2.4 The non-inclusive low growth model of Southern European countries

At the beginning of the 1980s, in terms of expenditure levels Spain and Italy appeared to be two somewhat different countries. The level of per capita expenditure in Italy was higher compared to that of Spain (the lowest of the eight countries), higher than that of the Anglo-Saxon countries and did not vary significantly from that of France. Expenditure in this model increased much faster (+54/65%) than in any other context. In the 1980s with regard to pensions Italy was still in a phase of expansion of public intervention. In contrast, in Spain the first measures of rationalisation but also of recalibration of the system were already in sight. A modernised vision of healthcare began to take shape with the substantial introduction and implementation of new national health services (NHS) (Vicarelli, 2005). In the matter of family policies, the approach adopted in Southern Europe resembled that of the Anglo-Saxon countries – lagging considerably in the development of early childhood services and with limited implementation of other reconciliation measures.

10.2.3 The 1990s: a decade of change

Overall, the considerable growth of expenditure on social protection continued during the 1990s in all four models and in practically all the policy areas analysed (see Figures 10.3a, 10.3b, 10.3c, and 10.3d).

10.2.3.1 The non-inclusive growth model of the Anglo-Saxon countries

Throughout the decade, total expenditure increased by about 32–39%. However, the level of this expenditure (both in per capita terms and as a share

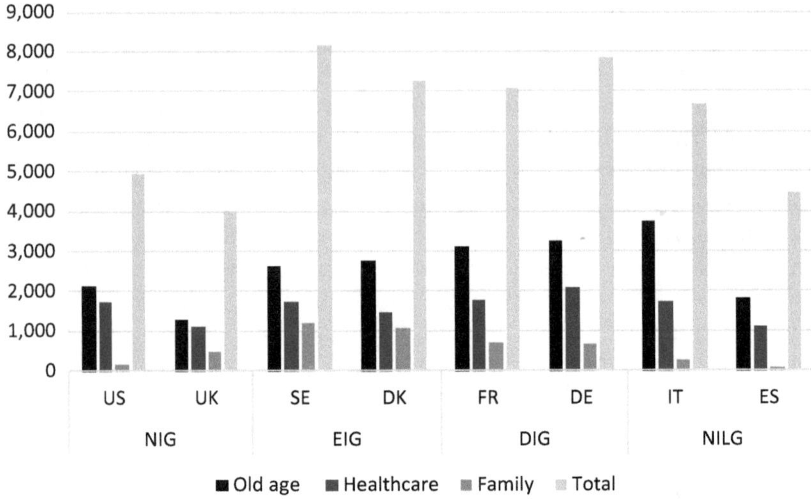

Figure 10.3a Public expenditure on social protection per capita in PPP (1990).

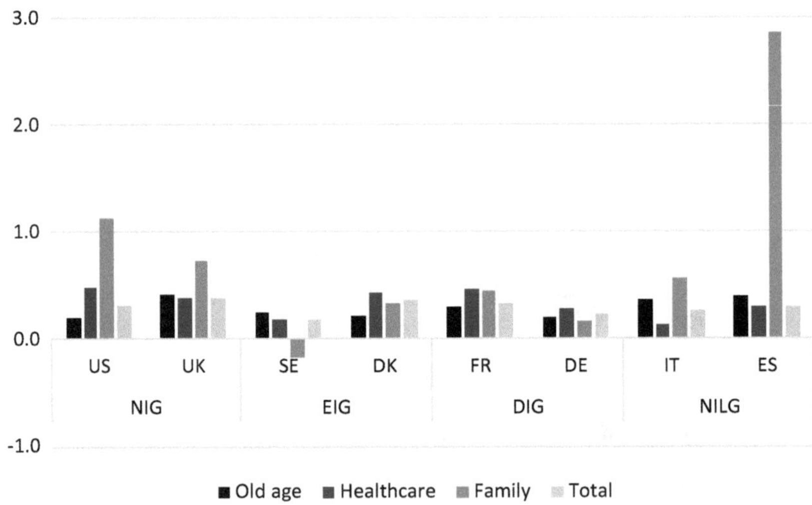

Figure 10.3b Percentage change in public expenditure on social protection per capita.

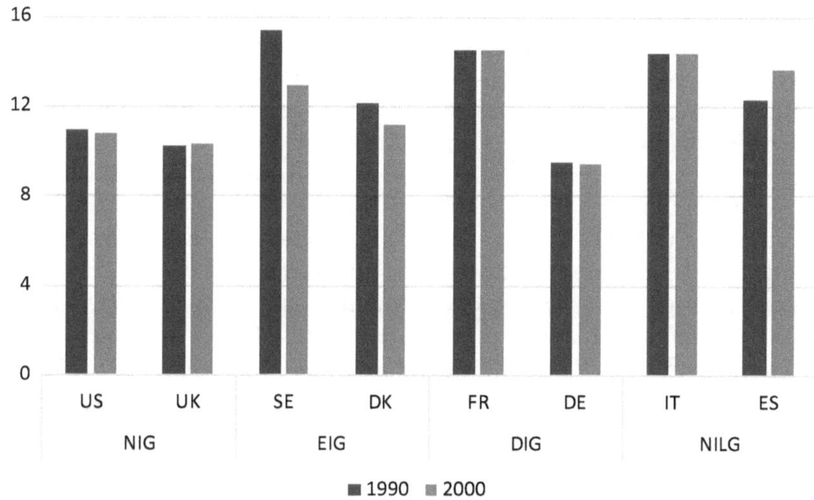

Figure 10.3c Generosity index of public pensions.

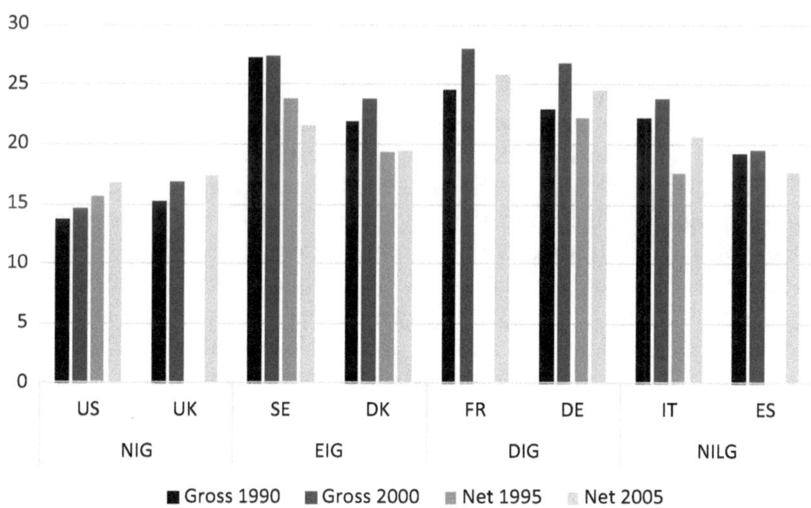

Figure 10.3d Public expenditure on social protection as a percentage of GDP.

Source: Elaboration on OECD data and Scruggs et al. (2017).

of GDP, gross or net) remained below that of the other models for the whole period under review.

In the UK, the Conservatives extended the retirement age for women from 60 to 65 in 1995 with the Pension Act, while Labour introduced a new Stakeholder Pension scheme in 1999, which made the contracting-out option more appealing to low wage-earners. In the USA, pension regulation remained unaltered in its main features. As the pension generosity index shows, there were no particular changes over the decade.

In healthcare, the 1990s were years of considerable transformation for the NHS in the UK, beginning with the radical reforms made by the Conservative government through the "NHS and Community Care Act" in 1991, which introduced the internal market, gave more power to NHS managers and reviewed administration of General Practitioner funding (Boyle, 2013). After the 1997 election, the Labour government initially focused on the accretion of public spending and regulation. 1999 was a crucial year, when the "Health Act 1999" replaced the notion of a quasi-market in the NHS with an approach of "integrated, partnership-based, performance-driven care" (Boyle, 2011). In the United States, the decade produced no new regulatory developments but public health was at the centre of one of the most heated policy debates. In particular, during the Clinton presidency, the Democrats attempted to expand public health coverage, which foundered due to Republican parliamentary opposition (Oberlander, 2016). Overall, per capita spending grew very significantly in both countries, especially in the United States (+49%).

Coinciding with the presence of centre-left governments, there was an expansionary phase in family policy. Spending increased significantly (+114% in the USA and +73% in the UK), partly as a result of starting from relatively low levels. In particular, in the UK, the Labour government launched a national strategy for children in 1998 with the aim of increasing the supply of services for early childhood with 1.6 million new places. The same government amended the tax credit legislation the following year, introducing a new instrument, namely the Working Family Tax Credit, which increased both the number of beneficiaries and the deductible threshold for care costs. In the USA in 1993, the Family and Medical Leave Act, one of the first measures adopted by the Clinton administration, introduced the right to 12 weeks of unpaid parental leave for all workers in the private sector employed in companies with at least 50 employees. The Democratic government also introduced other expansive measures, which were not particularly innovative from a regulatory perspective but were nonetheless significant in terms of disbursement (Michel, 2015).

10.2.3.2 The model of inclusive egalitarian growth in the Nordic countries

Investment of resources in welfare continued to increase in the Nordic countries, despite already relatively high levels of spending at the beginning of the decade. Significant reforms were introduced in the field of pensions, which lowered the level of generosity of the public system, offsetting it with the expansion of a widely spread and generous second pillar (Seeleib-Kaiser & Pavolini, 2018). In Sweden, the two reforms introduced by socialist governments in the 1990s still today form the support structure of the current Swedish multi-pillar pension system. In 1994 Sweden switched to a contributory system for the calculation of pensionable earnings in the first pillar and in 1998 a second pillar called Premium Pension was introduced, also contributory but funded. In Denmark, in the early 1990s conservative governments changed the indexation of pensions to real wages (1990) and introduced occupational pensions through collective agreements with trade unions (1991). In 1996 and 1998 the Social Democratic governments extended the coverage of occupational schemes in the case of illness, maternity or unemployment.

Several important innovations took place in the health sector, within a framework that saw significant accretion in expenditure levels (Blomqvist & Winblad, 2013). On the one hand, the two healthcare systems progressively opened up to more competition from private providers and a higher level of patient choice, and on the other hand, the central state started to take back some regulatory powers after decades of decentralisation. Patients' rights in the NHS were extended in various ways, from the right to choose a general practitioner without geographical restrictions to the right to express an opinion on treatment (in cases where several treatment options are available). The bottom-up managerial changes introduced were not only related to the patient's freedom of choice and the separation of purchaser and provider (following the model of British quasi-markets), but also to various forms of performance-related payment systems including DRGs (Diagnosis Related Groups). In the field of family policies, the decade did not see any particular institutional innovations at work, but a continuous and growing investment in the network of services and leave that had been established in both countries in previous decades.

10.2.3.3 The dualistic inclusive growth model of continental European countries

Expenditure continued to grow also in continental Europe, settling at levels not too dissimilar from those in the Nordic countries. In particular, the 1990s were a period of profound transformation in the field of pensions. In France the centre-right government adopted two important reforms. The Balladur Reform in 1993 increased both the reference period for calculating pay and the years of contributions required to qualify for a pension. In addition, the same reform indexed pensions to prices and introduced a state solidarity fund to finance the increase in non-contributory pensions. In 1997 the Thomas Act introduced voluntary supplementary pension schemes for private sector employees. In Germany in 1992 the so-called "Blum I reform" was introduced, indexing pensions to net wages and raising the retirement age for women. In 1997 the government formed by CDU and CSU introduced the Blum II reform: the introduction of the demographic factor in the indexation formula, the increase of pension credits for childcare, and the increase of the retirement age for disability pensions from 60 to 63 years.

This meant that the level of generosity of public pensions would remain largely unchanged in France while it declined in Germany (though partly offset by growth in private pensions).

In the healthcare sector, the first measures taken in the 1990s in France continued with retrenchment of costs by imposing low prices on health and pharmaceutical services and higher cost-sharing quotas (Palier & Davesne, 2013). From the mid-1990s onwards, the government strengthened state control and regulatory capacities over the financing and planning of the healthcare system. A major constitutional revision adopted in 1996 introduced the power for Parliament to determine each year the resources allocated to Sécurité Sociale funds and to set a limit on health insurance expenditure for the following year. In the hospital sector, a process of managerialisation was initiated. Reforms in Germany focused on healthcare governance with the intensification of competition between sickness funds, giving insured persons more freedom to choose between different funds, and superseding the principle of enrolment in the occupational fund closest to the worker's occupational profile (Health Reform of 1992) (Hassenteufel & Klenk, 2013).

With the expansion of state control under this reform, the traditional freedom of autonomous administration of German healthcare by health insurance funds and doctors' unions was curtailed. The other major reform of the decade, the law on the reorganisation of health insurance containing mainly cost-containment measures, came in 1997. Nonetheless, this was not sufficient to prevent per capita expenditure in these two countries from increasing substantially.

In the field of family policies, France and Germany continued to remain poles apart. A certain legislative inertia was manifested in Germany with regard to the services and reconciliation policies, despite a spread in expenditure (+17 per cent). In 1991 the French socialist government replaced AGED (the Child Homecare Allowance) with the more generous "*aide pour l'emploi d'une assistant maternelle agréé*" (AFEAMA). Moreover, the APE (*L'allocation parentale d'éducation* – Childcare Allowance) was extended to parents with two children and financial contributions were raised. A significant increase in per capita expenditure in the sector (+45%) took shape as a result of these innovations.

10.2.3.4 The non-inclusive low growth model of Southern European countries

On the whole per capita expenditure was distinguished by a continuous upsurge in Southern Europe in the 1990s (+26–30%). Here too pension reforms were introduced in the 1990s. In Italy, introduced by technical governments, these were oriented towards curtailing the very high burden of pension expenditure on the state budget. Key changes included the gradual raising of the retirement age to 65 years for men and 60 years for women, introduced by the Amato reform in 1992, and the shift to the contribution-based method for calculating pensionable earnings, a product of the Dini reform, along with the introduction of a multi-pillar system. In Spain in 1990 the socialist government introduced non-contributory pensions for poor, elderly, and disabled people and in 1997 the government led by the Popular Party passed the Law on the Consolidation and Rationalisation of the Social Security System, providing for several measures including the increase of the reference period for the calculation of pensionable earnings from 8 to 15 years. These reforms required a long implementation phase (especially in the case of Italy), and hence the level of generosity of the public pension system remained high, even increasing in Spain.

For the Spanish NHS the 1990s were the period in which important reforms introduced in the previous decade were implemented (Fidalgo & Ventura, 2013). The decentralisation process continued steadily and the scope of health coverage was widely extended to almost the whole of the Spanish population, reaching practically universal levels. A model of provision of free services was largely maintained. In Italy, important innovations were introduced with the reforms in 1992-93, which promoted an internal market and management processes inspired by the British model (Pavolini & Vicarelli, 2013). They also granted significant managerial autonomy to hospitals and local health units, transforming these into "*aziende*". The other main innovation concerned health decision-making powers, in particular correlated to the process of decentralisation, conceding even more to the Regions. If the political changes in the first part of the decade substantially regarded the internal market and the question of "competition", in the second part of the nineties the new centre-left government chose to fortify the role of the state in NHS regulation and proposed a model of "cooperation" among providers through the legislative decree approved in 1999. In terms of per capita expenditure, Italy was the country that grew the least (+ 13%), while Spain +30% was reached.

In the sphere of family policies, development continued to lag in Southern European countries. There were timid steps forward in Italy, while in 1990, the Spanish socialist government introduced a means-tested family allowance, very similar to the one developed two years earlier in Italy. It was, above all, Spain that sought to close the gap with Central and Northern Europe, increasing its level of per capita expenditure by 286% over a decade.

10.2.4 The new century: an adjustment phase

In the 2000s, spending on social protection continued to grow everywhere, especially in the Anglo-Saxon contexts, and there is no policy area where this upward trend did not manifest (Figure 10.4).

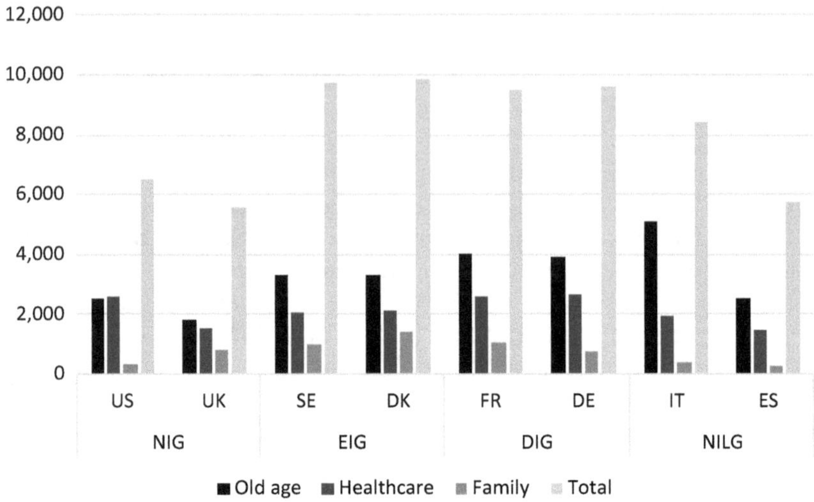

Figure 10.4a Public expenditure on social protection per capita in PPP (year 2000).

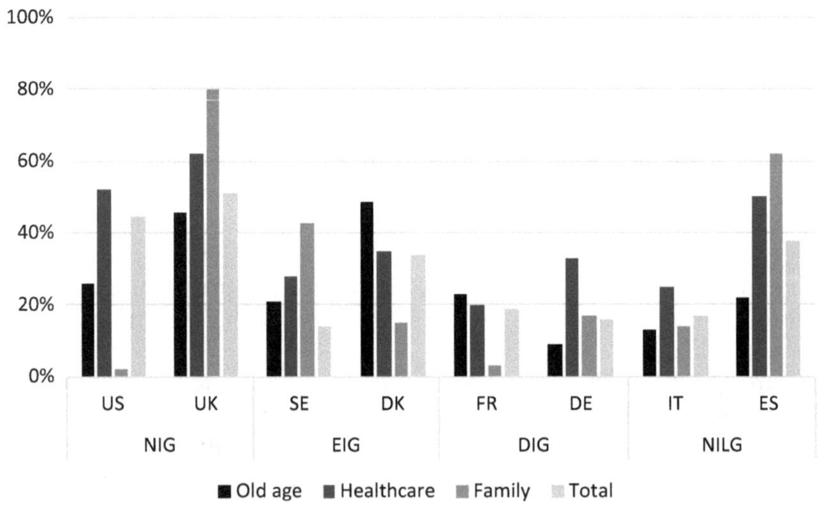

Figure 10.4b Percentage change in public expenditure on social protection per capita.

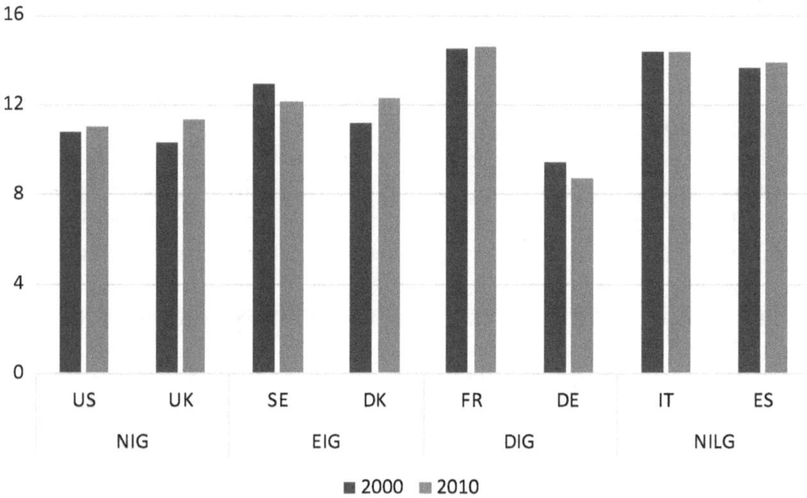

Figure 10.4c Generosity index of public pensions.

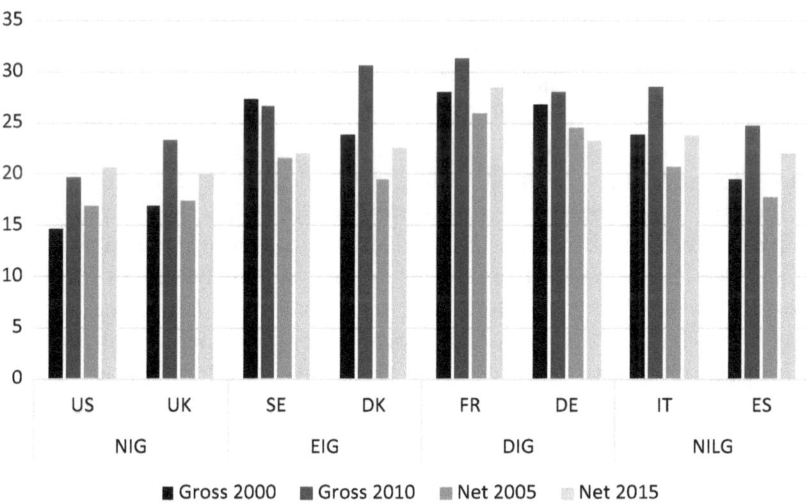

Figure 10.4d Public expenditure on social protection as a percentage of GDP.

Source: Elaboration on OECD data and Scruggs et al. (2017).

10.2.4.1 The non-inclusive growth model of the Anglo-Saxon countries

Total spending on welfare grew between 45% (USA) and 51% (UK) over the decade, generating a process of slow convergence in the levels of spending in these countries compared to those in Central and Northern Europe. In the case of pensions, there were no major changes in the US, while public intervention was expanded in the UK, as indicated by the generosity index. In 2008 important changes were introduced by the British Labour party to strengthen the first public pillar, including the abolition of contracting-out and the raising of the contribution rate linked to workers' earnings. The same reform also provided for voluntary self-enrolment in the second pillar. In the US Bush attempted a reform with a view to promoting privatisation, but the strength and resilience of the social security system outsmarted the centre-right government's aspirations and the design came to nothing (Berkowitz & De Witt, 2015).

For the British National Health Service, the decade represented a period of increasing investment of economic resources; on the one hand, the instruments of guidance and monitoring were reinforced, and on the other, decision-making power was devolved to Scotland, Wales, and Northern Ireland (Boyle, 2013). In addition, users' freedom of choice was amplified with the gradual opening up to the private sector from 2002 onwards. In the United States, there were no particular innovations. Nonetheless, public expenditure increased substantially (+52% in the USA and +62% in the UK), along with Spain, where it was relatively higher than in all other models.

With regard to family policies, in the UK the expansionary period under way since the mid-1990s continued with the promotion of four types of intervention. In 2000, a one-off cash transfer (Sure Start Maternity Grant) was introduced for each new birth. In 2002, the Child Tax Credit Act unified all previous tax credits into one single measure. In 2003, the Employment Relation Act increased both the pay and duration of the maternity grant. Finally, in 2004, the Sure Start programme allocated new resources for local governments to develop early childhood services. In the USA, the decade was largely marked by the Republican presidency and there were no particular innovations in this field (Michel, 2015). Also the trends in spending throughout the decade reflect the different choices in the two countries: virtually stable in the USA (+2%), growing by 80% in the UK.

10.2.4.2 The model of inclusive, egalitarian growth in the Nordic countries

During the decade under review, Danish expenditure continued to grow at a faster rate (+34%) compared to that in Sweden (+14%), while remaining below several other countries in terms of net impact on GDP. As far as pensions were concerned, Denmark was the only country to implement some major changes in in this period. In 2006, the Conservative government raised the retirement age for both early retirement and the first public pillar and supplementary pensions. Overall, the level of generosity of the pension system in both Nordic countries remained relatively high.

In healthcare, patients' rights to choose were extended in the Nordic countries, the partial privatisation of the primary care sector continued and there was a re-centralisation in the governance of the healthcare system (Anell, Glenngård, & Merkur, 2012). Nonetheless, spending increased substantially in any case in both countries. In the field of family policies, the well-established Scandinavian system continued to invest resources: while in 2000 per capita expenditure was about €1,000 in Sweden and €1,400 in Denmark, over the decade it increased by 43% and 15% respectively.

10.2.4.3 The dualistic inclusive growth model of continental European countries

The first decade of the new century represented a further moment of growth for the public social protection system on the continent (+16/19%). Regulatory interventions on the pension system had little impact in France while they were more marked in Germany, as illustrated in the generosity indices. In particular, the centre-right French government adopted in 2003, stipulating that from 2020 the number of contribution years required to access a pension would be 42. In 2007, the grand coalition government in Germany raised the retirement age from 65 to 67 with a very gradual entry into force between 2012 and 2029.

The health policies of the previous decade were essentially continued in France (Palier & Davesne, 2013). In 2003, a DRG-based system was introduced in relation to hospital care and a number of national agencies were endowed with more power to assess and monitor quality standards, chiefly in hospitals. In addition, forms of cost-sharing continued to be widespread. For Germany, too, the decade represented a period of continuity and further elaboration of the reforms conceived in the 1990s (Hassenteufel & Klenk, 2013). The reinforcing of free choice and competition between funds, introduced in the previous decade, took a further step forward with first the 2004 "Modernisation of Health Insurance" law, which allowed German health insurance funds to differentiate their services more, and then the 2007 "Strengthening of Competition" legislation. Expenditure in both countries grew significantly (+ 20% in France and +33% in Germany).

Within the continental welfare regime, France put into effect family policies that were already at an advanced level of development, while innovations in the decade were limited to measures for promoting part-time work in 2004–2005. In contrast, highly expansive interventions in services and leave were implemented in Germany. In 2004, the Social Democratic-led government adopted a national funding plan for the development of services. During the period of the grand coalition government, both parental leave and, most importantly, the right for every child aged one year and over to have a guaranteed place in early childhood services were introduced in 2007, representing one of the most important changes in German family policy in recent decades (2008).

10.2.4.4 The non-inclusive low growth model of Southern European countries

Expenditure trends followed different trajectories in this model: in Italy overall there was an increase of 17%, compared to 38% in Spain, (the highest relative change after the United States and the United Kingdom).

In the area of pensions, the centre-right government in Italy introduced in 2005 the "tacit consent" formula for the automatic transfer of severance pay or post-employment benefits to occupational pensions, later to be modified by the centre-left in 2006. Moreover, between 2009 and 2010 the centre-right government promoted an increase in the retirement age of female public sector workers from 60 to 65 with a phase-in period scheduled between 2010 and 2018. In Spain, the centre-right government took action in 2002 to encourage people to stay in the labour market beyond the age of 65 and to dissuade early retirement. Overall, in terms of generosity, the level of the pension system remained high in Italy while increasing only slightly in Spain.

In healthcare, Spain and Italy exerted more force in pushing towards the political-administrative decentralisation of the respective national health services. In particular, in Spain in 2002 the transfer of power to all the Regions was completed, with the role of the central government increasingly limited to ensuring equal access to health services throughout the country (Fidalgo &Ventura, 2013). Also in Italy the decade opened with another acceleration towards decentralisation, following the 2001 constitutional reform that ceded further power to the regions (Pavolini & Vicarelli, 2013). In the following years, however, the problem arose, in the absence of true fiscal autonomy, of how to avoid this transfer of powers turning into a mechanism generating autonomy at the local level but without accountability in terms of expenditure (Pavolini, 2011). To this end, the legislation of the past decade introduced the so-called "Deficit Recovery Plans", i.e. agreements between regions with health deficits and the central government, whereby the former committed themselves to implementing structural interventions in the network of health services in exchange for substantial aid from the latter to cover deficits. In terms of expenditure, Spain continued to invest more and more public resources (+38%) in comparison with Italy (+17%).

As far as family policies were concerned, Spain implemented more expansive interventions in the 2000s than Italy, as the relative change in per capita expenditure shows: +50% and +25% respectively. In 2007, the Zapatero government extended maternity leave to unemployed women and introduced a four-week paternity leave paid at 100%. In the same year, the same government adopted an expansion plan for early childhood services. In Italy, in 2001 the government introduced more flexibility in the use of maternity leave and adopted parental leave. In 2005, the centre-right government introduced a one-off monetary transfer (baby bonus) for all children born between 2003 and 2006.

10.2.5 The last decade: new acceleration and paradigm shifts

The decade that has just ended was one in which, for a short period in some countries and for a much longer time in others, the policy framework was marked by the crisis and the desire to introduce austerity policies. Compared to the periods considered so far, expenditure varied far less, and not only for the obvious reason of having been able to consider a five-year period (2010–2015) and not a decade. With the exception of the United States (and solely regarding public investment in the new health system), in all the other contexts the per capita expenditure increased at a very contained rate and even decreased in Southern Europe (Figures 10.5a, 10.5b, and 10.5c).

10.2.5.1 The pattern of non-inclusive growth in the Anglo-Saxon countries

Overall spending on social protection followed very different patterns in the Anglo-Saxon countries: strong growth in the USA (+34%) as opposed to virtually no growth in the UK (+3%).

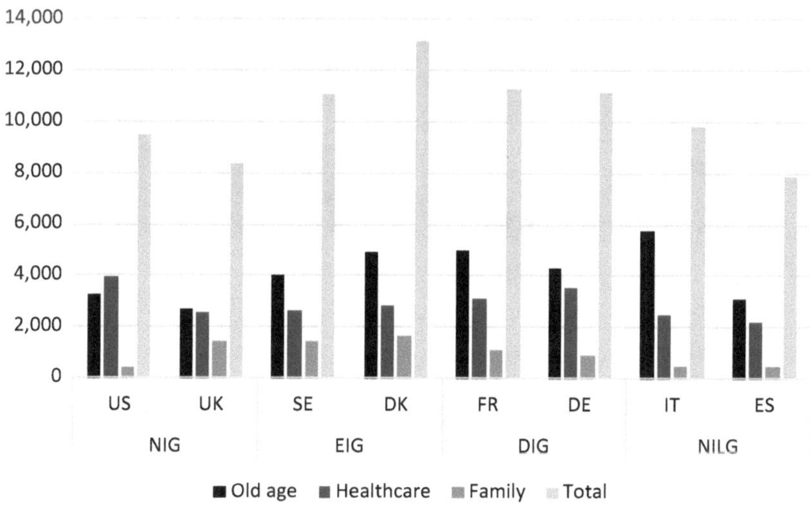

Figure 10.5a Public expenditure on social protection per capita in PPP 2010 (2015/18).

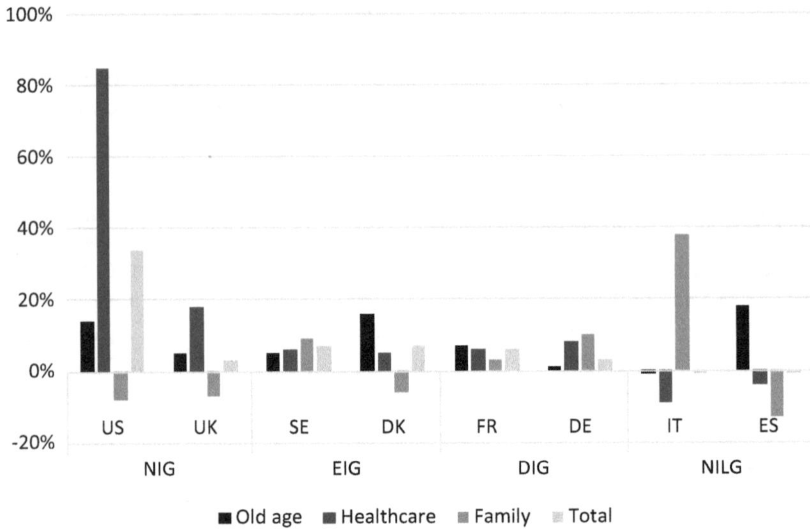

Figure 10.5b Percentage change in social protection expenditure per capita (2015/18).

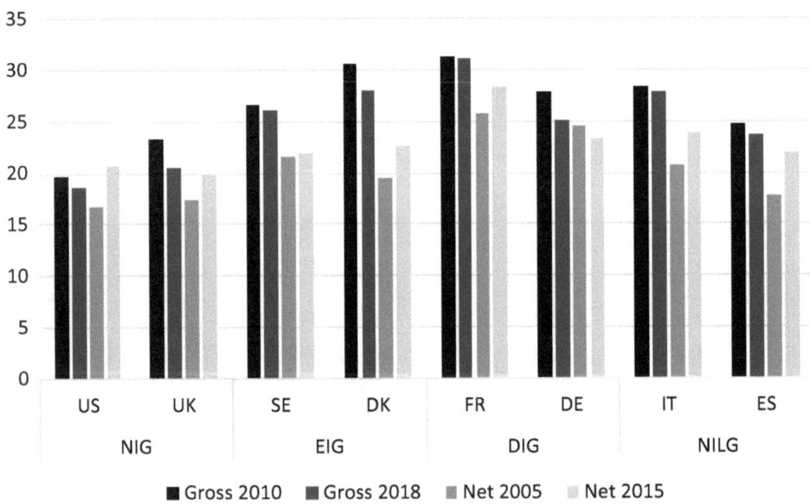

Figure 10.5c Public expenditure on social protection as a percentage of GDP.

Source: Elaboration of OECD data *online* and Scruggs et al. (2017).

In the area of pensions, the British Conservative government intervened in the first public pillar, raising the retirement age for men and women to 66 (Pension Reform 2011) and the number of contribution years to 35 (Pension Act 2014), while in the US there were no innovations.

Also in the health field the level of dynamism in the two countries followed opposite trends. In England the then Liberal–Conservative government decided to reintroduce innovations to the NHS with the reform "Health and Social Care Act 2012", again pushing the accelerator on quasi-markets in a version closer to that of the early 1990s. In the USA the most important public health reform since the 1940s was introduced: the Affordable Care Act (ACA) of 2010, mainly implemented from 2014 onwards. The goal of this reform was to significantly reduce the number of uninsured US residents (partly achieved with a reduction of more than half of the uninsured over a few years). The reform did not introduce a "European-style" healthcare system (either an NHS or mandatory health insurance), but it did allow for an increase in coverage through a combination of regulation and economic incentives that facilitated the expansion of eligibility for Medicaid and changes in individual insurance markets and Medicare. The ACA came up against strong political opposition from the Republicans, that persisted in the implementation phase of the legislation, even after the US Supreme Court's decision to allow individual states to opt out of Medicaid expansion. In family policies, there were no particular changes, except for cuts in the case of the UK: the expansionary period, which began in the mid-1990s, was interrupted between 2012 and 2013, when the then Conservative government retrenched funding for this type of intervention by around 32% as a result of the austerity measures it had launched. In both countries, per capita spending fell by around 7–8% over the five-year period.

10.2.5.2 The model of inclusive egalitarian growth in the Nordic countries

Expenditure on social protection in the Scandinavian countries increased by about 7% over a five-year period. This increase affected almost all policy areas considered here. In the field of pensions, only Denmark made some significant regulatory changes: the Social Democratic government in 2011 brought forward the increase in the retirement age for first-pillar pensions to the period between 2019 and 2022.

In healthcare, the agenda of the last decade in both countries focused more on quality of care, countering social exclusion and on patients' freedom of choice than on costs. In Sweden in 2010 the guarantee of a maximum waiting list, introduced in 2005, was made mandatory for the whole territory by setting a maximum waiting time of three months (Anell, Glenngård, & Merkur, 2012). Once this time limit has been exceeded, the patient may look for another facility and treatment costs are covered by the facility that did not comply with the waiting time. In 2015, a new patient protection law was introduced to widen the scope of patient autonomy and participation. Expenditure went up by about 5–6%.

With a consolidated tradition in the field of family policies, the Nordic countries have continued their efforts to make their system of intervention through early childhood services increasingly universalistic: this occurred especially in Sweden, where spending continued to rise (+9%), while it diminished in Denmark (to note: the level in 2010 was significantly higher than in all the other countries under review).

10.2.5.3 The dualistic inclusive growth model of continental European countries

Continental countries maintained a positive yet far more restrained pace of growth in overall spending compared to the previous decade. Changes in pensions were introduced only in France, where the 2014 socialist reform increased the contribution period required to access a pension by one year for those born from 1973 onwards.

Health insurance systems were characterised by a fair level of expenditure growth throughout the decade. In both cases, the agenda was centred more around access to and quality of care than (merely) cost control and efficiency. In France in 2016, the law for the "Modernisation of the health system" intervened in three directions: a reinforcing of prevention, the improvement of access to health services, especially in terms of their proximity (in rural areas) and opening hours of primary care, and the strengthening of territorial coordination between health facilities. In Germany, the increase in available healthcare resources was accompanied by regulatory interventions with the aim of reducing inequalities in access. Here too action was taken to ensure better access to health services in rural areas and to promote innovative interventions in healthcare (Busse & Blümel, 2014).

In both countries family policies showed substantial continuity from the previous decade: in France because the system was already sufficiently structured, while in the case of Germany spending increased by 10% over a five-year period as a result of the need to implement the major reform introduced at the end of the 2000s.

10.2.5.4 The non-inclusive low growth model of Southern European countries

The countries most affected by austerity were those in Southern Europe, where spending fell in the first five years. With regard to pensions, Italy introduced a drastic increase in the retirement age. To mitigate the effects of this reform, the subsequent Poletti-Renzi reform of 2016–2017 introduced the possibility of early retirement under certain conditions and only for some disadvantaged workers. In Spain, the 2011 reform adopted in the midst of the financial crisis increased the retirement age from 65 to 67 for retirement and from 61 to 63 for early retirement, as well as introducing the state of public finances and life expectancy into the pension indexation formula.

Both countries implemented stringent retrenchment in expenditure on healthcare. While in the case of Italy, the legislator intervened chiefly on the law of stability, providing for a reduction in spending in real terms at least until the middle of the current decade, in Spain the economic cuts were accompanied by some regulatory changes relating to rights of access to the NHS. In particular, in 2012 a fairly insurance-based logic was reintroduced in the right to access services. Irregular immigrants (with the exception of minors and pregnant women) were excluded from the system, except in cases of emergency or infectious diseases. Those with an annual income of more than €100,000 who were not part of the social security system, including family members, were considered not "insured" and excluded from the NHS. However, in 2016 the Spanish Constitutional Court declared this limitation illegal, reintroducing the universalism of the system through the courts. Other regulatory interventions in recent years have intervened on spending by providing new prescription charges, i.e. co-payments, and above all an automatic mechanism (as of 2014) that sets a maximum limit to the increase in public health spending, which cannot be higher than the medium-term Spanish GDP spending projections.

Lastly, family policies revealed a deceleration in spending in Spain and limited innovation in both countries.

10.3 Institutions and politics

How the reforms described in the previous paragraphs came about is not simple to interpret. Here the main actors operating in the field of welfare policies must be considered: the political ones in the strict sense (national parties and governments), the "traditional" social actors, historically recognised as counterparts in these fields (associations representing the interests of workers and enterprises), regional and local administrations, bureaucratic apparatuses, civil society and financial actors (insurance companies and banks).

The discourse here pertains to cases where institutions and actors, in particular politicians, have played a decisive role both in fostering and preventing institutional development. To start with, the various policy sectors should be examined, distinguishing between policy outputs, i.e. regulatory reforms actually adopted or significant increases/cuts in expenditure, and policy outcomes, that is, the more general effects that these policies have in relation to dimensions such as the universalism of enforceable social rights, the level of inequalities in access. The next concluding paragraph is devoted to the issue of outcomes. As far as policy outputs are concerned, we can distinguish three types of situations:

- *Institutional stability*: those cases in which despite governments' intentions and attempts at reform, they do not succeed in bringing about particular regulatory innovations (using Hall's terms, no third-order changes take place and only some first- and second-order changes are approved).

- *Incremental change*: those cases in which the regulations implemented simply try to adapt welfare systems to changed needs, without the aim of introducing deeper transformations (these are mainly first and second order changes).
- *Radical transformation*: those cases in which a combination of relevant changes are introduced to the institutional design of the social protection system, which change its overall functioning and logic (mainly third order changes).

In all the models the pension systems considered were subjected to strain linked to common phenomena (longer life expectancy, ageing of the population, etc.), which could have led to significant second- and third-order changes in the institutional design. If, however, we look at what has happened, we see that the various countries are distributed along all three of the situations indicated above: *institutional stability* in the US case where, despite the ambitions and attempts at reform by two Republican presidents (Reagan in the 1980s and Bush in the first decade of the new century), there have been no radical transformations in the system; *incremental change* in the cases of France and Denmark where the choices adopted over the 40-year period have had the effect of trying to adapt their respective pension systems to changed needs, without, however, introducing any III order transformations; *radical transformations* in Sweden, Germany, Italy, Spain and, to some extent, the United Kingdom (the latter astride the line between incremental change and radical innovation), have brought about a variety of significant changes to the institutional design of the pension system, both in terms of contribution and access to benefits and in terms of the nature of the system itself (with the shift from a single-pillar public model to a multi-pillar model, or the strengthening of the multi-pillar model, where already present). However, it should be borne in mind that in Southern Europe the shift to the multi-pillar model has in actual fact run aground.

In the field of healthcare, there have been no cases of institutional stability but rather of *incremental change*. This has led to the introducing of managerialisation, forms of competition between providers, also opening up to the private sector, decentralisation (and then re-centralisation) of the administration of the system, which have affected practically all European healthcare systems. Furthermore, it has also brought more radical transformation in the case of the United States, thanks to the reforms introduced in the past decade with Obamacare, and in the case of Spain, where in the 1980s the universalist model introduced in the Spanish Constitution at the end of the 1970s began to be implemented.

In the area of family policies, again all three types of situation emerge. *Institutional stability* can be found in the Anglo-Saxon model and to a large extent in the Italian model (with the latter and the British model on the line between *stability* and *incremental change*). In these countries, over a period of 40 years, few changes have been made to a public system that has only been able to support families with children to a residual (USA) or limited extent (Italy and the UK). The concept of *incremental change* accurately describes the situation in the Nordic countries, where innovations produced in the 1970s continued to be implemented and developed in the following decades. (At times more) *radical transformations* have occurred in the continental model (in France since the 1980s and in Germany since the 2000s) with a fair level of success, and in Spain, where less rewarding attempts have been made to promote ambitious policies to broaden public intervention both through services and through monetary transfers and leave. In the latter country, the aspiration to create a robust system of family support, developed in the 2000s, has been confronted with the cuts and austerity of the past decade, collocating the country somewhere between *incremental change* and *radical transformation*.

This brief synthesis of complex processes over a 40-year period affords a number of reflections (Table 10.1). First, there is no model among those considered that has not been affected by radical changes in at least one policy field. Second, incremental change remains the most widespread type of output in the field of welfare policy. Nonetheless, cases of radical transformation are numerous. Third, substantial institutional stability is the situation found least frequently (also because a relatively long time span is considered), but there are important cases (such as the US pension system) where reform ambitions have had to give way to the status quo.

What role have actors and institutions had in the various situations? The strength of institutional path dependency has been very intense in some cases (as in the case of the US pension system) and considerable in many others where policies have followed incremental changes. What has often been decisive is the initial institutional imprinting of the models. Institutions, and the actors associated with the status quo, undoubtedly set the course along

Table 10.1 Policy sectors and types of institutional change: a comparative view

	Institutional stability	*Incremental change*	*Radical Transformation*
Pensions	USA	Denmark, (United Kingdom), France	Sweden, (United Kingdom), Germany, Italy, Spain
Health		Nordic, continental and South European models, (United Kingdom)	USA, (Spain)
Family	USA, (United Kingdom), (Italy)	Nordic model, (United Kingdom), (South European model)	Continental Model (Spain)

which many policies evolved or remained relatively stable. However, this does not detract from the fact that parties, coalitions and social partners have not attempted to change the policy framework.

Generally, within the centre-right parties, there have been two major traditions relating to welfare during these decades: neo-liberal/conservative and Christian/conservative. The former has traditionally preferred, whenever possible, to attribute a more limited role to the state in terms of social protection, especially by framing welfare not as a tool for the redistribution and countering of inequalities, but rather as a way of collectively addressing social needs. In contrast, the latter has been more careful to mix conservative values with a focus on solidarity-based support for the less well-off. In the course of these decades, the parties that have embodied these two traditions have learned from the experience of attempted and sometimes failed reforms, especially those more oriented towards a neo-liberal/conservative perspective. In particular, the "revolutionary" attempts to dismantle welfare promised by Reagan and Thatcher in the 1980s met with frontal defeats (pension reform in the USA and to an extent in the UK) or were scaled down with respect to the objectives initially set (the health reform of the 1990s or the attempt to move to a model based on the Big Society in the UK). This was also due to the fact that many needs covered by welfare policies, in particular the three considered here (income in old age, health, and childcare), had the characteristic of not being typical only of certain social classes rather than others and this triggered consequences for the choices of political parties in terms of policy (ibid.). It was hence more problematic for centre-right parties to propose restrictive reforms in these areas. If anything, it was easier to resist raising expenditure and satisfying hitherto unprotected needs (again, the case of family policies in the USA).

This led to a change in the strategies of many of these parties, based on a twofold line of action. The first was an attempt to introduce changes (of first and second order) that had the capacity to transform the functioning of social protection systems in the medium term, without, however, having to openly promote unpopular reforms with precarious outcomes in terms of electoral support (through forms of *policy drift*). The second entailed transferring public resources as much as possible from direct management by the state or the social partners (as in the case of various systems based on compulsory social insurance with trade unions and employers' associations among the managers), to private actors and the market through various forms (tax concessions instead of services, competition for the management of services between public and private managers, etc.).

Looking at the situation of the left-wing parties, the picture appears just as convoluted for other reasons. In more recent decades, the electoral strength of these parties has often not been sufficient on its own to win elections, and coalitions with forces of the centre have been required, or there has been the necessity to propose electoral programmes capable of bagging a less progressive or more liberal electorate. This is partly due to how the social (and therefore electoral) structure of Western countries has changed over recent decades, with a crisis and a decline in industrial labour (the heart of factory unionism but also of a sizeable part of the electorate of left-wing parties) and a rise in both intellectual and professional work, perhaps self-employed, as well as in unskilled manual work. However, an explanation that is based exclusively on the transformations in the composition of the electorate overlooks an element that has been present in this policy field for a long time: at least in the most advanced experiences of universalistic welfare, or in any case welfare based on generous benefits, this goal has often been achieved through the construction of coalitions between left-wing forces and other more moderate political forces, in those cases where left-wing forces and socio-cultural conditions have made such coalitions possible. This ballgame occurred repeatedly in the Scandinavian case with alliances between left-wing and agrarian parties as early as the first half of the last century (Esping-Andersen, 1990). In contrast, it was precisely this inability to create such alliances in Southern Europe that made the competition in welfare between left and right more polarised (Manow, 2015) and also more difficult to achieve reforms in a universalist sense.

On the whole, therefore, in recent decades participation of the left-wing parties in reformist seasons has taken place but nonetheless in economic conditions that have since changed in comparison with the past (fewer resources to redistribute), and in the presence of a considerable rise in social needs. This changed context has often required more than just an expansionary policy, as was the case until the 1970s (and partly the 1980s); rather it has necessitated a policy of recalibration and readjustment, based on complex balances between what needs to be covered and to what extent. Overall, the strength of the left-wing parties seems to have carried weight above all in the initial phases of construction or consolidation of post-war welfare (up until the 1980s), while the different institutional setups achieved in those decades strongly influenced the subsequent evolutionary path.

The Anglo-Saxon model (above all the USA) is the one in which the different orientations between centre-left and centre-right governments are most clearly visible in terms of social policies, also because of the government systems and party structure that make the comparison and positions more coherent. Obamacare, amidst a thousand limitations and compromises, represented a clear victory for the reformist forces and a defeat for the conservatives who, even after the reform was approved, continued to fight to neutralise it.

In the Nordic countries the universalist tradition of welfare (and also citizenship that has acquired extensive social rights) made it extremely difficult for right-wing forces to try to change the institutional path, meanwhile paving the way for left-wing forces to continue in an inclusive but also reformist and pragmatic tradition, open to coalitions with centre forces (the development of family policies took place much earlier here than in any other country among those considered).

Continental Europe seems to have been able to count on a mix of strong welfare institutions but also on centre-right parties, often of Christian/conservative rather than neo-liberal inspiration, traditionally attentive to the needs of social protection, which have been accompanied by reformist, left-wing social-democratic parties to pursue a path of reform that is increasingly opening up to comply with "new" social needs (see the German reforms in the family sphere, in the wake of those already undertaken by the French).

The Southern European situation is the most challenging to construe. In this context, a traditionally unbalanced welfare system, to the advantage of some social groups (Ascoli & Pavolini, 2015) combined with the historical ideological opposition between the right (partly reactionary) and the left (partly maximalist) have made it more difficult to see reformist parties, both centre-right and centre-left, at work in recent decades and seriously motivated to find a common ground. In comparative terms, Italy is a country where many reforms have not been carried out, or in which the passage from one coalition of a certain political orientation to another has led to a significant change of direction in many welfare policies. Spain, for a whole series of reasons that are too intricate to summarise here, seems instead to have found its own way of promoting reforms in a more pragmatic and consensual way than Italy (Guillén & León, 2014). However, the reformist season in this country was forced to put the brakes on as a result of the crisis and austerity of the last decade (Burroni et al., 2021). Undoubtedly, the crisis and consequential austerity hit both countries with a force not seen in the other cases studied here, giving rise to a real exogenous shock in terms of the functioning of the social protection system.

10.4 The outcomes of welfare policies

By way of conclusion, some reflections can be made on the outcomes of the policies and in particular on the level of inequalities, as well as on the coverage of needs and on expenditure. In the course of a 40-year period, spending on social protection has continued to increase everywhere, both in relation to GDP and in per capita terms (Table 10.2).

In particular, it has at least doubled, if not tripled (Spain and the United States) in per capita terms in all four models, and the ratio to GDP has increased by several percentage points. Moreover, with the exception of Germany and Sweden, in all other countries and models the increase in welfare spending over almost four decades has been much greater than the increase in GDP. In relation to this phenomenon, Germany and Sweden show a more moderate growth in welfare spending, largely because they were already relatively "big spenders" on welfare in 1980 in comparison with all the other countries and, therefore, it is reasonable that these countries grew at a fast pace (Sweden

Table 10.2 Trend of public expenditure on social protection (1980–2018)

	Per capita at constant prices and at PPP				*% on GDP (gross)*	
	1980	*2015*	*Variation % 1980–2015*	*Variation % GDP 1980–2015*	*1980*	*2018*
United States	3.794	12.722	+235%	+153%	13.2	18.7
United Kingdom	3.177	8.654	+172%	+121%	15.8	20.6
Sweden	6.176	11.847	+92%	+110%	24.8	26.1
Denmark	5.464	14.058	+157%	+83%	20.3	28.0
France	4.802	11.884	+147%	+86%	20.1	31.2
Germany	6.592	11.548	+75%	+103%	23.6	25.1
Italy	4.339	9.798	+126%	+50%	18.2	27.9
Spain	2.681	7.832	+192%	+117%	15.0	23.7

Source: Elaboration on OECD data.

almost doubled its per capita spending), yet less intensively than the others. Overall, differences in expenditure levels between countries in the various models have declined over time: the coefficient of variation was seen to fall in the period from 1980 to 2015 (not shown in Table 10.2).

This trend in expenditure is not attributable only to demographic factors, such as the ageing of the population: while pension expenditure has certainly increased over a period of 40 years as a result of the progressive increase in life expectancy of individuals, all the other policy areas considered here have seen an increase in the level of real per capita expenditure (this figure is not shown in the table, but it may be obtained by comparing the graphs illustrated so far).

In net opposition to the idea of a generalised retrenchment of social protection as a result of neo-liberal policies, the picture that emerges from these pages is, instead, of a largely resilient welfare state that has absorbed an increasing share of public economic resources over time. In conclusion, however, our question concerns the effect on reducing inequality. Two types of exercises can be carried out here: one is to analyse the current level of inequality in access to welfare benefits, after decades of investment in public protection systems, while the other consists in considering the studies that offer information in relation to the policy areas discussed here.

The comparative analysis on distributional effects has been carried out by considering a series of indicators related both to the single policy areas considered (pensions, health, and family support policies) and to the total amount of resources transferred through welfare. Starting with the latter, we refer to Chapter 5 for a comparative understanding of how much the set of monetary transfers to households through public welfare in its various forms (from pensions to unemployment benefits to transfers for dependent family members), helps households to limit the risk of being poor. Here it is useful to bear in mind that the continental and Nordic one model, thanks to its welfare, reduces the risk of poverty the most, while the Anglo-Saxon model, in particular the United States, is that which manages to change people's starting conditions the least.

In the sphere of pensions, one way of appreciating the extent of generosity, but also fairness, of the social protection system is to consider the net replacement rates of pensions, i.e. how much pension income corresponds to when compared to the average salary obtained during the last years of work (Table 10.3). Two countries, Denmark and France, manage to achieve very low poverty rates among the elderly thanks to medium to high replacement rates, achieved in partially different ways. In Denmark an inclusive multi-pillar system is implemented (almost all active people on the labour market are covered), and higher net replacement rates for lower paid workers. France applies a slightly higher but similar average replacement rate among different profiles of workers within a system mainly centred around the public pillar. More horizontal redistribution takes place in Denmark than in France. The results in these two countries should hardly be surprising given the significantly higher per capita level of pension expenditure compared to all the remaining countries except Italy. This last country's result is, nonetheless, somewhat unexpected: while spending extensively on pensions, Italy has a significantly higher poverty rate among the elderly compared to the previous two countries. This is linked to the fact that of the eight countries surveyed, it has the highest replacement rates, with no greater attention paid to lower income earners (indeed the highest replacement rate is among workers with wages of 150% of the average wage). Hence, Italy emerges as a country that spends a considerable amount but fails to reduce poverty among the elderly and also inequality among pensioners in proportion to its expenditure. Denmark succeeds in both objectives, while France succeeds in reducing poverty but curtails inequality to a lesser extent.[2] The other countries are in different situations. The two Anglo-Saxon countries and Spain are characterised by substantial poverty rates among the elderly, which can be linked both to lower levels of public spending and also to a limited redistribution of resources among different profiles of workers (as can be deduced from replacement rates that grow as the worker's salary increases and, in the Anglo-Saxon countries, from the spread of the multi-pillar centred in the strongest sectors of the labour market[3]). Germany and Sweden lie somewhere between the latter group and the former.

Turning to family policies, in order to measure the diffusion but also the distributional effects of these interventions, it is useful to divide them into early childhood services (Table 10.4) and parental leave (Table 10.5). These services cover a relatively high percentage of children between 0 and 2 years of age in Denmark and France (around 55%), but require a certain economic sacrifice from families (especially couples) in order to be able to send their

Table 10.3 Income, pensions, and poverty

	Net replacement rate of pensions (men; %) (2018)						*Coverage rate of supplementary pensions (% active population 15–64 years) (2016)*			*Poverty rate among elderly (2016)*	*Per capita at fixed prices and at PPP (2015)*
	Public pillar			*Public and private pillars*			*Almost-compulsory*	*Occupa-tional*	*Indivi-dual*		
	50% of average salary	*100% of average salary*	*150% of average salary*	*50%of average salary*	*100% of average salary*	*150% of average salary*					
United States	61.2	49.4	42.7	94.1	83.7	79.0	0%	44%	19%	23.1	3.655
United Kingdom	51.0	28.4	20.2	82.3	61.0	47.4	46%	5%		15.3	2.806
Sweden	60.7	53.4	68.9	60.7	53.4	68.9	100%	24%		11.3	4.162
Denmark	104.5	70.9	63.3	104.5	70.9	63.3	85%	18%		3.0	5.713
France	71.4	73.6	69.0	71.4	73.6	69.0	0%	25%	8%	3.4	5.315
Germany	56.1	51.9	51.4	68.6	68.0	67.5	0%	70%		9.6	4.309
Italy	92.0	91.8	94.4	92.0	91.8	94.4	0%	21%		10.3	5.673
Spain	78.6	83.4	82.8	78.6	83.4	82.8	0%	26%		9.4	3.681

Source: OECD.

Table 10.4 Net costs for parents sending their children to early childhood education services (% of net household income) (2015)

	Single parent with 2 children		*Couple with 2 children and partner salary at 100% of average*		*Couple with 2 children and partner salary at 67% of average*		*Children aged 0–2 in socio-educational services for early childhood (%) (2017)*
	Main income earner with 100% of average salary	*Main income earner with 67% of average salary*	*Main income earner with 100% of average salary*	*Main income earner with 67% of average salary*	*Main income earner with 100% of average salary*	*Main income earner with 67% of average salary*	
United States	27	34	24	29	17	21	28.0*
United Kingdom	21	19	54	69	41	34	37.7
Sweden	5	4	3	4	4	5	46.6
Denmark	7	3	8	10	9	11	55.4
France	6	4	12	11	9	8	56.3
Germany	6	2	4	5	5	6	37.2
Italy	5	4	4	4	5	5	29.7
Spain	7	9	4	5	4	5	36.4

Source: OECD.

Note: * Data refers to 2011.

Table 10.5 Regulation of leave (2018)

	Length of leave (weeks)		*Replacement rate of monetary transfer linked to maternity leave*		
	Maternity leave	*Parental leave*	*50% of gross average salary*	*100% of gross average salary*	*150% of gross average salary*
United States	0	0	–	–	–
United Kingdom	39	0	48.4	31.1	25.4
Sweden	18	32	77.6	77.6	56.3
Denmark	12.9	42.9	100.0	53.3	35.5
France	16	26	100.0	100.0	98.8
Germany	14	44	100.0	100.0	100.0
Italy	21.7	26	80.0	80.0	80.0
Spain	16	0	100.0	100.0	100.0

Source: OECD.

children to nursery school or kindergarten. These countries are followed by Sweden, where around 47% of children go to nursery school and where the cost for families to access these services is lower for all family profiles compared to France and Denmark. Germany, the United Kingdom, and Spain provide coverage for about 37% of children but do so with different burdens on household budgets: in Germany and Spain through low levels of household expenditure, in the United Kingdom much higher levels, especially for families with lower incomes. The United States and Italy are in last place for the provision of early childhood services, but, at least in the case of Italy, families do not have to bear a high cost of accessing them.

A comparison of leave legislation shows a more easily classifiable situation. On the one hand, the two Anglo-Saxon countries reveal there is little or no incentive to take maternity leave (in the UK there are 39 weeks for maternity leave but with relatively low rates of replacement) or none at all (in the US, as pointed out in the previous paragraph). Spain comes closest to the Anglo-Saxon countries given the limited duration of maternity leave (although much better compensated for all worker profiles) and the absence of parental leave. The other countries are characterised by an overall broad coverage in terms of duration, adding up the different types of leave, and of the wage replacement rate, without differentiating between worker profiles (except for the Scandinavian countries where the replacement rate diminishes as the worker's wage increases).

In the case of healthcare, finally, it is useful to take up the main results of a recent OECD study (2019) dedicated specifically to the theme of access to healthcare according to economic situation, using the comparison between people belonging to the lowest quintile of income and those belonging to the highest quintile (Table 10.6). The United States, as it was easy to hypothesise,

Table 10.6 Inequalities in terms of access to health services (2018)

	Need-based standardised probability for care or visiting a doctor per income quintile (%)		*Need-based standardised probability of hospitalisation per income quintile (%)*		*Access to preventive (screening) services for breast cancer by income quintile (%)*		*Access to prevention (screening) services for colorectal cancer by income quintile (%)*	
	I quintile	*V quintile*	*I quintile*	*V quintile*	*I quintile*	*V quintile*	*I quintile*	*V quintile*
United States	59*	74*	12*	9*	71*	87*	51*	71*
United Kingdom	76	77	8	8	51*	62*	50*	45*
Sweden	62	65	6	8	74*	93*	43*	22*
Denmark	82*	76*	10	7	83	80	46	49
France	86*	91*	13	13	79*	90*	53*	67*
Germany	84*	88*	17*	14*	70	72	71*	77*
Italy	75*	83*	8	9	55*	75*	31*	50*
Spain	81	81	8	8	68*	86*	19*	35*

Source: OECD (2019).

Note: * Difference between I and V quintile statistically significant by 5%.

represents the context in which social class counts the most in significantly differentiating access to health services, including specialist facilities, hospitals and, above all, preventive care units. It should be remembered that this is the only country among those considered in this chapter in which a sizeable part of the population is not covered, except for emergency services (through the Medicaid programme). The country most similar to the United States is Italy where, in spite of the presence of the NHS, we find significant and wide differences per social class in all services, with the exception of hospitals. At the opposite end of the spectrum from the United States (and Italy) we find the Nordic countries, where no differences by social class can be observed. In the continental countries, with compulsory insurance systems, the differences are present but limited in the specialist-hospital field, while they become more marked in the field of prevention, especially in France. Two of the three remaining NHS systems (the UK and Spain) show no particular differences by social class in the specialist-hospital field, while these differences become more marked in the field of prevention, especially in Spain.

10.5 Concluding remarks

To summarise the results of the above tables, the data analysis confirms the traditional image of the various welfare systems, with some limited differentiations. The Anglo-Saxon welfare systems, especially the US and Southern European ones, are the contexts in which the social protection system succeeds least in reducing (or intends least to reduce) poverty and social inequalities. The Nordic countries are the opposite, followed by the continental countries.

Bearing in mind, however, that the data discussed concern the current phase, in which a high level of maturity has been reached in most of the social protection systems under review (also in terms of expenditure), it is difficult to imagine that in the past decades (at least since the 1980s), the inequalities created or not alleviated by welfare systems could have been greater than they are today, with some exceptions. In particular, in the field of pensions, the reforms that have affected European countries since the 1980s, and especially since the 1990s (in the USA very little has happened, as illustrated in the previous paragraph), have mainly concerned two aspects: the establishment of complementary pension schemes with (semi-)voluntary membership (the so-called multi-pillarisation) and the adoption of measures such as raising the retirement age or the years of contribution required to access a pension, with the aim of curtailing costs and guaranteeing the financial sustainability of pension systems. These reforms have not affected the universalism and overall largesse of the pension schemes in the Nordic countries or in France, but they have had different effects in other contexts. In particular, in the UK and Germany they have increased differences in the conditions of access to benefits on the basis of social class, creating the basis for the process of dualisation referred to in the introduction to this text, while in Southern

Europe the net effect they have had is not clear, although it would seem most likely to be that of increasing inequalities, at least in the case of Italy (Raitano & Jessoula, 2016).

In the sphere of family policies, with the sole exception of the Anglo-Saxon model (in particular the US) and, to a small degree, Italy (Pavolini et al., 2016), the expansion of interventions over the decades has brought with it greater universalism. More precisely, Daly and Ferragina (2018) identify the "founding phase" of family policies in the period between 1960 and 1980 in which welfare states mainly developed maternity leave for pregnant women in conjunction with monetary transfers and tax relief for families. From 1980 onwards, however, what Daly and Ferragina (2018) call the "consolidation phase" of family policies began, in which new policy instruments, such as care services, were introduced in addition to those already developed during the founding phase, forming the articulated range of family policies that includes: monetary transfers, care services, leave, promotion of flexible and part-time work. Over the years and decades, such interventions have become increasingly widespread in Europe.

A similar reasoning may be held as feasible also for healthcare. In this case, the United States represents a positive case starting from the phenomenon of "Obamacare", given the increase in coverage in the potentially universalistic direction of this intervention. All the other countries have seen an increase in the overall level of coverage and universalism over time, with Italy probably being the only European country among those considered where the combination of territorial inequalities between North and South in the functioning of the NHS and heavy spending cuts over the last two decades have in fact undermined the universalism of the system (Pavolini & Guillén, 2013; Pavolini & Seeleib-Kaiser, 2018).

Notes

1 To note: as this is an index covering only public compulsory pensions, it underestimates the level of generosity provided in those systems that have traditionally been multi-pillar (e.g. the UK) or that have become so in recent decades (e.g. Germany).

2 Other Eurostat data, not reported here and referring only to EU countries, show that Italy and France are among the Western European countries with the highest concentration of pension incomes in the highest quintiles of pensioners.

3 On this point see Seeleib-Kaiser and Pavolini (2018).

References

Adema, W., Fron, P., & Ladaique, M. (2011). *Is the European welfare state really more expensive?: Indicators on social spending, 1980–2012; and a manual to the OECD social expenditure database (SOCX).* OECD Social, Employment and Migration Working Papers, No. 124. Paris: OECD Publishing.

Anell, A., Glenngård, A.H., & Merkur, S. (2012). Sweden: Health system review. *Health Systems in Transition*, 14(5), 1–159

Anderson, K.M. (2005). Pension reform in Sweden: Radical reform in a mature pension system. In G. Bonoli (Ed.), *Ageing and pension around the world* (pp. 94–115). Cheltenham: Edward Elgar.

Anderson, K.M., & Immergut, H. (2007). *Sweden: After social democratic hegemony*. In E. Immergut, K., Anderson & I. Schulze (Eds), *Handbook of West European pension politics* (pp. 349–395). Oxford: Oxford University Press.

Ascoli, U. & Pavolini, E. (2015) (Eds). *The Italian welfare state in a European perspective*. Bristol: Policy Press.

Ascoli U. & Pavolini, E. (2016) (Eds). *The Italian welfare state in a European perspective: A comparative analysis.* Bristol: Bristol University Press.

Béland, D., Blomqvist, P., Andersen J.G., Palme J., & Waddan, A. (2015). The universal decline of universality?: Social Policy change in Canada, Denmark, Sweden and the UK. *Social Policy and Adminstration*, 48(7), 739–756. doi.org/10.1111/spol.12064

Berkowitz, E. & De Witt, L. (2015). Social security. In D. Beland, C. Howard, & K. Morgan (Eds), *The Oxford handbook of US social policy* (pp. 261–278). Oxford: Oxford University Press.

Boyle, S. (2011). *Health system in transition: United Kingdom (England)*. Brussels: European Observatory on Health System and Policies.

Boyle, S. (2013). England: Health reforms have improved the NHS. In E. Pavolini & A.M. Guillén (Eds), *Health care system in Europe under austerity* (pp. 31–56). London: Palgrave Macmillan.

Blome, A. (2017). *The politics of work-family reforms in Italy and Germany*. London: Routledge.

Blomqvist, P. & Winblad, U. (2013). Sweden: Continued marketization within a universalist system. In E. Pavolini & A.M. Guillén (Eds), *Health care system in Europe under austerity* (pp. 9–30). London: Palgrave Macmillan.

Bradshaw, R.J., Glendinning, C., Maynard, A.K., & Bennet F. (2015). *ESPN thematic report on social investment: United Kingdom*. Brussels: European Social Policy Network.

Burroni, L., Pavolini, E., & Regini, M. (2021) (Eds). *Mediterranean capitalism revisited: One model, different trajectories*. Ithaca: Cornell University Press.

Busse, R. & Blümel, M. (2014). Germany: Health system review. *Health Systems in Transition*, 16(2), 1–296.

Busse, R. & Riesberg, A. (2004). Health care systems in transition: Germany. *Health Systems in Transition*, 6(9), 1–234.

Chulià, E. (2007). Spain: Between majority rule and incrementalism. In E. Immergut, K. Anderson, & I. Schulze (Eds), *Handbook of West European pension politics* (pp. 499–554). Oxford: Oxford University Press.

da Conceicao-Heldt, E. (2007). France: The importance of electoral cycle. In E. Immergut, K. Anderson, & I. Schulze (Eds), *Handbook of West European pension politics* (pp. 150–202). Oxford: Oxford University Press,

Daly, M. & Ferragina, E. (2018). Family policy in high-income countries: Five decades of development. *Journal of European Social Policy*, 28(3), 255–270. doi:10.1177/0958928717735060

Emmeneger, P., Häusermann, S., Palier, B., & Seeleib-Kaieser, M. (2012). *The age of dualization: The changing face of inequality in deindustrializing society.* Oxford: Oxford University Press.
Esping-Andersen, G. (1990). *The three world of welfare capitalism.* Cambridge: Polity Press.
European Commission (2015). *The 2015 pension adeguacy report: Current and future income adeguacy in old age in the EU. Volume II*, Joint Report Prepared by the European Commission (DG EMPL) and the Social Protection Committee (SPC)
Ferrera, M., & Jessoula, M. (2005), Reconfiguring Italian pensions: From policy stalemate to comprehensive reforms. In G. Bonoli (Ed.), *Ageing and pension around the world* (pp. 24–46). Cheltenham: Edward Elgar.
Ferrera M., & Jessoula, M. (2007). Italy: A narrow gate for path-shift. In E. Immergut, K. Anderson, & I. Schulze (Eds), *Handbook of West European pension politics* (pp. 396–453). Oxford: Oxford University Press.
Fidalgo, E. & Ventura, J. (2013). Spain: Quo vadis? From cost containment to structural reforms. In E. Pavolini & A.M. Guillén (Eds), *Health care system in Europe under austerity* (pp. 82–101). London: Palgrave Macmillan.
Green-Pedersen, C. (2007). Denmark: A "world bank" pension system. In E. Immergut, K. Anderson & I. Schulze (Eds), *Handbook of West European pension politics* (pp. 454–498). Oxford: Oxford University Press.
Guillén, A.M. & León, M. (2014) (Eds). *The Spanish welfare State in European Context.* Farnham: Ashgate.
Guillén, A.M. & Pavolini, E. (2017). Spain: Regaining the confidence and legitimacy to advance social policy. In P. Taylor-Gooby, B. Leruth, & H. Chung, *After austerity: Welfare state transformation in Europe after the Great Recession* (pp. 136–154). Oxford: Oxford University Press.
Hall, P. (1993). Policy paradigms, social learning, and the state: The case of economic policymaking in Britain. *Comparative Politics*, 25(3), 275–296.
Hassenteufelf, P. & Klenk, T. (2013). Germany: Mixing rescaling, privatization and managerialism. In E. Pavolini & A. M. Guillén (Eds), *Health care system in Europe under austerity* (pp. 122–146). London: Palgrave Macmillan.
Hills, J. & Stewart, K. (2005) (Eds). *A more equal society? New Labour, poverty, inequality and exclusion.* London: Policy Press.
Hinrics, K. (2005). New century – new paradigm: Pension reforms in Germany. In G. Bonoli (Ed.), *Ageing and pension around the world* (pp. 47–73). Cheltenham: Edward Elgar.
Jansen, C. (2014). *The right and the welfare state.* Oxford: Oxford University Press.
Jessoula, M. & Raitano, M. (2016). I nervi scoperti del sistema pensionistico Italiano. *Il Mulino*, 3, 503–511.
Lewis, J. (2009). *Work-family balance, gender and policy*. Cheltenham: Edward Elgar.
León, M., Pavolini, E., Miro y Artigas, J., & Sorrenti, A. (2021). Policy change and partisan politics: Understanding family policy differentiation in two similar countries. *Social Politics: International Studies in Gender, State & Society*, 28(2), 451–476. doi.org/10.1093/sp/jxz025
Mandin, C. & Palier, B. (2005). The politics of pension reform in France: The end of exceptionalism? In G. Bonoli (Ed.), *Ageing and pension around the world* (pp. 74–93). Cheltenham: Edward Elgar Publishing.

Manow, P. (2015). Workers, farmers and Catholicism: A history of political class coalitions and the South-European welfare state regime. *Journal of European Social Policy*, 25(1), 32–49. doi:10.1177/0958928714556969.

Michel, S. (2015). Care and work-family policies. In D. Beland, C. Howard, & K. Morgan (Eds), *The Oxford handbook of US social policy* (pp. 491–509). Oxford: Oxford University Press.

Morgan, K. (2003). The politics of mothers' employment: France in comparative perspective. *World Politics*, 55(2), 259–289. doi:10.1353/wp.2003.0013

Morel, N., Palier, B., & Joakim, P. (2012). *Towards a social investment welfare state?* Bristol: Bristol University Press.

Naczyk, M. (2017). France: Squarinq the circle of unification in a fragmented pension system. In D. Natali (Ed.), *The new pension mix in Europe recent reforms, their distributional effects and political dynamics* (pp. 73–98). Brussels: Peter Lang.

Naldini, M. (2003) (Ed.). *The family in the Mediterranean welfare state*. London: Routledge.

Oberlander, J. (2016). Implementing the Affordable Care Act: The promise and limits of health care reform. *Journal of Health Politics, Policy and Law*, 41(4), 803–826. doi:10.1215/03616878-3620953

OECD (2019). *Health at a glance*. Paris: OECD.

Palier, B. & Davesne, A. (2013). France: Squaring the health spending circle?. In E. Pavolini & A.M. Guillén (Eds), *Health care system in Europe under austerity* (pp. 102–125). London: Palgrave Macmillan.

Pavolini, E. (2011) (Ed.). *Il cambiamento possibile/; La sanità in Sicilia tra nord & sud.* Fondazione RES, Rome: Meridiana Libri-Donzelli

Pavolini, E. & Guillén, A.M. (2013) (Eds). *Health care system in Europe under austerity*. London: Palgrave Macmillan

Pavolini, E. León M., Guillén M., & Ascoli, U. (2016). From austerity to permanent strain? The European Union and welfare state reform in Italy and Spain. In C. De La Porte, & E. Heins (Eds) *The sovereign debt crisis, the EU and welfare state reform* (pp. 131–157). London: Palgrave Macmillan.

Pavolini, E. & Seeleib-Kaiser, M. (2018). Comparing occupational welfare in Europe: The case of occupational pensions. *Social Policy and Administration*, 52(2), 477–490

Pavolini, E. & Vicarelli, M.G. (2013). Le due italia della sanitá. In S. Vassallo (Ed.), *Il divario incolmabile: Rappresentanza politica & rendimento istituzionale nelle regioni Italiane*,(193–222). Bologna: Il Mulino.

Pierson P. (1994). *Dismantling the welfare state?: Reagan, Thatcher and the politics of retrenchment*. Cambridge: Cambridge University Press.

Sabatinelli, S. (2017). *Politiche per crescere. La prima infanzia tra cura & investimento sociale*. Bologna: Il Mulino.

Sacchi, S. (2013). *La riforma del welfare nella crisi del debito Italiano: Pensioni, lavoro, ammortizatori sociali*. In A. Di Virgilio, & C. Radaelli (Eds), *Politica in Italia: I fatti dell'anno & le interpretazioni* (pp. 217–236). Bologna: Il Mulino

Saraceno, C. (2003). *Mutamenti della famiglia & politiche sociali in Italia*. Bologna: Il Mulino.

Seeleib-Kaiser, M. (2016). The end of conservative German model. *Social Policy and Administration*, 50 (2), 219–240. doi.org/10.1111/spol.12212

Scruggs, L., Jahn, D., & Kuitto, K. (2017). *Comparative welfare entitlements dataset 2. Version 2017-09.* University of Connecticut & University of Greifswald

Suarez Corujo, B. (2014). *El sistema público de pensiones: Crisis, reforma y sostenibilidad.* Valladolid: Lex Nova, Thomson Reuters.

Vicarelli, M.G. (2005). Control, competition and cooperation in European health systems: Points of contact between health policy and industrial policy. In M. Di Tommaso & S. Schweitzer (Eds), *Health policy and high-tech industrial development* (pp. 59–76). Cheltenham: Edward Elgar.

Weaver, R.K. (2005). Public pension reform in the United States. In G. Bonoli (Eds), *Ageing and pension around the world* (pp. 230–251). Cheltenham: Edward Elgar.

Whiteside, N. (2017). Britain's pension reform: A new departure. In D. Natali (Eds), *The new pension mix in Europe recent reforms, their distributional effects and political dynamics* (pp. 183–206). Brussels: Peter Lang.

Woods, D.R. (2012) (Ed.). *Family policy in transformation: US and UK policies.* London: Palgrave Macmillan.

Chapter 11

The influence of innovation and education policy on inclusive growth

Alberto Gherardini, Cecilia Manzo, and Dario Raspanti

11.1 Introduction

Linked indissolubly to the rise of ICT, the technological revolution has appreciably influenced advanced economies. Since the 1980s, firms relocate upstream or downstream the global value chains to face international competition from developing countries more effectively. The uncertainty in technological trajectories and the high degree of specialisation required to design new products and services has influenced innovation realisation. The conception and development of innovative products are no longer just the result of large firms' R&D investments but are fuelled by collaboration between different actors: large firms and SMEs, public and private research centres, and universities. In other words, the paradigm of open-innovation (Chesbrough, 2003) has steadily established itself and innovation is increasingly becoming a social construction (Trigilia, 2007).

In this scenario, the role of education and training institutions, and their relations with cutting-edge knowledge is becoming progressively more important. Universities' awareness to applied research demands, on the one hand, and firms' readiness to recognise the opportunities arising from the advancement of scientific research, on the other, are fundamental for generating innovation (Etzkowitz & Leydesdorff, 2000; Lawton-Smith, 2006; Gherardini, 2015). This has also changed the role of public policies for innovation. Today, governments actively support firms' basic and pre-competitive research by supporting investments, implementing network-building policies between firms and public research, and protecting intellectual property.

Hence innovation and education policies (IEP) have become increasingly fundamental development levers within the national political economy (Burroni, 2020). A country's level of welfare is conditioned by productivity, which in turn is closely linked to the innovative capacity of businesses and levels of education. Second, the sustainability of welfare systems, ever more costly due to the exacerbation of old social risks and the emergence of new ones, is influenced by the stability, if not the growth, of the financial bases of states, deriving from the taxation of the incomes of firms and individuals. But

DOI: 10.4324/9781003297130-14

the capacity of firms to bear the tax burden resulting from broad and inclusive welfare systems is in turn affected by the presence of a localised competitive advantage, aimed at avoiding flight to countries with lower tax burdens (Castells & Himmanen, 2002; Trigilia, 2016).

The aim of this chapter is to reconstruct the changes in the IEPs that take place in the wake of a shift beyond the Fordist–Taylorist paradigm, allowing the learning society paradigm to gain a foothold through the ICT revolution. In the following four paragraphs, the IEPs of the eight countries considered will be explored in depth. The sixth paragraph is devoted solely to education policies.

11.2 The Nordic countries

The economies of Sweden and Denmark at the beginning of the 1980s were in highly different conditions (Edquist & Lundvall, 1993; Fagerberg, 2016). While Denmark represented the paradigmatic case of the "small country in big trouble" because it was characterised by a fragile production system, chiefly rooted in the primary and agri-food sectors (Schwartz, 1994), the Swedish case was taken as a model of innovation-based development by international think tanks (OECD, 1997). Indeed, from the mid-1970s, Sweden began to lay the foundations of its systemic approach to innovation. However, in the early 1990s, both Scandinavian countries need to identify new development strategies.

11.2.1 The Danish responses to the challenges of the 1990s

Since the post-war period, the Danish economy has been governed by a dense network of horizontal and vertical relationships between policymakers, social partners, local stakeholders, and firms. For this reason, Denmark has been described as the country of the "negotiated economy" (Nielsen & Pedersen, 1991). A key feature of the Danish economic governance is the preponderance of organisations representing the interests of capital and labour, which use dialogue and compromise as the main instruments for resolving disputes at the central and, above all, at the local level. The state plays the role of intermediary and arbitrator. The development of the negotiated economy is closely linked to the particular Danish production structure, which consists mainly of networks of small enterprises, many of which are organised into cooperative societies (Kristensen, 1996; Iversen & Andersen, 2008). Moreover, interest representation organisations played a role in transforming Denmark into an innovation-driven economy. Darius Ornston (2012) coined the term "creative" neo-corporatism to describe social partners' involvement in creating the condition for Danish firms to enter high-tech markets.

While in other European countries, concertation served to defend constituent interests against external pressures, from the 1980s onwards in

Denmark it defined development strategies based on R&D training and support. This approach was inaugurated during the "blue period", namely, a decade of centre-right governments from 1982 to 1993 (Amin & Thomas, 1996) that continued after the return of a social-democratic coalition to government (1993–2001). Notwithstanding government alternation, this style of political economy has been not substantially altered, and now thus represents a strongly institutionalised practice.

The main achievements of creative corporatism were accomplished during the "blue period". One of these was to move beyond the sectoral and local approach to innovation using system-oriented national policies that promoted technology foresight (Amin & Thomas, 1996). Another successful feat involved the public support offered to the establishment and reproduction of local networks, both inter-firm and between firms and research centres, via the four-year Strategy 92 programme, launched in 1989 and developed by the Danish Technological Institute (Amin & Thomas, 1996, 267; Ornston, 2012, 109). This was the first of many clustering initiatives. Over time, succeeding governments have sought to build virtuous relationships with universities and technological assistance and training institutions (Edquist & Lundvall, 1993, 280; DASTI, 2016; Gergils, 2006). Finally, policies aimed at supporting start-ups in high-tech sectors were designed to create or attract venture capital funds, notably through the activation of private pension funds (Grimpe, 2015).

These interventions created some of the preconditions that would later give rise to the economic miracle of the early 2000s. Denmark witnessed the flourishing of high-tech companies, especially in the biotechnology and ICT sectors. The share of exports in highly innovative segments grew by 81% between 1985 and 2000 (Ornston, 2012, 94).

In more recent years, the Liberal government of Rasmussen launched the Danish Globalisation Strategy (2006) to increase the quality and international profile of Danish scientific research and its spillovers. This objective was pursued through the implementation of various strategies: increasing the share of competitive funding, upgrading doctorates and industrial doctorates, investing in long-life learning, merging processes between universities and, finally, the establishment of three "antennae" in highly innovative regions (Silicon Valley, Shanghai, and Munich), capable of offering internationalisation and opportunities for exchanging knowledge to Danish companies (Klitkou & Kaloudis, 2009; DFiR, 2018, 27; Aagaard & de Boer et al., 2017). The following Social Democratic government led by Thorning-Schmidt introduced the "Denmark–A Nation of Solutions" strategy (2013). In this case, the government first identified the general challenges (environment, energy, ageing population and digital security), and then the policy instruments, both in the innovation and tertiary education arenas, necessary to address them and, at the same time, promote economic growth and employment (Grimpe, 2015; Larousse, 2017). In both cases, the aim was to expand public investment in research and development from 0.7% to 1% of GDP.

Both strategies were the result of complex negotiation processes between the main actors of the national innovation system.

11.2.2 Innovation policy in Sweden

Due to the financial crisis of the 1990s and the subsequent takeover of many large Swedish companies by foreign multinationals, Sweden was forced to transform its governance style, passing from a sectoral to a systemic approach to innovation. The shift produced the Research and Innovation Act of 2008 and the Swedish Innovation Strategy of 2012. In both cases, these plans were drawn up following long preparatory phases of discussion between ministries, agencies and social actors. The first plan aimed to increase competition in the allocation of research funding (albeit in a context of increased ordinary funding), to push further towards the commercialisation of public knowledge and to fund strategic research areas (OECD, 2013; 2016), giving rise to a number of thematic policy-networks comprising universities, research centres and companies. By way of example, in the context of the so-called 4.0 transformations, a network (*Produktion 2030*) was set up between *Teknikföretagen* and IF Metall, i.e. the employers' associations representing respectively companies in the engineering and metalworking sectors, some multinationals in the technology and automotive sectors (including ABB, Alimak, Ericsson, Saab, Scania, and Volvo), many SMEs, and some universities and research institutions. In this case, the network aimed to develop innovation projects, disseminate the results to SMEs, provide vocational training, and learn about and disseminate good practices at a national level (Digital Transformation Monitor, 2017).

Swedish universities have a key role in the national innovation system. Public research closely adhered to the triple helix paradigm due to the centre-right government's 1992 Universities Act. The Act supported the promotion of university-industry consortia, entrepreneurship among university students and high-tech clusters (Etzkowitz, 2008). In terms of governance, this was achieved by activating national research funding foundations and venture capital funds. Universities and regional governments also gradually set up their own technology transfer foundations. Besides these, regional development agencies (*VINNOVA* and *Tillväxtverket*) were also included.

11.3 The countries of Continental Europe

France and Germany responded in markedly different ways to the major challenges of the end of the Fordist era. In France, the deindustrialisation process was more pronounced, similar in scope to that of the NIG countries. As will be seen, this initiated a public debate on re-industrialisation, which would have, above all, the effect of limiting the relocation of the R&D departments of French firms to other countries (Mustar, 2016). In contrast, in the 1990s, the German manufacturing system faced a competitiveness crisis. Here, governments used innovation policies to stimulate the development of high-tech sectors and limit the traditional propensity of German firms for incremental innovation, within a more comprehensive scenario of enhancement of the manufacturing sector.

In terms of policy trends, both countries introduced new approaches – clusters, the triple helix, strengthening entrepreneurship – but France showed more discontinuity with the past than Germany, radically changing its approach from *technological colbertism* (Chesnais, 1993) to an *innovation-pull* approach. In Germany, on the other hand, the changes were less radical, and, albeit there are recent changes, it still conserves a *manufacturing-led* approach.

11.3.1 The great transformation of French innovation policy

The aforementioned innovation-pull policies, which aim at supporting the R&D activities of companies, represent a key feature of the French approach to innovation today. These chiefly take the shape of direct fiscal incentives to companies, mostly tax offsets or credit support from public investment funds. However, there are also other measures such as policies for high-tech clusters and support for technology transfer.

All these measures have engendered a discontinuity from the 1980s (Larédo, 2016). In the past, public investment was indeed driven by sectoral investment programmes (Larédo & Mustar, 2001, 452). The model was that of technological colbertism, characterised by the state's dominant role in basic and applied research (Chesnais, 1993). However, exogenous pressures, such as the process of European integration and the constitution of the World Trade Organization (WTO), have weakened the driving force of dirigisme, bolstering the dismantling of sectoral planning and the privatisation, albeit tempered, of national champions (Cohen, 2007).

The sharp downtrend in military spending on R&D, falling from 40% to 18% of total public expenditure on R&D between 1990 and 1999 (Mustar & Wright, 2010), brought about the decline of technological colbertism. Nevertheless, the transformation took effect gradually. Already back in 1983, under the Mitterrand presidency, the main instrument of the new policy trend had been introduced: the Research Tax Credit. Even today, the CIR (*Crédit d'impôt recherche*) constitutes the main lever for promoting private innovation and is a significant locational factor for R&D departments of international companies (Mustar, 2016). After the 2004 CIR reform, France became the first country in the world in terms of volume of funding to support business R&D (OECD, 2014, 187).[1] By way of enhancing the logic of indirect R&D support, the year 2013 saw the introduction of two other instruments designed to support SMEs: the innovation tax credit (CII) and Bpifrance, the public investment bank offering innovation loans and venture capital.[2] In addition to the CIR, French governments also adopted other types of policies, though financially more limited. The best known is the *Pôles de compétitivité*, launched in 2004 to promote "innovation clusters" between companies and research centres, on the model of Silicon Valley (Larousse, 2017; Grivot, 2017).

France also boasts a long tradition of upholding the "valorisation" of public research results. In 1974, the National Agency for the Valorisation of Research (ANVAR) was created; in 1981, the structure and role of the CNRS (National Centre for Scientific Research) was modified, opening up the way for partnerships with private companies (Larédo & Mustar, 2001, 464). Nevertheless, it is since the end of the 1990s that these interventions have become firmly established (Bianchini & Llerena, 2016). The Allègre Law (1999) defined the regulatory framework for the transfer of research products from universities and public research institutions to enterprises. It gave researchers and academics to collaborate with firms, allowing the establishment of incubators and technology transfer offices (Muller et al., 2009), while the setting up of seed capital funds was facilitated (Gallochat, 2003; Mustar & Wright, 2010). A few years later, in 2006, the French government created the "Carnot" label, which endowed the collaborations for applied research between public R&D centres and companies with prestige and resources. To date, these centres continue to receive funding that is effectively comparable to the German Fraunhofer – institutes that inspired the Carnot policy – although their efficiency is still rather limited by comparison (Legait, Renucci, & Sikorav, 2015).

After the economic crisis of 2008, the French government increased investment in public resources and elaborated a systemic strategy for technological development. In December 2009, the Sarkozy presidency launched the *Programme d'investissement d'avenir* (PIA). The PIA was a heterogeneous plan in terms of its potential beneficiaries – universities, research centres, and businesses. It is also highly diversified as regards the financial instruments used (i.e. subsidies, loans, and direct investment managed by Bpifrance) and its aims, spanning from the development of new products to the creation of clusters (OECD, 2014).[3]

11.3.2 Manufacturing innovation in Germany

It is well known that German competitiveness is the rewarding outcome resulting from the coordination between private activities and public institutions (Hall & Soskice, 2001). Much has been written about the institutional factors that contributed to accomplishing this variety of capitalism (vocational training, industrial relations, corporate governance). However, less attention has been paid to collaborative networks between productive activities and public research, despite these having accompanied and shaped the emergence of German capitalism. This institutional framework allowed the large chemical and engineering companies to flourish, taking full advantage of in-house industrial research. At the same time, it also helped the rise of medium-sized companies (*Mittelstand*), whose competitiveness was based on a "learning by doing" approach.

The 1980s and 1990s represented a long period of economic difficulty for a development model that was institutionalised but tardy in responding to exogenous challenges, and which was burdened by the country's reunification (Giersch, Paqué, & Schmieding, 1992). In net contrast, the 2000s were a period of strong economic development. One of the key features to distinguish this rapid development was the high expenditure of German companies on R&D,[4] supported and stimulated by the actions of various governments. These can be divided into three different seasons: (1) the traditional manufacturing-led interventions (until the 1990s); (2) the policies for the promotion of high technology (1993–2003); and finally, (3) the more recent phase of extensive public spending in innovation strategies.

In the first season, few sectors and few large companies were parties to public intervention. As in France, together with a few large private companies, the state intervened to support the development of a limited number of strategic sectors (aerospace, telecommunications, the railway system). At the same time, those years saw the buttressing of research bodies that served the production system. These were the Fraunhofer, Helmholtz, and Leibniz institutes which, together with the university system and the Max Planck Institutes, increasingly constituted an essential resource for knowledge transfer to the production system (Schmoch, 2011).

The second season saw governments focus more on supporting high-technology sectors, which were underdeveloped compared to the United States. During the 1990s, policies promoted the emergence of start-ups in the new economy and in the field of biotechnologies. To this end, the government encouraged new entrepreneurship through support for specialised financing. In the same vein was the experience of the *Neuer Markt*, established in 1997 as a section of the Frankfurt Stock Exchange, inspired by the American Nasdaq. However, these instruments had less success than was expected (Vitols & Engelhardt, 2005).

As an initiative for promoting high technology, the technology cluster policy was more successful. Launched in 1995, the BioRegio programme was an effective model for the many clustering initiatives that followed, helping to establish some of Germany's leading biotechnology clusters (Dohse & Staehler, 2008). Lastly, the German government also focused on the triple helix model of innovation with the Exist programme (1998). The aim was to promote spin-offs from public research, help research organisations exploit the results of their research, and disseminate the entrepreneurial spirit among their students (Kulicke, 2014). Even today, it is still an active programme that has generated numerous entrepreneurial initiatives (EFI, 2019).

The third season began in 2004, with the second Schröder government (SPD) inaugurating the Year of Innovation. In the same year, it promoted the "Innovation and Future Technologies for SMEs" initiative, aiming to improve access to venture capital and increment interaction between businesses, research institutions and universities. However, it was not until the next Merkel government that a real strategy based on the close integration of innovation and industrial policies was launched. After a consultation with industrial and academic stakeholders, the first High Tech Strategy was introduced in 2006, a plan encompassing the three axes of German innovation policies: supporting new entrepreneurship and SMEs, increasing cooperation between science and industry, and enhancing human capital. To this end, the German government set itself the target of raising expenditure on research and development to 3% of GDP. This threshold was reached in the space of just a few years, and as such, the third High Tech Strategy, launched in 2018, would then raise the target to 3.5% of GDP. The main novelty of this policy approach lay in the definition of public–private roadmaps to bring innovation to some strategic regions for society (energy, health, mobility, security, and communication), combined with the high involvement of stakeholders in the decision-making and implementation process. With the 2006 strategy, formalised channels for dialogue between government, industry, and science were inaugurated (e.g. the *Innovationsdialog*, the Industry-Science Research Alliance, and the EFI-*Expertenkommission Forschung und Innovation*).

Several initiatives coalesced under the collective umbrella of the High-Tech Strategy, one of which was the *Excellence initiative* (active from 2005), inducing a radical reform of the public research system by promoting its internationalisation, the qualification of doctorates, competition between universities, academic entrepreneurship, and technology transfer. A second intervention included in the High-Tech Strategy was the *Industrie 4.0* initiative. Launched in 2011, the initiative aimed to upgrade the technology of German manufacturing by integrating cyber-physical systems and the "Internet of Things" into the production process. In this case, funding was earmarked for joint research projects between universities and businesses, for the creation of 15 competence centres and for co-financing projects by individual companies.

Yet the challenge for high-tech development was no longer only about promoting new entrepreneurship, as in the 1990s, or supporting manufacturing, but also about a new direct engagement of the state in creating new technologies. By way of illustration, in 2018 the Agency for Radical Innovation (under the control of the Ministry of Education and Research) was created on the model of the American DARPA, along with the Agency for Cybersecurity (EFI, 2019).

11.4 Southern European countries

Spain and Italy show the lowest public and private commitment to R&D and the lowest investment in the educational system among growth and inequality models. Nonetheless, they present appreciable differences from a qualitative standpoint. The two countries entered the 1980s with very different innovation systems. Spanish policymakers largely overlooked the support of firms' innovation during the Franco regime and the aftermath of the transition to democracy (Buesa Blanco, 2003). No specific item of expenditure in the general state budget was devoted to innovation up to 1986 (Muñoz, 2001, 364).

In contrast, Italy had two independent innovation systems at the same time (Malerba, 1993). The first system comprised large state-owned companies targeted by direct state investment in R&D and entailed collaborations with universities and public research centres (Antonelli, 2005). The second system was constituted by networks of SMEs located in industrial districts. This system lacked central state support but relied on territorially embedded resources. Local milieus provide SMEs with collective competition goods. SMEs triggered incremental innovation by deploying externally developed technologies through learning by doing processes.

Italy and Spain can therefore be said to have lacked in institutionalising the innovation system, yet without forestalling the innovativeness of many companies, which might be considered "hidden champions" (Donatiello & Ramella, 2017).

11.4.1 Italy from the 1990s to the present

In the 1990s, the two-engine growth model lost its propulsive capacity, thus initiating a slow but progressive decline (Toniolo, 2013). The abrupt privatisation of state-owned enterprises in the early 1990s weakened the innovation system based on large firms and public research centres (Artoni, 2013; Lucchese, Nascia, & Pianta, 2016). On the one hand, external pressures for a redefinition of state aid rules by the European Commission and European integration acceleration imposed a reduction of the national debt that was realised through state-owned firms selling. On the other hand, the disruptive landslide of the institutional and party system triggered by the *Tangentopoli* scandal changed public support for the State's direct presence in the economy. However, industrial districts displayed a capacity to adapt to the global challenge by rationalising the number of firms and consolidating some leading enterprises (Bellandi & Caloffi, 2014; De Marchi & Grandinetti, 2014; Belussi, 2015). In the years in which the country's competitive foundations were being redefined, incentives for business R&D were increasingly implemented in Italy, extending an approach already adopted with the reform of public R&D investment instruments. Governments, therefore, opted for incentives for industrial and pre-competitive research, or the support of highly skilled employment. Incentives, e.g. tax credits, were also employed to promote collaborations between firms and public research centres. Accordingly, from the 1990s onwards, Italy adopted an innovation-pull approach to innovation policies. However, the growing support for private and public innovation investments lacked a comprehensive strategic vision. The horizontal distribution of political competencies for innovation and research between several ministries hindered the emergence of a shared and coherent national strategy for innovation. The decentralisation of policy competencies to the regional and local levels contributed to fragmenting the policy supply to support innovation and thus increasing territorial inequalities.

In the 2000s, despite the steady expansion of funding, Italy failed to reach expenditure levels comparable with other countries, revealing a trend that was conditioned by the need to consolidate public spending. Nevertheless, at least three policies can be identified in this period to create a more articulated regulatory framework than the innovation-pull approach. First, "*Industria 2015*", a policy adopted by the Prodi government (2006), was inspired by the manufacturing-led model. The policy was aimed to facilitate the innovative leap of Italian SMEs operating in the automotive industry, household goods and green economy. The Ministry undertook to select and award "Industrial Innovation Projects" presented by partnerships between companies, universities and public research bodies that intended to invest in joint initiatives with a medium- to long-term horizon. Although *Industria 2015* was designed to be consistent with the characteristics of the Italian production system, it encountered significant obstacles in terms of implementation that were already endemic to national industrial policies, such as administrative stringencies in the assessment of projects and their application (Di Vico, 2014). The volatility of successive governments during the implementation phase and the effects of the economic crisis on public finances only added to the difficulties.

The second intervention was the Growth Decree 2.0 in 2012. It was introduced to support the creation and development of innovative start-ups through a set of tax benefits, incentives for capital investments, and ad hoc legislation on labour relations. In this case, the technical government led by Mario Monti reorganised the regulation of the new entrepreneurship sector within a more general framework through the retrenching of resources to the research system and rationalisation of tax incentives for R&D.

Finally, the last innovation policy intervention, launched by the Renzi government, also found continuity in the governments to follow. This was the manufacturing-led policy known as the 2017 Industry 4.0 Plan (Ramella & Manzo, 2021). The Plan was welcomed by companies and proved to be a success. In contrast with *Industria 2015*, in order to facilitate the smaller companies also, the government created streamlined measures consisting chiefly of incentives and tax breaks for those investing in 4.0 technologies, to which access was automatic. However, although the Plan with its set of concessions did effectively contribute to increasing investments in capital goods, it lacked the more general need to introduce radical innovation, generating instead effects that were, for the most part concentrated, in a few productive sectors (such as the metalworking sector) and in the most dynamic territories (Onida, 2017; Gherardini & Pessina, 2020; Ramella & Manzo, 2021).

11.4.2 The steady growth of the Spanish innovation system

The turning point of Spanish innovation policy was Law 13/1986, the so-called Law of Science. The law was created to endow the country with a national system of innovation that had largely been underdeveloped and inefficient during the years of the Franco regime (ERAC, 2014). It established new institutions to support public and private research (such as the CDTI), inter-ministerial coordination (CICYT –Interministerial Commission of Science and Technology – and the CACTI – Advisory Committee for Science, Technology and Innovation) and vertical coordination, following the attribution of shared competence in innovation to the Autonomous Communities (CCAA). The law also gave responsibility to the government to draft the National Plan for Scientific Research and Technological Development, which contained the government's multi-year objectives to coordinate national and regional programmes designed around R&D (health, defence, universities, infrastructure, and industry). However, this coordination activity was highly problematic and unstable (Gómez & Puente, 2007). The national plans were not binding for the CCAAs, and funds were allocated annually in the budget laws, contingent on the capacity of the parties involved (national and regional authorities) to respect the agreements stipulated in concertation, as is still the case today.

Nevertheless, as with Italy during the 1990s, the need to respect the parameters set down in the Maastricht Treaty induced a downtrend in spending. In Spain, convergence was achieved by using tripartite concertation to contain wage fluctuation and pension expenditure and introduce flexible forms of work (Molina & Miguelez, 2013).

Discontinuity in innovation policy characterised the 2000s. In 2005, the centre-left of Zapatero (PSOE) implemented a system-oriented policy called "*Ingenio 2010*" in response to the Lisbon Strategy (2000). *Ingenio* consisted of four programmes designed to improve collaboration between public research and business, basic research, and physical and digital infrastructure. The programme constituted an intermediate step in expanding public investment in innovation, which culminated in 2011 with the approval of the "New Science Law". This remodelled the governance of the Spanish system, qualifying it as a "system of systems", in view of the fundamental role attributed to policies at a regional level within national coordination instruments, such as the long-term Spanish Science and Technology Strategy (EECT), delineated in the three-year State Plans of Scientific and Technical Research and Innovation (Mineco, 2017).

In 2013, the Rajoy government (PP) implemented the Law to support entrepreneurs and firms' internationalisation. One of the key objectives was to disseminate entrepreneurial culture through the university system. Finally, the *Industria Conectada 4.0* Strategy revived the development of Spanish innovation policies after the interruption generated by the public debt crisis resulting from the global economic crunch. Strongly influenced by Germany's *Industrie 4.0*, the Strategy was based on an analysis of the Spanish manufacturing sector and its weaknesses, indicated in the dependence of SMEs on imported technologies from abroad. It represented part of a more comprehensive plan for developing the Spanish industrial sector, the Agenda for the Strengthening of the Industrial Sector in Spain (2014), which interacted, in turn, with both the Digital Agenda and the EECT. Despite the government's inclusive approach, the Strategy's budget was considerably lower than that of other similar interventions launched by other countries, including Italy (around €700 million over the 2016–2018 three-year period).

Lastly, the two Sanchez governments (PSOE) have recently signalled their wish to maintain a strategic approach about the Strategic Framework 2030, which incorporates 15 sectoral agreements signed by the previous governments and employers' organisations. The agreements set out a series of short- and medium-term measures, including those to further deploy 4.0 technologies in the Spanish economy.

11.5 The Anglo-Saxon countries

The United States and the United Kingdom crossed the threshold of the 1980s with two very different innovation systems underway. In the face of the challenge posed by the Cold War, the USA developed supremacy in all possible technological fields, with significant repercussions on the production system. This unfolded within the framework of the national security state (Weiss, 2014) under the massive funding of federal agencies – including NASA, the Department of Energy, the Department of Defence and the Defense Advanced Research Project Agency (DARPA) – which had the task of overseeing the technological frontier. Nevertheless, these agencies did not work in isolation but interacted with large technology companies and the research system. Justified by the need to ensure national security before economic development, the constant pursuit of technological and military hegemony thus indirectly created the basis for a comprehensive and highly connected innovation system that supported modernisation at all stages, from basic research to product commercialisation (*the extended pipeline model*).

In contrast, before the 1980s, the British government had intervened less systemically, supporting mainly the capitalisation and activities of large strategic firms, such as the General Electric Company, Imperial Chemical Industries and the military, aerospace, and pharmaceutical industries (von Tunzelmann, 2003). With the end of the Cold War and the liberal turnaround of the Reagan and Thatcher governments, a *laissez-faire* approach became the hallmark of economic policy in both countries (Wallace, 1995). Expenditure on research and development was progressively retrenched, accompanied by cutbacks in all interventions that were not aimed at primary and pre-competitive research, i.e. to solve market failures.

However, the two countries' positions at the pivotal moment of the 1980s were completely different: the United States could pride itself on highly competitive companies interconnected with public research and a highly developed financial system, all preconditions for the take-off of Silicon Valley and other high-tech districts. Inversely, high-tech firms in the United Kingdom lacked competitiveness while in the meantime, a surreptitious mistrust of technological development was progressively taking hold in the country in the wake of numerous nuclear accidents, the failure of the Franco-British Concorde project and concerns regarding bovine spongiform encephalopathy (or "mad cow disease").

11.5.1 The United States

At the turn of the Cold War, the innovation policies designed to counter the Soviet challenge became less relevant in the States. The Reagan presidency was determined to meet the challenge of the competitiveness of Japanese technological intervention with the boost of the *state-less political economy*. The cornerstone of this regulatory state approach comprised two acts: passing the Bayah-Dole Act (1980), which allowed universities to license intellectual property obtained through scientific research to companies (Mowery & Sampat, 2004). The second was the Presidential Commission on Economic Competitiveness in 1983, chaired by John Young, CEO of Hewlett-Packard, which further enhanced the protection of intellectual property for the protection and growth of the competitiveness of the US companies on an international scale. In 1986, when the Commission created the Council on Competitiveness (which still exists today), the second phase of support for precompetitive research was inaugurated through public–private partnerships to develop new technologies for innovation, computers, and energy and manufacturing. This approach would seem to tie in with the previous line taken by the government, namely the extended pipeline model, where the Department of Defense (DOD) supported innovation not only in the design phase but also in subsequent phases up to the potential purchase of the prototype. According to Bonvillian and Singer (2017) this model facilitates the combination of advanced research and technology implementation.[5]

The interventions implemented by the Clinton administration largely persevered with the programme of support for technological advancement initiated by the previous presidency. In those periods, the style of policymaking changed as several initiatives were taken with the explicit intention of consulting close to the industry and with a perspective to "regulatory negotiation" (Wallace, 1995). Moreover, the impact of the public and private investments of the previous years became apparent in this period. In fact, many high-tech districts, such as Silicon Valley, entered their phase of maturation and, in a short period, captured the attention of startups and the international community towards policies for innovation. (Audretsch, 2021).

Following the attack on the Twin Towers (2001), the issue of national security returned to the forefront of public discourse and, with it, the national security state approach. From 2001 onwards, spending on innovation policies increased. In parallel, the Department for Homeland Security was established, which also had the research and development of technologies to improve homeland security among its various responsibilities (Weiss, 2014).

In the following decade, the new "Asian challenge" replaced the challenge of terrorism. This time, China posed as a significant economic competitor and, at the same time, as the new contender for global hegemony. The Chinese threat was at the origin of the most recent debate in the United States on innovation and the adverse effects of the "invented-here, produced-there syndrome" (Bonvillain & Singer, 2017). These were the years of rising unemployment in manufacturing, a cause of concern for policymakers. Between 2011 and 2015, the Obama government made efforts to defend domestic production and face the challenge of re-shoring strategic manufacturing activities.

The debate on manufacturing had been initiated in previous years by MIT President Susan Hockfield (formerly on the General Electric board) together with Jeff Immelt (CEO of General Electric) when, in March 2009, an interdisciplinary working group comprising representatives of the 11 MIT faculties was set up. The debate continued, and from 2010 onwards, there were ideological divisions within Congress that decelerated (and at times stalled) decision-making. Despite this, Congress was able to pass one measure to support manufacturing on a highly bipartisan basis (ibid.). This was the establishment of the Advanced Manufacturing Partnership (AMP) to develop detailed plans to fortify the competitive advantage in advanced manufacturing. The aim, therefore, was to ensure US leadership in emerging technologies with the ultimate goal of creating high-quality manufacturing jobs and improving US global competitiveness.

Regeneration of the manufacturing industry was also one of the central points of Donald Trump's election campaign. The institutes supporting the advanced manufacturing requested by Obama continued to receive funding for 2017. From 2018 onwards, their future was not so clear. The government implemented the first cutbacks for several federal agencies with research, science, and technology programmes. In institutes on manufacturing, curtailment was not direct but rather a consequence of the downsizing of the departments with which the institutes of the NIST network were correlated.

11.5.2 The United Kingdom

The processes of privatisation that began in the 1980s in the UK had a different time scale and scope from those on the continent, giving rise to a model of a "regulatory state" that was reluctant to intervene directly in determining industrial choices, except in cases related to the defence sector (Thatcher, 2003). The industry support fell from about £20 billion in the late 1970s to around half a billion in the late 1990s. The Conservative government's answer to the loss of competitiveness was a policy by default and limiting support for private research and development to tax breaks for pre-competitive research. In those years, about half of public spending on R&D was absorbed by the Department of Defence, which then outsourced these activities to private firms, in what Edgerton (1991) called liberal militarism.

During the Thatcher administration, the government continued to fund some technology development programmes, such as the Product and Process Development Scheme (PPDS) and the Alvey Program, to develop microelectronics, telecommunications and robotics, albeit in a context of non-commitment. However, in 1988, the support was suspended when the government decided that these innovative actions had to be funded by industry rather than the government.

In the first half of the 1990s, the white papers on competitiveness published by the John Major's administration highlighted the government's approach in the three keywords: liberalisation, privatisation, and de-regulation (Sharp, 2003). Thus, the push for innovation as a driving force of competitiveness was not accompanied by public policies except through some incentives. On the contrary, the country's competitiveness was sustained by the investments of multinationals. The UK was the country that attracted the most foreign direct investment in Europe, a position that was stimulated by policies explicitly designed to invite capital (UK Trade and Investment 2015). By the mid-1990s, foreign-owned companies operating in the UK contributed 30% to output and 20% to employment in the manufacturing industries (Sharp, 2003).

At the same time, the government also came under increasing pressure to bring universities and industries closer together. The LINK programme (introduced by the Thatcher government to build research networks between business and universities) was complemented by two new programmes: the Teaching Company Scheme (TCS), stipulating those academics could work in innovative companies; and the Cooperative Awards for Science and Engineering (CASE), which funded doctoral scholarships on subjects chosen by private companies. Both programmes targeted companies and higher education research institutes to build partnerships and stimulate active participation in the technology transfer network and, at the same time, designated the companies as the ultimate beneficiaries of research funding. According to OECD data, the share of private research funding was higher than in the United States in those years.

Over the years, the Major government veered away from rigorous Thatcherism. The Minister for Science, William Waldergrave, launched a wide-ranging consultation that in 1993 gave rise to "Realizing our Potential: A Strategy for Science, Engineering and Technology", a programme which set out reforms to support biotechnology life sciences and manufacturing in general. The aim was to stay abreast of global technological change. To do this, "Fifteen Foresights Planning mechanisms" were set up to identify those areas in which new developments in science and technology opened new market opportunities and adopted a long-term perspective for investing in innovation.

The Blair government took a further step towards enhancing innovation in 1997 to create a new modernisation unit within the Treasury. The government identified five drivers of productivity: investment in physical capital, enterprise and innovation, education and skills, competition and regulation, and public sector productivity (HM Treasury, 1999). The Blair government made a mark, however, by setting up Regional Development Agencies (RDAs) in 1998, which were placed in charge of regional development policies, with particular reference to upgrading workers' skills and attracting foreign investment (FDI), also through the management of European structural funds. Industrial and innovation policies were thus integrated into the regional policy framework (Berry, 2016).

As in other European countries, from the 2000s onwards, the innovation agenda began to be influenced by the criteria for allocating European funds. Technological programmes promoting collaboration between science and industry (Callon et al., 1997) were enhanced, and at the same time, the tax credit dedicated to SMEs was incremented (Cunningham et al., 2016). In the meantime, following the model of the Manufacturing Extension Partnership (MEP) in the United States, the Manufacturing Advisory Service (MAS), commissioned by the Department of Trade and Industry (DTI), was established in England in 2002. The programme was managed at the regional level by the Centres of Manufacturing Excellence and was primarily aimed at supporting the SMEs.

Following Gordon Brown's appointment as prime minister in June 2007, public spending on R&D increased significantly. However, it did not (and would not) reach the levels of the pre-Thatcher period and remained below the expenditure invested in both the US and the inclusive growth countries. In the few years that Brown was prime minister (2007–2010), he endeavoured to change British innovation policies. In the first place, the Department of Education and Skills and the Department of Trade and Industry were merged into the Department for Innovation, Universities and Skills (DIUS). DIUS also worked closely with the new Department for Business, Enterprise and Regulatory Reform (BERR) until they merged in 2009. In terms of substance, the Brown government adopted a neo-Keynesian approach set out in the green paper "New Industry, New Jobs" (HM Government, 2009).

The considerable change imposed by the Cameron government entailed a reorganisation of the decision-making levels of government and, consequently, allocation of funds. Management control at the local level was "disrupted" by the abolition of RDAs in 2010. This consequence for manufacturing was a retrenchment of funding for the Centres of Manufacturing Excellence. In addition, the closure of the RDAs led to the transfer of functions (but not funds) to the Local Partnerships Enterprise (LPE), responsible for concluding agreements between local institutions and enterprises at the local level.

In 2012, the Cameron government launched the Advanced Manufacturing Supply Chain Initiative plan to strengthen collaborations between companies and universities for joint resources, funded first by the public and then by the private sector. In that year, 72% of total research and development spending was in manufacturing compared to 25% in services. The new strategy "Our Plan for Growth: Science and Innovation" (HM Treasury, 2014) ambitiously aimed to cast the UK in the role of the best country in the world for science and business through the implementation of six levers, among which also "Catalyzing Innovation" that included programmes to support SME research and development (High-Value Manufacturing Catapult).

Within a complex system of government-supported networking actions, university-industry links persisted. In 2015 the government promoted the Knowledge Transfer Network (KTN) programme operated by Innovate UK (formerly the Technology Strategy Board), the aim of which was to build better links between science, creativity, and enterprise by bringing together companies, entrepreneurs, academics, and funders to develop new products, processes, and services.

In June 2016, the British political landscape changed radically with the outcome of the referendum in favour of Brexit and the arrival of Theresa May in government. As Prime Minister, May proposed to integrate the competencies of the Department for Business, Innovation and Skills (BIS) and the Department of Energy and Climate Change (DECC) into the Department for Business, Energy and Industrial Strategy (BEIS). From the perspective of actions, it seems to have followed the line of the previous government: post-crisis industrial policy innovation was one of the critical points of the political discourse narrative not to be followed by substantial reforms, thus affording in practice more attention to the financial core of the country's economy, to the detriment of manufacturing (Berry, 2016).

11.6 Education policy

While innovation policy supports the economic system in its technological upgrading, the role of education in sustaining growth and reducing inequality is twofold. On the one hand, education systems affect firms' innovative capacity by providing qualified personnel. On the other hand, education fosters social mobility upward and can help reduce social inequalities by facilitating access to better-paid jobs. Nonetheless, this capacity depends on the education system's accessibility for students and their families, i.e. whether participation is guaranteed for all or limited to a proportion of citizens. However, this is true if the production system expresses a generalised demand for educated personnel. If this is not the case, the advantage of having a tertiary qualification is greatly diminished. Although the position in the labour market is more advantageous for graduates in all the models,[6] the countries with more traditional production systems have a higher share of skilled workers in jobs for which the skills they possess are not needed (OECD, 2015a).

This section focuses on selected countries' tertiary education, with particular attention to the means of access, the contribution required for enrolment and the resources invested by the public and private actors. Finally, we will look at the impact of any mismatch in skills.

In the EIG countries, an "education for all" approach, i.e. a system that aims to ensure that knowledge and skills are widely accessible, has prevailed for many years. The educational systems of Sweden and Denmark are characterised by some distinctive features. First, schooling is compulsory until the age of 16 and access to tertiary level education is not segmented, i.e. contingent on having chosen particular secondary education paths. In addition, university programmes are free for EU citizens, and a generous scholarship system to help defray the costs of student life for the less well-off exists in both countries. In recent years, the degree of universality in the Swedish university system has been significantly reduced: since 2014, Swedish universities could impose tuition fees reserved for non-European students only (Pinheiro, Geschwind, & Aarrevaara, 2014).

In NILG countries, there is a financing system in which students' contributions are proportional to their family household income. The average tax level is EUR 1,747 in Spain and EUR 1,926 per year in Italy – the highest level among the countries under scrutiny if the NIG countries are excluded (OECD 2019a). Moreover, the scholarship system is poorly funded and residual, linked mainly to the student's income (Viesti, 2016).

In France, the Ministry of Universities annually sets the amount for enrolment fees in three-year courses at public universities, which retain a margin of autonomy in determining the fee levels of subsequent pathways. In the 2019/20 academic year, the Ministry set the tuition fee for three-year courses for EU students at EUR 170 per student.[7] In the other DIG country, Germany, university enrolment is free.

NIG countries show significantly higher tuition fees for university courses than other models.[8] In the US, a variety of need- and merit-based scholarship programmes are implemented, reducing fees for around 89% of the student population in order to ensure access to more students (OECD, 2019). Despite this, the cost of enrolling in universities remains higher than in European countries, a factor that drives many students into private debt.

Resources for the tertiary system come from public budgets or private contributions. In NIG countries, most of these resources come from the private sector. In the US, household expenditure amounts to almost half of total funding (46.1%), as well as in the UK (49.1%), while the share of other private funding is just under 20% (OECD 2019a). The other two countries where households significantly finance the university system are Spain (29.2%) and Italy (29.9%), followed by France (11.2%). In the other countries considered, a household contribution is absent. EIG and DIG countries have significantly higher levels of expenditures on GDP than other countries.

The accessibility of the university system is not only conditioned by the level of the contribution required of students. It is also the design of the education system that allows access to a greater or lesser proportion of the population. Although there are no tuition fees in Germany, the design of the education system does not allow access to university for vocational school graduates, except in a few cases. This is also one of the reasons why the number of people with a university degree out of the total population (29.1% in 2018) is lower than the average for OECD countries (37.0%). The explanation for such a low level of degree attainment can be found in some of the elements inherent in the education system, which ascribes a series of responsibilities relating to education to the Länder (Powell and Solga, 2011; Döbert, 2015). The first is the distribution of students at the time of entry into lower secondary school, which guides their subsequent educational careers. Access to the different types of secondary school is determined by the results obtained during primary school, which ends at the age of 11. The early placement of students in pathways that prevent them from entering the tertiary system makes it more difficult for those from families with a low educational profile to access university, as they have more difficulty in achieving the results needed to enter grammar schools that grant access to university (Döbert, 2015). However, until recent years, the impact of this segmentation on inequalities was limited. Indeed, the vocational training system guaranteed access to well-paid jobs in the manufacturing sector. However, it is largely dependent on the willingness of enterprises to offer training to students, an element which has diminished over the years, with adverse effects on the system's ability to retrench disparities in wealth (Thelen, 2014).

In France, the tertiary education system is divided into two pillars: the university system, on the one hand, and the polytechnics and Grandes Écoles, on the other. The two sectors have different mechanisms of access, governance, and level of funding and confer different social prestige to those who attend them. A highly selective national examination regulates access to Grandes Écoles since they are responsible for the training of the French ruling class – i.e. public and private executives, high-profile professors and technicians. On the other hand, admission to universities is open to anyone with a secondary school diploma. Universities are also the preferred choice for those who fail the entrance exams to the Grandes Écoles (Hörner & Many, 2015).

Access to the best universities, therefore leading to higher wage expectancy, is based on both wealth and meritocracy in NIG countries: it is contingent on the possibility of paying high tuition fees or accessing scholarships based on merit or family income. In recent years, the economic burden of university education has increasingly shifted towards household savings and indebtedness. In the United States, national government allocations to public universities – those most affordable in terms of tuition costs – have fallen since 1992: spending per student has fallen in public colleges and universities by around 8%, while revenue (per-student tuition) has increased by 96%.[9] Likewise, in the UK the exponential increase in tuition fees has been matched by an overall decrease in exemption recipients and a marked increase in students applying for honour (or trust) loans (Bolton, 2018).

Except for Germany and Italy, where only 19.3% of 25–34-year-olds have a university degree, the other countries have a higher percentage of graduates in the total population than the OECD average. The other NILG country, Spain, now registers a value comparable to the average of the OECD countries (37.3%), because of the strong increase in graduates between 2000 and 2018 (14.6%), while in Italy this value was more contained (9.9% over the same period). Conversely, the United States, the United Kingdom, and Sweden show values that are strongly above average at just under 50% of the population.

Finally, it should be noted that not all national labour markets receive graduates in the same way. The NILG countries, along with the United States, have the lowest employment rates of graduates compared to the other countries considered. In 2018, Spain and Italy recorded an employment rate among those with a university education of 81.6% and 81.1%, respectively; in the United States, it is 82.2; while in the other countries considered, the value is in line with or higher than the OECD average value (85.3%). The productive fabric of the NILG countries, which is specialised in low-tech sectors and in which personal services prevail, requires few graduates. Spain and Italy are thus the two countries where the skills mismatch is most relevant (Burroni et al., 2019). The effects for the labour market are under-skilling (i.e. a workforce with skills lower than required), while the reflection on the education system is the abandonment of studies before graduation. The low

Table 11.1 Tertiary education policies in different growth models

Growth model	*Countries*	*Education policies*				*Mismatches in job market*
		Access	*Student contribution*	*Resources*	*Study grants*	
NIG	United States United Kingdom	*Income-related*	*High*	*Private*	*High*	*Medium-low*
EIG	Sweden Denmark	*Universalistic*	*None*	*Public*	*High*	*Low*
DIG	Germany	*Fragmented*	*None*	*Public*	*High*	*Low*
	France	*Meritocratic*	*Low*	*Mainly public*	*High*	
NILG	Italy Spain	*Universalistic*	*Medium*	*Mainly private*	*Low*	*High*

presence of graduates in firms then also has effects on economic development in terms of low productivity and low capacity to absorb knowledge from other organisations.

11.7 Concluding remarks

The review of the IEPs adopted in the four growth models has disclosed a variety of repertoires of action. Nevertheless, many elements of similarity emerge, both across and within models. Similarities arise from two types of factors. The first is that economies are subject to shared exogenous pressures. All European countries had to markedly discontinue aspects of their innovation policy models upon accession to the European Union in the 1990s. In those years, European legislation regulated the possibility for national governments to intervene directly in the economy through public enterprises or state holdings. From this point of view, the most striking example is the French case, which relinquished the approach of technological Colbertism in favour of an approach based on tax incentives. In addition, the European Council's soft policies, such as the Lisbon Strategy and Europe 2020, have promoted the repositioning of member economies in the most valuable stages of global value chains, with a focus on enhancing the skills possessed by the workforce. Finally, the programming of the European structural funds has also had common effects on the choices of the various countries, such as the regionalisation of innovation policies or the request to construct policies around societal challenges.

The second type of influencing factor revolves around the concept of "mimetic isomorphism" (Di Maggio & Powell, 1983), i.e. imitating other organisations as a cognitive shortcut to cope with situations of uncertainty. As illustrated, in an open and competitive economic system, national governments have been called upon to intervene in support of economic development. However, this intervention seems to have been influenced by a country's attempt to recreate the conditions that succeed in generating economic innovation in the most dynamic countries. Thus, the phenomenon of transferring policies from one context to another was fuelled, among other things, by international organisations, such as the OECD. The circulation and support of "good national practices" fostered the hybridisation of innovation policies.

The analysis of national cases has afforded the possibility to determine several waves of similar interventions adopted in different countries. For instance, since the second half of the 1990s, the main reference model has been that of the American high-tech districts. Clustering policies to support new entrepreneurship and, in parallel, the promotion of knowledge exchanges between universities and businesses have thus become widespread. Similarly, the publication in 2003 of the first international ranking of universities, drawn up by Shanghai Jiao Tong University, drew attention to the lower competitiveness of European research models. It was a real "Shanghai shock", which prompted substantial reforms in the financing and evaluation of the higher education system. Lastly, the brilliant performance of the German economy and the American "invented-here, produced-there" syndrome have more recently triggered the rediscovery of the strategic nature of manufacturing, hence promulgating initiatives to support industry, inspired precisely by the German *Industrie 4.0*.

These drives towards convergence have been moderated by the institutional specificities of individual countries and their economic structure (see Table 11.2). The EIG countries feature increasing public spending on research and development and a systemic approach to innovation policies, which evolves from strategies shared with key national stakeholders. The approach of creative corporatism, a style of the political economy adopted in the 1990s in EIG, has often withstood even the changing colour of governments. The innovation system's actors, especially universities, are at the centre of a coherent, cohesive and constant flow of policies. Regardless of the mode of implementation – more through agencies in Sweden, more characterised by project networks in Denmark – policies originate from forward-looking strategies and are implemented by highly collaborative public and private actors. The effects on the economic system have been distinctly positive, especially in Denmark, where the change of pace in promoting innovation in the 1990s was one of the prerequisites for the economic miracle of the following decade. The recent impact of Swedish interventions has been rather ambivalent. Despite the solid governmental impulse favouring innovation, the highly internationalised

Table 11.2 Innovation policies in the various growth models

Growth models	*Countries*	*Innovation policies*			*Integration with education policy*	*Type of state*
		Public spending	*Governance*	*Policy pattern*		
NIG	United States	*High*	*Federal agencies*	*Extended pipeline*	*Low*	*Innovator*
	United Kingdom	*Low*	*Minimal*	*Regulation*	*Low*	*Regulator*
EIG	Sweden	*High*	*Strategic negotiated*	*Systemic*	*High*	*Negotiator that leads*
	Denmark	*High*	*Strategic negotiated*	*Systemic*	*High*	
DIG	Germany	*High*	*Coordinated*	*Manufacturing-led*	*High*	*Institutionalised*
	France	*High*	*Minimal*	*Innovation pull*	*Average*	*Useful*
NILG	Italy	*Low*	*Fragmented*	*Hybrid*	*Low*	*Wasteful*
	Spain	*Low*	*Fragmented*	*Hybrid*	*High*	

companies seem to respond less and less to national regulation.[10] Overall, we have a *state that directs* innovative activities through *negotiated policies*.

Also, the DIG countries have seen an increase in innovation policy efforts over the years, especially in the wake of the 2008 economic crisis. In this case, France and Germany came from very different innovation policy traditions, respectively, *technological colbertism* on the one hand, and the *manufacturing-led* approach on the other. Already in the second half of the 1990s, both countries tried, with dubious success, to promote high-tech sectors and, more generally, the competitiveness of their firms. Although some of the instruments used are similar, the two approaches are still very different. French innovation policies revolved around R&D tax incentives, the aim of which was to invite and hold on to the most valuable activities of large firms in the country. In this case, governance was therefore *minimal*, and the state had the function of *facilitating* innovative activities. The German policies focused more on collaborations between companies and the many institutions for applied research. It is a decidedly *institutionalised* innovation system with *highly coordinated governance*, especially in manufacturing. Nevertheless, both countries have shared a progressive increase in public commitment to supporting innovation and the involvement of stakeholders in multi-year development strategies.

In contrast to the inclusive growth models, low levels of R&D expenditure, both public and private, distinguish the NILG countries, despite significant growth since the 1980s (although this trend was interrupted by the crisis in 2008). A second distinctive feature is the *fragmentation* of the innovation system, both on a horizontal level, between ministries responsible for innovation and research, and vertically between central and regional levels. Consequently, the resources allocated are fewer and subject to greater *dispersion*. In Italy, this fragmented system was not matched by a shared strategic vision of development. Moreover, relations between universities, research centres and businesses have also remained underdeveloped. The result is the persistence of divergence between businesses and the world of research, which hurts the inclination of companies towards innovation.

In the 1980s, the two NIG countries shared only one element in common regards innovation policy implementation – that of a period characterised by the mutual objective of withdrawing the state from supporting economic development. However, before and after the neo-liberal turning point, the two sides of the Atlantic were poles apart. In the United States, innovation policies significantly influenced the commercial success of American entrepreneurs in the sectors of telecommunications, biotechnology and digitalisation. However, federal investments in technology and innovation, fostered by a bipartisan commitment to national security were undermined by the waning of the Soviet challenge and the Reagan approach. Nevertheless, even in the 1980s, US innovation policies remained central to the development model, albeit with a shrinking budget, at least until the 2000s, when the new terrorist challenge reinstated the *extended-pipeline* model. The years of the Obama presidency nurtured a new approach that could justify federal spending on innovation policies from a bipartisan perspective: support for manufacturing in the face of competition from China. On the other hand, Trump's election led to a retrenchment of federal expenditure, including innovation policies, which did not fall below the lowest point reached during the Clinton and Bush presidencies. The state continues to play an important role in private innovation.

In contrast, Thatcherism had more persistent effects in the UK. This is especially so because the previous season of innovation policies had not produced a competitive innovation system. In this case, public spending on R&D fell dramatically, albeit with a slight reversal in the years of the Blair government's regional policies and, especially, in the post-financial crisis interlude handled by the Brown and Cameron governments. Thus, the state mainly developed a *regulatory* function, even though the government recently gave change signals by bolstering regional innovation systems.

As far as education policies are concerned, countries can be classified according to their characteristics in terms of conditions of access to universities, levels and origin of funding contributions and the spread of scholarships (see Table 11.1). At one extreme, EIG countries combine universalistic access, high spending and high levels of education. University enrolment is free and generous. Widespread subsidies that support students' living standards. This alone is enough to appreciate that the positive effects of policies aimed at economic growth are combined with more favourable conditions for greater upward social mobility in this model. On the other extreme, the NILG countries are characterised by similarly universalistic access but with high taxation, few and parsimonious scholarships. In these contexts, the university system is therefore seen to be more oriented towards the reproduction of inequalities than towards social mobility.

The DIG countries come between these two extremes. From the perspective of student expenditure on tuition fees and public expenditure in support of tertiary education, these countries resemble the EIG model, but rather tend towards the NILG countries in terms of the spread and generosity of scholarships. However, unlike in France, in Germany, access is not universal and produces labour market dualisation effects. Here, the early channelling of students into a segmented education system prevents the most disadvantaged students from reaching the highest levels of education. As a consequence, especially in more recent years, the contribution to social mobility is smaller.

Lastly, the NIG model shows a high incidence of graduates, although public spending is low, and the financing of studies is mainly left to the students themselves. Moreover, choosing the most prestigious universities, those that guarantee access to the best-paid jobs, depends on merit and/or the availability of significant private savings or capacity to incur debt.

In conclusion, the review of the policies on education and innovation shows the importance of the state's role in upholding economic development. Where innovation policies have been more intensely implemented, economic systems have reacted with greater competitiveness and productivity has increased. Yet, it cannot be argued that innovation policies are a necessary and sufficient condition for economic growth. Among others, a necessary condition is the co-existence of a productive fabric of large enterprises (Gherardini, 2021). Not only is their capacity to embrace innovation policies greater than that of the SMEs but, at the same time, they can exert influence on executives to invest in this policy arena.

Notwithstanding this, it appears difficult to find a direct relationship between innovation policies and the curtailment of inequality. From this point of view, education policies would seem to be of greater importance, showing stability over the period, and capable of anticipating the tendency to inclusiveness of the different models.

Notes

1 In 2013, the CIR absorbed 72% of public spending on research and development (Ministère de l'Enseignement supérieur, de la Recherche et de l'Innovation, 2016) amounting to about EUR 5.5 billion annually (Mustar, 2016).

2 Bpifrance, 'the entrepreneurs' bank', is the latest development in credit support for SMEs. It was founded in 2013 as a joint venture between the business section of the *Caisse des Dépôts et Consignations*, the *Fonds stratégique d'investissement* and *Oséo*, the public agency of private law created in 2005 to support credit and innovation for SMEs.

3 The first version of the PIA (2010) mobilised EUR 35 billion in addition to the existing funding, directing it towards four main axes of intervention: higher education (EUR 19 billion), production chains and SMEs (EUR 6.5 billion), sustainable development (EUR 5 billion) and the digital sector (EUR 4.5 billion). The second and third versions of the PIA also included direct funding for scientific research (Mustar, 2016).

4 Today, the private sector accounts for about two-thirds of total R&D expenditure, making it one of the highest in advanced economies.

5 One of the many initiatives launched in the 1980s was the National Institute of Standards and Technology (NIST), which promoted the participation of small businesses in research and development funding from federal agencies through the Small Business Innovation Research (SBIR). Finally, in the last years of the Reagan government, the Omnibus Foreign Trade and Competitiveness Act (1988–1999) was first approved, establishing the Manufacturing Extension Partnership (MEP), a national network involving universities, research centres and other players, aimed at bridging the gap between advanced technologies and the needs of small and medium-sized enterprises. Second, in 1991, the Advanced Technology Program (ATP) was launched to subsidise the adoption of high-risk technologies that promised significant economic and social benefits for the country.

6 Graduates have lower unemployment rates than those with secondary and elementary education; they also have higher employment rates (OECD, 2019a, 79).
7 Data from the French Agency for the Promotion of Higher Education, services to international students and international mobility (available at www.campusfrance.org/en/tuition-fees-France, consulted 17 March 2020).
8 According to Times Higher Education, annual fees at American universities vary between \$5,000 and \$50,000, reaching an average value of around \$33,000. Public universities generally charge lower tuition fees. In the UK, fees increased exponentially between 1998 and 2012 from a maximum of £1,000 set by the Blair government to a ceiling of £9,000 introduced by the Cameron government (Bolton, 2018). Although fees can vary from university to university, in the 2017/18 academic year, 121 of the 123 universities in the UK had raised tuition fees to the £9,000 annual cap for domestic students (ibid.).
9 Data provided by the State Higher Education Executive Officers Association.
10 For an attempt to explain the recent difficulties of Swedish enterprises in maintaining high levels of innovation, cf. Ornston (2018).

References

Aagaard, K. & de Boer, H. (2017). The Danish UNIK initiative: An NPM-inspired mechanism to steer higher education. In H. de Boer, J. File, J. Huisman, M. Seeber, M. Vukasovic, & D.F. Westerheijden (Eds), *Policy Analysis of Structural Reforms in Higher Education. Processes and Outcomes* (pp. 141–160). Basingstoke: Palgrave Macmillan.

Amin, A. & Thomas, D. (1996). The negotiated economy: State and civic institutions in Denmark. *Economy & Society*, 25, 255–281. DOI:10.1080/03085149600000012

Antonelli, C. (2005). Una strategia italiana verso l'economia della conoscenza, in M. Amendola, A. Antonelli & C. Trigilia (Eds), *Per lo sviluppo. Processi innovativi e contesti territoriali* (pp. 45–84). Bologna: Il Mulino.

Artoni, R. (Ed.) (2013). *Storia dell'IRI, vol. 4. Crisi e privatizzazione*. Bari: Laterza.

Audretsch, D.B. (2021). Have we oversold the Silicon Valley model of entrepreneurship?. *Small Business Economics*, 56, 849–856. DOI: 10.1007/s11187-019-00272-4

Bellandi, M. & Caloffi, A. (2014). *I nuovi distretti industriali. Rapporto di Artimino sullo sviluppo locale 2012-2013*. Bologna: Il Mulino.

Belussi, F. (2015). The international resilience of Italian industrial districts/clusters (ID/C) between knowledge re-shoring and manufacturing off (near)-shoring. *Investigaciones Regionales*, 32, 89–113.

Bianchini, S. & Llerena, P. (2016). Science policy as a prerequisite of industrial policy. *Economia e Politica Industriale*, 43, 273–280. DOI: 10.1007/s40812-016-0040-y

Bonvillain, W.B. & Singer, P.L. (2017). *Advanced manufacturing: The new American innovation policies*. Boston: The MIT Press.

Bolton, P. (2018). Tuition fee statistics, House of the Commons Library, Briefing Paper, n. 917, February 18th.

Bonvillian, W.B. & Weiss, C. (2015). *Technological innovation in legacy sectors*. Oxford: Oxford University Press.

Buesa Blanco, M. (2003). *Ciencia y tecnología en la España democrática: la formación de un sistema nacional de innovación*. Documentos de trabajo del IAIF 39.

Burroni, L. (2020). Stato, politiche per lo sviluppo e produttività. *Polis*, 34(2), 227–252. DOI: 10.1424/97772

Burroni, L., Gherardini, A. & Scalise, G. (2019). Policy failure in the triangle of growth: Labour market, human capital, and innovation in Spain and Italy. *South European Society and Politics*, 24(1), 29–52. DOI: 10.1080/13608746.2019.1575571

Castells, M. & Himanen, P. (2002). *The information society and the welfare state: The Finnish model*. Oxford: Oxford University Press.

Chesbrough, H.W. (2003). *Open innovation: The new imperative for creating and profiting from technology*. Brighton, MA: Harvard Business Press.

Chesnais, F. (1993). The French national system of innovation, in R.R. Nelson (Ed.). *National innovation systems: A comparative analysis* (pp. 192–229). New York: Oxford University Press.

Cohen, E. (2007). Industrial policies in France: The old and the new. *Journal of Industry, Competition and Trade*, 7(3–4), 213–227. DOI: 10.1007/s10842-007-0024-8

DASTI-Danish Agency for Science, Technology and Innovation (2016). *Cluster Strategy 2.0. Strategy for Denmark's cluster and network policy 2016–2018*. Copenhagen: DASTI.

De Marchi, V., Gereffi, G., & Grandinetti, R. (2017). Evolutionary trajectories of industrial districts in global value chains. In V. De Marchi, E. Di Maria & G. Gereffi (Eds), *Local clusters in global value chains* (pp. 33–50). New York: Routledge.

Digital Transformation Monitor (2017). *Sweden: Produktion 2030*. https://ec.europa.eu/growth/tools-databases/dem/monitor/content/sweden-produktion-2030.

Donatiello, D., & Ramella, F. (2017). The innovation paradox in Southern Europe. Unexpected performance during the economic crisis. *South European Society and Politics*, 22(2), 157–177.

DiMaggio, P.J. & Powell, W.W. (1983). The iron cage revisited: Institutional isomorphism and collective rationality in organizational fields. *American Sociological Review*, 48(2), 147–160. DOI: 10.2307/2095101

Di Vico, D. (2014). Politica industriale sì, ma on the road, in D. Di Vico & G. Viesti (Eds), *Cacciavite, robot e tablet. Come far ripartire le imprese*. Bologna: il Mulino.

DFiR-Danish Council for Research and Innovation Policy (2018). *World-class knowledge – why does Danish research perform so well?*. Copenhagen: DFiR.

Döbert, H. (2015). Germany. In W. Hörner, H. Döbert, L.R. Reuter, & B. von Kopp (Eds), *The education system of Europe. Second Edition* (pp. 305–333). New York: Springer.

Dohse, D. & Staehler, T. (2008). *BioRegio, BioProfile and the rise of the German biotech industry*. Kiel Working Paper, n. 1456.

Edgerton, D. (1991). *England and the aeroplane: An essay on a militant and technological nation*. Basingstoke: Macmillan.

Edquist, C. & Lundvall B. (1993). Comparing the Danish and the Swedish systems of innovation. In R.R. Nelson (Eds), *National Innovation Systems: A Comparative Analysis* (pp. 265–298). New York: Oxford University Press.

EFI (2019). *Research, innovation and technological performance in Germany: Report 2019*: Berlin: EFI.

ERAC (2014). *ERAC peer review of the Spanish research and innovation system: Final report*. Madrid: MINECO-ERAC.

Etzkowitz, H. (2008). *The triple helix: Industry-university-government innovation in action*. New York: Routledge.

Etzkowitz, H. & Leydesdorff, L. (2000). The dynamics of innovation: From National Systems and "Mode 2" to a Triple Helix of university–industry–government relations. *Research Policy*, 29(2), 109–123. DOI: 10.1016/S0048-7333(99)00055-4

Fagerberg, J. (2016). Innovation systems and policy: A tale of three countries. *Stato e Mercato*, 36(1), 13–40. DOI: 10.1425/82941

Gergils, H. (2006). *Dynamic innovation systems in the Nordic countries*. Stockholm: Studieförbundet Näringslive & Samhälle Förlag.

Gómez, M. (2007). Administración e investigación científica y técnica: veinte años después de la ley de la ciencia. *Revista d'estudis autonòmics i federals*, 5, 241–318.

Gallochat, A. (2003). French technology transfer and IP policies. In OECD. *Turning science into business: Patenting and licensing at public research organisations*. Paris: OECD Publishing.

Gherardini, A. (2015). *Squarci nell'avorio: Le università italiane e l'innovazione economica*. Firenze: Firenze University Press.

Gherardini, A. (2021). Perché investire in politiche per l'innovazione? Tre strade per otto economie avanzate. *Stato e Mercato*, 41(3), 351–388.

Gherardini, A. & Pessina, G. (2020). Cavalcare l'onda del cambiamento. Il Piano Impresa 4.0 alla prova dei distretti. *L'industria*, 2, 191–214. DOI: 10.1430/97562

Giersch, H., Paqué, K.H. & Schmieding, H. (1992). *The fading miracle: Four decades of market economy in Germany*. Cambridge: Cambridge University Press.

Grimpe, C. (2015). *RIO Country Report. Denmark 2014. JRC Science and Policy Report*. Luxembourg: European Commission.

Hall, P.A. & Soskice, D. (2001) (Eds). *Varieties of capitalism: The institutional foundations of comparative advantage*. Oxford: Oxford University Press.

HM Government (2009). *New industry, new jobs*. http://webarchive.nationalarchives.gov.uk/20100430155636/http://www.bis.gov.uk/files/file51023.pdf

HM Treasury (1999). *Budget 99: Building a stronger economic future for Britain*. https://assets.publishing.service.gov.uk/government/uploads/system/uploads/attachment_data/file/235397/0298.pdf

HM Treasury (2014). *The budget report*. https://assets.publishing.service.gov.uk/government/uploads/system/uploads/attachment_data/file/293759/37630_Budget_2014_Web_Accessible.pdf

Hörner, W. & Many, G. (2015). France. In W. Hörner, H. Döbert, L.R. Reuter, & B. von Kopp (Eds), *The education system of Europe, Second Edition* (pp. 269–292). New York: Springer.

Iversen, M.J. & Andersen, S. (2008). Co-operative liberalism: Denmark from 1857 to 2007. In S. Fellman, M.J. Iversen, H. Sjögren, & L. Thue (Eds), *Creating Nordic capitalism: The business history of a competitive periphery* (pp. 265–334). New York: Palgrave Macmillan.

Klitkou, A. & Kaloudis, A. (2009). *ERAWATCH Country Report 2008. Analysis of policy mixes to foster R&D investment and to contribute to the ERA: Denmark, Luxembourg. JRC Scientific and Technical Reports*. Luxembourg: European Commission.

Kristensen, P.H. (1996). On the constitution of economic actors in Denmark: Interacting skill containers and project coordinators. In R. Whitley & P. Kristense (Eds), *The changing European firm* (pp. 118–158). London: Routledge.

Kulicke, M. (2014). *15 Years of EXIST "University-based start-up programmes"*. Working paper. Munich: Fraunhofer Institute.

Larédo, P. (2016). Innovation policies: The national and regional dimensions. *Economia e Politica Industriale*, 43(3) 323–330. DOI: 10.1007/s40812-016-0038-5

Larédo, P. & Mustar, P. (2001). French research and innovation policy: Two decades of transformation. In P. Larédo & P. Mustar (Eds), *Research and innovation policies in the new global economy: An international comparative analysis* (pp. 447–496). Cheltenham: Edward Elgar.

Larousse, J. (2017). *Analysis of national initiatives on digitising European Industry. Denmark: Towards a digital growth strategy – MADE.* Brussels: European Commission.

Lawton-Smith, H. (2006). *Universities, innovation and the economy*. New York: Routledge.

Legait, B., Renucci, A. & Sikorav, J.L. (2015). *Les relations entre les entreprises et la recherche publique. Lever des obstacles à l'innovation en France*, www.economie.gouv.fr/files/files/directions_services/cge/recherche-publique-entreprise.pdf

Lucchese, M., Nascia, L. & Pianta, M. (2016). Industrial policy and technology in Italy. *Economia e politica industriale*, 43(3), 233–260.

Malerba, F. (1993). The national system of innovation: Italy. In R.R. Nelson (Ed). *National innovation systems: A comparative analysis* (pp. 230–238). Oxford: Oxford University Press.

MINECO (2017). *Plan estatal de política científica y técnica y de innovación 2017–2020*. Madrid: MINECO.

Molina, O. & Miguélez, F. (2013). *From negotiation to imposition: social dialogue in austerity times in Spain*. ILO Dialogue Working Paper, 51.

Mowery, D.C., Nelson, R.R., Sampat, B.N. & Ziedonis, A.A. (2015). *Ivory tower and industrial innovation: University-industry technology transfer before and after the Bayh-Dole Act.* Stanford: Stanford University Press.

Muller, E., Zenker, A. & Héraud, J.-A. (2009). *France: Innovation system and innovation policy*. Karlsruhe: Fraunhofer ISI Discussion Papers Innovation Systems and Policy Analysis, No. 18.

Muñoz, E. (2001). The Spanish system of research. In P. Larédo & P. Mustar (Eds), *Research and Innovation Policies in the New Global Economy. An International Comparative Analysis* (pp. 359–398). Cheltenham: Edward Elgar.

Mustar, P. (2016). Industrial policy in France: In search of lost time. *Economia e Politica Industriale*, 43(3), 305–313. DOI: 10.1007/s40812-016-0036-7

Mustar, P. & Wright, M. (2010). Convergence or path dependency in policies to foster the creation of university spin-off firms? A comparison of France and the United Kingdom. *The Journal of Technology Transfer*, 35, 42–65. DOI: 10.1007/s10961-009-9113-7

Nielsen, K. & Pedersen, O. (1991). From the mixed economy to the negotiated economy: The Scandinavian countries. In R. Coughlin (Ed.), *Morality, rationality and efficiency: New perspectives on socio-economics*. New York: M.E. Sharpe.

OECD (1997). *National innovation systems*. Paris: Organisation for Economic Cooperation and Development.

OECD (2013). *OECD reviews of innovation policy: Sweden, organisation for economic cooperation and development*. Paris: Organisation for Economic Cooperation and Development.

OECD (2014). *OECD reviews of innovation policy: France 2014*. Paris: Organisation for Economic Cooperation and Development.

OECD (2015). *Skills mismatch and public policy in OECD countries*. Economic Department Working Paper no. 120.

OECD (2016). *OECD reviews of innovation policy: Sweden 2016*. Paris: Organisation for Economic Cooperation and Development.

OECD (2019). *Education at a glance 2019: OECD indicators*. Paris: Organisation for Economic Cooperation and Development.

Onida, F. (2017). *L'industria intelligente: Per una politica di specializzazione efficace*. Milan: Università Bocconi Editore.

Ornston, D. (2012). *When small states make big leaps: Institutional innovation and high-tech competition in Western Europe*. Ithaca and London: Cornell University Press.

Ornston, D. (2018). *Good governance gone bad: How Nordic adaptability leads to excess*. Ithaca: Cornell University Press.

Pinhero, R., Geschwind, L. & Aarrevaar, T. (2015) (Eds). *Mergers in higher education: The experience from Northern Europe*. Heidelberg/New York/Dordrecht/London: Springer.

Powell, J.J.W. & Solga, H. (2011). Why are higher education participation rates in Germany so low? Institutional barriers to higher education expansion. *Journal of Education and Work*, 24(1-2), 49–68. DOI: 10.1080/13639080.2010.534445

Ramella F, Manzo C (2021) *The Economy of Collaboration: The New Digital Platforms of Production and Consumption*. Routledge, NewYork.

Schmoch, U. (2011). Germany: The role of universities in the learning economy. In B. Göransson & C. Brundenius (Eds), *Universities in transition: The changing role and challenges for academic institutions* (pp. 261–282). Ottawa: Springer.

Schwartz, H. (1994). Small states in big trouble: State reorganization in Australia, Denmark, New Zealand, and Sweden in the 1980s. *World Politics*, 46(4), 527–555. DOI: 10.2307/2950717

Sharp, M. (2003). The UK-experiment: Science, technology and industrial policy in Britain 1979–2000. In P. Biegelbauer & S. Borrás (Eds), *Innovation Policies in Europe and the US*. The New Agenda. Aldershot: Ashgate.

Thatcher, M. (2003). From industrial policy to a regulatory state. In H. Hayward & A. Menon (Eds), *Governing Europe* (pp. 313–329). Oxford: Oxford University Press.

Thelen, K. (2014). *Varieties of capitalism and the new politics of social solidarity*. New York: Cambridge University Press.

Toniolo, G. (2013). An overview of Italy's economic growth. In G. Toniolo (Ed.), *The Oxford Handbook of the Italian economy since unification* (pp. 3–36). Oxford: Oxford University Press.

Trigilia, C. (2007). *La costruzione sociale dell'innovazione: economia, società e territorio*. Firenze: Firenze University Press.

Trigilia, C. (2016). Tipi di democrazia e modelli di capitalismo: un'agenda di ricerca. *Stato e Mercato*, 36(2), 183–214. DOI: 10.1425/84067

Viesti, G. (2016). La compressione selettiva e cumulativa dell'università italiana. *Menabò di Etica ed Economia*, 27.

Vitols, S. & Engelhardt, L. (2005). *National institutions and high tech industries: A varieties of capitalism perspective on the failure of Germany's Neuer Markt*. Discussion Paper SP II 2005–03. Berlin: Wissenschaftszentrum.

Von Tunzelmann, N. (2003). Historical coevolution of governance and technology in the industrial revolutions. *Structural Change and Economic Dynamics*, 14(4), 365–384. DOI: 10.1016/S0954-349X(03)00029-8

Wallace, D. (1995). *Environmental policy and industrial innovation*. Oxford: Routledge.

Weiss, L. (2014). *America Inc.?: Innovation and enterprise in the national security state*. Ithaca: Cornell University Press.

Part III

Institutional structure, politics, and policies

Chapter 12

Processes of political convergence and divergence in advanced democracies

Alfio Mastropaolo, Franca Roncarolo, and Rocco Sciarrone

12.1 Dispersions

At the time of the English Civil War, Hobbes had postulated that as the upholder of a fundamental principle of order and governance of collective life, the state should be liable for counteracting the upheaval provoked by the conflict. Instead, legitimated by the principle of individual interest, the market, interwoven as one with the state, incorporated a controlled dose of disorder. By acknowledging pluralism, representative systems endorsed a further amount of turmoil, which was supervised too. While, on the one hand, through the post-war "socialdemocratic compromise", democratic systems indulged pluralism by giving prominence to political parties, on the other hand, they had to contend with the disorder brought about by the market by using state intervention. In a sense, some level of political disorder was accepted, while at the same time trying to curtail, control, or mitigate – as the case may be – the undesirable effects caused by market competition.

This task of supervision was assigned to the public authority by democratic systems, albeit with different national variations. As we know, state intervention in the economy was legitimised to a wide range of degrees. This intervention, while differing considerably from one context to another, was considered necessary, at times limiting and circumscribing, and at times explicitly controlling and administrating. In all cases, the idea of the primacy of politics over economics prevailed, that is, the conviction that the scope of the former should in some way contain, if not completely encompass, the latter. In other words, it was commonly thought that to produce social organisation, to not leave too much room for the automatic mechanisms of the market, to bring the economy and society together, politics were indispensable, alongside the more or less extensive intervention of the public authority (Bagnasco, 2003). As we know, the advance of neoliberalism has radically challenged this perspective.

The keystone of neoliberalism is to take the market as a model for associated life, incrementing *ad infinitum* the dose of creative disorder that characterises it, and trusting that it will spontaneously become ordered.

DOI: 10.4324/9781003297130-16

The naturalness, freedom, and *levitas* that neoliberalism attributes to market relations should be extended to the governance of associated life, dismissing the coercive heaviness, artificiality, sluggishness, and *gravitas* that it ascribes to the state. The state's foremost task is to ensure the minimum conditions for the market to function, while reducing its action to a minimum. This is an ambitious plan, and at the end of the twentieth century it galvanised an extraordinary upheaval, which involved the state, the market, but also the nation, the parties, the classes, i.e. the fundamental institutions that had hitherto governed modern collective life. One of the most prominent features, if not the most prominent one, that advanced societies have in common is the colossal and thorough reorganisation – or rescaling – that has heavily invested public authority, involving also the market at the same time.[1]

Public authority has undergone an extraordinary process of dispersion and externalisation, which, for the sake of simplicity, can be broken down into at least five non-contextual, non-symmetrical and often intertwined "movements": the first movement is lateral, and is precisely that which was instigated by the state in the direction of the market; the second moved upwards, in the direction of supranational institutions; the third downwards, towards subnational governments; while finally another lateral movement benefited the sphere of organised interests and so-called "civil society". A fifth movement of externalisation has been added: the revision of the chain of command in democratic societies. The division of tasks between parties, parliament, the executive, and public administration has become intricate. At first glance, it would appear that the executive has been strengthened. Yet this reinforcement is undermined by the weight of several encumbrances casting misgiving and mistrustfulness. As can easily be surmised, these five movements have hugely altered the institutional set-ups that historically had sought to reconcile capitalism and democracy, markedly affecting the relation between growth and inclusion that constitutes the focus of this book, not to mention challenging the categories with which political science and public law used to classify political regimes.

A few points can nevertheless be established, albeit with caution. As we shall see in the following pages, the dispersion of public authority generated by these movements brought the issues of growth and economic efficiency to the forefront, for a long time overshadowing those of inequality and social cohesion. It has not been a smooth process. On the contrary: while there has been a forceful thrust towards convergence, the counterthrusts have been just as vigorous. In other words, the democratic systems, institutions, and actors affected by these dispersive movements have welcomed them in very different ways, which are none too easy to reconstruct and classify. There remains no doubt that the policies adopted by each country, from those accepted without reserve to those endorsed with greater reluctance, if not for outright self-defence, have been conditioned by an extraordinary plurality of factors. In terms of administrative structures, of the greater or lesser autonomy of the market from the state and the form taken by the market itself, in terms of industrial relations, party systems, and therefore legitimisation processes, as well as political, bureaucratic, and entrepreneurial cultures and media/political relations, each country was initially different from the other. At times the state has manifested a readiness to forswear shares of authority, yet at other times the renunciation has been extorted; sometimes the new competences were admitted without demur, at other times they met with resistance: the state that received or renounced was never a unitary institution but then neither were the welcoming and receiving institutions, which are always divided between those willing to give in and receive and those who are opposed. Inevitably this was not without effects on the size and the trend of transfers, hence generating a variety of outcomes. Likewise, an analogous inference can be made about the market, the system of interests, and civil society. Each country had, and still has, its own capitalism, its own specific system of interests. Despite the convergences, the specificities still persist and are considerable.

This chapter will therefore pinpoint the changes that have impinged on the political sphere, shedding light on how the democratic systems and development models are intertwined. Our analysis will first focus on the movements mentioned above, i.e. the transformation processes that have led to a dispersion of public authority. As we shall see, these are processes that have exerted of pressure to transnational standardisation institutional frameworks and public policies. After describing this forceful drive towards convergence, consistent with the objectives of this research, our focus will shift to how different countries have reacted to these movements, with particular regard for their different forms of adaptation or opposition. Finally, the changes seen in politics will be related to the effects produced by the media system, another powerful factor that can determine significant differences in the various paths taken by political systems to contend with the problems linked to economic development and – at the same time, as far as possible – social cohesion. These attempts have come up against ever-increasing obstacles over time, but have also met with differentiated, albeit inevitably partial, responses.

The perspective adopted in this chapter shows, in short, the more political dimension of the complex links between growth and inclusion, all the more obvious if one considers the difficulty of reconciling policies constructed to pursue one or the other objective. As A.O. Hirschman has clearly pointed out:

> it would be disingenuous to pretend that stimulating economic growth and correcting or attenuating inequalities that arise in the course of growth require exactly the same policies. The problem rather consists in finding an optimal combination of policies that does as little damage as possible to either objective. We are more likely to find something close to this optimum if we admit from the outset that we are in the presence

> of two objectives between which there exists normally a good deal of tension and conflict.
>
> (Hirschman, 1995: 68)

Precisely for this reason, the relationship between economic development and social cohesion is a purely political issue, i.e. it invokes political action much more than policies, the configuration of public authority and its room for manoeuvre.

12.2 Towards the market

The first shift, not chronologically speaking but certainly the best known and most discussed, that has affected public authority and the governance of social life, went in the direction of the market. At the same time, the latter has undergone a far-reaching process of transformation and dispersion, countering the reorganisation that had taken shape during the period of "organised" capitalism.[2] It is a twofold re-designing, involving externalisation by the state and internalisation by the market, within which state-building and market-building have become intertwined – which is certainly nothing new.

Taking "organised" capitalism as our starting point, it is interesting to look at this process from the market perspective: partly organised by the state, partly self-organised. In that model, share ownership of companies was stable and long-lasting. At the same time, the Fordist factory, which organised production according to scale economies, grouped together and stabilised employees. It also provided for homogeneous wage conditions and standardised mass consumption, a powerful instrument of social integration, with a peculiar egalitarian component that rubbed off on the service sector and the public administration. Businesses and the state likewise legitimised the integrative and representative activity carried out by trade unions, which were also a principle of market organisation.

Quite another matter is "disorganised" capitalism (Offe, 1985).[3] The latter is in any case disorganised compared to the previous model, but, on closer inspection, not so much. It does not lack a hierarchical and a governmental structure, centred on financial institutions, banks, and rating agencies (Genschel & Zangl, 2017), and furthermore lacks neither rules nor customs. But it is nonetheless different. First and foremost a distinction can be seen in the transformation of the ownership and management of businesses, but also of the organisation of production, industrial relations, consumption, background, and culture of its employees, at all levels, and its users. Working hours and conditions, tasks, contract personnel, and wages have been disrupted. Unemployment is no longer a social or political issue and, with the active contribution of the public authorities, stable workers have diminished in number while fixed-term, precarious, flexible, part-time, on-demand, down to the so-called *gig economy* have all burgeoned (Crouch, 2019, chapters 4 and 9). The tertiary sector, whose workers have numerically surpassed those employed in manufacturing, is increasingly dispersed, even the advanced portion with the new professions serving businesses and financial institutions.

Technology and reduced transport costs have made it possible to shut down factories even more easily than laying off the workforce. The workforce has been transferred from the large Fordist factories to smaller production units that are easy to dismantle or to relocate across borders. Workers are no longer seen as a collective body but as a collection of individuals, with whom employers would prefer to negotiate individually. This dispersion has triggered an economic, social, and cultural destabilisation of the working and lower classes, as well as of the intermediate classes, implicating also a dispersion of the inequalities – there are many ways to be unequal, and they often overlap. All of which leads to the consequent decline not only of class identities, but also of the appeal of trade unions, along with their bargaining power and the indirect action of government brought to bear on their members. Also worthy of note is that the devitalisation of trade unions has corresponded to the weakening of business associations.

Public policy has had a decisive role in these changes. It has helped by adopting deregulation measures: promoting company bargaining over national bargaining, redesigning working conditions from a juridical viewpoint, allowing civil society to camouflage many forms of precarious and poorly paid work with solidarity and altruism. It has helped by allowing businesses to compete with national and local public authorities: in terms of labour costs, legal regulations, taxation, environmental protection, and so on. Who offers the most advantageous conditions? In the light of such offers, companies are free to set up their headquarters in one place, their registered office in another, their tax domicile in yet another, to be listed on the most promising stock market, to draw capital from heterogeneous sources and in diverse ways, and to expand their design and marketing activities in a multitude of different places.

Disencumbered from any social responsibility, not only from a cultural perspective but also from any action taken by the state, and in particular from the none-too-rigid constraints to which they had been subjected in the previous period, companies perceive competition differently in disorganised capitalism. The competition linked to their capitalising on the stock exchange and therefore to their capacity to be used for the purposes of financial speculation often manages to obscure the competition relating to investment, turnover, and often also profits, largely overlooking the effects on employment or on the local and social context in which they operate. The state has further helped enterprises by selling off activities previously considered as pertaining to the sphere of order and the general interest, and goods and services withdrawn from commodification because they are considered indispensable (Gallino, 2011). Among the many stories that can be told, two are emblematic: that of corporate welfare, or second welfare, and that of the munificent funding granted by corporations for cultural activities. The state saves money. In the case of corporate welfare, rather than a saving for the state, it is an expedient with which to remunerate employees thanks to the generous fiscal advantages that can be reaped.

Along the dividing line between them, or at the intersection where they meet, state and market eventually devised *in tandem* another technique of governing. Further portions of public authority ebbed away into that intermediate dimension often called governance. This is not all the doing of neoliberalism, but of subsequent modifications. Halfway between the state, as governmental technique based on authority and law, and the market, based on exchange and contract, the technique of horizontal coordination between public institutions and private actors was officially developed. Functional representation through neocorporative arrangements had, in the years of its implementation, unofficially become a *modus operandi* for governing major policy choices and for preventing and mediating conflicts. The great transformation of democratic regimes and capitalist economies has radically revised this technique, officially recognising the contractualisation of policies (Bobbio, 2000). Neocorporatism called for centralised negotiation between government, business organisations, and trade unions, which could be followed by local consultations, always on a triangular basis. Governance entails public institutions becoming partners, who sit down to negotiate together with local, business, trade union, and association interests, i.e. stakeholders,[4] rather than unilaterally making policy choices.

12.3 Supranational dispersion

The second shift, on the other hand, favoured the development of supranational institutions, with order, peace, cooperation, and integration comprising the rhetoric through which it took shape. In the aftermath of the First World War, the League of Nations and the Permanent Court of International Justice (or World Court) were its precursors. The Second World War moved in the same direction. The pledge made by democratic countries was to extend democratic principles and rules to relations between states. In fact, interdependencies multiplied during the war and the post-war period and it was now a question of governing them, until the end of the millennium when the dismantling of customs supervision and control, the liberalisation of the flow of capital, together with the abatement of transport and communication costs, allowed the surging tide of goods and people (also legitimised as contributing to peace and prosperity) to grow exponentially. Special institutions to govern these processes have gradually developed, while others, initially created for more limited purposes, have been redirected. The "intergovernmental" institutions have taken on the tasks of underpinning development, helping states in difficulty, protecting human rights, safeguarding cultural heritage, and so on.

At the same time, a network of supranational judicial institutions developed, while others set themselves the goal of regulating the globalisation of the economy, and since the 1990s pro-market reforms have actively been championed in the areas of public finance, development, good governance, and morality. Nor should we forget the multitude of agencies, both public and private, that have set about dictating norms, standards, and rules of conduct in a variety of fields, and thus supervising actual policies.

European countries have pursued a much more stringent and further-ranging collaboration, no longer intergovernmental. This is a well-known story, which unfolded far from smoothly. Coexistence and cooperation for over half a century has not served to eliminate competition or the hierarchies between states, nor is there any trace of a meta-state or anything resembling a state order. Moreover, any efforts to forge restrictions similar to those characterising federal regimes have so far been thwarted. Given that in particular the larger countries deemed it inopportune to relinquish of quotas of national sovereignty, this has inevitably generated a deliberately discontinuous public authority. Intermingling with that of the nation states, it has been completely redesigned. The Union has dispossessed the states of fundamental policies, or the states have surrendered them, in matters of competition, industrial policy, monetary policy, and so on. There is a formula that epitomises this process: there is no longer the nation-state, but instead the "member-state", in whose governance national and European institutions interpenetrate (Bickerton, 2017).

The mechanisms of this interpenetration and "Europeanisation" are complex. European governance is distributed over no less than four levels: the specifically European institutions, such as the Commission, the Court of Justice and the ECB itself; intergovernmental institutions, such as the Councils of Ministers; a multinational institution, such as the Europarliament; and finally an array of intergovernmental committees, where representatives of national public administrations interact (Cassese, 2017). Admittedly, the very architecture of Europe is labyrinthine and cumbersome, scarcely reflecting the conventional architecture of the democratic state. Not even a semblance of a common identity has evolved, despite the huge investments to this end. Yet the European Union is far from ineffective. The single currency and the central bank are constraints that could be described as "constitutional", as are the principle of free movement, the primacy of competition, the ban on state aid to companies, and the fiscal compact. In turn, the directives approved by the European Parliament and the Council of Ministers, the regulations, the standards, and the massive number of decisions taken by the Court of Justice, constitute the Union's governance. In this way, the European Union resembles the "regulatory state" coveted by neoliberalism rather than the interventionist state of the post-war compromise: dictating rules but not delivering services to citizens, let alone intervening in economic practices.

No coincidence, then, that not only has the Union, like the member states, made extensive use of new instruments – communication, information, incentives, standards, rules of conduct – rather than the usual legislative, economic and fiscal ones (Lascoumes & Le Galès, 2005; Halpern et al., 2014) – but its disciplinary capacity is limited to imposing fines on offenders. It was, after all, built on economic and financial foundations. The European institutions were designed to primarily address the problem of growth. First and foremost, we need to make the market work and thus affirm and defend the principles of competition and the free movement of goods, capital and labour. The so-called "cohesion policies" are compatible with this aim, seen as policies targeting the major territorial and social imbalances but set out in terms of development policies and not as redistributive policies. The failure to implement even a minimal common fiscal architecture only confirms the fact that the Union's concern is not to offset economic and social inequalities, nor indeed to avail itself of the opportunity offered to the member states to compete in this area.

The procedures of *multilevel governance* constitute another instrument of administration.[5] The European authorities and the European Parliament carry out a daunting amount of consultation, negotiation, hearing and coordination with the so-called stakeholders, organised interests, policy networks, lobbies, civil society and trade unions, regional and local authorities (Kriesi, Adam, & Jochum, 2006). The Commission instead pursues fundamental tasks of framing and agenda-building, bolstered by the distribution of ideas, expertise, and professionalism: this circulation of ideas, skills and therefore personnel between national and Community administrations, and between the public and private sectors, has favoured the emergence of a true Community administrative and technical elite, placed at the service of market growth and efficiency.

12.4 Subnational dispersion

Another act of dispersion of public authority has benefitted subnational institutions.[6] The reasons for devolution in favour of subnational governments are promoted and legitimised with quite different aims: on the one hand to acknowledge and regularise subnational peculiarities, on the other as a way of democratising public authority and bringing it closer to the citizens. From the 1960s onwards, at times in a dramatic fashion, "stateless nations" appeared – in Canada, the United Kingdom, France, Spain (Keating, 2001). Later, Reagan's New Federalism conferred a conspicuously fiscal connotation to self-government, overthrowing the centralising approach inherited from the New Deal and its welfare policies. Fiscal issues would also be significant for Blair's devolution, as well as many other cases.

In the face of the difficulty of coping with an increase in public spending, devolution appeared to be a means of better matching services to citizens' needs and at the same time allowing for a more effective and judicious use of public expenditure.[7] The national level of government was substituted by the local one, stimulated by a powerful cultural offensive: pursuing more restricted spaces of identity served to offset the displacement of shares of state authority in an upward direction. Regionally oriented parties and even the local enterprises have nonetheless been galvanised by decentralisation policies. The market, by rediscovering and exploiting the local dimension, also had a hand in contributing to the competition between territories, cities and regions.

This too constitutes no small turnaround. For centuries, the state was concerned with readjusting and recomposing territorial unbalances. It did so by levelling out cultural and economic differences, by bringing the peripheries closer to the centre, the countryside closer to the cities – using force if necessary. The territory covered by the state was a large and unitary space, symbolically represented by the nation, within which any unbalance appeared illegitimate and intolerable. In the season of state interventionism, national government action was officially given the task of redressing territorial inequalities: promoting the development of areas lagging behind, relieving the congestion of the most advanced areas, and ensuring that all citizens, wherever they lived, had the same rights and the same public services.

In recent decades, there has been a change in direction. To put it simply: the promotion and regulation of market competition have been targeted as the foremost mission of the state. Local areas compete, the regional divide has become legitimate, and the responsibility for the condition of these areas is attributed to their inhabitants and the ruling classes that they democratically select (Keating, 2013). Each territory, each local authority competes with the others on the basis of its productive structure, its natural resources, its "social capital", its political and administrative leaders, its entrepreneurs, its schools, universities and research centres. Competition will reward those who show themselves to be more adaptive, more creative, more productive, more responsible, while at the same time encouraging those who are lagging behind. It is up to local leaders to make the most of their territories: metropolises, major urban centres, suburbs, small and medium-sized towns, the countryside, plains, and mountains are all assets to be exploited (ibid.). Local governments are saddled with attracting investment and business, negotiating with enterprises with regard to their establishment in the area, offering them infrastructures and services, draining skills from other territories, and seizing the financial resources that the state – and the European Union – puts up for grabs (Rodríguez-Pose, 2018).[8]

The rediscovery of the local level is far from being uniformly distributed. It too is the result of disputes with different outcomes. There is competition between regions, cities, and intermediate spaces. What stands out is the supremacy of Saskia Sassen's "global cities" (Sassen, 2018; Iversen & Soskice, 2019), in which management, financial, and creative activities and advanced research are concentrated. As a result, these global cities have found themselves at an advantage in claiming reserved spaces of governance. A global city, or even a merely prosperous one, has capacities for self-government that others do not have, and local taxation provides it with opportunities that are denied elsewhere. It also has a different bargaining power. On a lower rung, we find large and medium-sized urban centres, which have progressed at times by galvanising the hinterland, at others by taking a step back (Iversen & Soskice, 2019: 224–229). More than the governing authorities, it is the economy that makes the difference. Often with very uncomfortable political effects (Iammarino, Rodriguez-Pose, & Storper, 2019).

12.5 Towards civil society

There is yet a fourth movement and a fourth externalisation to come, the one that has taken shape in favour of civil society. Only that, at this juncture, the formula has taken on a different meaning from the past: it is not the civil society of Hobbes or Locke, nor that of Hegel, let alone that of Gramsci, nor can it any longer be understood as a political space alternative to the state and parties, such as the one established in the period of collective movements after 1968. It still bears some traces of this, but it has become above all a space inhabited by private actors, in which the aim is to be free from unbalances, relations of supremacy and the shackles of bureaucracy, to be based rather on cooperation, generosity, altruism, spontaneity and civicness.[9] The welfare model conceived by Beveridge, that culminated in the recognition of "social" rights, promised universal protection for citizens, regardless of the circumstances. In its role as an agency providing collective protection, the state had promoted the establishment of a space of solidarity in which private institutions also participated, often with religious backgrounds, breaking out of the moulds of charity and philanthropy.

Unburdened of the imperative of profit and the opportunism of politics, civil society is the privately devised remedy for the excesses of individualism and selfishness, by virtue of the voluntary, disinterested, solidarity-based, moral relationships that are woven between those who participate in it. Civil society in the Thatcher era was at best reduced to philanthropy, regenerated in the new millennium under the guise of compassionate conservatism. New Labour also placed privatised civil society at the centre of its strategy by committing the state to support it, until it was officially recognised as the governing institution of collective life with the decisive contribution of the European Union. Public administrations, elected assemblies, national, and local executives, and parties all pay homage to it. It occupies a prominent place among the stakeholders invited to participate in decision-making regarding the management of public services or local governance.[10] As a matter of fact, with all due respect for its operators and their commitment to solidarity, civil society has actually become a surrogate for the state, which has relegated to it the low-cost provision of a significant proportion of public services. But the market has also had its say: the other relevant phenomenon is the imposing entry of business and finance within the confines of civil society, which have invented nothing less than what is defined as "*philanthrocapitalism*" (Arrigoni, Bifulco, & Caselli, 2020; Skocpol, 2016). This is another dispersive movement: bypassing conventional democratic procedures, donors contribute directly to policy making: they choose the sectors of intervention, set the agenda, and dictate the rules to be followed. Resources are allocated through organised competitive procedures, with all their accompanying forecasts and impact assessments, cost/benefit calculations, rankings, benchmarks, and audits.

"Philanthrocapitalism" and its rules also affect voluntary work, care for the poor, the sick, the elderly, children in difficulty, the disabled, migrants, ex-convicts and victims of racketeering and even exert rights protection. Philanthrocapitalism dictates models of action, demands specific professionalism and entrepreneurial skills, encourages business-oriented attitudes, and promotes cooperation between the public and private sectors. Camouflaged under the charitable image of the non-profit sector, private individuals obtain tax benefits, regulatory concessions, and financial resources,[11] perhaps with the commitment to reinvest in further philanthropic activities the services performed for profit (Eikenberry & Kluger, 2004).

12.6 An internal movement

These movements of dispersion did not, however, end with the depletion of state authority, to the benefit of supra- and sub-national institutions, the market, and civil society. There is a fifth, more complicated and ambivalent movement that took place in the heart of the state. The theories of overload and ungovernability formulated in the 1970s, advocating a revision of democratic systems to enhance their decision-making capacity, catalysed it. For the most part, adaptation ensued pragmatically, following other paths, i.e. updating the interpretation of written rules, or rethinking unwritten rules, particularly those concerning political competition and style of government. At times electoral legislation or even constitutional rules were revised. In any case, the shape of representation and parties, the shape of public bureaucracies and, finally, the link between parliament and the executive, and the latter's position, all met with change.

One general trend has been to strengthen the executive at the expense of representative assemblies. This adjustment, however, came about in a rather heterodox form, as well as with the usual notable national variations. An initial aspect is the multiplication of extra- and pre-political representation initiatives: this can be explained by the increase in social and political pluralism, but there is reason to think that this multiplication has served to dilute and debilitate representation itself. For their part, the parties have reduced their linkages with society and have long since given up assembling permanent collective bodies. Party systems are also breaking up, either because conventional ones are languishing, some even risking survival, or because of the emergence of outsider parties.

The inflation of pre-political and electoral representation was at first sight offset by the so called "presidentialisation" (Poguntke & Webb, 2005), all visibility in the leader of the executive. The drive coming from the media, and their *mise-en-scène*, contributed far more than formalised institutional adjustments (Mughan, 2000). The formula of presidentialisation is nevertheless inaccurate, as it wrongly evokes American presidentialism, an extremely complicated apparatus that is burdened by multiple counterweights and is unstable over time. In any case, this formula heralds a change of style in the running of the executive and in relations with the elected assemblies and public opinion, with serious consequences for the balance of power. A substantial share of power has been concentrated in the hands of the head of government, as well as part of the activity of representation: even in parliamentary regimes, the executive more than any other institution is credited with representing the will of the electorate.

Yet the authority that was supposed to be concentrated in the executive has in part been drained away elsewhere. First, because of the movements mentioned above, which have mitigated and externalised state authority. Second, because the chain of command of democratic systems has been complicated by at least four factors. The first of these is the supervisory, and sometimes guiding, action of independent authorities, including central banks: for almost all EU countries there is also the central bank in Frankfurt. The second factor is the excess of authoritativeness accorded to experts, some of whom operate within the authorities, others in the ministries and public administrations. The third factor is the space conquered by the judiciary and the constitutional courts, along the lines of the American model. The fourth factor involves the reforms inspired by the theory of New Public Management, which boosted competition within public administrations. What had been the backbone of the state for centuries was disarticulated. The culture of civil servants, in particular those at the top, increasingly interchangeable with those in the private sector, was transformed, importing market rationales. The structure of public administrations also changed, partly transformed into independent agencies (Christensen & Laegreid, 2001). The executive still appoints the members of the authorities, sometimes in conjunction with parliament. It also appoints the top managers in public administrations and does not lack defence from the judiciary. Nevertheless, if the constraints are slackened, the empowerment of the executive is biased to no small degree by the burden of coordination tasks it has the duty to perform.[12]

The dissociation between politics, staged for the benefit of the public, and policymaking, often conducted elsewhere, constitutes another reason for the greater load on the shoulders of the executive. It is not only a matter of backstage politics, which is a very obvious technique for dealing with conflict: it is not always a case of hidden interests. Policymaking has often become invisible – though not to the same extent in all countries – because it is overshadowed by the spectacle of overt politics, where disputants struggle to find reasons for agreement, even when compliance is needed, or would be possible. Nor should we forget the politics made invisible by the lack of transparency of the supra- and sub-national venues into which policy management has shifted. This severance between politics and policy does not create trust; indeed, it may give rise to misunderstandings. Some of these misunderstandings are easy to explain: in spite of all the promised answerability, how many citizens, and even professional observers, are able to attribute to each individual his/her responsibilities?[13] It goes without saying that in such conditions, the presidential executive occupies a less than comfortable position. Even if it now towers over every other public institution in the collective imagination, dispersion has not spared it.

12.7 Convergences, divergences, and resistance

There is no single, pre-established way of thinking and acting as a state; as such, to conclude that dispersion and decline of the state coincide would therefore be overly hasty.[14] The state as institution has always had variable configurations.[15] The assortment of its components, both material and symbolic, allowed it to be built and dismantled a thousand times, narrowing or widening the scope and intensity of its action. The application of the principle of sovereignty is far more complicated than the normative meaning of this concept.[16] Looking back over the history of the state, its areas of intervention have always been contested, both among its own and by other institutions, not only by the market.

If we compare different countries, the processes of state building and nation building, but also those of market building and society building, have learned from each other, but this learning has been asymmetrical. There is always a set of ideas and practices devised and tested somewhere, of which someone takes possession, applying it as they can in different conditions, as it suits them and above all as they succeed. The configurations appear when all is said and done. Professional bureaucracies, the representative regime, the division of powers, the nation, citizenship, the capitalist economy, market competition, but also nationalism, colonialism, and socialism, all correspond to ideas and practices shared throughout the West and beyond, but which have acclimatised differently from one place to another. The several dispersive movements are no exception. The state can act as such in many ways, at times through central bureaucracies, at times with the help of parties, and at others with the backing of big banking institutions, companies, and trade unions. Different actors have adopted the policies with which the state, the market, civil society and even the chain of command of democratic systems have been redesigned, with different aims, following different paths and with different consequences.

The driving forces exerted by the European Union on its member states, however powerful they may be, have produced different reactions according to the economic, political, and cultural conditions peculiar to each country. The multiple processes of adaptation have, for example, allowed Germany, alongside the northern European countries, to assume a pre-eminent position. In the first place, the economic weight of the Federal Republic transmuted into political influence and thus into the imposition of its rules and standards, starting with the euro, the profile of which was designed on that of the mark. All the same, what suited Germany and other northern European countries, such as constraints on public spending and liberalisation of competition, turned out to be indigestible for southern European countries.

The United Kingdom has also been at the forefront in dictating European competition policy and promoting the financialisation of the economy, favouring the service sector, which is the strongest point of its economy. Nonetheless, this has not managed to offset industrial decline, with serious damage to some sections of the population and some geographical areas, affected by both deindustrialisation and welfare cuts. In France, on the other hand, the centralist tradition and the *dirigisme* of the *grands corps* conditioned the rescaling processes: the divestment of state interventionism decelerated and thus so did the devolution towards sub-national authorities and civil society – only up to a certain point, however. The conversion of part of the *grands corps* to New Public Management and to the idea of the regulatory state was fundamental. The unexpected reconversion to free competition seen during Mitterand's first seven-year term in 1983 paved the way, and the rescaling took place largely in silence, fostered by the ever more intricate intertwining afforded by the status of member state.[17] Similarly, a downward dispersion was brought about by decentralisation measures adopted by the centre but even more so by a progressive erosion due to the leadership of certain mayors and local authorities. Other contributing elements included the action of the market and interests, which redesigned the national space, favouring the most dynamic areas, such as the Paris region and the southwest, and the regional policies initiated by the European Union. At the same time, concertation practices were encouraged throughout the country.[18]

Legal norms have not always been necessary. The status granted to London in 1999 by the Labour government extended the powers of the London authorities. But it is mainly thanks to the initiative of the financial sector, which found a favourable environment and considerable fiscal benefits there, that London has become a great global city. Instead, it was the identity claims flushed with North Sea oil that provided the premise for the wide-ranging independence claimed by Scotland. In Spain too, regionalism has progressed partly on identity grounds, but it is mainly the more vibrant regional economy that led Catalonia to claim autonomy from central power, later dramatised by local leaders with their separatist ambitions. Italian regionalism, from the 1990s onwards, has been legally reconfigured, not without heeding the claims of some political parties rooted in the more prosperous regions to relieve themselves of the burden of supporting Southern Italy. This has given rise to an extension perhaps even greater than that of German federalism, up to now more limited than the concept of federalism suggests, and for which instead attempts at reforming have been pursued for a decade.[19]

In keeping with its image, France has been somewhat hesitant in applying the rebalancing measures dictated by the European Union. On the other hand, neoliberalism and New Public Management have attracted much attention among the top public administrations, as evidenced by the even more frequent transfers from the public to the private sector.[20] In Italy, public sector divestments were instead carried out as a matter of urgency, with the aim of reducing the debt, following a bitter dispute that culminated in the dismissal of an entire political class as a result of judicial investigations. Valuable industrial activities at the heart of the national economy vanished, sold off to the private sector amid speculative manoeuvres by large private investors. In France, the United Kingdom, and Germany, the primary motive for privatisation was to expand and buttress the financial market. But the French state has also been cautious in conducting privatisation and deregulation policies and has maintained some ability to guide the national economy (Bortolotti & Siniscalco, 2004).

Moreover, an extraordinary example is presented by the European Union of the disempowerment of democratic politics conducted in recent decades in the name of its hopeless inefficiency. Thanks to the labyrinthine structure of its institutions, designed to harmonise or orchestrate the heterogeneous demands of the member states,[21] party politics plays only a secondary role. The Union's governance involves intense consultation activities on individual issues, with interest organisations, civil society, policy networks, and lobbies, which also infiltrate its bureaucracies, with the stakeholder democracy[22] often cooperating in its regulatory activity. Fritz Scharpf made the point very succinctly by contrasting democracy as "government by the people" with democracy as "government for the people". The people – needless to say – are still there. But if one democracy, the traditional one, legitimised itself as input-oriented, because it listened to the people, the other would be output-oriented. Without waiting to listen to the people, democracy is concerned – or promises to be concerned – with their well-being. The people, after all, are free to express *ex post* their approval, which, to be honest, appears at the moment to be not exactly enthusiastic (Scharpf, 1997: 6–13).

Institutions are forged by those who inhabit them, as well as by their critics and opponents. The movements that have shaken public authority could not fail to encounter movements of opposition and resistance. Some were successful, others completely ineffectual. The redistribution of national sovereignty through the European Union has long met with resistance within individual countries: the Italian communists opposed it for a long time, in 1954 France broke up the European Defence Community, the British parties also initially opposed it, then eventually agreed to join, and finally the opponents of the Union took over. The unification process met with much resistance from the United States. Despite appearances and concessions to neoliberal orthodoxy, there is probably some connection between the choice of the latter two countries to opt for non-inclusive growth and their reservations towards Europe, which constitutes an attempt to govern the continent.

Constrained by their traditions, the northern European countries, and to some extent the continental ones, have tried to reconcile growth and inclusion. But only some countries have managed succeeded to an acceptable degree to reconcile the imperatives of growth and the protection of social cohesion.

The descending movement towards local institutions has also represented a bone of contention. In France, public bureaucracies have opposed this downward trend, while in Italy, after the collapse, or disarmament, of the large national parties, regionalism has encountered no further obstacles, but it became just another thread in the web of stagnation and inequality. Increasingly depoliticised, the local government has also come into play, taking on more and more the characteristics of an "economic enterprise", one that controls public spending and makes its own territory competitive – more for businesses than for citizens, leaving yet again the problem of inequalities in the background. All this while giving rise to forms of resistance such as localism and identity claims, which end up accentuating the dispersion of public authority. In any case, the downward movement – on a par with the upward movement – contributes to depoliticising the links between growth and inclusion.

And so does the movement towards the market, severely testing the resistance of socialist parties, public bureaucracies, and collective movements. Not only has the market gained power, but it has taken on new implications, even a new symbolic and political significance, claiming to guide politics and inspire policies. Needless to say, markets differ from one country to another, and capitalism is never disorganised in quite the same way. Traces of neocorporative practices persist in Scandinavian countries (Christiansen, 2018). The reforms promoted by the Schröder government destabilised German corporate capitalism, but even now, at least for part of the labour market, the most protected, the trade unions still retain some influence and some negotiating capacity. In France capitalism is still supervised by the state, whereas in Mediterranean capitalisms the previous constraints have been ousted more radically. To a greater or lesser extent, however, labour unemployment has been depoliticised and with it the labour market, and this depoliticisation has not been offset by the other lateral movement towards civil society. On the contrary, one has reinforced the other. If in the 1970s civil society was an extension of the collective movements, the harbinger of critique and egalitarian claims, in recent years the shift towards civil society has served the processes of externalisation of public authority, fostering processes of interbreeding with organised interests. The forms of horizontal coordination promoted by governance, based on exchange and contract, between public and private actors, herald a type of inclusion once again conceived as a by-product of economic growth. National varieties of the last movement, the one that revolutionised the chain of command of democratic regimes, and its dovetailing with the other four, are no less heterogeneous. The original diversity of institutional architectures, party systems, administrative machinery and interest systems makes a great deal of difference. Even the memory of them counts, or the cultural resistance that this memory arouses. The buttressing of the executive was certainly not necessary in France, where many specialists have long been recommending a reparliamentarisation of the government of the Fifth Republic. In the United Kingdom, the role of the prime minister has been further boosted mainly by the media (Langer, 2011), while the Scandinavian countries have retained their parliamentary system, which, moreover, allowed minority governments to be formed that were still capable of governing. Nevertheless, it was in in Sweden that the role of experts in ministries became prominent. In Germany, entry into the euro has not disempowered the Bundesbank all that much and a certain tendency to delegate some crucial decisions to the Constitutional Court has been observed (Rothstein & Schulze-Cleven, 2020).

There are always cultural legacies that, far from being inconsequential, impinge on the ways in which New Public Management is implemented: it has imposed itself everywhere at the expense of "legalist" bureaucracies, but has been interpreted in a variety of ways. The top administration in France has been divided between sectors more exposed to the new doctrine, such as the economic ministries, and others more disinclined, such as the welfare administrations. In Denmark, to take another case, New Public Management is even being questioned, while in Italy the party system was reconstituted in the aftermath of an open, violent, and controversial diatribe against the consociational habits allegedly marking the party system eliminated by the 1994 elections.

12.8 Change, put to the test of the media

Another aspect that until now has remained latent is worthy of consideration: the way in which the functioning of the media has been interwoven with political changes, whether assenting to them or directing them but always – to some extent – shaping them. It is precisely the power of the effects produced by the media and the pervasive nature of their impact on the mechanisms of Western democracies that offer a sort of litmus test for the analysis of change, making it easier to appreciate the differences, helping to shed light on the continuity as well as the ruptures that characterise the processes. Those who have studied the processes of mediatisation[23] have repeatedly described the media as one of the main driving forces underlying the acceleration, intensification and diffusion of the changes that have taken place in Western democracies. Therefore, identifying the points where they come into contact is not difficult.

The commercial component that had always characterised communication in the United States, and was established in Europe from the second half of the 1970s onwards with the gradual end of the public monopoly in national broadcasting systems, accelerated the move towards the market (see Blumler, 1992; Blumler & Gurevitch, 1995), favouring the advent of a culture centred on economic exchange value. Among the decisive components of this culture, the metrics of success, as calculated in audience figures and converted into advertising investments, are accompanied by the appreciations in the polls that fuel the stock market of political quotations and the supply chain of communication. More recently, "likes" and preferences have been added, part of that ephemeral but nonetheless accredited currency in political-media arenas, that in this "society of platforms" (van Dijck, Poell, & De Waal, 2018) steer the "economy of attention" (Franck, 2019). They do so on the one hand by guiding the political flows of popularity and on the other by propelling choices and consumption by means of algorithms, with recommendations via increasingly personalised communication.[24]

This extreme versatility and a genetic propensity towards everything that is new – or at least that presents itself as such – have, moreover, fostered an unconditioned approval of the media, first the electronic ones and then the digital ones, by those who, over time, no longer felt adequately represented by a political system often in difficulty due to the complexity of increasingly multidimensional and global problems. The system was also overburdened by party apparatuses that were primarily concerned with their own self-reproduction. It is hardly surprising that this has given rise to additional motivations and reference models for that lateral thrust which, as we have seen, has dispersed democratic politics within civil society.

Furthermore, the interrelations between media and political movements on the vertical axis have been no less evident. On the one hand, in the age of communicative abundance (Blumler & Kavanagh, 1999), the need to differentiate targets and products has found an answer in narrow-casting communication that has favoured localisation processes, offering *ad hoc* showcases to segments of the public, micro-communities and representatives -political and otherwise- of local constituencies. On the other, intertwined with the trend towards globalisation, the drive to reach wider audiences, and the availability of the technologies necessary to achieve this, have contributed to making communication flows more transnational and the protagonists of a multi-level decision-making process, when not predominantly located outside the national arena, more familiar.[25]

Just how far the internal movement described in the preceding pages is closely intertwined with the effects of the mediatisation of politics has already been mentioned in the references to the processes of personalisation and presidentialisation of politics. Here, even more than with other dimensions, not only is the intensification produced by the media assessed, but also the scope of an environmental ecosystem that has facilitated both the emergence of a political stage crowded with actors and the verticalisation of the direct relationship between leaders and citizens (Swanson & Mancini, 1996).

It is precisely the extent of these changes, and the evidence of their widespread nature, that has led some scholars to hypothesise the systematic convergence of democracies towards specific models of mediatised politics. Hallin and Mancini, for example, by cross-referencing the variables relating to political systems with those relating to the distinctive features of the relations between politics and information environments,[26] distinguished three different models of relations. The first – typical of Mediterranean parliamentary democracies – is characterised by the parallelism[27] practised by the information system in relation to a political structure mainly governed by the logic of proportional electoral systems.[28] Here, unprofessionalised journalism, the historically elitist nature of printed media consumption, and the undisputed primacy of politics have relegated the sphere of public opinion to a condition tending towards marginality. This model – labelled "Mediterranean" or "polarised pluralist" model – is contrasted by the second "North Atlantic or Liberal" model, in which a majority electoral system fortifies the relationship with a public that historically experienced the early development of the mass press and finds support in the centrality of a journalism sustained by a deep-rooted culture of professional autonomy.[29] If the market is of little relevance in the first model, in the second the drive towards commercialisation is, on the contrary, so intense as to challenge politics and force it to accept the logic of the media as a reference. The model that Hallin and Mancini call "democratic-corporative", or Central-Northern European, in a position that is intermediate in many ways, includes those that in our research on the relationship between models of capitalism and models of growth have been identified as countries with inclusive egalitarian or dualistic growth.[30] First and foremost it is characterised by a feature that integrates the modernising dimension of media communication with the regulatory role of the state and the key role played by a substantial part of journalism in giving voice to the pluralism of interests. The original outcome is the coexistence of a highly professionalised journalism with a political parallelism historically rooted in the practices of consensual democracy.

Needless to say, these models only capture the dominant features and have exceptions. France, for example, is a borderline case of the Mediterranean model that clearly shares with other countries traits such as political parallelism and the significant role of the state – both as a financier of the press and as a censor, directly or indirectly, of certain journalistic narratives (the most controversial and sensitive) – but which enjoys the advantages of a more pronounced industrialisation and avails itself of a more solid information consumption by the public, as well as a better equipped rational-legal authority. In contrast, the UK case has certainly been characterised by an early development of the mass press and an almost ideal-type culture of journalistic autonomy, underpinned by strong professionalisation and the capacity for self-regulation. However, unlike the other countries of the North Atlantic model, the UK case (just as Ireland), has also been characterised by the presence of a strong public television and by some regulations intended to limit – at least in part – the space for the free market.

Notwithstanding the approximate nature of any classification, the models suggested by Hallin and Mancini at the beginning of the Millennium nevertheless offered a map for placing political-media systems within a space of correlations that up to that point had been relatively stable. In proposing them, however, the two authors did something more: they extended the diachronic perspective used to construct them and, searching for general tendencies, they looked ahead towards the future, identifying what to them appeared to be a common tendency towards homogenisation. Hallin and Mancini suggested that of the three models it appeared to be the North Atlantic one that acted as the pole of attraction in a magnetic field dominated by market forces and the logic of a modernisation process, understood as tending towards increased differentiation of the media from other institutions. Their hypothesis has, however, only partially been supported by the evidence gathered from subsequent investigations.

Partially, because – shortly afterwards – the framework of relations between journalism and politics was radically changed by the decisive entry of social media onto the scene, bringing into play new issues such as the new forms of production of information content through the digital participation of citizens, or individual and collective mobilisation within and outside the network.[31] And partially, in the second place, because local systems interpreted the North Atlantic model of modernisation, bending it to their own needs and characteristics[32] at times, even showing unexpected degrees of resilience.

While the United Kingdom followed the United States down the path of mediatisation, thus confirming its congruence with the liberal model, in Germany, for example, the party system put up more resistance to the wave of "commercial deluge". And although the effects of competition between the public and private television systems were significant (Pfetsch, 1996), the personalising drive in the media rationale have in fact been contained (Holtz-Bacha, Langer, & Merkle, 2014).

The deviation from their previous path towards the orbit of the liberal model shown by the Nordic countries was no less significant. Conceivable as a real bloc according to some, because of the specificities uniting them within the democratic-corporative model (Brüggemann et al., 2014), the Northern European countries have in fact maintained a substantial consistency with the original features of a relationship between media, citizens, and politics governed by the pluralistic principle of interest representation. As Strömbäck, Ørsten and Aalberg argued a few years ago:

> changes are not turning political communication or political journalism in the Nordic countries into a clone of the political journalism and

> political communication of the countries that are part of the liberal, or pluralistic-polarized model. Not least because systemic factors remain important in shaping the boundaries within which the news media, as well as political actors and citizens, operate.
>
> (2008: 271)

We might conclude that even in a framework of general orientation towards market models and a strong drive towards standardisation, the consolidated frameworks for relations between the media and politics, as well as the expectations nurtured by national cultures regarding the role of journalism, have continued to forge the practices of representation, along with public discourse. Hence, ultimately, it is possible to observe a scenario characterised by movements and counter-movements from the peculiar perspective of the relationship between media and politics as well. Alongside the strong movement towards convergence and standardisation, important processes of divergence and resistance between the different countries are once again emerging, reaffirming peculiarities that can be traced back to the characteristics of development paths and political-institutional arrangements.

12.9 Concluding remarks

In all the countries considered in our research, a dispersion of public authority can be discerned, albeit within a framework of specificities and divergences regarding both causes and effects. This point is crucial because, in the final analysis, only the public authority can be responsible for finding ways of adapting and reconciling the demands of economic development and those of social inclusion. The previous chapters have dwelt at length on different models of growth and inclusion, looking at them in relation to specific policy areas, analysing similarities and differences in the paths followed by different countries, taking into account their institutional and regulatory frameworks. In relation to the movements, we have illustrated in this chapter, each country shows a particular combination of adaptations, resistances, and effects. It is, of course, no coincidence that in countries with non-inclusive growth, the movement towards the market has been by far the dominant one, to which all others have adjusted. Thanks to the more powerful social democratic tradition and the persistent influence of trade unions, the strongest resistance has been in Northern European countries with inclusive and more egalitarian growth. In continental countries, with inclusive dualistic growth, and in Mediterranean countries, with low, non-inclusive growth, resistance proved to be ineffective, or soon gave way to adaptation processes, pursuing at times the upward movement, at times the downward movement, or thinking that the movement towards the market could be offset by with one towards civil society.

The scenario produced by these movements – especially with regard to redistribution and the containment of inequalities – therefore differs substantially from one country to another. In all the cases considered, it would not be far-fetched to claim that the majority of political actors have in any case supported, endorsed and, not infrequently, profited from them. At the political level, some variant of the trickle-down idea has prevailed across the board, together with the conviction that the sphere of action of public authority needs to be reduced. Not everything, however, has always consistently gone in the same direction. Not in all cases has the current moved with the same intensity, and neither has it produced the same results. Alongside the accelerating propulsion, the tide of shared dispersions has encountered decelerating factors – or even divergences – in the conformations of the different contexts and in the strategies of those who have tried to swim against the current, opposing some resistance to the movements considered so far, first and foremost the social democratic and left-wing parties, for whom the link between development and inclusion has historically been a constitutive identity trait and a principle of general orientation in political action.

Notes

1 For the concept of rescaling, see King and Le Galès (2017).
2 This concept can be found in Lash and Urry (1988). On Fordism, see Amin (1994).
3 A detailed description of market dispersion and disorganisation can be found in Streeck (2009).
4 For a general interpretation cf. Gaudin (1999), as well as Bobbio (2000) and Lascoumes (2003).
5 A theoretical elaboration can be found in Piattoni (2010).
6 See Keating (2017).
7 The Blair government promoted far-reaching devolution in favour of Scotland, one of the stateless nations, Wales, Northern Ireland and the London metropolitan government. In Spain, this was a way of defusing Catalan and Basque autonomist ambitions, above all. In Italy, regionalism was boosted to circumvent leftism.
8 An exemplary rebellion of disadvantaged areas led to Brexit (Becker, Fetzer, & Novy, 2017).
9 This formula was theorised by Giddens (1999, 78–86).
10 This is a narrow definition. According to the White Paper on EU Governance, civil society includes "trade unions and employers" associations (the "social partners"), non-governmental organisations, professional associations, charities, grassroots organisations, organisations involving citizens in local and municipal life, with a particular contribution from churches and religious communities".
11 On the effects that mingling with the private sector has on welfare, see De Leonardis (1998).
12 For a comparative survey see Peters, Rhodes, and Wright (2004).
13 A very circumstantial and comprehensive guide is in Papadopoulos (2013): on the dissociation between front and backstage see pp. 41–46 and 234–239; see also Culpepper (2011).
14 Indeed, Le Galès and Vezinat (2014) use another formulation: *l'État recomposé*.

15 This was well explained by Nettl (1968).
16 There is no vacuum beyond the state. There is still the state: Agnew (2013) speaks of "regimes of sovereignty".
17 Smith (2008) offers an interesting and critical exemplification of the "Europeanisation" of government action, albeit limited to the case of France.
18 Culpepper, Hall, and Palier (2008) are very informative; on devolution, in the same volume, see the chapter by Le Galès (2008).
19 On devolution in Germany see Burkhart (2009) and Auel (2014).
20 On France, see Rouban (2012).
21 Some of the essays in Vauchez and François (2020) deal with the European Union.
22 On this redefinition, and its political scope, cf. Aldrin and Hubé (2018).
23 Among the many works devoted to mediatisation, see the seminal essay by Mazzoleni and Schulz (1999) and the contribution to the systematisation of the concept by Strömbäck (2008).
24 For a critique of the concept based on classical economic theory that digital mass individualisation techniques necessarily offer better social and economic outcomes, see Mansell and Steinmueller (2022).
25 Among the most recent contributions on the topic of transnationalisation, see the volume edited by Neveu and Surdez (2020).
26 The reference is to the important contribution of Hallin and Mancini (2004), who report on research conducted on sixteen European and two North Atlantic countries, relating the different media systems to four strategic dimensions: the strength of the market, the typology of party systems, the role of the state, and the autonomy of journalism.
27 For a comparative study of the parallelism between media and politics, see van Kempen (2007).
28 In addition to Italy, this model includes Greece, Portugal, Spain and, as a case of many exceptions, France.
29 Here we find the United Kingdom, the United States, Canada, and Ireland.
30 According to Hallin and Mancini's analysis, Austria, Belgium, Denmark, Finland, Germany, the Netherlands, Norway, Sweden, and Switzerland are part of the democratic–corporatist model.
31 In this regard, see the update of Hallin and Mancini's analysis proposed by Mattoni and Ceccobelli (2018). However, it is interesting to note that the audience-oriented survey on the relationship between information consumption, political knowledge, and media systems in 17 European countries proposed by Castro et al. (2021) has recently provided insights that go in the same direction as Hallin and Mancini's analysis. From this perspective, significant differences also emerge between the democracies in which the Mediterranean journalism model operates and those in Northern Europe. In the former, in fact, there is a greater shift from traditional information media to social media, associated with a lower level of political knowledge, while where Hallin and Mancini had identified the "democratic corporatist model" the centrality of a more informative and inclusive system seems to persist.
32 For an overview see Esser and Pfetsch (2004). Interesting in this respect is what has been documented by Strömbäck, Ørsten, and Aalberg (2008) on the bloc of Nordic countries belonging to the democratic–corporatist model and, subsequently, by Brüggemann et al. (2014).

References

Agnew, J. (2013). *Globalization and sovereignty*. New York: Rowman and Littlefield.

Aldrin, P. & Hubé, N. (2018). From democracy by proxy to a stakeholder democracy: The changing faces of an EU founding value. In F. Foret & O. Calligaro (Eds), *European values: Challenges and opportunities for EU governance*. London: Routledge.

Amin, A. (Eds) (1994). *Post-Fordism: A reader*. Oxford: Blackwell Publishers.

Auel, K. (2014). Intergovernmental relations in German federalism: Cooperative federalism, party politics and territorial conflicts. *Comparative European Politics*, 12(4–5), 422–443. doi:10.1057/cep.2014.13

Bagnasco, A. (2003). *Società fuori squadra. Come cambia l'organizzazione sociale*. Bologna: il Mulino.

Becker, S.O., Fetzer, T., & Novy, D. (2017). Who voted for Brexit? A comprehensive district-level analysis. *Economic Policy*, 32(92), 601–650. doi.org/10.1093/epolic/eix012

Bifulco, L., Arrigoni, P., & Caselli, D. (2020). Perché e come studiare la filantropia. Appunti per un'agenda di ricerca. *Quaderni di Sociologia*, 82(64), 3–23. doi:10.4000/qds.3651

Blumler J.G. & Gurevitch, M. (1995). *The crisis of public communication*. London: Routledge.

Blumler, J.G. (1992). Public service broadcasting before the commercial deluge. In J.G. Blumler (Ed), *Television and the public interest: Vulnerable values in West European broadcasting* (pp. 7–21). London: Sage.

Blumler, J.G. & Kavanagh, D. (1999). The third age of political communication: Influences and features. *Political Communication*, 16(3), 209–230. doi:10.1080/105846099198596

Bobbio, L. (2000). Produzione di politiche a mezzo di contratti nella pubblica amministrazione italiana. *Stato e Mercato*, 58, 111–141.

Bortolotti, B. & Siniscalco, D. (2004). *The challenges of privatization: An international analysis*. Oxford: Oxford University Press.

Brüggemann, M., Engesser, S. Büchel, F. Humprecht, E., & Castro, L. (2014). Hallin and Mancini revisited: Four empirical types of Western media system. *Journal of Communication*, 64(6), 1037–1065. doi:10.1111/jcom.12127

Burkhart, S. (2009). Reforming federalism in Germany: Incremental changes instead of the big deal. *Publius: The Journal of Federalism*, 5(2), 341–65. doi:10.1017/S2071832200005447

Cassese, S. (2017). From the nation state to the global polity. In D. King & P. Le Galès (Eds), *Reconfiguring European states in crisis* (pp. 78–96). Oxford: Oxford University Press.

Christensen, T. & Laegreid, P. (Eds) (2001). *New public management: The transformation of ideas and practice*. Aldershot: Ashgate.

Christiansen, P.M. (2018). Still the corporatist darlings?, in P. Nedergaard & A. Wivel (Eds), *The Routledge handbook of Scandinavian politics* (pp. 36–45). Abingdon and New York: Routledge.

Crouch, C. (2019). *Will the gig economy prevail?* Cambridge: Polity Press.

Culpepper, P.D. (2011). *Quiet politics and business power: Corporate control in Europe and Japan*. Cambridge: Cambridge University Press.

Culpepper, P.D., Hall P.A., & Palier, B. (Eds) (2008). *Changing France: The politics that markets make*. Basingstoke: Palgrave Macmillan.

De Leonardis (1998). *In un diverso welfare. Sogni e incubi.* Milano: Feltrinelli.
Eikenberry, A. & Kluger, D. (2004). The marketization of the nonprofit sector: civil society at risk? *Public Administration Review*, 34(2), 32–40.
Esser, F. & Pfetsch, B. (Eds) (2004). *Comparing political communication: Theories, cases, and challenges*. Cambridge: Cambridge University Press.
Franck, G. (2019). The economy of attention. *Journal of Sociology*, 55(1), 8–19. doi:10.1177/1440783318811778
Gallino, L. (2011). *Finanzcapitalismo. La civiltà del denaro in crisi.* Torino: Einaudi.
Gaudin J.P. (1999). *Gouverner par contrat. L'action publique en question*. Paris: Presses de SciencesPo.
Genschel, P. & Zangl, B. (2017). The rise of non-state authority and the reconfiguration of the state. In D. King & P. Le Galès (Eds), *Reconfiguring European states in crisis* (pp. 62–77). Oxford: Oxford University Press.
Giddens, A. (1999). *The third way: The renewal of social democracy*. London: Polity.
Hallin, D.C. & Mancini, P. (2004). *Modelli di giornalismo: mass media e politica nelle democrazie occidentali*. Roma-Bari: Laterza.
Halpern, C., Lascoumes, P. & Le Galès, P. (Eds) (2014). *L'instrumentation de l'action publique: controverses, résistances, effets*. Paris: Presses de Sciences Po.
Hirschman, A.O. (1995). *A propensity to self-subversion*. Cambridge, MA: Harvard University Press.
Holtz-Bacha, C., Langer, A.I., & Merkle, S. (2014). The personalization of politics in comparative perspective: Campaign coverage in Germany and the United Kingdom. *European Journal of Communication*, 29(2), 153–170. doi.org/10.1177/0267323113516727
Iammarino, S., Rodriguez-Pose, A., & Storper, M. (2019). Regional inequality in Europe: Evidence theory and policy implications. *Journal of Economic Geography*, 9(2), 273–298.
Iversen, T. & Soskice, D. (2019). *Democracy and prosperity: Reinventing capitalism through a turbulent century*. Princeton: University Press, Princeton.
Keating, M.J. (2001). *Plurinational democracy: Stateless nations in a post-sovereignty era*. Oxford: Oxford University Press.
Keating, M.J. (2013). *Rescaling the European state: The making of territory and the rise of the meso*. Oxford: Oxford University Press.
Keating, M.J. (2017). The territorial state. In D. King & P. Le Galès (Eds), *Reconfiguring European states in crisis* (pp. 121–135). Oxford: Oxford University Press
King, D. & Le Galès, P. (Eds) (2017). *Reconfiguring European states in crisis*. Oxford: Oxford University Press.
Kriesi, H., Adam, S. & Jochum, M. (2006). Comparative analysis of policy networks in Western Europe. *Journal of European Public Policy*,13(3), 341–361. doi:10.1080/13501760500528803
Langer, A.I. (2011). *The personalisation of politics in the UK: Mediated leadership from Attlee to Cameron*. Manchester: Manchester University Press.
Lascoumes, P. (2003). Gouverner par les instruments. In J. Lagroye (Ed.), *La politisation* (pp. 387–401). Paris: Belin.
Lascoumes, P. & Le Galès, P. (Eds) (2005). *Gouverner par les instruments*. Paris: Presses de SciencesPo.
Lash, S. & Urry, J. (1988). *The end of organized capitalism*. Cambridge: Polity Press.
Le Galès, P. & Vezinat, N. (Eds) (2014). *L'État recomposé*. Paris: PUF.

Mansell, R. & Steinmueller, W.E. (2022). *Advanced introduction to platform economics*. Cheltenham: Edward Elgar.
Mattoni, A. & Ceccobelli, D. (2018). Comparing hybrid media systems in the digital age: A theoretical framework for analysis. *European Journal of Communication*, 33(5), 540–557. doi.org/10.1177/0267323118784831
Mazzoleni, G. & Schulz, W. (1999). "Mediatization" of politics: A challenge for democracy? *Political Communication*, 16(3), 247–261. doi.org/10.1080/105846099198613
Mughan, A. (2000). *Media and the presidentialization of parliamentary elections*. New York: Palgrave.
Nettl, J.P. (1968). The state as a conceptual variable. *World Politics*, 20(4), 559–592.
Neveu, E. & Surdez, M. (2020). *Globalizing issues: How claims, frames, and problems cross borders*. London: Palgrave.
Offe, C. (1985). *Disorganized capitalism: Contemporary transformations of work and politics*. Cambridge: MIT Press.
Papadopoulos, Y. (2013). *Democracy in crisis? Politics, governance and policy*. London: Palgrave MacMillan.
Peters, B.G., Rhodes, R.A.W., & Wright, V. (Eds) (2004). *Administering the summit: Administration of the core executive in developed countries*. Basingstoke: Palgrave Macmillan.
Pfetsch, B. (1996). Convergence through privatization? Changing media environments and televised politics in Germany. *European Journal of Communication*, 11(4), 427–451. doi:10.1177/0267323196011004002
Piattoni, S. (2010). *The theory of multi-level governance: Conceptual, empirical, and normative challenges*. Oxford: Oxford University Press.
Poguntke, T. & Webb, P. (2005). *The presidentialization of politics: A comparative study of modern democracies*. Oxford: Oxford University Press.
Rodríguez-Pose, A. (2018). The revenge of the places that don't matter [and what to do about it]. *Cambridge Journal of Regions, Economy and Society*, 11(1), 189–209. doi:10.1093/cjres/rsx024
Rothstein, S.A. & Schulze-Cleven, T. (2020). Germany after the social democratic century: The political economy of imbalance. *German Politics*, 29(3), 297–318. doi:10.1080/09644008.2020.1752677
Rouban, L. (2012). L'État à l'épreuve du libéralisme: les entourages du pouvoir exécutif de 1974 à 2012. *Revue française d'administration publique*, 142(2), 467–90. doi:10.3917/rfap.142
Sassen, S. (2018). *Cities in a world economy*. New York: Safe.
Scharpf, F. (1997). *Governing in Europe: Effective and democratic?* Oxford: Oxford University Press.
Smith A. (2008). The government of the European union and a changing France. In P.D. Culpepper, P.A. Hall, & B. Palier (Eds), *Changing France: The politics that markets make* (pp. 179–197). Basingstoke: Palgrave Macmillan.
Skocpol, T. (2016). Why political scientists should study organized philanthropy. *Political Science and Politics*, 3(4), 433–436.
Streeck, W. (2009). *Re-forming capitalism: Institutional change in the German political economy*. Oxford: Oxford University Press.
Strömbäck, J. (2008). Four phases of mediatization: An analysis of the mediatization of politics. *The international Journal of Press/Politics*, 13(3), 228–246. /doi.org/10.1177/1940161208319

Strömbäck, J. Ørsten, M., & Aalberg, T. (Eds) (2008). *Communicating politics, political communication in the Nordic countries*. Goteborg: Nordicom.

Swanson, D. & Mancini, P. (Eds) (1996). *Politics, media, and modern democracy: An international study of innovations in electoral campaigning and their consequences*. Westport, CT: Praeger.

Van Dijck, J., Poell, T., & De Waal, M. (2018). *The platform society: Public values in a connective world*. Oxford: Oxford University Press.

Van Kempen, H. (2007). Media-party parallelism and its effects: A cross-national comparative study. *Political Communication*, 24(3), 303–320. doi:10.1080/10584600701471674

Vauchez, A. & François, B. (Eds) (2020). *Politique de l'indépendance. Formes et usages contemporains d'une technologie de gouvernement*. Lille: Presses Universitaires du Septentrion.

Chapter 13

Social stratification and electoral behaviour

Alberto Gherardini and Giovanni Amerigo Giuliani

13.1 Introduction

Concomitantly with the end of Fordism in the 1970s, the transformations of the economic and labour market structure of Western countries substantially impacted social stratification and, consequently, "*class politics*" – that is, the presence of systematic links between the class of voters and the party they support (Oesch & Rennwald, 2018).

This chapter analyses the main changes of social stratification that took place between the beginning of the 2000s and the end of the 2010s. It also explores how such transformations correlate with the changes in the electoral behaviour of different occupational classes, with particular reference to voting for left-wing parties. We preferred to adopt a post-Fordist schema, recently used widely in the literature (Oesch, 2006; 2012; Schwander & Häusermann, 2013; Beramendi et al., 2015; Häusermann, 2020) instead of Erikson and Goldthorpe's traditional class schema (1993).

The analysis is constructed around two interconnected analytical dimensions. The first looks at the electoral behaviour of the different social groups in the four growth models. The aim is to show whether, and to what extent, the voting behaviour of social groups for left-wing parties follows a common trend or whether, on the contrary, specificities can be identified within the various models. Particular attention will be given to the electoral behaviour of the group of *production workers* – the historical constituency of the Western left-wing parties[1] – and to that of the new social groups created by the process of tertiarisation of the economy, namely *service workers* and *sociocultural professionals*. In the second dimension, the focus of the analysis shifts to changes in the constituencies of left-wing parties. Two aspects will be addressed. The first concerns the weight of the production worker class within the left-wing electorate and its change over time. The second regards the new configurations of social class coalitions supporting left-wing parties and their stability. The aim is to understand whether in the four growth models there has been a process of *"middle-classisation"* of the electorate or, on the contrary, *inter-class alliances* have formed in support of the left-wing parties.

DOI: 10.4324/9781003297130-17

From a theoretical and empirical perspective, the chapter links up with the final part of this volume (Chapter 14), which deals with the analysis of the policy proposals of left-wing parties and their change over time. The aim is thus to illustrate the changes in class politics in the post-Fordist era, considering both the demand and supply sides.

The chapter is divided into two parts.

In the first, after quickly referring to the debate in the literature concerning social stratification schemata, we will briefly expound on the new post-Fordist class scheme presented by Daniel Oesch and its main features. In this respect, through a quantitative analysis, we will show a change in production structure and social stratification between the Fordist and post-Fordist periods. Finally, relying on the well-informed literature in the field, we will develop hypotheses regarding the electoral behaviour of post-Fordist social groups, and in particular on their propensity to vote left parties.

In the second part, on the basis of longitudinal data provided by two international mass survey – the European Social Survey (ESS) and the International Social Survey Programme (ISPP) – we will empirically apply our theoretical framework and test the hypotheses.

13.2 New prerequisites for class politics

In the last decades, and more evidently since the 1990s, the concept of class – as well as that of "*class vote*" – has given rise to wide and heated debates in the comparative politics literature. The positions have been polarised among those who advocate for the end of class politics – the *dealignment thesis* (Dalton, 1996; Clark & Lipset, 1991) – on the one hand, and those who continue to emphasise the importance of the class variable in post-industrial societies, on the other (Pisati, 2010).

The first position can be traced back to the dealignment thesis, which argues for the downsizing of class voting in all advanced democracies (Rose & McAllister, 1986; Franklin, 1992). According to this thesis, citizens' electoral behaviour in post-Fordist societies is based mainly on their positions towards specific issues – changing over time and not linked to predetermined beliefs – and on the degree of liking for individual candidates. Several factors have determined this change in the voting behaviour: primarily, the development of a new *cultural* dimension of political conflict – responsible for obscuring the purely *economic* dimension – and the related post-materialist claims (Kriesi et al., 2008; 2012), as well as the fragmentation of public spaces and the detachment of citizens from trade unions and parties.

Inversely – while acknowledging that social class has become a less accurate predictor of voting intention – the second position argues that social class remains a relevant concept, since it continues to affect – positively or negatively – citizens' opportunities throughout their lives. In this regard, class inequalities – in terms of income distribution – not only persist but have increased in recent decades, particularly with the economic and financial crisis that began in the late 2000s. Therefore, social class would remain a key factor to explain electoral behaviour and its change over time (Erikson & Goldthorpe, 1993; Breen, 2005; Evans & Mills, 2000).

Nevertheless, even those who defend the class politics thesis claim that the conceptualisation and measurement of social class is inadequate in the post-Fordist age. For example, the Erikson and Golthorpe's (1993) class schema – which has been for many years a benchmark for the analysis of social stratification – still refers to blue and white collar workers as two homogeneous groups in mutual conflict. However, from the 1980s onwards, and increasingly so in the 1990s, the Fordist occupational system was significantly affected by structural changes in the economies and societies of Western countries. Broadly speaking, three interconnected adjustments have contributed to the transformation of the employment system.

The first adjustment concerns the process of de-industrialisation combined with the resulting tertiarisation of the economy (Freeman & Soete, 1994; Esping-Andersen, 1993; 1999; Pierson, 2001). The first phenomenon led to the massive decline of production workers, in particular, the unskilled ones. Development in production techniques also required an upgrading of the skills of industrial workers, and those who failed to do so have been pushed to the margins of the labour market. Tertiarisation has generated greater inequality in the employment system. The tertiary sector is highly polarised, with high-skilled and well-paid jobs at one end, and low-skilled and low-paid jobs at the other. These aspects will be further discussed below.

The second change involves the increase in the female employment rate in all advanced economies, primarily in the new service sector (Esping-Andersen, 1999; 2002).

The third change regards the expansion of tertiary education – no longer a privilege for a restricted segment of society – and the consequent updating and improvement of workers' skills – what is known as the *upgrading* of the labour market (Oesch, 2006; Beramendi et al., 2015). This upgrading of skills, however, was not generalised, but concerned a specific group of workers. Therefore, labour market polarisation has developed, with highly educated and skilled workers at the top of the hierarchy and low-skilled workers employed in low-paid jobs at the bottom. In short, the partial transition to a skills upgrade within the employment structure has not automatically improved working conditions (Oesch, 2012). On the contrary, the labour market is increasingly dualised, with growing inequalities in terms of income and job stability between high-skilled and low-skilled workers (Rueda, 2007; Crouch, 2010; Palier & Thelen, 2010).

The concept of class, therefore, needs to be reconceptualised through an "evolutionary" perspective that considers the paradigmatic changes in the occupational system and how these have modified – or "problematised" – the categories of the "working" and "middle" classes. In this regard, two preliminary reflections are necessary here.

First, low-skilled jobs have not disappeared, but they are no longer concentrated in manufacturing. In the post-Fordist era, the proliferation of low-skilled jobs took place in the service sector. In contrast with unskilled production workers, new service workers are less represented in trade unions and have little capacity for mobilisation (Bonoli, 2006). The result is lower protection in job contracts and more limited access to welfare (Palier & Thelen, 2010). With the emergence of this new category, the traditional division between manual and non-manual workers, between blue-collar and white-collar workers, is less straightforward. Service workers with low qualifications and low levels of education are placed in a new grey area, belonging neither to the middle class nor the traditional working class (Oesch, 2006).

Second, the middle class has become even more heterogeneous than in the Fordist period. The upgrading of skills within the occupational system and the expansion of the service sector – which now requires skilled and highly educated workers – have made the middle classes even less compact. In other words, the "occupational salad", as Wright Mills called the middle class, has become even more fragmented, with new interests and policy preferences to defend. A new class schema is needed to shed light on both the new grey area between the working class and the middle class, and the more composite nature of the latter. The new post-industrial class schema proposed by Daniel Oesch originates from these two points.

13.3 A new classification scheme

The *Fordist* social class schemata provided by the social stratification literature up to the 2000s are mainly based on a vertical type of stratification. For example, the aforementioned model proposed by Erikson and Goldthorpe (1993) was based on a hierarchical component that represents the rational behaviour of the employer: depending on the greater or lesser competitiveness of a worker's skills in the labour market, the employer would offer more or less advantageous employment relationships.

The *post-Fordist* class schema proposed by Daniel Oesch maintains this perspective but broadens it. The vertical axis of his scheme is based on skills: the higher the level of skills that can be used in the labour market, the greater the advantages of employment in terms of income and work autonomy. These competences can be identified in a hierarchical order: *professional/managerial, associate professional/managerial, generally/vocationally skilled*, and *low/unskilled*. In Oesch's schema, the skills criterion problematises the difference between blue-collar and white-collar workers, or between manual and non-manual work. Traditional Fordist class schemas assume that

Table 13.1 The 16-item post-Fordist occupational class schema proposed by Daniel Oesch

Independent work logic		*Technical work logic*	*Managerial work logic*	*Interpersonal work logic*	
Large employers (>9)	**Self-employed**	**Technical experts**	**Higher-grade managers and administrators**	**Sociocultural professional**	Professional/ Manager
Small business owners with employees (CA)		**Technicians**	**Lower-grade managers and administrators**	**Sociocultural semi-professionals**	Associate/ Professional Manager
Small business owners without employees (CA)		**Skilled manual**	**Skilled clerks**	**Skilled service**	Generally/ Vocationally Skilled
		Low-skilled manual	**Unskilled clerks**	**Low-skilled service**	Low/Unskilled

Note: The dotted lines indicate how the classes are to be grouped in the eight-item version. Compared to the original version (2006), some social class labels were changed in Oesch's subsequent work (see also Häusermann, 2010). In particular, the group of *skilled manuals* was called *skilled craft* and the *low-skilled manuals* were divided into *routine operatives* (e.g. assemblers) and *routine agriculture* (e.g. woodcutters). For this reason, the "extended" version of the class schema included 17 items, not 16. In the present work we use the updated version of the schema.

white-collar, non-manual workers were necessarily more privileged than blue-collar, manual workers. However, this advantage is no longer automatic in a post-industrial economy, given the increasing heterogeneity of non-manual work. Contracts in the low-skilled service sector offer lower benefits in terms of wage, access to welfare and job protection compared to those offered in the low-skilled manufacturing sector (Oesch, 2006).

In addition to the vertical perspective, Oesch includes a second dimension of a "horizontal" nature, a sort of "employee" perspective, which complements that of the employer. This horizontal differentiation is based on the work logic of employees. A job can thus be based primarily on technical competence (technical work logic), managerial power (managerial work logic), face-to-face interaction with customers (interpersonal work logic) or on self-employment (independent work logic). Differences in work logic, in turn, influence people's preferences and values.

Combining the vertical and horizontal perspectives, Oesch obtains a scheme comprising 16 social classes (Table 13.1), which can be further aggregated into eight broader groups.

Table 13.2 shows the eight-class "post-industrial" scheme used in this study. In contrast to Oesch's scheme, we have decided to include higher grade managers and administrators within the upper class. Although their work logic is officially managerial, over time this group has *de facto* increasingly followed an independent work logic, given their broad leeway at the firm level.

Table 13.2 Oesch's collapsed eight-class schema

Large employers, self-employed professionals, and high-grade managers (traditional bourgeoisie)	Technical (semi-) professionals	Associate managers	Sociocultural (semi-) professionals
Small business owners (*petty bourgeoisie*)	Production workers	Official clerks	Service workers

Note: Throughout the text, we simplified some labels for clarity and stylistic reasons. Accordingly, *traditional bourgeoisie* and *petty bourgeoisie* are used as synonymous respectively for the "large employers, self-employed professionals and high-grade managers" and for the "small business owners". Official clerks, technical (semi-) professional and sociocultural (semi-) professionals, and production workers are also referred as *clerks, technicians, sociocultural professionals, and blue-collar workers/working class*. Finally, similar to Häusermann (2010), to make clear that we are referring to unskilled workers, service workers are also labelled *low-skilled service workers*.

13.4 Changes in social stratification

We can now illustrate the main changes in the employment structure between the Fordist and post-Fordist periods, both in general terms and regarding the differences between the growth models used in our research framework.

As already pointed out, the long intersectoral transition from manufacturing to services had a considerable impact on the employment structure of the advanced economies. From 1970 to 2010, in the eight countries examined in this paper, the incidence of manufacturing employment halved, from 27.4% to 14% of the population. While the trend toward a shrinking manufacturing sector cuts across economies transversally, the phenomenon has been more robust in some countries in particular (Figure 13.1). Great Britain in 1970, for example, was the country with the second-largest share of manufacturing employment while, in 2010, only 8.7% of the employed worked in this segment of the labour market. Conversely, notwithstanding a decline, manufacturing employment continues to account for a significant share of the labour force in countries such as Germany and Italy, 22.4% and 18.6%, respectively.

In contrast, employment in services increased considerably, projecting the incidence of service sector workers from half the population to three quarters. Nevertheless, again, there are differences in employment levels achieved within growth models. In 2010, in the non-inclusive growth (NIG) countries, around eight out of ten workers were employed in services. Lower values are registered, however, in the neighbouring non-inclusive low growth (NILG) countries and Germany (Figure 13.2).

Nevertheless, the expansion of services has not had a homogeneous effect on social stratification but a dual trait. On the one hand, highly skilled, generally well-paid jobs have increased; on the other, low-skilled, low-productivity occupational segments have grown, with low wages and little protection

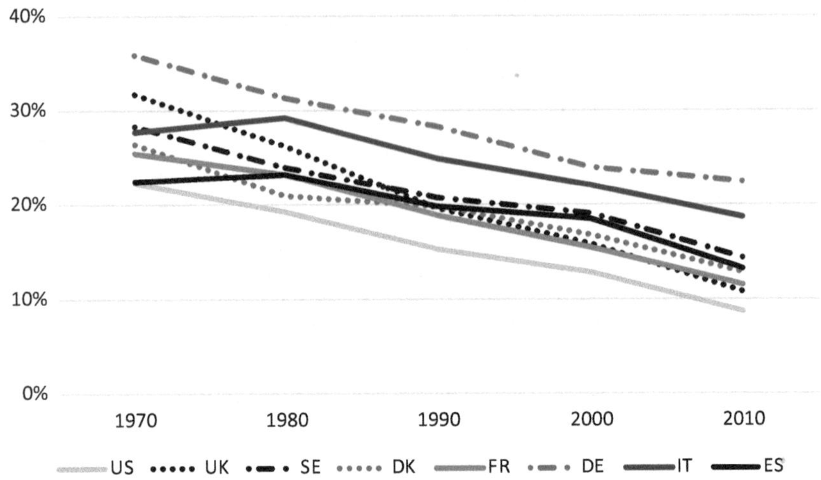

Figure 13.1 Share of workers in manufacturing sectors in the active population, percentage values (1970–2010).

Source: Our elaborations on GGDC 10-Sector Database. Timmer et al. (2015).

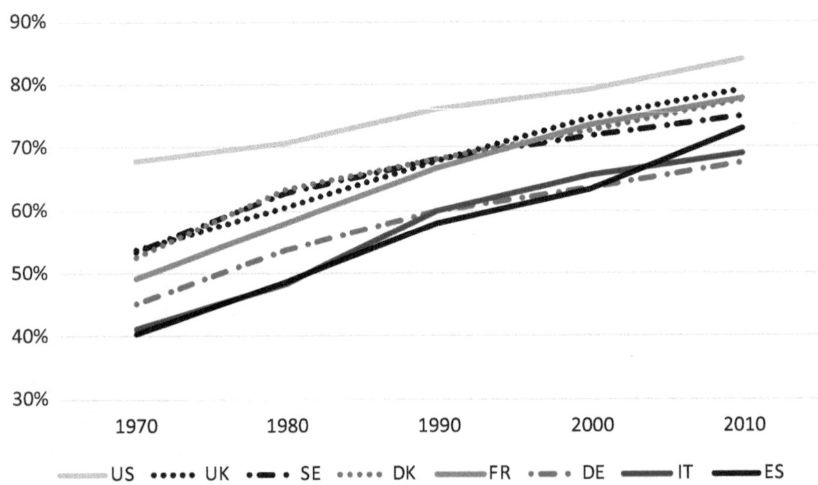

Figure 13.2 Share of workers in the service sectors in the active population, percentage values (1970–2010).

Source: Our elaborations on GGDC 10-Sector Database. Timmer et al. (2015).

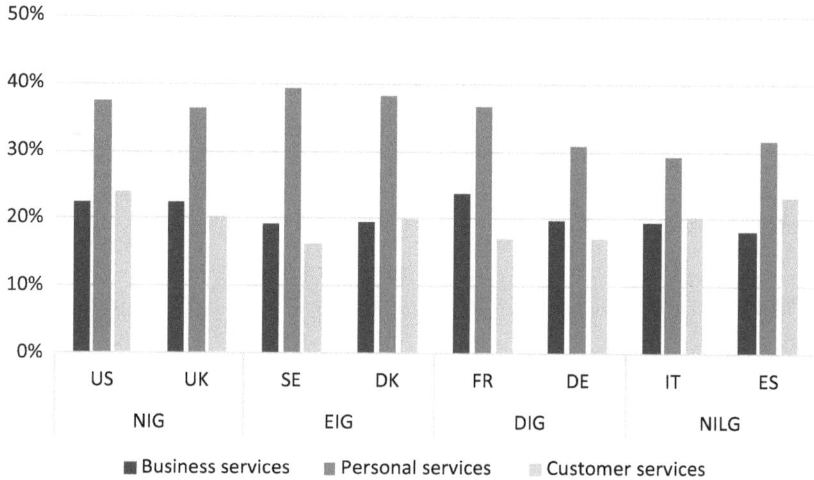

Figure 13.3 Incidence of service workers on the active population by type of service, percentage values (2010).

Source: Elaborations on GGDC 10-Sector Database. Timmer et al. (2015).

associated with them (Bonoli, 2006; Palier & Thelen, 2010). Moreover, especially in more recent years, intermediate positions have decreased due to the technological development of ICT (Wright & Dweyer, 2003; Autor, Katz, & Kearney, 2008; Goos & Manning, 2007).

In order to empirically evaluate these different types of service, we divided them into business services, which generally show the highest productivity and wage growth (e.g. finance, insurance, transport, telecommunications, etc.) and consumer and personal services,[2] i.e. occupations that generally show lower productivity and lower wages (Michaels, Natraj, & Van Reenen, 2014).

In this respect, the United States, the United Kingdom, and France show a high incidence of both high and low productivity services (Figure 13.3). In the Scandinavian countries, employment in personal services is the highest among the countries considered, also due to the central role of the public sector. On the other hand, Italy, Spain, and Germany show reduced employment shares in services, mainly personal services.

The post-Fordist transition has thus had influent effects on the productive structure in all advanced economies while, at the same time, also shaping their social framework. A recent picture of those effects is presented in Table 13.3, which applies the class scheme described in the preceding pages to some international surveys (the ESS and the ISSP). Significant differences in social stratification across countries emerged.

Table 13.3 Social stratification in some advanced democracies, percentage values (second half of the 2010s)

	NIG		*EIG*		*DIG*		*NILG*	
	UK	*USA*	*DNK*	*SWE*	*GER*	*FRA*	*ITA*	*SPA*
Traditional bourgeoisie	4.5	14.0	2.8	4.6	4.1	3.2	5.1	2.9
Petty bourgeoisie	11.0	9.8	5.2	6.1	5.8	8.0	17.1	13.4
Technical (semi-)professionals	9.2	9.7	11.6	12.7	11	11.2	7.1	7.5
Production workers	14.4	13.7	18.0	15.4	21.6	19.0	21.8	22.2
Associate managers	17.9	8.2	14.5	16.6	9.9	15.0	8.0	7.1
Office clerks	11.9	10.2	11.3	8.6	17.2	11.9	13.2	12.4
Sociocultural (semi-) professionals	12	11.7	16.1	15.5	14.5	11.8	9.7	10.5
Service workers	19.2	22.8	20.5	20.6	16.0	19.9	18.0	24.0
Total	*100*	*100*	*100*	*100*	*100*	*100*	*100*	*100*

Source: elaborations on ESS round 9 (Italy, Germany, United Kingdom, France) and ISSP 2017 (Denmark, Spain, Sweden, United States).

Note: Survey years vary between 2016 and 2018.

In the Scandinavian countries, transformations due to de-industrialisation have significantly strengthened the class of service workers. However, alongside this class, some social groups that have now become characteristic of the post-Fordist era, like sociocultural workers, low-level managers, and technicians, have significantly grown.

Unlike the Scandinavian countries, the United States and the United Kingdom show a more polarised class structure: at one extreme, a very high share of service workers, at the other, the traditional bourgeoisie and petty bourgeoisie are comparatively over-represented, especially in the United States.

In other cases, the post-Fordist transition seems to have been weaker. Traditional Fordist classes, such as clerks and blue collars, still represent a significant share of the social distribution. Nevertheless, social configurations vary from country to country. In Germany, production workers, office clerks and sociocultural semi-professionals are over-represented. The Italian class structure is distinguished by the remarkable of the petty bourgeoisie of self-employed workers and by a weaker role of the most qualified service workers, such as sociocultural semi-professionals, technicians, and associate managers. The case of Spain is quite similar to the Italian one, except for a more pronounced presence of low skilled service workers, who represent about a quarter of the Spanish population. Finally, France has a peculiar class structure, halfway between more post-industrial societies, such as those of the Anglo-Saxon and Scandinavian countries, and more traditional societies, as those of Italy and Germany. While production workers still account for almost a fifth of the population, there is a particular proportion of associate managers, technical semi-professionals, and low-skilled service workers.

13.5 How post-industrial social classes vote

The new post-Fordist social class schema allows us to undertake a proper investigation of more recent electoral behaviour and to assess the persistence or decline of class voting.

Based on the analyses conducted by Oesch and other scholars (e.g. Häusermann, 2010; 2020; Beramendi et al., 2015), we can formulate a series of hypotheses regarding the possible electoral behaviour of new classes in the post-Fordist period. Only those social classes in which voting for left-wing parties has been crucial in the past, or maybe relevant in the present, are debated.[3]

13.5.1 The "contended" class of production workers in the post-Fordist era

In the Fordist era, production workers were the key constituency of the left-wing parties. Accordingly, the Left pursued economic and social policies designed to defend the interests of this specific social class, particularly in the areas of labour regulation, access to welfare and education. However, since the 1990s, the policy proposals of the left-wing parties have gradually evolved, moving towards the centre of the political spectrum to broaden their consensus among the new social classes and compensate for the erosion of their historical working-class constituency (see Chapter 14). Moreover, the emergence of the new "cultural" dimension of political conflict has pressured left-wing parties to support liberal-oriented positions on civil rights, multiculturalism, globalisation, and environmental issue (Inglearth, 1990). The literature on comparative politics has illustrated that these two phenomena – the shift towards the centre in the economic dimension and the support for culturally liberal positions – have probably contributed to the alienation of left-wing production workers. As the transformations of the economic structure took effect, this group began to fear losing its status, perceiving itself as the real "loser" of the process of globalisation and modernisation (Lefkofridi & Michel, 2014). For these reasons, this social class, formerly more left-wing oriented, has become as a "contested stronghold" by the populist parties of the radical right. These latter ones have indeed developed a strategy based mainly on welfare chauvinism, in defence of the old social rights and benefits typical of the Fordist era (see Chapter 10). It is to be noted that in Germany, Spain, and Italy but also in other Mediterranean countries, for example, Greece – there are also new radical left-wing formations that attract the consensus of a share of production workers dissatisfied with the representation of left-wing parties.

Our first hypothesis is therefore the following:

> **H1**: *In the post-Fordist era, the vote of production workers for left-wing parties has decreased while their support for populist parties of the radical right has increased.*

13.5.2 The new area of possible influence of left-wing parties: the sociocultural (semi-)professional class

Comparative literature has revealed that the process of tertiarisation and skill upgrading of the labour market has increased the number of the sociocultural (semi-) professionals in most advanced economies. This social class represents a new type of middle class, culturally liberal and, at the same time, in favour of expanding welfare policies. Regarding this last point, the positions of sociocultural professionals represent an alternative to those of both the traditional bourgeoisie and managers, on the one hand, and those of the production workers, on the other. Indeed, the former tend to support more welfare cuts in exchange for tax cuts, while the latter would be more inclined to defend the *old social policies* (e.g. early retirement schemes, generous pensions and unemployment benefits), typical of the industrial period (Armingeon & Bonoli, 2006; Häusermann, 2010; 2012; 2018; Garritzmann, Häusermann, & Palier, 2019). In contrast, sociocultural professionals – referred in the literature as the new highly educated outsiders (Häusermann, Kurer, & Schwander, 2014) – are likely to be more supportive of expansions of *new social policies*, particularly social investment policies, even if this may imply cutting back on old social policies, such as, for example, an increase in retirement age (Häusermann, 2010; Garritzmann, Häusermann, & Palier, 2019). In terms of electoral behaviour, the literature has shown that this group has become the new key constituency of left-wing parties, although not exclusively the mainstream ones. Indeed, both New Left and the Greens have gained an increasing consensus from this new post-Fordist social class (Oesch & Rennwald, 2018).

Our second hypothesis is as follows:

> **H2**: *Sociocultural (semi-) professionals represent left-wing parties' new possible area of influence.*

13.5.3 The new grey area between blue-collar and white-collar workers: the service workers

The manufacturing sector's decline has not led to the disappearance of low-skilled jobs. On the contrary, such jobs have generally increased sharply in most advanced economies but have been concentrated in the new grey area represented by the service sector. The status of service workers is uncertain. On the one hand, they do not enjoy the same protection as production workers. They have been mainly entitled to need-based social policies while being excluded from the more generous social insurance programs (Palier & Thelen, 2010). On the other, while they are not negatively affected by the globalisation process – because they are employed in the sheltered sectors of the economy – they are not labour market insiders, given the precariousness of their job contracts (Häusermann, 2020). Moreover, in the low-skilled service sector, productivity cannot grow at the same level as in the manufacturing sector, which necessarily implies lower wages (Baumol & Bowen, 1966; Pierson, 2001). Furthermore, their degree of mobilisation and unionisation tends to be lower than that of blue-collar workers, given the fragmentation of preferences and interests to be defended and the more dispersed working conditions (Bonoli, 2006). In this regard, the literature shows that the poor unionisation of the service sector has made service workers' representation marginal for the trade unions (Rueda, 2007). In other words, unions in Western countries are less inclined to represent the fragmented interests of this group. Hence, service workers can be considered the new unskilled outsiders (Häusermann, 2010).

The electoral preferences of this group are therefore unclear. Recalling Oesch and Rennwald (2018) hypotheses, we can say that the vote of this class is fluid, open to possibilities of being gained by both left-wing and Christian-democratic or conservative parties, but also by the new radical right.

Our third hypothesis is as follows:

> **H3**: *The vote of unskilled service workers tends to be fragmented, with all major parties in open competition.*

13.5.4 The traditional bourgeoisie: area of influence of right-wing parties or new basin of the left?

The comparative party politics literature has consistently highlighted that the traditional bourgeoisie group constitutes the area of influence of centre-right-wing parties (Oesch & Rennwald, 2018). However, in the post-Fordist era, the emergence of a new dimension of conflict of a cultural kind has opened up the competition for the vote of this social class to other political actors. In other words, the traditional bourgeoisie may continue to have more market-oriented preferences in the economic dimension of political conflict but, at the same time, may support liberal positions on cultural issues, such as a multi-ethnic society and new civil rights. Given the realignment of left parties towards the centre, it is possible to hypothesise an increase in support from this group. However, empirical data have shown that a reconfiguration of preferences has also occurred in the centre-right pole, which, in any case, is not a heterogeneous bloc. Liberal parties have further accentuated their libertarian positions, while conservative or Christian-democratic parties have blunted their more authoritarian aspects, to use Herbert Kitschelt's terminology (2004). In view of this reflection, the chances of the traditional bourgeoisie vote being contended by left-wing parties are still low.

Our final hypothesis is the following:

> **H4**: *The bourgeoisie group remains the area of influence of the right-wing parties, and their support for left-wing parties is marginal.*

13.6 The electoral behaviour of the social classes

In this section, we will empirically test the previous hypotheses. The analysis is based on two international mass survey datasets, the European Social Survey (ESS) and the International Social Survey Programme (ISPP). Concerning time frame, the work compares the first round of surveys that took place in the early 2000s with the most recent rounds of surveys, held in the late 2010s, between 2017 and 2019.[4]

Table 13.4 shows the evolution of the vote of the eight post-Fordist social classes for left-wing parties between the early 2000s and the late 2010s. It highlights the sharp decline in the production worker vote for left-wing parties in all countries. Therefore, the downturn in support of the historical electorate of left-wing parties seems to be a generalised phenomenon. Nevertheless, it is possible to identify different patterns of decline among the four models.

In the NIG countries, the electoral fall is less marked. In the UK, the loss stands at less than six percentage points (hereinafter, pp), and the Labour Party managed to retain over 43% of the production worker vote in the late 2010s. In the US, blue-collar support for the Democrats remained relatively stable over the two decades under review, with only a slight decline (-3.5 pp) compared to the NILG and the dualistic inclusive growth (DIG) countries. However, it is essential to clarify at this point. The figures for these countries are strongly influenced by the majority voting system, which provides the electorate with fewer "political" alternatives. The majoritarian system thus indirectly helps left-wing parties to retain a larger share of votes, especially from historical constituencies, and to limit electoral losses (Lijparth, 1990). Two phenomena, however, are worth noting. On the one hand, the level of abstentionism in these countries (especially in the United States) is very high. In other words, in the absence of alternatives, those disappointed tend to take refuge in abstention (Plane & Gershtenson, 2004; Häusermann, 2020). On the other hand, the majoritarian system has fostered a re-polarisation of the party system, above all in the United States (see Girdon, Adams, & Horne, 2018; Rodden, 2019). In other words, while curbing the formation of new parties, and their chances of entering parliament, the majoritarian system provides strong incentives for the transformation and radicalisation of the traditional parties[5] (Kriesi et al, 2008).

Shifting the focus to the DIG and NILG countries, the decline in the working-class vote is particularly pronounced. In Germany and France, there

Table 13.4 Voting for left-wing parties of the post-Fordist social classes (early 2000s and late 2010s)

	NIG						*EIG*						*DIG*						*NILG*					
	UK			*USA*			*Sweden*			*Denmark*			*Germany*			*France*			*Italy*			*Spain*		
	t1	*t2*	*Dif.*	*t1*	*t2*	*Dif.*	*t1*	*t2*	*Dif.*	*t1*	*t2*	*Dif.*	*t1*	*t2*	*Dif.*	*t1*	*t2*	*Dif.*	*t1*	*t2*	*Dif.*	*t1*	*t2*	*Dif.*
Traditional bourgeoisie	26.1	27.9	1.8	49.9	41.6	-8.3	26.3	16.5	-9.8	14	19.4	5.4	14.7	17.2	2.5	20.6	9.4	-11.2	32	27.1	-4.9	20.6	13.3	-7.3
Petty bourgeoisie	30.4	24.9	-5.5	47.9	42.4	-5.5	18.1	25.2	7.1	12.6	18.6	6	25.1	14.5	-10.6	8.7	3.1	-5.6	24.9	16.2	-8.7	32.2	16.6	-15.6
Technical (semi-) professionals	28	41.5	13.5	42.7	52.2	9.5	36.2	21.6	-14.6	25	24.9	-0.1	60.4	24.4	-36	21.2	9.8	-11.4	38.5	20.1	-18.4	28.4	19,6	-8.8
Production workers	49.8	43.9	-5.9	55.4	51.9	-3.5	55	41.4	-13.6	36.7	36.5	-0.2	47.4	23.5	-23.9	41.3	7.6	-33.7	37.4	17.6	-19.8	47	32.6	-14.4
Associate managers	31.3	35.7	4.4	51.8	47.1	-4.7	39.2	20.3	-18.9	19.4	12.2	-7.2	34.1	19.2	-14.9	22.9	4.3	-18.6	34.7	15.9	-18.8	32.5	15.2	-17.3
Office clerks	24.9	36	11.1	63.3	56.8	-6.5	42.9	36.3	-6.6	26.5	30.9	4.4	24.7	21.4	-3.3	26.1	10.9	-15.2	33.5	22.9	-10.6	47	16.7	-30.3
Sociocultural (semi-) professionals	31.3	51.9	20,6	58.5	56.2	-2.3	33.2	33.4	0.2	24	32.8	8.8	42	16.9	-25.1	25.8	10.2	-15.6	47.1	32.3	-14.8	33.5	19.9	-13.6
Service workers	51.2	48.1	-3.1	57.6	58	0.4	47.4	42.4	-5	30.1	22.3	-7.8	52.4	18.1	-34.3	18.1	7.8	-10.3	39.9	17.1	-22.8	44.2	29.8	-14.4

Source: European Social Survey (ESS): round 1 (2001) and round 9 (2019); International Social Survey Programme: 2002 for France, 2002–2004 and 2014–2016 for the United States, 2017 for Denmark, Sweden, and Spain. Data are weighted.

Legend: t1=early 2000s; t2= late 2010s; Dif.: difference in percentage points.

was a decrease of 24 and 34 pp, respectively; in Italy and Spain, the value is slightly smaller (around -18 pp).

The downturn in production worker support for left-wing parties is evident if we look at the data from the late 2010s. In the last French elections, only 7% of workers voted for the French Socialist Party (PS), and in Germany only 23.5% chose the Social Democratic Party (SPD). Similarly, in Italy, working-class support for the Democratic Party (PD) was reduced by half in two decades, standing at below 20% in 2018.[6] In Spain, the Spanish Socialist Workers' Party (PSOE) has maintained a broader consensus than in other countries (32.6%) but still much lower than at the beginning of the 2000s.

The decline in working-class consensus for the left is evident though less pronounced in the egalitarian inclusive growth (EIG) countries. In Sweden, the downtrend in production worker support for the Social Democratic Workers' Party (SAP) has been more significant compared to that of the production workers for the Danish Social Democrats (SD). Nevertheless, the latter has limited its losses considerably over the last two decades. It should be noted that in both countries the percentage of production workers voting for the two social democratic parties has remained high – above 30%. In other words, notwithstanding a loss of support, both the SAP and the SD managed to contain their losses among their historical electorate.

Where did the production workers' votes go in the late 2010s?

Table 13.5 shows the first four parties voted for by this social class at the end of the 2010s. Left-wing parties continue to be the first choice in the NIG and EIG countries. On the contrary, in the DIG countries, the SPD is the third choice in Germany, after the CDU-UDC, while the PS in France is not included in the ranking. The situation in the NILG countries is more heterogeneous. In Spain, the PSOE continues, despite its decline, to be the most voted party among production workers. At the same time, while the PD in Italy is only the fourth choice, overtaken – as in Germany – by a centre-right party, Go Italy (FI).

It is interesting to note the degree of support of production workers for radical right-wing parties. In the DIG model, Alternative for Germany (AfD) and the National Front (FN) are the parties most voted by this group in Germany and France, respectively. In the Scandinavian countries, despite the resilience of the social-democratic parties, the Radical Right is the second choice in both Sweden and Denmark. Similarly, in Italy, the League is the second most voted party by the production workers. Finally, UKIP is the third most popular party among the working class in the UK.

These results would support the thesis that the Left has failed to maintain the loyalty of the production workers, which are now contested by the radical right-wing parties (H1). However, it is possible to identify different patterns of decline in support for left-wing parties. In the DIG and NILG countries, production workers have clearly moved away from the left. In contrast, the erosion of votes has been more contained – probably for different

Table 13.5 The most voted parties by the production workers, late 2010s

	CNI		*CIE*		*CID*		*BCNI*	
	NIG	*EIG*	*DIG*	*NILG*	*NIG*	*EIG*	*DIG*	*NILG*
1° Party	Labour Party, Labours (43.2%)	Democratic Party, Democrats (51.9%)	Swedish Social Democratic Party, SAP (41.4%)	Danish Social Democratic Party, SD (36.5%)	Alternative for Germany, AfD (25.2%)	National Front, FN (27.7%)	Movement 5 Stars, M5S (28,8%)	Spanish Socialist Workers' Party, PSOE (32,6%)
2° Party	Conservative Party, Tories (40.9%)	Republican Party, Republicans (48.1%)	Swedish Democrats – SD (21,9%)	Danish People's Party, DF (22.9%)	The Christian Democratic Union of Germany/ Christian Social Union in Bavaria CDU-CSU (24.4%)	The Republic on the Move, LaREM (14%)	The League (24,4%)	People's Party, PP (29,9%)
3° Party	United Kingdom Independence Party, UKIP (3.6%)		Moderate Party, M (17.7%)	Liberal Party, V (22.1%)	Social Democratic Party of Germany, SPD (23.5%)	France Unbowed, (12.3%)	Go Italy, FI (20,5%)	We can (13,9%)
4° Party	Liberal Democrats, LibDems (3.4%)		Green Party – MP (4.6%)	Liberal Alliance, LA (3.7%)	Free Democratic Party, FDP (10,4%)	The Republicans, LR (9.7%)	Democratic Party, PD (17,6%)	Citizens, Cs (9,4%)

Source: European Social Survey (ESS): round 1 (2001) and round 9 (2019); International Social Survey Programme: 2002 for France, 2002–2004 and 2014–2016 for the United States, 2017 for Denmark, Sweden and Spain. Data are weighted.

reasons – in the EIG and NIG countries. However, there has been a clear shift to the parties of the radical right in the Scandinavian countries.

The support of the sociocultural professionals for left-wing parties reveals marked differences between the four growth models (Table 13.4). In the DIG and NILG countries, voting for left-wing parties declined over the two decades under review. In Germany, this downswing was particularly marked. In 2017, Germany's sociocultural workers split over into the CDU-CSU (the most voted party by this social class, around 32%) and The Left (a radical left-wing party, which is the third option, with around 15.8% of the vote). In France, the decline in support was also severe, although slightly more contained than in Germany (-15.6 pp). In this country, sociocultural professionals opted for Emmanuel Macron's new party (35.0%), the most voted for The Republic on the Move (LaREM), followed by France Unbowed (FI, a radical right party, which obtained around 22% of the votes). A substantial decline in support for left-wing parties by sociocultural workers was also evident in Italy and Spain. In Italy, the PD did manage to keep more than 30% of the votes of this group – although in 2017 it turned out to be only the second choice of the sociocultural professionals, preceded by the Five Star Movement (M5S). In Spain, the party most voted for by sociocultural workers was the Popular Party (PP) (around 25%), while PSOE was only the second choice.

A different scenario can be seen in the EIG and NIG countries. Starting with the Scandinavian countries, in Sweden, the SAP continued to be the first party voted for by sociocultural professionals in the late 2010s (around 32%). In Denmark, the propensity of this class to vote for the SD increased in comparison with the early 2000s and, as in Sweden, the Social Democrats were the party most voted for by the group. A similar situation emerges when looking at the data for the Anglo-Saxon countries. In the United Kingdom, the vote of sociocultural professionals for the Labours increased significantly, attracting the consensus of more than 50% of those belonging to this social class. Finally, notwithstanding a limited decline in support, the Democrats continued to be the first choice of sociocultural professionals in the United States. However, it must again be remembered that the majority system heavily biases the data, so comparisons with other models must be made with care.

The hypothesis that sociocultural professionals represent a new area of influence of left-wing parties (H2) is only partially confirmed, especially if we consider the *time factor*. Nevertheless, our hypothesis is valid in the EIG models and in the NIG countries. In these countries, left-wing parties were able to maintain a high level of consensus among the working class and, at the same time, attract sociocultural professionals. This was not the case in the DIG and NILG countries, where losses among production workers and sociocultural professionals were matched.

With regard to low-skilled workers in the new services, the data in Table 13.4 show that in the DIG countries the decrease in support was particularly marked in Germany. In France – where the vote for this group had been more fluid also in the early 2000s – the downswing was more limited, but still considerable. In the NILG countries, Italy's decline is particularly evident (-22.8 pp). The PD is only the third most voted party, closely preceded by the Lega (18%) and by the M5S – this last being voted by more than 40% of low-skilled service workers. On the contrary, in Spain, the decline was more contained (about -8 pp). The PSOE managed to maintain the consensus of almost 30% of service workers, but, compared to the early 2000s, it was overtaken by the PP, albeit by a narrow margin.

A heterogeneous situation can also be observed in the EIG countries. The drop in consensus among low-skilled workers is evident in both Sweden and Denmark, though more remarkable in the latter. However, the downturn takes on a different significance in the two countries. In Sweden, the SAP continues to be the most popular party. In Denmark, on the other hand, the consensus is more limited (around 22.6%) and the SD, while also being the first most voted party, had only a slight advantage over the radical right-wing party at the end of the 2010s.

The NIG countries follow the opposite trend of the other three growth models. Finally, concerning the Anglo-Saxon countries, the Labours lost support in the UK but not significantly (only -3 pp of the consensus). On the contrary, the Democrats slightly increased their consensus among this social class in the USA.

In short, the hypothesis that the vote of low-skilled service workers turns out to be fragmented with all major parties in open competition (H3) is only partially confirmed. In the Anglo-Saxon countries, also because of the majority electoral system, this group's vote is stable or has even consolidated over time in favour of left-wing parties. In the Scandinavian countries, the propensity to vote for the social-democratic parties remains strong in Sweden, while it is weaker in Denmark, where the extreme right appears to obtain almost the same consensus within this group. Again, there is no open competition between all parties in the EIG countries. Workers in this sector seem to represent a stronghold of the left-wing party contended by the new Radical Right. Our hypothesis is confirmed in continental countries, especially Germany, where the vote is very fragmented. In France, fragmentation is more limited within the radical left, with the PCF and the FI in open competition. Finally, also in the Mediterranean countries, our hypothesis finds only partial confirmation. In Italy, at the beginning of the 2000s, low-skilled service workers represented an area of influence of the left-wing, but at the end of the decade, it was the M5S that attracted the most support, followed by the League. In Spain, the vote was more fluid: in this case, the two main parties, the PSOE and the PP, were in open competition for the vote of this group.

Finally, let us consider the electoral behaviour of the traditional bourgeoisie (Table 13.4). At the end of the 2010s, in the United Kingdom, Germany, and Denmark, the consensus of the traditional bourgeoisie towards left-wing parties increased. On the contrary, the left lost votes in the rest of the countries, especially France and Italy. However, such a loss was more modest than that displayed among the production workers. Table 13.6 shows that left-wing parties are among the top three parties voted for by the traditional bourgeoisie in all four growth models, albeit in different positions and with different intensities.

In the NIG countries, it is hardly surprising that Labour in the UK and the Democrats in the US are the second most voted party, considering the majority electoral system. It should be noted, however, that in both cases, the traditional bourgeoisie vote has remained firmly anchored to the Conservative parties, notwithstanding the fact that in the UK, Labour has managed to increase its support compared to the situation in the early 2000s.

Also, left-wing parties are the second vote choice in the EIG countries. Compared to the United States and the United Kingdom, this result is less obvious, considering that these countries are characterised by a proportional electoral law and a multi-party system. In other words, left-wing parties have managed to break through even among the upper class, in open competition with other right-wing parties. However, differences within the model can be noted. In Sweden, the Moderate Party (M) remain the first party voted by the traditional bourgeois class (37.3%) and the gap with the SAP is considerable. In Denmark, on the other hand, the gap between the Liberal Party (V) (around 23%) and the SD (around 19%) is narrow. It means that the upper class seems to have become a stronghold of the centre-right contended by the left wing in this country.

In the DIG countries, left-wing parties are the third most voted party of the upper class, but with substantial differences between Germany and France. In France, the majority of the votes of the traditional bourgeoisie were concentrated on Macron's centrist party (LaREM, 43%), which seems to have taken votes away from both Les Républicains (LR) and the PS. In Germany, on the other hand, the SPD has regained support among the upper class and the gap with the The Christian Democratic Union of Germany/ Christian Social Union in Bavaria (CDU-CSU) – although high – is smaller than that between the LaREM and the PS in France. Moreover, the SPD appears to be in open competition with the Greens and Liberal Party (FDP) for the upper-class vote. In other words, the SPD has lost support among the workers but has grown in the traditional bourgeoisie class – without, however, supplanting the CDU-CSU.

Finally, with regard to the NILG countries, substantial differences emerge between Italy and Spain. In Italy, despite a drop in support since the early 2000s,[7] the PD is the most voted party by the traditional bourgeoisie. In the face of a sharp drop in votes among the working class, the PD has become the upper-class party. However, the consensus achieved (27%) is much lower than that of the LsREM in France. In contrast, the traditional bourgeoisie has remained firmly anchored to the PP or has shifted towards Citizens (Cs) in Spain. Despite being the third most voted party, the PSOE obtains a limited

Table 13.6 The four most voted parties by the traditional bourgeoisie (late 2010s)

	NIG		*EIG*		*DIG*		*NILG*	
	UK	*USA*	*Sweden*	*Denmark*	*Germany*	*France*	*Italy*	*Spain*
1° Party	Tories (48.4%)	Republicans (58.4%)	M (37.3%)	V (23,2%)	CDU-CSU (30.3%)	LaREM (42.9%)	PD (27.1%)	PP (38.9%)
2° Party	Labour (27.9%)	Democrats (41.6%)	SAP (16.5%)	SD (19.4%)	Alliance 90/The Greens (17.6%)	LR (19.5%)	M5S (24.3%)	Cs (20.4%)
3° Party	LibDem (12.5%)		Liberal People's Party, L (12.9%)	DF (13.2%)	SPD (17.2%) FDP(17.1%)	PS (9.4%) FI (9.4%)	The League (16.4%)	PSOE (13.3%)

Source: European Social Survey (ESS): round 1 (2001) and round 9 (2019); International Social Survey Programme: 2002 for France, 2002–2004 and 2014–2016 for the United States, 2017 for Denmark, Sweden, and Spain. Data are weighted.

consensus among this class of voters (13%), and the distance with the PP remains high.[8]

Our hypothesis that the traditional bourgeoisie group is the area of influence of the centre-right parties (H4) is confirmed, although with exceptions. In Italy, the PD is the party most voted by the upper class. In France, Macron's centrist party gains the highest consensus among the bourgeois class, overtaking the Gaullist right. The analysis furthermore illustrates that support for left-wing parties from the traditional bourgeoisie varies between the countries examined. In the UK, US, Sweden, France, and Spain, the success of the left among the upper class is more limited – particularly in the last two ones.

13.7 Changes in the constituency of left-wing parties

Table 13.7 shows the changes in the constituencies of the left-wing parties in the four growth models. As explained above, the analysis will focus mainly on two aspects. The first concerns the weight of the production worker class within the left-wing parties' electorate, and its change over time. The second aspect regards the new configurations of social class coalitions supporting the left-wing parties. Our analysis aims to assess whether a *process of electorate middle-classisation* – which entails a marginalisation of lower social classes (production workers and low-skilled service workers) – may be identified.

Alternatively, whether inter-class alliances have formed between the new progressive middle class (the sociocultural professionals), the low-skilled outsiders (the service sector workers), and the historical blue-collar electorate (the production workers).

13.7.1 The weight of the production workers within the left-wing parties' constituency

Consistently with the data previously shown in Table 13.4, the weight of production workers in the constituency of the left-wing parties decreased in all four growth models. However, it is possible to identify substantial differences.

In the NIG countries, production workers' share within the constituency of Labour in the United Kingdom and the Democrats in the United States has diminished considerably (around -10 pp and -9 pp, respectively). Despite the fact that in these countries – also due to the majoritarian electoral system – the working class has continued to vote for the left over time, its weight within the electoral structure has shrunk. In contrast, in the EIG countries, the presence of the production worker has remained solid, notwithstanding a decline since the early 2000s. Production workers are still the class with the most significant weight within Denmark's SD constituency (around 25%) and represent 20.2% of the SAP electorate in Sweden, second only to low-skilled service workers. In the DIG countries, the downsizing of the working-class presence within the electorate of the SPD in Germany and the SP in France

Table 13.7 Changes in constituencies of left-wing parties in the four growth models (% of each class over the whole constituency), early 2000s, late 2010s

		Traditional bourgeoisie			*Petty bourgeoisie*			*Technical (semi-) professionals*			*Production workers*			*Associate managers*			*Office clerks*			*Sociocultural (semi-) professionals*			*Service workers*		
		t1	*t2*	*Dif.*	*t1*	*t2*	*Dif.*	*t1*	*t2*	*Dif.*	*t1*	*t2*	*Dif.*	*t1*	*t2*	*Dif.*	*t1*	*t2*	*Dif.*	*t1*	*t2*	*Dif.*	*t1*	*t2*	*Dif.*
NIG	UK-Lab.	9.8	3.4	-6.4	8.4	7.0	-1.4	4	10.3	6.3	23.2	13	-10.2	3.9	18.7	14.8	9.6	11.3	1.7	11.1	16.6	5.5	30	19.8	-10.2
	USA Dem.	20.6	12.6	-8	11.2	7.5	-3.7	7.1	9.7	2.6	22.3	12.9	-9.4	1.2	7.6	6.4	15.6	11.3	-4.3	11	17.3	6.3	11	21.1	10.1
EIG	SW-SAP	7.2	2.5	-4.7	3.7	4.8	1.1	7.5	9.2	1.7	22.6	20.2	-2.4	7	10.9	3.9	10.4	9.8	-0.6	11.7	17.1	5.4	29.9	25.6	-4.3
	DK SD	4.9	2.1	-2.8	3.6	3.8	0.2	7.8	11.4	3.6	31.5	25.4	-6.1	6.7	7	0.3	12.3	13.6	1.3	12.8	19.9	7.1	20.5	16.9	-3.6
DIG	GE-SPD	3.4	4.1	0.7	4.6	4.2	-0.4	14.9	15.4	0.5	30	20.9	-9.1	7.2	10.3	3.1	9.8	19.2	9.4	12.5	13.7	1.2	17.6	12.1	-5.5
	FR-PS	7.3	5.2	-2.1	3.6	3.5	-0.1	7.9	18.1	10.2	31.3	14.1	-17.2	7.9	9.4	1.5	17.4	16.3	-1.1	13.7	20.9	7.2	11	12.6	1.6
NILG	IT-PD	6.7	8.1	1.4	15.6	13.8	-1.8	4.9	10.2	5.3	24.2	16.7	-7.5	6.4	7.2	0.8	14	15.3	1.3	13.1	15.7	2.6	15.1	13.1	-2
	SP-PSOE	2.7	2.1	-0.6	14.9	9.9	-5	2.8	6.4	3.6	36.5	29.6	-6.9	5.6	5.4	-0.2	10.1	9.3	-0.8	8	11	3	19.6	26.4	6.8

Source: European Social Survey (ESS): round 1 (2001) and round 9 (2019); International Social Survey Programme: 2002 for France, 2002–2004 and 2014–2016 for the United States, 2017 for Denmark, Sweden and Spain. Data are weighted.

Note: For France, the data for the early 2000s refer to party affiliation (*party to which a person feels closer*) and not to the real electoral choice expressed at national elections. The values must therefore be read with caution.

is greater than in the Scandinavian countries. However, there are differences between the two countries. In Germany the downturn was less evident than in France, and the working class continued to be the most represented (20%) within the SPD electorate. In contrast, in France, the quota of production workers has decreased significantly, representing only 14% of the SPD constituency. Finally, in the NILG countries, the shrinking of the production workers' weight was more moderate than in the continental countries, but, again, with significant differences. The Spanish PSOE continued to represent the working class (30% of its electorate). In Italy, blue-collar workers are only 16.7% of the PD constituency. In other words, Spanish production workers continued to vote for the PSOE – despite a substantial decline – and retained a significant share within the party constituency. Inversely, in Italy, the PD lost support among production workers who jointly have a modest representation among the party electors.

13.7.2 Configuration of the coalitions supporting left-wing parties

In reference to Table 13.7, we notice that, despite a general decline in the vote of the sociocultural professionals (see Table 13.4), the latter have increased their weight within the constituencies of all the left-wing parties. This increase is more pronounced in the NIG and EIG countries and France, while it is more moderate in Germany and the NILG countries. Moreover, if we look at the values for the end of the 2000s, sociocultural workers represent a new area of influence of the left-wing electorate in the Scandinavian and Anglo-Saxon countries but also in Italy (where their weight is over 15%). In France, this group represents 20% of the PS electorate. Lower values can be observed in Germany and Spain. The data are consistent with the fact that, in Spain, the votes of sociocultural workers for the PSOE have halved over two decades, while, in Germany, those for the SPD have shrunk almost three-fold.

Moving towards the bottom of the social stratification, we can see a decline in the weight of low-skilled service workers in the EIG countries, but also in the UK, Germany, and Italy. However, at the end of the 2010s, in the NIG countries this class has the highest relative weight within the constituency of Labour in the UK (19.8%) – despite a distinct plunge since the early 2000s – and of the American Democrats (21%). In the EIG countries, the electoral weight of this group has declined over time, consistent with the fact that these workers have decreased their support for the SAP and SD. Nevertheless, the group has remained an area of influence for the left wing in Sweden (25% of the Sap constituency), hence becoming the class with the greatest relative weight – and has also maintained a crucial role in Denmark (17%, approximately). In the DIG countries, the service workers' share within the PS constituency has remained stable, while in Germany it decreased. However, the values stand at around 12% in both cases, considerably lower than in the NIG and EIG countries. Lastly, the situation is more heterogeneous in the NILG countries. In Italy, the weight of low-skilled service workers within the PD electorate has further declined over time and does not go any higher than 13% at the end of the 2010s. In contrast, in Spain, despite a downturn, the weight of the class remains significant (26.4%), second only to that of production workers.

The analysis of the weight of the traditional middle classes in the Left constituency leads to interesting results.

Except for Spain, the quota of technical professionals and associate managers has increased in all models concerning managers. At the end of the 2010s, the technical professionals represented a critical left electorate within the DIG countries – where their weight exceeded 15% in both Germany and France. In the NIG, EIG, and NILG countries, the role of this group was more modest, with values around 10%. The electoral weight of associate managers proved particularly significant in the United Kingdom (18%). In the EIG countries and Sweden, the share remained more contained (around 10%) and reasonably limited (below 10%) in the NILG countries and Denmark.

Finally, the weight of clerks within the constituencies of left-wing parties has diminished moderately in the United States, Sweden, Spain, and France, while it has increased in all other countries. Nevertheless, this group plays a crucial role in the left-wing constituencies in Germany, France, and Italy – exceeding 15% in all three cases.

The last group to be analysed is the bourgeoisie. As far as the traditional bourgeoisie is concerned, its weight within the left-wing constituency has dwindled in all the countries, with two important exceptions: Germany and Italy. In Germany, however, the increase has not affected its relative weight within the SPD constituency, which remains small (4.4%). On the contrary, in Italy, the weight of the traditional bourgeoisie within the PD electorate is relatively high (8.8%), second only to the USA, where the group represents 12% of the Democrat electorate.

Even the electoral weight of the petty bourgeoisie has decreased over time, except for the NIG countries. In general, the petty bourgeoisie does not represent a key constituency of the left-wing parties, except in the NILG countries. However, in Italy and Spain, the weight of this social class is above average, 13.8% and 9.9%, respectively, which are relatively high values for left-wing parties.

In the light of these data, it is possible to speculate on the *post-Fordist class coalitions* that were configured in the late 2010s to support the left wing. More specifically, it is interesting to assess whether the left-wing parties are supported by a coalition that includes the *historical* electorate of production workers, on the one hand, and the new groups of low-skilled service workers and sociocultural workers, on the other. Or whether the new structure of the left-wing constituency is based on a coalition comprising the middle classes (technical professionals, associate managers, and office clerks), with the support of the bourgeois classes as well.

Table 13.8 shows each social class's weight within the left-wing parties' constituency in the eight countries under review at the end of the 2010s. The first three social classes with the highest relative weight are in bold. Table 13.9

Table 13.8 Weight of each social class within the constituency of the left-wing parties in the eight countries, late 2010s (values)

	NIG		*EIG*		*DIG*		*NILG*	
	UK	*USA*	*Sweden*	*Denmark*	*Germany*	*France*	*Italy*	*Spain*
1° Party	**SWs (19.8%)**	**SWs (21.1%)**	**SWs (25.6%)**	**PWs (25.4%)**	**PWs (20.9%)**	**SCPs (20.9%)**	**PWs (16.7%)**	**PWs (29.6%)**
2° Party	**AMs (18.7%)**	**SCPs (17.3%)**	**PWs (20.2%)**	**SCPs (19.9%)**	**OCs (19.1%)**	**TPs (18.1%)**	**SCPs (15.7%)**	**SWs (26.4%)**
3° Party	**SCPs (16.6%)**	**PWs (12.9%)**	**SCPs (17.1%)**	**SWs (16.9%)**	**TPs (15.4%)**	**OCs (16.3%)**	**OCs (15.3%)**	**SCPs (11%)**
4° Party	PWs (13%)	TB (12.6%)	AMs (10.9%)	OCs (13.6%)	SCPs (13.7%)	PWs (14.1%)	PB (13.8%)	PB (9.9%)
5° Party	OCs (11.3%)	OCs (11.3%)	OCs (9.8%)	TPs (11.4%)	SWs (12.1%)	SWs (12.6%)	SWs (13.1%)	OCs (9.3%)
6° Party	TPs (10.3%)	TPs (9.7%)	TPs (9.2%)	AMs (7%)	AMs (10.3%)	AMs (9.4%)	TPs (10.2%)	TPs (6.4%)
7° Party	PB (7%)	AMs (7.6%)	PB (4.8%)	PB (3.8%)	PB (4.2%)	TB (5.2%)	TB (8.1%)	AMs (5.4%)
8° Party	TB (3.4%)	PB (7.5%)	TB (2.5%)	TB (2.1%)	TB (4.1%)	PB (3.5%)	AMs (7.2%)	TB (2.1%)

Source: European Social Survey (ESS): round 1 (2001) and round 9 (2019); International Social Survey Programme: 2002 for France, 2002–004 and 2014–2016 for the United States, 2017 for Denmark, Sweden, and Spain. Data are weighted.

Legend:

TB: Traditional bourgeoisie; TPs: Technical (semi-) professionals; AMs: Associate managers; SCPs: Sociocultural (semi-) professionals; PB: Petty bourgeoisie: PWs: Production workers; OCs: Official Clerks; SWs: Service workers.

Table 13.9 Composition of the coalition formed by the first three classes supporting the left-wing parties and overall weight on their electorate

	NIG		*EIG*		*DIG*		*NILG*	
	UK	*USA*	*Sweden*	*Denmark*	*Germany*	*France*	*Italy*	*Spain*
Class coalition	SWs+ AMs+ SCPs	SWs+ SCPs + PWs	SWs+ PWs+ SCPs	PWs+ SCPs + SWs	PWs+ OCs + TPs	SCPs+ TPs+ OCs	PWs+ SCPs + OCs	PWs + SWs+ SCPs
Overall weight	*55.1%*	*51.3%*	*62.9%*	*62.2%*	*55.5%*	*55.3%*	*47.7%*	*67%*

shows the coalition formed by the first three classes supporting the left wing and its overall weight in the constituency. The results are analysed for each growth model.

Starting with the NIG countries, in the UK the coalition of the three social classes with the highest electoral weight comprises low-skilled service workers, associate managers, and sociocultural professionals. This coalition of social classes achieves an electoral weight of 55% and, if we include production workers, it reaches 66%. In other words, the coalition supporting the Labours in the late 2010s includes both the new, libertarian, middle class – i.e. the sociocultural professionals – and the low-skilled, low-wage workers of the service sector. However, in the light of the downsizing of production workers, associate managers – which belong to the traditional middle class – represent now a key electoral group.

Inversely, the configuration of the coalition supporting the Democrats in the United States seems to have shifted more to the lower social groups. The top three social classes with the greatest weight within the party constituency are low-skilled service workers, sociocultural professionals, and production workers. Overall, this coalition represents 51% of the votes for the US left. Notwithstanding the lower value compared to the UK, the coalition seems to be more compact in terms of social policy preferences. In other words, the Democrats under Obama gained support from both the historical constituency of production workers and the new post-Fordist classes. However, the traditional bourgeoisie continues to have considerable weight. Presumably, the party is pressured to consider its policy interests, even if they diverge from those of the class coalition that now supports the Democratic Party.[9]

In the EIG countries, the coalition of service workers, sociocultural professionals and production workers is particularly powerful, representing well over 60% of the electorate of these parties. In other words, in the SAP and the SD, the production workers' representation crisis has been limited. At the same time, the two parties have succeeded in representing the new post-Fordist classes emerging from the process of globalisation and tertiarisation.

The coalitions in the DIG countries have displayed more instability. In Germany, the first three social classes in terms of electoral weight within the SPD constituency are production workers, clerks, and technicians. This coalition represents 55.5% of the party's electorate, with a weaker presence of low-skilled service workers and sociocultural professionals. The reconfiguration of the constituency structure since the end of the 2010s has thus pushed towards the traditional middle classes. Furthermore, though conserving a significant quota of production workers, their presence is nevertheless on the wane.

The situation is even more skewed towards the middle class in France, where the top three classes with the most significant electoral weight are sociocultural professionals, technical professionals, and clerks (55.3% of the SP electorate).

In this case, production workers and low-skilled service workers are under-represented. The party thus seems to have pursued a path of "*middle-classisation*", without, however, succeeding in winning over the loyalty of the middle and upper classes, who have flocked to Emmanuel Macron's centrist party.

Lastly, the reconfiguration of class coalitions is heterogeneous in the NILG countries, with Italy and Spain revealing significant differences. In Italy, the structure of the PD constituency is more fluid and consequently more fragile. The first three social classes – production workers, sociocultural professionals, and office clerks – do not amount to 50% of the party's electorate. The class of low-skilled service workers is marginal. Furthermore, unlike in other countries, the bourgeoisie in Italy (both traditional and petty bourgeoisie) has a significant weight (21.9%). In other words, the PD's class coalition formed on the "left" is weak. Besides, the significant weight of the bourgeois classes is supposed to affect the formulation of the party's policy proposals. Inversely, in Spain, we find a coalition of classes very similar to that of the DIG countries. The first three social classes by electoral weight – production workers, low-skilled workers, and sociocultural professionals – have an overall weight of 67%. In other words, the PSOE is supported by a *left-wing coalition*, which manages to hold together both the historical constituency of the production workers and the new post-Fordist social classes.

13.8 Concluding remarks

The chapter's goal has been to investigate the electoral behaviour of the post-Fordist social classes in eight advanced economies that occurred from the end of the 1970s onwards. Such changes have affected the political strategies of the political parties as the Glorious Thirties came to an end, especially those of the left-wing parties. More specifically, we tried to understand how the classes' support for the left was evolved between the early 2000s and the late 2010s and which kind of class alliances left parties can now rely on. Clearly, it cannot be assumed that changes in social structures have univocally and unilaterally influenced party strategies. Political parties have reacted in different ways, according to trajectories influenced by internal factors (history, ideology, organisational set-up) as well as external factors (above all, the characteristics of political competition, but also the economic situation of the countries). These trajectories are the consequence of the firm tensions and conflicts that have characterised the life of these parties everywhere.

However, the shrinking of the working class, the spread of high- and low-skilled workers in the service sector, and the upgrading in education levels all have undoubtedly conditioned the parties' strategies to widen or consolidate their consensus.

In the context of these transformations, the left-wing parties could have taken several paths, also in parallel. They could have tried to compensate for the diminution of production workers by appealing to low-skilled service workers. They might also have tried to broaden consensus among sociocultural professionals, typically more hostile to conservative parties from a cultural perspective. Finally, they could have gambled on the growing salaried middle classes (technicians, clerks) and the bourgeois electorate. In pursuing these goals, the left-wing had to focus on maintaining their traditional electorate – the production workers – who certainly could turn into a stronghold contended by other parties – first of all, the radical right, as indeed happened.

Data revealed that in the eight advanced economies under review, none of these possible paths was fully and univocally pursued by the left-wing parties. Different empirical responses emerged to the four initial hypotheses according to the growth models involved. The hypothesis that production workers' votes for left-wing parties decreased while their support for radical right-wing parties intensified (H1) found confirmation, but with substantial differences between models. On the one hand, the decline was more radical for the DIG and NILG countries and less so for the EIG countries. On the other, radical right-wing forces experienced growth in support among production workers in all the countries analysed, save in the case of Spain. Nonetheless, here too, the visibility of Vox – a new radical right-wing party – has recently increased.

The hypothesis that the traditional bourgeoisie group is the area of influence of centre-right parties has been confirmed (H4). Once again, however, there are exceptions. In Italy, the PD is the most voted party by the upper class.

Hypotheses H2 and H3, in contrast, were only partially confirmed. The empirical analysis suggests that sociocultural professionals represent the left parties' new area of influence (H2) only in the NIG and EIG models. On the contrary, the hypothesis cannot be confirmed in the DIG and NILG countries, especially considering the period after the economic crisis. As far as low-skilled service workers are concerned, their vote is particularly fragmented only in the DIG countries and Spain, with all the main parties in open competition (H3). In contrast, in the NIG and EIG countries, service workers' vote has been consolidated over time in favour of the left-wing parties – although in Denmark the group has moved closer to the radical right-wing parties. In Italy, the "populist" pole (M5S and Lega) has managed to attract most of the support of these workers.

It is time now for some conclusive remarks. First of all, the left-wing parties in the EIG and NIG countries are those that seem to have suffered the least enervation from the post-Fordist transition: not only have they managed to contain the loss of votes among production workers (albeit on the wane as an occupational class), but they have been increasingly able to replace them with the new growing service workers, both low and high-skilled. Nevertheless, it should be noted that this outcome issues from two very divergent paths. In the NIG models, the recovery of consensus among the lower classes was due only to Obama's high popularity among African American voters. On the contrary, in the case of the EIG countries, the left-wing parties were able to build a more consolidated bloc of high and low-skilled production and service workers. However, we should bear in mind that the results of the NIG countries are strongly conditioned by the majority electoral system which provides the electorate with fewer "political" alternatives and, at the same time, helps the left-wing parties to retain their historical constituencies more easily, thus containing centrifugal pressure. What is more, in the NIG countries, the abstention rate (especially in the United States) is very high. For this reason, the effect of the post-Fordist transition in NIG social classes is partly concealed by an electoral system that is difficult to compare with that of the other growth types.

The trajectory of the EIG left-wing parties toward a new post-Fordist social-democratic base is pretty unique. Indeed, in the NILG and DIG models, all countries, except for Spain, have in common their failure to represent low-skilled service workers and, to a lesser extent, sociocultural professionals. In these countries, left-wing parties undertook different paths. The first path is that of the French Socialist Party, which constitutes the emblematic case of a *leaking party*: not only did it fail to prevent losing its traditional constituency, comprising production workers (in any case smaller from the beginning, also due to the historical presence of the Communist Party), but it lost all its consent to the benefit of new parties that emerged on its right and left. Furthermore, it did not manage to attract service workers.

Italy and Germany share a more traditional social structure, instead. Production workers are still numerous and employment in service sectors is comparatively weaker. The weight of self-employed workers (petty bourgeoise) is also high, especially in Italy. This more traditional social structure undermined the post-Fordist challenges and, consequently, hindered the left-wing parties from recognising that service workers were more and more relevant in the post-Fordist social structure. German and Italian left-wing parties underwent two different paths. On the one hand, the SPD can be conceived as a *fortress party*, which tries to defend its traditional social bases (production workers, white-collar workers, technical professionals). However, SPD's effort is not that effective. It loses production workers' consent toward both its right and left and, at the same time, it fails to expand significantly in the direction of the new middle classes in the sociocultural sector. On the other hand, The PD can be defined as a *party that uproots itself*. In search of new social bases, chiefly in the salaried middle classes and the bourgeoisie, it relinquishes its roots in the working class while failing to create adequate appeal for the new low-skilled service workers.

In Spain, the PSOE adopts a different path that seems to bring it closer, in terms of electoral bases, to that of the Nordic countries. A sort of *post-Fordist Mediterranean social democracy* based on the electoral support of the traditional working-class, new service workers and professionals in the socio-cultural sector. It remains to be seen, however, to what extent the Spanish socialist party will be able to maintain and defend this coalition under attack from the new forces of the radical left and recently also from the radical right.

Notes

1 The term "main left-wing parties" is used here to refer to those parties labelled as social-democratic by Armingeon et al. (2018) and, in any case, to those parties representing the main left-wing force in the countries in question throughout the period examined here.

2 Consumer services include trade and repair of personal property, restaurants, and hotels (NACE Codes G–H). Business services include transport, storage, communication, financial activities, real estate, renting, information technology, research, and other business services (NACE Codes I–K). Finally, personal services include public administration, education, health and social work and household activities (NACE Codes L–P). The sectoral taxonomy used is ISIC rev. 3.1.

3 Concerning the other occupational classes, Oesch and Rennwald (2018) suggest that: (a) the consensus of the group of (semi-) professional technicians and office clerks is contended by all poles – left-wing, centre-right and radical right; (b) the group of associate managers should remain a predominantly centre-right party-oriented area; (c) as for the small business owners, the deterioration of their status, especially as a result of globalisation and the recent economic and financial crisis, could transform them from a predominantly centre-right oriented area into a stronghold contended by the radical right.

4 To use more homogenous data, we used three statistical weights: the first refers to the socio-demographic dimension: age, gender, geographical area, and educational qualifications. The second weight refers to the political dimension, namely the result of voting at the most recent elections when the interview was conducted. The third refers to social stratification. In this case, we used the extended Oesch' schema (16 social classes) based on the data from the European Labour Force Survey.

5 This transformation occurs for two reasons. First, since the number of traditional parties is limited, their internal composition tends to be heterogeneous. This encourages increasing competition between the various factions and thus generates changes, even radical, in political orientation. Second, elections in majoritarian systems are a zero-sum game. The opposition is more motivated to radicalise the conflict in order to differentiate itself from the government parties (Kriesi et al, 2008). In this regard, see the example of the Republicans in the United States following Donald Trump's victory and the British Conservatives after Brexit under the new leadership of Boris Johnson.

6 For the case of Italy, the votes of the Left Democrats (DS) and The Daisy were added together for the election results in the early 2000s. The two parties merged in 2007 to form the Democratic Party (PD).

7 As already indicated, for the early 2000s reference is made to the sum of the DS and The Daisy votes.
8 It should be noted that Spanish data refer to 2017 and therefore do not account for the last elections (2019), in which the far-right party Vox obtained 10.26% of the votes.
9 Voter turnout in the United States is historically low, especially when the lowest income quintile is considered (Mahler, 2008). See Dalton (2008) for more details.

References

Armingeon, K., Wenger, V., Wiedemeier, F., Isler, C., Knöpfel, L., Weisstanner, D., & Engler, S. (2018). *Supplement to the comparative political dataset – government composition 1960–2016*. Berne: Institute of Political Science, University of Berne.

Autor, D.A., Katz, L.F., & Kearney, M.S. (2008). Trends in US wage inequality: Revising the revisionists. *Review of Economics and Statistics*, 90(2), 300–323. doi:10.1162/rest.90.2.300

Armingeon, K. & Bonoli, G. (Eds) (2006). *The politics of post-industrial welfare states: Adapting post-war social policies to new social risks*. London and New York: Routledge.

Baumol, W.J, & Bowen, W.G. (1966). *Performing arts: the economic dilemma. A study of problems common to theater, opera, music and dance*. New York: The Twentieth Century Fund.

Beramendi, P., Häusermann, S., Kitschelt, H., & Kriesi, P. (Eds) (2015). *The politics of advanced capitalism*. New York: Cambridge University Press.

Bonoli, G. (2006). New social risks and the politics of post-industrial social policies. In K. Armingeon & G. Bonoli (Eds), *The politics of post-industrial welfare states: Adapting post-war social policies to new social risks* (pp. 3–26). London and New York: Routledge.

Breen, R. (2005). *Social mobility in Europe*. Oxford: Oxford University Press.

Clark, T.N. & Lipset, S.M. (1991). Are social classes dying? *International Sociology*, 6(4), 397–410. doi:10.1177/026858091006004002

Crouch, C. (2010). Flexibility and security on the labour market: An analysis of the governance of inequality. *Zeitschrift fur Arbeitsmarkt Forschung*, 43, 17–38.

Dalton, R.J. (1996). Political cleavages, issues, and electoral change. In L. LeDuc, R. Niemi & P. Norris (Eds), *Comparing democracies elections and voting in global perspective* (pp. 319–342). London: Sage.

Dalton, R.J. (2008). *Citizen politics: Public opinion and political parties in advanced industrial democracies*, 5th Ed., Washington, DC: CQ.

de Koster, W., Achterberg, P., & van der Waal, J. (2012). The new right and the welfare state: The electoral relevance of welfare chauvinism and welfare populism in the Netherlands. *International Political Science Review*, 34(3), 3–20. doi:10.1177/0192512112455443

Erikson, R. & Goldthorpe, J.H. (1993). *The constant flux*. Oxford: Oxford University Press.

Esping-Andersen, G. (1999). *Social foundations of postindustrial economies*. Oxford: Oxford University Press.

Esping-Andersen, G. (2002). *Why we need a new welfare state*. Oxford: Oxford University Press.

Evans, G. & Mills, C. (2000). In search of the wage-labour/service contract: New evidence on the validity of the Goldthorpe class schema. *British Journal of Sociology*, 51(4), 641–661. doi:10.1080/00071310020015307

Franklin, M. (1992). The decline of cleavage politics. In M. Franklin, T. Mackie, & H. Valen (Eds). *Electoral change* (pp. 383–405). New York: Cambridge University Press.

Freeman, C. & Soete, L. (1994). *Work for all or mass unemployment? Computerised technical change into the 21st century*. New York: Pinter.

Garritzmann J.L., Häusermann, S., & Palier, B. (2019). *The world politics of social investment*. Paper presented at the 17th ESPAnet-Europe Conference, 5–7 September 2019, Stockholm, Sweden.

Girdon, N., Adams, J., & Horne, W. (2018). How ideology, economics and institutions shape affective polarization in democratic polities. Paper presented at the annual "American Political Science Association" conference, Boston, Mass., 30 August – 2 September.

Goos, M. & Manning, A. (2007). Lousy and lovely jobs: The rising polarization of work in Britain. *The Review of Economics and Statistics*, 89(1), 118–133. doi:10.1162/rest.89.1.118

Häusermann S. (2020). Dualization and electoral realignment. *Political Science Research and Methods,* 8(2), 380-385. doi:10.1017/psrm.2018.48

Häusermann, S., Kurer, T., & Schwander, H. (2014). High-skilled outsiders? Labor market vulnerability, education and welfare state preferences. *Socio-Economic Review*, 13(2), 235–258. doi:10.1093/ser/mwu026

Häusermann, S. (2018). The multidimensional politics of social investment in conservative welfare regimes: Family policy reform between social transfers and social investment. *Journal of European Public Policy*, 25(6), 862–877. doi:10.1080/13501763.2017.1401106

Häusermann, S. (2010). *The politics of welfare state reform in Continental Europe: Modernization in hard times*. Cambridge: Cambridge University Press.

Häusermann, S. (2012). The politics of old and new social policies. In G. Bonoli and D. Natali (Eds), *The new welfare state in Europe* (pp. 111–132). Oxford: Oxford University Press.

Inglehart, R. (1990). Culture shift in advanced industrial society. Princeton, NJ: Princeton University Press.

Iversen, T. & Wren, A. (1998). Equality, employment, and budgetary restraint: The trilemma of the service economy. *World Politics*, 50, 507–46. doi:10.1017/S0043887100007358

Kitschelt, H. (2004). *Diversification and reconfiguration of party systems in post-industrial democracies*. Berlin: Friedrich Ebert Stiftung.

Kriesi, H., Grande, E., Lachat, R., Dolezal, M., Bornschier, M., & Frey, T. (2008). *West European politics in the age of globalization.* Cambridge: Cambridge University Press.

Kriesi H., Grande, E., Dolezal, M., Helbling, M., Hoglinger, D., Hutter, S., & Wuest, B. (2012). *Political conflict in Western Europe*. Cambridge: Cambridge University Press.

Lijparth, A. (1990). The political consequences of electoral laws, 1945–1985. *American Political Science Review*, 84(2), 481–496. doi:10.2307/1963530

Lefkofrid, Z. & Michel, E. (2014). *Exclusive solidarity? Radical right parties and the welfare state*. Florence: EUI Working Paper 120.

Mahler, V.A. (2008). Electoral turnout and income redistribution by the state: A cross-national analysis of the developed democracies. European *Journal* of *Political Research*, 47(2), 161–183. doi:10.1111/j.1475-6765.2007.00726.x

Michaels, G., Natraj, A., & Van Reenen, J. (2014). Has ICT polarized skill demand? Evidence from eleven countries over 25 years. *Review of Economics and Statistics*, 96(1), 60–77. doi:10.1162/REST_a_00366

Oesch, Daniel (2006). *Redrawing the class map: Stratification and institutions in Germany, Britain, Sweden and Switzerland*. London: Palgrave Macmillan.

Oesch, Daniel & Rodríguez-Menés, J. (2011). Upgrading or polarization? Occupational change in Britain, Germany, Spain and Switzerland, 1990–2008. *Socio-Economic Review*, 9, 503–531. doi:10.1093/ser/mwq029.

Oesch, D. (2012). The class basis of the cleavage between the new left and the radical right: An analysis for Austria, Denmark, Norway and Switzerland. In J. Rydren (Eds), *Class politics and the radical right* (pp. 31–51). London and New York: Routledge.

Oesch, D. & Rennwald, L. (2018). Electoral competition in Europe's new tripolar political space: Class voting for the left, centre-right and radical right. *European Journal of Political Research*, 57(4), 783–807. doi:10.1111/1475-6765.12259

Palier, B. & Thelen, K. (2010). Institutionalizing dualism: Complementarities and change in France and Germany. *Politics & Society*, 38(1), 119–148. doi:10.1177/0032329209357888

Pierson, P. (Eds) (2001). *The new politics of the welfare state*. Oxford: Oxford University Press.

Pisati, M. (2010). *Voto di classe. Posizione sociale e preferenze politiche in Italia*. Bologna: Il Mulino.

Plane, D.L. & Gershtenson, J. (2004). Candidates' ideological locations, abstention, and turnout in US midterm senate elections. *Political Behavior*, 26(1), 69–93. doi:10.1023/B:POBE.0000022344.05382.b4

Rose, R. & McAllister, I. (1986). *Voters begin to choose: From closed-class to open elections in Europe*. London: Sage.

Rueda, D. (2007). *Social democracy inside out: Partisanship and labor market policy in industrialized democracies*. Oxford: Oxford University Press.

Rodden, J. (2019). Keeping your enemies close: Electoral rules and partisan polarization. Paper presented at the "Seminar on the State and Capitalism since 1800", Boston, MIT, 1 March.

Schwander, H. & Häusermann, S. (2013). Who is in and who is out? A risk-based conceptualization of insiders and outsiders. *Journal of European Social Policy*, 23(3), 248–269. doi:10.1177/0958928713480064

Timmer, M., de Vries, G. J., & De Vries, K. (2015). Patterns of structural change in developing countries. In J. Weiss & M. Tribe (Eds), *Routledge handbook of industry and development* (pp. 79–97). New York: Routledge.

Wright E.O. & Dweyer, R.E (2003). The patterns of job expansions in the United States: A comparison of the 1960s and 1990s. *Socio-Economic Review*, 1(3), 289–325. doi:10.1093/soceco/1.3.289

Chapter 14

Politics and policies of left-wing parties

Alfio Mastropaolo, Vittorio Martone, Daniela R. Piccio, Rocco Sciarrone, and Luca Storti

14.1 The dilemmas of left-wing parties

This chapter discusses the relationship between the politics of left-wing parties from the 1980s up to the most recent phase, together with the policies that have determined paths of more or less inclusive growth. The focus therefore concerns how electoral consensus-building strategies have been intertwined with economic and social choices. Reference is made to left-wing parties in order to include not only parties belonging to the larger family of social democrats and socialists in this category but also to the smaller family of liberal left-wing democratic parties, such as the US Democratic Party (see Armingeon et al., 2018). Our analysis therefore concentrates on the broad area of the "left reformist" parties, including socialist and social-democratic, but in some cases also liberal-democratic, parties, i.e. the Labour Party (LP) in the United Kingdom and the Democratic Party (DP) in the United States, the *Sveriges socialdemokratiska arbetareparti* (SAP) in Sweden and the *Socialdemokratiet* (SD) in Denmark, the *Parti Socialiste* (PS) in France and the *Sozialdemokratische Partei Deutschland* (SPD) in Germany, the *Partido Socialista Obrero Español* (PSOE) in Spain and, in the case of Italy, the series of left-wing parties that have succeeded one another since the 1980s. Each of these actors, while internally heterogeneous, has its own cultural, organisational, and governmental traditions, which have contributed to forging the paths taken, as well as policy proposals and attitudes towards demands for redistribution. Obviously, in each case, the overall political-institutional framework (national, supra-, and sub-national), the choices made by other parties, and the electoral results are all important.

Another consideration for which it seemed appropriate to focus on left-wing parties draws on the hypothesis that they were the political actors most constitutively suited to promoting processes of redistribution and limiting inequalities in advanced economies. In fact, the options that have characterised the programmes of these parties and the actions taken by social democratic governments in Europe feature progressive taxation, the construction of the welfare state and labour protection. The data collected in the first

DOI: 10.4324/9781003297130-18

phase of our research suggest a clear association between inclusive socio-economic performance and the participation of left-wing parties in government. However, it is also evident that the more or less incisive and long-lasting presence of left-wing parties should be considered a necessary but not sufficient condition for approaching inclusive development. The weight and role of the left-wing actors in government has a special importance, especially in the constitutive phase of the welfare model, as does the degree of unity-division between these political forces, in terms of competition from "radical" left-wing formations and also in terms of relations with trade unions.

In this chapter we aim to explore the elements that emerged in the first phase of the research, using a comparative approach. In particular, the reactions of the left-wing parties to two sequences of problems are under scrutiny: the tensions deriving from the decline of Fordism, from the reorganisation of economic activities linked to the growth of globalisation, with notable consequences for employment, and at the same time the growing costs of the welfare instituted in the previous phase of the great post-war development. Clearly, left-wing parties are significantly concerned by these problems. On the one hand, they must contend with the collapse of their traditional industrial working-class constituency, while in terms of policymaking, they are forced to tackle changes in industrial relations and the reorganisation of welfare models. Faced with these challenges, a twofold movement appears: if parties tend to share similarities in their programmatic outlook, significant differences emerge in terms of the actual policies they advance. The hypothesis under discussion here is that the programme guidelines and messages addressed to the electorate essentially respond to the need to attract new consensus and thus counterbalance the crumbling traditional social bases. This fuels a stronger move towards policies that open up more to the market, include processes of de-regulation of the labour market, and target curtailed welfare costs – a proposal addressed above all to the new middle class, which at the same time gives greater attention to cultural issues related to the recognition of more extensive civil rights. However, once in government, responses from left-wing parties begin to diverge, because the programme offered has to reckon with the costs and benefits of certain choices. The institutional redistribution framework established in the previous phase heavily influences policymaking, and this in turn triggers a sort of resistance to – or adaptation of – previous forms of regulation, thus leading differences in development paths to persist.

14.2 Programmatic repositioning and personnel change

A large body of literature has revealed a refashioning of left-wing parties' programmes since the 1980s, upholding a move towards pro-market positions, alongside liberal policies and civil rights protection. What were the reasons behind this reshaping? An appraisal of the transition seen in the mid-1990s, and hence the role of the left within the "strategies of transition" away from the Fordist model, will reveal how the parties made a bid to counter the difficulties and the electoral decline they had experienced on the whole (albeit to varying degrees) in the previous decade. In that phase, left-wing parties partially regained consensus by adopting, almost unanimously, the "modernising" strategy known as the Third Way. This perspective, on the one hand, endorsed many of the criticisms launched by the neo-liberalism that had emerged in the 1980s against the welfare state and, on the other hand, aimed to temper its harshness by reconciling the free market, concern for social cohesion, and attention to education and training processes.

The programmatic repositioning of left-wing parties and the shift in their political proposal towards pro-market positions (Jobert, 1994) is mainly attributed to the changes that took shape in the 1980s. The decline of Fordism, globalisation, the evolution of the labour market and the redefinition of social stratification raised significant challenges for these parties, which came up against significantly transformed spaces in which to manoeuvre. Scholars in particular pointed to the following salient features: the drastic fall in the number of people employed in the primary sector, the constant decline in employment in the manufacturing sector and therefore the downsizing of the working class, accelerated by deindustrialisation and tertiarisation, the rise of social, business, and consumer services and the appearance of new cleavages (between public and private, high and low qualifications, natives and immigrants, etc.) (see, among others, Saunders, 1990 and Kriesi et al., 2008). Overall, the strain caused by traditional rifts gave rise to a progressive individualisation of electoral behaviour, which then became increasingly disengaged from class membership and more and more instrumental (see Chapters 12 and 13). As this new situation progressed, trade unions lost ground and the social roots of left-wing parties weakened, calling into question the social contract on which regulation was founded at the time of the great expansion (Bagnasco, 2016). At the same time, the way in which the political parties operated and the range of programmes they offered were also changing. The first signs of this change were pointed out in the late 1960s by Kirchheimer (1966), who theorised that parties were softening up the austerity of their previous ideological references in order to concentrate on broadening their potential electorate. In the case of left-wing parties, it was a question of paying more attention to the middle class, within which they already had a considerable following, and restyling – along with their programme priorities – the way in which they interacted with voters. This too was a long-lasting process: it covered almost a quarter of a century, eventually leading to a substantial metamorphosis of the parties, from the so-called "mass parties" to electoral-professional parties, increasingly oriented towards the electoral market and the expansion of their followers (Panebianco, 1982).

Hence, changes within the social structure were accompanied by changes within the political parties themselves. How much the former influenced the latter, and to what extent the parties were transformed regardless of changes in social stratification, has been widely discussed in the literature. Undeniably, if the social structure becomes more complex, parties cannot fail to take this into account, also by reworking the type of representation they supply. The issue of agency and political proposals is accentuated by top-down perspectives (cf. Evans & Tilley, 2012; Evans & De Graaf, 2013), according to which parties not only act as "interpreters" of ongoing transformations, but can also contribute in various ways to accelerating or hindering them. In other words, by setting out a specific vision of social transformations, parties modify categories and reference groups, aggregate different interests, sustain old and new divisions, and build different electoral coalitions (Beramendi et al., 2015). As regards left-wing parties in particular, there is a persistent bid to attract the middle class and remain electorally competitive; while on the one hand this fuels indistinctness among programmes (see, among others, Kitschelt, 1993; Renwald & Evans, 2014), on the other it also contributes to the political construction of the "middle class", in its internal composition and the criteria considered legitimate to be included or excluded from it (Sciarrone et al., 2011).

An interesting point to consider, in light of these references, is the evolution of left-wing parties' programmes over the long term, i.e. between the last elections held in the 1970s and those dating to 2015. Using the "Rile" index adopted by the Manifesto Research Project, it is possible to observe how electoral programmes can be placed on a left-right axis, where negative values indicate the left of the political spectrum. In Table 14.1 we have highlighted the years of major programmatic changes and the policy orientations that marked these transitions. As a rule, the most significant shifts occurred in the 1990s. The French Socialist Party is an exception, since its repositioning came about as early as the mid-1980s, when Mitterrand redefined his government's action on debt containment and the fight against inflation. Moreover, the most significant shifts transition towards the right of the political spectrum. The last column shows some of the main policy positions of the parties concerning growth (the economy, the role of the state, the labour market) and inclusion (welfare and social policies). This was the time of New Labour and the Third Way, which agreed with the viewpoint of supply side economics, and took increased (collective and individual) competitiveness as its fundamental programmatic objective, capable of fostering growth, reducing unemployment, and containing socio-economic inequalities in the era of globalisation. A more active industrial policy was therefore advocated, without the direct intervention of the state, but rather oriented towards promoting innovation, the use of technology, and skilled qualifications. The formulas shared by left-wing parties in the 1990s include competition, investment in training and reform in public administrations in the light of New Public

Table 14.1 Years of main programmatic shifts and policy positions

Parties	*Years*	*Main shifts*$_{(a)}$	*Distinguishing policy features*
LP	1992–1997	+ 38.5	Ideological shift (New Labour) Pro-market reforms, deregulation Revision of public spending on education and training Welfare to Work policies
DP	1988–1992	+ 19.5	Ideological shift (New Democrats) Public Administration reform (New Public Management) Work-first unemployment protection and poverty assistance measures Business creation and training oriented interventions
SAP	1991–1994	+ 30	Tax cuts for SMEs and support for ICT start-up companies Revision of R&D expenditure and reform of training in a pro-market and higher skill direction Re-introduction of apprenticeships Introduction of private welfare, workfare measures Partial privatisation of the pension system
SD	1994–1998	+ 16.6	Pro-market guidelines Deregulation and flexibilisation of employment and intermediary services Reducing unemployment benefits, investing in training and skills
PS	1981–1986	+ 19.2	Competitiveness, specialisation, and research, flexibilisation Protection of consumption, insurance, and social protection measures, accompanied by less public intervention and neo-liberal reforms (Rocard governments 1988–1993 and Jospin 1997–2002)
SPD	1994–1998	+ 16,6	Ideological shift (*Neue Mitte* – Agenda 2010) Labour flexibilisation for SMEs and low-skilled employees Hartz Reforms (2003–2005) and activation policies
PSOE	1993–1996	+ 19.1	Bureaucracy streamlining, competitiveness, liberalisation and privatisation Rationalisation of social spending and active labour policies Since 2000, renewal of the political class (*Nueva Via*) Austerity policies and electoral defeat (2010)
PDS$_{(b)}$	1994–1996	+9.7	Conversion of identity and strategy towards the centre Welfare state "of opportunities" Labour market flexibilisation

(a) Figures indicate programmatic shifts on the left-right axis, as measured by the Manifesto Project Database, 1978–2015. Higher numbers correspond to greater shifts towards the right of the political spectrum.

(b) Given the overlap of different leftist political families (in particular, socialists and ex-communists), the data regarding Italy only considers the post-1992 leftist parties (PDS/DS/PD). The major programmatic shift took place within the newly formed PDS.

Management (Osborne & Gaebler, 1992). Changes were also introduced in social protection models (segmentation and privatisation), labour policies (active policies and flexsecurity), and industrial and trade union relations.

The programmes offered were not the only element to be re-orientated in the course of the 1990s. Some significant changes can also be found in the personnel of the parties' Members of Parliament. As shown in Table 14.2, a downsizing of the working classes came into play, along with the rise of the middle class, especially civil servants and professionals. This development suggests two things: the concern shown for some social groups to the detriment of others, and the reorganisation of how parties functioned, with elected representatives increasing in importance compared to the old apparatus. Elected representatives are the ones who interact with voters, even on the ground. While the old apparatuses recruited their employees from the working classes, equipping them with the necessary skills themselves, the "post-apparatuses" (which, according to Kirchheimer, came onto the scene in the mid-1960s) preferred to recruit people who were already prepared to

Table 14.2 Social composition of the parliamentary groups of left-wing parties, comparison between "working class" and "middle class"[a] (percentages)

Country/period	*Glorious Thirties (1945–1973)*	*Neo-liberal shift (1979–1987)*	*Third Way (1992–1997)*	*Difference (1945–1973/1992–1997)*
United Kingdom				
Working class	38.05	31.86	18.55	-19.5
"Intellectual" middle class	26.21	28.36	33.15	6.94
Denmark				
Working class	8.88	1.79	1.3	-7.58
"Intellectual" middle class	22.09	32.78	42.66	20.57
France				
Working class	8.01	1.7	4.2	-3.81
"Intellectual" middle class	39.35	51.3	38.9	-0.45
Germany				
Working class	6.07	6.69	1.2	-4.87
"Intellectual" middle class	19.36	24.45	22.2	2.84
Spain				
Working class	/	6.33	4.05	-2.28
"Intellectual" middle class	/	36	37.25	1.25
Italy[b]				
Working class	/	/	5.4	/
"Intellectual" middle class	/	/	27.45	/

(a) Working class includes blue collars and primary sector workers; "intellectual" middle class includes teachers, professor, journalists and writers, as in Savage (2008).
(b) As for Table 14.1, data for Italy only refer to the post-1992 elections (here, PDS).

Source: Elaboration of CIRCaP and Datacube database, Cotta and Best [2007].

carry out representative action and government functions, opening up to new social groups.

On the other hand, "reformist" left-wing parties had always been very careful to reformulate their offer based on what was happening at the centre of the scale of social stratification, i.e. by contributing to the political construction of the middle class (Sciarrone et al., 2011). This was the main way in which opportunities for growth were declared, including in terms of social equity: precisely during the period of the great post-war social contracts, a political project that targeted full social citizenship was introduced with great strength.

The fundamental ingredients of this project, as we know, were social-economic conditions and institutional frameworks that combined the welfare state with collective processes of upward social mobility. Once this season passed, social-democratic parties – even more so when in government – tended rather to create privileged relationships with insiders (Rueda, 2008) having radically different socio-demographic profiles compared to those who acted as the driving forces behind economic development and the growth of the welfare state.

14.3 Institutional set-ups and electoral maximisation

Drawing on the path dependent perspective that that emphasises how trajectories of political change are dependent context-specific historical, economic, and political legacies (Pierson, 2004) in what follows we present the political context and institutional frameworks in which the "left reformist" parties that we observe operate. Let us start with the overall electoral weight of left-wing parties, which, as mentioned, has been in decline in all major countries, since at least the 1970s. Looking at the last four decades in the eight countries examined, the parties that were hegemonic in their national politics are precisely the ones that have lost the most support, such as the Sap in Sweden (-12.2), the SPD in Germany (-10.9), the SD in Denmark, the PSOE in Spain (-9.8), and the Labour Party in the United Kingdom (-8.5%).

In order to collocate the electoral fluctuations of the last quarter century and the strategies for programme repositioning within the political-institutional frameworks of reference, the following were taken into account: the electoral systems, classified according to their electoral disproportionality produced between the shares of votes and the shares of seats gained by each competing party (column 1); the average number of parties represented in Parliament, which refers to the extent of electoral competition and coalition space (column 2); the total number of centre-left parties, which indicates the room for coalitions within the left (column 3); the electoral success obtained by social-democratic parties, by the Democratic Party in the US case and, in the case of Italy, by the heirs of the Italian Communist Party (column 4); the last column indicates the votes obtained by the left as a whole, trends in which indirectly reflect the degree of fragmentation of the left-wing electorate (column 5).

Let us begin with the non-inclusive growth countries. In the United States, Jimmy Carter's defeat in the 1980 presidential election paved the way for the long Republican period, with the terms of office held by Ronald Reagan (1981–1989) and George Bush (1989–1993). The Democrats returned to the presidency only when Bill Clinton was elected in 1992, which coincided with the most profound redefinition of programmes witnessed in the period considered (+19.5 on Rile, Table 14.1). After two terms in office, the Democrats lost power in the 2000 presidential election, the outcome of which was actually decided by the Supreme Court, to a Republican majority, as well as by the votes Al Gore lost to a third force competing on the "left", the Green Party. The presidency was regained by the Democrats when Barack Obama was elected in 2008, once again with proposals comprising important welfare measures, such as healthcare reform, albeit still oriented towards the centre. In the United Kingdom, Labour suffered its second consecutive electoral defeat in 1983, partially due to a schism in its moderate wing, which merged with the Social Democratic Party (SDP): this was Labour's worst result until 2015 (26.7%), 10 percentage points lower than the previous electoral round in 1979 (36.9%), when the victory went to the Conservatives, led by Margaret Thatcher. The Labour Party returned to government only 14 years later, in the 1997 elections, after achieving its highest percentage of votes since 1980 (43.2%), thanks to a decisive repositioning of the programme and the personalisation of the political offer centred around the figure of Tony Blair, elected party leader during the July 1994 congress (+38.5 on Rile, Table 14.1). This was Labour's longest experience in government, lasting until 2010, in the aftermath of the 2007 financial crisis. In 2010 Labour recorded its second performance below 30% and returned to the opposition. In the history of the Labour Party, the 1997 election was a "critical" one (Evans & Norris, 1999), decisive in redefining the party's identity and affording the possibility to benefit from at least three factors: a re-orientation of the programme towards the centre, the promise to radically revise the policies adopted by the Conservative governments (allowing the loyalty of its traditional electoral base to be preserved) and, finally, the intolerance of part of the Tory electorate towards those policies.

Hence, a picture emerges of conservative governments associated with sustained growth performance and higher inequality, prevailing in countries with non-inclusive growth where majoritarian systems foster competition between two main political forces while others play a subordinate role. Most interestingly for the hypotheses put forward here, we can observe a tendency in two-party models for political proposals to converge towards moderate and centrist positions (Iversen & Soskice, 2001), corresponding to greater uncertainty with regard to the political programme (Evans & Tilley, 2012) and a stronger personalisation of political leadership (Aarts, Blais, & Schmitt,

Table 14.3 Average votes obtained by left-wing parties, comparison by decade (percentages, 1960–2015)

Countries/Parties	*1960–1979*	*1980–1989*	*1990–2000*	*2001–2015*	*Difference 1960–1979/ 2001–2015*
United Kingdom – LP	42.3	29.2	39.1	33.8	-8.5
United States – DP[a]	54.4	46.6	48.4	49.3	-5.1
Denmark – SD	36.1	30.9	36.0	26.3	-9.8
Sweden – Sap	45.7	44.5	39.8	33.5	-12.2
France – PS	10.9	34.8	22.3	26.9	16.0
Germany – Spd	41.3	39.4	36.9	30.4	-10.9
Spain – Psoe	29.9	44.1	38.2	34.3	-9.8[b]
Italy – Pds/DS/PD[c]	/	/	19.2	26.6	+7.4

(a) Only presidential elections are considered.
(b) Because of the weak institutionalisation of the Spanish party system in the late 1970s, for PSOE, differences are calculated based on the 1980s data.
(c) As for previous tables, data for Italy only refer to the post-1992 elections.

Source: Elaboration of the Comparative Political Data Set 1960–2015 [Armingeon et al., 2018].

2011). All these contextual elements allow us to better appreciate the strategic repositioning of the Democrats and Labour in the transitional phase of the 1990s.

The political and institutional framework for Scandinavian social democratic parties, the *Sveriges socialdemokratiska arbetareparti* (SAP) in Sweden and the Danish *Socialdemokratiet* (SD), stands in clear contrast. Both governed from the end of the Second World War until the 1970s, either in a majority or in coalitions. In the mid-1970s and up until the early 1980s, both parties suffered a pronounced rupture, and their electoral base was transformed as a consequence. From this moment on, their paths separated. The Danish Social Democrats suffered a series of defeats and had to wait until 1993 to participate in a new government coalition. According to Green-Pedersen (2001), their coalition partners were the ones who led them to more moderate positions. In 2001, for the first time in Danish political history, the Social Democrats lost their relative majority. For the next ten years, a centre-right coalition remained in power, supported by the radical populist Danish People's Party (PF).

In Sweden the SAP continued to win over 40% of the vote in the 1980s and has governed almost unremittingly since 1982, reaching 45% in the 1994 legislative elections. Unlike the SD, the SAP almost monopolised the left-wing electorate, partially by virtue of low intra-block electoral competition (Table 14.4). This fact persisted even in the 1990s, which was the time when European social democracies repositioned most noticeably: suffice it to say that in 1994 the SAP and the Left Party obtained an absolute majority

Table 14.4 Main features of political and institutional frameworks (1980–2015)

Countries	*Electoral Disproportionality*[a]	*ENPP*[b]	*No. of leftist parties*[c]	*Electoral support for left "reformist" parties*[d]	*Electoral sup port for centre-left parties*[e]	*Government Coalitions*
United Kingdom	15.8	2.3	1	34.0	34.0	Labour ('97–'10)
United States	11.6	1.65	1	50.0	0.0	Democratic Party ('93–'01) Democratic Party ('09–'15)
Denmark	1.3	5.1	2.7	30.3	42.4	SD ('80–'82) SD+RV ('93-'01)**** SD+RV+SPP ('11–'15)
Sweden	1.9	4.0	2.1	38.2	45.2	Sap ('82–'91) Sap ('94–'06) Sap + Green ('14–'15)
France	19.3	2.9	2.8	28.7	39.9	PS+PCF ('81–'84) PS (>'86) PS+MRG+Green ('90–'93) PS+PCF+Green+MRG ('97–'02) PS+ Green+PRG ('12-15)
Germany	4.0	3.5	1.5	35.0	39.5	Spd+Fdp ('80–'82) Spd+Green ('98–'05) Cdu/Cdu+Spd ('05–'09) Cdu/Cdu+Spd ('13–'15)
Italy	7.7	5.2	2.9	21.1	35.4	Pentapartito ('80–'92) Pds+Ppi+Udeur+Verdi+Pdci ('96–'01) Ulivo+Rif.Com.+Verdi+Udeur ('06–'08) Pd+Udc+SC+Ncd ('13–'15)
Spain	5.8	2.9	2.1	38.0	46.3	Psoe ('82–'96) Psoe ('04–'11)

(a) Degree of disproportionality based on Gallagher, Election indices dataset [2017].
(b) Effective number of political parties in parliament (1980–2015 averages) based on Gallagher, Election indices dataset [2017].
(c) For the United States we included the Democratic Party, despite its labelling as "liberal" by Armingeon et al. [2018].
(d) 1980–2015 averages based on Armingeon et al., Comparative Political Database [2018]. For the United States, the Democratic Party is considered.
(e) Electoral support for parties labelled as "social-democratic", "left-socialist" and "communist/post-communist" in Armingeon et al. [2018].

(51.4%) and governed without distractions. Subsequently, this success began to wane (Aylott & Bolin, 2007, 621), with progressive electoral losses: votes for the SAP in fact fell by 5 percentage points in the 2006 general election and by another 5 in the 2010 election, while votes for centre-right parties increased significantly, particularly Modraterna (+11% in 2006) and, above all, the populist right-wing party *Sverigedemokraterna*, which since its initial entry in the *Riksdag* in 2010 with 5.7% of the votes has seen its electoral base triple, obtaining 17.5% of votes in the 2018 general election.

In countries with egalitarian inclusive growth, the political-institutional context in which social-democratic parties operate presents unique traits in spite of these downward trajectories. In both Denmark and Sweden, these parties manage to govern for lengthy periods in coalitions with central groups (Christian-Protestant and liberal parties) or other left-wing actors (radical and green parties). The sheer scope of these coalitions, together with electoral strength and governmental functions, thus fuels a compromise, concocting a political proposal that mingles pro-market elements with more traditional ones and non-market coordination policies (Anderson, 2001; 2004). The conditions required to dismantle the fundamental features of the pre-existing inclusive growth models (Borioni, 2011), the foundations of which were laid in the 30-year post-war period, are not generated in this context.

With dualist inclusive growth, seen in countries of continental Europe, an intermediate situation prevails. With 40.9% in the 1998 general election, the German SPD returned to government (in a coalition with *Die Grünen*) after 16 years of opposition. The new leader, Gerard Schröder, presented himself as the candidate promoting renewal and a new centrist orientation: the *Neue Mitte*. Schröder took up part of New Labour's project of economic modernisation and technological reconversion, with the aim of improving German competitiveness in the global economy (Busch & Manow, 2001). However, the results were ambivalent among different groups of voters: while the party gained consensus among the middle class and in business circles, the privatisation of public services and the flexibilisation of the labour market alienated part of its traditional electorate. Partly as a consequence of these choices, in July 2005 a group of dissidents, together with former GDR communists (PDS), joined the Electoral Alternative for Work and Social Justice (WASG), which two years later engendered *Die Linke*. A shrunken consensus had already scaled down the SPD in the 2005 elections, when it consented to a *Große Koalition* with the CDU–CSU. Under the guidance of the CDU leader Angela Merkel as the first chancellor, since then the loss of support for the SPD has continued, as has the steady decline of the CDU–CSU alliance. An essential feature to underline here for our research is that, in the case of Germany, the transitional phase of the 1990s led to a repositioning that (partially) hinged on workfare policies and progressive cutbacks in the amount of social protection (Palier & Thelen, 2010), implemented in open conflict with trade unions (Streeck, 2005).

The electoral path followed by the French Socialist Party (PSF) is also closely linked to coalescing strategies within the left. As illustrated in Table 14.4, the relative weight of the Socialists is on average lower than elsewhere, and second only to Denmark and Italy, to which case we shall return presently. Unlike the SPD, the PSF governed during the 1980s and part of the 1990s (1981 to 1993). There was also a two-year period of co-existence between the Mitterrand presidency and the Chirac government (1986–1988). In 1981, France inherited the deflationary policies of the centre-right coalition led by Giscard d'Estaing and his mentor, prime minister and economist Raymond Barre. The programme of the presidential candidate Mitterrand, supported by the PSF in a coalition with the *Parti Communiste Français* (PCF), was inspired by the so-called "French-style Keynesianism" in opposition to the austerity of the liberal right, promising an agenda based on nationalisations and an "austerity with a human face", which coincided with the Mauroy government (until 1984). However, as early as 1984 the Fabius government, excluding the communists, abandoned the nationalisation plan and resumed a deflationary economic policy (Bliek & Parguez, 2008). Thus, when the legislative elections were held in 1986, the left suffered a defeat that led to an enforced *cohabitation* between Mitterrand and the Chirac government.

The PSF took the helm once again in 1988, when Mitterrand was re-elected and the Rocard government took office. Rocard, Mitterrand's rival in the PSF, would push the party towards even more centrist positions (Attali, 1995), forming a government with a socialist base but with members of civil society and personalities from centrist parties: the aim was to obtain a majority in parliament, which had been elected in 1986 and was dominated by the centre-right. The proposition was coolly received by the centrist parties and as a result Mitterrand decided to dismiss the *Assemblée Nationale*. In May 1988, the Socialists, together with their allied parties, obtained a narrower majority. Internal cleavages and discontent following the economic and fiscal crisis that was sweeping Europe at the turn of the 1990s was reflected at the ballot box, with 1993 turning out to be one of the worst years for the PSF. The outcome of the elections was a second co-existence (Balladur government) and the defeat of the socialist candidate in the 1995 presidential election, won by Jacques Chirac. The PSF returned to government in 1997 with a renewed *majorité plurielle*, with the Communists, the *Parti radical de gauche* and the Green Party. However, in the 2002 presidential elections, the first held since the 2000 constitutional reform, this coalition was unable to stand its ground; the PSF came third in the first round of the presidential election and Chirac and J.-M. Le Pen, the leader of the Front National, took part in the run-off. Subsequently, a decade led by the centre-right began, ending in 2012 with the election of Hollande and a new majority in the *Assemblée Nationale*. The strategies contained in the programmes of the SPD and the PSF in the countries showing the dualistic inclusive growth model seem to be characterised by internal cleavages within the centre-left. In these countries, the progressive dispersion of the socialist vote and the oscillating internal conflict within the left were superseded by governments of *Große Koalition* and co-existence, which endeavoured to preserve the model of the welfare state aimed mainly at the most organised component of labour, nevertheless exacerbating certain aspects of segmentation, and thus widening the gap between insiders and outsiders. The orientation of the socialists as of the late 1980s in France and the mid-1990s in Germany is ambivalent, with the objective of alleviating pro-market pressure by granting more attention (as in the case of Labour) to a distribution focused on consumption, or on financing social insurance benefits, in addition to universal minimum income measures (Palier, 2010).

Two different political and institutional scenarios emerge as we move on to study the Mediterranean countries with non-inclusive low growth: on the one hand, the electorally solid *Partido Socialista Obrero Español (PSOE)*, which ruled the country for more than half of the period considered, and on the other the Italian left, weakened by internal fragmentation. Until the 1990s, it hinged on the *Partito Socialista Italiano (PSI)* (Italian Socialist Party), a member of the Socialist International, with a modest electoral success (around 10%), which coexisted in government with the Christian Democrats and other minor parties. Moreover, the Communist Party as a major player undeniably held sway. In the wake of "Bribesville" corruption scandals, which swept away from parliament almost the entire political class, the Socialist Party together with the Christian Democrats (DC) left the stage. At this point, the Communist Party changed its name and political position, converging towards a programme akin to those presented by European social-democratic parties. But above all, the 1993 majoritarian electoral reform and the dissolution of the Christian Democratic Party paved the way to a scenario similar to a two-party system, claimed in the name of governability and public morality. On one side, led by Berlusconi, a composite, centre-right line-up, self-proclaimed liberal, appealed to a conspicuous share of the Christian Democrat electorate and assimilated a substantial part of the DC's politicians; on the opposite side, a centre-left line-up was split between the heirs of the PCI and the DC left, mostly aligned with the positions of European social democracy, and a variegated minority remained close to the positions of the radical left. This rupture that considerably undermined the competitiveness of the party, giving free range to the centre-right for quite some time.

The case of Spain shows both similarities and differences when compared to Italy: from 1980 to 2015, the PSOE obtained on average at least half of the total left-wing votes, assuming the role of dominant party. In fact, the PSOE held the absolute majority of seats for three consecutive elections (1982, 1986, and 1989), reaching its highest level of support after the so-called "electoral earthquake" of 1982 (57.7%), which not only laid the foundations of the long socialist dominance under Felipe Gonzales, but also constituted the Spanish bipartisanship, pivoting on the PSOE on one side and on *Alianza Popular* (*Partido Popular* since 1989) on the other. In this moment, the PSOE's advantage lay in the fact that its support extended more towards the right than the left (Gunther, Sani, & Shabad, 1986). Notwithstanding the fact that the Spanish social democracy managed to shed its traditional ideological heritage during 14 consecutive years of government (Sanchez Cuenca, 2014), it nevertheless gradually lost support (Table 14.3), to the point that in 1993 Gonzalez, in his fourth consecutive term as premier, found himself leading a minority government, externally supported by *Izquierda Unida*, a coalition of small parties headed by the communists (Field & Botti, 2013). The PSOE government was cut short in 1996: against a backdrop of economic crisis, inflation, and rising unemployment, not to mention embroilment in corruption scandals, it was narrowly defeated by the *Partido Popular*, which then formed a minority government with the support of Catalan and Basque nationalists. This experience came to an end in 2004, when the PSOE returned to power, led by José Luis Rodríguez Zapatero. The new government launched an anti-cyclical investment strategy to stem rising unemployment, but at the same time accentuated its turn towards the centre. Since the 2000s, *Nueva Vìa* has renewed its political figures and carried out a thorough programmatic and organisational revision of the party, aiming to recover the left and centre-left following that had gone adrift since the second half of the 1990s. And yet, the party appealed to the centre electorate with its programme and the policies implemented by its governments (Field and Botti, 2013). The financial crisis of 2007–2008 forced it to incontrovertibly change tack, which culminated in May 2010 with the adoption of drastic austerity measures, in accordance with European directives, which paved the way for the electoral defeats of 2010 and 2015 (Cordero & Montero, 2015).

On the whole, in the years in which the left-wing forces regained, at least in part, votes and went back to being active in government, the programmes they presented opened up to the role of the market, a deregulation of labour, and a downsizing of welfare. In Anglo-Saxon countries, where the electoral system tends to produce single-party majorities, the governing left-wing parties continue to pursue the privatisation and liberalisation policies implemented by previous governments. In countries where the left has been in government in coalitions with other parties, whether denominational, liberal, or green, a similar outcome can be observed. The implementation of pro-market policies is the result of changes in an approach to programmes that had already gained a foothold in the previous decade. In order to try and attract the middle-class vote, left-wing parties focus not only on new programmes but also on an internal organisational renewal and the modernisation of their image through a real incorporation of "auxiliary institutions" (Wring, 2007, 75) in the party structures: experts, journalists, economists coming from outside the relational network of reference, who focus on finding consensus among moderate voters and who, at the same time, acquire a growing influence on the party's strategic choices. In this context, the criteria through which to politically construct, represent and address the problem of inequality have also been manifestly overhauled (Webb, 1994; Holtz-Bacha, 2002; Mudge, 2018). From the constituency-oriented perspective, in which the target of the policy proposal was a sociologically defined constituency, the parties have shifted to an angle in which the offer is formulated on the basis of polls and market surveys, thus taking as its target the potential electorates identified from time to time through these surveys. In addition to the changes in the programmes proposed, in the distinguishing features of the political party and in their organisational structure, another significant turnaround can be seen in the relationship with trade unions, discussed below.

14.4 Relations with trade unions

One of the mainstays of European social democracy can be identified in the establishing of strong, stable and in some cases institutionalised relationships with trade unions (Mathers & Upchurch, 2011). Portrayed in the literature as "symbiotic", "Siamese twins", or "branches of the same tree" (Jansson, 2017; Mattina, 2018; Carrieri, 2019), parties and trade unions have been intertwined for decades through a rationale of reciprocity construed by some in a material sense, since parties offered trade unions the possibility to influence decision-making processes, obtaining in exchange a pool of members, potential voters, and even funders (Allern & Bale, 2017). Others, instead, have emphasised a shared feeling of upholding the same strain of values and identity (Carrieri, 2019).

In the 1980s, this link began to falter in many countries. Some held parties responsible for alienating trade unions, deeming them as remnants of the past, "useless burdens" that hindered the drive for modernisation (Kitschelt, 1994). According to others, it was trade unions that distanced themselves from parties as a consequence of their declining attention to the working class (Piazza, 2001; Parsons, 2015). However, there is unanimous agreement that relations between the social democratic parties and the trade unions deteriorated considerably (Howell, 2001, 7–8). This was no small decline, given that the synergy between parties and trade unions was in all likelihood decisive in improving the living conditions of workers and implementing the development of the welfare state, but also "for the equalising effects that resulted from policies aimed at a fairer distribution of the wealth produced by labour" (Mattina, 2018, 1). In other words, this synergy on the one hand bound social democratic parties to a commitment to reconciling development and redistribution, and on the other provided them with the political support necessary to promote such a reconciliation.

Historically, the relationship between parties and unions has taken the shape of a variety of traditions and institutional practices of concertation, the latter inevitably changing direction periodically. Fluctuations in the amount of common action agreed upon are likely to have an impact on the quality of relations between unions and political parties (Allern & Bale, 2017). In the rationale of exchange alluded to above, in countries where concertation is implemented on a regular and continuous basis, maintaining relations between unions and political parties was "crucial" for the latter, especially in cases where the rate of unionisation was high (Jansson, 2017). While high levels of concertation have been significantly correlated with solid bonds between parties and unions (see, among others, Padget & Paterson, 1991), it has also been pointed out that this interrelation should theoretically be invertible, i.e. the need for close relations between trade unions and political parties should be reduced when unions potentially have access to negotiations with government and employers. Notwithstanding certain similarities in approaches, here as well, we shall see that the paths that emerge are anything but linear. Against the backdrop of a prevailing tendency to significantly downsize the relationship between trade unions and social democratic parties, this drive towards uniformisation comes up against greater "resistance" in countries with inclusive growth, which uncoincidentally show higher levels of consultation. Relations between parties and trade unions becomes progressively weaker, on the other hand, where consultation is sporadic or absent, as in non-inclusive growth countries, even in the presence of organisations that are structurally interconnected from the outset, as in the case of the United Kingdom.

Studies offering an empirical survey of the types of relationship between trade unions and parties in diachronic and comparative terms have come up against the difficulty of summarising, in the different cases, the complexity, multiplicity and different degrees of formalisation and intensity of the relations existing between the two actors. We therefore propose once again the typology of Ludlam et al. (2002), which allows us to contemplate two important aspects of the relationship between trade unions and parties at the same time: the organisational integration of trade unions within parties (i.e. how much trade unions are represented in the internal organs of the parties) and their degree of influence on the decision-making processes of the parties themselves (Figure 14.1). Combining these two aspects, it is possible to outline four possible models of relations: (1) a "union-dominance" model, where unions occupy leading roles within the party's organisational structure and are at the same time in a position to influence its internal decision-making process; (2) a "party-union bonding type" model, when unions do not influence

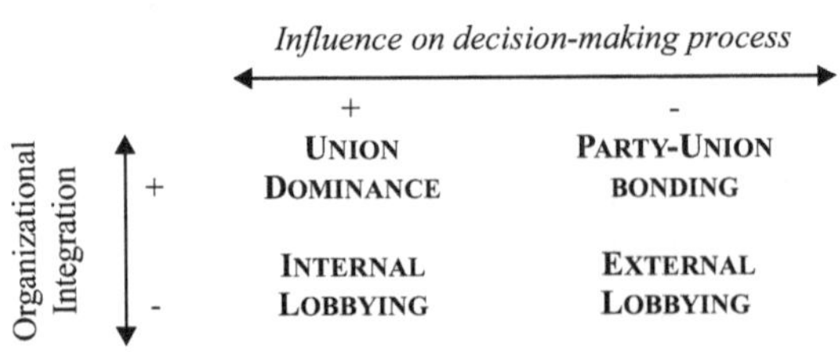

Figure 14.1 A typology of relations between left-wing parties and trade unions.

internal decision-making processes despite occupying high-status positions within the party; (3) an "internal lobbying" model, where trade unions are able to influence party decision-making without being integrated into organisational structures; (4) finally, an "external lobbying" model, which corresponds to a real distance between the two figures. Here, trade unions not only hold no high-ranking positions within parties but also have no ability to influence internal decision-making processes.

The analysis proposed here shows that, by the late 1990s, the prevailing relationship (with the exception of the relations between SAP, SD and the respective Swedish and Danish trade union confederations), falls into the fourth quadrant, with the unions reduced to the status of any other external interest group.

One of the first and most striking cases of a real distance is between Labour and the trade unions. From a context in which union members were automatically party members, where the Unions were organically represented with reserved seats in Labour's main decision-making bodies, and in which a strong influence on internal decision-making was exerted through a system of block voting (Koeble, 1987; Minkin, 1991; Ludlam et al., 2002), the trade unions' decision-making power was progressively weakened, following the modernisation sought by the leader Neil Kinnock during the 1980s, and proceeding to the abolition of trade union representation within the party's organisation (and block voting) after the 1993 statutory reforms. The Labour Party was relegated to the opposition, and the numerous focus groups established by communications experts, hired to recover electoral support, pointed towards an old, divided and excessively unionised party. If the aim was therefore to modernise the party and broaden its social base, there was no choice but to break the association between the party and the unions, so rooted in the English electorate and in the business community (Howell, 2001, 29). The breaking of the old bonds between party and unions in the UK case coincided with Labour's reformulation of the form of representation it offered.

In the case of the United States, due to the absence of a socialist tradition (Lipset & Marks, 2000) and the lack of organic links between unions and parties, the conditions at the outset were radically different from those in Europe. Yet this had not prevented, at the time of the New Deal, a preferential relationship to be forged between the Democratic Party and the American Federation of Labor and Congress of Industrial Organizations (AFL-CIO). For decades, the unions helped support the Democratic Party with substantial funding, volunteer work and electoral mobilisation, despite not being formally linked to the Democrats. The extent to which union backing was rewarded by the party is a matter of debate among scholars, who have sometimes described this relationship as "one-way" (Francia, 2010). What is certain is that these relations have deteriorated significantly since the 1980s.

Notwithstanding descriptions in the literature of the two Nordic countries, Sweden and Denmark, as examples of a strong relationship between social democracy and trade unions, the links between the two organisations in these countries have weakened considerably. As we shall see, however, this "divorce" (Aylott, 2003) does not seem as conspicuous as elsewhere. In both cases, as with the Labour Party and the Unions, it is a constitutive relationship, the two institutions being organisationally interconnected since their origins in the early twentieth century. As such, the decision to make membership in the Swedish Social Democratic Party (SAP) automatic for workers associated with trade union confederations (*Landsorganizationen, LO*) was made as early as the founding conference of the latter (Gidlung, 1992, 106). The founding leader of the SAP, Hjalmar Branting, also stated at one of the first national congresses that the trade union movement was, and would remain, a fundamental reference for the political action of the party (Aylott, 2003, 371). In both countries the bond was fortified by permanent trade union representation in the executive bodies of the two social democratic parties, and customary meetings with their representatives in parliament (Allern et al., 2007). As with Labour and the trade unions, signs of distancing became apparent towards the second half of the 1980s, with the SAP repealing the automatic membership rule, while the SD chose to shut down the channels of union representation within its executive bodies. Trade union influence on political decisions has nevertheless remained considerable, regardless of these changes, as have the contacts between the two organisations at both central and local levels (Christiansen & Rommetvedt, 1999; Aylott, 2003).

In contrast to the Nordic and Anglo-Saxon cases, the *Deutscher Gewerkschaftsbund* (DGB, German trade union confederation) and the SPD were never linked by formal inter-organisational relations, nor did trade union representatives ever wield any decision-making power within the party. The DGB was reconstituted after the Second World War according to a principle of non-partisanship, bringing together members of all political orientations. That said, the trade union and the SPD traditionally maintained special contacts between their leaderships. Informal contacts were the order of the day, especially with regard to policies that most closely affected trade union interests, such as labour, social and economic policies (Markovits, 1986). In the case of Germany, the rift came about in the second half of the 1990s, following the reform agenda advanced by the red–green coalition and the redefined programme of the SPD, which progressively ostracised the trade unions (Nachtway, 2013; Jackson & Thelen, 2015), so much so that the latter have been compared to an interest group seeking cooperation with any political figure (in the context of a splintered left) willing to promote their demands, first and foremost *Die Linke* (Spier, 2017).

In the case of France, among the factors that most jeopardised the establishment of formal links between trade unions and the PSF, we can observe the fragmentation of the political scene, including both the left wing and trade unions, as well as the significantly lower rate of unionisation compared to the European average. In determining the country's political and economic choices, the weight of the trade unions was thus rather marginal, only partly offset by the statist tradition. Nevertheless, as in the case of Germany, members of the executives of the two main trade unions (*Confédération Française Démocratique du Travail, CFDT*; *Confédération Générale du Travail, CGT*) were often called upon by socialist-led ministries as experts, especially with regard to matters of industrial policies (Parsons, 2017). Two key moments of estrangement are reported in the literature, which on closer inspection correspond to the two main re-positionings towards the centre of the PSF. The first dates to the mid-1980s, coinciding with the PSF's modernisation plans and the austerity policies pursued by the government; the second – which would actually go on to mark the PSF's official divorce from the trade unions (Parsons, 2015) – took place at the 1994 Congress, at which statements the trade unions' downsized role were made by the then Secretary Jospin.

More often than not, issues such as the fragmentation of the left, the exclusion of the Communist Party from the government, the plurality of trade unions and a system of industrial relations with little institutionalisation have led researchers to draw similarities between the Italian and the French cases, but the situation in this instance is more complex. Trade unions were stronger in terms of members and traditionally had preferential relations with certain parties: the Italian CGIL with the PCI and PSI, the UIL with the PSI and the minor parties of the centre, the CISL with the DC. These relations weakened with the strengthening of workers' organisations in the 1970s, alongside attempts to develop trade union unity (see, among others, Lange et al., 1982). After the attempt made by the technical government led by Ciampi in 1993 to institutionalise concertation, the reconfiguration of the party system thwarted, on the contrary, any sort of preferential relationship. While the CISL and UIL continued to communicate with the governing parties, relations with the CGIL remained problematical, even with the centre-left.

The relationship between the PSOE and the trade union confederation (*Unión General de Trabajadores*, UGT) is quite different, once again as a consequence of a feature unique to this country: the Spanish democratic consolidation following the Franco dictatorship was heavily influenced by socialist reformism. From the 1979 Congress onwards, the party secretary Gonzales was concerned with maintaining enough room for manoeuvre to deflect too much leverage from internal factions and the trade union confederations, despite these being historically very close to the socialist party (Puhle, 2001). Relations deteriorated with the first economic policies that characterised the PSOE government in the 1980s, until the general strike organised by the trade unions against the PSOE on 14 December 1988 and the abolition of automatic union membership, which had been established by the new statutory rules adopted by the party at the 1990 congress (Gillespie, 1990).

This distancing of social democratic parties from trade unions is consistent with their strategy of redefining their constituency at the expense of labour. For a long time, these parties had identified employment relations as the preferred area for politically reconciling the needs for economic development and social equity. The reconversion of the 1980s, the financial crisis of the early 1990s and the transition to post-Fordism all contributed to sparking off a general redefinition of the vocabulary and solutions proposed by left-wing parties to mediate between growth and inclusion, a mediation that represented one of their traditional and constitutive missions, albeit in different forms and with different intensity depending on the context. It was precisely the 1990s that represented a time of transition, but also a moment in which the fortunes of trade union relations in different countries started to diverge. The left wing governed almost uninterruptedly throughout the 30 years of post-war growth in the Scandinavian countries, where, in addition to laying the foundations of welfare, it consolidated its neo-corporatist tradition by fuelling the strength of the trade unions, which showed greater resilience even after the 1990s. In fact, the trade unions maintained their influence on the social democratic parties' internal decision-making processes, despite the slackening of their founding ties, forging their course of action and creating further incentives for negotiating policies (Burroni, 2016). Elsewhere, albeit with due differences, the left instead took on governmental roles precisely when capitalism was becoming "disorganised" and the economic competition induced by globalisation was intensifying, with significant transformations precisely on the organisation of labour, which was transfigured both in quantitative and qualitative terms. Industrial divestment and the legacy of privatisation had reduced employment rates, while technology, relocation and the financialisation of the economy opened the way to the dilemma of jobless growth. In response to this scenario, even the left-wing parties contributed to the rhetoric of the untenability of welfare costs: with the space for a proposal centred around full employment now ever narrower, the reformist proposals heeded the demands of the (labour) market, focusing on deregulation and the reduction of protection to favour employment (Gallino, 2007). The *fil rouge* linking these solutions lies in the fundamental shift from a collective to an individualised notion of work (Castel, 2004), two visions that refer to different models of social justice. The idea of "equality of positions", associated with a representation of society in terms of socio-professional stratification and/or social classes, was abandoned in favour of "equal opportunities" (Dubet, 2010, 49). The shift from one conception to another of work and equality strongly conditioned the political proposals made by left-wing parties: the idea of a society based on equality of positions requires a "general social contract" to be implemented through universalist policies, while the idea of equality of opportunity shifts the focus to individual "contracts". This same individualised and competitive conception of work favours the abandonment of neo-corporative regulation schemes and the adoption of de-collectivised criteria of bargaining, that is, forms of decentralised or, more precisely, individual negotiation (Regini, 2003).

One of the dominant features of European social democracy, i.e. its organic and institutionalised link with workers' representation associations (Taylor, Mathers, & Upchurch 2011, 287), was replaced, although in different forms (again depending on the national context), by more informal and discontinuous relations. Situations of strong organisational integration of trade unions within party organisations are no longer a part of political reality. The observations of Allern and Bale (2017, 329) regarding the effects of different levels of concertation on the "weak and insignificant" relations between trade unions and political parties, still need to be confirmed. In fact, with the exception, once again, of countries showing inclusive growth, there would seem to be no clear association between the degree of involvement of the social parties in policymaking activities and the relations between the two figures.

In conclusion, the redefinition of the programmes proposed by left-wing parties, which unfolded as we have seen chiefly from the 1980s onwards, was accompanied by significant changes in the selection of political personnel, in the internal organisational framework, and also in the traditional relations between these political formations and trade unions. But what are the links between this momentous shift and the policies actually pursued, particularly when these parties had governmental responsibilities? And what consequences does this bear for electoral results? These questions are addressed in the following pages.

14.5 Left-wing parties and the challenges of change

Programmes that undergo revisions, and also rifts, are a constitutive part of the history of political parties and in the case of left-wing parties they are far from exceptional. In the long term, they are by and large moderate reconsiderations, dictated by a fundamental motive. Left-wing parties were born as outsiders in relation to the political, but also economic establishment, and to get into government, they have to change their programmes, primarily to be recognised by the establishment, and secondly to increase their chances of electoral success. To name a few revisions: the Bad Godesberg congress in 1956 for the SPD, the Epinay congress in 1971, in which the SFIO became the PSF, or the Suresnes congress for the PSOE, which in 1974 even anticipated the fall of Francoism, or the PCI 1991 Congress, which dissolved the party and formed the PDS.

If the reasons as to why parties recalibrate their proposals are discernible, for electoral purposes and reasons of legitimacy, their amendments and reconsiderations are nevertheless complex. They are complicated internally because there is always a conflict between defenders of orthodoxy and innovators. There are always those who oppose rethinking, whether for idealistic reasons or simply to maintain positions of power. Revisions of the offer are also complicated from an electoral viewpoint: risks of dissatisfying a more or less significant part of the party's original electoral base are high and there are no certainties with regard to identifying a new electorate.

The script for party turnarounds is more or less pre-established: management teams are renewed and programmes revised while the political programmes are redesigned. The objective is twofold: to gain new voters while holding on to those at risk of leaving, or recuperating those who have already left. Nevertheless, renewing the constituency may be preferable to clinging to the old one. Generally speaking, parties may avoid making of overly drastic choices, endeavouring to reconcile their new offer with the former. It should be noted that, thanks to the mass media, contemporary parties are no longer oriented towards working on the loyalty of their constituency, nurturing it with care, or giving special attention to the local areas in which they are based. Their inclination is to acquire voters only with a view to the next election, without making too many commitments, focusing on the leadership or on some specific issue to which the electorate is more sensitive. Yet the problem of not losing the most loyal voters still arises and as such, there is always a substantial margin of ambivalence in any renewed political offer.

This ambivalence can be observed in the possible readings of the script for change. One interpretation is that the change is proposed to the original constituency precisely as a means of achieving traditional goals, while at the same time reaching out towards new segments of the electorate. A second interpretation consists in the old constituency being told it needs new goals that are more in line with its current needs. A third interpretation is that the old constituency is implicitly considered to be inessential, although the party will nevertheless claim to maintain its original vocation, that is, not preserve the established order of things but change it by persuading new portions of the electorate. Intertwining these interpretations is also possible, with emphasis on the renewal, or confirmation, of party leadership in the context of a more explicit or more circumspect renewal of the political programme.

The "about-face" concerning all major left-wing parties from the 1980s onwards should be re-read in the light of these principles. This phenomenon is worthy of note first and foremost for the direction taken by the change. The left-wing parties all shared the idea that the transition from Fordism to post-Fordism had renewed the social foundations and preferences of the entire electorate, including their own, and at the same time agreed on upgrading the policies that had prevailed until then, which consisted in the social-democratic-Keynesian compromise: the state's fiscal crisis had brought to light its problems in its sustainability.

Society had evolved, the economy was no longer the same, the labour market was different and, costs aside, the demand for welfare was also being updated. In short, it was convenient to conceive left-wing politics in a different way, closer to the market-oriented perspective. Not only that: according to a common diagnosis, the old working-class and popular electoral base was rapidly disappearing and new challenges arose for the left, addressing new classes, endeavouring to orient the transformations in such a way as to safeguard the principles of solidarity and justice that distinguish the party's history. Instead of adopting a strategy of direct resistance, Western leftists argued that a strategy of attack was preferable: not opposing change, but leading it.

The history of New Labour can be considered exemplary. Tony Blair, the party's leader, was an exponent of a new generation of politicians, alien to the old Labour tradition, which was strongly linked to the unions, and he staked his chances on an ambitious project of "modernisation" of the party and the country, in line with Anthony Giddens' Third Way doctrine (Giddens, 1999). Dismissing old Labour's egalitarian ambitions as obsolete, this tenet took into account some of Thatcherism's criticisms of the welfare state, but, rather than putting itself in the hands of the market, called for it to be reorganised and reconciled with social cohesion. Individualism was seen as a legitimate sentiment and individualisation an irreversible process. However, its potential could be exploited to promote growth by enhancing civil society and community ties for the benefit of social cohesion. Further ingredients included a break with the trade unions and their "corporatist" claims, a reform of public administrations in the light of New Public Management, giving ample space to experts and tapping into progressive liberalism (to protect minorities), which was already characterising the Clinton presidency (Fraser, 2017). In addition, now that welfare was considered inefficient, seen as a trap for the underprivileged classes, it had to be reformed. The cure for exclusion consisted in offering equal opportunities rather than assistance: the training required to operate autonomously in the market was promoted, as protection from its drawbacks and to climb the social ladder. The solution offered by workfare was to invest in training and facilitate access to employment.

This solution would soon set the standard. Not only did the leading Western left-wing parties agree with this sort of policies, they also implemented them. Each party obviously had its own history, its own symbols, its own codes, but the trend was general. In return, the repercussions were variable. In particular, this restyling of left-wing parties had an uneven impact on their action in government, their styles of governance, and, of course, on their policies.

This variety of outcomes is not easily explained. A great many factors come into play and the weight they exert varies according to the context. Drawing up an inventory for the last 30 years, we see an initial cluster of variables consisting of left-wing parties' positions in the party system: how long these parties have governed, the nature of their electoral following, what kind of relations they had with the opposing parties, and whether they had rivals on the left.

Duration in government turns out to be very diverse. In the 40-year period between 1980 and 2020, at one extreme we see the more favourable situation of the Swedish social democrats, who governed for 30 years, sometimes in coalition governments with centrist or more radical leftist formations. At the other end there are the Italian centre-left parties, which following the coexistence of the PSI with the DC until the early 1990s, have since governed under different guises for more or less 12 years, always in coalition governments, as composite as they were unstable, with centrist and radical leftist formations, at the same time or following one another. In the middle we find the Spanish Socialists, who were in government for 24 years; the French Socialists for 20 years having the presidency of the republic and for 7 years in the form of a coexistence; the Danish Social Democrats for 18; the American Democrats, who led the country for 16 years out of 40, even if only for short periods was the president backed by Congress and therefore able, if he so wished, to introduce a coherent inclusive policy; Labour, which governed the United Kingdom for 14 years; the German SPD, which governed for 10 years, plus 8 in a coalition with the CDU/CSU. A long presence in government is not in itself a guarantee of success, at least from an electoral viewpoint. For all the socialist parties, electoral results have been disappointing. The fact that Labour was able to implement its programme continuously from 1996 to 2010 did not prevent it from losing more than a third of its constituency.

The electoral outcomes of the left-wing parties are illustrated in Table 14.3. It is well known that, in addition to these results, the electoral system is very important. A significant difference exists between a first-past-the-post system, which almost necessarily produces single-party governments (as was generally the case with the American Democrats and Labour), or a system that favours them, such as the two-round system or run-off voting, adopted by the French, and proportional systems, the outcomes of which are more uncertain. The Spanish system, for example, proved highly selective up until the current Sanchez government, while elsewhere proportional systems have often led to coalition governments.

Equally influential are the similarities and differences in political programmes between the left-wing parties and their rivals, as well as their political styles. It is one thing to have a dialectic of opposing policies that intentionally contradict those of the previous government and quite another to have a less turbulent dialectic where, despite changes in government, some continuity, or some forms of incremental change, can be discerned. The gap between the American parties has grown wider and wider since the Reagan administration. The Republicans have become an ideological party, while the Democrats tend towards pragmatism. British Labour moved considerably closer to the programme of the Conservatives under Blair's leadership, only to break away again at the time of the Brexit. The French parties have had their ups and downs, but the statist orientation they share with their opponents has helped to narrow the gap, at least until the Sarkozy presidency. Divergences between the Scandinavian parties have been less dramatic, while a distinctive feature of Spanish and Italian politics has always been a marked polarisation.

A second cluster of variables refers to the history of the left within each democratic regime. Some left parties are united, some are splintered and some have recently disbanded. The American Democratic Party has never had any serious rivals on the left. Neither, with the exception of a brief period in the 1980s, has the Labour Party. *Die Linke* has provided competition for the German SPD since 2005, while the French Socialists have always suffered some rivalry on the left, first from the Communists and later from smaller formations. Modest competition on the left has come from the Scandinavian Social Democrats, while the dominance of the PSOE in Spain has been assured by the electoral system, which has long marginalised first the Communists, then *Izquierda Unida*. The Italian left was divided between socialists and communists until 1989, after which the former disappeared and the latter converted. But the cleavages widened from the 1990s onwards, until a part of the left was unified in the Democratic Party, incorporating other political cultures, in a somewhat precarious amalgam.

The history of welfare systems should also be taken into consideration. Scandinavia's welfare systems are old, solid, and well rooted in the very identity of the two countries mainly discussed in this research. Those who originally designed them with a universalist orientation, the social-democratic parties themselves, have considerably downsized them. However, the persistent influence of the trade unions and the consequent peculiar model of industrial relations have made it possible to maintain these systems, albeit at somewhat more modest levels of performance, partially thanks to the marketisation of many services, particularly in Sweden. The American welfare system has been neither as extensive nor as proficient as the those in Europe. Unprotected by trade unions, it has suffered above all from reduced financial resources, sometimes deliberately sought, sometimes fostered by conflicts between the presidency and Congress (Mettler, 2011). The UK once boasted an long-standing universalist welfare system, established in 1945 by the Attlee government, inspired by the Beveridge Report, and which from 1951 to 1979 was also confirmed by Conservative governments, constituting one of the keystones of the post-war consensus (Kavanagh & Morris, 1989). Since 1979, with no chance of resistance from either Labour's opposition or the Unions, welfare has been heavily slashed by financial cuts and Thatcher's policies, while its reconstitution by New Labour, which also increased public spending, was hampered by the restrictive prescriptions of the Third Way doctrine.

The post-war consensus, with regard to welfare and also a certain way of understanding the democratic regime, was a general trend. The Christian Democrats in Italy made their entry in 1949 with the Fanfani Plan, and further measures were adopted in the following years. However, it was only from centre-left governments onwards that the construction of welfare was further refined with doses of universalism, nevertheless remaining very dependent on the role attributed to families. Financial constraints, from the 1990s onwards, gave centre-right governments the opportunity to retrench. The left wing, in its periods of government, could do little to defend itself and the trade unions, moreover, were divided among themselves. In Spain more or less the same thing happened, where the PSOE was responsible for both reinforcing welfare and downscaling it, as later accentuated by the governments of the *Partido Popular*. Although curtailed by the centre-right parties in government, the role of trade unions in Germany and mass mobilisation in France allowed some resistance to the benefit of the protected segments of the labour market. In France, the cutback accelerated from the Sarkozy presidency onwards, after which Hollande didn't lift a finger to reverse the trend.

In conclusion, we shall now put our analysis in order, before mapping the points of our reasoning on left-wing parties onto the four models of more or less inclusive growth identified in our research.

14.6 Growth and inclusion in politics and policies

Governmental structures in democratic countries are highly complex machines. Describing how these machines run is oversimplified by isolating the state, representative institutions, and parties, drawing a clear line dividing them from the institutions that govern the market, the system of interests and the mass media. Put differently: the state, market, and media should be considered jointly and parties are located and operate within their interactions. This includes left-wing parties, which are constitutively oriented, as mentioned, towards offering some resistance to the pro-market orthodoxy that has inspired the policies applied since the 1980s. It goes without saying that the economic conditions of each country have also created, depending on varying viewpoints, opportunities and constraints that are not secondary.

The preceding paragraphs have attempted to illustrate how the challenges of growth and the erosion of traditional electoral bases have stimulated left-wing parties to reshape the programmes offered and adjust of their internal organisational structure and relations with unions. The result has been – in general – a convergence among parties towards a position more open to the market and oriented towards reducing welfare costs. The declared intention was to attract the consensus of the new middle class and (implicitly) compensate for the possible erosion of their traditional electoral bases, especially among workers and the middle class receiving welfare. Nevertheless, when it comes to assessing policies and outcomes in terms of more or less inclusive development, this convergence takes on different forms. In fact, in addition to the variables considered above, parties have to contend with the opportunities and constraints inherited from the institutional framework consolidated in the previous phase. Let us briefly review these effects in the light of our four models.

Starting with the non-inclusive growth model of the Anglo-Saxon countries, we first see significant differences in terms of ideological traditions and history between labour parties (as in Britain) and liberal democratic parties (as in America). In 1990, all these parties boasted a long tradition of participation in government – long in America, much shorter in Britain – within a context of political competition characterised by the majority electoral system. The United States has always been a liberal market economy. It is so by structure, but also in terms of culture. Belief in the free market, to which the State has no right to oppose any constraint, has deep roots. After the crisis (both economic and political) of the 1970s, the start of which coincided with the revocation of the Bretton Woods agreements, the Reagan administration put forward a very intense bid to promote this free market culture, which had been set back since the time of the New Deal, and which favoured its policies. This is the background against which Democratic administrations also moved. The initial attempt by the Clinton presidency to introduce an ambitious healthcare reform was rejected by Congress. Even in times of favourable economic conditions, minorities were rewarded by Clinton's progressive liberalism, which did not, however, address the social inequalities that had been growing since the early 1980s. The Obama presidency, once it had successfully dealt with the subprime mortgage crisis that exploded in 2006, managed with great difficulty to get Congress to approve a healthcare reform and certainly did not reverse the trend, leading to serious drawbacks, including political ones, in the areas with the oldest industrial settlements, victims of massive de-localisation processes.

Since the political culture had long accepted state intervention and distributional policies in the UK, more strenuous resistance was to be expected from Labour. But it is plausible that the Thatcherite movement was so strong that it prevented this resistance. By the time it had gained full momentum, the crisis in industry had been going on for at least a decade and one of the preferred topics of public debate was precisely the "intrusiveness" of the Unions.

In addition to promoting policies of deregulation and privatisation, Thatcherism in any case also gave rise to the deployment of a daunting cultural initiative: described by Stuart Hall as "authoritarian populism" (Hall, 1988), it extolled the healthy virtues of entrepreneurs, the self-employed, savers, investors large and small, and property owners. Labour's resistance was ineffective, with the leadership of Michael Foot culminating in the electoral disaster of 1983, preceded in 1982 by the split-off of the Social Democratic Party. The centrist leaders who took the helm were all culturally hostile to the unions, that is, until the arrival of Tony Blair and the establishment of New Labour. The economic record of Thatcherism was nevertheless considered positively on the whole, and it did not seem worth reversing the reasons for its success. Some of Labour's more traditional support was ultimately diverted to regional parties with social democratic roots, on the wave of support for Scottish and Welsh separatism. The Blair and Brown governments also did well as regards growth, albeit relying heavily on financial activities and the advanced services sector, yet their policies did not produce appreciable benefits in the area of socio-economic inequality, which actually increased. On the contrary, the persistent industrial decline and the deterioration of employment provoked conspicuous forms of regional dualism that proved decisive in offering support for Brexit.

In this model, we can therefore see that industrial relations were curtailed and welfare spending was essentially redirected towards workfare, as part of a broader push towards deregulation and the expansion of the market space, also on a global scale. Thus, the reorientation of the programmes offered and of the left-wing parties' governance did not challenge the policies of the conservative parties but limited itself to mitigating their social costs.

The situation in the inclusive growth model of the Nordic countries is completely different. In the Scandinavian countries analysed, social democratic parties have a long and entrenched history, as well as being traditionally more committed to redistribution through public policies, which, for Sweden, dates back as far as the 1930s. They have also always had a strong and institutionalised relationship with trade unions. In both Sweden and Denmark they governed during the years of intense post-war development and monopolised, or virtually, the executive leadership until the end of the 1970s.

However, the pro-market cultural campaign arrived here as well. Privatisation and deregulation policies were launched in these countries, along with attempts to debilitate the traditional model of interest representation based on centralised and multi-sectoral consultation, and the implementation of New Public Management. Nonetheless, some mechanisms came into play that diluted this movement. The Scandinavians' political culture seems to have remained attached to welfare, even if prevalently to the variant that privileges natives at the expense of immigrants, defined as "welfare chauvinism". This allowed the Danish and Swedish social democrats to maintain a good grip on their original working-class base, attracting support also from segments of the new middle class. While they have championed policies oriented towards innovation and the qualification of human capital, they have therefore chiefly promoted interventions to recalibrate welfare, albeit by privatising many services.

In recent times, social democrats in both countries have rethought their programmes offered, or rather they have convinced themselves of the need not to retreat any further, also in order not to increase the drive of right-wing populism. The very culture of the elites has, however, retained traces of the cooperative tradition of the two countries. The political debate has escalated, but only to a certain extent. As such, while the tradition of consultation is considered by some to belong to the past, others come to less drastic conclusions: the Scandinavian system of interests is quite robust and conflicts between employers and trade unions have always been handled, even in recent years, in an atmosphere of mutual respect. These elements, together with the persistence of favourable economic conditions over many decades, help to explain why the increase in inequality in the two countries has been more limited. The impressive egalitarian legacy of the golden age of welfare is ebbing away at a slower rate, thus helping to maintain more inclusive growth.

Looking at the dualistic inclusive growth model seen in continental countries, the picture changes. The French Socialist Party and the German Social Democratic Party have very different ideological traditions and histories. The participation in government of both these forces has been more moderate than that of the Scandinavian parties, especially in the period of great development and welfare construction. Reconstructing the actual influence exerted on the policies and the path of inclusive but dualistic development is hence more difficult in both cases. Thanks to the centre-right parties, the welfare system was developed in each country with protection and benefits for workers based on their professional position. The result was a social protection system that from the outset had less capacity to combat social inequalities, due to its fragmentation based on employment.

Notwithstanding the severe challenge that arose after 1989 with the laborious assimilation of the former GDR, the make-up of German society probably afforded a better chance of coping with the difficulties of the 1980s and 1990s. The well-established concertation institutions of the Rhineland capitalist model gave some extra protection to the working classes. Until the mid-1990s, when the economy was slowing down, it was the Social Democrats who adopted an aggressive strategy of pro-market reforms. Industrial companies reacted energetically to the difficulties by relocating. The haemorrhage was blocked by Schröder's reforms, which aimed at reducing costs for businesses and worker protection, as well as increasing competitiveness within German society itself, safeguarding the most technologically advanced companies. The enlargement of the European Union towards the East also helped, allowing for closer relocations, but at a great expense, both for the working classes and for the SPD. The latter paid dearly for its break away from the trade unions, followed by the secession of *Die Linke*, with an unrelenting series of electoral defeats that cast doubt on its position as Germany's second largest party, undermined by the *Grünen*. In addition, inequalities increased considerably. Above and beyond the serious territorial dualism involving the eastern *Ländern*, the concerted remnants of the Rhineland model protected a fairly large section of the labour market but at the expense of the least qualified and weakest workers. At the root of the SPD's electoral decline is the discontent produced by both forms of dualism.

In France, conversely, the Socialist Party found relief in the action of the public sector, both with trade unions and as the governing institution of French society. These two factors hindered pro-market reforms, prompting not only the Socialist Party, but the centre-right itself to move with some caution. As described above, Mitterrand, and the Fabius government in 1984, had triggered the French pro-market turnaround, disintegrating the coalition with the communists. This progressed after Chirac was elected as president, then lagged during the years of coexistence with the Jospin government until the Sarkozy presidency, coinciding with the 2008–2012 crisis and austerity measures, when market-centred reforms resumed. These would continue under the Hollande presidency, finding support in certain sectors of the public administration, whose managers had meanwhile become largely involved with the private sector and its spirit. This time, the old deterrents did not work and strong waves of discontent and protest were unleashed, for which the PSF, but also the centre-right (namely the UMP), paid a very high cost. The workers' base of the PSF had been shrinking for a long time, and they lost consensus among the middle class linked to welfare and the public sector, heavily penalised by the austerity measures. To the benefit of the new left of *La France Insoumise* (as well as Macron's *République en Marche*), the PSF even ended up "out of the market". Notwithstanding this, compared to Anglo-Saxon countries, the rise in socio-economic inequalities was more moderate, similar to Germany. The effects of the policies adopted by the Macron presidency remain to be seen. So far, the prodigious mobilisation of the trade unions against the reforms of the statute of railway workers and against pension reform, alongside the protests of the *gilets jaunes*, would not seem to bode well for the future.

Despite their significant differences, Germany and France share traits of the dualism represented by the insider area (large manufacturing companies and public employment) and the outsider area (mainly concerning young people and women employed in low-skilled services with low levels of protection and guarantees). Notwithstanding this dualism, however, both countries have managed, albeit in different forms and to different extents (Germany more so than France), to maintain moderate economic growth and a more contained increase in social inequalities. This outcome, as we have seen, seems nonetheless not to have benefited the left-wing parties.

Finally, let us consider the non-inclusive, low-growth model seen in Mediterranean countries, namely the cases of Spain and Italy. These two countries differ in many respects. Italy's industrial system is the second largest in Europe, while Spain's is undoubtedly more contained. The two countries' institutional frameworks and party systems are also different, as are their histories of the left; in the case of Spain, the PSOE has led the country for just over half of the last 30 years. Having buried its Francoist past, the country was admitted to the European Union, and promoted the modernisation of its infrastructures, accelerating a process that was initiated in the late Francoist period. It established a modern welfare system. However, even at the beginning of its term in government, the PSOE addressed its attention more towards the middle class than towards the lower classes, which tended to be championed by the Communist Party. Relations with trade unions have always been insignificant. In 1996, after 14 years of government, the socialists gave way to the *Partido Popular*, but the Gonzalez government had already begun to curtail welfare, in part due to the constraints imposed by the European Union and entry into the eurozone. The PSOE returned to government in 2004 with Zapatero, who also followed the pattern of progressive liberalism: this entailed considerable attention to civil rights, to fulfil the expectations of the more modern sectors of Spanish society, and a confirmation of the retreat introduced by Aznar, insisting on privatisation and deregulation measures, which gave rise to some discontent among the party's traditional electorate. Confirmed in the 2008 elections, Zapatero ceded power early in 2011 to the Rajoy government, following a dramatic worsening of the economic crisis. Affected by the severe austerity measures that were supported by financial and business circles in addition to being requested by the European Union, Rajoy's party governed during an economically problematic time as well. Once the phase of growth had come to an end in the 1990s, the Spanish economy was no longer able to promote the policies aimed at reducing inequalities that had marked the first Gonzalez governments.

This jeopardised the chances of the PSOE, which was nonetheless favoured by the peculiar Spanish electoral regime, which penalises minor parties. It is interesting to note the conclusion of this period of history, the most salient element of which was the appearance of a quite successful new left-wing political formation, which curtailed the lower-class electorate's willingness to vote for populist parties. This only came about in 2013 (with the formation of VOX), reawakening the ghosts of Francoism, but essentially eroding the constituency of the *Partido popular*.

Events in Italy were even more problematic, with the left initially divided between socialists and communists. As secretary of the PSI in 1976, Craxi tended to consolidate ties with the Socialist International and distance himself from the Communist Party. His party adopted an openly revisionist line, directed its attention to the centre, endeavoured to contend with the Christian Democrats for part of its electorate, and promoted a rift within the trade union movement, whose three main components had come closer together in the previous decade. In 1984, the Craxi government issued a decree blocking three points of the wage scale, in agreement with the CISL and UIL, preparing the ground for a referendum intended as a final confrontation with the PCI and CGIL. Having won the referendum, his party set out to follow in the footsteps of the French socialists, but its history came to an end with the "bribesville" investigations.

The Communist Party had a strong effect on the history of the Italian left. By the 1980s, this party had undergone a profound process of ideological revision, as was made clear among other things by its acceptance of Italy's adhesion to the process of European unification and the Atlantic Alliance. This revision did not suffice to afford it full legitimacy to participate in the national government, but its role was nonetheless extremely influential, consistent with its considerable electoral following. In the 1980s, the PCI could be considered a fully fledged socialist party of the traditional type, deeply rooted in the working-class electorate, but also among the middle class with close ties to welfare. Nevertheless, the ambiguous nature of the position imposed on the party by its competitors – neither fully in government, nor more firmly part of the opposition – would cost it a modest erosion of its constituency. The turning point for the PCI came with the fall of the Berlin Wall and a change in its name, which was accompanied by the secession of its left wing, giving rise to *Rifondazione Comunista*.

After the 1994 elections, the Italian left was profoundly renewed, not only as a consequence of the division of the PCI into two sections, but also thanks to the exodus of the Socialist Party and minor parties of the centre-left, as well as the dissolution of the Christian Democrats: much of this renewal was due to the new electoral law – three-quarters majority single-round and one-quarter proportional – and above all to the dichotomising effects produced when Berlusconi joined the fray, forming a centre-right alliance with *Lega Nord* and *Alleanza Nazionale.*

Compared to the left-wing parties of the other countries considered, there is no doubt that the Italian left came up against greater difficulties. Chiefly, because it governed less than any other left, but perhaps also because it was the most culturally uncertain and the most varied. With the exception of an interlude in the mid-1990s, the country's economic and financial conditions were never outstanding either, and as such, cutbacks to welfare came about in the most awkward conditions. The Italian left is still paying the price for its considerable cultural uncertainty, due to two fundamental factors: on the one hand, one of its component derives from the Christian Democrats, mostly descending from the DC left, which had played a leading role in introducing the variety of welfare often defined as "Mediterranean"; on the other hand, members with a Communist background, who have long felt the need to conceal their origins and convert with great zeal to pro-market policies. The portion of the working-class electorate (about two thirds) that had once backed the Communist Party progressively dwindled, as a consequence of both the restructuring of the industrial system and the progressive degeneration of the most radical component of the left: this took the form of abstentions or, to a modest extent, a shift towards the *Lega* party or, more recently, to the *Movimento 5 Stelle*.

How much have these limits suffered by the left affected the combination of low growth and increasing inequality? It is perhaps only responsible to a low degree. The right-wing coalitions have conducted pro-market policies unheeding the state of industrial relations and with even more indifference to the country's geographical dualism, in an atmosphere of unconcealed aversion towards members of the left wing, who are obviously all communists. The short-lived experiences of left-wing governments have therefore been of little use, not so much in terms of slowing down deregulation and privatisation, which was not part of their intention at all, but in terms of relaunching growth and reducing inequality, which has not ceased to escalate. All of which, from an electoral standpoint, has been to the distinct advantage of the populist right and the 5 Star Movement.

Overall, in both Spain and Italy, the dualism between insiders and outsiders has been even more pronounced than in continental countries. Implementing effective social protection measures has proven to be much more arduous given the budgetary constraints. Alongside the effects of an inefficient and underfunded welfare system, very limited resources have been allocated to active labour policies and investments in research, training, and innovation.

Despite these similarities, however, the paths followed in the two countries are substantially different. Since the 1990s, both Italy and Spain have had two social-democratic formations similar to those in other Western countries. Much as elsewhere, they have supported strategies aimed at reducing public intervention, privatisation, and liberalisation, making labour relations more flexible and breaking away from trade unions: all these strategies are aimed at supporting growth and economic efficiency. These orientations became stronger when both countries joined the single currency, and featured even more prominently after the 2008 economic crisis and austerity policies. Yet, the fundamental difference lies in the fact that the PSOE essentially dominated the Spanish left until 2015, when *Podemos* appeared on the scene and, in alliance with *Izquierda Unita*, succeeded in influencing its political programme.

The vicissitudes of the Italian left were far more intricate, and came to a climax with the birth of the Democratic Party in 2007, bringing together the last generation of communist leaders who had given rise first to the PDS and then to the Left Democrats, and the heirs of the Christian Democrat left. Their common ground consists essentially of Third Way positions. What further embroils the path followed by the left is the persistence of a more radical wing, or new left, alongside the Democratic Party. Thanks to its voters, this new left makes it possible to compete with the centre-right, but since it remains steadfastly embedded in the tradition of the interventionist state, divergences inevitably emerge regarding the political programme. This contradiction has considerably undermined the Italian left, compared to a right wing that is unquestionably more capable of overcoming its internal divisions and is therefore more successful in elections.

It should nonetheless be added that the very same left that went perhaps too hastily into government dismissed the issue of equality and social justice, recalibrating its own programme, also on a symbolic level, by putting the emphasis on the demands of economic development. As is well known, Italy failed to meet the challenge of inclusive growth and the Italian left has not been of much help.

Called upon to radically revise the relationship between the state and the market, in the last 30 years democratic countries have been subjected to a major challenge. After the stalemate of the 1970s, there was an urgent need to revive growth: all governments were convinced that the solution lay in favouring market competition and reducing state intervention in the economy and in collective life. The great gamble was whether or not growth would ensue. All the major left-wing parties took part in this wager, assuming that the conditions of the underprivileged classes would also be upgraded and enhanced. In fact, the results have been extremely modest for these classes, who are now indeed expressing their dissent in various ways. The outcomes, however, have not been the same everywhere, in terms of growth and even more so in terms of inequality. In our contribution, aiming our analysis towards the specific angle of the experiences of the left, we have therefore reconstructed the assortment of factors that have more or less favoured a combination of economic growth and social inclusion, aiming to understand which policies are responsible, but first and foremost which kinds of politics.

References

Aarts, K., Blais, A., Schmitt, H. (2011) (Eds). *Political leaders and democratic elections.* Oxford: Oxford University Press

Allern, E. & Bale, T. (2017) (Eds). *Left-of-centre parties and trade unions in the twenty-first century.* Oxford: Oxford University Press.

Allern, E.H., Aylott, N., & Christiansen, F.J. (2007). Social Democrats and trade unions in Scandinavia: The decline and persistence of institutional relationships. *European Journal of Political Research*, 46(5), 607–635. doi:10.1111/j.1475-6765.2007.00706.x

Anderson, K.M. (2001). The politics of retrenchment in a social democratic welfare state: Reform of Swedish pensions and unemployment insurance. *Comparative Political Studies*, 34(9), 1063–1091. doi:10.1177/0010414001034009005

Anderson, K.M. (2004). Pension politics in three small states: Denmark, Sweden and the Netherlands. *Canadian Journal of Sociology*, 29(2), 289–312.

Attali, J. (1995). *Verbatim*. Paris: Fayard.

Armingeon, K., Wenger, V., Wiedemeier, F. Isler, C., Knöpfel, L., & Weisstanner, D. (2018). *Supplement to the comparative political data set – government composition 1960–2015*. Zurich: Institute of Political Science, University of Zurich.

Aylott, N. (2003). After the divorce: Social Democrats and trade unions in Sweden. *Party Politics*, 9(3), 369–390. doi:10.1177/1354068803009003005

Aylott, N. & Bolin, N. (2007). Towards a two-party system? The Swedish parliamentary election of September 2006. *West European Politics*, 30(3), 621–633. doi:10.1080/01402380701276477

Bagnasco, A. (2003). *Società fuori squadra. Come cambia l'organizzazione sociale.* Bologna: Il Mulino.

Bagnasco, A. (2016). *La questione del ceto medio. Un racconto del cambiamento sociale.* Bologna: Il Mulino.

Beramendi, P., Häusermann, S., Kitschelt, H., & Kriesi, H. (2015) (Eds). *The Politics of advanced capitalism*. Cambridge: Cambridge University Press.

Bliek, J. G. & Parguez, A. (2008). Mitterand's turn to conservative economics: A revisionist history. *Challenge*, 51(2), 97–109.

Borioni P. (2011). Paesi nordici: campi, processi ed effetti della privatizzazione in corso. *Rivista delle Politiche Sociali*, 2, 235–255.

Burroni, L. (2016). *Capitalismi a confronto: istituzioni e regolazione dell'economia nei paesi europei.* Bologna: Il Mulino.

Busch A. & Manow, P. (2001). The SPD and the Neue Mitte in Germany. In S. White (Eds), *New Labour and the future of progressive politics* (pp. 175–189). London: Palgrave.

Carrieri M. (2008). *L'altalena della concertazione. Patti e accordi italiani in prospettiva europea*. Roma: Donzelli.

Carrieri, M. (2019). *Un lungo addìo? Come cambiano i rapporti tra i partiti e i sindacati.* Roma: Ediesse.

Castel, R. (2004). *L'insicurezza sociale. Che cosa significa essere protetti.* Milano: Università Bocconi Editore.

Christiansen, P.M. & Rommetvedt, H. (1999). From corporatism to lobbyism? Parliaments, executives, and organized interests in Denmark and Norway. *Scandinavian Political Studies*, 22(3), 195–220.

Cordero, G. & Montero, J.R. (2015). Against bipartyism, towards dealignment? The 2014 European election in Spain. *South European Society and Politics*, 20(3), 357–379. doi:10.1080/13608746.2015.1053679

Dubet, F. (2010). *Les places et les chances*. Paris: Seuil.

Evans, G. & Tilley, J. (2012). How parties shape class politics: Explaining the decline of the class basis of party support. *British Journal of Political Sciences*, 42(1), 137–161. doi:10.1017/S0007123411000202

Evans, G. & Norris, P. (1999). *Critical elections: British parties and voters in long-term perspective*. London: Sage.

Evans, G. & De Graaf, N.D. (2013). Explaining cleavage strength: The role of party positions. In G. Evans & N.D. De Graaf (Eds), *Political choice matters: Explaining the strength of class and religious cleavages in cross-national perspective* (pp. 3–26). Oxford: Oxford University Press.

Field, B.N. & Botti, A. (2013). *Politics and society in contemporary Spain from Zapatero to Rajoy*. London: Palgrave McMillan.

Francia, P.L. (2010). Assessing the Labor-Democratic party alliance: A one-sided relationship? *Polity*, 42(3), 293–303.

Fraser, N. (2017). The end of progressive liberalism. *Dissent*. www.dissentmagazine.org/.

Gallino, L. (2007). *Il lavoro non è una merce. Contro la flessibilità*. Roma-Bari: Laterza

Giddens, A. (1999). *The third way: The renewal of social democracy*. London: Polity.

Gillespie, R. (1990). The break-up of the "socialist family": Party-union relations in Spain 1982–89. *West European Politics*, 13(1), 47–62. doi:10.1080/01402389008424779

Green-Pedersen, C. (2001). Welfare-state retrenchment in Denmark and the Netherlands, 1982–1998: The role of party competition and party consensus. *Comparative Political Studies*, 34(9), 963–985. doi:10.1177/0010414001034009001

Gunther R., Sani, G., & Shabad, G. (1986). *Spain after Franco: The making of a competitive party system*. Berkeley and London: University of California Press.

Hall, S. (1988). *The hard road to renewal: Thatcherism and the crisis of the left*. London: Verso.

Holtz-Bacha, C. (2002). Professionalization of political communication. *Journal of Political Marketing*, 1(4), 23–37. doi:10.1300/J199v01n04_02

Howell, C. (2001). The end of the relationship between social democratic parties and trade unions? *Studies in Political Economy*, 65(1), 7–37. doi:10.1080/19187033.2001.11675218

Iversen, T. & Soskice, D. (2001). An asset theory of social policy preferences. *American Political Science Review*, 95(4), 875–893. doi:10.1017/S0003055400400079

Jackson, G. & Thelen K. (2015). Stability and change in CMEs: Corporate governance and industrial relations in Germany and Denmark. In P. Beramendi, S. Häusermann, H. Kitschelt & H. Kriesi, H. (Eds), *The politics of advanced capitalism* (pp. 305–331). Cambridge: University Press.

Jansson, J. (2017). Two branches of the same tree? Party–union links in Sweden in the twenty-first century. In E.H. Allern & T. Bale (Eds), *Left-of-centre parties and trade unions in the twenty-first century* (pp. 206–224). Oxford: Oxford University Press.

Jobert, B. 1994 (Ed.). *Le tournant néo-libéral en Europe*. Paris: L'Harmattan.

Kavanagh, D. & Morris, P. (1989). *Consensus politics from Attlee to Thatcher*. Oxford: Blackwell.

Kirchheimer, O. (1966). The transformation of Western European party systems. In J. LaPalombara & W. Myron (Eds), *Political parties and political development* (pp. 177–200). Princeton: Princeton University Press.

Kitschelt, H. (1993). Class-structure and social-democratic party strategy. *British Journal of Political Science*, 23(3), 299–337. doi:10.1017/S0007123400006633

Kitschelt, H. (1994). *The transformation of European social democracy*. Cambridge: Cambridge University Press.

Koeble, T.A. (1987). Recasting social democracy in Europe: A nested games explanation of strategic adjustment of political parties. *Politics & Society*, 20(1), 51–70. doi:10.1177/003232929202000l004

Kriesi, H., Grande, E., Lachat, R., Dolezal, M., Bornschier, S., & Frey, T. (2008) (Eds). *West European politics in the age of globalization*. Cambridge: Cambridge University Press.

Lange, P., Ross, G. & Vannicelli, M. (1982). *Unions, change and crisis: French and Italian union strategy and the political economy, 1945–1980*. London: Allen & Unwin.

Lijphart, A. (1999). *Patterns of democracy. Government forms and performance in thirty-six countries*. New Haven: Yale University Press.

Lijphart, A. (2012). *Patterns of democracy: Government forms and performance in thirty-six countries*, 2nd Ed. Yale: Yale University Press.

Lipset S.M. & Marks, G. (2000). *It did not happen here: Why socialism failed in the United States*. New York: W.W. Norton.

Ludlam, S., Bodah, M., & Coates, D. (2002). Trajectories of solidarity: Changing union-party linkages in the UK and the USA. *The British Journal of Politics and International Relations*, 4(2), 222–244. doi:10.1111/1467-856X.t01-1-00003

Markovits, A. (1986). *The politics of the West German trade unions: Strategies of class and interest representation in growth and crisis*. Cambridge: Cambridge University Press.

Mattina, L. (2018). Da fratelli siamesi a lontani parenti. La fine dell'alleanza privilegiata tra partiti e sindacati di sinistra. *Poliarchie*, 1, 139–160.

Mettler, S. (2011). *The submerged state: How invisible government policies undermine American democracy*. Ithaca: Cornell University Press.

Minkin, L. (1991). *The contentious alliance: Trade unions and the* Labour Party. Edinburgh: Edinburgh University Press.

Mudge, S.K. (2018). *Leftism reinvented: Western parties from socialism to neoliberalism.* Cambridge: Harvard University Press.

Nachtway, O. (2013). Market social democracy: The transformation of the SPD up to 2007. *German Politics*, 22(3), 235–252. doi:10.1080/09644008.2013.788153

Osborne, D. & Gaebler, T. (1992). *Reinventing government*. Reading: Addison-Wesley.

Padgett, S. & Paterson, W. (1991). *A history of social democracy in postwar Europe.* London: Longman.

Palier, B. (2010). *The dualization of the French welfare system.* In B. Palier (Eds), *A long goodbye to Bismarck? The politics of welfare reform in Continental Europe* (73–101). Amsterdam: Amsterdam University Press.

Panebianco, A. (1982). *Modelli di partito. Organizzazione e potere nei partiti politici.* Bologna: Il Mulino.

Parsons, N. (2015). Left parties and trade unions in France. *French Politics*, 13(1), 63–83. doi:10.1057/fp.2014.25

Parsons, N. (2017). *Left wing parties and trade unions in France*, in E.H. Allern & T. Bale (Eds), *Left-of-centre parties and trade unions in the twenty-first century* (pp. 112–129). Oxford: Oxford University Press.

Piazza, J. (2001). De-linking labour: Labor unions and social democratic parties under globalization. *Party Politics*, 7(4), 413–435. doi:10.1177/1354068801007004002

Pierson, P. (2004). *Politics in time: History, institutions and social analysis.* Princeton: Princeton University Press.

Puhle, H.-J. (2001). Mobilizer and late modernizers: Socialist parties in the new Southern Europe. In N. Diaamandouros & R. Gunther (Eds), *Parties, politics and democracy in the new Southern Europe* (pp. 268–328). Baltimore: The John Hopkins University Press.

Regini, M. (2003). I mutamenti nella regolazione del lavoro e il resistibile declino dei sindacati europei. *Stato e mercato*, 1, 83–108. doi:10.1425/8813

Rennwald, L. & Evans, G. (2014). When supply creates demand: Social democratic party strategies and the evolution of class voting. *West European Politics*, 37(5), 1108–1135. doi:10.1080/01402382.2014.920981

Rueda, D. (2007). *Social democracy inside out: Partisanship and labor market policy in advanced industrialized democracies*. Oxford: Oxford University Press.

Rueda, D. (2008). Left government, policy, and corporatism: Explaining the influence of partisanship on inequality. *World Politics*, 6(3), 349–389.

Sanchez-Cuenca, I. (2004). Party moderation and politicians' ideological rigidity. *Party Politics*, 10(3), 325–342. doi:10.1177/1354068804039120

Saunders, P. (1990). *Social class and stratification*, London: Routledge.

Savage, M. (2008). Culture, class and classification. In T. Bennet & J. Frow (Eds), *The Sage handbook of cultural ana*lysis (pp. 467–487). London: Sage.

Sciarrone R., Bosco N., Meo A., & Storti L. (2011). *La costruzione del ceto medio. Immagini sulla stampa e in politica*. Bologna: Il Mulino.

Spier, T. (2017). Growing apart? Trade unions and centre-left parties in Germany. In E.H. Allern, & T. Bale (Eds), *Left-of-centre parties and trade unions in the twenty-first century* (pp. 130–148). Oxford: Oxford University Press.

Streeck, W. (2005). Industrial relations: From state weakness as strength to state weakness as weakness: Welfare corporatism and the private use of the public interest.

In S. Green & W. E. Paterson (Eds), *Governance in contemporary Germany: The semisovereign state revisited* (pp. 138–164). Cambridge: Cambridge University Press.
Taylor, G., A. Mathers & M. Upchurch (2011). Beyond the chains that bind: The political crisis of unions in Western Europe. *Labour History*, 52(3), 287–305. doi:10.1080/0023656X.2011.600541
Webb, P. (1994). Party organizational change in Britain: The iron law of centralization?. In R.S. Katz & P. Mair (Eds), *How parties organize: Change and adaptation in party organizations in Western Democracies* (pp. 109–133). London: Sage.
Wring, D. (2007). Focus group follies? *Journal of Political Marketing*, 5(4), 71–97.

Index

Audretsch, D. B. 289
Auel, K. 331
Auroux, J. 210
Autor, D. A. 343
Aylott, N. 379, 386
Aznar, J. M. 399

Baccaro, L. 75, 79, 81–2, 181, 201
Bach, S. 199
Bagnasco, A. 9, 33, 309, 371
Bale, T. 383, 389
Balladur, É. 347, 380
Barbieri, P. 228
Barre, R. 380
Bassotti, M. 248
Becker, S. O. 330
Becker, U. 167
Béland, D. 242
Bellandi, M. 285
Belussi, F. 285
Beramendi, P. 30, 33, 53, 106, 111, 336, 338, 345, 372
Berger, S. 32
Bergholm, T. 179
Berkowitz, É. 252
Berlusconi, S. 226, 381, 400
Berry, C. 292, 293
Best, H. 374
Beveridge, W. 318, 393
Biagi, M. 226
Bianchini, S. 282
Bickerton, C. 315
Bieler, A. 179
Blair, T. 17, 224, 292, 300, 302, 316, 330, 376, 391–2, 395
Blais, A. 376
Bliek, J.-G. 380
Block, F. 132
Blomqvist, P. 247–8
Blümel, M. 258
Blumler, J. G. 326
Bobbio, L. 314, 330
Bodah, M. 384, 385
Bolin, N. 379
Bolton, P. 296, 302
Bongelli, K. 202
Bonoli, G. 32, 128, 339, 343, 346–7
Bonvillian, W. B. 289
Bordogna, L. 81, 199, 202
Borioni, P. 379
Bortolotti, B. 323
Bosetti, L. 64–6
Botti, A. 191, 202, 382
Bowen, W. G. 347
Bowman, J. R. 189
Boyer, R. 32, 71
Boyle, S. 307, 315
Branting, H. 386
Breen, R. 338
Brown, G. 292, 300, 395
Brüggemann, M. 328, 331
Buesa Blanco, M. 285
Burkhart, S. 331
Burroni, L. 32, 64–5, 71, 83–4, 89, 166, 174, 187, 264, 277, 296, 388, 403
Busch, A. 379
Busemeyer, M. R. 95
Busse, R. 243, 258

Callon, M. 292
Caloffi, A. 285
Cameron, D. 167
Cameron, D. W. 292–3, 300, 302
Carlin, W. 219
Carrieri, M. 191, 383
Carter, J. 215, 376

Cassese, S. 315
Castel, R. 388
Castells, M. 278
Castles, E. 152
Ceccobelli, D. 331
Cella, G. P. 74, 191, 200
Chesbrough, H. W. 277
Chesnais, E. 281
Chirac, J. 380, 397
Christensen, T. 320
Christiansen, F. J. 386
Christiansen, P. M. 324, 386
Ciampi, C. A. 212, 387
Cihák, M. 72
Clark, T. N. 337
Clegg, D. 220
Clinton, B. 17, 215, 225, 246, 289, 300, 376, 391, 395
Coates, D. 384–5
Cohen, E. 281
Colvin, A. J. S. 183–4
Corbyn, J. 18
Cordero, G. 382
Cotta, M. 374
Craxi, B. 399
Crouch, C. 10, 20, 32, 34, 77, 86, 178–9, 181–2, 187, 200, 312, 338
Culpepper, P. D. 330–1
Cunningham, L. 292

Dalton, R. J. 337, 366
Daly, M. 272
Davesne, A. 248, 253
Deaton, A. 32, 41
de Boer, H. 279
Dedoussopoulos, A. 89
Deeg, R. 65, 68–9, 71
De Graaf, N. D. 372
De Marchi, V. 285
Denozza, E. 65
de vries, G. J. 342–3
de vries, K. 342–3
De Winter, L. 166
De Witt, L. 252
DiMaggio, P. J. 297
Dini, L. 249
Di Vico, D. 286
Döbert, H. 295
Doellgast, V. 198–9
Dohse, D. 283
Dølvik, J. E. 178, 179, 222
Donatiello, D. 285
Dore, R. 32, 72
Dorigatti, L. 199
Drahokoupil, J. 198
Dubet, E. 388
Dumont, P. 166
Dweyer, R. E. 343

Edgerton, D. 291
Edquist, C. 278–9
Eichhorst, W. 199, 217
Eikenberry, A. 395
Emmenegger, P. 68, 296
Engelhardt, L. 319
Erikson, R. 316, 338–9
Esping-Andersen, G. 14, 32–3, 110, 119, 127, 226, 263, 338
Esser, E. 331
Estevez-Abe, M. 99
Etzkowitz, H. 277, 280
Evans, G. 338, 372, 376
Eydal, G. B. 128

Fabius, L. 380, 397
Fagerberg, J. 278
Fanfani, L. A. 393
Feenstra, R. C. 86
Fernández-Macías, E. 201
Ferragina, E. 272
Ferreira, E. 128
Ferrera, M. 23, 32–3, 110, 127
Fetzer, T. 330
Fidalgo, E. G. 249, 254
Field, B. N. 191, 382
Fillon, E. 190
Flora, P. 32, 94
Foot, M. 395
Fornero, E. 227
François, B. 331
Franklin, M. 337
Franzini, M. 32
Fraser, I. N. 391
Freeman, C. 338

Gaebler, T. 374
Gale, D. 64–5
Gallagher, M. 149–50, 378
Gallie, D. 167
Gallino, L. 313, 388
Gallochat, A. 282
Garritzmann, J. L. 95, 346
Gaudin, J. P. 330
Geering, D. 167

Genschel, P. 312
Gergils, H. 279
Gershtenson, J. 389
Geschwind, Ia. 294
Gherardini, A. 286, 301
Gibney, R. 183
Giddens, A. 330, 391
Gidron, N. 200
Giersch, H. 283
Gillespie, R. 387
Gingrich, D. W. 70
Girdon, N. 348
Giuliani, M. 166
Glenngård, A. H. 253, 257
Godard, J. 183
Godino, A. 84, 191, 199, 202
Goetschy, J. 181–2
Goldthorpe, J. H. 336, 338–9
Gómez Puente, M. 287
Goos, M. 343
Gore, A. 376
Gourevitch, P. 9
Grabka, M. 217
Gramsci, A. 318
Grandinetti, R. 285
Green-Pedersen, C. 127, 377
Greer, L. 198–9
Grimpe, C. 279
Grimshaw, D. 75, 201
Gualmini, E. 92
Guardiancich, L. 76, 199
Guillén, A. M. 128, 264, 272
Gumbrell-McCormick, R. 76, 85, 180–1
Gunther, R. 382
Gurevitch, M. 326

Hall, P. A. 17, 32, 60, 70, 94, 180, 183, 200, 260, 282, 331, 334
Hall, S. 395
Hallin, D. C. 327–8, 331
Halpern, C. 316
Hancké, B. 32
Hartz, P. 217, 219, 232, 373
Hassel, A. 231
Hassenteufelf, P. 248, 253
Häusermann, S. 30, 33, 53, 106, 111, 128, 167, 336, 338, 340–1, 345–8, 372
Havard, C. 199
Hegel, G. W. F. 318
Heidenheimer, A. J. 32
Hemerijck, A. 28, 33, 118, 128
Héraud, J.-A. 305
Hijzen, A. 103, 104
Himanen, P. 303
Hinrichs, K. 128
Hirschman, A. O. 311–12
Hobbes, T. 309, 318
Hockfield, S. 290
Hollande, E. 380, 390, 398
Hollingsworth, J. R. 32
Holtz-Bacha, C. 328, 383
Horemans, J. 206
Horne, W. 348
Hörner, W. 295
Howell, C. 75, 79, 81–2, 181, 183, 201, 383, 385
Hubé, N. 331
Hyman, R. 76, 85, 180–2

Ibsen, CL. 189
Ido, M. 32
Immelt, J. 290
Inglehart, R. 32, 200
Inklaar, R. 86
Iversen, M. J. 278
Iversen, T. 14, 19, 32, 43, 99, 149, 166, 317–18, 376

Jackson, G. 69, 71, 386
Jahn, D, 236
Jansson, J. 383–4
Jessoula, M. 126, 272
Jobert, A. 181, 182
Jobert, B. 394, 371
Jochum, M. 316
Johansson, E. 191
Johnson, B. 365
Jørgensen, C. 190
Jørgensen, H. 222
Jospin, L. 373, 387, 398

Kalleberg, A. L. 215
Kaloudis, A. 279
Kassalow, E. M. 183
Katz, H. C. 183–4
Katz, L. F. 343
Katzenstein, P. 179
Kaufman, B. E. 184
Kavanagh, D. 326, 393
Kearney, M. S. 343
Keating, M. J. 316, 317
Keller, B. K. 180
Keune, M. 198–200
Kinnock, N. 385

Kirchheimer, O. 14, 371, 374
Kirsch, A. 180
Kitschelt, H. 30, 33, 53, 106, 111, 336, 338, 345, 372–3, 383
Kittel, B. 75, 267
Kjellberg, A. 186
Klenk, T. 248, 253
Klitkou, A. 279
Kluger, D. 319
Knijn, T. 128
Kochan, T. A. 183
Koeble, T. A. 385
Kohl, H. 211
Korpi, W. 33, 93
Kriesi, H. 30, 33, 53, 106, 111, 316, 336–8, 345, 348, 371
Kristensen, P. H. 193, 278
Kuitto, K. 236
Kulicke, M. 283
Kurer, T. 346

Laegreid, P. 320
lammarino, S. 318
Lampousaki, S. 185
Lange, P. 76, 387
Langer, A. I. 325, 328
Larédo, P. 281–2
Larousse, J. 279, 282
Larsen, T. P. 198
Lascoumes, P. 316, 330
Lash, S. 330
Lawton-Smith, H. 277
Legait, B. 282
Le Galès, P. 20, 316, 330–1
Lehmbruch, G. 32, 166
Lenihan, H. 53
León, M. 264
Leonardi, S. 199, 201
Lewis, J. 110, 127
Leydesdorff, La. 277
Lijphart, A. 12–13, 32–3, 145–50, 162–4, 166–7
Lilja, K. 193
Lipset, S. M. 337, 385
Llerena, P. 282
Locke, J. 318
Lucchese, M. 285
Ludlam, S. 384–5
Lundvall, B. 278–9

Macron, E. 352, 354, 356, 362, 398
Mahler, V. A. 86, 366
Mahoney, J. 159
Mailand, M. 189, 191, 199
Maisonneuve, C. de la 128
Major, J. 291, 292
Malerba, E. 285
Mancini, P. 327–9
Manning, A. 343
Manow, P. 19, 23, 32–4, 162, 179, 219, 263, 379
Many, G. 317
Marchington, M. 183, 199, 201
Marginson, P. 201–2
Markovits, A. 386
Marks, G. 385
Martin, A. 222
Martin, C. J. 178
Martin, S. 103–4
Martínez Lucio, M. 76
Marx, I. 186
Marx, P. 199, 217
Masters, M. F. 183
Mathers, A. 383, 389
Mattina, L. 383
Mattoni, A. 331
Mauroy, P. 380
May, T. 293
Mayhew, K. 223, 224
Mazzoleni, G. 331
Mazzucato, M. 132
McAllister, I. 337
McDonough, T. 53
Meidner, R. 179
Merkel, A. 284, 379
Merkle, S. 328
Merkur, S. 253, 257
Mettler, S. 393
Michaels, G. 343
Michel, E. 246
Miettinen, R. 193
Miguélez, E. 287
Mills, C. 338
Mills, W. 339
Mingione, E. 94
Minkin, L. 385
Mitterrand, F. 210, 281, 372, 380, 397
Mjøset, L. 193
Molina, O. 76, 84, 88, 191, 199, 201, 287
Montero, J. R. 382
Monti, M. 227, 286
Morel, N. 28, 232
Moretti, E. 133
Morgan, K. 243

Morris, P. 393
Mowery, D. C. 289
Mudge, S. K. 33, 405
Mughan, A. 320
Muller, E. 282
Muñoz, E. 285
Muñoz de Bustillo, R. 201
Mustar, P. 280–2, 301
Mutti, A. 72

Nachtway, O. 386
Nascia, L. 285
Natali, D. 32, 128
Natraj, A. 343
Nelson, R. R. 132
Nettl, J. P. 331
Neveu, E. 331
Nielsen, K. 278
Niklasson, H. 189
Norris, P. 166, 200, 376

Obama, B. 33, 129, 225, 226, 290, 300, 361, 364, 376, 395
Oberlander, J. 246
Obinger, H. 167
Oesch, D. 336–41, 346, 347, 365
Offe, C. 312
Onida, F. 286
Ornston, D. 278, 279, 302
Ørsten, M. 328, 331
Osborne, D. 374

Paci, M. 33
Palier, B. 28, 32, 33, 46, 128, 210, 217, 220, 232, 248, 253, 331, 338, 339, 343, 346, 347, 379
Palme, J. 28, 232
Panebianco, A. 371
Papadopoulos, Y. 330
Paqué, K. H. 283
Parguez, A. 380
Parsons, N. 383, 387
Pasquino, G. 179
Paterson, W. 384
Pavolini, E. 200, 247, 249, 254, 264, 272
Pedaci, M. 88
Pedersen, O. 278
Pedersini, R. 79, 81, 181, 185, 199–202
Perez, S. A. 230
Pessina, G. 286
Peters, B. G. 330
Pfetsch, B. 328, 331
Pianta, M. 32, 285
Piattoni, S. 330
Piazza, J. 383
Pierson, P. 10, 32, 33, 94, 127, 128, 197, 242, 338, 347, 375
Piketty, T. 32
Pinheiro, R. 294
Piore, M. J. 209
Pisati, M. 337
Plane, D. L. 348
Poell, T. 326
Poguntke, T. 320
Poletti, G. 258
Pontusson, J. 86
Powell, J. J. W. 295
Powell, W. W. 297
Prodi, R. 286
Prosser, T. 201
Puhle, H.-J. 387
Pulignano, V. 199, 201

Raitano, M. 272
Rajan, R. 64
Rajoy, M. 229, 287, 399
Ramella, F. 131
Ramos Martín, N. 199
Rasmussen, L. 279
Raspanti, D. 88
Reagan, R. 184, 214, 215, 242, 260, 262, 288–9, 301, 316, 376, 392, 395
Regalia, I. 82, 191, 201
Regan, A. 78
Regini, M. 28, 32, 82, 191, 226, 289
Rehn, G. 179
Rennwald, L. 336, 346–7, 365
Renucci, A. 282
Renzi, M. 227, 258, 286
Reyneri, E. 92
Rhodes, M. 32–3, 35, 88, 230
Rhodes, R. A. W. 330
Riesberg, A. 243
Rizza, R. 61, 92
Rocard, M. 373, 380
Rodden, J. 348
Rodríguez-Pose, A. 317–18, 382
Rodrik, D. 41
Rommetvedt, H. 386
Rose, R. 337
Rostgaard, T. 128
Rothstein, S. A. 325
Rouban, L. 331
Rueda, D. 34, 46–7, 86, 338, 347, 375

Sabel, C. F. 209
Sacchi, S. 227
Sacconi, L. 65
Salvati, M. 8
Samek Lodovici, M. 92
Sampat, B. N. 289
Sánchez, P. 288, 392
Sánchez-Cuenca, I. 382
Sani, G. 382
Sanz, P. 185, 188
Sapir, A. 32, 61
Saraceno, C. 129, 13, 158
Sarkozy, N. 282, 392, 394, 398
Sassen, S. 317
Saunders, P. 371
Scalise, G. 174, 371
Scarano, G. 61
Scharpf, F. 323, 324
Schmalz, S. 89
Schmidt, M. G. 145, 279
Schmieding, H. 283
Schmitt, H. 376
Schmitter, P. C. 32, 166
Schmoch, U. 283
Schneider, F. 62
Schnyder, G. 69, 71
Schröder, C. 217
Schröder, G. 283, 324, 379, 397
Schulten, T. 198
Schulz, W. 331
Schulze, M. 222
Schulze-Cleven, T. 325
Schwander, H. 32–3, 219, 336, 346
Schwartz, H. 228, 278
Sciarrone, R. 372, 375
Scruggs, L. 236–7, 241, 245, 251, 256
Seeleib-Kaiser, M. 247, 272, 340
Serrano, A. 200
Shabad, G. 382
Sharp, M. 291
Shinkawa, T. 128
Sikorav, J. L. 282
Singer, P. L. 289–90
Siniscalco, D. 323
Skocpol, T. 33, 319
Smith, A. 331
Soete, L. 338
Solga, H. 295
Solow, R. 92
Somers, M. 33
Sorge, A. 71
Soskice, D. 14, 17, 19, 32, 94, 99, 149, 166, 183, 233, 282, 317–18, 376
Spier, T. 386
Stabilini, A. 91
Staehler, T. 283
Stiglitz, J. 32–3
Storper, M. 318
Streeck, W, 32, 35, 166, 174, 178, 180–1, 200, 330, 379
Strömbäck, E. J. 328, 331
Sullivan, R. 76
Surdez, M. 331
Swank, D. 178
Swanson, D. 327
Swyngedouw, M. 166

Talme, L. 191
Taylor, G. 389
Thatcher, Margaret 182, 215–16, 262, 288, 290–2, 318, 376, 393, 395
Thatcher, Mark 32
Thelen, K. 32–3, 46, 81, 94, 104, 107, 159, 166, 183, 217, 220, 223, 230–1, 295, 338, 339, 343, 347, 379, 386
Thiel, M. 89
Thomas, D. 279
Thomas, J.-P. 247
Thomsen, S. 71
Thorning-Schmidt, H. 280
Tilley, J. 372, 376
Timmer, M. P. 86, 342–3
Timming, A. 183
Titmuss, R. 110
Todor, A. 31, 166
Toniolo, G. 285
Toynbee, P. 224
Trampusch, C. 189
Traxler, F. 75, 86, 183
Trento, S. 64–5
Treu, T. 74, 191, 212
Trigilia, C. 32, 34, 76, 133, 149, 166, 277
Tros, E. 214
Trump, D. 18, 290, 300, 365
Tunzelmann, N. von 288

Upchurch, M. 383, 389
Urry, J. 330

Vandaele, K. 76, 89
van Dijck, J. 326
van Kempen, H. 331
van Kersbergen, K. 33, 167

Van Reenen, J. 343
van Rie, T. 186
Vassallo, S. 150, 166
Vauchez, A. 331
Venn, D. 104
Ventura, J. V. 249, 254
Vesan, P. 92
Vezinat, N. T. 330
Vicarelli, M. G. 243, 249, 254
Viesti, G. 294
Visser, J. 77, 79, 83, 151, 175, 186
Vitols, S. 283

Waddington, J. 183
Waldergrave, W. 291
Walker, D. 224
Wallace, D. 288–9
Watson, S. 34, 162
Webb, P. 320, 383
Weishaupt, J. T. 94
Weiss, L. 288, 290
Welz, C. 199, 201
Werquin, P. 97
Western, B. 114
Wheeler, H. 183
Wickham-Jones, M. 223–4
Wilensky, H. L. 167
Wilthagen, T. 214
Winblad, U. 247
Woods, D. R. 395
Wren, A. 183
Wright, E. O. 343
Wright, M. 281–2
Wright, V. 330
Wring, D. 382

Young, J. 289

Zangl, B. 312
Zapatero, J. L. R. 254, 287, 382, 399
Zattoni, A. 64–5
Zingales, L. 64

FSC
www.fsc.org
MIX
Papier | Fördert gute Waldnutzung
FSC® C083411

Kolibri 360 GmbH
Ferdinand-Jühlke-Straße 7
99095 Erfurt, Deutschland
produktsicherheit@kolibri360.de